Studies in Church History

61

(2025)

MARGINS AND PERIPHERIES
IN CHRISTIAN HISTORY

MARGINS AND PERIPHERIES IN CHRISTIAN HISTORY

EDITED BY

DAVID CERI JONES

PETER MARSHALL

CHARLOTTE METHUEN

PUBLISHED FOR
THE ECCLESIASTICAL HISTORY SOCIETY
BY
CAMBRIDGE UNIVERSITY PRESS
2025

Published by Cambridge University Press & Assessment
on behalf of the Ecclesiastical History Society
University Printing House, Cambridge CB2 8BS, United Kingdom

First published 2025

ISBN 9781009679404

ISSN 0424–2084

Bible quotations are taken from the following versions:

The Authorized (King James) Version. Rights in the Authorized Version in the
United Kingdom are vested in the Crown. Reproduced by permission of the Crown's
patentee, Cambridge University Press.

New Revised Standard Version Bible: Anglicized Edition, copyright © 1989, 1995,
Division of Christian Education of the National Council of the Churches of Christ in
the United States of America. Used by permission. All rights reserved.

SUBSCRIPTIONS: *Studies in Church History* is an annual subscription
journal (ISSN 0424–2084). The 2025 subscription price (excluding VAT), which
includes print and electronic access, is £156 (US $248 in the USA, Canada and
Mexico) for institutions and £85 (US $137 in the USA, Canada and Mexico) for
individuals ordering direct from the Press and certifying that the volume is for
their personal use. An electronic-only subscription is also available to institutions
at £88 (US $140 in the USA, Canada and Mexico). Special arrangements exist for
members of the Ecclesiastical History Society.

Previous volumes are available online at www.cambridge.org/StudCH

Printed in Great Britain by Henry Ling Limited, The Dorset Press, Dorchester, DT1
1HD

A catalogue record for this publication is available from the British Library

For EU product safety concerns, contact us at Calle de José Abascal, 56, 1°, 28003
Madrid, Spain, or email: eugpsr@cambridge.org

Contents

Contents

Contents

Preface

This, the sixty-first volume of Studies in Church History, presents papers given at the Summer Conference held at the University of Warwick in July 2023, and at the Winter Meeting held online in January 2024 under the presidency of Professor Peter Marshall. The articles in this volume provide a range of fascinating insights into the ways in which the marginal and the peripheral have been understood in Christian history, their relations to the centre (or their own sense of being at the centre), and the interactions between centre and margins. We would like to thank Professor Marshall for proposing this intriguing theme.

Academic publishing is dependent on the voluntary contributions of many people. The editors are grateful to all who offered contributions at the conference, to all who submitted papers for publication, and to those who peer reviewed the contributions. This volume has again benefitted from the meticulous work of Dr Alice Soulieux-Evans as assistant editor. The editors wish to thank the Society for funding her post. We would like also to express our gratitude to the Society's conference secretaries for the groundwork underpinning this volume: Professor Elizabeth Tingle for her detailed planning of the Summer Conference (and for driving home conference participants who found themselves stranded by a train strike) and Angela Platt for her equally careful planning of the Winter Meeting. Thanks are also due to the Society's secretary, Dr Joe Hardwick, and treasurer, Simon Jenkins, for all that they contribute to the Ecclesiastical History Society and its work.

In this volume, the Kennedy Prize, for the best contribution by a postgraduate student, has been awarded to Teodora Popovici, for her article 'Papal Indulgences and the Conversion of Schismatics in Late Medieval Transylvania (c.1350–c.1450)'. The President's Prize, for the best article by an early career scholar, has been awarded to Robert A. H. Evans for his essay '*Correctio* from the Margins: Geographical Peripheries and Moral Conformity in Later Carolingian Annals'.

David Ceri Jones
Aberystwyth University

Charlotte Methuen
University of Glasgow

Contributors

Lesley Abrams
    Emeritus Professor of Early Medieval History, University of Oxford, and Emeritus Fellow, Balliol College, Oxford

Miriam Adan Jones
    Independent Scholar

Aloysius Atkinson
    Postgraduate Student, University of Oxford

Emily J. Bailey
    Associate Professor, Towson University, MD

Alex Beeton
    Research Fellow, The History of Parliament Trust

Kateryna Budz
    British Academy's Researchers at Risk Fellow, School of Divinity, New College, University of Edinburgh

Manning Chan
    Postgraduate Student, The University of California, Santa Cruz

Shaun Church
    Parish Priest, St Francis de Sales, Hampton Hill, Middlesex

Robert A. H. Evans
    Senior Chaplain, Radley College, Abingdon

Lydia Fisher
    Honorary Research Fellow, University of Exeter

Alan Ford
    Emeritus Professor, University of Nottingham

John-Paul Ghobrial
    Professor of Modern and Global History, University of Oxford, and Lucas Fellow and Tutor in History, Balliol College, Oxford

Tim Grass
    Independent Scholar

Contributors

Mary Heimann
    Professor of Modern History, Cardiff University

Daniel Inman
    Associate Vicar, St Luke's and Christ Church, Chelsea

Jonathan Jarrett
    Associate Professor of Early Medieval History, Institute for
    Medieval Studies, University of Leeds

George Kam Wah Mak
    Associate Professor, Department of Religion and Philosophy,
    Hong Kong Baptist University

Dirceu Marroquim
    Permanent Associate, Instituto Arqueológico Histórico e
    Geográfico Pernambucano, Recife, Brazil

Peter Marshall
    Professor of History, University of Warwick

Teodora Popovici
    Postgraduate Student, University of Bucharest; Research
    Assistant, Institute for South-East European Studies,
    Romanian Academy

Catherine Rider
    Associate Professor in Medieval History, University of Exeter

Davide Salmoiraghi
    Honorary Research Associate, Department of Anglo-Saxon,
    Norse and Celtic, University of Cambridge

John W. Sawkins
    Professor of Economics, Heriot-Watt University, Edinburgh

Dongjun Seo
    Part-time Lecturer in Ecclesiastical History, Korean Bible
    University, Seoul

Anastasia Stylianou
    History Tutor, Astrophoria Foundation Year, University of Oxford

Martin Wellings
    Senior Research Fellow, Westminster College Oxford Trust

Abbreviations

ActaSS	J. Bolland and G. Henschen, eds, *Acta sanctorum* (Antwerp etc., 1643–)
AnBoll	*Analecta Bollandiana* (1882–)
AV	Authorized [King James] Version
ARG	*Archiv für Reformationsgeschichte* (1903–)
BAV	Biblioteca Apostolica Vaticana
BL	British Library
BN	Bibliothèque nationale de France
Bodl.	Bodleian Library
CathHR	*Catholic Historical Review* (1915–)
ChH	*Church History* (1932–)
CUL	Cambridge University Library
DIB	*Dictionary of Irish Biography*, 11 vols (Cambridge, 2009, 2018)
EETS	Early English Text Society
EHR	*English Historical Review* (1886–)
EME	*Early Medieval Europe* (1992–)
ET	English translation
HC Deb.	House of Commons Debates
HMC	Historical Manuscripts Commission
HR	*Historical Research* (1986–)
InR	*Innes Review* (1950–)
JBS	*Journal of British Studies* (1961–)
JEH	*Journal of Ecclesiastical History* (1950–)
JHC	*Journal of the House of Commons*
JMedH	*Journal of Medieval History* (1975–)
JMH	*Journal of Modern History* (1929–)
JRH	*Journal of Religious History* (1960–)
LPL	Lambeth Palace Library
MGH AA	Monumenta Germaniae Historica, Auctores antiquissimi, 15 vols (1877–1919)
MGH BdK	Monumenta Germaniae Historica, Die Briefe der deutschen Kaiserzeit (1949–)

MGH Capit.	Monumenta Germaniae Historica, Capitula regum Francorum, 2 vols (1883–97)
MGH Epp.	Monumenta Germaniae Historica, Epistolae (1887–)
MGH Epp. Sel.	Monumenta Germaniae Historica, Epistolae Selectae (1916–)
MGH Fontes n.s.	Monumenta Germaniae Historica, Fontes Iuris Gemanici Antiqui n.s. (1933–)
MGH LdL	Monumenta Germaniae Historica, Libelli de Lite Imperatorum et Pontificum, Saeculis XI et XII conscripti, 3 vols (1891–7)
MGH Poetae	Monumenta Germaniae Historica, Poetae Latinae Medii Aevi (1881–)
MGH SRG i.u.s.	Monumenta Germaniae Historica, Scriptores rerum Germanicarum in usum scholarum seperatum editi (1871–)
MGH SRG n.s.	Monumenta Germaniae Historica, Scriptores rerum Germanicarum, Nova series (1922–)
MGH SRM	Monumenta Germaniae Historica, Scriptores rerum Merovingicarum, 7 vols (1884–1951)
MGH SS	Monumenta Germaniae Historica, Scriptores (in folio) (1826–)
n.d.	no date
n.p.	non-paginated
n.pl.	no place
NRSV	New Revised Standard Version
n.s.	new series
OED	Oxford English Dictionary
ODNB	Oxford Dictionary of National Biography
o.s.	old series
P&P	*Past and Present* (1952–)
PL	J.-P. Migne, ed., Patrologia Latina, 217 vols + 4 index vols (Paris, 1844–65)
RH	*Recusant History* (1951–)
RSCHS	*Records of the Scottish Church History Society* (1923–)

s.a.	*sub anno* ('under the year')
SCH	Studies in Church History (1964–)
ScHR	*Scottish Historical Review* (1904–)
s.n.	*sub nomine* ('under the name')
TNA	The National Archives (Kew)
TRHS	*Transactions of the Royal Historical Society* (1871–)

Illustrations

Shaun Church, 'Experiencing Christian Sacred Space in the Roman Frontier Zones of the Fourth and Fifth Centuries'

aerial photo by Aerial Cam. © The Vindolanda Trust. Photo credit: Marta Alberti for the Vindolanda Trust.

Jonathan Jarrett, 'Priestly Provision at the Periphery: Building the Church in Tenth-Century Catalonia'

Lesley Abrams, Locations of Religious Encounter: The Scandinavian Diaspora in the Viking Age

Lydia Fisher, 'Illuminating Faith: Marginalized Stained-Glass Fragments and Lost Schemes in the Pre-Reformation Parish Church'

Introduction

A collection of scholarly articles on margins and peripheries in Christian history runs the risk of seeming almost wilfully diffident and restrained in ambition. The topic suggests a concern with places – as well as persons, concepts, themes – that, while perhaps interesting, are by definition subordinate and relatively inconsequential. As students of religious history – and perhaps as people too – our priorities are instinctively structured by metaphors of 'centrality'; one's valuable time is probably not best spent engaging with merely 'marginal' matters.

The contributions to this volume represent a resounding rejoinder to all such unexamined assumptions, and make a collectively compelling case for the importance of paying attention to a diversity of places, propositions and people that, over the long sweep of Christianity's historical development, have been considered marginal or peripheral. The articles here were originally presented as papers to the summer and winter conferences of the Ecclesiastical History Society, in July 2023 and January 2024, where participants, including an encouraging number of talented early career scholars, took up with alacrity an invitation to interrogate critically the concepts of 'marginality' and 'peripherality' in relation to Christian history, and to track their changing meanings and utility over time.[1]

It is important to state at the outset a fundamental premise of this collaborative endeavour: that the margins and peripheries of historical Christianity – whether geographical, societal or theological – have never been simply natural and God-given, but rather are subjective, contingent and socially constructed; they are always, to some degree or other, a matter of perspective. The processes of their construction, or imposition, often for implicitly or overtly ideological reasons, thus offer considerable insight into the workings of the churches as social institutions and the dynamics of religious life within them. A connected premise is that margins or peripheries are always, and

---

[1] In writing this introduction, I have benefitted from the comments of participants in a round-table discussion at the conclusion of the 2023 Summer Conference, and from a set of written reflections kindly forwarded to me by Robert Swanson.

Studies in Church History 61 (2025), 1–11 © The Author(s), 2025. Published by Cambridge University Press on behalf of the Ecclesiastical History Society.
doi:10.1017/stc.2025.1

of their very essence, relational. They have no intrinsic or autonomous meaning, and exist only in connection to some recognized moral fulcrum or known geographical centre. But where, in Christian terms, is the centre to be found?

A full account of the disputed attempts, over many centuries, to resolve that question might well require an entire historical survey of Christianity, a religion which traces its origins to the birth of a disadvantaged child in a subjugated province on the eastern periphery of the Augustan Roman empire. Jerusalem, the place of Christ's crucifixion, resurrection and expected Second Coming, was from the start the core of Christianity's eschatological imagination and the pivot of its moral geography. An ancient notion of Jerusalem as 'the navel of the world' was popularized by the biblical commentaries of Jerome, and the city was usually placed at the centre of medieval maps of the three known continents, a convention that has left its mark on modern cartography.[2] Yet Jerusalem, lost, regained, then lost again to the expanding forces of Islam, paradoxically became and remained a place on the margins of the Christian world.

A position of primacy, and of consequent centrality, was meanwhile claimed, and continues to be claimed, by the papacy in Rome – though one strongly disputed by the Orthodox churches, who looked to Constantinople (latterly, sometimes to Moscow) as first in honour among various institutional centres of the faith. With the split within Latin Christendom at the time of the Reformation, new centres of magisterial reform in Zürich, Geneva, London and other places established lines of connection and dependence with their own margins and peripheries, while an assortment of free-thinkers, dissidents and radicals planted their rival understandings of the faith in a variety of New Jerusalems or promised lands. The centre-periphery model of Christianity was reinforced in an age of global expansion and encounter, and through a European self-understanding of pre-eminence and centrality which largely shaped, and to an extent continues to shape, the subsequent historiography of religion. However, ancient churches in the Near and Middle East, in Ethiopia and in India, their establishment long predating the Christian ascendancy in Western Europe, certainly did not regard themselves as marginal or peripheral.

---

[2] Adriaan H. Bredero, *Christendom and Christianity in the Middle Ages*, transl. Reinder Bruinsma (Grand Rapids, MI, 1994), 95–6.

Christianity's margins have thus always been fluid and malleable, subject to sometimes contentious negotiation and to changing alignments over time. People and places once almost universally regarded as peripheral can suddenly find themselves at the centre of the action: in the early sixteenth century, the small-town backwater of Wittenberg, situated in thoroughly provincial Saxony, presents itself as a preeminent case. A more recent example of peripheries in motion is precisely identified by George Mak's article in this volume examining Bible publishing in mid-twentieth-century Hong Kong. As a result of the Communist Revolution of 1948–9, a small British colony, in a peripheral location off the coast of southern China, developed rapidly into the world centre for the printing and distribution of Chinese Protestant Bibles and other devotional works. These were aimed at an international diaspora which itself had once been marginal to Western missionary priorities, but, with access to mainland China now restricted, developed into a main focus for those efforts. In the case study presented in Alan Ford's insightful article, a place acknowledged to be on the extreme edge of Christian civilization became a focus of intense confessional debate precisely because of its peripheral character. The renowned pilgrimage site of 'St Patrick's Purgatory', a cave on a small island in Lough Derg, County Donegal, was believed in the Middle Ages to be a physical point of entry to the Otherworld. At the Reformation, Protestant polemicists blasted it as a symbol of popish obscurantism and corruption, while Roman Catholics hailed the remote location as a pristine repository of piety, tradition and faith.

Lines of connection between centre and periphery, and what happens in the course of these being traversed, is a theme of several of the articles in this volume. John Sawkins offers a meticulous examination of financial arrangements for the support of the ministry within the Free Church of Scotland created by the 1843 Disruption. He demonstrates how, through a system of cross subsidy, poorer rural parishes in the highlands and Northern isles were generously supported by wealthier urban ones in Glasgow, Edinburgh and Aberdeen. Here, the margins were being sustained, rather than neglected, albeit through a system that was itself a highly centralized one. A millennium and more earlier, in the emergent kingdom to the south, currency of a different kind was expended to strengthen links between the centre and margins. Miriam Adan Jones examines the distribution and extent of medieval church and chapel dedications to St Gregory, the pope who in the late sixth century initiated the Roman mission to the

English. The dedicatory process was overseen by political and ecclesiastical leaders who regarded the patronage of St Gregory as a powerful symbol of a not-always-obvious connectedness between the island kingdom on the western edge of Christian Europe and the mother church in Rome. There were fewer such dedications in the centuries after the Norman Conquest, but this development, Adan Jones intriguingly suggests, might indicate how England was becoming a less 'marginal' part of the Christian world, and more confident about its place within it.

Attempts by the 'centre', particularly the Roman papacy, to impose its authority and norms on peripheral territories usually relied on the co-operation of locally based agents, who often possessed their own priorities and agendas. Contrary to received wisdom, geographically distant territories were not necessarily resistant to new initiatives from the centre. The medieval church in Iceland, on the fringes of the Scandinavian world, and thus in Roman terms a periphery-within-a-periphery, has usually been seen by historians as a de facto independent entity, and one which was two centuries or so late in adopting the reforms of Gregory VII (1073–85). Davide Salmoiraghi provocatively argues, however, that Gizurr Ísleifsson, bishop of Skálholt between 1082 and 1118, was a remarkably effective agent of Gregorian reform in his diocese, dedicating his new cathedral to St Peter as a symbol of loyalty to far-off Rome. In one respect at least, however, Bishop Gizurr – married with six children – was hardly a model Gregorian. It would have been culturally and politically unthinkable for an early medieval Icelandic chieftain – which Gizurr was – to remain single and celibate. This is one example of a theme identified by several of the contributors to this volume: the periphery as a place for creative adaptation of universal norms to local needs and circumstances, and of periodic experiment and innovation.

Shaun Church, for example, draws on archaeological evidence in an ambitious attempt to reconstruct experiences of worship on the edges of the Roman empire in the fourth and fifth centuries, his analysis focusing on sites in the Egyptian western desert, on the border with Persia, and at the frontiers on the Danube and in northern England. He finds that the basilica form of ecclesiastical building, specified by Constantine for churches in Rome and the Holy Land, was widely and conscientiously adopted even on the outer fringes of the empire. But at the same time spatial designs were adapted in flexible and inventive ways to serve practical needs and reflect local cultural contexts.

The frontier as a place of creative institutional initiative features too in Jonathan Jarrett's detailed exploration of the region around Manresa in tenth-century Catalonia, on the boundary between Christianity and Iberian Islam. Sponsorship of settlement and provision of pastoral care in such contexts is conventionally attributed to covetous warlords and adventurous peasantry, with assistance from monastic churches. Jarrett, however, identifies a crucial role played by the secular collegiate church of Santa Maria, in a pattern displaying some similarities to, though also important differences from, the minster system operating in parts of Anglo-Saxon England. The frequently improvisational character of 'peripheral' Christianity stands in contrast to clichés about backwardness and stubborn resistance to change. This is seen too, in a very different context, in Daniel Inman's thoughtful account of intellectual culture in mid-eighteenth-century New England, a periphery of imperial Britain. Despite, or perhaps because of, colonial America's religious pluralism, many of its episcopal clergymen were precocious proponents of Enlightenment theology and philosophy, and active participants in an Anglican 'republic of letters'.

A conceptual difficulty with the terminology of 'periphery' is that it implicitly adopts the perspective of external authority, for whom the periphery was frequently conceived of as a challenge or problem, rather than of the people who actually lived in the places in question. It is incumbent upon us, as far as we can, to restore the agency of the periphery, and to understand the ways in which its inhabitants represented themselves, and identified and advanced their own communal and individual interests. Teodora Popovici, in her prize-winning article, explores this for the Catholic community of fourteenth- and fifteenth-century Transylvania, on the eastern edge of Latin Christendom. Her study focuses on indulgence requests directed to the papal chancery, a quintessential form of communication between centre and periphery in the late medieval church. In pursuit of the benefits such indulgences offered, petitioners (who were, in reality, often wealthy and powerful people) instrumentalized their own putative marginality, not in terms of physical distance from Rome, but by portraying themselves as vulnerable *fideles*, surrounded by 'schismatics' (Orthodox Christians), and increasingly at the mercy of Ottoman Turks.

As with medieval Transylvania, Christianity's – and particularly Catholicism's – historic margins and peripheries often turn out to be borders and boundaries, zones of exploratory encounter with a variety of perplexing 'others'. Such margins could be social and existential, as well as, or rather than, geographically outlying. Dirceu Marroquim's illuminating article contextualizes the life-story of a German Franciscan friar, Casimiro Brochtrup, who at the end of the nineteenth century emigrated as a missionary to Brazil. He initially worked in the rural hinterlands, but shifted his focus to working-class districts of the city of Recife, principally because the inhabitants there were increasingly susceptible to the blandishments of preachers belonging to the *nova-seita* ('new sect') of Pentecostalist Protestantism. Marroquim shows how this ministry to the marginalized and disadvantaged was entangled with the agenda of local political powerbrokers, but also how it anticipated the concerns of later liberation theology.

In perceived peripheral settings, relationships between self-identifying true Christians and supposedly deviant 'others' were often, but not always, contentious and confrontational. In his article on late seventh-century Wessex, Aloysius Atkinson persuasively argues that the conventional picture of unremitting hostility in this period, between Christians of native British descent and English churchmen who regarded the Britons as heretics, is misconceived, at least for southwestern Britain. Here, interactions between the churches remained surprisingly fraternal into the early eighth century, albeit the persistent English appeal to Roman endorsement and authority had an effect of marginalizing the British spiritually, a parallel to their increasing confinement to the island's geographical extremities. In Carolingian annals of the eighth and ninth centuries, as Robert Evans demonstrates in his prize-winning article, peoples from the geographical margins of Christian Europe might even be valorized rather than villainized, and held up as a mirror to Frankish society. Such texts regularly recounted improving episodes involving Greeks, Englishmen, Bulgars and Frisians, in which these stranger peoples were hailed as fellow Christians, and the periphery identified as a source of exemplary moral counsel.

Beyond the realms of rhetoric, actual relations between different ethnic and religious groups in peripheral settings can be difficult to reconstruct. Staying in the world of early medieval Europe, Lesley Abrams's article provides a compelling survey of patterns of conversion from paganism to Christianity within the Scandinavian diaspora during the so-called Viking Age, with a particular focus on England and Francia. Though the evidential problems are significant, and the voices of converts themselves almost entirely silent, Abrams identifies a 'striking creativity' on the part of ecclesiastics tasked with bringing

Northmen into the Christian fold. It is reflected in a flexible approach to the strict application of canon law, and, in the English case, in the survival of stone monuments mixing Christian and Norse mythological elements. These, Abrams suggests, may be not so much a sign of confused syncretism as of pagan narratives being purposively deployed to reinforce Christian truths.

'Accommodation' as part of a missionary or conversion strategy is a theme of several of the articles in this volume, again pointing us to margins and peripheries as places where Christian orthopraxis might prove particularly supple and imaginative. There were, of course, failures on this front. Tim Grass assiduously tracks the progress of Protestant reformation on the Isle of Man, from the late sixteenth to the late seventeenth century, and concludes that over the course of this period the island's religiously peripheral position was exacerbated rather than alleviated, principally due to a failure on the part of reformers to engage seriously with the Manx language. There were no published Manx translations of the Bible or Prayer Book in this period, and the religious formation of the laity and recruitment of suitable clergy was in consequence significantly hindered.

The travails of some Catholic clergymen in the same period are explored in John-Paul Ghobrial's absorbing article on French Capuchin missionaries operating in the seventeenth-century Ottoman empire, principally in territories corresponding to the modern states of Lebanon, Syria and Iraq. The mission they were engaged on might seem a clear instance of churchmen seeking to subordinate the periphery to the centre; its goal was to persuade a variety of Eastern Christians – Armenians, Copts, Jacobites, Nestorians and others – to acknowledge the supremacy of the papacy in Rome. Yet these representatives of an external and alien authority were usually, in Ghobrial's view, thoroughly 'rooted'. French Capuchins learned Arabic, co-operated with Ottoman officials, and often became closely integrated into the social and devotional lives of Eastern Christians, people who quite naturally did not regard themselves as in any way marginal. Indeed, the Capuchins in their letters made few references to conversion, and in practice made numerous accommodations to the social and religious cultures of the Middle East, not so much as a considered stratagem as out of pragmatic adaptation to the specific local contexts in which they lived and worked.

In a thought-provoking article dealing with another sphere of the Counter Reformation's evangelistic reach, Manning Chan takes a fresh look at perhaps the best-known case of accommodationism: the seventeenth- and early-eighteenth-century controversy over so-called 'Chinese Rites'. Jesuit missionaries, in the face of opposition from Dominican rivals, argued that Confucian patterns of ancestor veneration were civil ceremonies compatible with Christianity. Chan's account focuses on the writings in support of the Jesuit position produced by fourteen Chinese Catholic laypeople, another striking instance of the creative agency of the periphery. Her conclusion that both the missionaries and their Chinese allies failed to grasp the metaphysical meanings of Confucian ritual practice points, however, to some of the limitations of Christian peripheries as places of successful spiritual experiment.

A centre-periphery model of Christian cultural interaction needs to take account of the fact that the 'peripheries' sometimes spoke to each other. Two of the articles in this volume, by Anastasia Stylianou and Alex Beeton, address themselves to encounters in the sixteenth and seventeenth centuries between Greek Orthodox clergymen and representatives of the Church of England, two groups inclined to regard each other as exotic and geographically remote, but with a potential common interest in resisting the universalist aspirations of Rome. Beeton's informative study of the visit of two Orthodox priests to England in the late 1640s, and his chronicling of the warmth of welcome they received, suggests the ways in which marginal figures could become optimistic repositories of (probably unrealistic) hopes in a confessionally divided Europe. Stylianou's expansive account of the interest in England taken by two leading 'Venetian Greeks' explains how what might perhaps have ended as merely fleeting and contingent political contacts produced significant afterlives in print, promoting an enduring awareness, replete with potential, of religious difference at the opposing cartographic margins of European Christendom.

Marginality, in religion as in other spheres of life, can represent not only a geographical designation, but a social ascription, a lived experience and an unsettling state of mind. The sociological terminology around 'marginalization' is of relatively recent origins: the *Oxford English Dictionary*'s earliest example of, in this sense, 'to marginalize' dates only from 1970.[3] But the impulse itself is undoubtedly much older. In medieval Europe, as Catherine Rider demonstrates in her

[3] See 'Marginalize, verb', *OED*, online at: <https://www.oed.com/dictionary/marginalize_v?tab=meaning_and_use#38067264>, accessed 15 October 2024.

sensitive discussion of a still inadequately researched historical topic, a married couple's failure to reproduce was frequently a cause of spiritual disparagement and social stigma, a failing symptomatic of divine displeasure. Yet in some fourteenth- and fifteenth-century English sources dealing with the apparent infertility of Joachim and Anne, the later-life parents of the Virgin Mary, Rider finds more nuanced attitudes, and hints of a genuine pastoral concern about the distress caused to people by reproductive disorders.

The vicissitudes of another undoubtedly marginalized group are closely examined by Kateryna Budz, an early career scholar from Ukraine, whose research in the UK the Ecclesiastical History Society has been delighted to co-sponsor. Her article deals with priests of the underground Ukrainian Greek Catholic Church, who after 1946 defied orders from the Soviet authorities to 'reunite' with the Russian Orthodox. It is a story of remarkable resilience, fortitude and improvisation: Greek Catholic priests continued to serve clandestine congregations, while working in secular occupations and skilfully exploiting the deficiencies of the Soviet bureaucratic system. Fears about marginalization within an evolving ecclesiastical system feature too in Martin Wellings's intricate account of the mid-nineteenth-century Reform crisis within the Wesleyan Oxford Circuit, in the course of which rival parties tried hard to portray themselves as central to the doctrinal and institutional structure of Methodism, and their opponents as peripheral to it.

A strictly ecclesiastical marginality is not necessarily to be equated with impotence or obscurity. Emily Bailey's lively article focuses on the remarkable figure of Hannah Whitall Smith, a prolific writer, preacher and correspondent in the British and American Holiness movement of the later nineteenth century. Smith occupied no stable denominational position, but Bailey argues that her career suggests how margins and peripheries provide 'a fertile context for understanding religious dialogue, authority, innovation, and acceptance.' In more recent times, theologically liberal and socially progressive attitudes have often seemed distinctly marginal to mainstream evangelicalism. But this scarcely renders such voices unproductive or irrelevant. Our understanding of the 'evangelical left' in one Asian context is significantly enhanced by Dongjun Seo's article on the evangelical network formed in the 1980s at Seoul National University, in reaction to South Korea's authoritarian military regime. Although ultimately unable to transform the predominantly quietist and conservative tone of Korean evangelicalism, the movement in its heyday represented a vigorous and resourceful effort to redefine religion 'from the margins'.

Historians, of course, do not stand outside the parameters of centrality and marginality they purport to chronicle. Certain themes, topics and sources have been, and sometimes continue to be, marginalized within the study of religious history itself. One of these, so Lydia Fisher argues in her carefully researched contribution, is the profusion of fragments of stained glass to be found in English medieval parish churches. Though often neglected in favour of the handful of surviving complete sequences, or the elaborate schema located in cathedrals, such shards of evidence have the potential to tell us much about both collective religious culture and individual piety at the parish level. Another topic of relative historiographical neglect, as well as of cool condescension within mainstream churches, and frank bemusement from the secular world, is covered in Mary Heimann's fascinating article on the smuggling of Bibles into Eastern Bloc countries during the decades of the Cold War. Heimann shows how an initially small-scale and amateurish activity developed into an extensive, sophisticated and well-funded covert operation, comparable to, and in some ways more effective than, the work of the Western intelligence agencies. This allegedly 'peripheral' activity, Heimann argues, substantially helped to form the worldview of evangelical Christianity, and to shape the contemporary culture wars in which such Christians often feel themselves to be on the losing side.

The principal thread running through the highly diverse subject matters, chronologies and methodologies represented in this volume is the conviction that margins and peripheries deserve to be explored: not out of 'completism', or even a sense of moral responsibility towards the historically marginalized, but because their elucidation significantly enhances our understanding of the history of Christianity as a whole. The past, like a statue or painting, is always best viewed from a variety of angles, and the 'perspective of the periphery' usually has the potential to make us look more closely at, and think more carefully about, what we are seeing. My own contribution to the volume argues that a study of the British Reformations from the vantage point of Britain's off-shore islands can help move us away from 'diffusionist' models of religious change, and to appreciate more keenly the character of its locally negotiated reception, and the importance of its international dimensions.

In a speech to cardinals on the eve of his election in 2013, Pope Francis declared that 'the Church is called to come out of herself and go to the peripheries', explaining that he meant not just the geographical margins, but the 'existential peripheries' of pain, injustice, indifference and misery.[4] Historians might want to interject that the churches themselves have often been complicit in the construction and preservation of such peripheries, and arguably continue to be so. Nonetheless, it is an exhortation that scholars of religious history would be well advised to take to heart. As the articles in this volume ably demonstrate, Christianity has always been shaped, challenged, cheered and troubled by its margins and peripheries. They have proved to be founts of experiment, innovation and renewal; locations of encounter, conversion and resistance; and sites where meaning and worth have been negotiated and defined. Talk of 'cutting-edge' historical research has become a habitual scholarly cliché, but as these articles remind us, edges possess a persistent capacity to sharpen our analysis of the past.

Peter Marshall
University of Warwick
p.marshall@warwick.ac.uk

[4] Paul Philibert, 'When Not in Rome: Lessons from the Peripheries of the Church', *America: The Jesuit Review* (24 March 2014), online at: <https://www.americamagazi ne.org/issue/when-not-rome>, accessed 15 October 2024.

Experiencing Christian Sacred Space in the Roman Frontier Zones of the Fourth and Fifth Centuries

Shaun Church
Hampton Hill

This article argues that the spatial experiences created by the architectural features of Christian sacred spaces on the Roman frontiers of the fourth and fifth centuries were fundamental to how such spaces were perceived and engaged with. It suggests that the principles of spatial design established in Constantine's basilicas of Rome and the Holy Land influenced the experience of Christian worship, ritual and commemoration on the Roman frontiers. While these frontier Christian sacred spaces generally followed the architectural trends of Constantinian models, they also showed distinct local adaptations. This study highlights the important role of architectural spatial design in shaping religious experiences on the Roman frontiers, illustrating the dynamic relationship between architecture, worship and regional cultural contexts. It shows both continuity with Constantinian norms and evidence of adaptability and localized expressions of Christian sacred architecture on the Roman empire's peripheries.

INTRODUCTION

This article examines archaeological evidence to argue that Christian sacred spaces built along the Roman frontiers during the fourth and fifth centuries offered worshippers spatial experiences of worship, ritual and commemoration similar to those afforded by the Constantinian monumental churches of Rome and the Holy Land.[1] Previous

St Francis de Sales, Hampton Hill, Middlesex. E-mail: shaundchurch@yahoo.com.
This article stems from research conducted during my Master's dissertation in Roman Frontier Studies. I extend my gratitude to Dr Rob Collins and Dr Mark Jackson (The School of History, Classics and Archaeology, Newcastle University) for their guidance and encouragement to pursue publication. I also thank Marta Alberti-Dunn for her invaluable assistance in shaping this article, Lorena Hitchens for feedback on early drafts, and Rachel Kendall-Daw for constructive suggestions on the post-peer review draft. Lastly, I appreciate the peer reviewers whose critiques greatly refined the article's core arguments.
[1] Although the terms 'ritual' and 'liturgy' both reference structured and symbolic actions, they are not synonymous. While ritual is diverse and flexible, liturgy has more formal and

Studies in Church History 61 (2025), 12–47 © The Author(s), 2025. Published by Cambridge University Press on behalf of the Ecclesiastical History Society.
doi:10.1017/stc.2024.29

research has focused on individual frontier sacred spaces from this period. A study of how their architecture influenced worshippers' spatial experiences and the extent to which these were shaped by metropolitan ecclesiastical centres remains a potentially impactful and largely unexplored area.

For this article, 'spatial experience' is defined as the way in which the architectural elements of churches – such as entrances, exits, processional routeways and screening – together with the creation of funerary or cemeterial churches and external baptisteries, were perceived and engaged with by those gathered for worship, ritual or commemoration. It argues that these architectural features were important factors in how these sacred spaces were experienced, and that these elements of the Constantinian church-building programme influenced Christian worship practices across the Roman empire, including its frontiers. Furthermore, it will show that while Christian sacred spaces in frontier regions generally conformed to Constantinian architectural trends, they were also subject to local adaptations, demonstrating an interplay between sacred architecture, worship practices and cultural contexts.

CHRISTIAN SACRED SPACE PRIOR TO CONSTANTINE

As the church detached itself from temple and synagogue worship, early Christian communities gathered for worship in domestic settings, most probably in the *triniculum* (dining room).[2] They also met in rooms above shops, in tenements, apartments above baths, or other commercial spaces, with no particular setting being dominant.[3]

---

communal connotations relating to public worship. For the purposes of this article, the term 'liturgy' will be used solely in reference to the eucharistic liturgy. For a helpful discussion on the similarities and differences between ritual and liturgy, see 'Ritual vs. Liturgy: Understanding the Differences in Religious Practices', *LoreCat(alog)*, online at: <https://lore-cat.com/liturgy-vs-ritual/>, accessed 30 August 2024. This article will principally focus on spatial experience from the perspective of the lay worshipper, rather than of the celebrating clergy.

[2] Richard Krautheimer, *Early Christian and Byzantine Architecture*, 4th edn revised edition by Richard Krautheimer and Slobodan Ćurčić (New Haven, CT, 1986; first publ. 1965), 24; Michael White, *The Social Origins of Christian Architecture*, 1: *Building God's House in the Roman World. Architectural Adaptation Among Pagans, Jews and Christians* (Valley Forge, PA, 1990), 107.

[3] Jenn Cianca, *Sacred Ritual, Profane Space: The Roman House as Early Christian Meeting Place* (Montreal, 2018), 33.

Although these house churches were unrenovated rooms, much as they would have been in any private house, this did not negate a sacred connotation, and even though Christian worship spaces were materially unaltered from their day-to-day uses, they acquired temporary sacrality through ritual performance.[4]

Since the 1960s, the significance of a perceived intermediate architectural stage in the development of early Christian sacred space, believed to have emerged in the mid-third century, has been debated. This development, known as *domus ecclesiae* ('house of the church'), involved modifying domestic houses to accommodate evolving ritual practices.[5] The earliest known example was excavated in the 1930s at Dura-Europos (near modern-day Dayr al-Zawr in eastern Syria), a much-contested city in the border region between the Roman and Persian (Sassanian) empires, and dates to *c.*240, when a private residence was converted into a Christian assembly space, with a large meeting hall and a baptistery decorated with Christian murals.[6] However, the broader existence of the *domus ecclesiae* as a pre-Constantinian phenomenon is increasingly challenged. Critics argue that Dura-Europos was probably a unique local adaptation rather than a widespread trend.[7] Similarly, the *tituli*,[8] the local variation of the *domus ecclesiae* in Rome, purportedly renovated from private residences, lack solid literary or archaeological evidence from before the fourth century.[9] However, while debates continue around the evolution of Christian sacred spaces before Constantine (r. 306–37), this

---

[4] Ann Marie Yasin, *Saints and Church Spaces in the Late Antique Mediterranean: Architecture, Cult, and Community* (Cambridge, 2009), 14, 44; Cianca, *Sacred Ritual, Profane Space*, 135, 170.

[5] For the debate around the architectural category *domus ecclesiae*, see Krautheimer, *Early Christian and Byzantine Architecture*, 26–9; White, *Social Origins of Christian Architecture*, 20–5; Kim Bowes, 'Early Christian Archaeology: A State of the Field', *Religious Compass* 2 (2008), 576–617, at 579–82; Kristina Sessa, '*Domus Ecclesiae*: Rethinking a Category of Ante-Pacem Christian Space', *Journal of Theological Studies* 60 (2009), 90–108.

[6] For a detailed case study of the *domus ecclesiae* at Dura Europos, see Cianca, *Sacred Ritual, Profane Space*, 91–104.

[7] Sessa, '*Domus Ecclesiae*', 108.

[8] The term *tituli* originates from the marble slab inscribed with the property owner's name, establishing the claim to ownership. For a brief modern discussion of the titular churches, see Charles Stewart, 'Churches', in David Pettigrew, William Caraher and Thomas Davis, eds, *The Oxford Handbook of Early Christian Archaeology* (Oxford, 2019), 128–46, at 131–3.

[9] Sessa, '*Domus Ecclesiae*', 93–4, 106–8; compare also Bowes, 'Early Christian Archaeology', 580–1.

article focuses on the development of purpose-built Christian sacred spaces in the fourth and fifth centuries.

THE CONSTANTINIAN CHURCH-BUILDING PROGRAMME

In 313, the co-emperors Constantine and Licinius issued the Edict of Milan, legalizing Christianity. Christians were given the freedom to practise their faith openly without the threat of persecution, and Christianity was afforded the same legal status as other religions throughout the empire. This edict signalled the beginning of the so-called 'peace of the Church', a new era of church polity.[10] Under Constantine's reign, the church's position and organization became closely associated with the emperor's authority.[11] Constantine encouraged bishops to restore older churches and construct new ones; at the same time, he initiated a church-building programme. Although Constantine initially ruled only the West, upon gaining control of the East in 323, he urged Eastern bishops to undertake similar efforts, with materials to be supplied through the provincial governments.[12]

Constantine chose the basilica as the primary architectural form for his new churches, repurposing a structure rooted in secular Roman architecture to suit legalized Christianity. The basilica had undergone centuries of secular development, adopting various functions and architectural types, including as extensions to Roman *fora* and other public buildings, as places for commerce and the administration of justice, and as audience halls in imperial palace complexes.[13] The reasons for its selection are widely debated, but key theories include: the need for an architectural form untainted by the traditional temple architecture of the Greco-Roman world and Constantine's desire to draw upon the architecture of the imperial court (Ward Perkins); the basilicas' suitability to serve as 'meeting halls for congregations … or meeting halls for burial and funeral rites' and as 'audience halls of the Lord' (Krautheimer); their large, well-lit spaces, capable of extension and with a sense of movement along the longitudinal axis toward the

---

[10] Noel Lenski, 'The Significance of the Edict of Milan', in Edward Siecienski, ed., *Constantine: Religious Faith and Imperial Policy* (London, 2019), 27–56, at 27–9.
[11] Krautheimer, *Early Christian and Byzantine Architecture*, 39.
[12] Eusebius, *Vita Constantini* 2.4, 46.3; ET: Eusebius, *Life of Constantine*, transl. and commentary Averil Cameron and Stuart Hall (Oxford, 1999), 111.
[13] John Ward-Perkins, 'Constantine and the Origins of the Christian Basilica', *Papers of the British School at Rome* 22 (1954), 69–90, at 69–78.

apse, were well-suited for processions (Armstrong); the way in which basilicas (specifically the Lateran) 'thematized vision and (in)visibility' and highlighted such themes as magnificence, exclusiveness and power, highlighting the lordship of Christ (Dale); and that basilicas conveyed '*royal* splendor rather than *imperial* ideology' (Stewart).[14]

Constantinian church ritual required significant 'concerted movement' by its participants.[15] The multi-aisled basilica was well-suited for processions within the eucharistic liturgy. Even in frontier areas with smaller Christian communities, such processions were probably an important ritual experience. Processions were more than a practical means of movement from one place to another. They also created an atmosphere of celebration and solemnity for both participants and observers.[16] Literary evidence of processions within the liturgy is found in the writings of the late-fourth-century pilgrim Egeria, who described the liturgies she witnessed in the Holy Sepulchre and elsewhere in Jerusalem, in which worshippers moved in procession while singing psalms and hymns.[17] Egeria's account offers insights into how Christian sacred space was experienced ritually.

Archaeological evidence from the Lateran Basilica in Rome (often referred to in the scholarship as the Constantinian Basilica), probably the first built under Constantine's patronage, reveals how architectural elements were utilized to enhance spatial and ritual experience.[18] The *fastigium*, an ornate pediment adorned with silver statues of Christ and the apostles and supported by four bronze columns, separated the nave from the *presbyterium* (sanctuary).[19] The *solea*, a corridor-like fence, extended down the central aisle of the nave, forming a processional

---

[14] For the debate around the Christian basilica, see Ward-Perkins, 'Constantine and the Origins of the Christian Basilica', 69–90; Richard Krautheimer, 'The Constantinian Basilica', *Dumbarton Oak Papers* 21 (1967), 115–40; Gregory Armstrong, 'Constantine's Churches: Symbol and Structure', *Journal of the Society of Architectural Historians* 33 (1974), 5–16; Dale Kinney, 'The Church Basilica', *Acta ad archaeologiam et artium historiam pertinentia* 15 (2001), 115–35; Stewart, 'Churches', 134–41.

[15] Gregory Dix, *The Shape of the Liturgy*, 2nd edn (London, 1945; repr. London, 1993), 397.

[16] Ibid. 397, 448–9; Yasin, *Saints and Church Spaces*, 290.

[17] Anne McGowan and Paul Bradshaw, *The Pilgrimage of Egeria: A New Translation of the Itinerarium Egeriae with Introduction and Commentary* (Collegeville, MN, 2018), 68–101.

[18] Ward-Perkins, 'Constantine and the Origins of the Christian Basilica', 87.

[19] Krautheimer, *Early Christian and Byzantine Architecture*, 48. It is noteworthy that Eusebius, in his first-hand description of the new church at Tyre, speaks of the physical division of the church: 'In the middle he [Bishop Paulinus] placed the holy of holies – the altar – excluding the congregation from this area by surrounding it with wooden latticework

corridor for the entrance of the clergy.[20] Together, these elements influenced the spatial dynamics of experience within the basilica. The *fastigium* partially obscured the view of the apsidal *presbyterium* from the nave, drawing the laity's attention towards the *solea*. However, only those in the front rows, on either side of the *solea*, would have had a clear view of the procession, suggesting that those who secured a vantage point near it would have enjoyed a more participative experience in the liturgy, including a full view of the liturgical procession of the clergy, and a partial view of the altar and the ceremonies occurring beyond the *fastigium*.[21]

The basilica was to become the dominant form of church architecture across the empire, although Constantine's churches varied in style. Notable examples include old St Peter's in Rome, the Holy Sepulchre in Jerusalem and the Church of the Nativity in Bethlehem. These churches marked the emergence of architectural structures known as *martyria*, designed to commemorate significant biblical events and the veneration of the relics of the saints.[22] Innovations at St Peter's were the incorporation of an atrium and a transverse hall (transept) separating the nave and the apse, immediately in front of which was a *baldachino* (a free-standing canopy) over the altar, above the shrine believed to mark St Peter's grave.[23] St Peter's was laid out on a grander scale than the Lateran Basilica and was richly embellished.[24] Understanding the archaeology of Constantine's original Holy Sepulchre complex in Jerusalem is challenging, as much of it lies beneath or is incorporated into the present building. Constantine built a five-aisled basilica, the *Martyrion*, accessed via a triple-entranced atrium with a colonnaded courtyard to the east of the *Aedicule* (an ornate structure covering the tomb of Christ) and possibly a baptistery south of the church.[25] The Church of the Nativity in Bethlehem, like the

---

of marvelous artistry.' Eusebius, *The Church History* 10.4.44, transl. and commentary Paul Maier (Grand Rapids, MI, 2007), 317.

[20] Lex Bosman et al., 'Visualising the Constantinian Basilica', in Lex Bosman, Ian P. Haynes and Paolo Liverani, eds, *The Basilica of Saint John Lateran to 1600* (Cambridge, 2020), 134–67, at 156–62.

[21] Dale Kinney, 'The Church Basilica', 131–2.

[22] White, 'Architecture: The First Five Centuries', 735.

[23] Ibid. 728.

[24] Krautheimer, *Early Christian and Byzantine Architecture*, 57.

[25] McGowan and Bradshaw, *The Pilgrimage of Egeria*, 61–2; Justin Kelly, *The Church of the Holy Sepulchre in Text and Archaeology* (Oxford, 2019), 10–11, 109.

Holy Sepulchre, drew upon St Peter's basilical architecture, featuring five aisles and an atrium, but focused on an octagonal chamber memorializing Christ's birthplace, instead of an apse.[26]

Between the fourth and the sixth centuries, octagonal churches became popular for *martyria*, often incorporating the basilica's rectangular shape to create grand, domed churches.[27] This innovation distinguished the *martyria* from rectangular basilicas, such as the Lateran Basilica, which were associated with regular worship and assembly.[28] Another development was the construction of cemeterial basilicas outside the walls of Rome, including the Basilica Apostolorum (San Sebastiano) on the Via Appia, and the Basilica Sant'Agnese on the Via Nomentana.[29] These were associated with the Christian catacombs, whose origins can be traced to the early third century.[30] By the late fourth century, the catacombs were increasingly linked to the cult of martyrs, leading to a growing desire for burials *ad sanctos* ('near the saints').[31]

Monumental baptisteries also emerged in the fourth century, some as freestanding structures, and others as an intrinsic but distinct part of a church building. This separation emphasized the foundational nature of baptism as the entry point into the Church, and maintained the distinction between the baptized and those preparing for baptism (catechumens).[32] Typically, the baptismal font was placed at the centre of the baptistery, which could take a square, circular or polygonal shape, with a central, often octagonal, plan being common in many baptisteries in Italy and the East. The earliest documented central plan baptistery is the octagonal Lateran baptistery built next to the Lateran Basilica late in Constantine's reign.[33] Its octagonal design probably influenced that of the baptistery of St Giovanni alle fonti at St Thecla's Church, Milan, built *c.*350 by St Ambrose (*c.*339–97) and other baptisteries constructed in northern Italy in the fourth

---

[26] White, 'Architecture: The First Five Centuries', 730.

[27] Ibid.

[28] Ibid. 735–6.

[29] Vincenzo Fiocchi Nicolai, 'The Catacombs', in Pettigrew, Caraher and Davis, eds, *The Oxford Handbook of Early Christian Archaeology*, 67–84, at 73.

[30] Ibid. 67.

[31] Ibid. 75.

[32] Olof Brandt, 'Understanding the Structures of Early Christian Baptisteries', in David Hellholm et al., eds, *Ablution, Initiation, and Baptism: Late Antiquity, Early Judaism and Early Christianity* (Berlin and Boston, MA, 2011), 1587–610, at 1588.

[33] Ibid. 1592–3.

and fifth centuries.[34] The significance of the octagonal design is debated: traditionally, the number eight symbolized the renewal and resurrection, new beginnings and rebirth associated with baptism, but the popularity of octagonal halls in the fourth century suggests that caution is necessary in assuming a purely theological motivation.[35]

Constantine's church-building programme was marked by experimentation and creativity, producing diverse architectural forms, including multi-aisled basilicas, with or without apses, ambulatories and atria; centrally planned churches; and polygonal structures like *martyria* and baptisteries. Constantinian church architecture established a wide variety of church designs, and it was only in the fifth century that more stable regional norms and distinct building types began to emerge. Consequently, it is unsurprising that a significant degree of diversity and innovation can be also observed in the Christian sacred spaces of the frontier regions alongside continuity with and reinterpretation of those of Rome and the Holy Land. The case studies that follow will examine the implications of how these trends influenced the spatial experiences of sacred spaces on the Roman frontiers.

CASE STUDIES

Methodology

Four case studies have been selected from frontier sites: Kellis, in Egypt's Dakhleh Oasis; Nisibis, near the border with the Persian empire; Novae, on the Danube frontier; and Vindolanda, on the northern frontier of Britain (Figure 1). These sites were chosen due to the presence of archaeological evidence of two or more Christian sacred spaces from the fourth or fifth centuries, and the availability of modern archaeological research associated with recent excavation of the sites. An additional incentive for selecting these sites is their archaeological complexity, which makes them fascinating and compelling research material. The lack of comprehensive modern archaeological research on Christian sacred spaces on other frontiers, such as the Rhine and Roman North Africa, limited the range and number of suitable case studies. However, the selected sites offer a robust

---

[34] Ibid. 1593.
[35] Ibid. 1601–2.

19

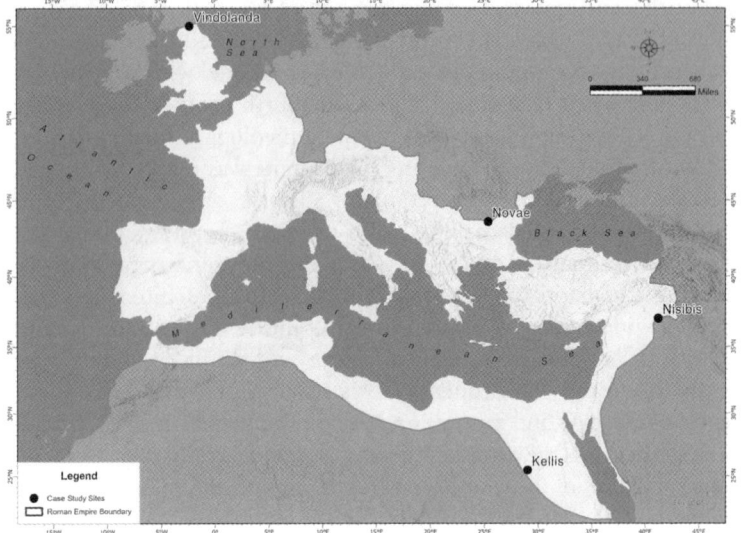

Figure 1. Map of Roman Empire in the Fourth Century CE, showing the proximate locations of the four case study sites. Figure design: Dr. Ayoub Lahlouh, Abdelmalek Essaâdi University, Tetouan, Morocco.

dataset for investigating the spatial experience of Christian practice and worship on the Roman frontiers during this period.

Case Study 1: Kellis, The Dakhleh Oasis, Egypt

The Dakhleh Oasis, one of seven in Egypt's Western Desert, was perceived as a 'border-like' environment in the fourth century despite not being a formal Roman frontier.[36] Seven churches in the Dakhleh Oasis are securely dated to the fourth century, with two more tentatively so.[37] Kellis (modern-day Ismant el-Kharab) was chosen as a case

[36] Anna Boozer, 'Frontiers and Borderlands in Imperial Perspectives: Exploring Rome's Egyptian Frontier', *American Journal of Archaeology* 117 (2013), 275–92; Paul N. Kucera, 'An Oasis Border in the Fourth Century CE: The Evidence from Dakhleh', in Ashten Warfe et al., eds, *Dust, Demons and Pots: Studies in Honour of Colin A. Hope* (Leuven, 2020), 425–36, at 434.

[37] Gillian Bowen, 'Christianity in Dakhleh Oasis: An Archaeological Overview', in eadem and Colin Hope, eds, *The Oasis Papers, 9: A Tribute to Anthony J. Mills after 40 Years of Research in Dakhleh Oasis. Proceedings of the Ninth International Conference of the Dakhleh Oasis Project* (Oxford, 2019), 367–80, at 367.

study due to the early date of its churches and the proximity and interrelationship between its small and large east churches.[38] Furthermore, the West Church Complex, a funerary church, offers a fascinating insight into how Christian sacred space was possibly used for the commemoration of the dead. There is no known literary or archaeological evidence for Christianity in the oasis much before the fourth century, when a robust Christian community is attested at Kellis. In addition to the surviving archaeology, textual sources, including fragments of a liturgical codex, papyrus and wooden boards bearing Christian prayers, epistles, personal letters and references to various bishops and priests, confirm the presence of a Christian community at Kellis by the early fourth century.[39]

The Small East Church (20 m x 5.5 m) (Figures 2 and 3) consists of two rooms, with the church to the south (Room 1) and an adjoining room (Room 2) to the north.[40] Ceramic and numismatic evidence suggests a *terminus post quem* of 306–12 for the building's modification.[41] Room 1 was transformed from a simple room lined with brick benches into a church, probably serving a public function before its adaptation. The excavators conclude that it may have initially been a *domus ecclesiae* that evolved over time to meet the community's needs.[42]

The main alteration involved the construction of a raised sanctuary with an apse and vaulted side chambers (*pastophoria*) for storage.[43] Access to the church was through Room 2, with a double door probably serving as the clergy's processional route, while the congregation probably used the western door.[44] The rapid conversion of the building, including the creation of a nave and distinct sanctuary within

---

[38] Ibid. 378.

[39] Gillian Bowen, 'The Christian Monuments of Kellis: Churches and Cemeteries', in Colin Hope and eadem, eds, *The Excavations at Ismant Al-Kharab*, 2: *The Christian Monuments of Kellis: The Churches and Cemeteries* (Oxford, 2024), 414–8. There is literary evidence for the presence of a Manichean community at Kellis. As there is no evidence to suggest a connection between the three Kellis churches, this community is not discussed here. It is, however, possible that members of the Manichean community were buried in the Christian cemeteries of Kellis: see Bowen, 'The Christian Monuments of Kellis', 419.

[40] Gillian Bowen, 'The Small East Church at Ismant el-Kharab', in eadem and Colin Hope, eds, *The Oasis Papers*, 3: *Proceedings of the Third International Conference of the Dakhleh Oasis Project* (Oxford, 2003), 153–65, at 154.

[41] Gillian Bowen, 'The Churches', in Colin Hope and eadem, eds, *Kellis: A Roman-Period Village in Egypt's Dakhleh Oasis* (Cambridge, 2022), 269–88, at 274.

[42] Bowen, 'Kellis: A Roman Village', 163–4.

[43] Bowen, 'Small East Church', 158–9; Bowen, 'The Churches', 271.

[44] Bowen, 'The Churches', 273.

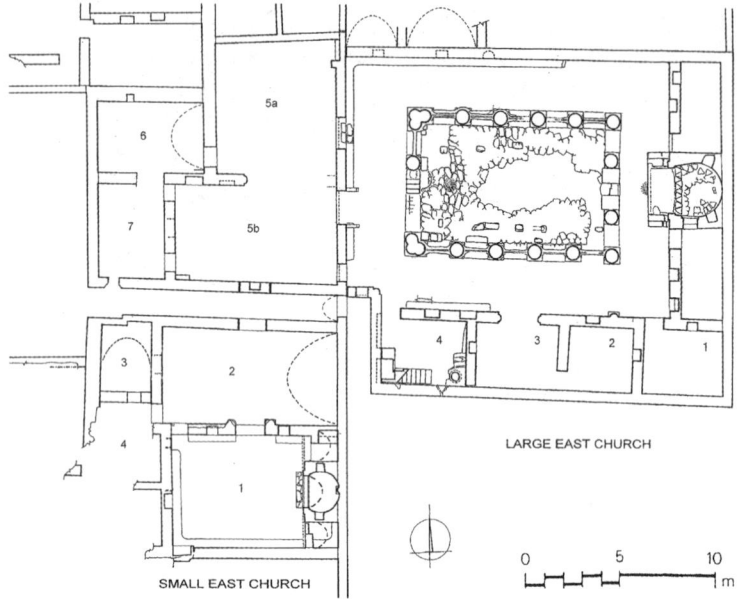

Figure 2. Kellis, Plan showing the relation of the Large East Church to the Small East Church; from Gillian Bowen, 'The Christian Monuments of Kellis', 66 (figure II.1). Copyright: Colin A. Hope and Dakhleh Oasis Project. Drawings: J. Knudstead, J. Dobrowolski and B. Rowney, modified by B. Parr.

an apsidal area, probably indicates a deliberate effort to create a more distinctive space for the celebration of the eucharistic liturgy. Such enhancements would have allowed for a visually richer spatial experience of worship beyond what the simpler space of a *domus ecclesiae* could offer. The transition of the Small East Church from a *domus ecclesiae* to a more formal ecclesiastical structure illustrates an early intentional enhancement of worship space. This transition, marked by the introduction of a raised sanctuary and defined processional routes, reflects a sophisticated approach to spatial organization designed to create a more immersive and orderly environment for worship.

The intention to enhance the spatial experience is even more evident in the construction of the Large East Church (20 m x 17 m) (Figures 2 and 4). Numismatic evidence suggests this purpose-built basilica, the earliest known in Egypt, was founded before Constantine died

Figure 3. Kellis, Room 1 of the Small East Church: the nave, following its conversion for Christian worship, looking east; in Gillian Bowen, 'The Christian Monuments of Kellis', 17 (plate I.2). Copyright: Colin A. Hope and Dakhleh Oasis Project. Photo: Colin A. Hope.

in 337.[45] The church has three doors – two double and one single – and the central doors probably served as the clergy's processional route.[46]

The Large East Church features a four-sided ambulatory defined by a four-sided mudbrick colonnade. While Egyptian churches followed the same basic ground plan as three or five-aisled basilicas elsewhere, they also incorporated a complete ambulatory. This ambulatory, formed by lateral aisles joined to transverse aisles, created a distinctive walkway encircling the nave.[47] Ambulatories are a recognized feature of the traditional Roman *basilica forensic*, or a forum-style basilica, a form that appears to have been adopted in church construction in several parts of Egypt.[48]

---

[45] Gillian Bowen proposes a *terminus post quem* of 313–31: see Bowen, 'The Christian Monuments of Kellis', 138–40.

[46] Ibid. 177.

[47] Peter Grossmann, 'Early Christian Architecture in Egypt', in Roger Bagnell, ed., *Egypt in the Byzantine World 300–700* (Cambridge, 2007), 103–36, at 104.

[48] Ibid. 104–15. Whilst highlighting this retention of an earlier architectural tradition in parts of Egypt, Grossman also recognizes that comparison with other parts of the empire is challenging, as the abandonment of the transverse aisles in the construction of churches in the rest of the empire may have occurred at an earlier date, but for which archaeological evidence is now scant.

Figure 4. The Large East Church: the nave and north aisle, looking south-west; from Gillian Bowen, 'The Christian Monuments of Kellis', 84 (plate II.27). Copyright: Colin A Hope and Dakhleh Oasis Project. Photo: Colin A. Hope.

The church was accessed via a short flight of steps leading down to the return aisle, a feature that may have held liturgical significance (perhaps related to processions) by the fourth century.[49] Mudbrick bases and gouges in the columns suggest that wooden screens, at least one metre high, partitioned the lateral ambulatory aisles and the northern section of the return aisle (Figure 4).[50] These screens predate the previously known earliest examples from the Eastern empire and North Africa by 125 years.[51] There is no substantial evidence that fourth-century congregations were confined to the lateral aisles, suggesting that these screens perhaps served a decorative purpose, rather than dividing the room.[52] A

[49] Bowen, 'The Churches', 275–6.
[50] Ibid. 276.
[51] Urs Peschlow, 'Dividing Interior Space in Early Byzantine Churches: The Barriers between the Nave and Aisles', in Sharon Gerstel, ed., *Thresholds of the Sacred: Architectural, Art Historical, Liturgical and Theological Perspectives on Religious Screens, East and West* (Washington, DC, 2006), 53–71; Bowen, 'The Churches', 276.
[52] Krautheimer, *Early Christian and Byzantine Architecture*, 486 n. 14; Robin Jensen, 'Recovering Ancient Ecclesiology: The Place of the Altar and the Orientation of Prayer in the Early Latin Church', *Worship* 89 (2015), 99–124, at 103–13.

screen of undetermined height once stood across the apse's entrance, identifiable now only by its emplacement. Like the *fastigium* of the Lateran Basilica in Rome, it potentially restricted the congregation's view of the sanctuary and, consequently, their experience of the eucharistic action.[53] The screening in the Large East Church was clearly an intentional and significant factor of its design. The division of space created by this screening, aesthetic or otherwise, will inevitably have restricted access and sightlines and, consequentially, influenced the spatial experience of worship. Screening might have created a sense of mystery within the eucharistic liturgy, but it might equally have created a sense of spatial exclusion or detachment for the laity in the nave.

An *ambo* or chancel, a raised platform for reading and preaching, stands in front of the main doorway, built against the western colonnade's single column. Although only an outline remains, a semicircular component of the *ambo* that projected into the nave suggests this was originally an elaborate structure (Figure 5).[54] Oriented towards the nave, this feature would have enhanced the spatial experience of the laity by making the proclamation of Scripture and preaching more directly accessible and audible to those assembled in the nave.[55] The addition of an *ambo* suggests an attempt to make aspects of the eucharistic liturgy more accessible, which might be interpreted as reflecting a balance between maintaining sacred boundaries and ensuring a level of inclusivity in worship.

A pair of mudbrick pedestals at the eastern end of the nave, covered with oil residue and positioned directly in front of the *bema* (a raised platform associated with the sanctuary area), suggests a ceremonial function, though their precise purpose is uncertain.[56] These pedestals may have served as tables for the laity's offerings to be selected and blessed for the eucharist.[57] Given the central location of these pedestals at the nave's eastern end, directly in front of the *bema*, they possibly played a role in the laity's experience of the eucharistic liturgy. We know regrettably little about the laity's expectations regarding their ability or inability to view the ritual performed in the sanctuary, but if

[53]   Elizabeth Bolman, 'Veiling Sanctity in Christian Egypt: Visual and Spatial Solutions', in Gerstel, ed, *Thresholds of the Sacred*, 73–104, at 760.

[54]   Bowen, 'The Churches', 276.

[55]   Bowen, *The Christian Monuments of Kellis*, 177.

[56]   Ibid. 87, 177.

[57]   Peter Grossman, 'Typological Considerations on the Large East Church at Ismant el-Kharab', in Hope and Bowen, eds, *Dakhleh Oasis Project*, 153–6, at 153 n. 2.

Figure 5. Kellis, The Large East Church: column 2A and the chancel (ambo); from Gillian Bowen, 'The Christian Monuments of Kellis', 85 (plate II.29). Copyright: Colin A. Hope and Dakhleh Oasis Project. Photo: Colin A. Hope.

the screen obstructed the laity's view of the sanctuary, these pedestals may have been one of the few significant points for the laity's inter-action with the liturgical action of the eucharist, bridging the division, both real and perceived, between the laity and the sanctuary.

The eastern transverse aisle, combined with the placement of two stone steps on either side of the platform, influenced the processional approach to the apse. Instead of accessing the apse from the front, it was approached via these steps on either side of a platform projecting into the transverse aisle. Access from the west end remained possible through the eastern end of the nave, which lacked a screen. However, the placement of these steps suggests the possibility that the lateral and transverse aisles forming the ambulatory might have served a processional function. The incorporation of an ambulatory at Kellis, as well as elsewhere in the Dakhleh Oasis and other parts of Egypt, suggests the possibility of a localized adaptation of the processional liturgy associated with the Constantinian basilicas.

Rooms 5a and 5b may have served as the church's *narthex*, or vestibule, where catechumens usually received instruction before baptism. Catechumens probably used the double-doored entrance from the courtyard, while the entrances in Room 5b may have been reserved for the clergy and the baptized.[58] The Large East Church appears to have incorporated specific areas, access points and routeways intended for different echelons of the community. Entrances appear to have been designated according to the ecclesial status of clergy, laity and catechumens. Entrances reserved for clergy will also have emphasized ecclesiastical hierarchy. How, where and when one entered a Christian sacred space had experiential implications for every worshipper. The design and positioning of entrances and the division of sacred space based on ecclesial status and ritual considerations were clearly as significant considerations at the frontiers as they were in major ecclesiastical centres. While individual reactions to this are challenging to discern or interpret, the very presence of distinct entrances probably impacted a person's sense of status within the community, creating a variety of spatial experiences of worship, not least those of inclusion or exclusion.

No evidence indicates the presence of a baptistery at Kellis or elsewhere in the Dakhleh and Kharga Oases. Although bishops had traditionally reserved the celebration of baptism to themselves, from the fourth century onwards, there is evidence that priests increasingly conducted baptisms, leading to the construction of baptisteries in both rural and urban settings, albeit not usually as separate buildings.[59] Fourth-century wooden tablets from Kellis mention a bishop (*episkopos*), but it is unclear whether a bishop resided there.[60] Given the absence of unexcavated structures near the east churches that could have served as a baptistery and a complete lack of evidence for baptisteries throughout the villages and small settlements of the oases, it is more plausible that the bishop resided in Mothis

---

[58] Bowen, *The Christian Monuments of Kellis*, 177.
[59] Olof Brandt, 'Understanding the Structures of Early Christian Baptisteries', 1597–8.
[60] Roger Bagnall, *The Kellis Agricultural Account Book (P. Kell. IV Gr. 96)* (Oxford, 1997), 81.

(modern-day Mut al-Kharab) and that catechumens from Kellis and other Dakhleh settlements travelled there for baptism.[61] As the capital of the oasis during the fourth century, Mothis was an episcopal see and had at least one church serving its dependent villages and settlements.[62]

The mudbrick West Church Complex (7.4 m x 5.3 m), located on the edge of the settlement, comprises a church, a western outer room and six additional rooms integrated as a unit (Figure 6). Numismatic evidence indicates that the church's construction dates to the mid-fourth century, with a possible *terminus post quem* before 340.[63]

The sanctuary area features an apse flanked by two *pastophoria*. The *bema*, positioned at the front of the nave and in front of the centre of the apse, was accessed from the west by two steps, with additional steps on either side of the *bema* leading to the sanctuary. There is no evidence that the sanctuary was screened.[64] In the nave, two pit graves, probably fourth century, were discovered near the sanctuary, suggesting that the church served a funerary purpose.[65] This theory is supported by the presence of a small Christian cemetery with nine graves within an enclosure to the east.[66] All the graves were simple pit burials aligned with Christian east-west orientation, with the head aligned to the east.[67] The cemetery enclosure also incorporated two tombs in classical style, with one, West Tomb One, reused for eleven secondary burials, all oriented in the Christian east-west alignment. This reuse suggests that the Christian community at Kellis regarded these individuals as Christians, possibly even attributing to them a particular sanctity. Consequently, burial in proximity to these

---

[61] Gillian Bowen, Personal communication by email, 25 August 2024.

[62] Gillian Bowen, 'Christianity at Mut al-Kharab (ancient Mothis), Dakhleh Oasis, Egypt', in Camilla Di Bianse-Dyson and Leonie Donovan, eds, *The Cultural Manifestations or Religious Experience: Studies in Honour of Boyo Ockinga* (Münster, 2017), 241–8, at 243.

[63] Bowen, *Christian Monuments of Kellis*, 138.

[64] Bowen, 'Fourth Century Churches', 77.

[65] Bowen, 'The Churches', 284.

[66] Bowen, *Christian Monuments of Kellis*, 305. In addition to the cemetery attached to the West Church Complex, a large cemetery (K2) has also been discovered at Kellis. Over 700 graves, predominantly simple pit graves but also a few small tombs, have been excavated. All the graves were consistent with Christian burial practice: see Gillian Bowen, 'Christian Burial Practices', in Hope and eadem, eds, *Kellis: A Roman-Period Village*, 343–66.

[67] Bowen, 'Fourth Century Churches', 78; eadem, 'Christian Burial Practices', 358–60. Christians were traditionally buried facing east due to the scriptural teaching that Christ's second coming would be from the east. Burial facing east meant that Christians would be ready to meet their saviour.

Figure 6. Kellis, The West Church Complex, looking south-east; from Gillian Bowen, 'The Christian Monuments of Kellis', 268 (plate III.1). Copyright: Colin A. Hope and Dakhleh Oasis Project. Photo: Colin A. Hope.

tombs may have been believed to confer an element of sanctity or protection.[68]

The graves in the West Church were identified as those of a male and an infant.[69] The only other known funerary church in the Dakhleh Oasis is at Trimithis (modern-day Amheida), also from the fourth century, which contained eight burials.[70] Understanding the spatial experiences of worshippers and mourners in this space is challenging because a specific Christian burial liturgy did not exist before the seventh or eighth centuries.[71] However, the presence of pit graves within the church and in the nearby cemetery enclosure suggests a community engaged in honouring their dead, possibly attributing special sanctity to this site.

The West Church Complex may have initially served as a private chapel for the celebration of the eucharistic liturgy, where intercessory

---

[68] Bowen, *Christian Monuments of Kellis*, 306.

[69] Ibid. 328.

[70] Ibid. 305.

[71] Alexandra Plesa, 'Religious Belief in Burial: Funerary Dress and Practice in Late Antique and Early Islamic Cemeteries at Matmar and Mostagedda (Late Fourth-Early Ninth Centuries CE)', *Ars Orientalis* 47 (2017), 18–42, at 34.

prayer for the dead would have been an element. It may have only later accommodated burials and memorial meals (*refrigeria*) associated with the dead.[72] Regardless of its precise functions, its existence as a funerary church, with its dual role as a place of worship and burial, reinforces the significance of Christian burial sites and the commemoration of the dead, paralleling the practices associated with cemeterial churches elsewhere in the empire, not least in the cemeterial churches above the Roman catacombs.

The churches of Kellis offer valuable insights into the spatial experience of early Christian worship, ritual and commemoration at this periphery of the Roman empire. The architectural evolution of these churches reveals a refinement of sacred space that shaped the experience of space and worship. The spatial developments observable in the Kellis churches provide insights into how early Christians in the Dakhleh Oasis adapted and refined their sacred spaces to enhance the experience of space, worship, ritual and commemoration. These appear to have been as significant on the empire's boundaries as in its metropolitan cities.

Case Study 2: Nisibis, Mesopotamia

Nisibis (modern-day Nusaybin in Turkey) was a key military and commercial hub on the Roman-Sassanian (Persian) border. Epigraphic evidence indicates the presence of Christians at Nisibis by the early third century.[73] Bishop Jacob (Mar Yaqub) of Nisibis is traditionally credited with building a cathedral between 313 and 320, but it is likely that his successor, Volagesos, built the cathedral discussed here *c.*359, on the site of Jacob's earlier church. The Byzantine monk and ascetical writer John Moschos (*c.*550–619) described the cathedral as having five doorways in a portico, suggesting a five-aisled structure with a courtyard.[74] Though excavation of the basilica is incomplete, and its precise date and full extent are unknown,

---

[72] Peter Grossman, 'Churches and Meeting Halls in Necropoleis and Crypts in Intramural Churches', in Elisabeth O'Connell, ed., *Egypt in the First Millennium AD – Perspectives from New Fieldwork* (Leuven, 2014), 93–123, at 93, 97; Bowen, *Christian Monuments of Kellis*, 306.

[73] Paul Russell, 'Nisibis as the Background to the Life of Ephrem the Syrian', *Hugoye: Journal of Syriac Studies* 8 (2011), 179–236, at 218.

[74] Elif Keser-Kayaalp and Nihat Erdoğan, 'The Cathedral Complex at Nisibis', *Anatolian Studies* 63 (2013), 137–54, at 140.

partial excavation has revealed the foundations of a five-aisled building approximately 90 m x 50 m, a genuinely monumental church given its early date (Figure 7).[75]

Despite uncertainties in its architectural details, it is clear that the cathedral was designed on a scale resembling that of the Constantinian basilicas in Rome and the Holy Land. Its five-aisled basilical hall would have provided an impressive experiential 'theatre' for both the participants and observers of the processional liturgies for which such a massive building was so well-suited. The cathedral's monumental scale suggests a well-established Christian community situated on a key route for both pilgrimage and trade. When Egeria visited Edessa, she wrote that she was within 'five staging posts' of Nisibis. During periods of peace, it is probable that large numbers of Christians from Sasanian Persia passed through the city.[76]

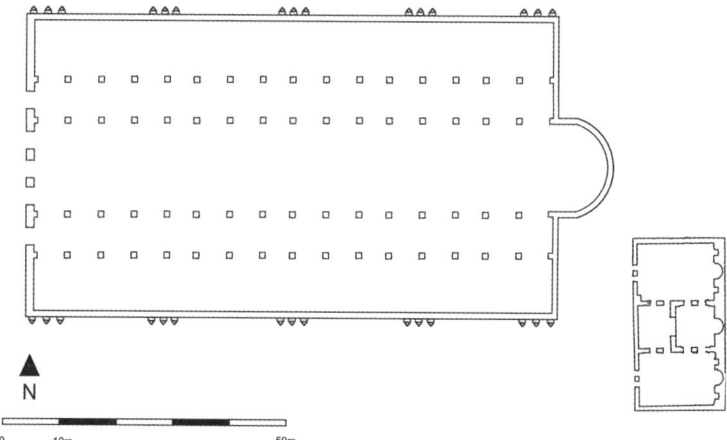

Figure 7. Nisibis, Reconstruction of the Cathedral as a five-aisled basilica and the Baptistery as a three-hall structure; from Elif Keser-Kayaalp and Nihat Erdoğan, 'The Cathedral Complex at Nisibis', 142 (figure 7). Copyright: Elif Keser-Kayaalp and Nihat Erdoğan. Plan credit: Elif Keser-Kayaalp.

[75] Ibid. 143.
[76] Egeria, *Itinerarium Egeriae* 20.12, in McGowan and Bradshaw, *The Pilgrimage of Egeria*, 144; Timothy Barnes, 'Constantine and the Christians of Persia', *The Journal of Roman Studies* 75 (1985), 126–36, at 131.

Today, although only the cathedral's foundations remain, the nearby so-called Church of St Jacob is contemporaneous with the basilica (Figures 8 and 9).[77] Originally a triple-hall building, it now comprises only the northern and central sections. An *in situ* inscription from 359 identifies this edifice as a baptistery.[78] The central section was probably the actual baptistery, with the northern and southern spaces serving as integrated spaces with direct access to the baptistery.[79] These areas may have been used for elements of the baptismal rites, such as the administering of the pre-baptismal oil of catechumens and the provision of a space for catechumens to disrobe before baptism. As with other baptisteries, the exact arrangement and function of each room remain uncertain.[80] Beneath the eastern part of the original central structure

Figure 8. Nisibis, the Western and Southern Facades of the standing of the Church of St Jacob (Mor Yakub); from Elif Keser-Kayaalp and Nihat Erdoğan, 'The Cathedral Complex at Nisibis', 143 (figure 8). Copyright: Elif Keser-Kayaalp and Nihat Erdoğan. Photograph credit: Elif Keser-Kayaalp.

[77] Keser-Kayaalp and Erdoğan, 'Cathedral Complex at Nisibis', 143.
[78] Ibid. 148.
[79] Lale Karataş and Murat Dal, 'A Proposal for the Restitution of the World's First Baptistry and University, Mor Yakup Church, Turkey', *Journal of World Architecture* 7 (2023), 72–82, at 75.
[80] Everett Ferguson, *Baptism in the Early Church: History, Theology, and Liturgy in the First Five Centuries* (Grand Rapids, MI, 2009), 820.

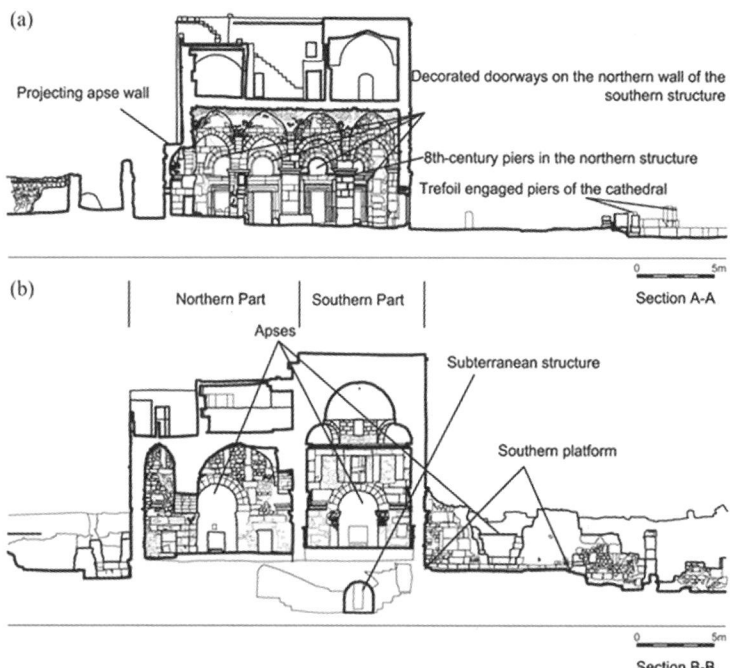

Figure 9. Nisibis, the Church of St Jacob (Baptistery): sections of the two storeys (the upper floor is a modern addition); from Elif Keser-Kayaalp and Nihat Erdoğan, 'The Cathedral Complex at Nisibis', 145 (figure 7). Copyright: Elif Keser-Kayaalp and Nihat Erdoğan. Plan credit: Elif Keser-Kayaalp.

(now the southern section) is a cistern-like crypt now containing Bishop Jacob's sarcophagus, possibly relocated here after the cathedral's destruction.[81] It has been proposed that catechumens may have descended into and ascended from this crypt during the baptismal ceremonies in a ritual representing the baptismal theology of dying and rising, and the womb of rebirth.[82]

An often-overlooked aspect of the baptismal ritual was the post-baptismal procession from the place of baptism to the basilica, where

---

[81] The exact date of the cathedral's destruction remains uncertain, with theories suggesting it may have been destroyed by the Persians in 573 or the early 800s, or as a result of the 717 earthquake: Keser-Kayaalp and Erdoğan, 'Cathedral Complex at Nisibis', 143.

[82] Keser-Kayaalp and Erdoğan, 'Cathedral Complex at Nisibis', 152; Ferguson, *Baptism in the Early Church*, 819.

the neophytes would for the first time join the congregation to partake in the eucharist. Before baptism, catechumens were excluded from the eucharistic liturgy, making their post-baptismal entry into the cathedral particularly significant. Egeria's account of the Easter vigil in Jerusalem vividly captures the power of this transitional moment, describing how the newly baptized were ceremoniously led by the bishop from the baptistery to the site of Christ's tomb in the Holy Sepulchre, prior to returning to the *martyrion* basilica to participate in the eucharist.[83] This processional movement was probably a key element of the post-baptismal ritual in Nisibis as well, reflecting how sacred space could be ritually utilized.[84] In what would have been the grand, candlelit, colonnaded basilica of Nisibis, the experience for the neophytes in white baptismal robes processing to receive the eucharist for the first time must have been equally powerful, highlighting the potential of monumental sacred space to enhance the experience of ritual.

The Christian sacred spaces at Nisibis reveal a connection between architectural design and spatial experience. The monumental basilica, with its expansive five-aisled layout, would have enhanced the ritual experience by creating a grand setting for processions. As in the Kellis Large East Church, this grandeur was probably both aesthetic and functional. However, unlike at Kellis or the Lateran Basilica in Rome, no record or archaeological evidence for the church's interior furnishings has been discovered which could shed light on how this vast space might have been further partitioned and decorated, limiting a further consideration of the possible impact of other elements of the architecture and decoration on the spatial experience of the basilica's interior. The baptistery, with its distinctive architectural features, illustrates the increasing importance given to baptismal ritual from the fourth century onward. The potential ritualistic use of the crypt demonstrates how physical spaces could symbolize important theological concepts. Both the basilica and the baptistery in Nisibis show how early Christian communities used architecture to enrich their expressions of worship and theology. These spatial elements transformed architecture into an active participant in the experience of sacred space, shaping and reflecting the community's experience of the sacred.

[83] Egeria, *Itinerarium Egeriae* 38.1–2 (McGowan and Bradshaw, *The Pilgrimage of Egeria*, 179).
[84] Richard Rutherford, 'Baptisteries in Ancient Sites and Rites', in Pettigrew, Caraher and Davis, eds, *The Oxford Handbook of Early Christian Archaeology*, 167–87, at 176.

Case Study 3: Novae, Moesia Secunda

The legionary fortress and late antique town of Novae, located near Svištov on the Danube in north-western Bulgaria, offers some of the earliest reliable evidence for Christianity's expansion along the Lower Danube, dating from the second half of the third century and the beginning of the fourth. Novae is believed to have been a site of persecution, with the martyrdom of St Luppos at Novae probably taking place as a result of the Diocletian edicts of 303–4.[85] The Byzantine historiographer Theophylact Simocatta (d. *c.*640) confirms that the commemoration of Luppos was important in late antique Novae. Simocatta recounts how Peter, the brother of Emperor Maurice (*r.* 582–602), was urged by the citizens of Novae to stay in the town for the celebration of the martyr's festival.[86]

Excavations at Novae have revealed four late-fourth- or fifth-century churches inside the town walls and one cemeterial church just outside them (Figure 10). Basilica One (25.5 m x 15 m), the earliest, is a single-apse, three-aisled church with a narthex.[87] Basilicas Two (26 m x 15.6 m) and Three (31 m x 15.6 m), constructed one on top of the other, are also single-apse, three-aisled churches with a narthex, the latter being the larger and later. Their similar architectural features suggest a construction date in the mid-fourth to early fifth century.[88] The spatial distribution of the basilicas around the town may imply a parochial function, serving the town's local communities.[89] A detailed analysis of these three basilicas is challenging since the archaeological reports have not been published.[90]

North-west of Novae, a fifth-century three-aisled, single-apse basilica (20.8 m x 13.3 m), with a narthex probably added in the sixth century, is

---

[85] Atanassov, 'Christianity along the Lower Danube Limes in the Roman Provinces of *Dacia Ripensis, Moesia Secunda* and *Scythia Minor*', in Liudmil Vagalinski, Nicolay Sharankov and Sergey Torbatov, eds, *The Lower Danube Limes (1st-6th C. AD)* (Sofia, 2012), 327–80, at 327.

[86] *The History of Theophylact Simocatta* 7.2.17, transl. Michael and Mary Whitby (Oxford, 1986), 182.

[87] Maria Čičikova, 'La basilique et la nécropole paléochrétiennes extra muros de Novae (Mesie Inferieure)', in Andrzej Biernacki and Piotr Pawlak, eds, *Late Roman and Early Byzantine Sites on the Lower Danube* (Poznan, 1997), 57–69, at 61–2.

[88] Ibid. 62.

[89] Ibid. 61.

[90] Andrzej Biernacki, 'A City of Christians: Novae in the 5th and 6th C. AD', *Archaeologia Bulgarica* 9 (2005), 53–74, at 54.

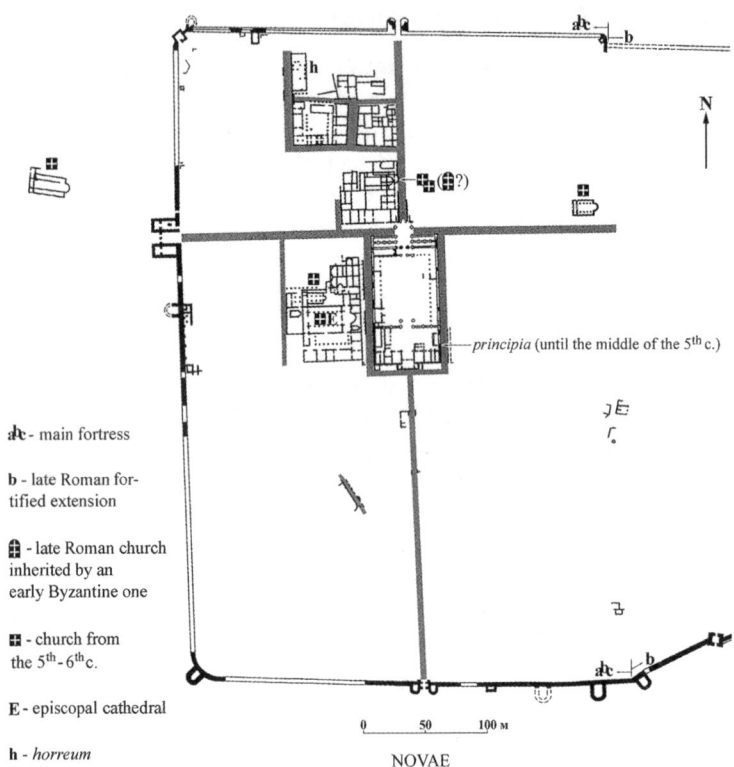

Figure 10. Novae, Plan of Late-Antique Novae, showing the location of the fifth and sixth-century churches; from Ventzislav Dintchev, 'Town and Church in Late Antiquity: Architectural and Urbanistic Dimensions', in Lyudmil Vagalinski et al., eds, *Proceedings of the First International Roman and Late Antique Thrace Conference 'Cities, Territories and Identities'* (Sofia, 2018), 357–70, at 362 (figure 7). Copyright: Ventzislav Dintchev. Drawing credit: Ventzislav Dintchev.

associated with a Christian necropolis containing over sixty graves and reminiscent of the West Church Complex at Kellis.[91] Evidence from the late fourth and early fifth centuries elsewhere in the empire suggests that by then some communities were holding funerary rituals for prominent individuals inside church buildings. Gregory of Nyssa (*c.*335–*c.*394), in his account of the funeral of his sister, Macrina,

---

[91] Čičikova, 'La basilique et la nécropole paléochrétiennes', 59; Biernacki, 'A City of Christians', 56.

recounts how the church vestibule could not accommodate the gathered crowd. He describes the community's overnight vigil, during which they sang hymns and psalms around her body.[92] It is notable that the church served as the space for these rituals, which were choreographed by Gregory as the bishop.[93] The cemeterial basilica at Novae may have also served a commemorative function, potentially housing the relics of St Luppos in a tomb in the apse. It is possible that in the early fourth century Luppos was initially buried in the necropolis, with a *martyrium* subsequently built over his grave. The potential development of Christian worship in Novae, centred around the necropolis and its cemeterial church, seems to parallel the practice and experience of worship and commemoration as well as the tradition of *ad sanctus* burials observed in the suburban cemeterial basilicas and catacombs outside Rome.

In the fifth century, the simple *martyrium* may have been replaced by the cemeterial basilica, with the altar situated above Luppos's tomb. The relics of St Luppos may have been transferred to a martyrial chapel within the episcopal basilica in the late fifth or early sixth centuries.[94] Prior to the late fifth century, burials within churches inside the walls of towns and cities were largely forbidden, and although the observance of this ban became somewhat more flexible, the practice remained unusual.[95] Accordingly, if Luppos' body were indeed transferred to the episcopal basilica, this would have been a rare and exceptional event, significantly elevating the sanctity of the episcopal basilica and establishing it as a place of veneration and pilgrimage. While the saint's relics were not the primary focal point of the basilica, their translation may have shaped ritual practices, especially on the saint's feast day, when a procession to the martyrial chapel could have formed an important element of the celebrations.[96] The significance attached to the relics of St Luppos and their possible translation to the episcopal basilica highlights how the cult of saints played a role in the articulation and shaping of sacred space.[97]

Novae's episcopal basilica (40.26 m x 22.32 m), a three-aisled church with a single apse and a narthex, ranks among the largest

---

[92] Gregory of Nyssa, *Life of Saint Macrina*, transl. with introduction and notes by Kevin Corrigan (Toronto, 1996), 49.

[93] Yasin, *Saints and Church Spaces*, 65.

[94] Atanassov, 'Christianity along the Lower Danube Limes', 348.

[95] Grossman, 'Churches and Meeting Halls', 111.

[96] Yasin, *Saints and Church Spaces*, 287.

[97] Ibid.

basilicas on the middle and lower Danube dating to this period.[98] Archaeological evidence indicates that it was constructed and modified in phases from the late fourth to late sixth century.[99] Besides the possible martyrial tomb for St Luppos, the discovery of another burial vault within the basilica provides evidence for intra-ecclesial burial in funerary churches in this period, reminiscent of the situation observed at West Church Complex in Kellis.[100]

In the atrium of the episcopal basilica was a freestanding baptistery (7.4 m x 5.05 m), probably added in the last quarter of the fifth century.[101] The baptistery featured a baptismal basin or tank, accessible by dual stone steps on its east and west sides, and was adorned with marble slabs. The tank is rectangular in shape, inscribed within a circle with an internal diameter of 1.65 meters. As a result, the overall layout of the tank complex has a hexagonal floor plan. The hexagon may have symbolized Christ's death on the sixth day, while the circle may have represented the womb of new birth, reflecting the baptismal theology of dying and rising.[102] However, the cautionary caveat offered in the discussion of the Nisibis baptistery concerning the theological interpretation of the shape of baptisteries should be kept in mind.[103]

Positioned in the atrium, the baptistery offered a direct route for catechumens arriving from the west and facilitated their processional movement to the basilica after baptism. Two of the three doorways may have been designated for catechumens and neophytes, marking their entry and exit, while the third was perhaps reserved for the bishop and clergy.[104] The possible creation of entrances and exits for specific echelons of the community to be used at specific ritual moments highlights the significance of the spatial experience of sacred space, similar to the Large East Church at Kellis, and probably reinforced ecclesiastical status and

---

[98] Biernacki, 'A City of Christians', 57.

[99] Andrzej Biernacki, 'The Bishopric of Novae (Moesia Secunda, 4th-6th Cent.): History, Daily Life', in Olof Brandt, ed., *Acta XV Congressus internationalis archaeologiae christianae: Toleti (8–12.9.2008). Episcopus, civitas, territorium*, 2 vols (Vatican City, 2013), 1: 895–914, at 737.

[100] Biernacki 'Bishopric of Novae', 739–40; Yasin, *Saints and Church Spaces*, 70.

[101] Biernacki, 'City of Christians', 60.

[102] Ferguson, *Baptism in the Early Church*, 819.

[103] Brandt, 'Structures of Early Christian Baptisteries', 1601–2; Biernacki, 'A City of Christians', 60.

[104] Yasin, *Saints and Church Spaces*, 287.

precedence. As at Nisibis, the spatial transition from the baptistery to the basilica at Novae was probably an important element of the baptismal experience. The neophytes' ascent from the baptismal basin symbolized their spiritual rebirth. Passing through designated doorways – perhaps one designated specifically for their exit from the baptistery and entry into the main basilica – ritually and symbolically reinforced their transition from catechumens to full members of the Church. The strategic placement of the baptistery relative to the basilica demonstrates how sacred spaces were adapted to enhance the sanctity of worship and reinforce hierarchical, ecclesial and communal identities.

As at Kellis and Nisibis, the spatial arrangement and architectural features of Novae's basilicas and the external baptistery reflect the Christian community's evolving ritual and commemorative practices. Novae's sacred architecture not only facilitated but actively shaped the practices of worship, ritual and commemoration of its Christian community, reflecting broader trends in early Christian worship across the empire.

Case Study 4: Vindolanda, Britannia Secunda

On the frontier in Britannia Secunda, northern England, along Hadrian's Wall, potential churches have been identified at the forts at South Shields, Housesteads and Birdoswald.[105] Most notably, at Vindolanda, the apsidal design and dating of several structures from the sub-Roman (409–600) and post-Roman (600–800) periods indicate the possibility of up to five early Christian churches (Figure 11). However, as Andrew Birley and Marta Alberti observe in their report of the excavation, the evidence is 'extremely fragmentary in nature and much debated'.[106]

Excavations have revealed that the demolition of three of the four wings of the *praetorium* (commanding officer's house) around the

---

[105] Paul Bidwell and Stephen Speak, *Excavations at South Shields Roman Fort*, vol. 1 (Newcastle upon Tyne, 1994), 103–4; James Crow, *Housesteads: A Fort and Garrison on Hadrian's Wall* (Stroud, 2004), 114; Tony Wilmott, Hilary Cool and Jerry Evans, 'Excavations at the Hadrian's Wall Fort of Birdoswald (Banna), Cumbria', in Tony Wilmott, ed., *Hadrian's Wall: Archaeological Research by English Heritage 1976–2000* (Liverpool, 2009), 395.
[106] Andrew Birley and Marta Alberti, *Vindolanda Excavation Research Report* (Bardon Mill, 2021), 6, 68.

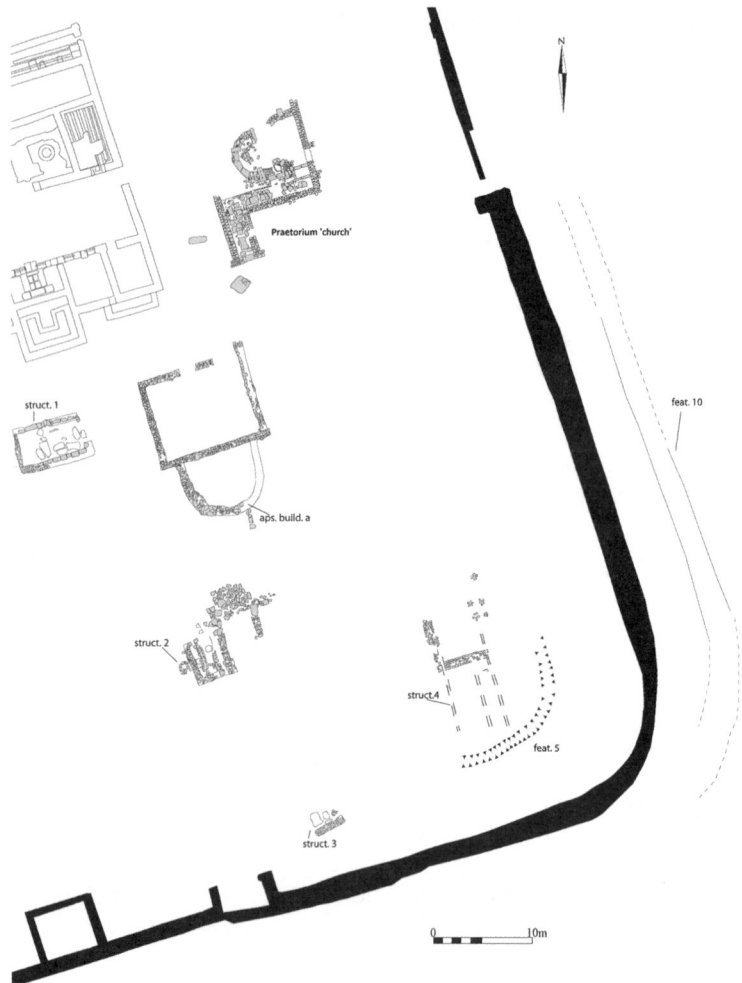

Figure 11. Vindolanda Fort, the sub-Roman buildings in the south-eastern quadrant as they would have appeared in period IXA (the sub-Roman period), *c*.409–600 CE; after Andrew Birley and Marta Alberti, *Vindolanda Excavation Research Report*, 40 (figure 23). Copyright: Vindolanda Trust. Plan credit: Marta Alberti for the Vindolanda Trust.

360s or 370s would probably have rendered it uninhabitable, with the commanding officer and his family perhaps taking up residence in the *principia* (headquarters building). In the southern part of the *praetorium* courtyard and the remains of the east wing, a 'church-like' structure with an apse was built (Figure 12).[107] Stratigraphic evidence indicates that this structure was erected some time after the alterations undertaken *c.*360–70. The date of construction of the *praetorium* 'church' (6.5 m x 3 m nave, with a 5 m diameter apse) remains uncertain, but can be estimated at *c.*400 or shortly thereafter.[108] There is debate regarding the nature and purpose of the alterations to the *praetorium*. One recent counter-argument to the 'church' theory is that the apsidal structure could have served as an extension of the eastern wing of the *praetorium* into the courtyard, perhaps functioning as a reception room, and compensating for lost rooms due to deterioration elsewhere in the *praetorium*.[109]

The *praetorium* 'church', like other sub-Roman structures at Vindolanda, generally adhered to the pre-existing layout.[110] Only a single

Figure 12. Vindolanda, the *praetorium* 'church'. © The author.

[107] Ibid. 22.
[108] Robin Birley, Andrew Birley and Justin Blake, *The 1998 Excavations at Vindolanda: The Praetorium Site Interim Report* (Greenhead, 1999), 21.
[109] Rob Collins, 'The Culture of Command in the 4th and 5th Centuries in Northern *Britannia*', in Nick Hodgson and Bill Griffiths, eds, *Roman Frontier Archaeology in Britain and Beyond* (Oxford, 2022), 243–55, at 251–2.
[110] Birley and Alberti, *Vindolanda Excavation Research Report*, 23.

course of masonry remains, leaving the nature of the upper structure, whether timber or stone, uncertain. The excavators currently consider a part-stone, part-timber construction more probable.[111] Just inside the building's entrance, an altar dedicated to Jupiter and the genius of the *praetorium* was repurposed as a paving stone. With its inscribed side facing downward, it perhaps represented a deliberate religious and ceremonial act symbolizing the triumph of Christianity. The *praetorium* 'church' probably remained in use throughout the sub-Roman period.[112]

Another apsidal building, referred to as 'Apsidal Building A' (8.7 m x 11 m nave-like space, with a 9.3 m diameter apse), was discovered within a fourth-century cavalry barracks (Figures 11 and 13). This structure, also interpreted as a possible church, features a semi-circular apse and a square nave, with numismatic evidence providing a *terminus post quem* for the laying of the apse's foundation of *c.*364–78. Like the *praetorium* 'church', there is no evidence of subsequent modifications, suggesting that it may have been abandoned only at the end of the post-Roman period.[113]

Significant parallels exist between Apsidal Building A and the *praetorium* 'church', particularly in their incorporation of pre-existing fourth-century masonry to transform square rooms into nave-like spaces. In addition, their foundations rest directly above demolished fourth-century contexts; the apse walls are constructed of facing stones; and the apses are set slightly off-centre with the naves to create a basilical-type layout.[114] These similarities suggest a consistent construction pattern and a level of continuity in architectural development at Vindolanda in the sub-Roman period.[115]

The spatial experiences for worship and ritual in these two modest buildings would inevitably have been simpler than the sacred spaces of Kellis, Nisibis and Novae. The diminutive size of the Vindolanda structures would have limited the potential for spatial division and distinct entrances and routeways. Nevertheless, the attempt to replicate

[111] Birley, Birley and Blake, *The 1998 Excavations at Vindolanda*, 20–1; David Breeze, *Collingwood Bruce's Handbook to the Roman Wall*, 14th edn (Newcastle upon Tyne, 2006; first publ. 1885), 441–2; Andrew Birley, Personal communication by e-mail, 23 June 2022.
[112] Birley and Alberti, *Vindolanda Excavation Research Report*, 23.
[113] Ibid. 49.
[114] Ibid.
[115] Part of another apse was excavated nearby, but as the majority of the rest of the building fell outside the 2008–12 Scheduled Monument Consent, full investigation is yet to be undertaken: ibid. 34, 68.

Figure 13. Vindolanda, the stone-by-stone plan of the foundations of Apsidal Building A (shaded in grey), overlaid with an aerial photo by Aerial Cam. © The Vindolanda Trust. Photo credit: Marta Alberti for the Vindolanda Trust.

the basilical shape of Christian sacred space, even on a modest scale, is significant, perhaps reflecting a desire by the Vindolanda community to incorporate elements of Christian architecture and the rituals associated with it, as known from other regions.

Nearby, an originally third-century rectangular building was demolished in the fourth century, and part of its outer wall was repurposed into a rectangular water tank clad with well-cut, reused ashlar sandstone blocks (Figure 14). A smaller flagstone-floored space in front of the main tank extended into the street, forming an access point for drawing water.[116] By the end of the fourth century, the tank seems to have been converted into a roofed building with numismatic evidence suggesting a *terminus post quem* of 321–23 for its construction.[117] This modification may have corresponded with the creation of a walk-in water tank capable of both practical and ritual use, with access to the water enhanced by levelling the eastern wall and adding a step. This tank would have been contemporaneous with the *praetorium* 'church' and possibly the Apsidal Building A.[118]

The interpretation of the water tank as a baptismal tank or font is speculative, but plausible. As at Kellis, catechumens at Vindolanda possibly went elsewhere for baptism. However, despite its much simpler design compared to the ornate baptisteries at Nisibis and Novae, the tank's enclosed structure, convenient stepped access, and its proximity to both the *praetorium* church and Apsidal Building A suggest that it could have served as a site for the baptismal rituals. Such an arrangement would have also allowed for the possibility of a short post-baptismal procession to either of the adjacent proposed churches.

Interpreting the water tank as a potential baptismal font raises the question of who might have performed baptisms at Vindolanda. As noted above in relation to the absence of a baptistery at Kellis, evidence from the fourth century onwards suggests an increase in baptisms performed by priests and the construction of small, though usually not separate, baptisteries in rural areas.[119] This trend may inform our understanding of the water tank at Vindolanda, suggesting its potential for functioning as a place for the celebration of baptism.

At the beginning of this case study, it was noted that evidence for ecclesiastical structures at Vindolanda is both fragmentary and debated. While the *praetorium* 'church' and Apsidal Building A cannot be definitively confirmed as churches, evidence from post-Roman buildings and material culture supports the interpretation that they were. Although Vindolanda's Christian context may not be as

---

[116] Ibid. 41.

[117] Ibid.

[118] It is unclear whether the enclosed tank continued to serve a practical purpose, if and when it was used for baptism. However, it seems at least plausible that the sacred nature of the baptismal rituals might have led to the tank's being reserved for this sacred purpose.

[119] Brandt, 'Understanding the Structures of Early Christian Baptisteries', 1597–8.

Figure 14. Vindolanda, the water tank was possibly converted into a baptismal tank/font and was perhaps associated with the *praetorium* 'church' and Apsidal Building A. © The author.

clear-cut as sites such as Kellis, Nisibis or Novae, the cumulative evidence makes a compelling case for a Christian presence.

Two further structures – Apsidal Buildings B and C – deserve mention, even though they fall outside the chronological scope of this article. Stylistic analysis suggests that these buildings belong to the post-Roman period, and they may represent a new type of church-like structure with an elongated, 'rocket-shaped' apse and rectangular nave.[120] If this identification is correct, it indicates a significant new phase in the development of Christian sacred spaces within the fort, supporting the continuation of an already established Christian environment.

In addition to the excavated buildings, numerous artefacts excavated at Vindolanda strengthen the Christian interpretation of the site. These include stone carvings with Christian motifs, a portable altar stone incised with a *chi-rho* cross, and a copper alloy nail-cleaning strap-end decorated with a possible depiction of a figure in the *orans* position of prayer. This last artefact was found near Apsidal Building A. Additionally, a remarkable lead vessel covered inside and out with Christian symbols was excavated within Apsidal Building B.[121]

Examining the architectural and spatial experiences of potential early Christian structures at Vindolanda reveals a complex and debated picture of religious transformation. Despite the fragmentary nature of the evidence, it suggests intriguing possibilities for the presence of Christian sacred spaces in this frontier community. Although alternative interpretations are possible due to the incomplete evidence and ongoing debates, these buildings, especially when considered alongside the Christian artefacts found on the site and the architectural continuity, suggest that they were structures which might well reflect an evolving experience of Christian sacred space at Vindolanda in the sub-Roman and post-Roman periods.

Conclusion

The study of fourth- and fifth-century spatial experiences associated with worship, ritual and commemoration in frontier settlements like Kellis, Nisibis, Novae and Vindolanda reveals the intricate relationship between architecture and religious practice. Constantine's basilicas in Rome and the Holy Land marked a shift towards the centralization

---

[120] Birley and Alberti, *Vindolanda Excavation Research Report*, 55–8, 68–71.

[121] Images of these buildings and artefacts can be found in Birley and Alberti, *Vindolanda Excavation Research Report*, Apsidal Building b, 56 (figure 36); Apsidal Building c, 57 (figure 37); Christian symbols and markings, 172 (plate 14); the nail-cleaning strap-end, 49 (figure 31); the lead vessel, 38, 120–1 (figure 38 and plates 12 and 13).

and monumentalizing of Christian worship, creating a template that influenced Christian sacred architecture, worship and ritual practice throughout the empire. At the frontiers, Christian sacred spaces followed trends from Rome and the Holy Land, whilst remaining adaptable to local innovations. Features such as basilical church layouts, cemeterial and funerary churches, designated entrances, processional routeways, screening and freestanding baptisteries illustrate how architectural innovations were tailored to fit local contexts. These sacred spaces integrated diverse worship, ritual and commemorative practices, demonstrating that flexibility in sacred architecture was as evident at the empire's peripheries as at its core. The case studies highlight the dynamic relationship between sacred architecture and religious practice at the Roman frontiers, showing that the foundational model provided by the monumental basilicas of Rome and the Holy Land was dynamically reinterpreted rather than rigidly adopted, balancing continuity and innovation.

Future research would benefit from a more comprehensive, interdisciplinary approach to the study of the spatial experience of Christian sacred spaces and worship, ritual and commemoration, especially in frontier contexts. Further study of both similarities and divergences in the creation and experience of these spaces has the potential to yield further insights into how frontier Christian communities engaged with and experienced their sacred spaces. This is a field of Roman frontier studies that merits more attention.

British and English Churches in Late-Seventh-Century Wessex: Who was Peripheral?

Aloysius Atkinson [ID]

University of Oxford

Late-seventh-century texts from south-western Britain, especially a letter addressed by Abbot Aldhelm of Malmesbury to a British king and his clergy, offer a different perspective on relations between the British and English churches to that provided by eighth-century Northumbrian authors. The writings of Bede and Stephen of Ripon have cast a long shadow by suggesting that hostility between British and English Christians was the norm. The 660s have been interpreted as a turning-point, with the arrival of Theodore of Tarsus as archbishop of Canterbury leading to the Britons being branded as heretics and impeding any interaction between British and English churches. This article argues that, in the South-West, relations remained warm until the final years of the seventh century, notwithstanding differences over the date of Easter and the tonsure. Dumnonia's political decline was principally responsible for British Christianity's ultimate marginalization.

INTRODUCTION

In south-western Britain, British and West Saxon Christians enjoyed warm relations into the late seventh century. The writings of Aldhelm of Malmesbury (*c.*642–709), a leading West Saxon churchman, display his regard for British Christianity and attest to extensive contacts, including hospitality and joint worship. Texts from Wessex contrast with sources, notably works by influential early-eighth-century Northumbrian authors, which have created an impression of profound hostility between the British and English churches, particularly from the 660s.

Foremost among these, Bede's *Historia Ecclesiastica* presented the Britons negatively, as a 'nation of heretics' (*gentis perfidae*) opposed to

St John's College, St Giles, Oxford, OX1 3JP.
E-mail: aloysiusatkinson@gmail.com.

Studies in Church History 61 (2025), 48–70 © The Author(s), 2025. Published by Cambridge University Press on behalf of the Ecclesiastical History Society. This is an Open Access article, distributed under the terms of the Creative Commons Attribution licence (http://creativecommons.org/licenses/by/4.0), which permits unrestricted re-use, distribution and reproduction, provided the original article is properly cited.
doi:10.1017/stc.2024.31

both the Catholic Church and the English. He alleged that they refused to evangelize the Angles and Saxons, and highlighted Britons' ongoing rejection of Roman practice in respect of the date of Easter and the tonsure.[1] The reasons for Bede's animus against the Britons have been vigorously debated, the interpretation most favourable to him suggesting that he simply adopted Gildas's line in the late-fifth- or early- to mid-sixth-century *De Excidio Britanniae*.[2] Alternatively, literary imperatives may have required that the Britons provide a 'foil' for the virtues of the English and Irish.[3] The suspicion that the *Historia* reflects Bede's own ethnic antipathy has been especially influential.[4] This antipathy appears to be connected to his perception of a contemporary British threat, plausibly emanating from the kingdom of Strathclyde.[5] Bede's commentary on the First Book of Samuel may also reflect Northumbrian divisions, with some of its elite collaborating with Britons.[6]

Alexander Murray's argument that Bede saw the Britons as an 'unchosen' people depends on Bede's casting the English as God's chosen people, a new Israel.[7] Gildas had referred to the Britons as 'latter-day Israel' (*praesens Israel*), apparently considering them a new chosen people.[8] However, the notion that Bede saw the English as the new chosen people has been criticized, since his and other early medieval

---

[1] Bede, *Historia Ecclesiastica gentis anglorum* [hereafter: *HE*] 2.2, 5.23; ET: *Bede's Ecclesiastical History of the English People*, ed. and transl. Bertram Colgrave and Roger Mynors (Oxford, 1969), 140–3, 560–1.

[2] T. M. Charles-Edwards, 'Bede, the Irish and the Britons', *Celtica* 15 (1983), 42–52.

[3] Clare Stancliffe, *Bede and the Britons*, Whithorn Lecture 2005 (Whithorn, 2007), 11–12.

[4] Alan Thacker, 'Bede, the Britons and the Book of Samuel', in Stephen Baxter, ed., *Early Medieval Studies in Memory of Patrick Wormald* (Farnham, 2009), 129–47, at 134; W. Trent Foley and Nicholas J. Higham, 'Bede on the Britons', *Early Medieval Europe* 17 (2009), 154–85, at 157–9; Stancliffe, Bede and the Britons, 12; Nicholas Brooks, 'From British to English Christianity: Deconstructing Bede's Interpretation of the Conversion', in Catherine E. Karkov and Nicholas Howe, eds, *Conversion and Colonization in Anglo-Saxon England* (Tempe, AZ, 2006), 1–30, at 7.

[5] Stancliffe, *Bede and the Britons*, 23–30.

[6] Thacker, 'Bede, the Britons', 142–4.

[7] Alexander Murray, 'Bede and the Unchosen Race', in Huw Pryce and John Watts, eds, *Power and Identity in the Middle Ages* (Oxford, 2007), 52–67, at 59.

[8] Gildas, *De Excidio Britanniae* [hereafter: *DEB*] 26, in *The Ruin of Britain and Other Works*, ed. and transl. Michael Winterbottom, rev. edn (London, 2002), 13–79, 87–142, at 28, 98; George Molyneaux, 'Did the English Really Think they were God's Elect in the Anglo-Saxon Period?', *JEH* 64/4 (2014), 721–37.

writers' fundamental concern was with the universal Church.[9] None-theless, the *Historia*'s English-British dichotomy perpetuates the question of how Bede perceived each people's providential status, particularly given his assertion that 'God in his goodness did not reject the people whom he foreknew'.[10] Unusually, W. Trent Foley and Nicholas Higham interpreted this as referring not to the English but to the Britons, suggesting Bede saw them as analogous to the Jews, with the English analogous to the Church.[11] For Samuel Cardwell, however, Bede took the Britons as a 'cautionary tale' for the English, viewing the former as a chosen people violating their covenant.[12]

Stephen of Ripon, Bede's contemporary and Wilfrid's hagiographer, likewise assumed that hostility characterized English-British relations. His *Vita Wilfridi* offered two vignettes showing Northumbrian destruc-tion of the British church. In the first, Wilfrid, standing in his church at Ripon, recited 'a list of the consecrated places in various parts which the British clergy had deserted when fleeing from the hostile sword wielded by the warriors of our own nation.'[13] He related, moreover, how Wilfrid, having restored a British woman's child to life, seized him by force, renamed him 'Eodwald Bishop's Son' and committed him to the minster-community at Ripon.[14] Eodwald's baptism at English hands made him a true Christian, unlike his mother, whom Stephen likened to the Syro-Phoenician woman in Mark's Gospel: a 'dog', outside Israel and the normal scope of divine grace.[15]

Such hostility was not confined to eighth-century Northumbrian texts. Penitential texts associated with Theodore, archbishop of Can-terbury (r. 669–90), survive in seven recensions, some dating from

---

[9] Molyneaux, 'Did the English?', 726–9; Conor O'Brien, 'Chosen Peoples and New Israels in the Early Medieval West', *Speculum* 95 (2020), 987–1009.

[10] '[N]on tamen divina pietas plebem suam, quam praescivit, deseruit': *HE* 1.22 (*Ecclesiastical History*, ed. Colgrave and Mynors, 69).

[11] Foley and Higham, 'Bede on the Britons', 165–70, 184–5. Compare Charles-Edwards, 'Bede, the Irish', 52; Stancliffe, *Bede and the Britons*, 5; Molyneaux, 'Did the English?', 729.

[12] Samuel Cardwell, 'The People Whom He Foreknew', *Journal of the Australian Early Medieval Association* 11 (2015), 41–66, at 42, 58–9.

[13] '[E]a loca sancta in diversis regionibus quae clerus Bryttannus, aciem gladii hostilis manu gentis nostrae fugiens, deseruit': Stephen, *Vita Wilfridi* [hereafter: *VW*] 17, ed. and transl. Bertram Colgrave, *The Life of Bishop Wilfrid by Eddius Stephanus* (Cambridge, 1927), 37.

[14] *VW* 18 (*Life*, ed. Colgrave, 41).

[15] Ibid.; Mark 7: 24–30.

Theodore's lifetime.[16] These texts include some stringent rulings against the 'Quartodeciman' heretics, that is, those who did not observe the 'Roman' Easter.[17] However, other rulings take a more moderate stance, leading to contradictory statements, even within some recensions, on the validity of sacraments performed by those who rejected the Roman Easter.[18] Clare Stancliffe has explained this as Theodore softening his previously hard-line stance *c.*678.[19] However, only the less severe rulings appear in the recension of Theodoran penitential rulings known as the *Capitula Dacheriana*, which appears to reflect Theodore's pre-673 teaching.[20] Moreover, views represented in these penitential texts cannot simply be attributed to Theodore himself. The rulings' corrupt transmission was already recognized as a problem in the early eighth century.[21] More fundamentally, Theodore's approach to teaching involved commenting on canonical traditions he had encountered, including sharing contradictory rulings.[22] The harsher canons may represent his commentary on Eastern canonical discipline, not necessarily intended as prescriptions for contemporary England.[23]

Nonetheless, Theodore's arrival as archbishop has been considered significant in marginalizing British Christians who did not accept the Roman Easter.[24] Thomas Charles-Edwards has emphasized the paschal controversy's role in foreclosing the Britons' claim to *Romanitas* ('Roman-ness'), including in Frankish and even some Irish eyes, across the seventh century; while Theodore regarded the Britons as both

---

[16] Roy Flechner, 'The Making of the Canons of Theodore', *Peritia* 17–18 (2003–4), 121–43, at 123–6.

[17] *Die Canones Theodori Cantuariensis und ihre Überlieferungsformen*, recension U [named for its eighth-century compiler, the 'Discipulus Umbrensium'; hereafter: U] 1.5.1–13; recension G [after its manuscript heading, 'Canones Gregorii'; hereafter: G] 26–28, 48–53, ed. Paul Willem Finsterwalder (Weimar, 1929), 255, 257–8, 295–7.

[18] Ibid. U 2.9.1–3; G 187, 189; recension D [the 'Capitula Dacheriana', seemingly comprising rulings given pre-673; hereafter: D] 116–17, 124 (ed. Paul Willem Finsterwalder, 248–9, 270, 323–4).

[19] Clare Stancliffe, *Bede, Wilfrid and the Irish*, Jarrow Lecture 2003 (Jarrow, 2003), 16–17.

[20] Flechner, 'The Making of the Canons of Theodore', 125.

[21] Ibid. 126.

[22] Roy Flechner, 'An Insular Tradition of Ecclesiastical Law: Fifth to Eighth Century', in James Graham-Campbell and Michael Ryan, eds, *Anglo-Saxon/Irish Relations before the Vikings* (Oxford, 2009), 23–46, at 38–9.

[23] Compare Stancliffe, *Bede, Wilfrid and the Irish*, 15.

[24] See, for instance, T. M. Charles-Edwards, *Wales and the Britons, 350–1064* (Oxford, 2013), 239–41, 396–410; Henry Mayr-Harting, *The Coming of Christianity to Anglo-Saxon England*, 3rd edn (University Park, PA, 1991; first publ. 1972), 112, 122–3.

heretics and schismatics.[25] However, the treatment of Irish Christianity in Northumbria suggests that the 660s may not have marked an irrevocable turning-point in relations with those who did not observe the Roman Easter. Stancliffe developed Charles-Edwards's proposal that a 'middle party', accepting the Roman Easter but favourable towards the Irish tradition, dominated the Northumbrian church from c.678 until the early eighth century, suggesting that some at least of this party remained openly in communion with those who rejected the Roman Easter.[26] This article presents a similar argument for south-western Britain, suggesting that here British and English Christians maintained good relations, despite the paschal controversy. The British church only became peripheral in the 690s, when political shifts critically weakened the Britons' position.

The strongest evidence for these relationships comes from the letter written by Aldhelm to Geraint, king of Dumnonia, a British kingdom comprising Cornwall and probably most of Devon, to urge acceptance of the Roman Easter and tonsure.[27] This offers an invaluable glimpse of ecclesiastical relations in action in the early days of Theodore's archiepiscopate, decades before Bede's *Historia Ecclesiastica* and Stephen's *Vita Wilfridi* were composed. Michael Lapidge and Michael Herren posited that the 672 Council of Hertford probably commissioned the letter.[28] However, Lapidge subsequently accepted Catherine Cubitt's argument that the synod responsible cannot be identified, and thus came to consider a precise dating of the letter as impossible.[29] In my view, however, Lapidge's revised position should not be accepted. As he and Herren showed, Aldhelm closely echoed Theodore's words, recorded in Hertford's *acta*. Both emphasized fidelity to the Fathers' decrees, and referred to council participants' collective discussions regarding how it could be achieved. This congruity goes beyond the general themes of charity and unity which Cubitt highlighted as far from unique to these

[25] Charles-Edwards, *Wales and the Britons*, 239–41, 396.

[26] T. M. Charles-Edwards, *Early Christian Ireland* (Cambridge, 2000), 320–1, 336–43; Stancliffe, *Bede, Wilfrid and the Irish*, 17.

[27] Aldhelm, *Epistola ad Geruntium* [hereafter: *Ep. Ger.*], in Rudolf Ehwald, ed., *Aldhelmi Opera*, MGH AA 15 (Berlin, 1919), 480–7; ET: *Aldhelm: The Prose Works*, transl. Michael Lapidge and Michael Herren (Cambridge, 1979), 155–60.

[28] *Aldhelm: The Prose Works*, transl. Lapidge and Herren, 142–3.

[29] Michael Lapidge, 'The Career of Aldhelm', *Anglo-Saxon England* 36 (2007), 15–69, at 67–8.

texts.[30] Further, Aldhelm's hyperbolic depiction of the council's 'innumerable' company of bishops tallies with Bede's estimation of Hertford's importance.[31] Duncan Probert's argument that the letter was written in the mid-690s relied on unsafe assumptions that this letter was the book by Aldhelm to which Bede referred, that it was composed contemporaneously with the acceptance of the Roman date for Easter by Britons under West Saxon rule, and that this took place *c.*695–7.[32] By contrast, the textual evidence adduced above suggests that the letter was indeed commissioned by Hertford. The influence of Theodore, under whom Aldhelm had studied, may also be visible in its overall approach, which was critical of certain British practices without reflecting antipathy towards the British church.

While Aldhelm's respectful tone and moderate manner have been widely recognized, Martin Grimmer adduced the letter to argue that the intolerant English mounted a hostile takeover of British churches within their territory and marginalized as heretics those British Christians whom they did not control, including Geraint's subjects.[33] However, the letter reveals more than courtesy or even respect. Particularly when viewed in its broader literary context, it shows that the West Saxon church was no more 'central' than that of the Britons, and perhaps rather less so. In south-western Britain, English and British Christian communities existed side-by-side for at least a generation after the synod of Whitby (664), the council at which the Roman Easter gained acceptance in Northumbria. This was the case, despite the fact that following the synod an important segment of Northumbrian churchmen sought actively to marginalize those Christians who did not adopt the Roman Easter.

---

[30] Catherine Cubitt, *Anglo-Saxon Church Councils c.650–c.850* (London, 1995), 63, 261.
[31] *Ep. Ger.*, 481 (*Aldhelm: The Prose Works*, transl. Lapidge and Herren, 155); *HE* 4.5 (*Ecclesiastical History*, ed. Colgrave and Mynors, 349–53).
[32] Duncan Probert, 'New Light on Aldhelm's Letter to King Gerent of Dumnonia', in Katherine Barker and Nicholas Brooks, eds, *Aldhelm and Sherborne: Essays to Celebrate the Founding of the Bishopric* (Oxford, 2010), 110–28, at 119–23.
[33] Barbara Yorke, 'Aldhelm's Irish and British Connections', in Barker and Brooks, eds, *Aldhelm and Sherborne*, 164–80, at 176; Samuel Cardwell, '"What Sort of Love will not Speak for a Friend's Good?": Pastoral Care and Rhetoric in Early Anglo-Saxon Letters to Kings', *JMedH* 45 (2019), 405–31, at 411; Probert, 'New Light', 116; Martin Grimmer, 'Saxon Bishop and Celtic King: Interactions between Aldhelm of Wessex and Geraint of Dumnonia', *The Heroic Age* 4 (2001), electronic journal online at: <https://www.heroicage.org/issues/4/Grimmer.html>, accessed 31 August 2023.

Aldhelm's Relationship with the Britons

Aldhelm valued ties with his British counterparts. He took for granted that West Saxon and Dumnonian clerics were in communion with each other, but bitterly lamented that 'bishops of Dyfed … glorying in the private purity of their own way of life, detest our communion to such a great extent that they disdain equally to celebrate the divine offices in church with us and to take courses of food at table for the sake of charity'.[34] Grimmer suggested that the difference between the attitudes in Dumnonia and Dyfed, a British kingdom in modern south-west Wales, to which Aldhelm alluded was merely one of degree.[35] However, a poem in which Aldhelm described staying in a monastery while passing through Cornwall seems to confirm the warmth of his relations with Dumnonian churchmen.[36] Aldhelm recalled how he prayed matins with his hosts, showing that they celebrated the liturgical hours together.[37]

Indeed, Aldhelm's letter reflects respect for British ecclesiastics well beyond simple camaraderie. Among his complaints against the clergy of Dyfed was that 'should any of us, I mean Catholics, go to live with them, they do not deign to admit us to the company of their brother-hood until we have been compelled to spend the space of forty days in penance'.[38] Aldhelm seems here to be describing adherents to Roman

---

[34] 'Demetarum sacerdotes de privata propriae conversationis munditia gloriantes nostram communionem magnopere abominantur in tantum, ut nec in ecclesia nobiscum orationum officia celebrare nec ad mensam ciborum fercula pro caritatis gratia pariter percipere dignentur': *Ep. Ger.*, 484 (*Aldhelm: The Prose Works*, transl. Lapidge and Herren, 158).

[35] Martin Grimmer, 'Bede and the Augustine's Oak Conferences: Implications for Anglo-British Ecclesiastical Interaction in Early Anglo-Saxon England', *Journal of the Australian Early Medieval Association* 2 (2006), 103–19, at 116.

[36] Aldhelm, *Carmen Rhythmicum*, in Rudolf Ehwald, ed., *Aldhelmi Opera*, MGH AA 15 (Berlin, 1919), 524–8; ET: *Aldhelm: The Poetic Works*, transl. Michael Lapidge and James L. Rosier (Cambridge, 1985), 177–9; Probert, 'New Light', 113–14. Katherine Barker interpreted 'Usque … Domnoniam / Per … Cornubiam', as meaning 'from Cornwall to the borders of Dumnonia': Katherine Barker, '*Usque Domnoniam*: the Setting of Aldhelm's Carmen Rhythmicum, Literature, Language and the Liminal', in Barker and Brooks, eds, *Aldhelm and Sherborne*, 15–54, at 24. However, this reading seems quite forced.

[37] Aldhelm, *Carmen Rhythmicum*, 527–8 (*Aldhelm: The Poetic Works*, transl. Lapidge and Rosier, 178–9).

[38] '[S]i quilibet de nostris id est catholicis ad eos habitandi gratia perrexerint, non prius ad consortium sodalitatis suae adsciscere dignantur, quam quadraginta dierum spatia in penitendo peragere compellantur': *Ep. Ger.*, 484 (*Aldhelm: The Prose Works*, transl. Lapidge and Herren, 158).

practices entering religious communities in Dyfed, perhaps renowned monasteries such as that on Ynys Bŷr (Caldey Island, Pembrokeshire). These were not necessarily West Saxons: Aldhelm's designation of them as 'Catholics' (*catholicis*) could hint that they were not, but instead British subjects of the West Saxons. What is clear is that Aldhelm saw nothing strange or reprehensible in those who shared his theological standpoint seeking to live the monastic life in Dyfed, despite the local church's non-acceptance of the Roman Easter and tonsure. This implies that Aldhelm recognized and affirmed these monasteries' reputation for holiness, and perhaps particularly the antiquity of their saints' cults and monastic tradition.

Aldhelm's respect for British monasteries seems significantly greater than that which Bede expressed for early-seventh-century Bangor. Bede's praise was juxtaposed with Æthelfrith's slaughter of its members and could be taken to demonstrate how even monastic excellence could not avert divine vengeance for their disobedience to Rome.[39] In contrast, Aldhelm's acceptance that 'Catholics' might enter monasteries in Dyfed where objectionable (to him) liturgical practices were maintained shows that he did not make continued religious fellowship conditional on the renunciation of these practices. Aldhelm's emphasis on unity seems consistent with an early, and moderate, Theodoran penitential ruling stipulating that chrism and the eucharist be given to non-conforming Britons providing they first professed their desire 'to be with us in the unity of the Church'.[40]

Even in admonishing Geraint and his Dumnonian bishops about their liturgical errors, Aldhelm avoided unequivocal affronts.[41] His primary concern, raised before Easter or the tonsure, was 'the unity of the Catholic Church and the harmony of the Christian religion, without which an indifferent faith grows sluggish and future gain is exhausted'.[42] Aldhelm's point should not be construed overly positively: it intimated that Geraint and his bishops risked a schism. Nonetheless, he avoided directly attacking their traditions and implied

---

[39] *HE* 2.2 (*Ecclesiastical History*, ed. Colgrave and Mynors, 137-143); Foley and Higham, 'Bede and the Britons', 175.

[40] '[S]e nobiscum esse in unitate aeclesie': *Die Canones Theodori*, D 124 (ed Paul Willem Finsterwalder, 249).

[41] Compare Cardwell, 'What Sort of Love?', 418; Probert, 'New Light', 116.

[42] '[E]cclesiae catholicae unitate et christianae religionis concordia, sine quibus fides otiosa torpescit et merces futura fatescit': *Ep. Ger.*, 481 (*Aldhelm: The Prose Works*, transl. Lapidge and Herren, 155).

that the English clergy sought to prevent such a rift. Aldhelm thus presented his concern about their errors as stemming from his feeling of comity towards them. Whereas Bede located the roots of their downfall in their sinful conduct after the collapse of Roman rule and their rejection of Augustine of Canterbury, for Aldhelm, the Britons' peril lay in the future.[43]

In one significant respect, Aldhelm softened potential criticism of the British church in a similar manner to Bede and the Irish. Aldhelm raised the spectre of Quartodecimanism, an Eastern heresy of which those who refused to adopt the Roman Easter were accused. Describing its adherents as a 'certain type of heretic among the Orientals', he mentioned them only in the context of the Council of Nicaea (325), without directly accusing Geraint or his bishops of Quartodecimanism.[44] Regarding the Irish, Bede omitted the charge altogether.[45] Stephen of Ripon, by contrast, accused not just the Britons and Irish, but also those English clergy who were in communion with them, of Quartodecimanism.[46] Quartodecimanism was also invoked by Theodoran penitential rulings, although none is known to derive from his earliest teaching.[47] Thus Aldhelm admonished his readers as the council had instructed him, without unequivocally alleging heresy.

Aldhelm suggested that, these matters apart, the Britons might even be superior to the West Saxons as Christians. Having attacked the particularly stringent line taken by British churchmen in Dyfed, calling them Pharisees, Aldhelm referred to Christ's example in forgiving the reformed sinner, or prostitute, mentioned in Luke's Gospel, who was associated with Mary Magdalene.[48] Probert's suggestion that she represented the Britons cannot be accepted.[49] She was contrasted with the Pharisees, who represented the misguidedly rigorist clergy of Dyfed, excessively proud of their pristine traditions. She was not a Pharisee who had moved from pride to true faith, as Nicodemus had,

---

[43] Stancliffe, *Bede and the Britons*, 8.

[44] '[G]enus quoddam hereticorum aput orientales': *Ep. Ger.*, 483–4 (*Aldhelm: The Prose Works*, transl. Lapidge and Herren, 157–8).

[45] Alan Thacker, 'Bede and the Irish', in L. A. J. R. Houwen and A. A. MacDonald, Beda Venerabilis: *Historian, Monk & Northumbrian* (Groningen, 1996), 31–59, at 38–40.

[46] *VW* 12, 14–15 (*Life*, ed. Colgrave, 25, 31–3); Stancliffe, *Bede, Wilfrid and the Irish*, 6.

[47] *Die Canones Theodori*, U 1.5.3; G 48, 53 (ed Paul Willem Finsterwalder, 257–8, 295).

[48] *Ep. Ger.*, 485 (*Aldhelm: The Prose Works*, transl. Lapidge and Herren, 159); Luke 7: 37–50; Philip Almond, *Mary Magdalene: A Cultural History* (Cambridge, 2022), 3, 58.

[49] Probert, 'New Light', 118.

but instead represented those belatedly converted from depravity and sinfulness.[50] Thus, the repentant sinner symbolized Aldhelm's people, so recently converted from paganism.

PAGANISM AND THE BRITONS

The explanation for Aldhelm's startling analogy can be found in a British hagiography, *Vita Samsonis*, which provides a valuable insight into the seventh-century British church.[51] The extant text seems to have been compiled in Brittany in the later seventh or very early eighth century, reworking an earlier *Vita* composed *c*.600 in Cornwall.[52] Material cannot be specifically assigned to the original text, but the Breton writer stressed his reliance on mainland British tradition and had visited sites in Britain associated with this Samson.[53] An anecdote related by *Vita Samsonis* seems to reflect British attitudes to, and polemics against, paganism, probably in mainland Britain as well as Brittany.

En route to Brittany, Samson passed through Cornwall, where he came across 'men worshipping a certain idol after the custom of the Bacchantes'.[54] Appalled, he observed their veneration of this 'abominable image'.[55] The language used here is strikingly similar to the terms in which Aldhelm's writings depicted paganism. Aldhelm consistently focused on idols and images, portrayed worshippers as Bacchic revellers and generally avoided mentioning pagan gods. His account of the fourth-century Egyptian ascetic Apollonius in his prose treatise *De virginitate* offers a good example of this approach. Aldhelm's source, Rufinus's *Historia Monachorum*, had described paganism as 'demon-worship', instantiated in the 'demonic superstition' of a god's

---

[50] See John 3: 1–2.

[51] See Nancy Edwards, 'Perspectives on Conversion in Wales', in Roy Flechner and Máire Ní Mhaonaigh, eds, *The Introduction of Christianity into the Early Medieval Insular World: Converting the Isles* (Turnhout, 2016), 93–107, at 94.

[52] Lynette Olson, 'Introduction: "Getting Somewhere" with the First Life of St Samson of Dol', in eadem, ed., *St Samson of Dol and the Earliest History of Brittany, Cornwall and Wales* (Woodbridge, 2017), 1–18; Richard Sowerby, 'The Lives of St Samson: Rewriting the Ambitions of a Medieval Cult', *Francia* 38 (2011), 1–31, at 28–30.

[53] Sowerby, 'Lives of St Samson', 29.

[54] '[H]omines bachantum ritu quoddam fanum … adorantes': *Vita Samsonis* 48, ed. Pierre Flobert, *La Vie ancienne de Saint Samson de Dol* (Paris, 1997), 216; ET: *The Life of St. Samson of Dol*, transl. Thomas Taylor (Felinfach, 1991), 49.

[55] '[S]imulacrum abominabile': *Vita Samsonis* 48, ed. Flobert, *La Vie ancienne*, 216 (*Life of St. Samson*, transl. Taylor, 49).

temple.[56] In Aldhelm's account, however, Apollonius encountered 'some crowds of pagans revelling [*debachantes*] everywhere around an effigy'.[57] The cult-image was merely 'the worthless statue of their idol'.[58] While praising the early martyr Julian, Aldhelm again employed terminology for pagan worship closely similar to that used by *Vita Samsonis*, referring to 'more than five hundred impious statues of idols, to which temple-priests were offering incense, offering up libations like dervishes [*bachantum ritu*]'.[59] Similarly, Aldhelm's account of the martyrdom of Cosmas and Damian avoided explicitly mentioning pagan gods, attributing it rather to unwillingness 'to burn incense at the petty little statues of the pagans'.[60] Thus, Aldhelm repeatedly imposed on his material an understanding of paganism as idolatry strikingly similar to the line taken by *Vita Samsonis*.

This use of *bacchari* and *debacchari* (both meaning 'to rage' or 'rave', with strong Bacchic connotations) to describe pagan worship was absent from Aldhelm's main patristic sources, notably Augustine and Jerome, and lacks parallels in other texts to which he had access.[61] Gildas, for instance, used *debacchari* to depict Maximus's fourth-century usurpation.[62] Venantius Fortunatus used it for drunken merriment.[63] Gregory of Tours – whom Aldhelm never cited – used the word frequently, but for demonic possession and its consequences, rather than for pagan worship.[64] The usage found in Aldhelm seemingly enjoyed very limited

---

[56] '[C]ulturam daemonum', 'daemoniaca superstitio': Rufinus, *Historia Monachorum*, 7.2.1, 7.7.1, in *Tyrannius Rufinus: Historia Monachorum sive de Vita Sanctorum Patrum*, ed. Eva Schulz-Flügel, (Berlin, 1990), 287, 294; ET: *Inquiry about the Monks in Egypt*, transl. Andrew Cain (Washington, DC, 2019), 105, 111.

[57] '[G]entilium turmas circumquaque ... debachantes': Aldhelm, *De Virginitate Prosa* 38, ed. Scott Gwara, *Aldhelmi Malmesbiriensis Prosa de Virginitate: cum Glosa Latina atque Anglosaxonica* (Turnhout, 2001), 559; ET: *Aldhelm: The Prose Works*, transl. Lapidge and Herren, 59–132, at 104.

[58] '[F]rivolam simulacri effigiem': ibid.

[59] '[N]efandas simulacrorum effigies plus quam quingentas, quibus pontifices delubrorum libamina litantes bachantum ritu turificabant': ibid. 36, ed. Gwara, 511–13 (*Aldhelm: The Prose Works*, transl. Lapidge and Herren, 101).

[60] '[A]d turificandum statunculis ethnicorum': ibid, 34, ed. Gwara, 443 (*Aldhelm: The Prose Works*, transl. Lapidge and Herren, 95).

[61] Compare Michael Lapidge, *The Anglo-Saxon Library* (Oxford, 2006), 178–91.

[62] *DEB* 13 (ed. and transl. Michael Winterbottom, 21 [ET], 93).

[63] Venantius Fortunatus, *Carmina, praefatio* 5, ed. Marc Reydellet, *Venance Fortunat. Poèmes – livres I–IV* (Paris, 1994), 5.

[64] Gregory of Tours, *Vitae Patrum* 4.4, 16.4, 17.4, ed. Giselle de Nie, *Gregory of Tours: Lives and Miracles* (Cambridge, MA, 2015), 54, 232, 248; idem, *Liber de Virtutibus Sancti Martini* 2.20, 2.25, 4.21, ed. de Nie, *Gregory of Tours*, 572, 582, 808; idem,

contemporary currency. Bede's use of *debacchari* to depict Cadwallon of Gwynedd's onslaught against the Northumbrians came in a passage apparently inspired by Gildas's treatment of Maximus, while his verse *Life of Cuthbert* used *bacchari* of demonic possession.[65] The West Saxon cleric Boniface used *bachari* to add colour to a depiction of greed, with no hint of pagan worship.[66] Therefore, the characterization of idolatry as Bacchic revelry was unusual. That it features in both *Vita Samsonis* and Aldhelm's writings suggests that British discourse on paganism influenced Aldhelm.

West Saxon texts also represented arguments against paganism in the same way as *Vita Samsonis*. *Vita Samsonis* showed the saint upbraiding the idolaters that 'they ought not to forsake the one God who created all things and worship an idol'.[67] Similar lines of argument featured consistently in West Saxon writings. In the early eighth century, Bishop Daniel of Winchester advised Boniface, then missionizing among continental pagans, to contrast their 'begotten gods' with the universe's need for a creator.[68] Aldhelm's student Æthilwald expressed the same contrast in a poem for his friend Offa, an East Saxon sub-king who abdicated in 709. He dismissed the pagan gods from whom early English royal houses claimed descent and emphasized the Christian God's role as creator.[69] The similarities between *Vita Samsonis*'s perspective on paganism and those expressed by West Saxon authors are clear, involving both terminology and ideas. These parallels could derive from British criticism of West Saxon paganism, before Wessex's mid-seventh-century conversion and perhaps even thereafter.

A further indication that Aldhelm was familiar with British critiques of paganism emerges from his letter to Heahfrith, a prospective student.

Decem Libri Historiarum 7.35, 8.34, 10.25, ed. Bruno Krusch and Wilhelm Levison, MGH SRM 1.1 (Hanover, 1951), 356, 403, 519.

[65] *HE* 2.20; Charles-Edwards, 'Bede, the Irish', 46–7; Bede, *Vita Metrica S. Cudbercti* 13, ed. Michael Lapidge, *Bede's Latin Poetry* (Oxford, 2020), 234–5.

[66] Boniface, *Aenigmata* 13, in *The Old English and Anglo-Latin Riddle Tradition*, ed. Andy Orchard (Cambridge, MA, 2021), 208.

[67] '[N]e idolum, unum Deum qui creavit omnia relinquentes, colere deberent': *Vita Samsonis* 48, ed. Flobert, *La Vie ancienne*, 216 (*Life of St. Samson*, transl. Taylor, 49).

[68] '[G]enitis diis': *Die Briefe des Heiligen Bonifatius und Lullus* 23, ed. Michael Tangl, MGH Epp. Sel. 1 (Berlin, 1916), 39; ET: *The Letters of Saint Boniface*, transl. Ephraim Emerton (New York, 2000), 26.

[69] Æthilwald, *Carmina Rhythmica* 4; ET in: Brent Miles, ed. and transl., 'The *Carmina Rhythmica* of Æthilwald: Edition, Translation, and Commentary', *Journal of Medieval Latin* 14 (2004), 73–117, at 95.

In a rare depiction of early English paganism, Aldhelm described how 'once the crude pillars of the same foul snake and the stag were worshipped with coarse stupidity'.[70] He borrowed 'coarse stupidity' from Gildas's description of the pagan Balaam cursing the Israelites, while the statement as a whole recalls Gildas's portrayal of Romano-British idolatry.[71] Aldhelm had probably read Gildas during his early education and his considerable literary debt to him suggests Aldhelm's respect for British scholarship.[72] Aldhelm may even have brought *De Excidio Britanniae* to Theodore's school at Canterbury, where he was among the earliest students, and where *De Excidio* was used for Latin teaching and as a rare Latin source for the *Laterculus Malalianus*, a theological text which its editor has described as 'an historical exegesis of the life of Christ'.[73] Stancliffe's hypothesis that Bede acquired information about Augustine of Canterbury's second encounter with British bishops from a British text preserved at Malmesbury further suggests West Saxon interest in British perspectives on recent ecclesiastical history.[74] Aldhelm's awareness that Britons had criticized West Saxon paganism implies that he would not have shared Bede's assessment of their greatest sin, failing to preach to the English.[75]

Aldhelm's consciousness of British perspectives on paganism thus provides the context for his presentation of the West Saxons as the repentant sinner. He acknowledged thereby that the Britons had been Christians much longer and that he risked ridicule by criticizing British liturgical practice when the West Saxons were recent pagans. The metaphor was, however, also subtly threatening. Aldhelm quoted Christ's rebuke of the Pharisees for judging the sinful woman.[76] Moreover, her frequent identification as Mary Magdalene, who stood

---

[70] '[P]ridem eiusdem nefandae natricis ermula cervulusque cruda … colebantur stoliditate': Aldhelm, *Epistola ad Ehfridum*, in Rudolf Ehwald, ed., *Aldhelmi Opera*, MGH AA 15 (Berlin, 1919), 488–94, at 488; ET: *Aldhelm: The Prose Works*, transl. Lapidge and Herren, 160–4, at 161.

[71] Neil Wright, 'Aldhelm, Gildas and Acircius', in idem, *History and Literature in Late Antiquity and the Early Medieval West* (Aldershot, 1995), n.p. [1–28], 7 [NB: the volume's pagination is not continuous].

[72] Compare ibid.; Yorke, 'Aldhelm's Irish', 175.

[73] Brian Christopher Hardison, 'Words, Meanings and Readings: Reconstructing the Use of Gildas's *De Excidio Britanniae* at the Canterbury School', *Viator* 47 (2015), 1–22.

[74] Clare Stancliffe, 'The British Church and the Mission of Augustine', in Richard Gameson, ed., *St Augustine and the Conversion of England* (Stroud, 1999), 107–51, at 126–8.

[75] Stancliffe, *Bede and the Britons*, 5, 8.

[76] *Ep. Ger.*, 485 (Lapidge and Herren, *Aldhelm: The Prose Works*, 159).

by Christ's cross and became the first witness to his resurrection, hinted that the West Saxons could achieve far greater honour than the Britons, their earlier sins notwithstanding.[77] If some Britons, at least, were ill-fated Pharisees, the West Saxons stood for the fresh start Christ offered sinners. They attained this status as adherents to Roman practices and members of the universal Church. Implicit within Aldhelm's superficially humble metaphor was Bede's later perception of the Britons as having forfeited their divine election, though, in contrast to Bede's generalized denunciation, Aldhelm's perspective seems narrowly concerned with specific shortcomings.

Indeed, Aldhelm sought to appropriate the Britons' Christian heritage, which he did not consider fundamentally compromised. Aldhelm staked a claim to British Christianity by stressing that he wrote at the behest of 'an episcopal council, where, out of almost the entirety of Britain an innumerable company of the bishops of God came together'.[78] This description was scarcely accurate. Only five bishops seem to have attended the Council of Hertford, all from south-eastern and south-central Britain, representing churches in the early English kingdoms of Kent, East Anglia, Mercia and Wessex.[79] Moreover, the council apparently acknowledged that its jurisdiction only encompassed Canterbury's ecclesiastical province, excluding the Northumbrian see at York.[80] The salience of Aldhelm's claim stemmed from its assertion that a single British church existed, from which he hoped that the Britons would not separate.

Bede also appropriated Britain's Christian heritage, particularly in Book I of his *Historia Ecclesiastica*.[81] However, whereas Aldhelm seems to have associated the Britons with an image of sinful Israel indirectly, Bede did so unambiguously. He compared the Germanic migration to Britain with the Babylonian conquest following Israel and Judah's long moral decline, again borrowing the analogy from Gildas,[82] but

---

[77] Compare Matt. 27: 56, 28: 1–10; Mark 15: 40, 16: 1–11; Luke 24: 1–11; John 19: 25, 20: 1–18.

[78] '[C]oncilio episcoporum, ubi ex tota paene Brittania innumerabilis Dei sacerdotum caterva confluxit': *Ep. Ger.*, 481 (Lapidge and Herren, *Aldhelm: The Prose Works*, 155).

[79] *HE* 4.5 (*Ecclesiastical History*, ed. Colgrave and Mynors, 349–51).

[80] Alan Thacker, 'Wilfrid: His Cult and his Biographer', in Nicholas J. Higham, ed., *Wilfrid: Abbot, Bishop, Saint* (Donington, 2013), 1–16, at 6–7.

[81] *HE* 1.16–1.22 (*Ecclesiastical History*, ed. Colgrave and Mynors, 53-69).

[82] *HE* 1.15 (*Ecclesiastical History*, ed. Colgrave and Mynors, 53); *DEB* 24 (ed. and transl. Michael Winterbottom, 27, 97–8).

using Gildas quite differently to Aldhelm. Whereas Aldhelm had respected Gildas as an authoritative Christian teacher, in line with contemporary British and Irish opinion, Bede reframed his prophetic lament as historical description, asserting that their 'unspeakable crimes … Gildas their own historian describes in doleful words'.[83] Treating Gildas as an historian allowed Bede to argue that the Britons had forfeited their position through their sinfulness.[84] Aldhelm's letter shows that the seeds of this logic had been sown in Wessex by the late seventh century, but had not yet fully germinated. West Saxon Christianity's relative novelty remained the dominant context for church relations, while Aldhelm continued to respect the British Christian tradition.

ROME AS CENTRE

Given this religious environment, Aldhelm's criticisms of British practice required him to appeal beyond local tradition and authority, grounds on which the Britons were undeniably stronger. Thus, he framed his argument in Roman terms, adjuring Geraint 'that you no longer detest with swollen pride of heart and with scornful breast the doctrine and decrees of blessed Peter'.[85] The letter repeatedly appealed to Petrine and Roman authority, which both Bede and Stephen of Ripon suggested had been decisive at Whitby.[86] Aldhelm concluded his letter with a reference to Christ's entrustment of the keys to Peter and his naming him as the rock on which the church was built.[87] According to Bede, Wilfrid similarly rested his case with the entrustment of the keys to Peter.[88] Aldhelm also criticized the Dumnonians

---

[83] '[I]nenarrabilium scelerum facta … historicus eorum Gildas flebili sermone describit': *HE* 1.22 (*Ecclesiastical History*, ed. Colgrave and Mynors, 69); Stancliffe, *Bede and the Britons*, 2–11. See also Stephen J. Joyce, *The Legacy of Gildas: Constructions of Authority in the Early Medieval West* (Woodbridge, 2022), 36–42.
[84] *HE* 1.22, 2.2 (*Ecclesiastical History*, ed. Colgrave and Mynors, 69, 141–3); Cardwell, 'The People Whom He Foreknew', 42.
[85] '[U]t ulterius doctrinam et decreta beati Petri contumaci cordis supercilio et protervo pectore non abominemini': *Ep. Ger.*, 485 (Lapidge and Herren, *Aldhelm: The Prose Works*, 159).
[86] *HE* 3.25 (*Ecclesiastical History*, ed. Colgrave and Mynors, 294–309); *VW* 10 (*Life*, ed. Colgrave, 21–3).
[87] *Ep. Ger.*, 485–6 (Lapidge and Herren, *Aldhelm: The Prose Works*, 159–60).
[88] *HE* 3.25 (*Ecclesiastical History*, ed. Colgrave and Mynors, 306–7); compare *VW* 10 (*Life*, ed. Colgrave, 23).

for rejecting 'the tonsure of St Peter, prince of the apostles' and for not observing Easter in line with the Council of Nicaea, whose participants were 'the bishops of the Roman church'.[89]

Aldhelm's insistence on an all-encompassing understanding of Petrine authority implies that he knew it would strike Dumnonian readers as novel and unwarranted. Indeed, *Vita Samsonis* articulated an ecclesiology based on an annual episcopal synod.[90] The Britons' response to Augustine also emphasized synodical governance, while Gildas applied Christ's grant of the keys to Peter to every 'holy bishop'.[91] Aldhelm's criticism of British liturgical customs, from a consciously marginal position in terms of tradition and authority, needed to redefine ecclesial centres and peripheries. The similarities between his approach and that attributed to Wilfrid may be connected to Agilbert, who was both Wilfrid's senior colleague at Whitby and bishop of Wessex during Aldhelm's youth.[92]

Aldhelm may also have been influenced by Theodore's introduction of a significant ecclesiological development to the insular world. The contemporary papacy actively promoted Rome's significance as a holy city and its own unique status as the 'institutionalization' of Christ and the apostles' work, via the apostolic succession.[93] Papal claims to be defending orthodoxy were central to a bitter mid-seventh-century rift with Constantinople over Monotheletism, which the emperors promoted as a Christological compromise to heal the Eastern split over Miaphysitism. Pope Martin I was arrested in 649 for his opposition to imperial religious policy and died in exile, leading to his veneration as a martyr. The venerable monk-theologian Maximus was subsequently seized from Rome and exiled, dying following the mutilation of his arm.[94] Theodore belonged to the same circle as Maximus and was present in Rome as these shocking

---

[89] '[T]onsuram sancti Petri, apostolorum principis'; 'ecclesiae Romanae pontifices': *Ep. Ger.*, 482–3 (Lapidge and Herren, *Aldhelm: The Prose Works*, 156–7).
[90] *Vita Samsonis* 42–3, ed. Flobert, *La Vie ancienne*, 206–10 (*Life of St. Samson*, transl. Taylor, 43–5).
[91] Stancliffe, 'The British Church', 132–3.
[92] *HE* 3.7, 3.25 (*Ecclesiastical History*, ed. Colgrave and Mynors, 298–301); *VW* 10 (*Life*, ed. Colgrave, 21).
[93] Rosamund McKitterick, *Rome and the Invention of the Papacy* (Cambridge, 2020), 35–6, 228.
[94] W. Trent Foley, *Images of Sanctity in Eddius Stephanus' Life of Bishop Wilfrid: An Early English Saint's Life* (Lampeter, 1992), 80–3, 99; Catherine Cubitt, 'Appendix 2: The Chronology of Stephen's Life of Wilfrid', in Higham, ed., *Wilfrid*, 334–47, at 342.

events unfolded.[95] Their consequence was a new definition of *Romanitas* as theological orthodoxy in line with papal Rome. This obviated the significance of the Britons' own ancient tradition and their status as (arguably former) imperial *cives*.[96] Obedience to papal Rome provided Aldhelm's argument's touchstone, notwithstanding his respect for British Christianity.

Thus, in south-western Britain *c.*672, neither British nor English Christians could effectively establish a claim to ecclesiastical centrality. The Britons' much longer Christian tradition was being undercut by the increasing emphasis on papal authority. The West Saxons were recent converts, and their ecclesiological assertions had limited efficacy faced with a local church confident in its own bishops' authority. Aldhelm's response was to preserve strong ties with the Britons, even while articulating an ecclesiology which pushed them to the margins.

The Britons become Peripheral

From the 690s, the Britons' political failure seems to have rendered the British church peripheral, no longer a recognized counterpart to the church of the West Saxons, to which it was losing adherents. The West Saxons had encroached westwards for much of the seventh century, apparently winning key victories over the Britons in 658 and 682.[97] The chronology of this expansion cannot be determined precisely, but Wessex's primary mid-century concern remained the Mercian threat.[98] The career of Ceadwalla – the best-documented seventh-century West Saxon ruler by far – indicates that in the late 680s, Wessex's key interests lay further east. Ceadwalla conquered Sussex, Surrey and the Isle of Wight and clashed with Kent.[99] Only under his successor Ine (r. 689–726) was Wessex able to concentrate on the

---

[95] Phil Booth, *Crisis of Empire: Doctrine and Dissent at the End of Late Antiquity* (Berkeley, CA, 2014), 135–6.

[96] Charles-Edwards, *Wales*, 239–41.

[97] *Anglo-Saxon Chronicle* [hereafter: *ASC*], *s.a.* 658 and 682, in *The Anglo-Saxon Chronicle: A Collaborative Edition*, ed. David Dumville and Simon Keynes, 9 vols (with a volume for each textual variant, customarily designated by letters) (Cambridge, 1983–2005), A: 30, 32; B: 21, 23; C: 39, 41; E: 29, 33; Probert, 'New Light', 111–12; Bruce Eagles, *From Roman Civitas to Anglo-Saxon Shire: Topographical Studies on the Formation of Wessex* (Oxford, 2018), 139.

[98] Barbara Yorke, *Wessex in the Early Middle Ages* (London, 1995), 57–62; D. P. Kirby, *The Earliest English Kings*, rev. edn (London, 2000; first publ. 1991), 46–9.

[99] *HE* 4.15–4.16 (*Ecclesiastical History*, ed. Colgrave and Mynors, 381–5).

Britons to its west.[100] The frontier zone probably consisted of multiple, localized borders between 'Englishries' and 'Britishries', meaning that increasing numbers of British communities and their churches fell under West Saxon rule.[101] Early in his reign, Ine issued a law code which codified his British subjects' second-class status and provided for their assets' long-term transfer to the English, through ethnically-differentiated compensation tariffs.[102] Military, legal and economic repression seems to have been matched by a harsher political culture. John-Henry Clay has argued that Ine promoted a dynastic identity founded upon the Britons' defeat and dispossession, traced back to Cerdic centuries earlier.[103]

This deteriorating socio-political situation may have engendered serious ecclesiastical consequences.[104] Bede praised Aldhelm, because he 'led many of those Britons who were subject to the West Saxons to adopt the catholic celebration of the Easter of the Lord'.[105] That is, Aldhelm converted residents of 'Britishries' under West Saxon control, presumably in tandem with their secular subordination.[106] Although the passage only dates their conversion to the period of Aldhelm's abbacy, it may be possible to situate it more specifically. Three chapters earlier, Bede had referred to the adoption of the Roman Easter by 'the greater part of the Irish in Ireland and some of the Britons in Britain'.[107] These may be the same Britons, namely many of

---

[100] Thus John-Henry Clay's proposal that the Gewisse 'annexed' Dorset, Somerset and Devon during 652–61 cannot be accepted: John-Henry Clay, '*Adventus*, Warfare, and the Britons in the Development of West Saxon Identity', in Walter Pohl and Gerda Heydemann, eds, *Post-Roman Transitions: Christian and Barbarian Identities in the Early Medieval West* (Turnhout, 2013), 169–213, at 191.

[101] Barker, '*Usque Domnoniam*: Sherborne', 91–2; Alex Woolf, 'Apartheid and Economics in Anglo-Saxon England', in Nicholas J. Higham, ed., *Britons in Anglo-Saxon England* (Woodbridge, 2007), 115–29, at 128; Eagles, *From Roman Civitas*, 138. Linguistic data may corroborate such socio-cultural enclaves: Duncan Probert, 'Mapping Early Medieval Language Change in South-West England', in Higham, ed., *Britons*, at 231–44, at 243.

[102] Woolf, 'Apartheid and Economics', 127–9; Martin Grimmer, 'Britons in Early Wessex: The Evidence of the Law Code of Ine', in Higham, ed., *Britons*, 102–14.

[103] Clay, '*Adventus*, Warfare', 202–4.

[104] Woolf, 'Apartheid and Economics', 127–9.

[105] '[M]ultos ... eorum, qui Occidentalibus Saxonibus subditi erant Brettones, ad catholicam dominici paschae celebrationem ... perduxit': *HE* 5.18 (*Ecclesiastical History*, ed. Colgrave and Mynors, 515). See Stancliffe, 'The British Church', 110; Cardwell, 'What Sort of Love?', 407.

[106] Charles-Edwards, *Wales*, 428. Compare Probert, 'New Light', 115; Stancliffe, *Bede and the Britons*, 17.

[107] '[P]lurima pars Scottorum in Hibernia, et nonnulla etiam de Brettonibus in Brittania': *HE* 5.15 (*Ecclesiastical History*, ed. Colgrave and Mynors, 505).

those under West Saxon rule.[108] Charles-Edwards suggested that the 'Quo tempore' which opened this chapter referred to Theodore's death in 690.[109] However, Theodore's death's significance as the chronological anchor to which it might refer seems diluted by the precise dates for his successor's election, consecration and enthronement in 692–3 which Bede had also provided.[110] Probert proposed Willibrord's consecration, which Bede dated to 696. Probert argued that the northern Irish probably adopted the Roman Easter in 697, based on the presence of Adomnán of Iona at the Synod of Birr.[111] However, Armagh had apparently done so by 688, undermining the case for Irish and British conversions c.695–7.[112] All that can be shown is that Bede located these conversions in the 690s or perhaps late 680s. If the Britons in question were those converted by Aldhelm, he was apparently able to take a much more direct and successful approach in this period than he had done in c.672, which would be consistent with the Britons' weakened socio-political position.

The Britons' situation continued to worsen thereafter, with the *Anglo-Saxon Chronicle* depicting warfare between Ine and Geraint in 710, the year after Aldhelm died. This may provide the context for Geraint's grant of an estate in Cornwall to the West Saxon church at Sherborne (Dorset), further suggesting that the English church was becoming established as the ecclesiastical centre.[113] Charles-Edwards interpreted the *Annales Cambriae*'s reference to a battle among the *Cornuenses* in 722 as suggesting that Dumnonia probably fell to the West Saxons in the early eighth century.[114] Thus, from the 690s, the south-western Britons' political standing was in decline for a generation. By contrast, Aldhelm's letter to Geraint did not speak to total Dumnonian disintegration. Aldhelm wrote before it was clearly established, theologically or politically, who was peripheral, and at a time when Theodore's ideas still seemed novel, thus further strengthening the case that it was commissioned by the Council of Hertford.

---

[108] Charles-Edwards, *Wales*, 403.

[109] Ibid. 403 n. 135.

[110] *HE* 5.8 (*Ecclesiastical History*, ed. Colgrave and Mynors, 473–5).

[111] Probert, 'New Light', 121.

[112] Charles-Edwards, *Early Christian Ireland*, 428.

[113] *ASC*, s.a. 710 (*The Anglo-Saxon Chronicle*, ed. Dumville and Keynes, A: 33; B: 24; C: 43; D: 10; E: 35); *Charters of Sherborne*, ed. M. A. O'Donovan (Oxford, 1988), xlii, xlviii, 81; Barker, '*Usque Domnoniam*: Sherborne', 82–3.

[114] *Annales Cambriae, s.a.* 722, in *Nennius: British History and the Welsh Annals*, ed. and transl. John Morris (London, 1980), 45–9, 85–91; Charles-Edwards, *Wales*, 429–30.

Wider Perspectives

Neither the British nor the West Saxon church was marginalized in south-western Britain until the Britons' political collapse, seemingly in the 690s and early years of the eighth century. In the 670s and probably also the 680s, ecclesiastical relations were far from the antipathy represented by Bede and Stephen. West Saxon attitudes to British Christianity in this period appear comparable to those many Northumbrians held towards the Irish tradition. Aldhelm respected the Britons intellectually and shared hospitality with them, while some adherents of Roman practice were sufficiently attracted by British monasticism to undertake penance and enter a British monastery. West Saxon clerics remained in communion with their British neighbours and, to some extent, continued to respect their claim, as long-standing Christians, to a certain spiritual centrality. Aldhelm, at least, remained conscious that the Britons had been Christian long before his own people and had made forceful criticisms of paganism. His letter recognized the British church's tradition, while nonetheless demanding full conformity with papal Rome, the centre of authority.

The South-West may not have been typical, as substantial regional variation seems likely.[115] Nonetheless, this study shows that here, at least, the 660s was not a caesura in relations between adherents of the two Easters and tonsures. Moreover, the career of Wine, Wessex's most infamous early bishop, may imply that the early English more widely continued to respect the British church into the 670s.

Apart from two brief references in the *Anglo-Saxon Chronicle*, Wine is only known from Bede's *History*, which painted a deeply unflattering portrait.[116] Bede's most serious charges were that, having left Wessex, Wine purchased the see of London and that he had earlier consecrated Chad bishop with the assistance of two British co-consecrators, rendering Chad's orders defective.[117] Yet, as this article has argued, when Wine requested his British confrères' assistance, concelebration with clergy from the British church was unproblematic in the South-West. Wine made that request to comply with the Council of Nicaea's requirement for at least three episcopal consecrators, reiterated in

---

[115] See Stancliffe, *Bede and the Britons*, 17.

[116] *ASC, s.a.* 656 (E text only) and *s.a.* 660 (*The Anglo-Saxon Chronicle*, ed. Dumville and Keynes, E: 29–30; and A: 30; B: 21; C: 39).

[117] *HE* 3.7, 3.28; 4.2, 4.12 (*Ecclesiastical History*, ed. Colgrave and Mynors, 235, 317, 335, 369). Compare *VW* 15 (*Life*, ed. Colgrave, 33).

Gregory the Great's *Libellus Responsionum*, regarded as authoritative in the contemporary English church.[118] Wine's appointment as bishop of London by Wulfhere of Mercia seems murkier. Barbara Yorke initially suggested that, while still Wessex's bishop, Wine had colluded with Wulfhere, its archenemy, but more recently has presented Wine as a victim of Mercian abduction.[119] The allegation of simony seems a later imputation. Aldhelm told Geraint that his clerics' un-Roman style of tonsure was devised by Simon Magus.[120] As attitudes towards the Britons hardened, the charge of simony might have been levelled against the defector Wine in view of his co-operation with British colleagues.

The unreliability of the simony charge indicates that Wine's collaboration with British bishops did not make him unsuitable for the episcopate in Wulfhere's eyes, suggesting that late 660s Mercian attitudes to the British church may not have been dissimilar to those in Wessex. However, following Theodore's arrival in 669, Wine's actions must have appeared more questionable, as the new archbishop insisted that Chad's consecration be regularized, due to the British bishops' participation.[121] Nonetheless, Theodore's view of Wine is hard to gauge. He was not removed as bishop of London, yet did not attend the Council of Hertford.[122] In eighth-century Northumbria, Bede and Stephen presented Chad's consecration and, in Bede's case, Wine himself, as profoundly problematic.[123] The transformation of

---

[118] *HE* 1.27 (*Ecclesiastical History*, ed. Colgrave and Mynors, 87); Norman Tanner, ed., *Decrees of the Ecumenical Councils*, 1: *Nicaea I to Lateran V* (London, 1990), 7; Flechner, 'An Insular Tradition', 32–7; Michael Elliot, 'New Evidence for the Influence of Gallic Canon Law in Anglo-Saxon England', *JEH* 64 (2013), 700–30, at 706. Compare Grimmer, 'Bede', 117 n. 66.

[119] Yorke, *Wessex*, 172; eadem, 'Competition for the Solent and 7th-century Politics', in Ben Jervis, ed., *The Middle Ages Revisited* (Oxford, 2018), 35–43 at 38.

[120] *Ep. Ger.*, 482 (Lapidge and Herren, *Aldhelm: The Prose Works*, 156–7).

[121] *HE* 4.2 (*Ecclesiastical History*, ed. Colgrave and Mynors, 335); *VW* 15 (*Life*, ed. Colgrave, 33). Stancliffe argued that Stephen of Ripon's account, in which Chad was fully reordained by Theodore and Wilfrid, was probably accurate, rather than Bede's, in which he was not, citing reasons why Bede would have suggested reconciliation rather than reordination: Stancliffe, *Bede, Wilfrid and the Irish*, 16. However, the *Capitula Dacheriana* recension of Theodore's Penitential contains only the ruling requiring reconciliation, not that requiring reordination, while Aldhelm's letter and poem, by condoning joint liturgy, assumed the validity of Britons' orders. It therefore seems more likely that Theodore reconciled Chad, in line with Bede's account.

[122] *HE* 3.7, 4.5 (*Ecclesiastical History*, ed. Colgrave and Mynors, 235, 349–51).

[123] *HE* 3.7, 4.2 (*Ecclesiastical History*, ed. Colgrave and Mynors, 235, 335); *VW* 14–15 (*Life*, ed. Colgrave, 31–3).

attitudes towards the British church was gradual, yet radical. Recognizing that, Bede's twin imputations against Wine should be set aside. Wine's career suggests that, after Whitby and even after Theodore's arrival, his concelebration with British bishops was not generally seen as blame-worthy.

An obscure comment in Stephen's *Life of Wilfrid* may suggest that, notwithstanding the strength of eighth-century anti-British discourse in Northumbria, even there, relations were not unambiguously antagonistic in the late seventh century. After Wilfrid's release from prison in Dunbar, East Lothian, in 681, 'he was driven from his own province in such a way that no rest was allowed him even in the land of strangers on either side of the sea, wherever the power of Ecgfrith prevailed'.[124] This suggests that Wilfrid considered exile on both sides of the Firth of Forth, in Pictish and British territory.[125] Although Wilfrid's monastic confederation had expanded among the Britons, Picts and Scots, the possibility of his exile there seems not to have been considered, perhaps due to his self-presentation as an arch-romanist.[126] Nonetheless, on a recent visit to Rome, Wilfrid had subscribed to the anti-Monothelete synod on behalf of 'all the northern part of Britain and Ireland and the islands, which are inhabited by the races of Angles and Britons as well as Scots and Picts'.[127] This suggests that he saw himself in some form of ecclesial relation to British Christians. This could be simply staking a claim for York to be recognized as the metropolitan see for northern Britain and Ireland because of local churches' heterodoxy on Easter.[128]

---

[124] '[D]e propria provincia expulsus erat, ita ut nec in aliena regione ultra vel citra mare, ubi potestas Ecgfrithi praevaluit, requiem habere permiserit': *VW* 41 (*Life*, ed. Colgrave, 81).

[125] Stephen of Ripon's account of Wilfrid's first imprisonment had a certain British undertone, giving British names for two places under Northumbrian control: *Dynbaer* (Dunbar) and *Broninis*: *VW* 36, 38 (*Life*, ed. Colgrave, 73, 77); Leslie Alcock, *Bede, Eddius and the Forts of the North Britons*, Jarrow Lecture 1988 (Jarrow, 1988), 4–6. Andrew Breeze proposed that *Broninis* means 'meadow hill' and was Durham's British name: Andrew Breeze, 'Was Durham the *Broninis* of Eddius's Life of St Wilfrid?', in Richard Coates and Andrew Breeze, *Celtic Voices, English Places* (Stamford, 2000), 147–9.

[126] *VW* 21 (*Life*, ed. Colgrave, 43).

[127] '[O]mni aquilonali parte Brittanniae et Hiberniae insulisque quae ab Anglorum et Brittonum necnon Scottorum et Pictorum gentibus colebantur': *VW* 53 (*Life*, ed. Colgrave, 115).

[128] T. M. Charles-Edwards, 'Wilfrid and the Celts', in Higham, ed., *Wilfrid*, 243–59, at 257–9.

Indeed, Wilfrid's monastic family's northward expansion seems to have been associated with Northumbrian imperialism.[129] Nevertheless, Wilfrid apparently considered British and Pictish areas to be potentially suitable places of exile. While in his eyes undoubtedly peripheral, the Britons were not yet entirely beyond the pale.

---

[129] Ibid.; Sarah Foot, 'Wilfrid's Monastic Empire', in Higham, ed., *Wilfrid*, 27–39, at 33–5.

Correctio from the Margins: Geographical Peripheries and Moral Conformity in Later Carolingian Annals

Robert A. H. Evans

Radley College

This article explores how accounts of those living on the periphery of the Carolingian empire were used by authors at the centre as good examples, in order to promote the lessons of religious reform. Scholarship has primarily focused on how early medieval authors elided geographical distance and a lack of moral probity. In many cases, this helped to construct a sense of a geographically bounded Christian people defined by their moral conformity. The cases in this article, however, demonstrate a willingness – especially in the later ninth century – to take lessons from people who were strange and different, and even to use these as critiques of those at the centre who ought to have known better.

The Carolingian reforms presented themselves, at least superficially, as about centralization.[1] From the late eighth century onwards, Frankish kings and churchmen sought to bring conformity and unity wherever there was error and diversity. For these reformers, the deviances of paganism, heresy and immorality – not to mention ecclesiastical incompetence – all needed to submit to correction from the centre.[2] Indeed, the term *correctio* has often been used as a scholarly shorthand for the drive to improve Christian life and thought in the light of standards set by the court.[3] Just as the Frankish kingdoms had military

History Department, Radley College, Abingdon, OX14 2HR. E-mail: rahe.evans@radley.org.uk.

I should like to thank the audience at the EHS Winter Conference in January 2024 and the anonymous peer reviewers for their helpful feedback and comments. I should also like to express my gratitude for the help and encouragement provided by Lesley Abrams, Katy Cubitt, Carey Fleiner and Sam Ottewill-Soulsby. Any errors remain, as ever, my own.

[1] Thomas F. X. Noble, 'Carolingian Religion', *ChH* 84 (2015), 287–307, at 295–300.

[2] For key accounts, see Rosamond McKitterick, *Charlemagne: The Formation of a European Identity* (Cambridge, 2008), 306–20; Mayke de Jong, *The Penitential State: Authority and Atonement in the Age of Louis the Pious*, 814–840 (New York, 2009), 112–47.

[3] On the vocabulary of the Carolingian reforms and its pitfalls, see Carine van Rhijn, 'Introduction: rethinking the Carolingian reforms', in Arthur Westwell, Ingrid Rembold and Carine van Rhijn, eds, *Rethinking the Carolingian Reforms* (Manchester, 2023), 1–30,

Studies in Church History 61 (2025), 71–94 © The Author(s), 2025. Published by Cambridge University Press on behalf of the Ecclesiastical History Society.
doi:10.1017/stc.2024.30

frontiers, so did Christian orthodoxy and morality have boundaries that included and excluded. At the same time, however, conformity did not equate to the unilateral and top-down process that might be assumed.[4] In Rutger Kramer's words, 'the Frankish Church thrived on diversity and had the ability to accommodate many different varieties of the same core message'.[5] Those at the centre allowed for greater variety of expression than a cursory reading of their ideals might suggest. Conformity did not mean uniformity. Carolingian rulers and their advisers even valued debate and the expression of alternative viewpoints (drawing heavily on Roman models of rhetoric).[6] As this article will explore, such open-mindedness extended to what lessons could be learned from those living on the distant peripheries of the Frankish kingdoms.

The early medieval periphery has attracted considerable recent attention in two ways.[7] The first has been the political, military and diplomatic management of geographical frontiers and the extent to which, for example, the Carolingians successfully incorporated them into their realms.[8] The second has been how the geographical margins and their inhabitants spurred reflections about identity and community at the centre.[9] Through 'strategies of distinction' and perceptions of moral and cultural difference, 'group identity could be strengthened

---

especially at 16–18. Although the term *correctio* can be overly elastic, it remains a convenient shorthand that the Franks themselves actually used.

[4] Rutger Kramer, *Rethinking Authority in the Carolingian Empire: Ideals and Expectations during the Reign of Louis the Pious (813–828)* (Amsterdam, 2019), 49–57; van Rhijn, 'Introduction', 26–9.

[5] Rutger Kramer, 'Monasticism, Reform, and Authority in the Carolingian Era', in Alison Beach and Isabelle Cochelin, eds, *The Cambridge History of Medieval Monasticism in the Latin West*, 1: *Origins to the Eleventh Century* (Cambridge, 2020), 432–49, at 433.

[6] Irene van Renswoude, *The Rhetoric of Free Speech in Late Antiquity and the Early Middle Ages* (Cambridge, 2019), 180–205; Mayke de Jong, *Epitaph for an Era: Politics and Rhetoric in the Carolingian World* (Cambridge, 2019), 102–31.

[7] Walter Pohl, 'Frontiers and Ethnic Identities: Some Final Considerations', in Florin Curta, ed., *Borders, Barriers, and Ethnogenesis: Frontiers in Late Antiquity and the Middle Ages* (Turnhout, 2005), 255–65.

[8] Julia M. H. Smith, '*Fines Imperii*: The Marches', in Rosamond McKitterick, ed., *The New Cambridge Medieval History*, 2: *c.700–c.900* (Cambridge, 1995), 169–89; Sam Ottewill-Soulsby, *The Emperor and the Elephant: Christians and Muslims in the Age of Charlemagne* (Princeton, NJ, 2023), 114–15, 151–2.

[9] Pohl, 'Final Considerations', 265.

by emphasis of what did not belong'.[10] The elision of an early medieval ethnic identity with a sense of moral rectitude depended partly on the vilification of those 'strange peoples' (*exterae gentes*) beyond the frontiers.[11] A combined moral and political centre – centred upon royal courts and associated ecclesiastical networks – made sense if those who were geographically distant were also morally beyond the pale.

Carolingian thinkers, however, did not necessarily envisage the boundaries of Christianity and the military frontiers of the empire as coextensive. As various scholars have stressed, the Franks did not think that they – as an ethnic group – had a monopoly on 'good Christianity'.[12] Theodulf of Orléans, writing in the early 790s, wrote that 'almost the entire world is filled with Christ's people'.[13] By definition, Christian identity had permeable edges, capable of including ethnic variations and those at or beyond geographical frontiers. This article explores how, perhaps surprisingly, the geographical periphery furnished some Carolingian authors with positive moral counsel and exemplars. Those at the geographical margins exemplified views and behaviours that conformed precisely to the moral ideals which these authors wished to press upon their readers. The geographically peripheral, yet morally conformist, could admonish those at the centre who deviated from the core message of contemporary reform. This strategy of admonition, which echoed the 'valorisation of the barbarians' by Roman historians such as Tacitus, found particular expression in Frankish annals.[14]

---

[10] Walter Pohl and Ian Wood, 'Introduction: Cultural Memory and the Resources of the Past', in Clemens Gantner et al., eds, *The Resources of the Past in Early Medieval Europe* (Cambridge, 2015), 1–12, at 10. See also essays collected in Walter Pohl and Helmut Reimitz, eds, *Strategies of Distinction: The Construction of Ethnic Communities, 300–800* (Leiden, 1998).

[11] Hans-Werner Goetz, '*Gens*: Terminology and Perception of the "Germanic" Peoples from Late Antiquity to the Early Middle Ages', in Richard Corradini et al., eds, *The Construction of Communities in the Early Middle Ages: Texts, Resources and Artefacts* (Leiden, 2003), 39–64, at 58–9.

[12] Conor O'Brien, 'Empire, Ethnic Election and Exegesis in the *Opus Caroli* (*Libri Carolini*)', in Stewart J. Brown, Charlotte Methuen and Andrew Spicer, eds, *The Church and Empire*, SCH 54 (Cambridge, 2018), 96–108; Gerda Heydemann and Walter Pohl, 'The Rhetoric of Election: 1 Peter 2.9 and the Franks', in Rob Meens et al., eds, *Religious Franks: Religion and Power in the Frankish Kingdoms. Studies in Honour of Mayke De Jong* (Manchester, 2016), 13–31.

[13] O'Brien, 'Empire, Ethnic Election and Exegesis', 108.

[14] Eric Adler, *Valorizing the Barbarians: Enemy Speeches in Roman Historiography* (Austin, TX, 2011).

Structured according to the years of the Incarnation, annals had emerged in the late eighth century.[15] As with all early medieval histories, they did not simply describe their world and its events (mimetically), but sought to show their readers how to navigate them (prescriptively).[16] Frankish annalists became increasingly prescriptive as the ninth century wore on, especially as moral rhetoric intensified during the reign of Louis the Pious (814–40).[17] Part of this was the depiction of moral 'otherness' against or through which valid norms could be taught. This article looks at four annalists from the 840s to the 890s, who contributed to the so-called *Annals of St Bertin* and *Annals of Fulda*. Each of these annalists were, broadly speaking, close to the courtly centres of the Carolingian kingdoms. The *Annals of St Bertin* were written first by courtiers of Louis the Pious, followed by Prudentius, bishop of Troyes, and then finally by Hincmar, adviser to Charles the Bald (r. 840–77).[18] The *Annals of Fulda*, meanwhile, were written at one of the foremost monasteries of the East Frankish kingdom with excellent links to the court of Louis the German (r. 840–76).[19] These authors enjoyed proximity to royal power but also – as part of the upper echelons of the Frankish church – helped to generate the normative centre against which moral non-conformity was measured.

The article considers these annalists because they all depicted marginal groups who endorsed – by word or deed – Carolingian moral norms, as part of a wider didactic strategy to conform their own audiences to that imagined moral centre. These episodes are complex, and the groups involved were marginal to different extents. Some were

---

[15] Helmut Reimitz, *History, Frankish Identity, and the Framing of Western Ethnicity 550–850* (Cambridge, 2015), 293–443.

[16] Gabrielle Spiegel, 'History, Historicism, and the Social Logic of the Text in the Middle Ages', *Speculum* 65 (1990), 59–86.

[17] De Jong, *Penitential State*, 59–111; compare Robert Evans, 'The Writing of Annals in the Frankish Kingdoms after 829', in Sören Kaschke and Bart van Hees, eds, *Annals in Carolingian Europe: A Genre in Motion* (forthcoming).

[18] *Annales Bertiniani*, ed. Félix Grat, Jeanne Vielliard and Suzanne Clémencet, Société de l'histoire de France 470 (Paris, 1964) [hereafter: *AB*, followed by year of entry and page number]; Janet L. Nelson, 'Annals of St. Bertin', in Margaret Gibson and eadem, eds, *Charles the Bald: Court and Kingdom*, 2nd edn (Aldershot, 1990; first publ. 1981), 23–40.

[19] *Annales Fuldenses*, ed. Friedrich Kurze, MGH SRG i.u.s. 7 (Hanover, 1891) [hereafter: *AF*, followed by year of entry and page number]; Timothy Reuter, *The Annals of Fulda: The Ninth Century Histories*, vol. 2 (Manchester, 1992), 1–14; Eric J. Goldberg, *Struggle for Empire: Kingship and Conflict under Louis the German, 817–876* (Ithaca, NY, 2006), 14–15.

simply far from wherever the annalist wrote, others were physically beyond Carolingian territory. They were all, however, proximate to the annalists' own communities and in correspondence with them (unlike, for example, the twelfth-century legend of Prester John, a Christian king in the distant Orient). Their inclusion reveals something important about the kind of unity and conformity desired by Carolingian reformers. They aimed not at a chauvinistic uniformity but made space for ethnic and geographical diversity under a broader Christian fellowship. Despite the apparent self-confidence of Frankish churchmen, they proved open to lessons on *correctio* from 'strange peoples'.

English and Greek Counsel

The first case study concerns the closing year of the reign of Louis the Pious. Louis' reign had been characterized by dynastic infighting and an intensifying moral discourse, centred upon the need for counsel and admonition.[20] The *Annals of St Bertin*, which would eventually provide a narrative from the year 830 to 882, began as an anonymous effort by those close to the emperor to continue a set of annals associated with the imperial court.[21] In the early 840s, these annals came to be written by Prudentius, bishop of Troyes, until his death in 861.[22] Based on various thematic consistencies, however, Prudentius may have been involved in its writing at the palace as part of a wider team.[23] Intriguingly, Prudentius was himself from the margins: one of several Iberians who had made a career in the Frankish church.[24]

The lengthy entry for 839 recounts various catastrophes and dynastic struggles that plagued the emperor. Among these, a deacon from the palace named Bodo had converted to Judaism, taken the name Eleazar, and fled to Spain.[25] This is an excellent example of, firstly,

---

[20] De Jong, *Penitential State*, 112–47.

[21] Reimitz, *History, Frankish Identity, and the Framing of Western Ethnicity*, 432–3.

[22] Nelson, 'Annals of St. Bertin', 34.

[23] Ibid. 25–8; Reimitz, *History, Frankish Identity, and the Framing of Western Ethnicity*, 427. On Prudentius, see Jared Wielfaert, '*Prudentius of Troyes and the Reception of the Patristic Tradition in the Carolingian Era*' (PhD thesis, University of Toronto, 2015).

[24] Ottewill-Soulsby, *Emperor and Elephant*, 24.

[25] On whom, see Frank Riess, *The Journey of Deacon Bodo from the Rhine to the Guadalquivir: Apostasy and Conversion to Judaism in Early Medieval Europe* (London, 2019).

'otherness' being used negatively as a warning and, secondly, ideological marginality being paralleled by a movement to the geographical periphery. Bodo begins in close proximity to the emperor and represented the best of a Christian education: 'imbued in the Christian religion from almost the very cradle by the instruction [*eruditionibus*] of the palace clergy'.[26] The author even noted his ethnic identity from within the Frankish kingdoms as an 'Aleman by birth'.[27] He ends beyond salvation and on the far side of the Pyrenees, in Zaragoza, 'along with some Jews'.[28] The author also stressed the contrast in behaviour. As a Christian, he had learned and studied and went on pilgrimage; as a Jew, he changed his hair, took up arms and married. Significantly, Bodo was 'seduced by the enemy of the human race' despite all his learning.[29] The annalist warned that even those closest to the centre – those who had received the best education – could slip away to the ideological (and in this case geographical) margins.

Moreover, the account has a strongly affective dimension. Bodo's apostasy was to be 'most tearfully bemoaned by all sons of the Catholic Church'.[30] It was 'grievous for the Emperor and Empress and indeed for all those redeemed through the grace of the Christian faith'.[31] The interplay between centre and margins mattered and reinforced the contrast in the emotions of the reader, who was encouraged to sympathize with the imperial family. Throughout, the author defined Christianity clearly, both with reference to salvation (redeemed by grace) and as belonging to the visible church (as children thereof). Bodo's ideological marginalization, therefore, served to clarify the identity of the centre. This is a typical example of how vilification served to emphasize a group's identity by way of contrast. Importantly, however, the author did not elide Christianity with either the Franks or the Carolingian empire, a move which seems intended to set up what follows.

The entry continued with more constructive moral counsel, also from beyond the frontiers. Æthelwulf, king of Wessex, sent envoys to the emperor warning him 'to devote even more careful attention and

[26] '[A]b ipsis paene cunabulis in christiana religione palatinis eruditionibus ... aliquatenus inbutum': *AB*, *s.a.* 839 (ed. Grat, Vielliard and Clémencet, 27).
[27] 'Alamannica gente progenitum': ibid.
[28] '[C]um Iudaeis': ibid.
[29] '[H]umani generis hoste pellectum': ibid. 28.
[30] '[L]acrimabile nimiumque cunctis catholicae aecclesiae filiis ingemescendam': ibid. 27
[31] '[A]ugustis cunctisque christianae fidei gratia redemptis luctuosum extiterit': ibid.

concern to the salvation of the souls of those subject to him'.[32]
Æthelwulf's envoy also passed on a letter which contained a striking
vision of impending judgement, a letter which the annalist inserted
into their narrative.[33] This vision was given to 'a certain religious priest
… while seized out of his body'.[34] A guide showed the priest a heavenly
world where children wrote out books in letters of black ink and blood,
representing the 'various sins of Christian men' and 'sins and crimes of
Christians', specifically the breaking of the Sabbath.[35] The letter
warned the emperor that 'unless the saints cried out to God so
incessantly with tears, there would already have been an end to so
many evil [Christians]',[36] and that 'if Christian men do not quickly do
penance … the greatest danger will intolerably come quickly upon
them'.[37] Specifically, a dense fog would cover the land for three days,
followed by pagan men laying waste to Christian lands. This all but
named the Vikings – who had already begun raiding both Frankish
and English shores – as the agents of judgement.

Neither the English nor their kings had featured in Frankish annals
up to this point. Indeed, Charlemagne had expressed little interest in
diplomacy with those north of the Channel.[38] Here, however, a West
Saxon king offered fulsome counsel to the emperor, quoted at length
by a source close to the court. Although the letter (which shows no
signs of fabrication) originated in a different context, its content and
tone overlapped significantly with the moral discourse of Louis' reign,
chiefly the concerns around sin and divine judgement through military
defeat. This discourse had included admonitory visions, a general

---

[32] '[M]onens etiam curam subiectorum sibi erga animarum salute solicitius impenden-
dam': ibid. 29
[33] Paul Dutton, *The Politics of Dreaming in the Carolingian Empire* (London, 1994), 107–
12; although compare de Jong, *Penitential State*, 136–7: 'Dutton tends to overestimate the
political nature of these dream texts'. On visions more generally, see Jesse Keskiaho, *Dreams
and Visions in the Early Middle Ages: The Reception and Use of Patristic Ideas, 400–900*
(Cambridge, 2015).
[34] '[C]uiusdam religiosi praesbiteri … ei rapto a corpore': *AB, s.a.* 839 (ed. Grat, Vielliard
and Clémencet, 29).
[35] '[D]iversa hominum christianorum peccata … christianorum peccatis et
facinoribus': ibid.
[36] '[N]isi istae animae sanctorum tam incessanter cum fletu ad Deum clamarent, iam
aliquatenus finis tantorum malorum': ibid.
[37] '[S]i cito homines christiani … non egerint poenitentiam … cito super eos maximum et
intolerabile periculum veniet': ibid. 30.
[38] Joanna Story, *Carolingian Connections: Anglo-Saxon England and Carolingian Francia,
c.750–870* (Aldershot, 2003), 169–213.

concern over sin and divine judgement, and a specific concern about the Sabbath.[39] In fact, the vision of the demon Wiggo (found in Einhard's *On the Translation of Marcellinus and Peter*) had urged obedience on this specific point.[40] Visions, in themselves, have a marginal quality. They feature marginal figures, whether human ascetics or spiritual agents, and come from beyond normal life. This vision, however, took place within the context of diplomatic communication between royal centres across the very tangible physical boundary of the English Channel. Crucially, the vision elided Frankish and English territory into 'the lands of the Christians', equally vulnerable to sin and sharing a common pagan threat. This further developed the construction of a Christian identity begun in the Bodo episode, which had also transcended identification of Christians with particular ethnic groups. The marginal, in this case positively, helped to create an inclusive Christian identity: one that had been called into question by Bodo's apostasy.

The very next passage also described diplomacy, this time from the Greeks, on the opposite border to that of the English. Named envoys arrived from Constantinople to express friendship and affection between the two emperors.[41] They also congratulated Louis on recent victories won 'from heaven'.[42] They encouraged him to 'give thanks to the Giver of all victories'.[43] In a very different way to the letter from Æthelwulf, this also paralleled aspects of Carolingian moral discourse: the need to ascribe victories to God.[44] Indeed, the annalist would do so at the very end of the entry, when a Saxon army sent by Louis defeated the Sorbs while 'supported by heavenly help'.[45] This replicated the language of 'heaven' used by the Greek envoys and put their advice into practice, by recognizing what God had done. This added to the

---

[39] De Jong, *Penitential State*, 132.

[40] Ibid. 162–3.

[41] For this embassy, see Philip Grierson, 'The Carolingian Empire in the Eyes of Byzantium', in *Nascita dell' Europa ed Europa Carolingia. Un'equazione da verificare*, Settimane 27 (Spoleto, 1981), 885–918, at 912.

[42] '[C]aelitus … assecutus … in Domino exultatio ferebatur': *AB, s.a.* 839 (ed. Grat, Vielliard and Clémencet, 30).

[43] 'Datori victoriarum omnium gratias referre': ibid.

[44] Robert Evans, '"Instructing readers' minds in heavenly matters": Carolingian History Writing and Christian Education', in Morwenna Ludlow, Charlotte Methuen and Andrew Spicer, eds, *Churches and Education*, SCH 55 (Cambridge, 2019), 56–71.

[45] '[C]aelestibus auxiliis fulti, victoriam adepti sunt': *AB, s.a.* 839 (ed. Grat, Vielliard and Clémencet, 33–4).

sense of a Christian identity that included other Christian kingdoms and rulers, this time defined not by shared sinfulness, but by their recognition of heaven's mercies. Significantly, this attribution of military victories to divine agency had fallen out of favour with Frankish annalists during Louis' reign.[46] It may be that the Greeks' counsel provided implicit justification for restoring what the author regarded as an important part of his role.

Louis, therefore, received advice from two fellow Christian rulers, from opposite borders of his empire. Their advice complemented one another very precisely, especially on this latter point of recognizing and talking about divine agency. The English, through an epistemologically murky vision, implied and inferred the possibility of divine judgement and the dangers of sin. Divine agency, however, remained very implicit, appearing only as the recipient of saintly intercession in the English vision. Agency instead lay with the sins of the Christians. The Greeks, by contrast, openly attested the agency of God in the emperor's recent military successes, which was to be celebrated. Both passages, importantly, articulated the response expected from Louis and (by extension) the reader. In the former, Louis needed to look to the salvation of his people, specifically through the observance of the Sabbath. In the latter, Louis needed to recognize and give thanks for what God had done. The annalist did not want to risk their readers taking divine favour for granted, but nor did they want them to think that God only came in judgement. By using voices from the periphery, the annalist could offer variegated yet coherent advice to the centre. This involved both a sense of Christian identity, which (although shaken by Bodo) remained secure and founded upon a shared recognition of the problems of sin and the mercy of divine agency.

Prudentius of Troyes explicitly took up these themes as he continued the annals, by repeatedly depicting divine activity beyond the borders of the Frankish kingdoms. As an Iberian among the Franks, he had every reason to encourage an ethnically inclusive understanding of Christian identity. Specifically, he ascribed the military successes of other Christian societies to God. The Beneventans, for example, defeated the Saracens 'with God's help' in 843.[47] The Irish and English both defeated the Northmen 'by the help of our Lord Jesus

---

[46] Robert Evans, 'A Secular Shift in Carolingian History Writing?', *EME* 29 (2021), 36–54.
[47] 'Dei auxilio': *AB*, *s.a.* 843 (ed. Grat, Vielliard and Clémencet, 45).

Christ'.[48] This created a sense of a coherent Christian world of which the Frankish kingdoms formed only a part. What gave this urgency was the constant fear of non-Christian aggression – whether Scandinavian, Slavic or Saracen – shared across the Christian world. In the entry for 845, the year in which the Northmen first attacked Paris (less than 100 miles from Troyes), Prudentius made this explicit. He asserted that 'the equity of divine goodness, offended so greatly by our sins, wore down the Christians' lands and kingdoms'.[49] What Prudentius offered his community was a reminder that all remained within God's power. As they read the annals, however, they would have first encountered those ideas in the messages of foreign kings from beyond Frankish borders, yet who participated in the same Christian identity under God's care.

BULGAR DEVOTION

In 861, the *Annals of St Bertin* passed into the hands of Hincmar, archbishop of Reims – a key royal adviser and major figure in Frankish politics – who continued them until his death in 882.[50] Although he despised Prudentius (on doctrinal grounds), he shared his interest in how Christians from the geographical margins could provide models for those at the centre. This centre included Hincmar's own clergy at Reims, but also the court of Charles the Bald (840–77). In his entry for 866, Hincmar drew their attention east, to the Bulgars, whose king oversaw the conversion of his people 'with God inspiring him, and with the signs and afflictions on the people of the kingdom warning him'.[51] However, the king's 'leading men, being troubled, incited the

---

[48] '[A]uxilio domini nostri Ihesu Christi': *AB*, s.a. 848 (ed. Grat, Vielliard and Clémencet, 55); 'auxilio domini nostri Ihesu Christi': *AB*, s.a. 850 (ed. Grat, Vielliard and Clémencet, 60).

[49] '[P]eccatis nostris divinae bonitatis aequitas nimium offensa taliter christianorum terras et regna attriverit': *AB*, s.a. 845 (ed. Grat, Vielliard and Clémencet, 50).

[50] Marlene Meyer-Gebel, 'Zur annalistischen Arbeitsweise Hinkmars von Reims', *Francia* 15 (1987), 75–108. On Hincmar's career more generally, see Rachel Stone and Charles West, eds, *Hincmar of Rheims: Life and Work* (Manchester, 2015).

[51] 'Deo inspirante et signis atque afflictionibus in populo regni sui monente': *AB*, s.a. 866 (ed. Grat, Vielliard and Clémencet, 133). For discussion of this conversion, see Richard Sullivan, 'Khan Boris and the Conversion of Bulgaria: A Case Study of the Impact of Christianity on a Barbarian Society', *Studies in Medieval and Renaissance History* 3 (1966), 55–139; Peter Barford, *The Early Slavs* (London, 2001), 221–2; Henry Chadwick, *East and West: The Making of a Rift in the Church from Apostolic Times until the Council of Florence* (Oxford, 2003), 113–18.

people against him'.[52] Whereas the entry for 839 had provided counsel, the episode provides a positive example of robust Christian leadership in the face of catastrophe.

The king – now named Boris-Michael – found himself surrounded in his palace by 'however many there were in the ten counties'.[53] When he counter-attacked, Hincmar stressed the sheer impossibility of the odds: 'he set out against all that multitude with only 48 men'.[54] Boris-Michael, however, did so 'having invoked Christ's name' and his few men, 'fervent towards Christian devotion, remained with him'.[55] There are several exemplary actions here. Firstly, Boris-Michael stood firm for Christ's name despite the odds and did so by praying. Secondly, his faithful men remained loyal despite the pressure of their peers, and as a result of their own devotion. Loyalty (or *fides*) had a dual meaning for the Franks, capturing both faith in God and loyalty to the king.[56] Whereas earlier annals had looked at how other groups had simultaneously become Christian and become loyal to Carolingian kings, Hincmar conveyed that sense in an entirely foreign context. Boris-Michael's men were good Christians and loyal warriors, regardless of their relationship to the Franks. Hincmar, therefore, presented a royal household – new to the faith, remote from the West Frankish kingdom – functioning exactly as a Christian political society ought to.

What happened next vindicated their devotion. The king's warband saw 'seven clerics and each held a burning candle in his hand, and thus preceded the king and his men'.[57] The rebels, however, saw 'a great flaming *villa* was falling upon them, and the horses of the king's

---

[52] '[P]roceres sui moleste ferentes, concitaverunt populum adversus eum': *AB, s.a.* 866 (ed. Grat, Vielliard and Clémencet, 133).

[53] 'Quotquot igitur fuerunt intra decem comitatus, adunaverunt se circa palatium eius': ibid. Compare Daniel Ziemann, 'The Rebellion of the Nobles against the Baptism of Khan Boris (865–866)', in Joachim Henning, ed., *Post-Roman Towns, Trade and Settlement in Europe and Byzantium*, 2: *Byzantium, Pliska, and the Balkans* (Berlin, 2007), 613–24, who discusses both Hincmar's sources and complementary Byzantine evidence.

[54] '[C]um quadraginta tantum octo hominibus … profectus est contra omnem illam multitudinem': *AB, s.a.* 866 (ed. Grat, Vielliard and Clémencet, 133).

[55] '[I]nvocato Christi nominee … qui erga christianam devotionem ferventes sibi remanserant': ibid.

[56] Kramer, *Rethinking Authority*, 41–2. On loyalty, see essays in Jörg Sonntag and Coralie Zermatten, eds, *Loyalty in the Middle Ages: Ideal and Practice of a Cross-social Value* (Turnhout, 2015).

[57] '[S]eptem clerici, et unusquisque eorum tenebat cereum ardentem in manu sua, sicque praecedebant regem et illos qui cum eo erant': *AB, s.a.* 866 (ed. Grat, Vielliard and Clémencet, 133).

men ... advanced upright and struck them with their fore-hooves'.[58] It is worth noting again the importance of the visionary, which furthered the sense of distance from the everyday experience of Hincmar's readers, while simultaneously validating the moral norms which governed it. The rebels tried to flee in terror but found themselves rooted to the ground. Boris-Michael, tempering justice with mercy like a good Christian king, killed fifty-two of the leading men but released the remainder unharmed. From start to finish, the king and his men acted in ways which would have gladdened the heart of any Carolingian palace chaplain.

Hincmar, however, did not leave the Bulgars on the margins, but related their experience to the geographical and political centres of Christian Europe. Firstly, Boris-Michael asked the Carolingian kings for help setting up ecclesiastical life in his kingdom. Louis the German sent bishops and priests, while Charles the Bald sent liturgical vessels, vestments and books, funded by his bishops (that is, Hincmar and his colleagues). This tied Hincmar to events among the distant Bulgars. They were not merely a helpful allegory for Christian kingship, but part of the same ecclesiastical structures as the Franks. Secondly, Boris-Michael sent his son and some leading men to Rome. To St Peter (by name), he also sent gifts and 'the arms with which he had being clothed when in Christ's name he triumphed over his adversaries'.[59] The importance of gift-giving has repeatedly been stressed in scholarship, and victorious generals sometimes sent captured trophies to their kings.[60] For Boris-Michael to send his trophies to the pope made a comparable, but actually more powerful, statement about hierarchy and submission to the church. That Hincmar repeated the phrase 'in Christ's name' to describe the armour furthered the sense of a Christian victory. As a gift to Rome, however, it pulled the reader's perspective out to encompass Christianity understood universally and centred upon Rome. Hincmar thus established – as the earlier *Annals of St Bertin* had done – a clear overarching sense of Christian identity and showed the reader what it meant to live correctly within it, just as the entry for 839 had done.

---

[58] '[M]agna villa ardens super eos caderet, et equi eorum qui cum rege errant ... erecti incedebant et cum anterioribus pedibus eos percutiebant': ibid.

[59] '[A]rma, quibus indutus fuerat, quando in Christi nomine de suis adversariis triumphavit': ibid. 134.

[60] Compare a Frankish example, *AB*, *s.a.* 865 (ed. Grat, Vielliard and Clémencet, 122).

As in the previous case study, this passage picked up themes in the entry for the year (and indeed Hincmar's annals) as a whole. In the West Frankish kingdom, there had been repeated clashes within the aristocracy and between members of the Carolingian family in recent years.[61] The divided loyalty of Boris-Michael's men may have resonated with this. At the same time, Hincmar's relationship with Charles the Bald had become strained in 865, because of a dispute over the appointment of Wulfhad to the see of Bourges.[62] Boris-Michael allowed Hincmar to present an ideal of Christian kingship which was dependent on and obedient to the church. Such resonances are, of course, merely suggestive. Stronger literary links, however, appear in the contrast between Boris-Michael's success and the defeat of West Frankish forces at Brissarthe by the Northmen in the same entry. The Frankish commanders – Robert the Strong and Ranulf of Poitou – were important members of the West Frankish aristocracy and had featured prominently in Hincmar's narrative. Hincmar pointedly wrote that they would have defeated the Vikings 'if God had been with them'.[63] Instead, their forces were defeated, Robert was killed, and Ranulf died of his wounds because, 'refusing to be corrected [*castigare*]', they 'deserved to experience vengeance'.[64] (Their sin was to hold lay abbacies.[65])

The episodes of Boris-Michael and Robert and Ranulf thus complement one another, showing positive and negative examples of Christian militarism. Importantly, Hincmar stopped short of ascribing Boris-Michael's victory explicitly to God. Hincmar rarely did this anyway, but the explicit denial of divine help to Robert and Ranulf brought this into sharper relief. In both cases, victory or defeat hinged on the spiritual and devotional attitudes of Boris-Michael and his men (positively) and Robert and Ranulf (negatively). Whereas other Carolingian historians – including Prudentius – had explicitly ascribed Christian victories to God, Hincmar may have felt that this downplayed the spiritual responsibilities of the Christian soldier. What is remarkable is that he explored this lesson by inverting the centre and

---

[61] Geoffrey Koziol, *Politics of Memory and Identity in Carolingian Royal Diplomas: The West Frankish Kingdom (840–987)* (Turnhout, 2012), 97–211.

[62] Nelson, 'Annals of St. Bertin', 37.

[63] '[S]i Deus cum eis esset': *AB, s.a.* 866 (ed. Grat, Vieillard and Clémencet, 131).

[64] '[C]astigari noluerunt, in se ultionem experiri meruerunt': ibid.

[65] On which, see Gaëlle Calvet-Marcadé, *Assassin des pauvres. L'Église et l'inaliénabilité des terres à l'époque carolingienne* (Turnhout, 2019).

the margins. The central and courtly figures of Robert and Ranulf failed, whereas the king of a distant land, a new Christian, succeeded. The foreign king thus behaved in a manner that fulfilled the highest ideals of Carolingian *correctio*.

Before moving on, it is worth interrogating briefly the role of Rome itself. The see of St Peter was central as an authority in Hincmar's annals (both in the Bulgar episode and elsewhere) and in Carolingian Christianity. As a city, however, Rome was a geographically marginal location and remote from the experience of West Frankish audiences. As Jan Clauß has noted, respect for Rome's apostolic authority did not preclude Frankish suspicion of the city itself with its infighting and conspiracies.[66] It is, therefore, significant that, like Boris-Michael, Pope Nicholas provided Hincmar with another example of Christian leadership in the face of the catastrophe, ironically when the (Carolingian) Emperor Louis II threatened Rome in 864. Nicholas proclaimed a fast so that God 'might give the Emperor a good mind' towards 'the authority of the apostolic see'.[67] Louis II arrived to find 'the clergy and people of Rome' carrying out Nicholas's instructions by 'celebrating their fast with crosses and litanies'.[68] His men attacked the worshippers and smashed their crosses, and then desecrated the Holy Cross in St Peter's itself. Pope Nicholas, learning of Louis' plan to imprison him, secretly escaped across the Tiber, 'where he stayed for two days and nights without food or drink'.[69] The passage is chiastic: the prayers of the Romans and Nicholas frame the iconoclasm by Louis' men. In the end, Louis II fell ill and one of his iconoclastic soldiers died, and Rome was saved.

The episodes are implicitly connected by Louis II's appearance in the entry for 866, demanding the Bulgar trophies from Pope Nicholas. No doubt Louis sought to contest Nicholas's centrality in a broader Christian world, but the pope 'made excuses'.[70] Like the Bulgar episode, the events in Rome in 864 also involved the marginal

---

[66] Jan Clauß, 'Imports and Embargos of Imperial Concepts in the Frankish Kingdom: The Promotion of Charlemagne's Imperial Coronation in Carolingian Courtly Culture', in Christian Scholl et al., eds, *Transcultural Approaches to the Concept of Imperial Rule in the Middle Ages* (Frankfurt, 2017), 77–116, at 109–10.

[67] '[U]t imperatori mentem bonam … donaret': *AB*, *s.a.* 864 (ed. Grat, Vielliard and Clémencet, 106).

[68] '[C]lerus et populus Romanus cum crucibus et laetaniis ieiunium celebrantes': ibid.

[69] '[U]bi duobus diebus ac noctibus sine cibo ac potu mansit': ibid.

[70] *AB*, *s.a.* 866 (ed. Grat, Vielliard and Clémencet, 132).

and the central. Papal authority represented the centre of Hincmar's religious world, yet Rome lay beyond the geographical scope of his readers' experience, in distant Italy. They are threatened, meanwhile, not by pagans (as with Boris-Michael's opponents) but by a Carolingian ruler, who ought to have conformed to Christian norms. Nicholas himself was forced to the edge of the city, alone, to escape Louis' fury. Only there, in prayer and fasting, did deliverance eventually come. Hincmar's emphasis, as among the Bulgars, was on prayerful submission to God in the face of wickedness. This shared focus – and the importance of Rome to both narratives – shows how Hincmar used geographical marginality to convey Christian norms. In both cases, the marginality destabilized expectations. Even the pope might seem marginalized or distant to the experience of those in Reims. Even a recently converted king proved a better Christian than the Carolingians. Hincmar's point in both episodes is that what mattered was steadfast humility before God in the face of adversity, in a way which built upon themes already present in the *Annals of St Bertin*.

FRISIANS AND NORTHMEN

The *Annals of Fulda* represented an alternative annalistic tradition originating in the East Frankish kingdom. This began in the 830s at the monastery of Fulda, which enjoyed close connections to the court of Louis the German (r. 840–76). Its various authors often explored moral questions facing those involved in contemporary politics and warfare. One of these annals' lengthiest episodes concerned a conflict on the north-west margins of Louis' kingdom, in northern Frisia. Even after their conquest in the eighth century, Frankish historians still referred to the *Frisiones* as a distinct ethnic group, as in this entry.[71] It had only recently joined Louis' kingdom, as part of the Treaty of Meerssen (870). The annalist thus specified the region, but added that it was still part of 'Louis' kingdom'.[72] The region and its inhabitants, therefore, were peripheral to the annalist's audience without being as remote as the English, Greeks or Bulgars considered so far. A Viking

---

[71] See, for instance, *Annales Regni Francorum, s.a.* 789, ed. Friedrich Kurze, MGH SRG i.u.s. 6 (Hanover, 1895), 84.
[72] '[I]n regnum Hludowici regis, in comitatum videlicet Albdagi': *AF, s.a.* 873 (MGH SRG i.u.s. 7: 80).

leader, called Rudolf, attacked the region, demanding tribute.[73] The Frisians replied, as loyal subjects, 'that they were not bound to pay tribute to anyone except to King Louis and his sons'.[74] This emphasized at the outset that these remote Frisians shared the same political identity as the monks at Fulda (unlike the purely religious solidarity of previous cases studies).

As with the Bulgars, the annalist used the Frisians to set forth how to respond correctly to a pagan onslaught. Rudolf swore to kill the men, enslave the women and children, and seize their treasure. In response, 'invoking the Lord, who had very often rescued them from their enemies', the loyal Frisians joined battle, killing Rudolf and eight hundred Northmen.[75] The Frisians here remembered God's help to them in the past and depended on Him in the present. This was something Carolingian rulers had done earlier in the *Annals of Fulda* (Charles Martel in 726 against the Saracens; Charles the Fat in 869 against the Moravians).[76] Conversely, in 849, a Frankish army – sent by Louis the German – had been defeated by the Bohemians precisely because they had not feared God.[77] Fulda numbered East Frankish generals among its patrons, and its abbots sometimes commanded the king's armies. As a result, they cared about a correct attitude to military operations and the need to depend on God. The annalist, as Hincmar had done, located such positive exemplars of this among those on the distant periphery of their kingdom. The Frisians' invocation of God is vindicated, as it had been for Carolingian princes. The Viking survivors were cut off from their ships and took shelter, while 'the Frisians' besieged them and took stock.

Only at this point does the annalist mention the Frisians' commander: 'A Northmen, who had become a Christian and for a long time lived with these Frisians, had led their attack'.[78] Strikingly, this anonymous captain was himself marginal to the group he commands. Indeed, ethnically, he had more in common with the enemy. Yet his

---

[73] Simon Coupland, 'Poachers and Gamekeepers: Scandinavian Warlords and Carolingian Kings', *EME* 7 (1998), 85–114, at 101–3.

[74] '[R]espondissent se non debere tributa solvere nisi Hludowico regi eiusque filiis': *AF, s.a.* 873 (MGH SRG i.u.s. 7: 80).

[75] '[I]lli autem Dominum invocantes … qui eos saepius ab hostibus liberaverat': ibid.

[76] *AF, s.a.* 726 (MGH SRG i.u.s. 7: 2); *s.a.* 869 (MGH SRG i.u.s. 7: 69).

[77] *AF, s.a.* 849 (MGH SRG i.u.s. 7: 39).

[78] '[U]nus Nordmannus, qui christianus effectus longo tempore cum eisdem Frisionibus conversatus est et eiusdem certaminis duxerat': *AF, s.a.* 873 (MGH SRG i.u.s. 7: 80).

faith and long-term loyalty to the Frisians had clearly allayed any suspicions about divided loyalty. In his address to his men, his ethnic marginality contrasted with his moral conformity as he exemplified contemporary norms of humility and gratitude to God. As I have argued elsewhere, this speech (as recorded) fulfils Cicero's criteria for persuasive rhetoric, albeit from a Christian perspective.[79] The oration argues, firstly, that 'we few have prevailed against many enemies, not regarding our own strength, but God's grace'.[80] Behind this statement lies an allusion to 1 Maccabees 3: 18–19, which contrasted numerical superiority in battle with dependence on God. Other Carolingian historians (including the current annalist) used these verses to describe military successes, albeit usually Frankish ones.[81] It also featured in contemporary texts on kingship, such as Sedulius Scottus' *On Christian Leaders*, written for Charles the Bald in 869.[82] Hincmar himself had used the same verse to warn Charles the Bald not to trust (or conversely to fear) military strength.[83] This is not to suggest that the annalist knew these West Frankish texts, but he certainly held similar convictions. Sedulius wrote, for example, that a leader 'ought to establish their whole confidence not in themselves nor the strength of their men but in the power and grace of the Most High'.[84] That this annalist presented an ex-Viking as espousing the same moral views as such palace advisers is remarkable.

This statement about divine agency, however, informed his second piece of advice: the Frisians should not recklessly try to improve on what they had already accomplished. Instead, they should take hostages and oaths from the Vikings, and let them go rather than risk

---

[79] Robert Evans, '"Words that supply valour": God, Warfare, and the Rhetoric of Persuasion in Carolingian History Writing', in Matthew Rowley and Natasha Hodgson, eds, *Miracles, Political Authority and Violence in Medieval and Early Modern History* (London, 2021), 29–47, at 37–8.

[80] '[Q]uod modo nos pauci contra plurimos praevaluimus hostes, non nostris deputandum est viribus, sed Dei gratiae': *AF, s.a.* 873 (MGH SRG i.u.s. 7: 80).

[81] See, for instance, *AF, s.a.* 876 (MGH SRG i.u.s. 7: 87–9); *AF, s.a.* 900 (MGH SRG i.u.s. 7: 134).

[82] Sedulius, *De Rectoribus Christianis* 15; ET: *Sedulius Scottus: De Rectoribus ('On Christian Rulers')*, ed. and transl. Robert Dyson (Woodbridge, 2010), 144–6.

[83] Hincmar, *De regis persona et regio ministerio* 14, PL 125, col. 843.

[84] '[N]on in se nec in suorum fortitudine … totam confidentiam stabilire debent … sed in Altimissi virtute et gratia totam confidentiam stabilire debent': Sedulius, *De Rectoribus*, 14 (ed. Dyson, 137).

defeat.[85] This was a sensitive issue for those fighting the Northmen. Should battle be joined against the odds, risking defeat and (by extension) giving the invaders freedom to raid? Or was negotiation and caution acceptable if it mitigated that impact? As Rachel Stone has argued, these were moral issues, relating to courage and cowardice.[86] It directly affected the discharge of the aristocracy's obligations to protect the Christian people from attack. Later on, different authors of the *Annals of Fulda* would condemn two different commanders for attacking Viking warbands 'rashly' (*incaute*).[87] The Frisians' anonymous leader contrasted the possibilities open to his men. Although exhausted, they could keep fighting their enemies who had been pushed to desperation. Or they could negotiate a return of treasure and the Vikings' exit with little risk, which seemed the 'more sensible' (*consultius*) option. As Mayke de Jong and Irene van Renswourde have argued, such debates and methods of persuasion pervaded the high politics of the Carolingian court.[88] Here, such strategies appear on the lips of an outsider to those on the margins. Above all, the narrative shows the wisdom of such counsel: the others agree, the Vikings hand over hostages and treasure, make oaths and leave 'with great confusion and loss of men'.[89] This is perhaps the most successful encounter with the Northmen in any set of annals for some decades. They are defeated in battle, their leader killed, and they leave with nothing. And yet that honour goes to an anonymous leader and a group distinct from the annalist's own people, although part of his kingdom.

As with the examples from the *Annals of St Bertin*, the episode derived even greater force from its position within the overall entry for 873, which it concluded. This began with a starkly different tone and troubling moral warning. In January, the annalist recounted, King Louis held an assembly at Frankfurt with men from all over the kingdom to discuss 'the state of the realm' (*statu regni*). The entry began in the political heart of the kingdom, with the king, his sons and his leading men. Yet here, of all places, the demonic burst in and possessed Charles the Fat, Louis' youngest son, who thrashed around

---

[85] '[I]lli autem miserunt pecuniam multam valde et obsides, quos dederant, receperunt, prius tamen, ut dixi, praestito': *AF, s.a.* 873 (MGH SRG i.u.s. 7: 81).

[86] Stone, *Morality*, 94–101.

[87] *AF* [Mainz continuation], *s.a.* 882 (MGH SRG i.u.s. 7: 97–8); *AF* [Bavarian continuation], *s.a.* 891 (MGH SRG i.u.s. 7: 119).

[88] Van Renswoude, *Rhetoric of Free Speech*, 180–205; De Jong, *Epitaph for an Era*, 71–101.

[89] '[I]n cum magna confusione ac sui detriment': *AF, s.a.* 873 (MGH SRG i.u.s. 7: 81).

while those around wept with fear.[90] As the Fulda annalist explained, Charles had himself been deceived and ensnared by Satan, just as he had conspired to deceive his father. There are parallels with the episode of Bodo-Eleazar, involving both the courtly, the demonic and the affective response of those involved. Louis then addressed another son, Louis the Younger, who had conspired with Charles, in direct speech. There is '*nothing … hidden which will not be revealed*' (Matthew 10: 26) and advised him to 'confess … do penance, and pray humbly to God'.[91] The episode captured the familiar themes of loyalty and humility, and the need for practical submission to God, unfolding at the centre of the East Frankish kingdom.

Three interrelated aspects connected this to the later episode in Frisia. Firstly, divine agency conditioned the course and outcome of both episodes very explicitly. The annalist announced that Charles's possession unfolded 'with the Lord doing it'.[92] He had conspired against the king 'chosen and ordained by God'.[93] He was possessed so as to 'learn' (*disceret*) that there is 'no counsel against God'.[94] In an important sense, Charles here parallels Rudolf's attack on Frisia, 'ignorant of the revenge that would pursue him from heaven'.[95] Moreover, where Charles failed to submit to God and suffered, the Frisians invoked God and triumphed. Secondly, both episodes highlight the knowledge (or ignorance) of spiritual realities. Rudolf was ignorant, Charles needed to learn, Louis the Younger needed to 'see' (*videsne*) where conspiracy leads, and what has been hidden was now revealed. Even the heroic Frisians needed persuading by their commander not to presume God's continued grace.

Finally, and closely related to this, both episodes involve communication. It was unusual for annalists to include direct speeches, yet this entry contained two, both urging their listeners to take counsel. Charles's possession means that he is unable to communicate properly.

---

[90] For a detailed discussion, see Simon MacLean, 'Ritual, Misunderstanding, and the Contest for Meaning: Representations of the Disrupted Royal Assembly at Frankfurt (873)', in Björn Weiler and idem, eds, *Representations of Power in Medieval Germany, 800–1500* (Turnhout, 2006), 97–119.

[91] '*[N]ihil opertum est, quod non reveletur* … confitere ergo peccata tua et age poenitentiam et Deum humiliter postula': *AF, s.a.* 873 (MGH SRG i.u.s. 7: 77).

[92] 'Domino faciente': ibid.

[93] '[A] Deo electum et ordinatum': ibid.

[94] '[N]on esse consilium contra Deum': ibid.

[95] '[I]gnarus vindictae quae eum de caelo erat secutura': ibid. 80.

'Shouting, now quietly, now in a loud voice, he threatened with open mouth to bite those holding him'.[96] While counsel leads to correction, the demonic obscures knowledge and hinders communication. What is so striking, however, is the contrast in good counsel at either end of the episode. On the one hand, the East Frankish king must warn his son about conspiracy and the demonic and to undertake penance. On the other, an anonymous ex-Viking urges the simple recognition of God's help, humbly sought and graciously provided. Both were touchstones of Carolingian ideals, but their juxtaposition at the centre and periphery here threw them into stark relief. The periphery put the centre to shame.

THE BULGARS RETURN

In the closing decades of the ninth century, what was 'central' to Frankish society began to change. The monopoly of the Carolingian dynasty over royal power gave way to an increasingly fragmented political landscape ruled by competing dynasties.[97] The very nature of the periphery thus altered dramatically. Nonetheless, in some quarters, including the later *Annals of Fulda*, the relevance of marginal communities to the normative function of historiography persisted. By the 890s, one version of these annals had come to be written in Bavaria, with possible links to the court of Arnulf of Carinthia (887–99).[98] The Bulgars, so distant from Hincmar in Reims, now served as valued Christian allies just across the frontier. What made their example perhaps more pressing was that in 896, Arnulf had suffered a stroke, and the annalist now lacked a clear Christian king to provide coherence to his narrative. In the elderly Boris-Michael, the Bavarian annalist found one who could at least provide moral instruction, in a manner which echoed the entry for 873.

In 896, the Bulgars found themselves bested by Hungarian invasions (backed by the Byzantines). 'Miserable and uncertain', they ran 'to the feet of their old king, Michael, who had first converted them to

---

[96] '[N]unc exili nunc grandi voce clamitans morsum se tenentibus aperto ore minabatur': ibid. 77.
[97] See Stuart Airlie, *Making and Unmaking the Carolingians, 751–888* (London, 2021), 273–318.
[98] Evans, 'Writing of Annals'.

the truth of the Christian religion'.[99] They specifically sought his 'advice' (*consulere*), highlighting once again the importance of counsel. The king told his men to 'seek help from God', which they duly did.[100] More intriguingly, he enjoined penance 'for the injury inflicted upon Christians'.[101] This pointed to the perennial ninth-century issue of Christian kingdoms fighting one another instead of their pagan enemies. East Frankish texts in the 890s, such as the acts of the Council of Tribur (895), strongly emphasized the primacy of a unifying Christian identity.[102] Indeed, the Bavarian annalist has to be adamant that Arnulf's campaigns in Italy were against 'bad Christians' to avoid compromising this.[103] Boris-Michael's counsel here both illustrated the fragility of Christian identity while illustrating the religious solidarity between the Bulgars and the eastern Franks.

The Bulgars nonetheless followed Boris-Michael's advice and 'by God's mercy, victory … fell to the Christians' against the 'gentile [Hungarians]'.[104] The Bulgars thus prove to be morally instructive neighbours for the annals' Bavarian readers. This echoed the entry for 873 in various ways: it was located in a proximate region among a neighbouring yet distinct ethnic group, who took counsel and triumphed over their pagan enemies through divine agency. What distinguished the Bavarian annalist from his 870s predecessors was that he elsewhere used 'Christian' to denote East Frankish or Bavarian armies (including against the Hungarians). In this entry, and those for 891 and 900, armies identified by their ethnic group set out to fight (East Franks and Alemans in 891, and Bavarians in 900). On joining battle, however, the annalist switched to calling them 'Christians', all helped by God. He thus showed how disparate ethnic groups – some marginal and some central – could all be contained in the same Christian identity against pagan threats. This was a new development in Carolingian historiography and showed how, as the Carolingian

---

[99] '[M]iseri, inscii … ad vestigia vetuli illorum regis Michaelis qui eos primum ad christianae religionis veritatem convertit': *AF* [Bavarian continuation], *s.a.* 896 ((MGH SRG i.u.s. 7: 130).

[100] '[A]uxilium a Deo querendum esse': ibid.

[101] '[D]e inlata christianis iniuriae': ibid.

[102] See, for instance, *Concilium Triburiense*, c. 34, ed. Alfred Boretius and Victor Krause, MGH Capit. 2 (Hanover, 1897), 233.

[103] See, for instance, *AF* [Bavarian continuation], *s.a.* 893 (MGH SRG i.u.s. 7: 122): 'malis christianis'.

[104] '[M]isericordia Dei victoria … christianis concessa est … gentilium Avarorum': ibid. 130.

hegemony fragmented, the importance of a shared Christian self-consciousness became more pressing. At the same time, this approach shared elements already apparent in the *Annals of St Bertin* in the 830s and 840s. As the Carolingian world changed, established constructions of Christian identity and its relationship to moral conformity continued to provide traction on contemporary issues.

CONCLUSION

Space forbids the discussion of many further lines of inquiry: the Iberian and Mediterranean frontiers, and the distant margins of Christianity in the Holy Land, for example, or the appearance of margins in other Frankish historians. Before suggesting why annalists used marginal characters in the ways discussed, two further observations are necessary. Firstly, the prescriptive and idealized nature of these narratives should not preclude their basis in reality. Evidence abounds not only of cultural and religious conflict across the Carolingian frontier, but also of accommodation and cultural exchange between centres and peripheries.[105] Although such exchanges were certainly complex and fluid, they also gave rise to important and lasting affinities between the Franks and their various neighbours. The Normans are simply the most famous example of 'strange peoples' who – like the anonymous hero of the *Annals of Fulda* – entered a Frankish cultural world. Such exchange and accommodation sustained the annalists' evident curiosity about what those distant from themselves got up to and what this might teach their audiences.

Secondly, although based on the reception of rumours and reports from afar, the annalists seem to have integrated these episodes into their narratives with considerable ingenuity. It often remains unclear how far early medieval historians – especially annalists – intended to juxtapose seemingly random episodes to achieve a greater narrative impact.[106] Some combinations hint at deeper arguments, others may simply reflect the order that information reached the author. The examples considered here could, theoretically, have stood alone and still made valuable moral arguments to their readers. Nonetheless, their thematic coherence with other episodes within a single entry is

---

[105] McKitterick, *Charlemagne*, 288–91. For the later example of the Vikings, see especially Pierre Bauduin, *Le monde franc et les Vikings, VIIIe–Xe siècle* (Paris, 2009).

[106] James Palmer, *The Apocalypse in the Early Middle Ages* (Cambridge, 2014), 165.

suggestive of wider authorial planning in these particular cases. At the very least, such events gained relevance because they spoke to concerns already embedded within the narrative. More generously, they reinforce the sense that annalists – just as much as biographers or epic poets – knew how to assemble their material with both literary and didactic skill.

The consistent thread running through these episodes, and examples of accommodation more broadly, was Christianity. This gave the Franks and their converted (or converting) neighbours a shared vocabulary and a vision of community which they could share without abandoning their own particular identities. This made marginal communities didactically valuable, and related to two further developments. Firstly, Carolingian ideas about ethnicity were changing. As Helmut Reimitz has demonstrated, Charlemagne's reign had seen an attempt to create a single Frankish identity into which the king's subjects could be elided.[107] As Charlemagne conquered more regions, that Frankish identity proved too narrow to gain traction among such a diversely-peopled empire. By *c*.800, Frankish historians began searching for alternative, broader visions of community, in which different ethnicities could coexist rather than being invalidated.[108] Christianity, and especially the concept of the *ecclesia* as discussed by Mayke de Jong, provided coherence and unity across ethnic diversity (as it had done in the New Testament) and allowed for individuals and communities to operate with several layers of identity.[109] The examples considered in this article were the next step. If other ethnic identities were valid because they shared their Christian faith with the Franks, then strangers from the periphery could provide valuable moral advice and counsel. It is worth pointing out how remarkable this is. These examples demonstrate a potent de-centring of the Franks within their own social imagination.

This would have been unlikely, however, without a second important condition which made strangers, if anything, better than those at the centre. As van Renswoude has shown, late antique Christianity had a long tradition of the outspoken outsider – the prophet and the

---

[107] Reimitz, *History, Frankish Identity, and the Framing of Western Ethnicity*, 344–5.

[108] Ibid. 8–9; compare O'Brien, 'Empire, Ethnic Election and Exegesis', 98–9.

[109] Mayke de Jong, '*Ecclesia* and the Early Medieval Polity', in Stuart Airlie and Walter Pohl, eds, *Staat im frühen Mittelalter: Forschungen zur Geschichte des Mittelalters* (Vienna, 2006), 113–32; O'Brien, 'Empire, Ethnic Election and Exegesis', 108; Heydemann and Pohl, '1 Peter 2.9', 26–30; Kramer, *Rethinking Authority*, 39–40.

ascetic – speaking truth to power. In Merovingian culture, holy men were often marginal to the royal court and yet had enormous rhetorical and persuasive authority precisely because they operated in a liminal world, out in the wilderness but close to God.[110] Under the Carolingians, that inspired and ascetic dimension of monasticism became more routinized and institutionalized, and the court became far less indulgent of marginal voices.[111] Outspoken bishops could easily find themselves cold-shouldered by the courtly establishment and so had to find other ways to counsel and persuade that followed a new set of rules.[112] Carolingian historians, however, did not want their audience to become complacent; they did not want their very centrality to blind them to the need for humility. This, after all, was the key message behind each of the episodes considered above.

Geographical strangers, therefore, provided perfect foils. There was a literal distance between them and the authors who used them to criticize and counsel. There was a great difference between saying how the current bishop, abbot or king should rule – with all the controversy that entailed – and pointing to how sensibly a distant Christian leader seemed to be leading their people. These distant characters had no direct stake in the political life of the texts' audiences. They were safe to listen to and admire. Criticism of colleagues or patrons could remain implicit. Discussions about what it meant to lead well as a Christian could be abstracted by making them geographically remote. At the same time, however, the shared Christian identity and military experiences of these peripheral Christians overlapped sufficiently with the audiences of these texts to prove instructive. They fought the same enemies and battled the same temptations, and thus had something valuable to say. Marginal Christians provided yet another way for the Frankish church to debate and negotiate its way towards wiser and stronger pastoral leadership.[113] Their distance made them excellent if implicit critics of Frankish arrogance. Their shared Christianity made them worthy exemplars to follow. By their very marginality, they sustained the moral core of the Carolingian *correctio*.

---

[110] Renswoude, *Rhetoric of Free Speech*, 133–60.

[111] Albrecht Diem, 'Monks, Kings, and the Transformation of Sanctity: Jonas of Bobbio and the End of the Holy Man', *Speculum* 82 (2007), 521–59, at 555–6.

[112] Renswoude, *Rhetoric of Free Speech*, 206–29.

[113] Kramer, *Rethinking Authority*, 19–29.

Medieval English Church Dedications to St Gregory: Connecting Centre and Periphery

Miriam Adan Jones

Newcastle upon Tyne

This article examines the distribution of medieval English churches and chapels dedicated to St Gregory, arguing that this distribution reflects Gregory's symbolic significance in the pre-Conquest church as a figure who could connect centres and margins. Early dedications in ecclesiastical and royal centres recall the Gregorian mission and the connection it forged between Britain, on the margins of Christian Europe, and Rome at the centre. Concentrations of later dedications in East Anglia and the South-West asserted the connection of these more peripheral regions with the newly formed English nation, through veneration of its patron saint. The decline in numbers of Gregory dedications after the Conquest reflects the transfer of Gregory's status as founder of the English church and patron of the English nation to other saints.

Bede's *Ecclesiastical History of the English People*, completed in 731 at Bede's monastery in Jarrow on the south bank of the Tyne, famously opens by positioning Britain and its inhabitants at the edge of the world.[1] Bede's purpose in the five books that follow is to show how the Christian faith arrived, took root and flourished in this most marginal of places.[2] For Bede, none had played a more significant part in bringing this about than Pope Gregory I (590–604), who had initiated the Roman mission to the *Angli* in the late sixth century, thus forging a direct link between Britain and Rome, margin and centre, and becoming the spiritual father of the English church.[3] Seeing Rome as the centre and themselves as peripheral had a profound effect on the self-understanding

---

24 Hepple Way, Newcastle upon Tyne. E-mail: miriamadanjones@gmail.com.

[1] Bede, *Historia Ecclesiastica gentis anglorum* [hereafter: *HE*] 1.1; ET: *Bede's Ecclesiastical History of the English People*, ed. and transl. Bertram Colgrave and Roger Mynors (Oxford, 1969), 14–17.

[2] Jennifer O'Reilly, 'Islands and Idols at the Ends of the Earth: Exegesis and Conversion in Bede's *Historia Ecclesiastica*', in Stephane Lebecq, Michel Perrin and Olivier Szerwiniack, eds, *Bède le vénérable. Entre tradition et posterité*, Histoire et littérature de l'Europe du Nord-Ouest 34 (Lille, 2005), 119–45.

[3] *HE* 2.1 (*Ecclesiastical History*, ed. Colgrave and Mynors, 124).

Studies in Church History 61 (2025), 95–115 © The Author(s), 2025. Published by Cambridge University Press on behalf of the Ecclesiastical History Society.
doi:10.1017/stc.2024.32

of the early English church and on the formation of English identity.[4] As the key figure in their Christian origin story, Gregory himself became an emblem both of the idea of the English as a united people and of their connection with Rome and the wider Christian world.[5] Accordingly, although Gregory was remembered with respect in Rome and beyond as a theologian, exegete, liturgist and administrator, it was in the English church that his cult was most enthusiastically promoted in its earliest stage.[6] The first *Life of Gregory* was produced at the double monastery at Whitby (now in Yorkshire) near the turn of the eighth century, and this text also gives us the earliest evidence of an altar dedicated to Gregory, located in the monastery's church.[7] In 747, the Council of Clofesho legislated that Gregory's feast day should be kept throughout the English church and his name included in the litany.[8] Gregory was venerated throughout the pre-Conquest period as the 'apostle of the English', as reflected in liturgical calendars, hymns, letters and other sources.[9]

However, these relatively few textual sources can offer only a partial picture of the spread of Gregory's cult in early medieval England. For a fuller analysis, we must turn to other types of evidence. This article will use dedication patterns to offer new insights into where, when and

---

[4] Nicholas Howe, 'Rome: Capital of Anglo-Saxon England', *Journal of Medieval and Early Modern Studies* 34/1 (2004), 147–72; Nicholas Brooks, 'Canterbury, Rome, and the Construction of English Identity', in Julia M. H. Smith, ed., *Early Medieval Rome and the Christian West: Essays in Honour of Donald A. Bullough*, The Medieval Mediterranean 28 (Leiden, 2000), 221–46.

[5] Anton Scharer, 'The Gregorian Tradition in Early England', in Richard Gameson, ed., *St Augustine and the Conversion of England* (Stroud, 1999), 187–201; Alan Thacker, '*Peculiaris Patronus Noster*: The Saint as Patron of the State in the Early Middle Ages', in John Robert Maddicott and David M. Palliser, eds, *The Medieval State: Essays Presented to James Campbell* (London and Rio Grande, 2000), 1–24, at 17–22; Erin Thomas A. Dailey, 'The *Vita Gregorii* and Ethnogenesis in Anglo-Saxon Britain', *Northern History* 47 (2010), 195–207; Catherine Cubitt, 'Universal and Local Saints in Anglo-Saxon England', in Alan Thacker and Richard Sharpe, eds, *Local Saints and Local Churches in the Early Medieval West* (Oxford, 2002), 423–53, at 447–8.

[6] Alan Thacker, 'Memorializing Gregory the Great: The Origin and Transmission of a Papal Cult in the Seventh and Early Eighth Centuries', *EME* 7 (1998), 59–84.

[7] Anon., *Vita Gregorii*, c.19; ET: *The Earliest Life of Gregory the Great by an Anonymous Monk of Whitby*, ed. and transl. Bertram Colgrave (Cambridge, 1985), 104; Wilhelm Levison, *England and the Continent* (Oxford, 1946), 264–5.

[8] Arthur West Haddan and William Stubbs, eds, *Councils and Ecclesiastical Documents relating to Great Britain and Ireland*, 3: *The English Church, 595–1066* (Oxford, 1871; repr. Oxford, 1964), 368 (canon 17).

[9] Mechtild Gretsch, *Ælfric and the Cult of Saints in Late Anglo-Saxon England*, Cambridge Studies in Anglo-Saxon England 34 (Cambridge, 2006), 21–64.

why Gregory was commemorated. By the end of the Middle Ages, churches, chapels and altars dedicated to Gregory could be found throughout England. Although their total number remained small, their distribution, and changes to that distribution over time, points to the symbolic meaning of Gregory's cult as a means of connecting centres and margins. This study will attempt to identify all known pre-Reformation Gregory dedications and analyse both their geographic and chronological distribution. These findings will be brought into conversation with what we know from other sources about the spread and significance of Gregory's cult in medieval England, to argue that Gregory dedications are most prevalent where invoking his patronage served to assert the connection between periphery and centre. In particular, I will suggest that dedications to Gregory are predominantly a feature of two periods and contexts: in the pre-Viking era, in early ecclesiastical centres that traced their origins to Gregory's Roman mission; and during the expansion and consolidation of West Saxon rule, in places newly incorporated into the English kingdom. By comparing the English dedications with a sample from the European continent, I will argue that the smaller set of dedications from post-Conquest England should be interpreted not as a reflection of Gregory's importance to the English church as such, but of his status in the wider church as a pope, doctor of the Church, promotor of monasticism and worker of eucharistic miracles.

DISTRIBUTION PATTERNS

Before analysing the distribution of dedications to Gregory, it is worth making some general points about the nature of the evidence. A distribution map of church dedications is always an interpretation of partial and sometimes conflicting evidence. It is also a palimpsest, from which the individual chronological layers cannot wholly be recovered. Over the course of centuries, new churches and chapels were constructed, existing structures expanded or rebuilt, new patrons added to old, old dedications forgotten, and lost dedications recovered (not always accurately).[10] A church where all these stages are well documented would be a rare find indeed. Often, we may guess that the earliest evidence for a dedication significantly post-dates the dedication itself,

---

[10] For an overview of English dedications and their study, see Nicholas Orme, *English Church Dedications: With a Survey of Cornwall and Devon* (Exeter, 1996), 3–58.

and yet changes to dedications were frequent enough that we cannot always be sure the earliest known dedication is the original dedication. These factors mean that, in each individual case, establishing the medieval dedication and when it was chosen relies on a balance of probabilities. Nevertheless, standing back to look at the distribution as a whole rather than at individual cases, it is possible to discern meaningful patterns.[11] Some saints' dedications cluster heavily in particular regions: for example, dedications to Swithun in the south, and dedications to Cuthbert in the north.[12] As I will show below, Gregory dedications are not restricted to a particular region, but they do occur more frequently in some regions than in others. Dedication patterns may also reveal changes to a saint's popularity over time, and part of this article's argument is that dedications to Gregory are concentrated in the period before the Norman Conquest. Sometimes, it is also possible to detect patterns in how dedications to a saint sit within the landscape. For example, the archangel Michael was associated with hilltops and waterways, while Mary was a popular choice as the patron of a second church within a larger ecclesiastical complex.[13] Several of the Gregory dedications discussed below have in common that they are associated with dedications to either Peter or Paul, or both, implying a conceptual link between these saints.

Undergirding church dedication research is the understanding that the choice of patron held significance, with certain saints being seen as desirable or appropriate because of their associations with particular places or people.[14] For local saints, such as founders and leaders of religious communities, or local holy men and women, this was on account of their personal connections. However, most of the dedications of medieval England were to saints whose cult had a wider reach, and who were chosen for the symbolic meanings they invoked.[15] The choice of dedication, therefore, could function as a statement about the identity, ideals and affiliations of a community. It was the bishop who supplied the chrism for the consecration of a church and officiated at the service, and he would therefore have been well placed to

[11] Graham Jones, 'Comparative Research Rewarded: Religious Dedications in England, Wales and Catalunya', in idem, ed., *Saints of Europe: Studies Towards a Survey of Cults and Culture* (Donington, 2003), 210–60, at 254.
[12] Graham Jones, *Saints in the Landscape* (Stroud, 2007), 168–9.
[13] Ibid. 70, 74–6; Helen Gittos, *Liturgy, Architecture and Sacred Places in Anglo-Saxon England* (Oxford, 2013), 111–12.
[14] Jones, 'Comparative Research', 259–60.
[15] Cubitt, 'Universal and Local Saints', 446–7.

influence the selection of a patron saint. Donors and land-owners could also be influential figures.[16] Their choice was not constrained by the availability of relics: these were not essential to the rite (although they were considered desirable) and, if they were used, did not have to be those of the saint invoked as patron.[17] However, the presence of an important relic could influence the dedication.[18] In early medieval England, dedications to universal saints were, by far, more common than to local saints, with a clear preference for biblical saints and Roman martyrs.[19] That Gregory appears in this company from an early date underscores his importance in the early English church.

The earliest dedications to Gregory are known from narrative sources, like the altar in the monastery at Whitby already mentioned. Bede records another altar dedicated to Gregory in the north portico of the monastery of SS Peter and Paul, Canterbury, and a portico dedicated to Gregory in the cathedral of St Peter at York.[20] Other sites are not documented until later but may belong to the pre-Viking age as well. These include St Gregory by St Paul's in London, documented by the early eleventh century, but possibly an early foundation;[21] Rendlesham in Suffolk, which was an important settlement in the early kingdom of East Anglia;[22] and Kirkdale in Yorkshire, where an inscription commemorates the restoration of 'St Gregory's minster' shortly before the Norman Conquest, and archaeological

[16] Jones, 'Comparative Research', 232; Charles L. S. Linnell, *Norfolk Church Dedications* (York, 1962), 8–9.

[17] Gittos, *Liturgy*, 216–19; Alison Binns, *Dedications of Monastic Houses in England and Wales, 1066–1216*, Studies in the History of Medieval Religion 1 (Woodbridge, 1989), 13–14.

[18] Binns, *Dedications*, 45.

[19] Levison, *England and the Continent*, 259–65; Michael Hicks, 'Leavings or Legacies? The Role of Early Medieval Saints in English Church Dedications beyond the Conquest and Reformation', in Alexander James Langlands and Ryan Lavelle, eds, *The Land of the English Kin: Studies in Wessex and Anglo-Saxon England in Honour of Professor Barbara Yorke* (Leiden, 2020), 582–601, at 583; Alan Thacker, 'In Search of Saints: The English Church and the Cult of Roman Apostles and Martyrs in the Seventh and Eighth Centuries', in Smith, ed., *Early Medieval Rome and the Christian West*, 247–78.

[20] *HE* 2.3, 2.20 (*Ecclesiastical History*, ed. Colgrave and Mynors, 144, 204); Thacker, 'Memorializing', 75; Levison, *England and the Continent*, 264–5.

[21] Thomas Arnold, ed., *Memorials of St Edmund's Abbey*, 3 vols (London, 1890–3), 1: 42–3; Thacker, 'Memorializing', 79.

[22] Christopher Scull and Gabor Thomas, 'Early Medieval Great Hall Complexes in England: Temporality and Site Biographies', *Anglo-Saxon Studies in Archaeology and History* 22 (2020), 50–67, at 62; Christopher Scull, Faye Minter and Judith Plouviez, 'Social and Economic Complexity in Early Medieval England: A Central Place Complex of the East Anglian Kingdom at Rendlesham, Suffolk', *Antiquity* 90/354 (2016), 1594–612, at 1602.

evidence suggests a thriving ecclesiastical site by the mid-eighth century, which can probably be identified with the place known as *Cornu Vallis* in the textual record.[23] In York, early origins have been suggested for the church of St Gregory, Micklegate (now destroyed), as a subsidiary church that formed part of a group of churches connected to Christ Church, alias Holy Trinity; the dedications of these churches together mirrored the dedications of the altars at Christ Church in Canterbury, and were perhaps chosen following the promotion of York to metropolitan status in 735.[24] Early origins have also been suggested for the only church dedicated to Gregory in the medieval diocese of Durham: Kirknewton (Northumberland), although the earliest extant church fabric and written records date only to the early twelfth century.[25]

Among the medieval churches dedicated to Gregory, there are twenty for which there is pre-Conquest evidence, whether documentary, archaeological or architectural. The preponderance of these is found in the dioceses along the eastern seaboard, reflecting the origins of Gregory's cult in the Roman mission to the kingdoms of Kent and Northumbria and its spread from these centres. In Canterbury diocese, in addition to the chapel to Gregory at St Augustine's priory, there was a church in Wye that was probably dedicated to Gregory.[26] The East Anglian diocese of Elmham, into which the earlier diocese of *Dommoc*

---

[23] Elizabeth Okasha, *Hand-List of Anglo-Saxon Non-Runic Inscriptions* (Cambridge, 1971), 87–8 (no. 64); Philip Rahtz and Lorna Watts, 'Three Ages of Conversion at Kirkdale, North Yorkshire', in Martin Carver, ed., *The Cross Goes North: Processes of Conversion in Northern Europe, AD 300–1300* (York, 2003), 289–309, at 301; Richard Morris, 'Landscapes of Conversion amongst the Deirans: Lastingham and its Neighbours in the Seventh and Eighth Centuries', in Paul S. Barnwell, ed., *Places of Worship in Britain and Ireland, 300–950* (Donington, 2015), 119–51, at 143–5.

[24] Richard Morris, 'Alcuin, York, and the *alma Sophia*', in Lawrence A. S. Butler and Richard K. Morris, eds, *The Anglo-Saxon Church: Papers on History, Architecture, and Archaeology in Honour of Dr H. M. Taylor*, Council for British Archaeology Research Report 60 (London, 1986), 80–9, at 84, 86–7, 88 n. 21.

[25] Eric Cambridge, 'Archaeology and the Cult of St Oswald in Pre-Conquest Northumbria', in Catherine E. Karkov, ed., *The Archaeology of Anglo-Saxon England: Basic Readings* (New York, 1999), 233–78, at 256. Rosemary Cramp, *Corpus of Anglo-Saxon Stone Sculpture*, 1: *County Durham and Northumberland* (Oxford, 1984), 251, lists the sculpture of the Magi found here as 'wrongly associated with the pre-Conquest period'. The church was surrendered to the bishop of Durham by Kirkham Priory in 1154x9. M. G. Snape, ed., *English Episcopal Acta*, 24: *Durham, 1153–1195* (Oxford, 2002), 72–3.

[26] Ann Williams and Geoffrey H. Martin, eds, *Domesday Book: A Complete Translation* (London, 2002), 13; C. Paul Burnham, *A Window on the Church of England: The History of Wye Parish Church* (Wye, 2015), 5.

was amalgamated, had churches of St Gregory in Pentlow in Essex (joint dedication with George);[27] in Sudbury,[28] Barnham,[29] and Hemingstone[30] in Suffolk (as well as Rendlesham already mentioned); and in Heckingham[31] and Norwich[32] in Norfolk. In the East Midlands, in the expansive diocese of Dorchester, which encompassed the earlier bishoprics of Leicester and Lincoln, the church at Fledborough (Leicestershire) is documented by the eleventh century, although its dedication only enters the record later.[33] Graham Jones has suggested Ratby (also Leicestershire) as another early Gregory dedication.[34] St Gregory's, Northampton (now destroyed), is documented from the eleventh century. Saxon burials were found near it, and its proximity to St Peter's, where archaeologists have uncovered remains of an eighth-century hall complex, has led John Blair to suggest an earlier church of St Gregory contemporary with that complex.[35] However, because sites like this tended to develop over time, it is also possible that the church of St Gregory was constructed at a later date to complement the existing church, hall and cemetery.[36] In York diocese, in addition to

---

[27] G. C. Alston, 'St Gregory's Patrimony', *The Downside Review* 23 (1904), 269–80, at 279; Harold M. Taylor and Joan Taylor, *Anglo-Saxon Architecture*, 3 vols (Cambridge, 1965–78), 2: 491.

[28] Dorothy Whitelock, ed. and transl., *Anglo-Saxon Wills* (Cambridge, 1930), 38–43 (nos 15 and 16).

[29] Williams and Martin, eds, *Domesday Book*, 1244; Thomas Astle, Samuel Ayscough and John Caley, eds, *Taxatio ecclesiastica Angliæ et Walliæ auctoritate P. Nicholae IV, circa A.D. 1291* (London, 1802), 120; Linnell, *Norfolk Church Dedications*, 44.

[30] Williams and Martin, eds, *Domesday Book*, 1233; Taylor and Taylor, *Anglo-Saxon Architecture*, 1: 295.

[31] Williams and Martin, eds, *Domesday Book*, 1124; Alston, 'Patrimony', 275.

[32] Brian Ayers, 'The Growth of an Urban Landscape: Recent Research in Early Medieval Norwich', *EME* 19 (2011), 62–90, at 82; Astle, Ayscough and Caley, eds, *Taxatio*, 78.

[33] Williams and Martin, eds, *Domesday Book*, 764.

[34] Graham Jones, 'The Origins of Leicestershire: Churches, Territories, and Landscape', in Katherine Elkins, ed., *Medieval Leicestershire: Recent Research in the Medieval Archaeology of Leicestershire* (Leicester, 2015), 13–40, at 20. The settlement is early and had a priest by the time of Domesday; the church was said in the thirteenth century to have received a pension from nearby Markfield on the feast of St Gregory *ab antiquo* ('from ancient times'). Williams and Martin, eds, *Domesday Book*, 633; William P. W. Phillimore, ed., *Rotuli Hugonis de Welles, Episcopi Lincolniensis*, 3 vols (London, 1909), 1: 247.

[35] John Blair, 'Palaces or Minsters? Northampton and Cheddar Reconsidered', *Anglo-Saxon England* 25 (1996), 97–121, at 104–8; idem, 'Anglo-Saxon Minsters: A Topographical Review', in idem and Richard Sharpe, eds, *Pastoral Care Before the Parish*, Studies in the Early History of Britain (Leicester, 1992), 226–66, at 261.

[36] Blair, 'Anglo-Saxon Minsters', 250–6; idem, *The Church in Anglo-Saxon Society* (Oxford, 2005), 201; Gittos, *Liturgy*, 90, remarks on 'a continued desire to add new churches to existing sites' evident from *c.*950 onwards.

the dedications mentioned above, the church of St Gregory at Bedale has pre-Conquest masonry.[37]

Moving westward, in Winchester, as in London, there was a church of St Gregory adjacent to the cathedral of SS Peter and Paul; this church was documented by c.901.[38] The church of Welford (Berkshire) is recorded in the Domesday book.[39] In the diocese of Worcester, the only church of St Gregory was at Tredington. Here, there is stonework from the late Saxon period and the Domesday book records the presence of a priest.[40] Located by the river Stour, this may be the property 'by the Stour' which was disputed between King Offa of Mercia and Bishop Heathored of Worcester in 781. Property in Tredington was certainly given to the bishop of Worcester in 747. These early legal records, together with the traces of tenth-century church fabric, have led scholars to suggest that St Gregory's may have originated in the eighth century as a monastery with links to the cathedral.[41] The only medieval Gregory dedication in Lichfield diocese is Offchurch (Warwickshire); pre-Conquest origins for the church have been suggested on the basis of some of the architectural features and traces of a Saxon cemetery, although the place-name ('Offa's church') is suggestive of the type of private church more frequently established in the eleventh and twelfth centuries.[42] Lastly, in the diocese of Hereford, the church of St Gregory at Morville (Shropshire) is exceptional in that the Domesday survey records not

[37] Hardy Bertram McCall, *The Early History of Bedale in the North Riding of Yorkshire* (London, 1907), 74–9, 101–2; Taylor and Taylor, *Anglo-Saxon Architecture*, 1: 57.

[38] Alexander R. Rumble, *Property and Piety in Early Medieval Winchester: Documents Relating to the Topography of the Anglo-Saxon and Norman City and its Minsters*, Winchester Studies 4.3 (Oxford, 2002), 50–6.

[39] Williams and Martin, eds, *Domesday Book*, 142; Frederick Arthur Crisp, *Fragmenta Genealogica* 7 (London, 1902), 78.

[40] Taylor and Taylor, *Anglo-Saxon Architecture*, 2: 623–6, with 1: xxv (key to periods); Williams and Martin, eds, *Domesday Book*, 478.

[41] Patrick Sims-Williams, *Religion and Literature in Western England 600–800*, Cambridge Studies in Anglo-Saxon England 3 (Cambridge, 1990), 159, 162; Francesca Tinti, *Sustaining Belief: The Church of Worcester from c.870 to c.1100*, Studies in Early Medieval Britain 5 (Abingdon, 2010), 116.

[42] Louis F. Salzman, ed., *The Victoria History of the County of Warwick*, 6: *Knightlow Hundred* (London, 1951), 195, 197; Blair, *Church in Anglo-Saxon Society*, 386 and 386 n. 70. The connection with King Offa of Mercia is legendary: Wiesje Emons-Nijenhuis, 'St Fremund, Fact and Fiction', *Revue bénédictine* 123 (2013), 99–127, at 107 n. 56.

only the church and its staff of eight canons, but also its dedication to Gregory.[43]

A relatively large number of churches dedicated to Gregory are found in the South-West, in the area that had originally been the diocese of Sherborne and which was later repeatedly divided and reorganized. Many foundations cannot be securely dated, but Norman architecture or sculpture is found at Treneglos (Cornwall),[44] Weare (Somerset),[45] and Marnhull (Dorset).[46] Treneglos in particular is probably earlier: the place-name element *eglos* ('church') suggests an early ecclesiastical site, perhaps with an original dedication now unknown.[47] In Devon, the churches of Dawlish,[48] Goodleigh[49] and Venn Ottery (a chapel of Harpford)[50] are documented by the late thirteenth century.[51] Older origins are of course possible, and I will suggest below how these dedications may fit into a pre-Conquest political context.

There is evidence that dedications to Gregory continued after the Conquest. Cropton (Yorkshire) is unlikely to be older than the twelfth century, since at the time of the Domesday survey the settlement had no recorded population and consisted mainly of woodland.[52] The church, which stands beside the remains of a Norman motte-and-bailey castle,[53] was rebuilt in the nineteenth century, but a twelfth-century font

---

[43] Williams and Martin, eds, *Domesday Book*, 692.

[44] Orme, *English Church Dedications*, 120. Orme records that there is also evidence for St George, whom on balance he prefers as the medieval patron.

[45] Alston, 'Patrimony', 273.

[46] Royal Commission on Historical Monuments (England), *An Inventory of the Historical Monuments in Dorset, 3: Central* (London, 1970), 148–9; available on *British History Online*, at: <http://www.british-history.ac.uk/rchme/dorset/vol3/pp148-160>, accessed 10 February 2024.

[47] Orme, *English Church Dedications*, 120.

[48] Ibid. 153.

[49] Ibid. 165.

[50] The dedication feast was held on the feast of St Gregory until 1410, but this by itself is inconclusive; the earliest record of the dedication is from the eighteenth century. Orme, *English Church Dedications*, 213.

[51] Francis C. Hingeston-Randolph, *The Registers of Walter Branscombe (A.D. 1257-1280), and Peter Quivil (A.D. 1280–1291) Bishops of Exeter, with some Records of the Episcopate of Bishop Thomas de Bytton (A.D. 1292–1307), also the Taxation of Pope Nicholas IV, A.D. 1291 (Diocese of Exeter)* (London and Exeter, 1889), 131, 332–3, 346.

[52] Williams and Martin, eds, *Domesday Book*, 790.

[53] Historic England, *National Heritage List for England*, entry no. 1011624, online at: <https://historicengland.org.uk/listing/the-list/list-entry/1011624>, accessed 26 June 2024.

survives.[54] Eight miles from Kirkdale, its dedication may have been influenced by that of the older church. From the thirteenth century, as the medieval parish system solidified, the construction and dedication of new parish churches virtually came to a halt, but chapels continued to be built, and side-chapels, aisles and altars to be added to existing churches, some of which had Gregory as their patron. In Somerset, Stoke St Gregory enters the historical record in 1233 as a chapel in North Cory parish, and there was a chapel of St Gregory in Whitchurch by 1544.[55] Preston Patrick (Cumbria) was originally a chapel dependent on Burton; the earliest recorded dedication (in 1331) is to Gregory, but it was later dedicated jointly to Gregory and Patrick, and still later Patrick became the sole patron.[56] On the whole, chapels are less well documented than churches, making patterns in their dedications more difficult to discern. These examples show that dedications to Gregory did continue into the later Middle Ages, but their relatively small number suggests that Gregory was not an especially popular choice of patron in this period.

Monastic communities provide the context for another set of post-Conquest Gregory dedications. At the monastery of SS Peter and Paul, Canterbury (which by the late tenth century was known as St Augustine's, after its founder), the old altar dedicated to Gregory in the north *porticus* remained in place until 1091, when it was demolished in order to complete the rebuilding of the abbey, and a new Gregory chapel was constructed.[57] Archbishop Lanfranc (d. 1089) founded St Gregory's Priory, Northgate, Canterbury, around 1085.[58] In Christ Church Cathedral, Archbishop Anselm (d. 1109) undertook extensive rebuilding, after which the southernmost chapel off the south-east transept

---

[54] Ibid., entry no. 1281522, online at: <https://historicengland.org.uk/listing/the-list/list-entry/1281522>, accessed 5 February 2024.

[55] Historical Manuscripts Commission, *Report on the Manuscripts of Wells Cathedral* (London, 1885), 6; compare Nicholas Orme, 'The Medieval Church Dedications of Somerset', *Proceedings of the Somerset Archaeological and Natural History Society* 160 (2017), 83–94, at 93.

[56] Alston, 'Patrimony', 279.

[57] Crook, *English Medieval Shrines*, 52, 133; Richard Sharpe, 'The Setting of St Augustine's Translation', in Richard Eales and idem, eds, *Canterbury and the Norman Conquest: Churches, Saints and Scholars, 1066–1109* (London, 1995), 1–14, at 1–2; Robin Fleming, 'Christ Church Canterbury's Anglo-Norman Cartulary', in Charles Warren Hollister, ed., *Anglo-Norman Political Culture and the Twelfth Century Renaissance: Proceedings of the Borchard Conference on Anglo-Norman History, 1995* (Woodbridge, 1997), 83–156, at 100 n. 89.

[58] Paul Antony Hayward, 'Gregory the Great as "Apostle of the English" in Post-Conquest Canterbury', *JEH* 55 (2004), 19–57, at 37–8.

contained an altar dedicated to Gregory.[59] The Augustinian priory at Frithelstock (Devon), founded *c.*1220, had Gregory and Mary as its patrons.[60] An altar was dedicated to Augustine and Gregory in Christ-church priory at Twynham (Dorset) in 1214.[61] York Minster had an altar in the crypt dedicated jointly to Nicholas and Gregory by 1364, when it was apparently replaced by separate altars for each in the minster's transepts.[62] The late-sixteenth-century compilation known as *The Rites of Durham* records an altar dedicated to Gregory at Durham Cathedral before the Reformation.[63]

What patterns can we detect in this distribution? The earliest documented dedications to Gregory are located in important ecclesiastical centres: Canterbury, York and the influential monastery of Whitby. Other early, possibly pre-Viking, dedications are also found in high-status locations. Some are associated with a cathedral (London, Winchester, York Micklegate, possibly Tredington); others appear to have been important ecclesiastical or monastic centres in their own right (Kirkdale, Morville). Rendlesham was a royal estate, and Kir-knewton is a mile from the seventh-century royal palace at Yeavering. Taking the pre-Conquest evidence as a whole, dedications are concentrated in the east, and especially in East Anglia, together with the middle Anglian zone around the great rivers. The antiquity of these dedications is difficult to assess, because the disruptions to church life in the Danelaw make it hard to establish continuity or discontinuity of ecclesiastical foundations across this ninth-century caesura.[64] Some may be survivals from the seventh or eighth century, with their origins in the early Roman mission to East Anglia. On the other hand, some or

---

[59] John Crook, *English Medieval Shrines* (Woodbridge, 2011), 137–8.

[60] Orme, *English Church Dedications*, 164; Alston, 'Patrimony', 271.

[61] Islwyn Geoffrey Thomas, '*The Cult of Saints Relics in Medieval England*' (PhD thesis, Queen Mary University of London, 1974), 257, 525; compare Binns, *Dedications*, 14.

[62] Philippa Margaret Turner, 'Image and Devotion in Durham Cathedral Priory and York Minster, *c.*1300–*c.*1540: New Contexts, New Perspectives' (PhD thesis, University of York, 2014), 124.

[63] Joseph T. Fowler, ed., *Rites of Durham: Being a Description or Brief Declaration of All the Ancient Monuments, Rites, & Customs Belonging or Being Within the Monastical Church of Durham Before the Suppression*, Surtees Society 107 (Durham, 1903), 23.

[64] Dawn M. Hadley, *The Vikings in England: Settlement, Society and Culture* (Manchester, 2006), 192–227. The Danelaw refers to the area under Danish control following Viking incursion and settlement in the eastern and northern part of England.

all of them may belong to the tenth century. The group of dedications in the south-western peninsula likewise cannot conclusively be assigned to a particular era. The evidence is Norman or later, but the churches and their dedications may be earlier than the evidence. Finally, there is a scattering of chapels and monastic dedications from the post-Conquest period. We can therefore trace in the dedication patterns the first flourishing of Gregory's cult in high-status centres, its later concentration in areas more removed from both royal and ecclesiastical power, and finally its tapering popularity over the later Middle Ages.

NATIONAL PATRON

To understand these patterns, we must examine how Gregory functioned within the communion of patronal saints. As noted above, narrative and liturgical sources suggest that Gregory personified the connection between the English church and the Church universal, but was also seen as the particular patron of the people whose conversion he had initiated. We can see this understanding reflected in the dedication evidence, too. Initially, the emphasis appears to have been on Gregory's Roman and apostolic connections. Many of the earliest dedications to Gregory are of altars, side-chapels or ancillary churches attached to main churches dedicated to Peter or Paul. This is true of the dedications at Canterbury, York and Whitby, as well as London, Winchester and Northampton. Helen Gittos has argued that church dedications were 'used to embody relationships between churches' in a number of ways, expressing the connections of churches to one another as parts of a single complex, elements in a larger urban setting, or affiliated institutions in different locations.[65] Assuming that the arrangement of dedications was significant, the pattern of juxtaposing Gregory with Peter and Paul points to a conceptual association between these saints. As pope, Gregory had been Peter's successor as head of the Roman church, and just as Paul was the apostle to the Gentiles, Gregory was apostle of the English. The arrangement of the dedications, with Peter or Paul chosen as patron of the more important structure and Gregory as that of the lesser, reflects the relationship of the English church on the margins, to the Roman church at the centre.

---

[65] Gittos, *Liturgy*, 95.

Dedications to Gregory thus expressed a particular self-understanding on the part of those who chose them. They recalled the Roman origins of their church, and signalled an ongoing allegiance to Rome as the centre to which the churches of the English should look. At the same time, Roman sympathies could also be expressed through other dedication choices: King Offa (d. 796) showed his loyalty to Rome with a series of dedications to St Peter;[66] Bishop Wilfrid (d. 709/10), echoing the dedication of Gregory's own monastery on the Caelian Hill in Rome, dedicated both Hexham and Oundle to St Andrew;[67] likewise, the dedications in Canterbury mirrored the dedications of Roman churches.[68] Dedications to Gregory must therefore have been chosen in part for the additional meaning they carried, conveying a sense of the English as a single people with a shared spiritual identity and history represented by their apostle.

Gregory's association with English identity undoubtedly helps to account for the almost total lack of dedications to him in Wales and Scotland.[69] I would suggest it also contributed to the relatively high number in Middle and East Anglia, and in the South-West. In both these regions, those responsible for choosing a saintly patron could use Gregory to assert the place of their local church within the wider English church and nation. In the eastern group of dedications, as mentioned, most Gregory dedications appear to be pre-Conquest, a trend perhaps associated with the integration of this region into the English kingdom following Danish incursions and then settlement in the ninth century.[70] West-Saxon control of the south-western peninsula was also cemented in the ninth and tenth centuries.[71] Although, as

[66] Levison, *England and the Continent*, 29–31; Catherine Cubitt, *Anglo-Saxon Church Councils*, *c.650–850*, Studies in the Early History of Britain (London and New York, 1995), 226.

[67] James E. Fraser, 'Rochester, Hexham and Cennrigmonaid: The Movements of St Andrew in Britain, 604–747', in Stephen I. Boardman, John Reuben Davies and Eila Williamson, eds, *Saints' Cults in the Celtic World* (Woodbridge, 2009), 1–17, at 6–7.

[68] Gittos, *Liturgy*, 61–6, 95–6; Thacker, 'In Search of Saints', 256–8; Brooks, 'Canterbury, Rome', 221–47.

[69] See 'The Survey of Dedications to Saints in Medieval Scotland', online at: <https://saints.hca.ed.ac.uk/dedication/DE/JD/779>, accessed 10 February 2024; 'Dioceses of Wales and the Marches', *Transnational Atlas and Database of Saints' Cults*, online at: <https://graham-jones.info/data-and-other-resources/tasc-datasets/>, accessed 10 February 2024.

[70] See Dawn M. Hadley, 'Viking and Native: Re–thinking Identity in the Danelaw', *EME* 11 (2002), 45–70, at 52–3, on 'Danishness' and 'Englishness' in the Danelaw.

[71] Orme, *English Church Dedications*, 13.

noted above, the Gregory dedications in this region only enter into the evidence in the Norman period or later, they may in fact have earlier origins in the centuries of West-Saxon expansion and consolidation. Nicholas Orme has observed how 'kings and Church leaders in the late Anglo-Saxon period encouraged the cults of English saints as a means of extending political power, religious influence, and even national integration.'[72] His examples include Cuthbert, Edmund of Bury and Swithun. Although Gregory was not an English saint in the sense of having English origins, his symbolic representation of a united English church and nation meant he might well be considered an English saint for such integrative political purposes.

That the West-Saxon kings were interested in the patronage of Gregory for their nation-building project is suggested by the second English coronation *ordo*, a liturgical order composed in the early tenth century, which invokes Gregory's intercession, along with that of the Virgin Mary and St Peter, during the blessing of the newly invested ruler.[73] This reference to Gregory's patronage of the royal house of Wessex sits within a wider literary context in which the role of Gregory as a foundational figure in the history of the English people was repeatedly underscored. Following Bede, the *Anglo-Saxon Chronicle* (first composed *c*.890, then expanded and reworked in multiple versions) makes the Gregorian mission an integral part of the early history of the English.[74] That foundation narrative was rehearsed again in the preface to Æthelwold's translation of the *Rule of Benedict*, which drew on Gregory's spiritual authority to promote the (royally sanctioned) monastic reforms of the tenth century.[75] The lavishly illustrated Benedictional of Æthelwold, possibly produced for King Edgar's coronation in 973, depicts Gregory in a prominent position alongside Benedict and Cuthbert, all leading saints for the English church.[76]

---

[72] Ibid. 17.
[73] Thacker, '*Peculiaris Patronus Noster*', 21–2; David Pratt, *English Coronation Ordines in the Ninth and Early Tenth Centuries*, Henry Bradshaw Society 125 (London, 2023), 38, 168–9.
[74] Courtnay Konshuh, 'Constructing Early Anglo-Saxon Identity in the *Anglo-Saxon Chronicles*', in Alexander James Langlands and Ryan Lavelle, eds, *The Land of the English Kin: Studies in Wessex and Anglo-Saxon England in Honour of Professor Barbara Yorke* (Leiden, 2020), 154–79.
[75] Gretsch, *Ælfric*, 43.
[76] Ibid. 45.

The tenth century therefore provides a plausible historical context for a wave of dedications to Gregory. The analysis above has shown that these dedications were concentrated in precisely those areas where English identity could not be taken for granted, but needed to be asserted. As Sarah Foot has pointed out, in the late ninth century, 'Alfred's English were the Christian people of Kent, Wessex and western Mercia,' but by the early eleventh century, the people of East Anglia and Northumbria were also included in the English people and polity.[77] In these newly incorporated and marginal regions of what became England, Gregory dedications could serve to cultivate a sense of national unity, connecting the peripheries of the kingdom to its centres through a shared story of salvation.

After the Norman Conquest, the cult of Gregory was taken up and promoted by the new elites, especially by archbishops Lanfranc (1070–89) and Anselm (1093–1109).[78] Yet, as Paul Hayward has argued, by the 1120s 'Gregory seems to have been dropped as England's apostle almost everywhere, though his cult was still accorded great respect at most abbeys and monastic cathedrals.'[79] We have seen above some examples of dedications to Gregory in these contexts. The epithet 'apostle of the English', however, came to be attached more and more often to Augustine of Canterbury.[80] Gregory's role as national patron thus came under pressure from rival saints. While, following his arrival at St Augustine's, Canterbury, Benedictine hagiographer Goscelin was promoting Augustine, Herman the archdeacon, from the abbey at Bury St Edmunds, was working to raise the profile of Edmund, the martyred king, and to position him as a patron saint for the nation.[81]

Between the thirteenth and fifteenth centuries, the role of national patron was gradually transferred to George.[82] Graham Jones has suggested that many church dedications to Gregory were subsequently changed to George.[83] Documented instances of this are scarce, but it is

---

[77] Sarah Foot, 'The Making of *Angelcynn*: English Identity before the Norman Conquest', *TRHS* 6th series 6 (1996), 25–49, at 47.

[78] Hayward, 'Gregory the Great', 19–21, 48–54.

[79] Hayward, 'Gregory the Great', 56.

[80] Ibid. 56–7.

[81] Tom Licence, 'The Cult of St Edmund', in idem, ed., *Bury St Edmunds and the Norman Conquest* (Woodbridge, 2014), 104–30, at 114–15.

[82] Jonathan Good, *The Cult of St George in England* (Woodbridge, 2009), 19–20, 52–94.

[83] Jones, *Saints*, 37, 158–60.

not difficult to imagine confusion arising between the two saints, who had similar names and functions. Seaton (Devon) is now St Gregory's, but medieval records all agree that the church's patron was George.[84] The only evidence for Gregory as the medieval patron is a charter of 1267, granting rights to hold a fair on the feast of 'Gregory the Martyr', most likely a scribal error.[85] There is evidence for both Gregory and George at Treneglos.[86] There may indeed be cases where an earlier dedication to Gregory has left no record. George was clearly far more popular at a later stage: medieval churches dedicated to George number over one hundred, more than double the tally of those dedicated to Gregory, despite Gregory's cult being better established at an earlier date.[87] Coming at the problem from a different angle, Lawrence Butler has noted that, of the total number of English churches dedicated to George, only a small proportion – he calculates 2.3 per cent – have surviving pre-Conquest fabric. While Butler allows that this might be the result of rebuilding, he also points out that for Gregory the proportion of churches still showing pre-Conquest fabric is much higher (14 per cent), suggesting 'a pre-conquest preference' for Gregory, while George enjoyed 'a predominantly late medieval popularity'.[88] We might wonder whether the transfer of national patronage was the cause or the effect of Gregory's tapering popularity over the course of the Middle Ages. What is clear is that, from the twelfth century, Gregory faced significant competition in his role as the patron of the English.

Gregory's cult therefore underwent a transformation, emphasizing new aspects of his sanctity. In the thirteenth century, it was strengthened by the spread of images of St Gregory's vision, showing an apparition of Christ to Gregory during his celebration of the mass.[89] In addition, in late medieval England, 'St Gregory's Trental' became a popular form of devotion. Involving the celebration of thirty masses over the course of a year, it was believed to be a highly effective form of

---

[84] Orme, *English Church Dedications*, 198.

[85] Samantha Letters, *Gazetteer of Markets and Fairs in England and Wales to 1516* (London, 2003), n.p.

[86] Orme, *English Church Dedications*, 120.

[87] Good, *Cult of St George*, 162.

[88] Lawrence Butler, 'Church Dedications and the Cults of Anglo-Saxon Saints in England', in idem and Morris, eds, *The Anglo-Saxon Church*, 44–50, at 44.

[89] Kathryn M. Rudy, *Rubrics, Images and Indulgences in Late Medieval Netherlandish Manuscripts* (Leiden, 2017), 101–36.

intercession for the dead.[90] Although Gregory's contribution to the conversion of the English was still remembered, he now became more strongly associated with eucharistic devotion.

As in post-Conquest England, so too on the European continent the cult of Gregory was found primarily among the clerical hierarchy and in monasteries.[91] In certain contexts, Gregory's role in the spread of the Christian faith to the far corners of the world was commemorated, often when it could serve as an example. Pope Nicholas I deliberately emulated Gregory's *Libellus Responsionum* to Augustine in his approach to Khan Boris of the Bulgarians in 866.[92] Missionaries in the sixteenth century would later draw on Gregory's advice to Augustine and his company, seeing parallels with their own work to convert the indigenous peoples of the Americas.[93] Usually, however, it was Gregory's contributions to monasticism, liturgy, scholarship and church order that provided the primary reasons for his veneration.[94] Among the poems of Alcuin (d. 804) are three for altars to Gregory in unspecified continental locations: in each of these, it is Gregory's role as *doctor* that is noted.[95]

A full inventory and analysis of continental dedications to Gregory would be beyond the scope of this article, but some examples may offer a point of comparison for the English dedications. The medieval lists of church dedications collected and edited by Oswald Holder-Egger

---

[90] Eamon Duffy, *The Stripping of the Altars: Traditional Religion in England, 1400–1580*, new edn (New Haven, CT, 2022; first publ. 1992), 293–4.

[91] For some examples, see Bruno Judic, 'Le culte de saint Grégoire le Grand et les origines de l'abbaye de Munster en Alsace', in Martin Heinzelmann, ed., *L'hagiographie du haut Moyen Âge en Gaule du Nord. Manuscrits, textes et centres de production*, Beihefte der Francia 52 (Stuttgart, 2001), 263–95.

[92] Conrad Leyser, 'The Memory of Gregory the Great and the Making of Latin Europe, 600–1000', in Kate Cooper and Conrad Leyser, eds, *Making Early Medieval Societies: Conflict and Belonging in the Latin West, 300–1200* (Cambridge, 2016), 181–201, at 192.

[93] Lesley Abrams, *Bede, Gregory and Strategies of Conversion in Anglo-Saxon England and the Spanish New World* (Jarrow, 2013), 26–30.

[94] For Gregory's literary legacy, see Constant J. Mews and Claire Renkin, 'The Legacy of Gregory the Great in the Latin West', in Bronwen Neil and Matthew Dal Santo, eds, *A Companion to Gregory the Great*, Brill's Companions to the Christian Tradition 47 (Leiden, 2013), 315–42. Leyser, 'Memory', 188–201, highlights the influence of Gregory's *Register*, a text with a very limited reception in early medieval England. See also Benjamin Savill, 'The Consul Vanishes? On Using and Not Using Gregory the Great's *Register* in Early Medieval England', *EME* 32 (2024), 106–27.

[95] *Poeta Latini aevi Carolini*, ed. Ernst Dümmler, *MGH Poetae* 1 (Berlin, 1881), 310, 317, 341. The first of these is from a set of inscriptions intended for a church of St Vedast; the other two are also for large churches with multiple altars.

are remarkable in the level of detail they provide, and can serve as a sample representing wider trends.[96] In these texts, Gregory appears in a handful of dedication ceremonies. Usually, these involved the use of his relics, alongside those of other saints, in the consecration of an altar which is then given a different dedication.[97] Sometimes, the presence of his relics implied his joint patronage as part of a collective such as 'all saints' or 'all confessors'.[98] In a few instances, there were altars assigned to Gregory specifically: an altar dedicated in 949 at St Maximin's Abbey, Trier; an altar to Gregory at St Eucharius' Abbey, Trier, dedicated in 1148; and one of six altars in a crypt in the monastery of Emmeram, dedicated in 980.[99] Gregory was also the joint patron of the church of the Benedictine monastery of Petershausen, outside Konstanz, founded in the tenth century and rededicated in 1085, which had a head relic housed in the main altar.[100] Julia Smith has argued that in Petershausen the relic of Gregory served to underscore the connection of the monastery with Rome, a connection that was also symbolically manifested in other ways, including the monastery's layout and location in relation to the city.[101] Gregory was therefore deployed there in a similar way to early medieval England, personally embodying a community's links with Rome. It is notable that these examples, few as they are, are all found in monastic contexts. This is not to say there were no parish churches dedicated to Gregory on the continent. One such is San Gregorio Nelle Alpi, Veneto (Italy), documented in the late twelfth century.[102] Another is the church of Saint-Grégoire, Ille-et-Vilaine (France), which was donated to the chapter of Rennes cathedral by a man named Halenaldus in the eleventh or twelfth century and later became parochial.[103] A

---

[96] *Fundationes et dedicationes ecclesiarum*, ed. Oswald Holder-Egger, *MGH SS* 15.2 (Hanover, 1888), 960–1125, 1269–88, 1315.

[97] Ibid. 965 (Benedict), 993 (unknown), 1078 (Otto), 1097 (Oswald), 1108 (Trinity, the Holy Cross, John the Baptist, John the Evangelist, Philip and James), 1273 (Michael), 1283 (unknown).

[98] Ibid. 971 (Christ and the Holy Cross, and Mary and all Saints, 'especially those whose relics are in the church'), 976 (all confessors).

[99] Ibid. 1095, 1270, 1279.

[100] Ibid. 1023–4; Alison I. Beach, *The Trauma of Monastic Reform: Community and Conflict in Twelfth-Century Germany* (Cambridge, 2017), 9.

[101] Julia M. H. Smith, *Europe After Rome* (Oxford, 2005), 288–9.

[102] R. P. D. Aloysius Tomasetti, ed., *Bullarum diplomatum et privilegiorum sanctorum romanorum Pontificum, 3: A Lucio III (1181) ad Clementium IV (1268)* (Turin, 1858), 28.

[103] Guillotin de Courson, *Pouillé historique de l'archevêché de Rennes*, 6 vols (Paris, 1886), 6: 64.

systematic study of the continental dedications and their distribution would be desirable, helping us to better understand the spread of Gregory's cult.

What appears to be distinctive about the English dedications, compared to the continental evidence, is their relative frequency at a comparatively early date. The popularity of Gregory in pre-Conquest England reflects a context in which it made sense, to those building and dedicating churches, to recall the origins of their church in the Gregorian mission. That mission had been sent to them directly from the heart of the Christian world and had given a powerful impetus and legitimization to the formation of English identity.[104] The Gregorian mission had brought the marginal people of Britain into communion with the centre, and indeed had recast them for a central role in salvation history, as in them the command to bring the gospel to the 'ends of the earth' was fulfilled.[105] This narrative was put to good use by those who, from the late ninth century onwards, began to envision the English not only as a spiritual, but also as a political community, with Gregory as its patron. Such considerations increased Gregory's appeal as a choice of dedication beyond that which he held more generally as a holy man and teacher of the faith.

CONCLUSION

The evidence of church dedications surveyed here has confirmed but also nuanced the picture offered by textual sources of the spread of Gregory's cult in early medieval England. Mechtild Gretsch has argued, based on the great distances between the earliest known dedications at Canterbury, York and Whitby, 'that the cult of St Gregory, from its very beginnings, was a pan-English cult, not a local affair.'[106] The distribution pattern analysed here suggests that, while the cult of Gregory was indeed not restricted to a particular locality, it was also not taken up in the same way across all the early English

---

[104] Patrick Wormald, 'The Venerable Bede and the "Church of the English"', in Geoffrey Rowell, ed., *The English Religious Tradition and the Genius of Anglicanism* (Wantage, 1992), 13–32; Anton Scharer, 'Die Rolle der Kirche bei der Identitätsbilding der Angelsachsen', in Walter Pohl, ed., *Die Suche nach den Ursprüngen: von der Bedeutung des frühen Mittelalters* (Vienna, 2004), 255–60.

[105] O'Reilly, 'Islands and Idols', 119–45; Nicholas Howe, *Writing the Map of Anglo-Saxon England: Essays in Cultural Geography* (New Haven, CT, 2008), 107–11.

[106] Gretsch, *Ælfric*, 25.

kingdoms. The earliest altars and churches dedicated to Gregory were in important centres of the early English church that traced their origins to the Gregorian mission. As the cult was diffused from these centres, dedications to Gregory could be found in an ever wider geographic area, but they are not distributed uniformly across all early English kingdoms or dioceses. The distribution pattern thus reveals regional variations which are harder to identify from the textual evidence. The lack of early dedications to Gregory in the Mercian heartlands suggests that perhaps attitudes to the saint – and to what he represented – were different here than in other early English king-doms. The low number of dedications in Kent, despite the leading role played by Canterbury in the promotion of Gregory's cult, serves as a reminder that the ideals of leading churchmen were not always taken up by local communities. The group of dedications to Gregory in the South-West, on the other hand, appears to reflect a successful pro-gramme of assimilation into the English kingdom from the tenth century onwards. I have proposed here that the same may be true of the cluster in the East Midlands and East Anglia, areas which had been part of the Danelaw. This study therefore contributes to a more textured understanding of the ways in which English identity was constructed and promoted across a range of times and places.

Dedications to Gregory, as to any saint, were polyvalent, and will have meant different things to different people at different times. In the tenth century, Gregory's long-standing association with monasti-cism took on fresh relevance in the context of the Benedictine reforms, and after the Conquest, his cult flourished especially in monastic circles. Later medieval dedications to Gregory reflect the significance he still held as a universal saint, revered in England as elsewhere in Europe as a doctor of the Church, proponent of monasticism, key figure in the development of the papacy, and worker of miracles, but no longer as the apostle or patron of the nation.

Within the complex landscape of the medieval cult of saints, Gregory's place was central in some ways and marginal in others. Among a cast of almost exclusively biblical saints, Gregory was one of the few less traditional dedications to flourish during the earliest phase of English church-building. Yet in that period he was almost never the main patron but rather the dedicatee of side-chapels, porticos and secondary churches. His cult was promoted by senior ecclesiastical leaders, but limited in its popular appeal. His churches were concen-trated in early ecclesiastical and royal centres, but later also in the more peripheral medieval dioceses of Exeter and Norwich. I have suggested that Gregory was useful in all these contexts as a representation of the connection between centre and margin: between Rome and the English church, between the nation and its regions. The driving force behind the development of his cult had been church leaders and secular rulers, who saw in him a patron for their vision of a united English church and later nation, and who wished to emphasize – precisely because it was not always obvious – the intimate connection between their insular church and its distant parent church in Rome. Gregory's diminishing popularity over time, conversely, may reflect the extent to which both the idea of England itself, and England's place within the Christian world, were increasingly seen as self-evident.

Priestly Provision at the Periphery: Building the Church in Tenth-Century Catalonia

Jonathan Jarrett [iD]

Keighley, West Yorkshire

In standard accounts of Christian expansion into the frontier with Islam in early medieval Iberia, if the church plays a role, it is the monastic church, operating as frontier land developer. Alternatively, this action is left to a pioneer peasantry or to acquisitive warlords, with the church only following. A close-up study of the activities of priests around the Catalan frontier town of Manresa, however, shows a collegiate secular church structure building up frontier infrastructure well in advance of developing monasticism. These peripheral priests wove neighbourhoods into larger church networks which were the first institutional structures to develop in this area. Such a pattern may also be characteristic in similar areas elsewhere.

INTRODUCTION

Catalonia's position on the frontier between what have become Spain and France has made it the sort of periphery which can be critical to a ruling core, but which rarely directs core policy, despite some

Institute for Medieval Studies, University of Leeds

75 Exley Road, Keighley, West Yorkshire, BD21 1LT, UK. E-mail: jjarrett@chiark.greenend.org.uk.

This article represents research undertaken at the Universities of Oxford and Birmingham in 2013–14. An initial version was presented at the International Medieval Congress, University of Leeds, in July 2014. I must thank all those who commented on it at these stages, especially Professors John Blair and Julia Barrow, and the College of Arts and Law at Birmingham for helping me obtain facsimiles of crucial documents. The present article also owes much to the critique of Dr Rebecca Darley, as well as the reviewers and editors of SCH. Only I can be held responsible for its failings, however. I must also thank the organizers of the 2023–4 meetings of the Society for their repeated kind consideration of my personal circumstances.

Studies in Church History 61 (2025), 116–141 © The Author(s), 2025. Published by Cambridge University Press on behalf of the Ecclesiastical History Society.
doi:10.1017/stc.2024.33

economic importance.[1] Only in the Middle Ages can a Catalonia be found that was not governed either from a distant centre to which its counties were, if not peripheral, at least secondary – such as the united Spanish Crown – or by a Catalonia-based power whose legitimacy derived from elsewhere, such as the kings of Aragón. To complicate matters, medieval Catalonia was not a unit, but a disparate set of counties initially grouped under rival families of counts, not all related.[2] Nonetheless, from the tenth century, the growing importance of the count-marquises of Barcelona gave this 'pre-Catalonia' its own peripheries, initially in the Pyrenees, but more famously thereafter in the 'no-man's land' between Christian and Muslim polities to the south-west.[3] Over the following centuries, accelerated by the collapse of Umayyad rule at Córdoba after 1013, that space was closed up by colonization and military take-over, in a process many scholars no longer call *Reconquesta* (Sp. *Reconquista*; 'reconquest').[4] But in the tenth century, the south-western edge of this cohering space was substantially ungoverned, and subject to pioneer efforts by various agencies, although which agencies is a matter of historiographic debate. This article's task is to reassert the secular church as a factor in that debate.

A good place to start is the city of Manresa. One of the Catalan counties' more substantial urban foci, Manresa was also one of the

---

[1] For some outlines within a huge literature, see Peter Sahlins, *Boundaries: the Making of France and Spain in the Pyrenees* (Berkeley, CA, 1989); Flocel Sabaté, 'Catalonia Among the Long-Standing Regions of Europe', in idem, ed., *Historical Analysis of Catalan Identity* (Bern, 2015), 13–28.

[2] An accessible account is Thomas N. Bisson, *The Medieval Crown of Aragon: A Short History* (Oxford, 2000).

[3] Both the terms 'pre-Catalonia' and, in this context, 'no man's land,' originate in the work of Ramon d'Abadal i de Vinyals, for which, see especially Ramon d'Abadal, 'La pre-Catalunya (segles VIII-XI)', in Ferran Soldevila, ed., *Història dels Catalans*, 5 vols, 2nd edn (Barcelona, 1970; first publ. 1961), 2: 601–991; Abadal, *Els primers comtes catalans*, Biografies catalans: sèrie històrica 1, 2nd edn (Barcelona, 1965; first publ. 1958), esp. 73–114. For the most recent account of the area in this period, see Cullen J. Chandler, *Carolingian Catalonia: Politics, Culture, and Identity in an Imperial Province, 778–987*, Cambridge Studies in Medieval Life and Thought 4th series 111 (Cambridge, 2019); and for historiography, see idem, 'Carolingian Catalonia: The Spanish March and the Franks, *c.*750–*c.*1050', *History Compass* 11 (2013), 739–50.

[4] Alejandro García Sanjuán, 'Cómo desactivar una bomba historiográfica: la pervivencia actual del paradigma de la Reconquista', in Carlos de Ayala Martínez, Isabel Cristina Ferreira Fernandes and J. Santiago Palacios Ontalva, eds, *La Reconquista: ideología y justificación de la Guerra Santa peninsular*, Historia & Arte 5 (Madrid, 2019), 99–119.

furthest-flung, an originally Roman town deep in the Llobregat valley.[5] It was neither the seat of a count, the centre of a county nor an episcopal see. For these functions, Manresa looked to the older city of Vic d'Osona to its north-east.[6] Vic's bishop acted as the distant head of Manresa's clergy and, to some extent, as the local count; mostly, however, the town and its church were left to govern themselves.[7] It is, nonetheless, quite well documented, which allows a close study of how the church was established, or re-established, in this peripheral zone.

Debate over Frontier Settlement

There already exist competing answers for how this happened.[8] Peasants might begin a settlement venture themselves, or with capital provided by an aristocrat or monastery with conditions involving dependence or renders. Once established, they might demand or even construct protection through fortifications. Alternatively, deeper needs of defence against Muslim raids might press the authorities to establish fortifications first, after which settlers would move in under their protective shadow or because of incentives offered by relevant patrons. Either way, before long they would need a church. With that

---

[5] Philip Banks, 'Las ciudades y su papel', in Jordi Camps, ed., *Cataluña en la época carolingia: arte y cultura antes del románico (siglos IX y X)* (Barcelona, 1999), 65–71; ET: idem, 'The Cities and their Role', in Camps, ed., *Cataluña en la época carolingia*, 451–55. For Manresa specifically, see below, nn. 26 and 27.

[6] On Vic, see Ramon Ordeig i Mata, *Els orígens històrics de Vic (segles VIII–X)*, Osona a la butxaca 1 (Vic, 1981), online at: <http://www.patronatestudisosonencs.cat/uploads/files/Els_origens_historics_de_Vic.pdf>, accessed 30 July 2018; M. Dolors Molas i Font, Imma Ollich i Castanyer and Antoni Caballé i Crivillés, 'De l'Auso romana al Vicus Ausonensis medieval', *Ausa*, 33/161–2 (2008), 719–22, online at: <http://raco.cat/index.php/Ausa/article/view/128429>, accessed 17 October 2014.

[7] The bishop's position is clear in *Catalunya carolingia*, 4: *Els comtats d'Osona i Manresa* [hereafter: CC4], ed. Ramon Ordeig i Mata, 3 vols, Memòries de la Secció Històrico-Arqueològica 53 (Barcelona, 1999), 1: 365–77 (no. 182). Digital access is via 'CatCar' (December 2019), online at: <https://catcar.iec.cat/documents/edicio/llistaMan.action?request_locale=en>, accessed 25 October 2024. This edition contains almost all the primary material for the rest of the paper; references to documents in it hereafter are abbreviated as CC4, followed by the document number. Secondary commentary from the edition is cited by volume and page number.

[8] Compare Paul Freedman, *The Origins of Peasant Servitude in Medieval Catalonia* (Cambridge, 1991), 56–88, for peasant initiative; with Flocel Sabaté Curull, 'Las tierras nuevas en los condados del nordeste peninsular (siglos X–XII)', *Studia Historica: Historia Medieval* 33 (2005), 139–70, online at: <https://dialnet.unirioja.es/servlet/articulo?codigo=1704747>, accessed 9 March 2014, for military and aristocratic priorities.

church's (re-)establishment, Christianity's periphery was extended another step closer to Islam's.

The agencies that founded churches in this zone are also debated. It is accepted that monasteries, aristocrats and bishops all did so,[9] but the balance between them is contested. Moreover, some communities took the initiative themselves, as shown by the acts of consecration of the resulting churches.[10] These documents, almost unique to Catalonia, show bishops being brought out to areas that are sometimes not subsequently documented for decades, but which on such occasions still engaged with central authority.[11] The church on the periphery was thus one engine of that authority's expansion.

NATURE OF THE FRONTIER

There is, of course, an extensive historiography about the nature of frontiers, now and in the Middle Ages.[12] Its competing typologies of the frontier suggest the need to make clear what kind of frontier is

---

[9] Bishops in early medieval Catalonia were sometimes aristocrats, of course, but we can rarely show this. I prefer here to separate laymen, who held the rights to land on which churches stood but did not supervise the ministry, from bishops, whose business was the ministry and who did not need rights over the land to have rights over its churches.

[10] On these, see Ramon Ordeig i Mata, 'La consagració i la dotació d'esglésies a Catalunya en les segles IX–XI', in Frederic Udina i Martorell, ed., *Symposium internacional sobre els orígens de Catalunya (segles VIII–XI)*, 2 vols (Barcelona, 1991), 2: 85–101, online at: <http://www.raco.cat/index.php/MemoriasRABL/article/view/202475>, accessed 1 July 2014.

[11] Wendy Davies, 'Local Priests in Northern Iberia', in Steffen Patzold and Carine van Rhijn, eds, *Men in the Middle: Local Priests in Early Medieval Europe*, Ergänzungsbände zum Reallexikon der Germanischen Altertumskunde 93 (Berlin, 2016), 125–44, online at: <https://library.oapen.org/handle/20.500.12657/24650>, accessed 28 November 2023. Davies cites three from further west in the Iberian Peninsula: ibid. 137 and n. 55. One Catalan example is studied in Jonathan Jarrett, 'Centurions, Alcalas, and *Christiani perversi*: Organisation of Society in the pre-Catalan "Terra de Ningú"', in †Alan Deyermond and Martin Ryan, eds, *Early Medieval Spain: A Symposium*, Papers of the Hispanic Research Seminar 63 (London, 2010), 97–127, at 104–08.

[12] This immense literature cannot be summarized in a note. A recent introduction to each of global, medieval and Iberian levels is found respectively in Brett Bowden, 'Frontiers: Old, New, and Final', *The European Legacy: Toward New Paradigms* 25 (2020), 671–86; Giles Constable, 'Frontiers in the Middle Ages', in O. Merisalo, ed., *Frontiers in the Middle Ages*, Textes et études du Moyen Âge 35 (Turnhout, 2006), 3–28; and Philippe Sénac, 'En guise d'introduction. Quelques observations sur l'historiographie récente de la frontière dans l'Espagne médiévale (VIIIe–XIIIe siècles)', in Sébastien Gasc et al., eds, *Las fronteras pirenaicas en la Edad Media (siglos VI–XV). Les frontières pyrénéennes au Moyen Âge (VIe–XVe siècles)* (Zaragoza, 2018), 13–24.

envisaged in this article.[13] Likewise, in the light of anthropologically informed scholarship suggesting that borders have meaning only because of being enacted, it is worth asking who, in this article's understanding, did the 'borderwork' of constructing a periphery as different from the spaces on either side of it.[14]

The traditional dyad of open or closed frontiers, usually but wrongly attributed to Frederick Jackson Turner, is of limited help here.[15] The space beyond the developing edge of the Catalan counties clearly had geographical depth. The distance from Manresa to the nearest then-Muslim city, Lleida, was and is 100 km, and Manresa was itself somewhat of an outpost; from Lleida to both Barcelona and Vic, governmental centre to governmental centre, is 160 km. Much of the space between them was thinly populated, settled only by dispersed *villa* communities arrayed over some distance around their notional centres (often churches), or in isolated homesteads not part of wider units (and thus usually unknown to us except through archaeology).[16] What Turner called 'free land' was widely available, but the people to exploit it were not.[17] In this sense, this frontier was 'open'; but since there was also a substantial power on its far side, it was finite and therefore also 'closed'. On the Christian side, a network of fortresses spread into this zone from points of established government; some also existed outside central control.[18] The historiography in recent decades has de-emphasized emptiness, instead emphasizing the existence of 'unconnected' populations in these zones, whom sources from the centre considered bandits or heretics, if they were even mentioned.

---

[13] For some theoretical approaches, see Emmanuel Brunet-Jailly, 'Theorizing Borders: An Interdisciplinary Perspective', *Geopolitics* 10 (2005), 633–49.

[14] Chris Rumford, 'Citizen Vernacular: The Case of Borderwork', in idem, ed., *Cosmopolitan Borders* (London, 2014), 22–38.

[15] This is not in fact present in Turner's essay, which has many versions. Here I use Frederick Jackson Turner, 'The Significance of the Frontier in American History', in idem, *The Frontier in American History* (New York, 1921), 1–38, online at: <https://www.gu tenberg.org/files/22994/22994-h/22994-h.htm>, accessed 28 June 2021.

[16] Eduardo Manzano Moreno, 'Christian-Muslim Frontier in al-Andalus: Idea and Reality', in Dionisius Agius and Richard Hitchcock, eds, *Arab Influence upon Medieval Europe*, Folia scholastica mediterranea 18 (Reading, IL, 1994), 83–96, at 94–6.

[17] Turner, 'Significance', 18–22; compare David A. Nichols, 'Civilization Over Savage: Frederick Jackson Turner and the Indian', *South Dakota History* 2 (1972), 383–405.

[18] Sabaté, 'Las tierras nuevas'. For a castle outside central control, see *Cartulario de 'Sant Cugat' del Vallés*, ed. José Rius [Serra], 3 vols, Textos y Estudios de la Corona de Aragón 3–5 (Madrid, 1945–7), 2: 94–6 (no. 449); and index volume, ed. Federico Udina Martorell (Barcelona, 1981).

Even so, few would deny a lower population density in these areas than in those under more established governmental, and ecclesiastical, provision.[19] As to the enaction of this frontier, such 'bordering' was partly done by scribes who referred to such locations as being in *marcis, marginis, limitibus* ('marches', 'margins', 'limits') and so on, even though they also recorded established land tenure and boundaries there. However, it was also done by settlers who moved there to occupy land under favourable conditions which did not pertain closer to home, even though they probably had to compete for such lands with locals.[20] A difference regarding these spaces was recognized, if sometimes exaggerated, by contemporaries.[21] In accordance with the writings of those contemporaries, this article therefore understands this frontier as a space of low population density, with its population grouped sporadically, unrecognized by most wider governmental structures.

THE CHURCH AND THE HISTORIOGRAPHY

There is, as has already been noted, a reasonably settled paradigm that describes how and whence that population was increased and brought under authority.[22] The settling agency is almost always reckoned as monastic. This paradigm is quite easy to substantiate in the sources, but raises two problems which this article seeks to address.[23]

---

[19] Manzano, 'Ideal and Reality', 93–6; Jarrett, 'Centurions, Alcalas, and *Christiani perversi*', esp. 111–15.

[20] For charter language, see Julia M. H. Smith, '*Fines Imperii*: The Marches', in Rosamond McKitterick, ed., *The New Cambridge Medieval History*, 2: c.*700*–c.*900* (Cambridge, 1995), 169–89, at 176–7. For settlers, see Freedman, *Peasant Servitude*, 56–88. For competition, see Jonathan Jarrett, 'Settling the Kings' Lands: *Aprisio* in Catalonia in Perspective', *EME* 18 (2010), 320–42.

[21] Jarrett, 'Centurions, Alcalas and *Christiani perversi*', esp. 98–9, 105–8, 117–9.

[22] Jonathan Jarrett, 'Engaging Élites: Counts, Capital and Frontier Communities in the Ninth and Tenth Centuries, in Catalonia and Elsewhere', *Networks and Neighbours* 2 (2014), 202–30, online at: <https://nnthejournal.files.wordpress.com/2018/05/nn-2-2-jarrett-engaging-elites1.pdf>, accessed 5 September 2024.

[23] The idea of the monastery as frontier developer probably originates, albeit in passing, with Charles Julian Bishko, 'Salvus of Albelda and Frontier Monasticism in Tenth Century Navarre', *Speculum* 33 (1948), 559–90; reprinted in idem, *Studies in Medieval Spanish Frontier History*, Collected Studies 124 (London, 1980), n.p. (no. 1). However, this has been developed particularly by scholars of Cistercians, both in Catalonia: Lawrence J. McCrank, 'The Cistercians of Poblet as Medieval Frontiersmen: An Historiographic Essay and Case Study', in *Estudios en homenaje a don Claudio Sánchez-Albornoz en sus 90 años:*

The first is the peripheral church itself. The standard paradigm tends to assume a starting position of no church presence. Some outside agency would then have established churches and these, eventually, became sufficiently numerous to develop something like a parochial structure.[24] This presents two difficulties. Firstly, it is clear from the archaeology, especially from Santa Margarida de Martorell north-north-east of Barcelona, that churches could and did operate in these unconnected areas despite the lack of a supporting ecclesiastical structure; in Santa Margarida's case, for six centuries before making it into the written record.[25] Ecclesiastical ground zero should therefore not always be assumed. Secondly, there is an intermediate step which is left unexplored: what happened between the first church consecration and the completion of the parish structure, and who brought it about? In this, the first churches and their incumbent clergy must have been critical.

MANRESA AND ITS CHURCH

These are issues that the records from around Manresa can help us address. Hundreds of documents survive covering the city's area following the Frankish conquest of the area in the early ninth century. Despite this, only one scholar has written about Manresa in this era, Albert Benet i Clarà.[26] Benet catalogued the area's churches as they appear in the documentary record, but for the processes behind their

---

anexos de Cuadernos de Historia de España, 6 vols (Buenos Aires, 1983), 2: 313–60; and more widely, Emilia Jamroziak and Karen Stöber, eds, *Monasteries on the Borders of Medieval Europe: Conflict and Cultural Interaction*, Medieval Church Studies 28 (Turnhout, 2013). Two local studies of monasteries doing such work, among others, are David Guasch i Dalmau, 'L'activitat repobladora del monestir de Sant Cugat del Vallès vers el Penedès al darrer quart dels segle X i primer de l'XI', *Miscel·lània penedesenca* 26 (2001), 111–40; Jonathan Jarrett, 'Power over Past and Future: Abbess Emma and the Nunnery of Sant Joan de les Abadesses', *EME* 12 (2003), 229–58, at 240–8.

[24] For example, Ramon Ordeig i Mata, 'Cel les monàstiques vinculades a Guifré el Pelós i a la seva obra repobladora (vers 871–897)', ed. S. Claramunt and A. Riera, *Acta Historica et Archaeologica Mediaevalia* 22 (2001), 89–119.

[25] For Santa Margarida, see Centre d'Estudis Martorellencs, 'Santa Margarida', 7 August 2020, online at: <https://sites.google.com/a/intranetcem.net/santa-margarida/>, accessed 17 July 2024; ET: 'The Archaeological Site', 3 January 2011, online at: <http://www.infocem.net/publicacions/guiasm-ang.pdf>, accessed 17 July 2024.

[26] See especially Albert Benet i Clarà, *L'expansió del comtat de Manresa*, Episodis de la història 255 (Barcelona, 1982); idem, *Història de Manresa, dels orígens al segle XI* (Manresa, 1985).

appearance, he was reliant on the paradigm outlined above.[27] Despite his close acquaintance with the city, Benet did not make it one of his case studies of frontier development, focusing instead on the county around Manresa and the development of lay jurisdictions there. This makes sense for frontier development as Benet understood it: its first step was fortification, which was for him primarily the task of lay noble landowners, not the church.[28]

Since Benet wrote, two things have happened which allow for a more detailed treatment of Manresa as a peripheral church in development. The first is a swing in the wider scholarship of frontiers and borderlands from studying processes of political control and settlement by outsiders, to studying the experiences and everyday strategies of the emplaced inhabitants of the border.[29] The second is the full publication of almost every surviving document covering the area up to the year 1000 as part of the century-long *Catalunya Carolíngia* project, with painstaking indices and now a digital search, making available to all data that even Benet did not have.[30] The area has also been mapped in the ongoing *Atles dels comtats de la Catalunya*

---

[27] Albert Benet i Clarà, 'Castells i línies de reconquesta', in Udina, ed., *Symposium internacional*, 1: 365–91, online at: <http://www.raco.cat/index.php/MemoriasRABL/article/view/202539>, accessed 1 July 2014, is as clear a formulation of that paradigm as exists. For the church catalogue, see Benet, *Història de Manresa*, 63–80. Much rescue archaeology has been carried out around Manresa, but it has yet to be synthesized: Jordi Gibert Rebull, 'L'alta edat mitjana a la Catalunya central (segles VI–XI): Estudi històric i arqueològic de la conca mitjana del Riu Llobregat', *Butlletí de la Societat Catalana d'Estudis Històrics* 23 (2012), 353–85, is a beginning.

[28] Benet, *L'expansió del comtat de Manresa*, focuses on rural settlement, and is very short. Benet's other studies include *Sallent, dels orígens al segle XIII*, Episodis de la història 220 (Barcelona, 1977); idem, 'La repoblació de la Segarra a l'alta Edat Mitjana (segles IX–XI)', *Palestra universitària* 3 (1988), 279–95; idem, 'La repoblació del Bages a l'alta Edat Mitjana', in *XXVI Assemblea intercomarcal d'estudiosos: Manresa, 17–18 octubre, 1981*, 2 vols (Manresa, 1984), 1: 39–47; as well as innumerable articles in Jordi Vigué and Antoni Pladevall, eds, *Catalunya romànica*, 27 vols (Barcelona, 1984–97). For his frontier development paradigm, see Benet, 'Castells i línies de reconquesta'; idem, 'Castells, guàrdies i torres de defensa', in Udina, ed., *Symposium Internacional*, 1: 393–407, online at: <http://www.raco.cat/index.php/MemoriasRABL/article/view/202540>, accessed 1 July 2014.

[29] This is a literature too vast to be summarized here, especially since this development has largely taken place outside medieval studies. Two good illustrations are Sahana Ghosh, 'Cross-Border Activities in Everyday Life: the Bengal Borderland', *Contemporary South Asia* 19 (2011), 49–60; Karin Dean, 'Borders and Bordering in Asia', in Alexander Horstmann, Martin Saxer and Alessandro Rippa, eds, *Routledge Handbook of Asian Borderlands* (London, 2018), 56–72.

[30] CC4 (see above, n. 7).

carolíngia, thereby fixing many obscure locations.[31] With that apparatus to hand, it is possible to identify some of the local church's principal figures, determine their spheres of action and rebalance the agency in their organization, between the usually-dominant monastic colonization and the organic expansion of local secular church provision.

METHODOLOGY AND MATERIAL

The record is, however, neither straightforward nor narrative. There is no chronicle evidence beyond a few notes in Frankish sources; there are no episcopal or abbatial *gesta* or other forms of ecclesiastical history; there is not even much hagiography, and what does exist is of uncertain date or focused primarily on externalities.[32] Instead, the historian must work with hundreds of charters, detailing land sales and donations, wills, disputes and so forth.[33] This privileges the visibility of not just certain forms of social action, but also of certain social strata, the landed and respectable, with the poor or subject making few appearances. It also privileges men over women, although not to exclusion. And, perhaps surprisingly, it preserves lay interests over ecclesiastical ones. The preservation of this material, however much is now in public archives, has almost all been due to the church at some point, and it is therefore an understandable starting assumption that it concerns property that was of interest to, or ultimately owned by, the church, monastic or secular.[34] It is often possible to disprove that, however,

---

[31] Jordi Bolòs and Víctor Hurtado, *Atles del comtat de Manresa (798–993)* (Barcelona, 2004).

[32] On the lack of narrative, see T. N. Bisson, 'Unheroed Pasts: History and Commemoration in South Frankland before the Albigensian Crusades', *Speculum* 65 (1990), 281–308. The hagiography is primarily constituted by the *Life* of Saint Eulalie, probably fourteenth-century as we have it, and focused on Barcelona: see Joan-F. Cabestany i Fort, 'El culte de Santa Eulàlia a la Catedral de Barcelona [S. IX–X]', *Lambard: estudis d'art medieval* 9 (1996), 159–65; and on the *Life* of Peter Orseolo, earlier but focused on a foreign visitor to Saint-Michel de Cuxa: see Abadal, *L'Abat Oliba*, 44–8. Neither is a frontier story.

[33] See Jonathan Jarrett, 'Introduction: Problems and Possibilities of Early Medieval Charters', in idem and Allan Scott McKinley, eds, *Problems and Possibilities of Early Medieval Charters*, International Medieval Research 13 (Turnhout, 2013), 1–18.

[34] A discussion of the preservation can be found in Ramon Ordeig i Mata, 'Introducció', in CC4, 1: 11–52, at 33–45.

and safer to say that the evidence we have was collected by people, or families, whose materials subsequently came to the church or were at some time stored in churches.[35]

The major preserving institution in this article is the monastery of Sant Benet de Bages.[36] Sant Benet was founded in 950 by a magnate called Sal·la, who was a comital deputy (*vicarius*) and was responsible for many frontier building projects.[37] Of these, Sant Benet was probably the most enduring and successful. Admittedly, by the time the church there was consecrated in 972, Sal·la and one of his sons were already dead, and the other soon followed. The one grandson seems not to have taken an interest in the monastery, which was thus left unexpectedly independent, and in difficulties, by the 990s. Monks only begin to be recorded there after the consecration and, in general, development there seems to have been slow. Yet it survived, in some form or another, until 1835, along with most of its archive. That archive was scattered during the Spanish Civil War, but much has been reassembled at Santa Maria de Montserrat or in the Archivo de la Corona de Aragón in Barcelona.[38]

I take as my area the *terminium* or jurisdictional limit of the city church of Santa Maria, defined in a papal privilege of 978 and mapped by Bolòs and Hurtado (Figure 1).[39] Using this and the indices of the

---

[35] Compare Adam J. Kosto, 'Laymen, Clerics, and Documentary Practices in the Early Middle Ages: The Example of Catalonia', *Speculum* 80 (2005), 44–74; idem, '*Sicut mos esse solet*: Documentary Practices in Christian Iberia, c.700–1000', in Warren C. Brown et al., eds, *Documentary Culture and the Laity in the Early Middle Ages* (Cambridge, 2013), 259–82; Jonathan Jarrett, 'Ceremony, Charters and Social Memory: Property Transfer Ritual in Early Medieval Catalonia', *Social History* 44 (2019), 275–95.

[36] Sant Benet is studied in, *inter alia*, Fortià Solà, *El monestir de Sant Benet de Bages* (Manresa, 1955); Xavier Sitges i Molins, *Sant Benet del Bages* (Manresa, 1975); Francesa Español, *Sant Benet de Bages* (Manresa, 2001). However, none is easily obtainable; more accessible is Francesc Junyent i Mayou et al., 'Sant Benet de Bages', in Vigué and Pladevall, eds, *Catalunya Romànica*, 11: *El Bages*, ed. Antoni Pladevall (Barcelona, n.d.), 408–38, online at: <https://www.enciclopedia.cat/catalunya-romanica/sant-benet-de-bages-sant-fruitos-de-bages>, accessed 6 September 2024.

[37] Jordi Gibert Rebull, 'Del Conflent a la conca d'Òdena: La família del veguer Sal·la dins el marc de l'expansió del comtat d'Osona-Manresa al segle X', *Miscellanea Aqualatensia* 16 (2015), 121–56, online at: <https://www.raco.cat/index.php/MiscellaneaAqualatensia/article/view/312477>, accessed 22 July 2019; Jonathan Jarrett, *Rulers and Ruled in Frontier Catalonia, 880–1010: Pathways of Power* (Woodbridge, 2010), 144–51.

[38] Ordeig, 'Introducció', 41–3.

[39] Bolòs and Hurtado, *Atles del comtat de Manresa*, 52–3, after CC4 1247.

Figure 1 Map of the assigned territory of Santa Maria de Manresa, with locations mentioned in the text shown where known; after Bolòs and Hurtado (see n. 39). © The author.

Catalunya Carolíngia establishes the documentary sample set out in Table 1.[40]

This naturally involves some duplication, as several documents feature more than one place. The actual number of individual documents from between 898 and 1000 tabulated above includes 253 documents from Sant Benet de Bages, as opposed to fifteen from

[40] Rafel Ginebra and Ramon Ordeig, 'Índex alfabètic de noms', in CC4 3: 1355–63. In Table 1 can be found the numbers of all the documents used as evidence here. To save space and avoid indigestible lists of numbers in notes, subsequent citations only cover instances where the table does not show which documents are involved.

Table 1 Documentary sample from the *terminium* of Santa Maria de Manresa as found in CC4 (see n. 7).

Documents in CC4 (see n. 7)	Settlement
476, 663, 975, 995, 1180, 1263, 1280, 1305, 1316, 1409, 1461, 1473, 1478, 1481, 1534, 1665, 1701 & 1825	L'Angle
1187, 1417, 1580	L'Arca
38, 403, 438, 476, 532, 538, 610, 663, 666, 691, 835, 838, 882, 903, 951, 1024, 1091, 1153, 1256, 1279, 1327, 1362, 1417, 1419, 1466, 1472, 1486, 1614, 1638, 1658, 1699, 1720, 1739, 1741, 1742, 1790, 1815, 1819, 1836, 1852, 1856	Bages
939, 1161, 1425, 1528	Barrí de Todsèn
678, 680, 797, 809, 813, 885, 921, 983, 1008, 1068, 1147, 1165, 1190, 1284, 1307, 1334, 1433, 1529, 1568, 1781, 1830	El Buc
881, 1059	El Ceguer
1109, 1156, 1181, 1183, 1267, 1278, 1286, 1297, 1299, 1346, 1422, 1432, 1456, 1527, 1551, 1713, 1750, 1777, 1841	La Celada
1247, 1263	Cornet
1478, 1592	Espinavessa
1273	Figuerola (not located)
932	Fitor (not located)
1193	Font de Sant Benet
1247	la Guàrdia
1209, 1257	la Guardiola (Sant Fruitós)
692, 779, 953, 996, 1201, 1247, 1263, 1510	la Guardiola (Sant Salvador)
1183, 1267, 1430	el Guix
881	el Gradel
1614	el Guadel
1452	*villa de* Guisardino
293, 373, 403, 474, 558, 668, 733, 877, 939, 955, 989, 1007, 1127, 1157, 1257, 1256, 1270, 1283, 1299, 1335, 1360, 1402, 1412, 1475, 1486, 1604, 1810, 1840, 1846	Manresa (city proper)
719, 747, 1866	Matadars
1247	Moial
438, 473, 474, 476, 663, 666, 715, 733, 833, 843, 875, 884, 949, 955, 958, 977, 985, 995, 1021, 1024, 1032, 1063, 1099, 1100, 1101, 1117, 1124, 1141, 1142, 1151, 1154,	Montpeità

(*Continued*)

Table 1 *Continued*

Documents in CC4 (see n. 7)	Settlement
1157, 1158, 1160, 1171, 1172, 1184, 1224, 1225, 1251, 1252, 1279, 1305, 1316, 1348, 1363, 1413, 1424, 1426, 1427, 1429, 1447, 1461, 1473, 1480, 1486, 1488, 1489, 1504, 1506, 1507, 1522, 1599, 1629, 1630, 1637, 1641, 1645, 1646, 1665, 1685, 1693, 1695, 1721, 1728, 1731, 1741, 1752, 1764, 1769, 1796, 1806, 1817, 1827, 1851, 1857, 1870	
473, 852, 881, 982, 995, 1014, 1059, 1108, 1113, 1114, 1119, 1225, 1256, 1405, 1534, 1657, 1832, 1861	Navarcles
38, 1247, 1475, 1739	Olzinelles
1143	Ordeos
1180, 1196, 1197, 1567, 1632, 1818, 1825, 1864	la Palanca
975, 982, 1108, 1405	el Pont (Navarcles)
1115, 1184, 1249, 1257, 1466, 1815	el Pujol
877	*Qulga*
918	Rafecs
898, 1416, 1439, 1549, 1636bis	Salelles
440, 818, 1040, 1247, 1552, 1840	Santa Maria de Manresa
663, 1412	Sant Iscle de Bages
995, 996, 1127	Sant Benet de Bages
501, 958, 988, 995, 1063, 1143, 1225, 1251, 1261, 1348, 1360, 1363, 1427, 1438, 1504, 1665, 1737, 1769, 1816, 1819	Sant Fruitós de Bages
967, 1431	Sant Valentí de Montpeità
903	Torre d'Ília
1401	*Turre de Seniofredus vicario*
386, 981, 1464, 1531	Ullastrell
1229, 1247	Vallformosa
1047, 1164, 1344, 1448, 1514, 1516, 1544, 1603, 1814	Vilapicina

all other sources. Of these, however, only seventy-six mention Sant Benet or its lands, and a number actually predate the monastery.[41]

---

[41] The monastery or its lands appear in CC4 861, 949, 951, 955, 967, 975, 982, 995, 996, 1014, 1021, 1022, 1032, 1059, 1063, 1083, 1113–5, 1127, 1143, 1148, 1151, 1172, 1180, 1184, 1193, 1225, 1247, 1263, 1305, 1316, 1334, 1360, 1402, 1413, 1424–6, 1428,

Those presumably survive because they were somehow associated with documents that did relate to the monastery's rights; but some of our evidence has only passed through that filter by association, which gives us some chance of seeing beyond the monastery's concerns.

This is also shown by mapping the areas concerned in the documents, which has been done by Bolòs and Hurtado. (Figure 2) While the monastery's interests are certainly represented in that map, there are substantial foci where the house itself did not, as far as can be seen, hold any substantial property. In fact, although it originated many of the documents, the monastery's own territory hardly features in the sample. And while Bages, Montpeità and Navarcles loom large in the monastery's property, none of the other stand-out areas in Figure 2 were particular foci for that property.

A considerable difference is, however, noticeable between the settlement to the north and east of the city, and that to the south and west. The former zone presents a relatively crowded picture, in which communities, albeit quite small ones to judge from the recurrences of witnesses and neighbours, jostled for space and for access to the city. To the south and west, settlements seem sparser and smaller, without the same sense of who the people who usually took part in things were. This may be because there simply were fewer of those people, or because they were not engaged in the land transactions that would have brought them into the records, or because they did not archive the charters with our institutions if they were. Even these latter options, however, suggest an earlier stage of settlement here, in which the inheriting generations who might be selling, rather than clearing, land had not yet arisen. These differences remind us that Manresa itself denoted the edge in terms of the kind of civil operations that generated our source material, and thus demonstrates its peripheral location with respect to both church and government.

Delving more deeply into demography, the sample records 5,264 appearances of persons. That includes many people occurring more than once, but it is still a large number, of whom 807 used a clerical title, in 468 cases a priestly one (*presbyter, sacer* or *sacerdos*). These numbers illustrate the lay predominance in the record. They also

---

1430, 1461, 1472, 1475, 1478, 1481, 1489, 1504, 1522, 1534, 1549, 1612, 1614, 1629, 1632, 1641, 1645, 1658, 1665, 1721, 1731, 1737, 1741–3, 1752, 1796, 1806, 1816, 1819, 1824, 1846, 1852, 1859, 1864 and 1870. Everything earlier in the sample therefore predates the monastery.

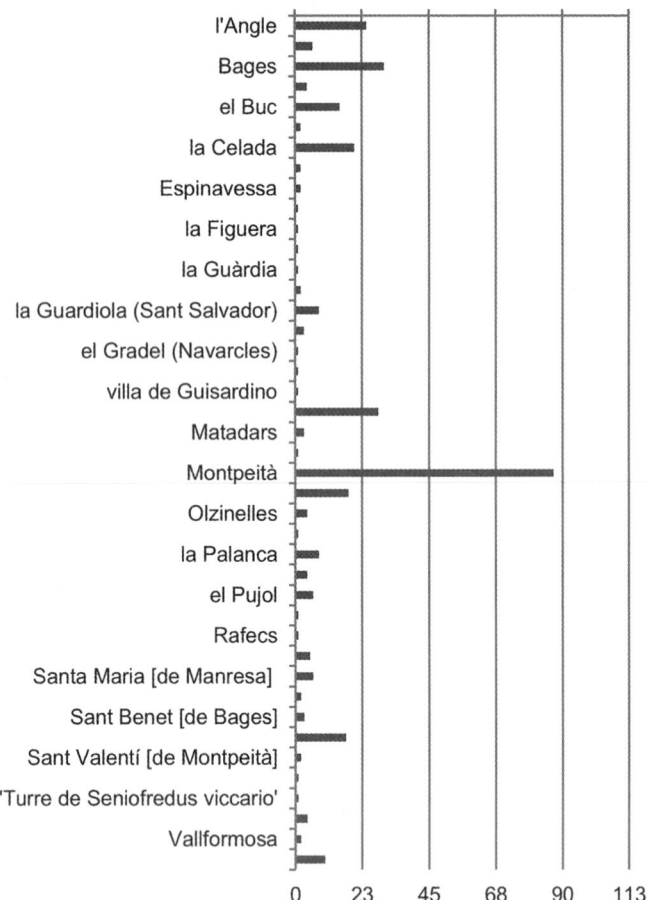

Figure 2 Settlement foci in the Manresa documentation. © The author.

demonstrate that the area was far from deserted, and while they give us no basis for guesses at local population figures, there is a difference between this landscape and that around the more northerly frontier redoubt of Cardona, where a city population had repeatedly to be re-established over the ninth and tenth century; or even places in other parts of the Iberian frontier, such as Castilian Sepúlveda, whose relatively early *fuero* or town law code records a similarly small scale community.[42] This part of the frontier was admittedly governmentally peripheral, but still fairly populous, with connections to central hierarchies through the city.

On the other hand, no documentation survives from what should be the most important institution in this study, the city church of Santa Maria.[43] It is mentioned here and there in what we have and, as shown below, must have maintained a reasonably numerous staff of clergy; but, in its perilous frontier location, the city was sacked at least once and possibly twice by Muslim armies between 997 and 1003, and this appears to have destroyed the church's archives.[44] It was sacked again during the War of the Spanish Succession (1701–14), with similar effects.[45] We are, therefore, trying metaphorically to see into the next room through a door that is only ajar, and must be thankful that the view is even this good.

CHURCHES AND CLERGY

None of the churches recorded in the documents of the area show any pre-Romanesque fabric, so their dates can only be suggested from the charter evidence, whose first mentions may considerably postdate their actual establishment.[46] By that inadequate metric, the oldest was Santa Maria de Manresa itself, whose consecration can probably be dated to 937.[47] Outside the city, Sant Fruitós de Bages, the most north-

[42] For Cardona, see Victor Farías, 'Guerra, llibertat i igualitarisme a la frontera', in Josep Maria Salrach, ed., *La formació de la societat feudal, segles VI–XII* (Barcelona, 1998), 112–13. For Sepúlveda, see Manzano, 'Christian-Muslim Frontier', 95–6.

[43] Our sample includes a *regestum*, or abstract of the church's consecration, in *c.*937 (CC4 440), which is attested only from a reference to the document, lost even then, in the act of reconsecration of the church in 1020. For more on the church, see Francesc Junyent i Mayou et al., 'Santa Maria de Manresa o de la Seu', in Vigué and Pladevall, eds, *Catalunya Romànica*, 11: 513–15, online at: <https://www.enciclopedia.cat/catalunya-romanica/santa-maria-de-manresa-o-de-la-seu>, accessed 6 September 2024.

[44] The dates are disputed. Dolors Bramon, *De quan érem o no musulmans: textos del 713 al 1010. Continuació de l'obra de J. M. Millàs i Vallicrosa* (Vic, 2000), 342 and n. 310, collects both primary and secondary references. Benet, *Història*, 86–8, mounted a sustained argument for 999, but 997 or 1003 have a clearer basis in the evidence.

[45] Benet, *Història*, 11.

[46] A photograph exists of a now-vanished church at Santpedor that may have been pre-Romanesque. See Antoni Gallardo, 'Portal de l'antiga església', n.d., online at: <https://mdc.csuc.cat/digital/collection/afcecemc/id/5114>, accessed 1 March 2024. This church is not included in the *Catalunya Romànica*.

[47] See above, n. 43.

Jonathan Jarrett

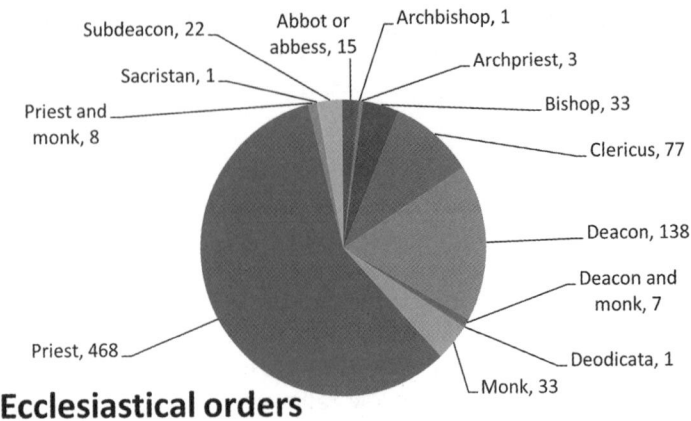

Ecclesiastical orders

Figure 3 Chart of clerical titles in the documentary sample for Manresa, 898–1000. © The author.

easterly, is first recorded in 942, and Sant Iscle de Bages in 950.[48] No other church is mentioned until after 1000. The pattern thus matches that of settlement, suggesting that churches were established on the city's 'homeward' side early on, but not in the zone between it and the far frontier until after the turn of the millennium and the unexpected collapse of the Andalusī caliphate after 1009.[49]

The ratio of known clergy to known churches in the Manresa area is therefore quite high, suggesting that most churchmen were otherwise organized. The material does not identify clergy as belonging to particular churches, so affiliations can only be deduced by association. Several other features of the evidence deserve note before that is attempted, however.

In the first place, the visible structure of the clergy is strongly top-heavy (Figure 3). The material records 476 appearances of priests, as opposed to 145 of deacons, twenty-two of subdeacons and seventy-seven of *clerici* (various other grades of cleric). Examining these clerical appearances by role suggests a reason for this, which is the pre-eminence of priests as agents of the written record. It is not only that priests were literate; fragmentary evidence, including some non-

[48] Sant Fruitós in CC4 501; Sant Iscle in CC4 663.
[49] Peter C. Scales, *The Fall of the Caliphate of Córdoba: Berbers and Andalusis in conflict*, Medieval Iberian Peninsula 9 (Leiden, 1994).

clerical scribes attested writing charters, suggest that writing was not a clerical monopoly here.[50] It seems clear from our sample, however, that it was usual and perhaps preferable for a priest to write one's charter.[51] This is true in sixty-nine per cent of our documents, with deacons, *clerici* and subdeacons writing in rough proportion to their overall frequency of occurrence, among a few other scribal dignities, including apparent laymen. This, of course, means that most charters show us at least one priest, but often involve no other churchmen. If we saw priests only when they were actually party to, witnesses of or neighbours in the transaction of land, more than half our count would disappear.

Even then, though, the number of priests would nearly equal appearances of all other ecclesiastical orders combined and be double the next most numerous one (deacons), so there seems genuinely to have been a large proportion of priests in the clergy here (Figure 3). Perhaps this was because, unlike other dignities, it is one which could be held for decades.[52] It is also possible, however, that priests appear in such numbers because they were the basic unit of ecclesiastical provision. A rural church could be operated by a single priest. He might prefer to have a deacon or two, a doorkeeper and so on; but without a priest, the others would probably not be there.[53]

Because of their predominant role in documentary production, however, priests naturally appear first and foremost as scribes, three times more often than as witnesses, their next most commonly recorded activity (Figure 4). They were directly party to transactions much less often. Were the priests working as scribes associated with the communities who thus enlisted them? If so, we would expect consistent appearances of a given priest in a particular area. It transpires, however, that things were not that simple.

---

[50] Michel Zimmermann, *Écrire et lire en Catalogne (IXe–XIIe siècle)*, 2 vols, Bibliothèque de la Casa de Velázquez 23 (Madrid, 2003). Compare also for laypersons, Jonathan Jarrett, 'Nuns, Signatures, and Literacy in late-Carolingian Catalonia', *Traditio* 74 (2019), 125–52. More broadly, see Roger Collins, 'Literacy and the Laity in Early Medieval Spain', in Rosamond McKitterick, ed., *The Uses of Literacy in Early Mediaeval Europe* (Cambridge, 1990), 109–33; reprinted in Roger Collins, *Law, Culture and Regionalism in Early Medieval Spain*, Variorum Collected Studies 356 (Aldershot, 1992), no. 16, 109–33.
[51] Jesús Alturo i Perucho, 'Le statut du scripteur en Catalogne (XIIe–XIIIe siècles)', in Marie-Clotilde Hubert, Emmanuel Poulle and Marc H. Smith, eds, *Le statut du scripteur au Moyen Age*, Matériaux pour l'histoire 2 (Paris, 2000), 41–55.
[52] I have not found any cases as extreme as the centenarian priest in Marco Stoffella, 'Local Priests in Early Medieval Rural Tuscany', in Patzold and van Rhijn, *Men in the Middle*, 98–124, at 105–6, but several thirty-year careers are demonstrable.
[53] Compare Davies, 'Local Priests in Northern Iberia', 131–2.

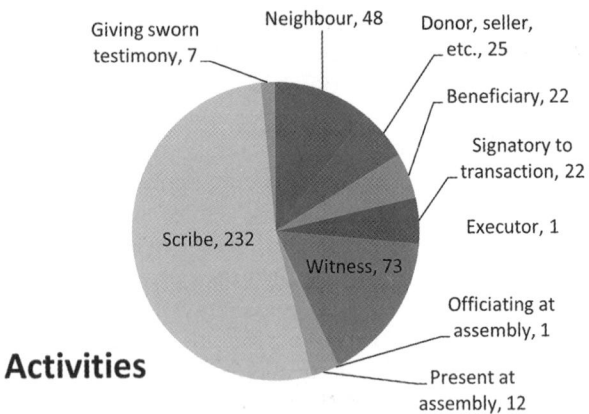

Figure 4 Activities of priests in the documentary sample for Manresa, 898–1000. © The author.

Priestly Profiles

Some places do indeed seem to have had associated clergy. The strongest case is Santpedor, in whose territory a settlement called el Buc shows nine priests: firstly Arduin in 957; then, in the period 958–63, one Abo, who would later join Sant Benet de Bages; with some interleaved appearances by one Sendred. In 963, there is a single appearance by Eliseu; then Esteve in 966–87, as well as Sesgut in 970–80 and Julià in 990–1000, with two further priests mentioned later.[54] They all appear as scribes, and several occur nowhere else. It thus seems reasonable to assume that Santpedor had a steady establishment of one, and perhaps sometimes two, priests, including at least Abo, Esteve and Julià.

It is possible to attempt the same exercise with the two secular churches of Bages, although their proximity to each other adds to the problems caused by their closeness to the monastery. Montpeità also offers a plausible sequence, although complicated by the fact that almost all the priests involved, and all the scribes, became monks at Sant Benet and were involved with the house before joining it. There seems to have been some kind of church at Montpeità, but its

---

[54] See Table 1, *s.n.* 'el Buc'.

ministry was being delivered by priests connected to Sant Benet.[55] These two to four churches supply the only cases where the presence of established clergy is even this plausible.

Indeed, when the exercise is performed within the city limits of Manresa, the result is quite different: nineteen priests in total, of whom twelve wrote documents, none more than one each.[56] That suggests that many priests were available in the city. If Santa Maria's archive had survived, these men might be more clearly recorded; but, as it is, they might either be very local to the places with which their appearances are associated, or, conversely, associated with the city church rather than any specific locale outside.

The latter suggestion can be supported by looking at some specific priests. A problem is that those associated with the monastery appear most in our record, not because the monastery employed them, but because they apparently deposited their documents in its archive. Two in particular have to be ignored: Baldomar, one of the confusing presences at Montpeità, apparently himself from Balsareny to the north-west, but not clearly the priest there; and the slightly older Badeleu, whose origins are obscure. Both had comital connections; both became stalwart, if perhaps retired, members of the monastic community at Sant Benet; and both fail to help us with this question, because the material they deposited at the monastery had more to do with their landholding interests than their pastoral roles.[57] A more helpful example is Sunyer, who wrote, among many other documents, the monastery's 972 endowment.[58] His hand is recognizable in extant autograph documents, and he spelled his name unusually (*Sunierius*), which helps identify him in others.[59] Despite his presence in their archive, and an evidently important role there, he does

---

[55] Sant Benet seems to have recruited among active clergy, which complicates its members' attestations considerably. It would take a separate article to demonstrate this, but many of the monks involved in the election of Abbot Ramio in 1002 can also be found in our sample as priests. For the list of those involved, see Jaime Villanueva, *Viage á la iglesia de Vique, año 1806*, Viage literario a las Iglesias de España 7 (Valencia 1821), 281–3 (apéndix 13), online at: <https://www.google.co.uk/books/edition/Viage_literario_%C3%A1_las_iglesias_de_Espa/Sa3uYC1tU80C>, accessed 13 October 2013.

[56] See Table 1, *s.n.* 'Santa Maria de Manresa'.

[57] On them, see for now Bolòs and Hurtado, *Atles*, 79.

[58] CC4 1127.

[59] I also attribute to him CC4 949, 958, 985, 997, 1113, 1119, 1141 and 1142. A Sunyer spelt thus also appears in CC4 1117, 1143, 1161, 1171, 1172, 1180, 1193 and 1246.

not seem to have been either a monk or a client of Sant Benet's founders; he is never entitled *monachus* and does not otherwise appear with Sal·la's family.

Sunyer is not the only such priest. One Esclúa is attested between 982 and 1000 in seven documents.[60] Two late ones concern property at Montpeità, but the others do not. One deals with Sant Fruitós de Bages and one with la Palanca, which were close by, but another is focused far off to the north at l'Arca. Two more tie him to Manresa itself. An explanation for this diffuse focus is that interests were coming to the priest rather than the other way round, and the obvious locus is the city church. Whether transactors knew Esclúa because he sometimes ministered to their areas, or whether he was simply on duty as notary when they came into town to have their transaction solemnized, cannot be known. Similarly unclear is whether Sunyer was chosen to write prestigious documents because he was a close connection of someone important, or because his importance was institutional, but the town is likely to have been the significant location in all cases.

It is perhaps also possible to see a process of change, from provision orchestrated out of Santa Maria, to ministry by a fixed incumbent of a rural church. At la Celada, close to the city, seven priests occur, three of them more than once, all as scribes.[61] The scribes overlap, and while a sequence is possible to construct, it is broken, with one Eldovigi appearing discontinuously and much scribal work being done by a deacon, Elies. All the priests appear in connection with other places, as does Elies. This looks like a collegiate operation in which duty at or concerning la Celada fell to outside clergy, presumably from the city, on some kind of rotation. After a while, however, only one priest appears, Llobet. He also appears elsewhere, but between 984 and 997, he was the priest who wrote documents about la Celada. Had he been assigned there on an ongoing basis? La Celada never acquired its own church, but it may have been given its own part-time priest.

---

[60] CC4 1381, 1438, 1580, 1632 and 1641 (as *presbiter*) and 1796 and 1815 (as *sacer*).

[61] Scribes for la Celada occur in CC4 as follows: 1109 (Eldovigi *sacer*); 1156 (Elies *levita*); 1181 (Bonfill *presbiter*); 1183 (Elies *levita*); 1267 (Elies *levita*); 1278 (Ermengol *presbiter*); 1286 (Eldovigi *sacer*); 1297 (Elies *levita*); 1299 (Joan, no title); 1346 (Ansulf *sacer*); 1422 (Ansulf *sacer*); 1432 (Oruç *sacer*); 1456, 1527 (Llobet *sacer*); 1551 (Badeleu *presbiter*); 1713 (Adroer, no title); 1750, 1777 (Llobet *sacer*); 1841 (Sunifred *presbiter*).

CATALONIA AND ELSEWHERE

So far, these pre-Catalan priests have been considered in splendid isolation, but they were part of a wider church, indeed of a church much affected by the eighth- to ninth-century Carolingian conquest of the area and its alterations, as some argue, to religious, intellectual and scribal culture.[62] Moreover, a recent store of scholarship on local priests of this era makes possible a comparison between the Catalan material and findings from elsewhere.[63]

Many contributors to this recent scholarship have been concerned with the question of priests' learned apparatus, in the form of education and books.[64] Michel Zimmermann's expansive study of the Catalan evidence reveals a priesthood with something like a standard equipment of texts.[65] This picture is harder to get in Manresa, because it derives principally from church consecrations and priests' wills, neither of which survive in any number through Sant Benet. The observance by our scribes of what, it has been suggested, was a Carolingian modification of local charter formularies, however, implies that that was enforced here too (although with a sample dominated by documents from after 940: we see the results only several generations later).[66] This may also explain some negative features of our evidence, which studies of other areas make ours seem peculiar. There are, for example, no families of clergy in the Manresa evidence, though these were common in Italy and not unknown elsewhere. Even away from the frontier, there seem to be only

---

[62] Compare Zimmermann, *Écrire et lire*, broadly in favour of a lesser presence compared to works of patristics and surviving Visigothic texts; and Chander, *Carolingian Catalonia*, in favour of deeper Carolingian impact.

[63] Patzold and van Rhijn, *Men in the Middle*. The present author was kindly invited to participate in this project but was unfortunately unable to do so due to other commitments. See also Francesca Tinti and Carine van Rhijn, 'Shepherds, Uncles, Owners, Scribes: Priests as Neighbours in Early Medieval Local Societies', in Bernhard Zeller et al., *Neighbours and Strangers: Local Societies in Early Medieval Europe* (Manchester, 2020), 120–49, which I have not been able to consult directly.

[64] Davies, 'Local Priests in Northern Iberia', 140–1; Yitzhak Hen, 'Priests and Books in the Merovingian Period'; Carine van Rhijn, 'Manuscripts for Local Priests and the Carolingian Reforms'; Steffen Patzold, '*Pater noster*: Priests and the Religious Instruction of the Laity in the Carolingian *populus christianus*', all in Patzold and van Rhijn, eds, *Men in the Middle*, 162–76, 177–98, 199–221, respectively.

[65] Zimmermann, *Écrire et lire*, 1: 526–30.

[66] Jonathan Jarrett, 'Comparing the Earliest Documentary Culture in Carolingian Catalonia', in idem and McKinley, eds, *Problems and Possibilities*, 89–126.

occasional uncle-nephew successions, with nothing like the clerical dynasties visible in Tuscany.[67] Likewise, there is almost no record (here or in Catalonia more widely) of priests owning their own churches. The sole case known to me, not from Manresa, involves a priest who was appointed by someone else (the count of Urgell, to the north of our area, at his chief castle's church).[68]

Instead, the weight of power in the appointment of priests seems to have lain with bishops.[69] The possibility that such priests were trained at the cathedrals also raises the likelihood of episcopal preferment. This may be why the counts of Urgell, where more direct comital control of appointment is apparent, came in for occasional critique in their cathedral's documentation.[70] If Urgell is the exception that proves the rule, then the silence of the quite voluminous evidence perhaps suggests this was a church established on fairly canonical lines, arguably even more so than some closer to the core. One might suppose that a frontier church would be unguided and anarchic, but the process of establishment visible here seems to have set things up as reformers would have wanted.

One place, however, where the wider scholarship does find an echo in Catalonia in general, and Manresa specifically, is the idea of superior churches below cathedral rank. The model of the early English minster seems relevant here, even if disputed. This proposes a pastoral structure in the early English church centred on large, collegiate churches, each covering a wide area in which, locally, there might only be chapels or outdoor locations of worship.[71] In this respect, it is not unlike the

---

[67] For Tuscany, see Stoffella, 'Local Priests in … Rural Tuscany', 121–4; compare Davies, 'Local Priests in Northern Iberia', 131, for north-western Iberia (no father-son succession); and, more broadly, Julia Barrow, *The Clergy in the Medieval World: Secular Clerics, their Families and Careers in North-Western Europe, c.800–c.1200* (Cambridge, 2015).

[68] *Catalunya carolíngia*, 8: *Els comtats d'Urgell, Cerdanya i Berga*, ed. Ramon Ordeig i Mata, 2 vols, Memòries de la Secció Històrico-Arqueològica 111 (Barcelona, 2020), 1: 408–9 (no. 433).

[69] Pierre Bonnassie and Jean-Pascal Illy, 'Le clergé paroissial aux IXe–Xe siècles dans les Pyrénées orientales et centrales', in Pierre Bonnassie, ed., *Le Clergé rural dans l'Europe médiévale et moderne*, Flaran 13 (Toulouse, 1995), 153–66, online at: <https://books.ope nedition.org/pumi/23166>, accessed 25 March 2024.

[70] Jarrett, 'Comparing the Earliest Documentary Culture', 125–6. For criticism of the count, see *Catalunya carolíngia* 8/1: 416 (no. 444).

[71] John Blair, 'Minster Churches in the Landscape', in Della Hooke, ed., *Anglo-Saxon Settlements* (Oxford, 1988), 35–58; Eric Cambridge and David Rollason, 'The Pastoral Organization of the Anglo-Saxon Church: A Review of the "Minster Hypothesis"', *EME* 4 (1995), 87–104; John Blair, *The Church in Anglo-Saxon Society* (Oxford, 2005). For a more neutral view, see Christopher Andrew Jones, 'Minsters and Monasticism in Anglo-Saxon

Italian system of *plebes* or baptismal churches, with plural priests, each holding rights over smaller, more local churches with fewer and more dependent clergy.[72] The newer English system naturally had fewer churches, and over the tenth to twelfth centuries, it is argued, the establishment of local churches broke the early minster territories up into parishes that largely still exist.[73]

This model, and the less disputed Italian structure, have obvious resemblances to the situation outlined in Manresa, with Santa Maria as minster or *plebs*. There are, nonetheless, four important differences. Firstly, Santa Maria seems to have been quite a large establishment, functionally a delegated episcopal outpost that furnished clergy for pastoral operations near and far, although there is no sign that it had any kind of canonry. It may be unhelpful to compare Santa Maria with any but the largest minsters, or with any *plebs*. Secondly, Santa Maria sat in a town. The size of that town is a mystery, although it had at least one suburb (Barri de Todsèn), but Santa Maria was not its only component, or even its only church, and was not therefore a settlement centre in its own right, like some English minsters.[74] Thirdly, both in Blair's English hypothesis and in the Italian layout of *plebes*, the system was stable and not intended to develop, whereas there are signs here, both in the priestly provision and the subsequent parish map, that part of the role of Santa Maria de Manresa and its clergy was to generate new parish foci. Fourthly, in the minster hypothesis, as in the Italian context, there was little difference between a collegiate church of priests and a monastery.[75] In the Catalan counties, however, those institutions had different jobs.[76] Sant Benet de Bages may have largely drawn its community from among the pastoral clergy, but the monastery itself had no *parrochia* (parish) and no visible ministry outside its own confines (except,

---

England', in Alison I. Beach and Isabelle Cochelin, eds, *The Cambridge History of Medieval Monasticism in the Latin World*, 2 vols (Cambridge, 2019), 1: 502–18. For Iberia, see Wendy Davies, 'Where are the Parishes? Where are the Minsters? The Organization of the Spanish Church in the Tenth Century', in David Rollason, Conrad Leyser and Hannah Williams, eds, *England and the Continent in the Tenth Century: Studies in Honour of Wilhelm Levison (1876–1947)* (Turnhout, 2010), 379–97.

[72] For Italian *plebes*, see Stoffella, 'Local Priests in … Rural Tuscany'.

[73] Blair, *Church in Anglo-Saxon Society*, 426–504.

[74] Benet, *Historia de Manresa*, 123–38.

[75] For Italy, see Paul Aebischer, '*Monasterium* dans le latin de la Tuscie longobarde', *Anuario de Estudios Medievales* 2 (1965), 11–30.

[76] Ordeig, 'Cel les monàstiques'.

perhaps, at Montpeità). Everywhere else's ministry was handled from the city.

All this offers another, more or less Carolingian, micro-Christianity that might be added to our bank of comparative studies of the early medieval church, but there was something distinctively peripheral about priestly provision around, and especially beyond, Manresa.[77] Firstly, it was more thinly churched than most places, except the mission ground of early England; and priests from a large, but vulnerable, sub-cathedral in an insufficiently fortified town did much of the work. Secondly, the visible churches around Santa Maria de Manresa, even behind the frontier from it, seem to have been small; none of them except the monastic Sant Benet seem to have had more than two priests or other clergy visibly assigned, although plenty more priests can be seen. While it is possible that the lack of detectable dynastic or aristocratic control of churches or priestly office reflected the rigour of Carolingian reform in the area, the fact that what reformers would have considered failings are easier to find further east and north also points to the small size and newness of churches here; there were probably just not sufficient clergy established long enough to have built such structures of patronage or reproduction. As in England, albeit in a different context, we are seeing a church forming at its own edge.

Conclusion

Catalonia – and specifically the Manresa area – remained a frontier. The destruction of Santa Maria around the year 1000 shows this clearly, but even without it, our limited map of church provision on this periphery underlines Manresa's pivotal position. Beyond it were communities cut off by stretches of no-man's land (and considerable geographical obstacles); behind it were communities in development, both secular and pastoral, as well as a coalescing monastery.

In standard accounts of the extension of control on the Catalan frontier, monasteries, such as that one, perform a central function as colonizers of wasteland and sponsors of settlement, and indeed churches. Bishoprics are given a lesser role, more reactive to demands from settlers than actually responsible for settlement (though bishops are in fact

---

[77] Rob Meens, 'Conclusion: Early medieval Priests – Some Further Thoughts', in Patzold and van Rhijn, eds, *Men in the Middle*, 222–8.

documented awarding frontier development concessions).[78] Frontier churches like Santa Maria de Manresa are, however, absent from such accounts. These churches, collegial or otherwise, may also have been sponsors of development, settlement and pastoral provision, which would, when the military context allowed, be bases for the next steps in the return of organized Christianity to this area, and perhaps others like it elsewhere.

Supplementary Material

To view supplementary material for this article, please visit http://doi.org/10.1017/S0424208424000330.

---

[78] See *inter alia* the discussion in Gaspar Feliu, 'El bisbe Vives de Barcelona i el patrimoni de la catedral (974–995)', in *Miscel·lània d'Homenatge a Miquel Coll i Alentorn en el seu vuitanté aniversari* (Barcelona, 1984), 167–91.

Locations of Religious Encounter: The Scandinavian Diaspora in the Viking Age

Lesley Abrams
Balliol College, Oxford

This article examines the process of conversion to Christianity of Scandinavians who left their homelands in the ninth and tenth centuries and settled in Christian societies in the West. The churches that were involved left us no accounts, but fragments of evidence ranging from papal letters to stone sculpture help to construct a picture of diversity, wherever routes to conversion can be glimpsed across this Scandinavian diaspora. Two contrasting settings – Normandy, soon after the Viking Rollo was put in charge in 911, and northern England, under the authority of Scandinavian kings from the late ninth to the mid-tenth century – are discussed, highlighting the agency of churchmen at the interface between paganism and Christianity. The sources hint at contrasting dynamics and a range of strategies, from creativity to coercion, as churches faced the challenge of bringing immigrant Scandinavians into the Christian centre.

During the so-called Viking Age – from the late eighth century to around 1050 – Scandinavians travelled far afield, and many settled permanently overseas. Over time, the emigrant populations became Christian, a conversion that was only later followed in the emerging kingdoms of their homelands of Norway, Denmark and Sweden. Thanks to the preservation of a repertoire of Norse mythological and cosmological lore by later medieval writers, especially in Iceland, we think we know a great deal about the religious world that

Balliol College, Oxford.
E-mail: lesley.abrams@balliol.ox.ac.uk.
To conform to SCH House Style, this article will use upper-case 'Viking'; in my own practice, I prefer 'viking', to avoid the misleading national or ethnic implications that the upper-case noun can carry.

Studies in Church History 61 (2025), 142–167 © The Author(s), 2025. Published by Cambridge University Press on behalf of the Ecclesiastical History Society. This is an Open Access article, distributed under the terms of the Creative Commons Attribution licence (http://creativecommons.org/licenses/by/4.0/), which permits unrestricted re-use, distribution and reproduction, provided the original article is properly cited.
doi:10.1017/stc.2024.34

Christianity replaced. However, the process of leaving it behind took place largely in darkness, and, when written traditions developed at a later time, even constructed conversion narratives are few and far between. Norway celebrated the brutal triumphal campaigns of St Olaf, a missionary king par excellence, and Iceland developed a literature harking back to the adoption of Christianity by arbitration.[1] However, where Scandinavian populations settled overseas in Christian societies – whether Britain, Ireland or Normandy – the churches that absorbed these newcomers seem to have shown little interest in recording or commemorating their conversion history.

The Scandinavians of the diaspora occupy a complex position in relation to this volume's theme of 'Margins and Peripheries'.[2] As, initially, followers of traditional polytheistic religions, in Christian terms their paganism made them outsiders, alien and threatening. Military, political and economic success nevertheless gave them dominant roles in many new environments, often placing them at the centre of highly Christianized societies, and their impact as immigrants remained significant even where independent Scandinavian political power was overturned. Some of the mobile army members and later settlers could have been converts, but even after they had been overseas for some time it is arguable that the majority remained pagan. That they became Christian tends to be taken for granted, but in the absence of conversion narratives, the mechanisms that brought this transformation about are often assumed to be irrecoverable. Bringing these communities of outsiders into the Christian fold must nevertheless have offered a challenge to all the churches. Some are known to have actively cooperated with the regimes the Scandinavians established, but it is difficult to envisage the pastoral response of religious establishments to the influx of incomers, as the sources are so few, so fragmentary and so random. In consequence, the religious interface between the Scandinavians and the churches where they settled has remained largely unprobed. Even if these conversions can only be construed from indirect evidence, I would like to argue that the

[1] The relevant bibliography is extensive. See, for example, Nora Berend, ed., *Christianization and the Rise of Christian Monarchy: Scandinavia, Central Europe and Rus'* c.900–1200 (Cambridge, 2007); Ildar Garipzanov and Rosalind Bonté, eds, *Conversion and Identity in the Viking Age* (Turnhout, 2014).
[2] For the use of the term 'diaspora' for communities of Scandinavian heritage settled overseas and retaining connections of various kinds with their homelands, see Lesley Abrams, 'Diaspora and Identity in the Viking Age', *EME* 20 (2012), 17–38.

sources are sufficient to reveal a diversity of experience for the new Christians and a striking creativity of approach by at least some of the churchmen faced with the task of converting them.

No single template of conversion could have fit all the Scandinavians of the diaspora. In addition to the obvious differences in political organization, social structure and economic practices in the zones of settlement, the churches of the regions where Viking armies were active and Scandinavian settlers made permanent homes were distinctly varied, with strong or weak episcopacies, dynamic or decadent monastic communities, and significantly different local cults. Some were clearly seriously weakened by years of war followed by hostile takeover; others were apparently robust. The nature of the Scandinavian immigration – elite takeover, peasant migration, urban or maritime mercantile communities – also differed, and all these factors conditioned the process of religious interaction. Each region therefore had its own chemistry, and locations of encounter between pagans and Christians spanned the economic, social, political and ecclesiastical spheres. The categories are overlapping, of course, but investigation of the economic context could lead us to the merchant quarter allocated to the Rus' nation in Constantinople, where traditional Rus' laws and pagan religious protocols were respected in the heart of Eastern Christendom. The social route could take us to an Icelandic farm where everyday non-Christian religious rituals were performed by households which included Christian Irish slaves.[3] The canvas is too vast to consider fully here, so I will focus on the interface between Scandinavian pagans and native Christians in political and ecclesiastical encounters and on two settings: Francia and northern England in the ninth and tenth centuries.

But first: what would have been involved in Christianizing immigrant Scandinavian populations? Conversion narratives usually describe missionaries going to do God's work among the heathen, not what Christians should do when the heathen come and live next door. The terrain of investigation into the process of conversion can be a methodological and terminological minefield. At least four different criteria have been used to identify converts: is it sufficient merely to have received the sacrament of baptism, or is it the performance of Christian ritual that indicates that people have converted? Does

---

[3] See above, n. 1.

conversion entail the taking onboard of a system of belief, or does it mean a life lived according to a new set of rules and moral guidelines? Understanding what Scandinavian pagans were converting from is similarly problematic. The term 'pagan' is loaded with judgements and pre-conceptions, and while one alternative, 'pre-Christian', may avoid this baggage, categorizing practices and beliefs with reference to what came to replace them is not ideal. Recently adopted by the noteworthy collaborative project, 'The Pre-Christian Religions of the North',[4] it nevertheless has the advantage of indicating the plurality of practice, whereas 'paganism' and other alternatives – 'traditional' religion, 'Old Norse' religion – mislead by implying a non-existent uniformity; regional variation was evidently standard also in the homelands.

Although contemporary evidence is far from plentiful, it does allow us to see that, in the ninth and tenth centuries, forms of religious practice brought from home were followed by Scandinavians in diaspora locations. Even this scarce and uneven evidence reveals traditional religious themes, but with overseas variations that stemmed from military campaigning, migration and exposure to Christianity in different locations, reflecting the diversity of local experience. It has been said that by the ninth century, Scandinavian paganism was 'degenerate' and 'run-down', ready to submit to Christianity,[5] but reconsiderations of the nature of religion have prompted something of a rethink of this assumption.[6] The recovery by metal-detectorists of increasing numbers of apparently pagan amulets has also changed the picture of religious life on the road. Almost identical images representing gods and mythical figures are found across the Scandinavian world, in the homelands and overseas alike: forty-one Thor's hammers

---

[4] Margaret Clunies Ross, ed., *The Pre-Christian Religions of the North: Research and Reception*, 2 vols (Turnhout, 2018–19); Jens-Peter Schjødt, John Lindow and Anders Andrén, eds, *The Pre-Christian Religions of the North: History and Structures*, 4 vols (Turnhout, 2020).

[5] David Wilson, 'The Vikings' Relationship with Christianity in Northern England', *Journal of the British Archaeological Association* 3rd series 30 (1967), 37–46.

[6] In addition to the volumes cited in n. 4, recent studies include Margaret Clunies Ross, 'Archaeology and Textuality in the Study of Pre-Christian Religion', in Nicolas Meyland and Lukas Rösli, eds, *Old Norse Myths as Political Ideologies: Critical Studies in the Appropriation of Medieval Narratives* (Turnhout, 2020), 117–28; Andreas Nordberg, 'Some Thoughts on the Category of Religion in Research of Viking Age Scandinavia', in Daniel Sävborg, ed., *Crossing Disciplinary Boundaries in Studies of the Viking Age* (Turnhout, 2022), 253–76.

in England to date, for example.[7] I have argued elsewhere that an active and dynamic paganism underpinned the lives of the men, women and children who made up the army communities that led semi-nomadic lives overseas during the course of the ninth century.[8] When they gave up mobile warfare and settled, maintaining their religion could help sustain immigrants' sense of connection with their homelands; losing it could help them assimilate.[9]

Some scholars are cynical about the process. The few Viking-Age conversions outside Scandinavia that are recorded in contemporary texts took place in the diplomatic sphere in connection with peace agreements between Christian rulers and Viking leaders.[10] This was politics, of course, and therefore – the sceptical thinking goes – these so-called converts are not to be taken seriously *as* converts; Vikings agreeing to be baptized by kings must have been unscrupulous and opportunist. Dyspeptic Frankish churchmen first voiced this view. Vikings were feckless, sneaky and unreliable; they were too stupid to understand Christianity; they were only motivated by self-interest and greed, accepting conversion for the rich gifts handed out by royal sponsors; *convertis de façade*, in François Neveux's telling expression, they failed to take their new religion seriously.[11] Variations on this theme appear in annals, narratives, poetry, sermons, exegesis and liturgical texts, where Vikings were seen to fulfil the prophecy in Jeremiah 1: 14, that evil shall come from the North. Comments such as these were not impartial: annalists and other writers often had political agendas, and colourful tabloid-style Vikings were useful weapons for critics of the king. In the 880s, Notker's biography of

---

[7] Tim Pestell, 'Imports or Immigrants? Reassessing Scandinavian Metalwork in Late Anglo-Saxon East Anglia', in David Bates and Robert Liddiard, eds, *East Anglia and its North Sea World in the Middle Ages* (Woodbridge, 2013), 230–55. My thanks to Tim and to Gareth Williams for confirming the figures in 2023.

[8] Lesley Abrams, 'The Religious Life of Viking Armies', in Charlotte Hedenstierna-Jonson and Irene García Losquiño, eds, *Viking Camps: Case Studies and Comparisons* (London, 2023), 240–57.

[9] For one collection of papers from a large bibliography on the subject of identity in the Viking Age, see Garipzanov and Bonté, eds, *Conversion and Identity*.

[10] Lesley Abrams, 'The Scandinavian Encounter with Christianity Overseas: Diplomatic Conversions in the 9th and 10th Centuries', in Anne Pedersen and Søren Sindbaek, eds, *Viking Encounters: Proceedings of the 18th Viking Congress* (Aarhus, 2020), 30–42.

[11] François Neveux, 'L'héritage des Vikings dans la Normandie ducale', in Élisabeth Ridel, ed., *L'héritage maritime des Vikings en Europe de l'Ouest* (Caen, 2002), 101–18, at 104; Olivier Guillot, 'La conversion des Normands à partir de 911', in Brigitte Beaujard, ed., *Histoire religieuse de la Normandie* (Chambray, 1981), 25–53, esp. 26–30.

Charlemagne caricatured Vikings who presented themselves for baptism at the court of his son, Louis the Pious: one Viking complained about the quality of the white baptismal robes, which were, he grumbled, inferior to those he had been given on many previous occasions.[12] Presented as 'comically unchanged by their encounter with Frankish Christianity',[13] Vikings were not just ridiculous, however; they were also dangerously duplicitous. Pierre Bauduin has argued that in Francia, throughout many decades of warfare punctuated by truces and alliances, stories of suspect and fraudulent Viking converts reveal significant anxiety among the Franks about the collaborative relationships engendered by the turbulent military and political situation.[14] In the 990s, Richer of Reims's *Historia* featured an anecdote in which a retainer of King Odo (r. 888–98) killed a Viking chief just as the king was about to lift him from the font; the murderer defended himself by arguing that the Viking would have been 'the cause of future calamity', and he was later rewarded with land and honours by the king.[15] Vikings who failed to take their conversion seriously were not only denying God, they were deceiving the Frankish establishment by pretending to be allies, integrated into Christian society.

There were doubtless Vikings who were feckless, greedy, ignorant and unreliable, but to my mind the tetchiness and satirical tendencies of these clerical authors have had a disproportionate impact on scholars. So has another argument, that as Scandinavian paganism was polytheistic it had 'room for another god', and Viking-Age converts simply 'added Christ to their pantheon'.[16] Converting, according to this thinking, would therefore have involved little change.

---

[12] *Gesta Karoli Magni* 2.19, ed. Hans F. Haefele, MGH SRG n.s. 12 (Munich, 1980), 89–90; ET: *Two Lives of Charlemagne*, transl. Lewis Thorpe (Harmondsworth, 1969), 168–9.
[13] Paul Kershaw, 'Laughter after Babel's Fall: Misunderstanding and Miscommunication in the Ninth-Century West', in Guy Halsall, ed., *Humour, History and Politics in Late Antiquity and the Early Middle Ages* (Cambridge, 2002), 179–202, at 197.
[14] Pierre Bauduin, *Le monde franc et les Vikings VIIIe–Xe siècle* (Paris, 2009), e.g. 128–30.
[15] Richer of Reims, *Historiae* 1.9–11, ed. Hartmut Hoffmann, MGH SS 38 (Hanover, 2000), 45–7; ET: *Richer of Saint-Rémi: Histories*, ed. and transl. Justin Lake, 2 vols (Cambridge, MA, 2011), 1: 30–9.
[16] Wilson, 'The Vikings' Relationship', 46; David Stocker, 'Monuments and Merchants: Irregularities in the Distribution of Stone Sculpture in Lincolnshire and Yorkshire in the Tenth Century', in Dawn M. Hadley and Julian D. Richards, eds, *Cultures in Contact: Scandinavian Settlement in England in the Ninth and Tenth Centuries* (Turnhout, 2000), 179–212, at 194–5.

I would question this too: for one thing, the church taught an extensive programme of regulated Christian living in the early Middle Ages, at least as an aspiration. Furthermore, 'just adding another god' inaccurately reduces Scandinavian paganism to the worship of gods and goddesses. Scandinavians did worship a range of deities, and their religion lacked Christianity's single creed, authoritative scriptures and standardizing institutional infrastructure. However, like contemporary Christianity, traditional pagan religions were a way of life: daily interactions with the transcendental in the form of public and domestic ritual provided the contours of the political, social and physical landscape in which people lived.[17] The subject is admittedly obscured by the lack of contemporary evidence, making conclusions hypothetical, and (as we shall see) substitutions of one (Christian) thing for another (pagan) one certainly helped ease the process of change. Nevertheless, unexplored assumptions continue to have too much influence on perceptions of religious life in this period which then cloud our understanding of conversion. The premise that faith and doctrine are the essence of religious identity, for example, is not helpful here.

This is made clear in a source relating to the Bulgars, not Scandinavians but a contemporary people living on the Volga river. Their ruler, Khan Boris, was considering accepting Christianity from Rome, and he wrote to Pope Nicholas I in the 860s with one hundred and six questions. Can a man have two wives, he asked; and would it still be forbidden to eat near the king at his table? Just one wife, said Nicholas, and while the current practice of sitting on stools far away from the king and eating off the ground was, in his view, bad manners, it was not 'against the faith'.[18] The implications of being Christian were troubling Boris, as Bulgar religious identity was linked to a wide range of everyday behaviour. The pope was reassuring. Asked whether the Bulgars could continue to wear trousers, he replied that 'we do not wish the exterior style of your clothing to be changed, but rather the behavior of the inner man within you' – unless what they were doing was a sin.[19] The pope's answers make it clear that the complete

---

[17] See, for further discussion, Nordberg, 'Some Thoughts'.

[18] *Epistolae Karolini aevi*, ed. Ernest Perels, MGH Epp. 6 (Berlin, 1925), 568–600, at 586, 583; ET: 'The Responses of Pope Nicholas I to the Questions of the Bulgars', transl. William L. North, online at: <https://sourcebooks.fordham.edu/basis/866nicholas-bulgar.asp>, accessed 27 November 2023.

[19] Ibid. 588. Trousers on women were undesirable, however (though not forbidden).

transformation of social customs was not a prerequisite for a good Christian life. On the other hand, the workings of the devil that were manifested in 'observations of days and hours, the incantations, the games, iniquitous songs, and auguries' were to be entirely abandoned.[20]

Contemporary Scandinavian concerns are unfortunately not so richly documented. As Francia shared a border with Denmark, however, it was on the receiving end of Viking activity for many years before the conversions of the homeland kingdoms, and Frankish observers of politics and war occasionally offer glimpses of their pagan neighbours' religious protocols. Casual details in the record of events show that religious difference was no obstacle to treaty-making between pagans and Christians, for example: each side sealed contracts with their own religious rituals.[21] In England, King Alfred (r. 871–99) famously made a treaty which Viking leaders confirmed with oaths on a holy ring.[22] However, sometimes Christian kings, including Alfred, made baptism a condition of defeat or alliance, a strategy that is attested in Viking-Christian military and diplomatic relations for almost two hundred years.[23] It had its successes, though as we have seen, failure made better copy. Standing sponsor at baptism made kings the spiritual fathers of Viking leaders, establishing a dominance through religious and social ties that aimed to make the baptized subject to their military and political authority as well.

In the 860s, one Viking found this out the hard way. A letter to Roric, a 'Northman converted to the Christian faith', from Hincmar, archbishop of Reims (845–82), shows how churchmen could act as the

---

[20] Ibid. 581.

[21] For example, *Annales de Saint-Bertin*, s.a. 862, ed. Félix Grat, Jeanne Vieillard and Suzanne Clémencet (Paris, 1964), 89; ET: *The Annals of St-Bertin*, transl. Janet L. Nelson (Manchester, 1991), 98. See also Lesley Abrams, 'Cross-Cultural Oaths: King Alfred the Great, Emperor Leo V, and the Rus' in Byzantium', in Constantin Zuckerman, ed., Ποιμὴν καὶ διδάσκαλος: *Studies in Honour of Jonathan Shepard*, Occasional Monographs 7 (Paris, forthcoming 2025).

[22] *Anglo-Saxon Chronicle*, s.a. 876; ET in: *English Historical Documents, c.500–1042* [hereafter: *EHD*], transl. Dorothy Whitelock, 2nd edn (London, 1996; first publ. 1968), 199 (no. 1), online at: <https://search-ebscohost-com.ezproxy-prd.bodleian.ox.ac.uk/login.aspx?direct=true&AuthType=ip,shib&db=nlebk&AN=94643&site=ehost-live>, accessed 12 July 2023.

[23] Abrams, 'The Scandinavian Encounter'; Simon Coupland, 'From Poachers to Gamekeepers: Scandinavian Warlords and Carolingian Kings', *EME* 7 (1998), 85–114.

Frankish king's party whips.[24] Hincmar warned Roric not to help Baldwin, count of Flanders, who had been excommunicated for seizing Charles the Bald's daughter Judith and marrying her. In Hincmar's framing of the situation, it was Roric's conversion that had committed him politically: it was his responsibility as a Christian to toe the party line and support the king. The letter points out the religious consequences of disobedience: if he goes against the king's wishes, Roric's baptism will count for nothing, says Hincmar, and the prayers of the saints will be useless and unable to help him.

Roric seems to have complied; he had been given a grant of land and he had a territory to run, sufficient motive, presumably, to submit to the king's command. For leaders of Viking armies whose baptisms had sealed more temporary arrangements, however, religious commitments need not have lasted long. In 876, 'a group of Northmen were baptised ... but afterwards, like typical Northmen, they lived according to pagan custom just as before', grumbled a Frankish annalist.[25] The complaint that Vikings were being baptized more than once was a repeated charge. However, if this was so and (as I believe) serial baptism was not just a trope but a real strategy for difficult times, the instigators of this practice are unlikely to have been ignorant and untrustworthy Vikings. Baptisms, after all, were performed by bishops and priests, and kings and other great men acted as sponsors. Despite being deplored by vocal anti-Viking churchmen, such a practice must have been implemented by their fellow bishops and royal patrons. This was a politically volatile time in the Frankish empire, and many peace agreements and alliances – with or without baptism – were made and unmade soon thereafter. When agreements broke down or outgrew their usefulness, Viking bands moved on, whereupon other lords might seal further short-term arrangements at the font. This was a violation of canon law, but churchmen were expected to be loyal to their lords and leaders, and the usefulness of baptism as a political instrument could override other considerations. There were also relationships between Viking bands and Frankish lords lower down the social ladder, although whether baptism was ever involved there is unknown. These relationships were similarly condemned for religious reasons. Fulk, archbishop of Reims (883–900), complained that local

---

[24] Flodoard, *Historia Remensis ecclesiae* [hereafter: *HRE*] 3.26, ed. Martina Stratmann, MGH SS 36 (Hanover, 1998), 336.

[25] *Annales de Saint-Bertin*, *s.a.* 876, 206 (*The Annals*, transl. Nelson, 195).

lords submitting to the protection of Vikings were abandoning their Christian religion; and in a fiery letter to Charles the Simple he condemned the king's alliance with a Viking army in the 890s as an association that would corrupt the purity of Christians.[26]

Another way kings attempted to subdue the Viking threat was by granting land and power, delegating the task of ruling small polities in their name to Viking chiefs like Roric, who thereby acquired a political identity and a place (admittedly precarious) amongst the elite.[27] The best attested example – and the most successful – is the grant of Frankish territory to Rollo in 911. While Rollo and his men may have been baptized to seal the political deal that put them in power in their *terra Normannorum*, no treaty-text or contemporary reference survives, and a gap in the annals leaves us ignorant of the arrangement that created Normandy and reliant on later, tendentious, sources. Although it may have increased the chances that the venture would succeed, it was apparently not always the case that land grants required the Viking recipient to convert.[28] Chronicles and hagiographies claimed that Rollo showed himself to be a glorious Christian, but they are all late, partisan and unreliable, especially on this religious question.[29] One contemporary survival, however, offers a snapshot of the early days of his regime. Some five to ten years after the grant to Rollo, Wido, the archbishop of Rouen, wrote to his colleague Herveus, archbishop of Reims (900–22). In turn, Herveus wrote to the pope, John X (914–28), who replied:

> Concerning the Northmen, recently converted to the faith … . So brother, what should be done with regard to this that you have made known to us, that the Northmen have been baptised and rebaptised, and after baptism they have lived like heathens, and that in a pagan fashion [*paganorum more*] they have killed Christians, slaughtered priests, and eaten food sacrificed to the idols they worship?[30]

[26] *HRE* 4.5 (ed. Stratmann, 380, 384–5).

[27] Coupland, 'From Poachers to Gamekeepers'.

[28] Ibid. 98.

[29] Mark Hagger, *Norman Rule in Normandy 911–1144* (Woodbridge, 2017), 186–208; Mathieu Arnoux, 'La conversion des Normands de Neustrie et la restauration de l'église dans la province de Rouen', in François Bougard, ed., *Le christianisme en Occident du début du VIIe siècle au milieu du XIe siècle. Textes et documents* ([Paris], 1997), 269–81.

[30] *Papsturkunden 896–1046*, ed. Harald Zimmermann, 3 vols (Vienna, 1984–9), 1: 65–7 (no. 38); Olivier Guillot, 'La conversion des Normands peu après 911', *Cahiers de civilisation médiévale* 14 (1981), 101–16, 181–219, at 105; my translation. The correspondence is undated but must have been written between 914 and 922.

Wido's letter has not been preserved, but he had evidently reported that while some of the neophyte Viking Christians were compliant, others were baulking at the constraints of their new religion. How should he and his clergy deal with the crisis? In reply, the pope sketched out the guiding principles of a pastoral programme:

> If they were not in fact novices in faith, they should face canonical judgment. However, since they are immature in faith, we entrust to your deliberation and judgement how to judge, since you, having that people in your neighbourhood, can better than anyone else seek to convert them and understand their ways and likewise all their deeds and how they live.

> ... For you well know that one should proceed with them more gently than holy canons decree, lest burdens of which they have no previous experience prove (God forbid) too heavy for them, and ... they relapse into the old ways of their former life, which they had abandoned.[31]

At least some of the bad behaviour mentioned – attacking churches, killing priests – may have been the collateral damage of war and political infighting; but the qualifying *paganorum more* might suggest something more sinister, and the reference to sacrifices to idols gives the actions of the Viking forces an explicitly religious definition. The pope made it clear that even in these less-than-ideal circumstances churchmen had the responsibility of making good Christians out of the kind of rough converts created by political settlements. Neverthe-less, he acknowledged that the situation required special measures, and he recommended a lenient, flexible and accommodating approach, where it was not always necessary to obey canon law, and where converts were not to be judged by the standards applied to the local flock. The real burden of reply, however, fell not on the pope but on the archbishop of Reims. Herveus assembled for his colleague in Rouen a dossier of twenty-three chapters containing extracts 'from the sentences of the Fathers and from the canons and decretals of the Roman pontiffs' which offered guidance to Wido's clergy.[32]

---

[31] Ibid.

[32] Beb28, in MGH Epp. 9 (forthcoming), online at: <https://data.mgh.de/databases/epp9/bin/epp_ft_search_2.xql?id=BEb28&q=Heriveus>, accessed 14 April 2022; my translation. This is discussed in detail in Guillot, 'La conversion des Normands peu après 911'. See also Marie-Céline Isaïa, 'Hagiographie et pastorale. La collection canonique d'Hervé, archevêque de Reims (†922)', *Mélanges de science religieuse* 67 (2010), 27–48.

Authorities cited range from Scripture through late antique texts to Bede, covering a variety of topics relevant to a pastoral programme. There is nothing in the collection about what the converts are to be taught to believe, however: the focus is discipline, not doctrine. Running themes include the authority of bishops and the vocation of the clergy, past measures for dealing with idol worship and pagan feasts, apostasy, serial baptism,[33] repentance and redemption. Penance is frequently recommended and is central to the approach. One extract specifies that it should be tailored to personal circumstances, including sex and age.[34]

I have so far discovered nothing from the period to match this dossier's snapshot of uncooperative Viking-Age converts in collision with Christian expectations, nor its outline of a pastoral programme specifically designed to absorb them into the church. Its message of leniency and tolerance, however, had many precedents, often building on Paul's observation in 1 Corinthians 3: 2 that 'babes in Christ' should be fed milk, not meat. In early England, for example, the 'milk of simpler teaching' had been recommended as appropriate until the ignorant 'grew strong on the food of God's word … [and] were capable of receiving more elaborate instruction and of carrying out the more transcendental commandments of God'.[35] While the approach articulated by the pope and the archbishop in the dossier shares this vision of gentle progress, it is striking how much it contrasts with the uncompromising anti-Viking line expressed by other churchmen in the public sphere. Herveus's brief prefatory remarks do include a conventional denunciation of apostates (the lapsed Viking converts are like dogs returning to their vomit) which may reflect the lost letter from the beleaguered local churchman, Archbishop Wido. However, the correspondence between Pope John and Archbishop Herveus seems to be intended to inform, not express judgements; its matter-of-factness is far removed from political point-scoring and that rhetorical device, the imagined Viking. This dossier appears to be a thoroughly practical

[33] About ten of the extracts relate to baptism; intriguingly they all take the line (in different ways) that serial baptism is unacceptable.

[34] Beb28, ch. 23 (MGH Epp. 9, n.p.).

[35] Bede, *Ecclesiastical History of the English People* [hereafter: *HE*] 3.5, ed. and transl. Bertram Colgrave and Roger Mynors (Oxford, 1969), 228–9; Katherine Cross, 'Moving on from the "Milk of Simpler Teaching": Weaning and Religious Education in Early Medieval England', in Thijs Porck and Harriet Soper, eds, *Early Medieval English Life Courses: Cultural-Historical Perspectives* (Leiden, 2021), 210–28, esp. 213–20.

piece of ecclesiastical business, churchman to churchman, in which, I would argue, we are hearing the authentic voice of experience at the interface between pagan and Christian, a voice notably silent elsewhere. If so, it is a rare contemporary witness to an active religious life in a Viking army. The dossier's seemingly unprejudiced snapshot of pagan activity among Rollo's followers and the responses of these senior clerics to the request for help offer unusual insight into ecclesiastical thinking about how one location of encounter could theoretically be navigated.

Unfortunately, there is no way of knowing how far – or even whether – the proposed programme was implemented. There is no trace of the dossier in Normandy. The surviving manuscript, copied at Reims in the tenth century, is now in Paris.[36] The ninth century had seen significant disruption in Francia, and opinions differ as to the degree of continuity of infrastructure in the region after its cession to Rollo, including the state of the church led by the province's archbishop.[37] Throughout the tenth century, archbishops were apparently in post in Rouen, where they had close relations with the Scandinavian ruling regime, but the restoration of other dioceses was very slow: bishops were not in place everywhere until the 990s, many years after the Viking takeover,[38] suggesting that the episcopal church at least may have struggled to assert itself across the province. The picture is obscured by the fact that by c.1000, when the church emerged from an almost invisible first century of Norman rule, the written record was largely monopolized by its patrons, the powerful dukes who were Rollo's descendants.[39]

Across the Channel, a different dynamic was in place, as resistance to Viking attack had largely failed everywhere but in the Wessex of King Alfred. The rulers of England's three other kingdoms had been defeated in the 860s and 870s by Viking armies who then seized

---

[36] Paris, BN, Lat. 4280A; see above, n. 32. The pope's letter also survives in another contemporary Reims manuscript, now Rome, BAV, Reg. lat. 418.

[37] David Bates, *Normandy before 1066* (Harlow, 1982), 2–43, sets out the problem. For a range of views, see Felice Lifshitz, 'La Normandie carolingienne. Essai sur la continuité, avec utilisation de sources négligées', *Annales de Normandie* 48 (1998), 503–24; and Pierre Bauduin, *La première Normandie (Xe–XIe siècles)* (Caen, 2004), 13–34.

[38] Lucien Musset, 'Un millénaire oublié. La remise en place de la hiérarchie épiscopale en Normandie autour de 990', in Pierre Guichard et al., eds, *Papauté, monachisme et théories politiques, 2: Les Églises locales. Études d'histoire médiévales offertes à Marcel Pacaut* (Lyon, 1994), 563–73.

[39] Lesley Abrams, 'Early Normandy', *Anglo-Norman Studies* 35 (2012), 45–64.

power, after which substantial areas of eastern and northern England were settled by their followers. In the 890s, Pope Formosus threatened 'all the bishops of England' with anathema, having heard that 'the abominable rites of the pagans have sprouted again in your parts and that you have kept silent, like dogs unable to bark', a lack of bishops being apparently partly to blame.[40] Since they had 'awakened' and 'begun to renew the seed of the word of God', Formosus had withdrawn his threat of excommunication, he said; but he gave no explanation of how the bishops' seed was being sown, and there is no further correspondence, no other record, and no dossier on the Reims model to help construct a picture of how change was being pursued.

While the conversion of those Scandinavians who settled in England may be unrecorded in the archives, it is nevertheless highly visible in the landscape in the form of carved stone monuments. Before the Viking Age, the English church had a longstanding tradition of sophisticated stone sculpture tied to devotional and funerary practices; after the Scandinavian settlement, this art was transformed, especially in northern England. Devotional monuments continued to be raised, but sculpture became increasingly important in secular society as a means of commemorating the dead in a Christian setting. The Scandinavian homelands had no comparable tradition of carved stone at this time, but political change and new patrons brought new ideas and aesthetics which, combined with the models and inspiration of the preceding 'Anglian' period, led to significant innovation. The technology, material and form of the many crosses and grave-slabs erected were largely local, but the ornament and iconography introduced were in many cases inspired by Scandinavian connections and radically different from previous English norms.

One striking subgroup of sculptures in northern England, for example, incorporated characters and scenes from Norse mythology, images that would have been immediately recognizable to a Scandinavian audience. The god Thor, his line baited with an oxhead, is shown fishing for the World Serpent on a fragment of a slab or frieze at Gosforth in Cumbria (Figure 1).[41] Stones with mythological references such as these

---

[40] Echoing Isa. 56: 10; William of Malmesbury, *Gesta pontificum Anglorum*, 1: *Text and Translation*, ed. and transl. Michael Winterbottom (Oxford, 2007), 79–83; *EHD* 955–6 (no. 227).
[41] Richard N. Bailey and Rosemary Cramp, *Cumberland, Westmorland and Lancashire North-of-the-Sands*, Corpus of Anglo-Saxon Stone Sculpture 2 (Oxford, 1988), 108–9.

Figure 1. Fragment of a slab or frieze, Gosforth, Cumbria. Copyright: Corpus of Anglo-Saxon Stone Sculpture, University of Durham. Photograph credit: Tom Middlemass.

are all preserved in church settings and also bear conventional Christian imagery. Above Thor on the Gosforth fragment, a hart, a symbol of Christ, is entangled in the coils of a snake: on this one stone, therefore, 'two gods struggle with evil in serpent form'.[42] Interpretation of these monuments has varied: it has sometimes been assumed that the people who put them up 'weren't really Christian'; or they were so ignorant of Christian teaching that they failed to realize that Thor was incompatible with Christ, that one God meant just that. The decorative scheme has also been seen as evidence of a hybrid religion, a regional amalgam of Christianity and Norse paganism.[43] While there may of course have been pressure from below, from Scandinavians unwilling to give up their religion, stones like these are unlikely to have been raised without ecclesiastical involvement. The specialized craft of production, the appropriation of religious space and, most importantly perhaps, the thinking that is represented by these images strongly

[42] Richard N. Bailey, *England's Earliest Sculptors* (Toronto, 1996), 90.
[43] Stocker, 'Monuments and Merchants', 194–9; see below, 161.

Figure 2. Cross, Gosforth, Cumbria. Copyright: Corpus of Anglo-Saxon Stone Sculpture, University of Durham. Photograph credit: Tom Middlemass.

suggest that the church was involved. Analysis by Richard Bailey and Lilla Kopár has proposed that the mythological references to gods and heroes were actually in dialogue with Christian content: their pagan narratives were conscripted to a new purpose and were deployed to illustrate Christian truths.[44]

Norse mythology and Christian images are also paired on the large cross in Gosforth churchyard (Figure 2).[45] Here, Christ stands within a frame, blood pouring from his side. Above him (mid-cross), Viðar, the son of the god Oðin, prises open the jaws of the wolf that had killed his

---

[44] Richard N. Bailey, *Viking Age Sculpture in Northern England* (London, 1980), and *England's Earliest Sculptors*, 77–94; Lilla Kopár, *Gods and Settlers: The Iconography of Norse Mythology in Anglo-Scandinavian Sculpture* (Turnhout, 2012).
[45] Bailey and Cramp, *Cumberland, Westmorland*, 100–4; Kopár, *Gods and Settlers*, 90–104.

father, poised to tear it apart.[46] Viðar's act belongs to a central narrative of Norse mythology, Ragnarøk, the apocalyptic battle between the gods and the forces of evil, and Bailey has argued that the images on the Gosforth Cross represent an eschatological programme that visualized victory over evil and chaos and aimed to inspire 'reflective contemplation' by evoking Ragnarøk together with the crucifixion and the Second Coming.[47] The ring-chain decoration on the lower section of the shaft recalls both Yggdrasil, the earth-tree where Oðin died, and the *treow* or *beam* (Old English 'tree') on which Christ was crucified.[48] Viðar and Christ both sacrificed themselves to defeat evil; both nonetheless emerged victorious. The complementary images offered a kind of commentary between two cosmic perspectives, although the driving force was Christian thinking. The juxtapositions invited the onlooker to reflect on the parallels and contrasts, but their presence was purposeful, not simply 'cultural fusion': the images are a 'pagan iconography of Christian ideas', the approach one of 'speculative theology'.[49]

Even an image as iconic as the crucifixion, Bailey has argued, could be adapted, and its meaning tailored. In most representations of Christ on the cross, the paired figures in attendance are either Longinus and Stephaton, or John and the Virgin Mary; the two attendant figures on the Gosforth Cross, however, have been identified as Longinus and Mary Magdalene, both arguably archetypes of the converted (Figure 3).[50] Mary's dress and hair are Scandinavian in style, familiar from contemporary metal amulets.[51] Bailey has suggested that the choice of Mary Magdalene and Longinus was intended to further shape the cross's iconographic programme, enhancing its power to address a newly Christian community more directly.

Bailey has described the Gosforth Cross as 'an extreme visual response to the advice given by Pope Gregory' three hundred years earlier, during the Anglo-Saxon conversion, recorded in Bede's

---

[46] Bailey, *Viking Age Sculpture*, 125–9; Kopár, *Gods and Settlers*, 89–90.

[47] Bailey, *England's Earliest Sculptors*, 88–9.

[48] Kopár, *Gods and Settlers*, xx, 99; Bailey, *Viking Age Sculpture*, 146–7.

[49] Bailey, *England's Earliest Sculptors*, 84, 93 (borrowed from the nineteenth-century scholar Sophus Bugge), 85. These images were carved hundreds of years before the Norse narratives they represent were written down, so the reverse flow of influence, of Christianity on paganism and on the Christian authors who recorded and preserved it, is difficult to trace, although it was doubtless significant: Kopár, *Gods and Settlers*, 89, 103–4.

[50] Bailey, *England's Earliest Sculptors*, 88–9; Kopár, *Gods and Settlers*, 94–9.

[51] This could have evoked another association, with the goddess Hel, ruler of the underworld: Kopár, *Gods and Settlers*, 99–101.

Figure 3. Detail of Gosforth Cross, Gosforth, Cumbria. Copyright: Corpus of Anglo-Saxon Stone Sculpture, University of Durham. Photograph credit: Tom Middlemass.

Historia ecclesiastica.[52] 'What I have decided after long deliberation about the English people', Gregory had written to the missionary Mellitus in 601, is 'that the idol temples of that race should by no means be destroyed, but only the idols in them'; Gregory instructed Mellitus to build altars with relics on the sites of pagan shrines.[53] This is what God did for the Israelites in Egypt, wrote Gregory: 'he preserved in his own worship the forms of sacrifice which they were accustomed to offer to the devil.'[54] Festivals, where animals had been sacrificed to pagan gods, could carry on after conversion because what

[52] Bailey, *England's Earliest Sculptors*, 89. Gregory's advice was also known through collections of his correspondence, its probable route of transmission into Herveus's dossier: Beb28, ch. 3 (MGH Epp. 9, n.p.).
[53] *HE* 1.30 (*Ecclesiastical History*, ed. and transl. Colgrave and Mynors, 106–7).
[54] Ibid. (108–9), referring to Lev. 17: 1–7.

had been a pagan ritual, killing and eating animals to worship idols, could be continued as a Christian one, killing and eating animals in praise of God. It would not take much to extend this message from rituals and sites to narratives and imagery; they could likewise be allowed to remain unchanged in form, as their meaning was transformed. Bailey has observed that monuments such as the Gosforth Cross, erected centuries after Gregory's advice, may be the only evidence to survive that people in northern England 'were capable of this type of radical thinking' at this time.[55]

How the thinking behind these iconographic schemes went from theory to practice – how it filtered down to parish priests, for example – is obscure. Educated northern churchmen could have been familiar with Gregory's letter through Bede, although other authorities for this reinterpretation of pre-Christian forms through a figurative lens would have been available. It is sometimes assumed that English, Irish and Frankish clergy knew little about contemporary paganism; but whoever created these decorative programmes must have been sufficiently well informed about pagan gods and myths to make them serve a Christian purpose, pairing that knowledge with Christian teaching, converting Sigurd and Viðar to the service of the true God (as Gregory would have it) and representing them locally in stone.[56]

Monuments like these presumably had a devotional function, but they may also have served as teaching aids, important items in the preacher's toolkit. The hero Sigurd, who appears on a number of stones – including an elaborate grave-slab from the cemetery at York Minster which featured many episodes of his life – was able to understand the language of birds after defeating a dragon, roasting its heart and tasting its blood.[57] Might this have helped explain the eucharist to Scandinavian converts?[58] If, however, we think of the monuments of this subgroup as just static representations of a theological vision of correspondences, we may be missing something about the way sculpture was experienced. Stone monuments may not have been simply 'monumental'. While surviving Old Norse mythological

[55] Bailey, *Viking Age Sculpture*, 132.
[56] Direct evidence of such knowledge is scarce and mainly from southern England; see Audrey L. Meaney, 'Æthelweard, Ælfric, the Norse Gods and Northumbria', *JRH* 6 (1970), 105–32.
[57] James Lang, *York and Eastern Yorkshire*, Corpus of Anglo-Saxon Stone Sculpture 3 (Oxford, 1991), 71–2. For Sigurd, see Kopár, *Gods and Settlers*, 23–41.
[58] Bailey, *England's Earliest Sculptors*, 93.

lore has largely been preserved on the page, it was originally performed.[59] Viking-Age religion in Scandinavia, it has been argued, was a 'behavioural experience'; surviving rich textiles show elaborate scenes of what seems to be highly performative spiritual practice.[60] Moreover, in England, stone could be imagined as animated: in the Old English poem *Andreas*, the figure of an angel on a frieze not only speaks but leaps from the wall and walks out along the road 'to take God's mission' into the world.[61] If we think of sculpture as static, we are surely underestimating its performative role and undervaluing its experiential and communicative power.

We can only speculate about how the images on these stones were decoded by contemporaries, however, and interpretations along these lines, postulating a strategy of purposeful, sophisticated, theological thinking, go too far for some. The sculpture nevertheless shows a church readily recruiting and adapting imported images and ornament and apparently comfortable with correspondences from the immigrants' traditional thought-world. David Stocker has taken a more secular line, suggesting that while the archbishops of York were 'closely involved' in the development of iconography 'pandering to [the] pagan background' of the settlers, the collaboration was motivated by political necessity: he has argued that these monuments served to articulate the archbishops' alliance with Scandinavian kings in northern England, a coalition which lasted until the latter's final defeat by the West Saxons in 954.[62] A political interpretation would certainly enhance understanding of the ostentatiously Scandinavian iconography on the grave-slab from York, although it is far from clear that it would apply to distant Gosforth, which may or may not have been within York's jurisdiction.[63] Unfortunately, these sculptures are also difficult to

---

[59] Brian McMahon and Annemari Ferreira, eds, *Old Norse Poetry in Performance* (London, 2022), esp. Terry Gunnell, 'Introduction', 1–15.

[60] Neil Price, 'Performing the Vikings: From Edda to Oseberg', in Karen Bek-Pedersen et al., eds, *The Wild Hunt for Numinous Knowledge: Perspectives on and from the Study of Pre-Christian Nordic Religions in Honour of Jens Peter Schjødt*, Religionsvidenskabeligt Tidsskrift 74 (Aarhus, 2022), 63–88, at 69 and 73–80.

[61] Michael D. J. Bintley, '"The Stones of the Wall Will Cry Out": Lithic Emissaries and Marble Messengers in Andreas', in Meg Boulton and idem, eds, *Insular Iconographies: Essays in Honour of Jane Hawkes* (Woodbridge, 2019), 61–79, at 61–5.

[62] Stocker, 'Monuments and Merchants', 195–6.

[63] For a recent reassessment of the region's complicated diocesan history, see Neil McGuigan, 'Cuthbert's Relics and the Origins of the Diocese of Durham', *Anglo-Saxon England* 48 (2019), 121–62.

date,[64] and art historians' preference for date-ranges as unspecific as 'tenth-century' makes linking monuments and politics problematic. Furthermore, theologically creative decorative programmes as proposed by Bailey need not have been formulated solely for the first generation experiencing religious change. While the pagan-Christian juxtapositions had the potential to speak to converts, the message of correspondence and cultural connection could also have resonated at a later time, well after the initial settlement, when other kinds of capital (nostalgia, ethnic consciousness and regional solidarity) had accrued to the Scandinavian heritage in England.

Ecclesiastical initiatives – pastoral and political – remain hypothetical, and there were other ways in which conversion could occur. More organic and ad hoc forms of religious accommodation between incomers and locals, not driven from above, were no doubt also in play and instrumental in encouraging change. Local Christians and Christianity did not disappear, and there were many ways of attracting newcomers to the faith. Local saints could have drawn pagans into Christian worship, for example, their status as spirits of place akin to Scandinavian animistic traditions. English Christians could have befriended and then sponsored their pagan neighbours at the font. Churchmen were best placed to make decisions about what images could communicate the desired religious message, however,[65] and, as far as sculpture is concerned, they were the most likely to have spotted the potential of using the Scandinavian inheritance to articulate Christian teaching in material form in this way.

Monuments with mythological images represent only one, relatively small, regional manifestation of a revolution in sculpture that took place in northern England. The stone crosses of the pre-Viking period had been highly stylized, dense with liturgical and scriptural references, sometimes inscribed with Latin or Old English commemorative or devotional texts. After the Scandinavian settlement, another kind of radically different look was introduced. The occasional

---

[64] Bailey, *Viking Age Sculpture*, 45–75.

[65] Just as decisions were made regarding images in art in Constantinople in 692 at the Quinisext Council, decreeing that the image of Christ as a lamb should be replaced with Christ 'in human form', 'so that all may understand by means of [the human figure] … his redemption which was wrought for the whole world': see Canon 82, Quinisext Council, online at: <https://www.newadvent.org/fathers/3814.htm>, accessed 20 April 2023.

Figure 4. Cross, Middleton, Yorkshire. Copyright: Corpus of Anglo-Saxon Stone Sculpture, University of Durham. Photograph credit: Tom Middlemass.

lapidary inscription in Norse and/or runes survives,[66] but much more common were crosses and grave-slabs with men on horseback, men with weapons, men with drinking horns; men hunting, standing, sitting: a cross from Middleton (Yorkshire; Figure 4), for example, shows a man with four bladed weapons, a helmet and a shield.[67] These monuments in local churches or churchyards portraying proudly armed men were a significant innovation, material signs which could combine declarations of lordship with allegiance to the Christian religion. This unprecedented secular self-representation expressed as

---

[66] Eleanor Rye, 'A New Runic Inscription from Sockburn Hall, County Durham: E 19 Sockburn', *Futhark* 8 (2017), 89–110.
[67] Lang, *York and Eastern Yorkshire*, 182–4; Dawn M. Hadley, 'Warriors, Heroes and Companions: Negotiating Masculinity in Viking-Age England', *Anglo-Saxon Studies in History and Archaeology* 15 (2008), 270–84, esp. 275–8.

Christian piety allowed individuals to advertise publicly their incorporation into the society of Christians. Christian art no longer provided the models for Christian monuments in other ways as well: while pre-Viking Christian sculpture had been decorated with ornament that reflected the art of the scriptorium, the large corpus of post-settlement sculpture is exuberantly decorated with art styles modelled on those current in Scandinavia. The Gosforth Cross's Borre-style ring-chain motif, for example, appears on Scandinavian metalwork and textiles.[68] These changes in mortuary practice signalled the affinities of a new Anglo-Scandinavian elite in ways that combined elements of their Scandinavian heritage with established conventions of the English church.

In a perfect world, the two halves of this short study would now come neatly together. The strategy of openness, tolerance and accommodation outlined for Rouen's Viking converts would be seen to manifest itself in material culture resembling these accommodating carved stones from northern England. On present evidence, however, there is nothing in Normandy that exhibits this kind of cultural mix in material form. Scandinavian place-names and personal names are abundant, as is evidence of pride in a Nordic heritage in sources as early as the eleventh century, but Normandy has no comparable corpus of monuments reflecting the Scandinavian origins of its founders.[69]

The contrast is striking, and some of the explanation must lie with ecclesiastical actors. Stone sculpture was a highly developed element of England's Christian heritage. Faced with a challenge, the church in northern England drew on this cultural inheritance and reworked it to suit a society absorbing newcomers and experiencing change. After the settlement, patrons were not necessarily all of Scandinavian descent, but the new classes of monuments with mythological and secular images allowed immigrants (and descendants of immigrants) to proclaim their new identities and anchor themselves in Christian society without losing everything that recalled their past lives as pagans: neither their language, their visual culture, nor the universe of their imagination. The Norman church must have found a way for its Scandinavian immigrants to become Christian that drew them into the indigenous religious identity,

---

[68] James Graham-Campbell, *Viking Art* (London, 2013), 63–81. Portable objects may have provided models for the motifs and designs on stone.

[69] Abrams, 'Early Normandy'; Mavis Baylé, 'Réminiscences angloscandinaves dans la sculpture romane de Normandie', *Anglo-Norman Studies* 13 (1990), 35–48.

but whether or not that way allowed the converted immigrants to express their difference from the surrounding populations who had been Christian for so long is unclear. Is it significant that in England, the son of a member of the Viking Great Army of the 860s became not just a bishop but archbishop of Canterbury, whereas the earliest known bishop in Normandy with a Norse name was not in post until *c.*990 at the earliest?[70] Apart from the archbishops of Rouen, senior churchmen are noticeably absent from the record throughout the tenth century, and it is unclear how many priests remained in place in Normandy to minister to their flocks and apply the dossier's programme.[71]

The political matrix in which religious change took place nevertheless differed significantly in these two locations and doubtless affected the dynamic between pagans and Christians. The Scandinavian regime in Rouen soon came to identify itself vigorously with the church, and it may have used its new religion as an instrument in the drive to establish control over other communities of Scandinavians settled in the region. Pressure to convert in western Normandy, for example, could have been a reflex of Rouen's ambitions and – if achieved – unwelcome, a sign of the loss of independence. Since both sides of this particular interface between paganism and Christianity traced their origins to the same homelands, allusions to Scandinavian heritage carried more complications than in England. Only when Normandy's young leader Richard I (r. 942–96) found himself dependent on unconverted Viking warbands in the mid-tenth century, Fraser McNair has argued, did his court in Rouen develop a language of overarching Norman ethnicity, creating 'a powerful if rather incoherent sense of group solidarity' to appeal to the new arrivals.[72] By the time Dudo of St Quentin finished his history of the Norman dukes in the early eleventh century, Rouen's supremacy was well established, inter-Scandinavian rivalries were conveniently obscured, and *Dacigena*, 'Scandinavian-born', had become a synonym for 'Norman'.[73]

---

[70] Oda, bishop of Ramsbury, *c.*900x27–41, was archbishop of Canterbury from 941 to 958. On Norgod, bishop of Avranches, see Richard Allen, 'The Norman Episcopate, 989–1110', 2 vols (DPhil thesis, University of Oxford, 2009), 31–44, esp. 31–2.

[71] Abrams, 'Early Normandy', 61.

[72] Fraser McNair, 'The Politics of Being Norman in the Reign of Richard the Fearless, Duke of Normandy (r. 942–996)', *EME* 23 (2015), 308–28, at 310.

[73] *De moribus et actis primorum Normanniae ducum*, ed. Jules Lair, Mémoires de la Société des Antiquaires de Normandie 23 (Caen, 1865); *Dudo of St Quentin: History of the Normans*, transl. Eric Christiansen (Woodbridge, 1998); McNair, 'Politics of Being Norman', 322.

We do not know whether the strategy of conversion by accommodation recommended to the archbishop of Rouen by the pope was a resounding success, or abandoned in despair, but there are hints that the approach across Normandy may have been fiercer and more coercive. Samantha Herrick's study of eleventh-century saints' lives has highlighted a distinctive regional interest in conversion, suggesting that the issue remained live long after Rollo's takeover.[74] In these hagiographical narratives, holy men of the distant past battle pagan shrines and convert populations by force brutally sustained by royal power. Herrick has observed that this implies that, at least in parts of the Norman province, the process of conversion had also been unwelcome in more recent times.[75] Mark Hagger has argued that conversion was slow and 'not easily achieved' in Normandy because 'coercion could take the process only so far'; 'hearts and minds' were only won 'with the passing of generations'.[76] What was also required was a reconstruction of the infrastructure of the institutional church, but this was entirely dependent on the extension of ducal political control and far from rapidly achieved.

What did the Scandinavians make of their conversion, however it came about? We can only speculate, but we might wonder whether some of those who experienced a more accommodating strategy could have felt the adaptation of their cultural property as a loss, or perceived in the process an injury inflicted by what we would now call cultural appropriation. Christianity's attitudes to other religions – its propensity to 'ingest' and 'transform' them in its own image while insisting on its superiority and separateness – is not universally admired;[77] nor can its introduction have always been perceived as entirely beneficial by those who accepted it. However, Viking-Age pagans are largely silent, their perspective lost; and the majority of sources relevant to their conversion – whether contemporary or retrospective – were written by churchmen whose work abounds with tabloid-style clichés or tendentious revisionism. Furthermore, in Normandy the origins of the province became entangled in ducal propaganda, and although its

---

[74] Samantha Kahn Herrick, *Imagining the Sacred Past: Hagiography and Power in Early Normandy* (Cambridge, MA, 2007), esp. 125–7.

[75] Ibid. 83–8.

[76] Hagger, *Norman Rule*, 211–13.

[77] Nora Berend, 'Interconnection and Separation: Medieval Perspectives on the Modern Problem of the "Global Middle Ages"', *Medieval Encounters* 29 (2023), 285–314, at 285 and 309.

Scandinavian heritage came to define its identity, nothing was to be gained by retailing the religious struggles and institutional setbacks that probably characterized the Norman church in its first Scandinavian century. In England, Scandinavian regimes were everywhere replaced in the tenth century by a West Saxon king from southern England, ruling a single unified kingdom. It was consequently not in the interests of churches and churchmen in zones of Scandinavian settlement to talk about old allies; collaborations and compromises might have been better forgotten. In addition to the voice of the Scandinavian convert, we are therefore also missing – with the exception of the Norman dossier – the voice from the ecclesiastical coalface.

Outsiders in religious terms when interactions first began, Scandinavians nevertheless achieved notable power and were major actors in significant settings, as military enemies and allies, kings, merchants and settlers. Religious conversion was a crucial means of bringing them further inside the tent. Without narrative evidence – indeed, without conventional evidence of any sort – an unproblematized idea that conversion 'just happened' has taken root, but this tendency to see the transition from paganism to Christianity as an organic development conflates the diverse routes to conversion and ignores their singularity. A focus on the interfaces between pagan and Christian gives more room to the agency of churchmen, although the energy and creativity with which they faced their local challenges can generally only be imagined. The institutional church was not the only agent that brought Christianity to the Scandinavians of the diaspora, but even the scanty sources that we have show churchmen at work with strikingly different solutions to this task.

The Pope of Iceland? Gizurr Ísleifsson and the Gregorian Reform in the Medieval North

Davide Salmoiraghi [iD]

University of Cambridge

In 1053, the archdiocese of Hamburg-Bremen became patriarchate of the North as part of a process of centralization with which the Curia sought control over Scandinavia and the North Atlantic. Although these ambitions risked being cut short by the German archbishops, who aspired to larger margins of independence, Gregory VII (1073–85) was able to secure the Icelandic diocese of Skálholt as a supporter of Roman reforming ideals. Bishop Gizurr Ísleifsson (1082–1118) maintained direct contacts with the Curia and organized the Icelandic church as a loyal Gregorian agent. In the absence of royal and archepiscopal authority in Iceland, Gizurr was considered 'king and bishop over the country': arguably, the pontiff of his own diocese. Through the analysis of Latin and Norse sources, this article explores how Gregorian ideals reached Iceland during the Investiture Controversy and how papal supremacy was built into the foundations of the northernmost diocese of Christendom.

The movement of church reform that started with the pontificate of Gregory VII in the late eleventh century reached Iceland, the northernmost province of Christendom, with considerable delay. Since the conversion of the island in the year 1000, the first century of the church in Iceland was characterized by a profound interplay between the secular and the religious, so much so that scholars have argued for its nationalistic and semi-secular nature, more or less free from papal control.[1] It was only in the late twelfth century that bishops started

---

E-mail: ds938@cam.ac.uk.

[1] On the organization of the church in medieval Iceland, see Einar Ól. Sveinsson, *The Age of the Sturlungs: Icelandic Civilization in the Thirteenth Century*, transl. Jóhann S. Hannesson (Ithaca, NY, 1953); Jón Viðar Sigurðsson, 'Islanske storkirker før 1300', in Helgi Þorláksson, ed., *Church Centres: Church Centres in Iceland from the 11th to the 13th*

Studies in Church History 61 (2025), 168–185 © The Author(s), 2025. Published by Cambridge University Press on behalf of the Ecclesiastical History Society.
doi:10.1017/stc.2024.36

fighting for the freedom of the church from the interference of secular chieftains.[2] The Gregorian movement towards ecclesiastical independence was first promoted by the Norwegian archdiocese of Niðaróss, which, since 1152, had overseen and administered the two dioceses of Iceland: the southern diocese of Skálholt and the northern diocese of Hólar. After its introduction in the 1170s, it took another century before the reform was successfully settled in favour of the church by Bishop Árni Þorláksson of Skálholt (1269–98), who won over the chieftains with the support of the Norwegian monarch, under whose authority Iceland had passed in 1262.

In this article, I investigate the existence of Gregorian tendencies in the Icelandic church prior to this first movement and around the time of the namesake of the reform, Pope Gregory VII (1073–85), and question the extent to which Rome shaped the episcopal authority of its northern representatives, especially during the episcopate of Gizurr Ísleifsson of Skálholt (1082–1118), Iceland's second bishop. Previous scholarship has focussed on the uniqueness of the church of Iceland, stressing how its complete independence from Rome shaped its origins and development. In particular, Magnús Stefánsson did not see Gizurr's effort as a valuable contribution to the Gregorian reform and deemed further speculation on the subject as pointless.[3] While I agree with the conclusions of the scholars on the secular nature of the early period of the church in Iceland, I challenge the claim that it was absolutely independent of Rome. Rather, I shall argue that through a careful negotiation between the Icelandic system and the rules of the

---

century and their Parallels in other Countries (Reykholt, 2005), 157–66; and Jan Brendalsmo and Jón Viðar Sigurðsson, 'The Social Elites and Incomes from Churches *c.*1050–1250', in Bjørn Pouslen, Helle Vogt and Jón Viðar Sigurðsson, eds, *Nordic Elites in Transformation, c.1050–1250*, 1: *Material Resources* (New York, 2019), 248–74.

[2] Old Norse texts refer to this movement as *staðamál* (the question of the properties), as the clergy was mainly concerned with the ownership of the churches that had been built on chieftains' estates. For an overview of the Icelandic bishops' efforts to reform the church according to the tenets of the Gregorian reform and of the controversy over ecclesiastical property, see Magnús Stefánson, 'Frá Goðakirkju til Biskupskirkju', in Sigurður Líndal, ed., *Saga Íslands*, 4 vols (Reykjavík, 1974–89), 3: 111–260; Orri Vésteinsson, *The Christianisation of Iceland: Priests, Power, and Social Change 1000–1300* (Oxford, 2000), 210–23, 286–90; Gunnar Karlsson, *The History of Iceland* (Minneapolis, MN, 2000), 38–43, 96–9; Erika Sigurdson, *The Church in Fourteenth-Century Iceland: The Formation of an Elite Clerical Identity*, Northern World 72 (Leiden and Boston, MA, 2016), 32–43; Gottskálk Jensson, 'Íslenskar klausturreglur og libertas ecclesie á ofanverðri 12. Öld', in Haraldur Bernharðsson, ed., *Íslensk klausturmenning á miðöldum* (Reykjavik, 2016), 9–57.

[3] Magnús Stefánson, 'Kirkjuvald eflist', in Sigurður Líndal, ed., *Saga Íslands*, 2: 55–144, at 62.

church, Gizurr was able to take advantage of the interests of the chieftains to further the organization of the church in Iceland, implementing most of the pope's directives, but adapting them to the social system of his land. The sources allow for a Gregorian reading of the life of Gizurr Ísleifsson and an interpretation of his deeds that indicates the bishop's attention to the guidelines of the Curia around his time.

My interpretation of the relations between Rome and its northern suffragans begins by illustrating the anti-papal sentiments of the clergy of Hamburg-Bremen, Iceland's first archbishopric, and the propaganda that was produced under the direction of Archbishop Liemar. I then contrast the attitude of the archdiocese with the conciliatory approach of the Icelandic bishops, and the consequences it had for the Icelandic church. Furthermore, I argue that Bishop Gizurr Ísleifsson not only shaped the church of Iceland according – as best he could – to the directives of the Curia, but also embraced Gregory VII's conception of papal authority and reproduced it in his own country. I suggest that the absence of royal or direct superior ecclesiastical authority in Iceland allowed Gizurr to act and present himself as the pontiff of his own diocese. Finally, I address the issue of Gizurr's marriage and interpret it as the result of a compromise between Roman aspirations and Icelandic customs, rather than a contradiction of the bishop's Gregorian outlook.

I. Gregorian Reform and the Archdiocese of Hamburg-Bremen (1056–1101)

The archdiocese of Hamburg was founded in 831 by Pope Gregory IV as part of a mission to convert Denmark, Norway and Sweden. After the Danish King Horik I sacked the city in 845, the archbishopric was moved to Bremen, creating the larger archdiocese of Hamburg-Bremen, with jurisdiction over the whole of Scandinavia.[4] As a sign of its strategic importance, in 1053 Pope Leo IX bestowed upon Archbishop Adalbert (1053–72) the dignity of apostolic legate and vicar of the North, including the Atlantic settlements of the Faroe

---

[4] On the process of Christianization of Scandinavia, see, among others, Birgit Sawyer, Peter Sawyer and Ian Wood, eds, *The Christianization of Scandinavia: Report of a Symposium Held at Kungälv, Sweden, 4–9 August 1985* (Alingsås, 1987); Alexandra Sanmark, *Power and Conversion: A Comparative Study of Christianization in Scandinavia* (Uppsala, 2004); Nora Berend, *Christianization and the Rise of Christian Monarchy* (Cambridge, 2007).

Islands, Greenland and Iceland.[5] However, the centralizing tendency of the papacy clashed with the aspirations of the archbishops themselves. During his years of office, Adalbert acted as the chief adviser to the young King Henry IV of Germany (1056–1105), who satisfied Adalbert's appetite for expansion by granting lands and privileges to the archbishopric. Strengthened by this support, Adalbert's ambition was for Hamburg-Bremen to become a reference point in northern Europe, with a level of independence that would have rivalled that of Rome.[6] The pope was therefore cautious, granting the legatine dignity on condition of the steadfast obedience (*debita subjectione*) of Adalbert and his successors to the Apostolic see.[7]

Adalbert extended his authority of apostolic legate to the northern edges of Christianity in 1056, when he consecrated the first bishop of Iceland. Ísleifr Gizurarson belonged to the prominent chieftain family of the Haukdælir and had been educated and ordained priest at Herford in Saxony. According to Old Norse-Icelandic sources, Ísleifr was chosen by the Icelanders, who sent him abroad to be consecrated. In his journey, he met the Holy Roman emperor, Henry III (1046–56), who gave him safe passage to Rome, from where Pope Victor II (1055–7) sent him in turn to his metropolitan, Archbishop Adalbert, who consecrated him on 25 May 1056. *Hungrvaka* ('Hunger-Waker'), the early-thirteenth-century Old Norse collection of bishops' lives, records traces of the archbishop's direct interest in the affairs of the newly established Icelandic church,[8] which he wanted to free from the influence of those 'bishops' who had not been appointed by the archdiocese. Despite being considered the first official bishop, Ísleifr's position was still precarious. He was technically a missionary bishop *in partibus infidelium* ('in the region of the infidels'), with neither an official see, nor an officially determined diocese. He also had

---

[5] *Diplomatarium Islandicum* [henceforth: *DI*] 18, in *Diplomatarium Islandicum: Íslenzk fornbréfasafn*, ed. Jón Sigurðsson, 16 vols (Copenhagen and Reykjavik, 1857–1952), 1: 57–60.

[6] Iain S. Robinson argues that the independence and immunity of Hamburg-Bremen was part of Adalbert's conception of 'freedom of the church': Iain S. Robinson, *Henry IV of Germany, 1056–1106* (Cambridge, 1999), 58.

[7] *DI* 12 (*Diplomatarium Islandicum*, ed. Jón Sigurðsson, 1: 50).

[8] After his consecration, Bishop Ísleifr took back with him to Iceland a letter from the archbishop promising a personal visit to the new members of his archdiocese: compare *Hungrvaka* 2, in *Biskupa sögur II*, ed. Ásdís Egilsdóttir, Íslenzk Fornrit 16 (Reykjavík, 2002), 8–9; and Adam of Bremen, *Gesta Hammaburgensis ecclesiae pontificum* [henceforth: *GHEP*] 4.36.

competition: *Hungrvaka* registers that, in this period, at least six clergymen came to Iceland to proselytize from different lands. All of them are referred to as bishops; all stayed in Iceland for many years, and at least one of them, Bishop Bjarnvaðr, was remembered for his remarkable zeal.[9]

Relations between Scandinavia and Rome increased during the papacy of Gregory VII (1073–85), who was in direct contact with Scandinavian sovereigns. To counter Adalbert's self-centred belief in the freedom of the church, Gregory VII corresponded with King Sweyn Estridsson of Denmark (1047–76), with whom he discussed the foundation of an independent metropolitan see.[10] While this project would become reality only after Gregory's death, with the foundation of the archdiocese of Lund (1104), the relationship between Hamburg-Bremen and Rome became increasingly tense during the tenure of Adalbert's successor, Archbishop Liemar (1072–1101). Like his predecessors, the archbishop was an important supporter of Henry IV, to whom Liemar owed his election. Liemar openly showed his hostility to the pope's understanding of the bishops' role and their prerogatives when Gregory intervened directly in the running of his metropolitan see. In 1074, two papal legates, Hubert of Palestrina and Gerald of Ostia, were sent to Germany to convene a general reforming synod, usurping a legal prerogative of the archbishop, who was only asked to assist the papal envoys. When he refused, Liemar was suspended from office and summoned to Rome to explain his conduct at the Lenten synod the following year.[11] Eager to secure the claims of his see in the North, he obeyed the summons and went to Rome, there expressing his opposition to the pope's infringement of his own authority as metropolitan and the authority of his bishops in general.[12] Despite his attempts to mediate with the

---

[9] *Hungrvaka* 3 (*Biskupa sögur II*, ed. Ásdís Egilsdóttir, 11–13).

[10] *Das Register Gregors VII.* 2.51 and 2.75, ed. Erich Caspar, MGH Epp. Sel., 2 vols (Berlin, 1920–3), 1: 192–4, 237–8; Herbert E. J. Cowdrey, 'The Gregorian Reform in the Anglo-Norman Lands and in Scandinavia', in Alphons Maria Stickler, ed., *La Riforma Gregoriana e l'Europa, 1: Congresso Internazionale, Salerno, 20–25 maggio 1985* (Roma, 1989), 321–52, at 323–34.

[11] *Register* 2.28 (MGH Epp. Sel., 1: 160–1).

[12] *Hildersheimer Briefe* 15, in *Briefsammlungen der Zeit Heinrichs IV.*, ed. Carl Erdmann and Norbert Fickermann, MGH BdK 5 (Weimar, 1950), 33–5; Ian Stuart Robinson, '"Periculosus Homo": Pope Gregory VII and Episcopal Authority', *Viator* 78 (1978), 103–32, at 109–10 and 113.

pope on behalf of the emperor at Canossa (1077) and Rome (1080), Liemar remained a firm opponent of the pope's authoritarian views. He was the only German archbishop to take part in the Brixen Synod in June 1080, which saw the deposition of Gregory VII and the election of the antipope Clement III, and he later acted as chief adviser to Henry IV during the siege of Rome in 1083.

The anti-papal attitude of the archbishopric within which Iceland's church fell is well illustrated by two works associated with Archbishop Liemar at the time of the consecration of Bishop Gizurr of Skálholt. Liemar is the dedicatee of Adam of Bremen's *Gesta Hammaburgensis ecclesiae pontificum*, which was completed around the time of his suspension.[13] The work not only claims the independence of the archiepiscopal see but celebrates it as a second Rome.[14] Together with Bishop Benno of Osnabrück (1067–88), himself a staunch supporter of the rights of the emperor,[15] Liemar sponsored the composition of a treatise entitled *Liber de controversia inter Hildebrandum et Henricum imperatorem*.[16] This work figures among the royalist pamphlets of the collection known as *Libelli de lite imperatorum et pontificum* (pamphlets on the controversy between emperors and popes) that were written by members of the clergy, which Robinson defined as 'episcopal polemics'.[17] The treatise was composed between 1084 and 1085 by Wido, canon and bishop of Osnabrück after Benno's death (1093–1101), who was also active in the royalist party as an advisor to Henry IV. It defends the election of Clement III after the Synod of Brixen, arguing against the legitimacy of Gregory's election, and

---

[13] For a recent overview of Adam of Bremen's work, see Bartusik et al., *Adam of Bremen's* Gesta Hammaburgensis Ecclesiae Pontificum*: Origins, Reception and Significance* (London, 2022).

[14] Adam of Bremen, *GHEP* 3.24, 3.73.

[15] On Benno's career, see Edgar N. Johnson, 'Bishop Benno II of Osnabrück', *Speculum* 16 (1991), 380–403.

[16] *Excerpta ex Widonis Osnabrugensis libro de controversia inter Hildebrandum et Heinricum imperatorem*, ed. Lothar von Heinemann, MGH LdL 1 (Hanover, 1891), 461–70. On Wido's career, see Detlev Jasper, 'Die Papstgeschichte des Pseudo-Liutprand', *Deutsches Archiv für Erforschung des Mittelalters* 31 (1975), 12–107.

[17] Iain S. Robinson, *Authority and Resistance in the Investiture Contest: The Polemical Literature of the Late Eleventh Century* (Manchester, 1978), 100. According to Robinson, these treaties had a smaller circulation than the more 'official' works of propaganda produced on both sides of the controversy, being distributed among groups of sympathisers in the monasteries or cathedral chapters at a local level.

criticizes the latter's misuse of the instrument of excommunication against the emperor and his bishops.

II. Gizurr the Gregorian

While Wido's text and his sponsorship are exemplary of the climate of tension at the archepiscopal see of Hamburg-Bremen, the career of Bishop Gizurr Ísleifsson (1082–1118) offers evidence of the position that the episcopal see in Iceland took vis-à-vis the demands of the Curia. The connection between the bishop of Iceland and the pope, alongside the importance of Roman approval, are particularly stressed in *Hungrvaka*,[18] in which Gizurr is the most extensively discussed of the earliest bishops of Iceland.[19]

After the death of Bishop Ísleifr in 1081, the people of Iceland requested the election of Gizurr, his son, then forty years of age. Like his father, Gizurr had received his education in Herford in Saxony; he had also travelled to Rome with his wife and spent a year in Denmark before being consecrated bishop of Iceland.[20] His connection to the Gregorian cause is evident from the time of his consecration. Due to Archbishop Liemar's suspension, Gizurr could not be consecrated in Hamburg-Bremen and went directly to the pope. Gregory VII had him consecrated by the archbishop of Magdeburg, Hartwig of Spanheim (1079–1102), a trustworthy spokesman of the papal party in the investiture controversy (1076–1122).[21] According to *Hungrvaka*, the

[18] Compare Hjalti Hugason, ed., *Kristni á Íslandi*, 1: *Frumkristni og upphaf kirkju* (Reykjavík, 2000), 258–81, at 262–3.

[19] Aside from *Hungrvaka*, information about Gizurr is recorded in *Íslendingabók*, the story of the settlement and the first institutions of Iceland written by Ari Þorgilsson around 1122–33 and in *Kristni saga*, the narrative of the conversion of Iceland, composed in the early thirteenth century: *Íslendingabók* 10, in *Íslendingabók – Landnámabók*, ed. Jakob Benediktsson, Íslenzk Fornrit 1 (Reykjavík, 1986), 21–6; *Kristni saga* 15–8, in *Biskupa sögur I*, ed. Sigurgeir Steingrímsson, Ólafur Halldórsson and Peter Foote, 2 vols, Íslenzk Fornrit 15 (Reykjavík, 2003), 2: 40–4. These sources are related to one another and, for the purpose of the present study, are treated as synoptic texts.

[20] On Gizurr, see Ármann Jakobsson, 'Hinn fullkomni karlmaður: Ímyndarsköpun fyrir biskupa á 13. Öld', *Studia theologica islandica* 25 (2007), 119–30; on Gizurr's marriage in relation to the Gregorian programme against clerical marriage, see below.

[21] Hartwig was the dedicatee of Bernhard of Hildesheim's *Liber canonum contra Heinricum IV* (1085) and the object of harsh criticism in the pro-imperial *Liber de unitate ecclesiae convervanda*, composed by an anonymous monk of Hirsau in the 1090s: see Melve, *Inventing the Public Sphere*, 529–33. On the extension of Hartwig's authority over Scandinavia in place of Liemar, see Wolfgang Seegrün, *Das Papsttum und Skandinavien bis zur Vollendung der nordischen Kirchenorganisation* (Neumünster, 1967), 99; and Erich

archbishop received Gizurr with honour and distinction, and consecrated him on 4 September 1082; he also provided him with 'everything that was needed', possibly robes and other episcopal
paraphernalia, or material relating to canon law.[22] Before returning
to Iceland, Gizurr spent a further year in Norway, where he accomplished his first duty on behalf of his people, confirming his father's
oath to King Óláfr *kyrri* Haraldsson (1066–93), and thus accepting the
provisions regarding the rights of the Icelanders in Norway.[23]

It seems that Gizurr travelled to Rome during the peak of the
controversy between pope and emperor, and that he told the pope
all the troubles he had suffered on the way.[24] In Rome, it is possible
that Gizurr was subjected to the Gregorian proselytizing and 'charismatic leadership' to which the pope exposed many foreign visitors with
the hope of turning them into trusted Gregorians.[25] Gregory VII's
persuasion may have been even more convincing in the case of Gizurr,
who met the pope during or immediately after Henry IV's second siege
of Rome (summer 1082).[26] Gizurr's two visits to Rome may also be
interpreted as signs of personal obedience to the pope, who had often

---

Hoffmann, *Die heiligen Könige bei den Angelsachsen und den skandinavischen Völkern*
(Neumünster, 1975), 545. It is significant to the discussion of the relations between Rome
and Scandinavia to note that, after Henry IV deposed him in 1085 on account of his
involvement in the Saxon opposition, Hartwig took refuge in Denmark, in the kingdom of
Cnut IV (1080–6), the last of a long line of Danish kings with whom the pope had
personally corresponded and the first Danish saint to be canonized (1101): *Annales
Magdeburgenses, s.a.* 1085, ed. George H. Pertz, MGH SS 16 (Hanover, 1859), 178.

[22] *Hungrvaka* 4 (*Biskupa sögur II*, ed. Ásdís Egilsdóttir, 15–6); compare *Jóns saga helga* 6, in
Biskupa sögur I, ed. Sigurgeir Steinsgrímsson, Ólafur Halldórsson and Foote, 2: 191–2. A
similar phrase is found in *Árna saga*, where it is also said that the Norwegian archbishop gave
the bishop-elect Árni 'decretales cum apparatu' (decretals) at the moment of his consecration: *Árna saga* 8, in *Biskupa sögur III*, ed. Guðrún Ása Grímsdóttir, Íslenzk Fornrit
17 (Reykjavík, 1998), 24.

[23] *DI* 21 (*Diplomatarium Islandicum*, ed. Jón Sigurðsson, 1: 64–8); *Grágás* 248, in *Laws of
Early Iceland: Grágás*, ed. Andrew Dennis, Peter Foote and Richard Perkins, 2 vols
(Winnipeg, 1980), 2: 213.

[24] 'Fór hann þá á fund Gregorii páfa ok sagði honum allan málavöxt sinnar ferðar ok svá
vandræði þau sem um var at vera ámarga vegu' ('He then went on to meet with Pope
Gregory VII and gave him a full account of his travels and the manifold difficulties
involved'): *Hungrvaka* 4 (*Biskupa sögur II*, ed. Ásdís Egilsdóttir, 15); ET: *Bishops in Early
Iceland*, transl. Theodore M. Andersson (London, 2021), 11.

[25] Iain S. Robinson, 'The Friendship Network of Gregory VII', *History* 63 (1978), 1–22,
at 5. See also Kriston R. Rennie, 'Extending Gregory VII's "Friendship Network": Social
Contacts in Late Eleventh-Century', *History* 93 (2008), 475–96.

[26] On the question of Gizurr's involvement in the controversy, see Jón Helgason, *Islands
Kirke fra dens Grundlaeggelse til Reformationen: En Historisk Fremstilling* (Copenhagen,
1925), 63; Jón Jóhannesson, *Íslendinga Saga*, 2 vols (Reykjavík, 1958), 1: 176.

stressed that bishops should demonstrate their devotion to Peter and his vicar by coming *ad limina apostolorum* (to the threshold of the apostles).[27]

Once back in Iceland in 1083, it is apparent that Gizurr organized and strengthened the church in Iceland according to the directives of the Roman church. First, the bishop had a church built and attached to his ancestral land at Skálholt, which he intended to become the bishop's see 'for as long as Christianity was maintained in Iceland'.[28] The association between the Icelandic and the Roman church was strengthened by the dedication of this new cathedral to the Virgin and St Peter. Iceland thus became the first country in Scandinavia to have a (cathedral) church dedicated to the Apostle Peter,[29] a significant move at a time when Gregory VII was giving particular importance to the prince of the apostles and to his own role as his vicar.[30] *Hungrvaka* defines Skálholt as 'the spiritual mother of all the other consecrated buildings in Iceland', and its implicit association with St Peter's Basilica in Rome is made explicit in *Petrs saga postola II*, the thirteenth-century hagiographical saga of the apostle.[31]

Bishop Gizurr also successfully established the payment of Peter's pence. Again, Iceland was the first Scandinavian country to introduce tithing into the official laws of the land.[32] Most scholars overlook the importance of this accomplishment, arguing that the introduction of the tithe benefitted the chieftains, enabling them to access revenues of churches that stood on their lands.[33] In fact, owning churches and cashing their revenues was not the only

---

[27] Compare *Register* 9.1 and 9.20 (MGH Epp. Sel. 2: 569–9, 600–1).

[28] The church was consecrated on Holy Cross Day (14 September), but it is not known when Gizurr had started building the church. For an assessment of the archaeological evidence for this phase of the cathedral church, see Hörður Ágústsson, *Skálholt. Kirkjur* (Reykjavík, 1990), 297–8.

[29] On the cult of saints in post-conversion Scandinavia, see Haki Antonsson, 'Saints and Relics in Early Christian Scandinavia', *Mediaeval Scandinavia* 15 (2005), 51–80.

[30] In his epistles, Gregory VII referred to the saint not just according to the standard practice of the papal chancellery but instrumentally, according to what has been defined his own personal 'Petrine modulation' of the practice: see Michele Maccarrone, 'I Fondamenti "Petrini" del Primato Romano in Gregorio VII', *Studi Gregoriani* (1985), 55–122, at 109.

[31] *Petrs saga postola II* B4, in *Postola Sögur: Legendariske Fortællinger Om Apostlernes Liv Deres Kamp for Kristendommes Udbredelse Samt Deres Martyrdød*, ed. Carl R. Unger (Christiania [Oslo], 1874), 215.

[32] Compare *Hungrvaka* 4 (*Biskupa sögur II*, ed. Ásdís Egilsdóttir, 16–17); *DI* 22 (*Diplomatarium Islandicum*, ed. Jón Sigurðsson, 1: 70–162).

[33] For a comprehensive overview of the establishment of the tithe and its interpretations, see Orri Vésteinsson, *Christianisation*, 67–92.

source of power for the chieftains, who were very limited in how they could dispose of these assets. The law prescribed that church properties were to be listed in cartularies (*máldagar*), that they could not be sold,[34] and that the churches and their priests had to be maintained.[35] The tithe payments also encouraged the formation of parishes, as those who attended a church would pay the tithe there. In this regard, Gizurr ordered a count of farm owners in Iceland, probably in order to establish the distribution of churches and ensuring lay support in their construction. This is evidenced in the foundation of the second diocese of Iceland, Hólar, which Gizurr ordered at the request of his countrymen in 1106.[36] Finally, Magnús Stefánsson has pointed out that the rapid development of the organized system of the church under Gizurr led to the inclusion of a separate section of ecclesiastical laws when the first Icelandic legal code was committed to parchment in the winter of 1117–8.[37] It is significant that the recording of the laws was supervised by Sæmundr Sigfússon, a powerful chieftain and priest. Sæmundr had also supported Gizurr's introduction of the tithe alongside the lawspeaker and poet Markús Skeggjason, who in turn had accompanied Gizurr to the court of the Norwegian king to confirm the rights of the Icelanders in the country. Thus, Sæmundr' and Markús's involvement in Gizurr's decisions exemplifies the support that chieftains gave to the bishop's organization of the church in Iceland.

The extant sources unanimously stress the exceptional prestige of Gizurr's position and present his years of office as a golden age of peace. In contrast to the lack of a central power in Iceland, his authority was so well established, that Norse and foreign accounts – without exception – refer to Gizurr as both king and bishop in his own country:

---

[34] The Old Norse-Icelandic law code known as *Grágás* prescribed that every church keep a record of its property in its register (*máldagi*), which was to be updated regularly and read aloud to the congregation once a year: see *Laws of Early Iceland: Grágás*, ed. Dennis, Foote and Perkins, 1: 32–3.

[35] After their consecration, churches were nominally owned by the bishop, who in turn acted as warden for the patron saint. On the concept of *loca sanctorum* ('places of the saints'), see Paul J. Fouracre, 'The Origins of the Carolingian Attempt to regulate the Cult of Saints', in Paul Hayward and James Howard-Johnston, eds, *The Cult of Saints in Late Antiquity and the Middle Ages: Essays on the Contribution of Peter Brown* (Oxford, 1999), 143–65.

[36] *Hungrvaka* 4 (*Biskupa sögur II*, ed. Ásdís Egilsdóttir, 17–18).

[37] Magnús Stefánson, 'Kirkjuvald eflist', 66.

All the chieftains promised him to be submissive to all of God's ordinances and do whatever he commanded.[38]

He gained great honour and respect from the very outset of his career as bishop, and everybody wished to do exactly as he ordered, young and old, rich and poor, women and men, and it was proper to say that he was both king and bishop over his country as long as he lived.[39]

[After his death] it was the consensus of everyone that there would never be a replacement for him. It was also the view of all prudent men that, by dint of God's benevolence and his own achievements, he was the most distinguished man in Iceland, both among clerical and secular men.[40]

---

[38] 'Allir höfðingjar hétu honum at halda hlýðni um öll Guðs boðorð, þau er hann byði, ef honum yrði byskupsvíglu auðit': *Hungrvaka* 4 (*Biskupa sögur II*, ed. Ásdís Egilsdóttir, 15; *Bishops in Early Iceland*, transl. Andersson, 11).

[39] 'Hann tók tign ok virðing svá mikla þegar snemmendis byskupsdóms síns, ok svá vildi hverr maðr sitja ok standa sem hann bauð, unger ok gamall, sæll ok fátœkr, konur ok karlar, ok var rétt at segja at hann bar bæði konungr ok byskup yfir landinu meðan hann lifði': *Hungrvaka* 4 (*Biskupa sögur II*, ed. Ásdís Egilsdóttir, 16; *Bishops in Early Iceland*, transl. Andersson, 12). Compare 'Episcopum suum habent pro rege; ad illius nutum respicit omnis populus; quicquid ex Deo, ex scripturis, ex consuetudine aliarum gentium ille constituit, hoc pro lege habent' ('They hold their bishop as king. All the people respect his wishes. They hold as law whatever he ordains as coming from God, or from the Scriptures, or even from the worthy practices of other peoples'): Adam of Bremen, *GHEP* 4.36; ET: *History of the Archbishops of Hamburg-Bremen*, transl. Francis J. Tschan, Columbia Records of Civilization 53 (New York, 1959), 217–8.

[40] 'En þat kom ásamt með öllum mönnum at hans þóttusk aldregi iðgjöld fá. Þat hefir ok verit allra vitra manna mál at hann hafi af Guðs góðgipt ok sjálfs sinni atgørvi göfgastr maðr verit á Íslandi, bæði lærðra manna ok ólærðra': *Hungrvaka* 5 (*Biskupa sögur II*, ed. Ásdís Egilsdóttir, 20; *Bishops in Early Iceland*, transl. Andersson, 15). *Morkinskinna*, the ealry thirteenth-century collection of lives of kings of Norway, further elaborates the description of Gizurr as king and bishop by adding the secular dimension of chieftaincy to the praise: 'Þá er Gizurr Ísleifsson kom á fund Haralds konungs var rœtt um at hann vári merkiligr maðr. Þá sagði Haraldr konuungs: "Svá er þat sem ér segið, en þar má gøra vel af þrjá menn. Hann má vera víkingahöfðingi, ok er hann vel til þess fenginn. Þá má hann ok vera konungr af sínu skaplyndi ok er vel fengit. Með þriðja hætti má hann vera byskup, ok þat mun hann helzt hljóta ok mun vera inn mesti ágætismaðr".' ('When Gizurr Isleifsson came to King Haraldr, the king was told that he was a distinguished man. Then King Haraldr said: "What you tell of him could be made into three men. He could be a viking chieftain and has the makings for it. Given his temperament, he could be a king, and that would be fitting. The third possibility is a bishop, and that is probably what he will become, and he will be a most outstanding man."') *Morkinskinna* 46, ed. Ármann Jakobsson and Þórður Ingi Guðjónsson, Íslenzk Fornrit 23 (Reykjavík, 2011), 289–90; ET: *Morkinskinna: The Earliest Icelandic Chronicle of the Norwegian Kings (1030–1157)*, transl. Theodore M. Andersson and Kari Ellen Gade (Ithaca, NY, 2018), 255.

These extracts suggest that Gizurr was considered to exercise a power and authority over both ecclesiastical and secular matters that were pivotal to the establishment of the Roman church in Iceland. The way he achieved this was by negotiating between his role as chieftain and his role as bishop, and by adapting the directives of Rome to the social and cultural context of his homeland, thus achieving the church's goals, while preserving Iceland's peace. While there is no indication that he ever fought for the Gregorian cause in Iceland as other bishops were doing elsewhere,[41] Bishop Gizurr can be regarded as a Gregorian agent in the sense of a bishop who obeyed the directives of the pope and furthered them in his own diocese as best he could. This paralleled the strategy of Gregory VII, who was himself proceeding with care in his correspondence with the Scandinavian kings.[42] Moreover, while elsewhere in Europe the authority of the bishops was undermined by secular rulers, in Iceland, bishops exercised their authority in a context characterized by relatively weak chieftains who were also involved in internal conflicts.[43] Most importantly, the Icelandic bishops were themselves chieftains. Consequently, as in the case of Gizurr, they were able to acquire an authority that was unprecedented. In a sense, through the nationalistic character of combining the secular and the religious, 'Christianity remained on the whole palatable to the Icelanders and in some respects vanquished its own victors.'[44]

If, in the absence of a king, Gizurr himself often acted as one, in the absence of superior religious authority, he also acted as his country's archbishop, dealing personally with the Curia and furthering the pope's directives. As chieftain and bishop, he acted as *primus inter pares* ('first among equals') in both systems, while his double status raised him above both groups. This was necessary if he wanted to succeed in establishing the tenets of the church of Rome in the northernmost province of the church. Some elements of Gizurr's biography are suggestive of his quasi

---

[41] On the importance of the local contexts of action of the bishops in defining their attitude towards enforcing and acting on the tenets of the reform, see, amongst others, Maureen C. Miller, *The Formation of a Medieval Church: Ecclesiastical Change in Verona, 950–1150* (Ithaca, NY, 1993); and John Howe, 'St Berardus of Marsica (d. 1130) "Model Gregorian Bishop"', *JEH* 58 (2007), 400–16.
[42] Cowdrey, 'The Gregorian Reform', 326–34.
[43] Hjalti Hugason, ed., *Kristni á Íslandi*, 218.
[44] Sigurður Nordal, *Icelandic Culture* (Ithaca, NY, 1990), 236–53, esp. 241, 245 (quotation at 245).

papal (self-)representation in the eyes of his contemporaries, and especially in the late-twelfth-century sources. In a sense, the bishop is seen as establishing Iceland's own *Patrimonium sancti Petri* ('the patrimony of St Peter'), donating his own estate and other property to the church he himself had built and dedicated to St Peter, and encouraging others to follow his example.[45] Among Gizurr's donations to his newly built cathedral, *Hungrvaka* mentions a precious purple-white chasuble ('purpurahökul hvítan') that would have been worn by Gizurr and his successors.[46] Although white became the distinctive pontifical colour only later, visual emblems of distinction such as this were important for signalling a special authority.[47] Finally, by far the most significant praise for Gizurr in his role of king, bishop and pope of Iceland, is the interpretation of the events following his death:

> The wisest of men thought that Iceland seemed to decline after the death of Bishop Gizurr just as Rome declined after the fall of Pope Gregory. The loss of Bishop Gizurr pointed in the direction of all the decline in Iceland, both in shipping losses and loss of life with the resulting loss of revenue, and beyond that hostility and lawlessness as well as mortality in the whole country such as had not occurred since the country was settled.[48]

Here, *Hungrvaka* seems not only to be suggesting Gizurr's holiness, but also to be claiming that, in the minds of his countrymen, his

---

[45] Two early-twelfth century charters report that farmer Tanni Tordason and his wife Hallfríðr made donations of land and wealth to the almshouses at Bakka, in the west of Iceland, 'at the advice of Bishop Gizurr': *DI* 24, 25 (*Diplomatarium Islandicum*, ed. Jón Sigurðsson, 1: 167–9, 172–4).

[46] *Hungrvaka* 4 (*Biskupa sögur II*, ed. Ásdís Egilsdóttir, 16).

[47] Gregory VII stressed the papal prerogative of wearing the imperial insignia in his *Dictatus papae*, relying on a tradition that dated to the Donation of Constantine: *Constitutum Constantini* 16, in *Das* Constitutum Constantini, ed. Horst Fuhrmann, MGH Fontes n.s. 10 (Hanover, 1968), 91–3. See also Maureen C. Miller, *Clothing the Clergy: Virtue and Power in Medieval Europe*, c.800–1200 (Ithaca, NY, and London, 2014), 191–2. Among the privileges given to Adalbert in 1059, Leo IX granted his vicar of the North permission to wear a mitre on special occasions of the liturgical calendar: *DI* 18 (*Diplomatarium Islandicum*, ed. Jón Sigurðsson, 1: 59–60).

[48] 'Svá hugðisk at inum virtustum mönnum, at svá þótti drúpa Ísland eptir fráfall Gizurar byskups sem Rómaborgarríki eptir fall Gregorii páfa. En fráfall Gizurar byskups bendi til ættar um öll óhœgendi á Íslandi af óáran, bæði í skipabrotum ok manntjóni ok fjárskaða er því fylgði, en eptir þat ófriðr ok lögleysur ok á þat ofan manndauði sá um allt landit at engi hafði slíkr orðit síðan er landit var byggt': *Hungrvaka* 5 (*Biskupa sögur II*, ed. Ásdís Egilsdóttir, 21; *Bishops in Early Iceland*, transl. Andersson, 16).

authority and power was one and the same with those of the pope. Although here the reference is most probably to Gregory I rather than to Gregory VII, it is worth noting that parallels between the two popes were cited in defence of the legitimacy of the election of Gregory VII, who, like his predecessor, had been a monk, and that these soon became a constituent part of contemporary biographies of the pope, where they had both a laudatory and a legitimizing purpose.[49] It is therefore all the more significant that this parallel is used, apparently for the first time, to highlight Gizurr's prestige and his exceptional role as the founder of the church in Iceland and the establisher of it ecclesiastical tradition.

III. Gizurr and Clerical Marriage

Clerical marriage is another area where Bishop Gizurr seemingly had to compromise his Gregorian identity. Contrary to the multiple prescriptions against clerical marriage promoted by the Curia since the mid-eleventh century, the sources register that Gizurr was married.[50] Like his father Ísleifr, Gizurr married once he came back to Iceland after his ordination as priest in Saxony. His wife was Steinunn Þorgrímsdóttir, a widow, and the couple had five sons and one daughter.[51]

In marrying, Gizurr was following what had been common practice among the Western clergy until the mid-eleventh century, and

---

[49] On the parallels between Gregory I and Gregory VII in the polemicists, see Robinson, *Authority and Resistance*, 31–9. The reception of Gregory I's ecclesiology during the pontificate of Gregory VII has been investigated in Gerhart B. Ladner, 'Gregory the Great and Gregory VII: A Comparison of Their Concepts of Renewal', *Viator* 4 (1973), 1–26; Ovidio Capitani, 'La ricezione di Gregorio Magno durante il pontificato di Gregorio VII', in *Convegno internazionale Gregorio Magno nel XIV centenario della morte: Roma, 22–25 ottobre 2003* (Rome, 2004), 291–319.

[50] For an overview of the issue of clerical marriage during the pontificate of Gregory VII, together with an analysis of the previsions that predate and follow it, see Anne Llewellyn Barstow, *Married Priests and the Reforming Papacy: The Eleventh-Century Struggle* (New York, 1982), 19–45; and Helen Parish, '"A Concubine or an Unlawful Woman": Celibacy, Marriage, and the Gregorian Reform', in eadem, *Clerical Celibacy in the West: c.1100–1700* (Burlington, VT, 2010), 99–134.

[51] All of Gizurr's sons but one (Böðvarr) died young, before their father. His daughter Gróa married Ketill Þorsteinsson, who became the second bishop of Hólar (1122–45). *Hungrvaka* reports that Gróa later became a nun and lived until the days of Bishop Klœngr Þorsteinsson of Skálholt (1152–75). It is unknown whether she took the veil when her husband was elected bishop or perhaps after his death in 1145. We know that Ketill moved north to administer his diocese but died at Skálholt, where Gróa is also said to have died.

what would remain an Icelandic custom amongst clergymen and monastics until the late thirteenth century.[52] Clerical marriage was tolerated if the union had taken place before ordination, otherwise priests were expected and required to abstain sexually from their wives. Some canons even forbade married priests to separate from their wives, since this would be likely to leave their wives and children destitute.[53] Since Gizurr was consecrated bishop when he was forty years old, it is possible that he abstained from intercourse with his wife afterwards, but the sagas do not report this.[54] If that was the case, Gizurr might have been following similar guidelines to those issued by Hamburg-Bremen around the time that his father held office. Unable to limit the lust of his clergy according to the Roman Synod held in Easter 1049, Archbishop Adalbert urged them to exercise caution, if not chastity.[55]

Another feature that is in contrast with Gregorian attitudes, but rather in tune with the tolerance of former times, is that Gizurr neither repudiated nor enslaved his wife. According to the 1051 Roman Synod, the wives and mistresses of the clergy became *ancillae* (servants) of the Lateran.[56] In contrast, *Hungrvaka* reports that Steinunn Þorgrímsdóttir was in charge of the episcopal household at Skálholt while Bishop Gizurr attended to the see.[57] Far from being in a position of servitude, the Old Norse text uses the term 'household management' (*búsforráð*) to refer to

---

[52] On clerical marriage in medieval Iceland, see Jenny M. Jochens, 'The Church and Sexuality in Medieval Iceland', *JMedH* 6 (1980), 377–92, at 382–3; Sigurdson, *The Church in Fourteenth-Century Iceland*, 130–6. Iceland was not the only country where clerical marriage continued to be practised well into the thirteenth century: see, among others, Filippo Liotta, *La Continenza dei chierici nel penserio canonistico classico da Graziano a Gregorio IX* (Milan, 1971).

[53] Michel Dortel-Claudot, 'Le Prêtre et le marriage. Évolution de la législation canonique des origines au XIIe siècle', *L'Année canonique* 17 (1973), 319–44.

[54] Jón Helgason (*Islands Kirke*, 63) expressed his doubts on this matter.

[55] 'Si non caste, tamen caute': Adam of Bremen, *GHEP* 4, schol. 76 [77]. Horst Fuhrmann, 'Adalberts von Bremen Mahnung: "Si non caste, tamen caute"', in Martina Hartmann et al., eds, *Papst Gregor VII. und das Zeitalter der Reform: Annäherungen an eine europäische Wende. Ausgewählte Aufsätze* (Wiesbaden, 2016), 492–99.

[56] Dyan Elliott, 'The Priest's Wife: Female Erasure and the Gregorian Reform', in eadem, *Fallen Bodies: Pollution, Sexuality, and Demonology in the Middle Ages* (Philadelphia, PA, 1998), 81–106.

[57] *Hungvaka* 4 (*Biskupa sögur II*, ed. Ásdís Egilsdóttir, 15). The text presents this arrangement as a practice that had been put in place by Gizurr's own mother, Dalla Þorvaldsdóttir.

Steinunn's role in the household at Skálholt, which echoes the scriptural role of a wife according to Genesis 2: 18 and Titus 2: 4–5.[58]

Rather than representing an explicitly anti-Gregorian stand, Gizurr's marriage seems to reflect older ecclesiastical provisions and probably also the requirements of his own status as chieftain. Following the prescriptions of the pastoral epistles (1 Timothy 3: 2, 12; Titus 1: 5–6), Gizurr only married once and initiated disciplinary action against those members of the clergy who married multiple times. His respect for orthopraxis is evident in the case of Jón Ögmnudsson, the first bishop of Hólar (1106–21), who had married twice, a situation that rendered him unfit for consecration.[59] According to the early-thirteenth-century saga of Bishop Jón, Gizurr referred the matter to the archbishop in Lund, to whom he sent the bishop-elect with a letter that detailed his status.[60] In turn, the archbishop sent Jón to Rome, where the Icelander pleaded his case in front of Pope Paschal II. The saga reports that the pope was astounded by Jón's respect for spiritual marriage, which had brought him to openly confess his sin to the pope himself. Finding that losing such an exemplary bishop would be worse than diverging from orthopraxis, Paschal II set aside 'the objections of the laws' and issued a dispensation to the Icelander.

Jón's case is therefore exemplary of Bishop Gizurr's attitude towards clerical marriage, which he tried to enforce in his own country according to pre-eleventh-century provisions. Furthermore, it shows that papal dispensation was open to the Icelandic clergy, perhaps in consideration of their place at the edge of the Christian world. It is also possible that similar dispensations had been issued to Ísleifr and Gizurr themselves during their visits to the Curia.[61]

---

[58] On the role of women in Norse society, especially after the conversion, see Else Mundal, 'The Double Impact of Christianization for Women in Old Norse Culture', in Kari E. Børresen, Sara Cabibbo and Edith Specht, eds, *Gender and Religion: European Studies* (Rome, 2001), 237–53. A classic study of Norse women remains Jenny Jochens, *Women in Old Norse Society* (Ithaca, NY, 1995).

[59] Joseph Vergier-Boimond, 'Bigamie', in *Dictionnaire de droit canonique* 2 (1947), 853–88.

[60] *Jóns saga* 20–2, in *Jóns saga Hólabyskups ens Helga*, ed. Peter Foote, Michael Chesnutt and Jonna Louis-Jensen (Copenhagen, 2003), 77–81. On this episode, see Joel Anderson, 'Disseminating and Dispensing Canon Law in Medieval Iceland', *Arkiv För Nordisk Filologi* 128 (2013), 79–95.

[61] Jochens, 'Church and Sexuality', 382.

Conclusion

To be 'king of Iceland' is a recurrent sub-theme in Old Norse literature, where it is used to praise or mock the abilities of Icelanders in hyperbolic terms.[62] In the case of Bishop Gizurr Ísleifsson of Skálholt, the sources are unanimous in granting him the title of king in a most laudatory sense, implying a fullness of secular power that transcended the hierarchy of the Icelandic system. With this article, I have provocatively suggested that Bishop Gizurr would equally deserve the title of pope: that is, in recognition of the highest authority in both the secular and the spiritual sphere. This is based on a reading of the sources and an interpretation of the bishop's acts in the context of the Gregorian reform.

Despite the secular nature of the early Icelandic church, *Hungrvaka* stresses Gizurr's connection to the Roman church and suggests that the bishop was, if not a trusted Gregorian agent, at least an aspiring Gregorian bishop with the most powerful say in both the ecclesiastical and secular spheres. This focus on Gizurr's obedience to Rome may be explained in light of the process of interpretation that Haraldur Hreinsson has defined as 'Gregorian hermeneutics': a framework for understanding the discourses of the Christian religion promoted by the archbishopric of Norway in the late twelfth century through texts of ecclesiastical literature.[63] It is not unlikely that the early-thirteenth-century authors of *Hungrvaka* may have shared in this interest and elaborated a Gregorian reading of Gizurr's episcopate that would illustrate the themes of papal and episcopal authority, and the demand for obedience to the Icelandic chieftains.[64]

---

[62]   Theodore M. Andersson, 'The King of Iceland', *Speculum* 74 (1999), 923–34, at 923. The theme was first explored in Hermann Pálsson, 'Brands þáttur örva', *Gripla* 7 (1990), 117–30.

[63]   Haraldur Hreinsson, 'The Apostles and Ecclesiastical Elites in Medieval Iceland: A Gregorian Hermeneutic Turn in the Medieval North', in Grzegorz Pac, Steffen Hope and Jón Viðar Sigurðsson, eds, *The Cult of Saints and Legitimization of Elite Power in East Central and Northern Europe up to 1300*, Comparative Perspectives on Medieval History 2 (Turnhout, 2024), 113–34.

[64]   *Hungrvaka* may have been first authored by Gizurr's own great-nephew, the lawspeaker Gizurr Halsson (1133–93), who 'was held in high esteem at Rome, more so than any other Icelander before him' (*Sturlunga saga*, ed. Jón Jóhannesson, Magnús Finnbogason and Kristján Eldjárn, 2 vols [Reykjavík, 1946], 1: 60). This may also explain the Gregorian agenda behind its composition. On Gizurr Halsson, see Gottskálk Jensson, 'Latin Oratory at the Edge of the World', in Dario Bullitta and Kirsten Wolf, eds, *Saints and their Legacies in Medieval Iceland* (Cambridge, 2021), 99–134.

Although it is clear that Gizurr's actual Gregorianism was far from perfect, I have argued in this article that the bishop was bound to compromise with the system of his land if he wanted to gain the powerbase to organize the church according to the directives of Rome. While he did not fight for ecclesiastical ownership of chieftains' churches, his position as a chieftain was itself instrumental for the success of the church in Iceland, and so were the chieftains that constituted his network of support, such as Sæmundr Sigfússon and Markús Skeggjason. As for clerical marriage, if he deviated from Gregorian demands, Gizurr strictly enforced the orthopraxis that the church had prescribed for centuries, both in his own marriage and in the case of Jón Ögmnudsson's two marriages. In this area too, Gizurr followed ecclesiastical guidelines, which, though pre-Gregorian, were more applicable to his role as chieftain. This suggests that he acted with a pragmatism that was pivotal for furthering the establishment and institutionalization of the church in Iceland.

In conclusion, Bishop Gizurr successfully founded the church in Iceland on the obedience due to St Peter and his vicar. He was also responsible for the enforcement of the tithe payment, which had not been introduced before in Scandinavia. Both these aspects introduced tenets of contemporary papal reform that would be settled in the struggle between bishops and chieftains two centuries later. His attitudes to church ownership and to marriage show a pragmatic ability to adapt the needs of the church to his own context. The respect and devotion Gizurr received from both secular and religious authorities in Iceland and abroad are the signs of his unprecedented authority. If, according to Gregorian formulations, the pope should expect the same obedience that a subject would give to a king, the lack of central authority in Iceland allowed Bishop Gizurr to receive the same obedience as both king and pope.

Infertility and the Margins of Society: Medieval Churchmen think about Reproductive Disorders

Catherine Rider ⓘ

University of Exeter

The history of infertility is a rapidly growing field but the relationship between infertility and religion remains under-studied. This article investigates the ways in which religious writers in the European Middle Ages thought about infertility, focusing (in keeping with the theme of 'margins and peripheries') on how far these sources presented reproductive disorders as leading people to be marginalized or stigmatized. It examines several key sources discussed by earlier scholars before moving on to a detailed analysis of late medieval English retellings of the story of the birth of the Virgin Mary, who was born to her parents in old age. The article argues that there is some evidence that infertility could be viewed as a source of stigma and infertile people as marginalized. However, the narratives of the birth of the Virgin offered a more inclusive view, and were modified by different authors to reflect different experiences of infertility.

The history of infertility is a rapidly growing field, ranging from the ancient world to the twenty-first century. Scholars have shown that experiences of involuntary childlessness are not constant; rather, they are shaped by a host of factors, including a person's gender, age, social group, and the rules for marriage and divorce operating in their society.[1] However, some experiences are recorded relatively frequently, across different societies. One of them is a feeling of marginalization, of being left on the periphery of society and of 'normal' family life. Work that has gathered testimonies from people

Department of Archaeology and History, University of Exeter, Mail Room, Old Library, Prince of Wales Road, Exeter, UK EX4 4SB. E-mail: c.r.rider@exeter.ac.uk.

[1] For overviews, see Gayle Davis and Tracey Loughran, eds, *The Palgrave Handbook of Infertility in History: Approaches, Contexts and Perspectives* (London, 2017); Zubin Mistry, 'Review Essay: Infertility in History and the History of Reproduction', *Gender & History* 32 (2020), 657–75.

Studies in Church History 61 (2025), 186–207 © The Author(s), 2025. Published by Cambridge University Press on behalf of the Ecclesiastical History Society. This is an Open Access article, distributed under the terms of the Creative Commons Attribution licence (http://creativecommons.org/licenses/by/4.0), which permits unrestricted re-use, distribution and reproduction, provided the original article is properly cited.
doi:10.1017/stc.2024.37

who have experienced infertility speaks to these feelings of marginalization. When the American historian Elaine Tyler May advertised for people who were childless (for any reason) to write to her about their experiences for her 1995 history of childlessness in the USA, *Barren in the Promised Land*, she received letters describing a wide range of feelings and situations. Some people had chosen at an early age not to have children, while others found that the children they wanted never came, sometimes despite extensive fertility treatment. Several spoke of feeling marginalized or isolated. For example, Marie Gutierrez wrote that: 'I can't accept the fact that I feel like some sort of alien, all women who are "normal" have children'.[2] Sharon Stoner complained: 'I just wish our society would not look upon us as incomplete people because we did not have children.'[3] A few men recorded similar feelings: Dave Crenshaw wrote that he felt 'alienated from the rest of society, as I knew I never could be one of them'.[4]

In part, these letters reflect a particular moment, and Tyler May argued that the USA in the 1980s saw what she called a 'new pronatalism':[5] having a child was often presented as the moment when you became a real adult, and US media warned of an 'infertility epidemic', especially among educated women who delayed parenthood. However, experiences of marginalization do not only reflect that particular context and have been noted in many different places in the contemporary world.[6] The issue has been less explored historically, however, especially for premodern societies such as those of the Middle Ages. In part, this is because medieval experiences of infertility are difficult to recover. There is much medieval writing about infertility, including treatises on reproductive medicine, saints' lives and miracle narratives, but there are very few first-hand testimonies from people who experienced fertility challenges. One exception – discussed by several scholars – is the letter collection of Francesco and Margarita Datini, wealthy merchants based in fourteenth-century Italy. The couple's marriage remained childless (although Francesco had an

---

[2] Elaine Tyler May, *Barren in the Promised Land: Childless Americans and the Pursuit of Happiness* (Cambridge, MA, 1995), 220.
[3] Ibid. 223.
[4] Ibid. 221.
[5] Ibid. 213.
[6] Lorna Gibb, *Childless Voices: Stories of Longing, Loss, Resistance and Choice* (London, 2019), gives a series of examples throughout her book.

illegitimate child), and several letters contain advice from friends and family, directed to both Francesco and Margarita, on how to conceive.[7] The Datinis, a wealthy couple at the heart of a network of correspondents, do not seem to have been marginalized, but their childlessness was nonetheless noted and discussed by their circle, an experience that may not always have been comfortable. However, it remains difficult to generalize from this one case.

Thinking about infertility in terms of religious history offers a different perspective on medieval experiences of infertility, one that speaks to the issue of margins and peripheries. Religion is a lens through which people think about fertility – and other life experiences – in many societies. In the European Middle Ages, it was particularly important, because of the church's role in shaping marriage law and attitudes to sexuality, but using faith to make sense of fertility issues is not purely a medieval phenomenon. A recent book by two US-based theologians, Candida Moss and Joel Baden, highlights the diverse ways in which the Bible continues to shape experiences of infertility.[8] Moss and Baden argue strongly that biblical views of infertility are not monolithic. They observe that even when the Bible praises fertility as a gift from God, it does not generally present infertility as a sign of divine punishment or blame infertile people for their own childlessness. They also highlight passages, such as Isaiah 54: 1, 'Sing, O barren one, who did not bear' [NRSV], which suggest that not everyone is expected to reproduce and that, in some circumstances, infertility might not be a terrible outcome. For Moss and Baden, this is not just an academic exercise: one aim of the book is to give Christians experiencing reproductive difficulties, and the clergy, therapists and medical professionals who work with them, more diverse ways to think about their experiences.[9]

Religious and biblical views of infertility therefore remain relevant and have the potential to influence people's marginalization, or feelings of marginalization, in a variety of different ways. This in turn suggests a way to approach the medieval evidence. Much of it was

[7] Katharine Park, 'Managing Childbirth and Fertility in Medieval Europe', in Nick Hopwood, Rebecca Flemming and Lauren Kassell, eds, *Reproduction: Antiquity to the Present Day* (Cambridge, 2018), 162–63; Ann Crabb, 'Ne pas être mère. L'autodéfense d'une Florentine vers 1400', *Clio* 21 (2005), 150–61.

[8] Candida R. Moss and Joel S. Baden, *Reconceiving Infertility: Biblical Perspectives on Procreation and Childlessness* (Princeton, NJ, 2015), 16–20.

[9] Moss and Baden, *Reconceiving Infertility*, ix–x.

written by clergy, who were celibate and expected to be childless. Most of these men are unlikely to have had direct experience of seeking children within marriage, although it is nevertheless possible that they felt their lack of children, as some of the men who wrote to Tyler May did. However, clergy who ministered or preached to laypeople probably encountered men and women who were involuntarily childless, and when they retold stories of miraculous fertility, clerical authors sometimes imagined what the experience of infertility might be like. In doing so, they drew on earlier biblical and apocryphal sources, but they varied in their emphasis and details. To explore further how clerical authors might imagine these experiences, this article focuses on a series of later medieval versions of a story that depicts infertility and marginalization: the birth of the Virgin Mary to her parents, Joachim and Anne, who had been married for twenty years without having a child. These retellings, aimed often at a wide audience, described the social exclusion that Mary's parents experienced, and their sadness and anger. This picture of stigma and marginalization can be found in some other medieval sources, as we will see. However, these same narratives of Mary's birth also argued against marginalizing infertile couples in this way, and described a range of possible experiences.

In discussing medieval religious texts relating to infertility, this article will speak to, and extend, the small but growing body of scholarship on infertility and religion in premodern Europe. The subject is still relatively neglected, as most work on medieval and early modern infertility (including my own previously published work) focuses on medical texts and ideas, for which there is a large and well-defined body of evidence. We now have a good understanding of the medical theories relating to infertility, which often ascribed the problem to imbalances in the humours, especially a lack of heat in the man's or woman's body. We can also see how these theories interacted with ideas about gender and age; the range of possible treatments; the transmission of texts on reproductive medicine; and the ways in which this knowledge circulated in the vernacular for lay audiences.[10]

---

[10] Joan Cadden, *Meanings of Sex Difference in the Middle Ages: Medicine, Science, and Culture* (Cambridge, 1995); Monica Green, *Making Women's Medicine Masculine: The Rise of Male Authority in Pre-Modern Gynaecology* (Oxford, 2008); Sarah Toulalan, '"To [o] Much Eating Stifles the Child": Fat Bodies and Reproduction in Early Modern England, *HR* 87 (2014), 65–93; Sarah Toulalan, '"Elderly Years Cause a Total Dispaire of Conception": Old Age, Sex and Infertility in Early Modern England', *Social History of Medicine* 29 (2016), 333–59; Jennifer Evans, 'Female Barrenness, Bodily Access and

By contrast, religious texts have received less attention. Daphna Oren-Magidor, working on sixteenth- and seventeenth-century England, has explored how men and women used the Bible to make sense of their own infertility, but for the Middle Ages, work remains piece-meal.[11] In the 1980s, two pioneering monographs by Sylvie Laurent (on childbirth) and Jean-Claude Bologne (on infertility, contraception and abortion) gave an overview of some of the religious texts that discussed fertility and birth.[12] More recently, Regina Toepfer has examined some of the most influential theological works relating to infertility, as well as medieval and early modern German retellings of the story of Anne and Joachim.[13] Meanwhile, studies of pregnancy and childbirth miracles have considered the relatively small number of conception miracles recorded at saints' shrines.[14] Some of this work investigates the marginalization and stigma that might go with infertility, as we will see below. However, because so many texts remain

---

Aromatic Treatments in Seventeenth-Century England', *HR* 87 (2014), 423–43; Jennifer Evans, '"They Are Called Imperfect Men": Male Infertility and Sexual Health in Early Modern England', *Social History of Medicine* 29 (2016), 311–32; Catherine Rider, 'Men and Infertility in Late Medieval English Medicine', *Social History of Medicine* 29 (2016), 245–66; eadem, 'Men's Responses to Infertility in Late Medieval England', in Davis and Loughran, eds, *The Palgrave Handbook of Infertility in History*, 273–90; eadem, 'Gender, Old Age, and the Infertile Body in Medieval Medicine', in Sara Ritchey and Sharon Strocchia, eds, *Gender, Health, and Healing, 1250–1550* (Amsterdam, 2020), 267–90.

[11] Daphna Oren-Magidor, 'From Anne to Hannah: Religious Views of Infertility in Post-Reformation England', *Journal of Women's History* 27 (2015), 86–108.

[12] Jean Claude Bologne, *La naissance interdite. Stérilité, avortement, contraception au moyen-âge* (Paris, 1988); Sylvie Laurent, *Naître au moyen âge. De la conception à la naissance, la grossesse et l'accouchement (XIIe-XVe siècle)* (Paris, 1987).

[13] Regina Toepfer, *Kinderlosigkeit: Ersehnte, verweigerte und bereute Elternshaft im Mitte-lalter* (Heidelberg, 2020), 23–49, 187–213; ET (of first half): eadem, *Infertility in Medieval and Early Modern Europe: Premodern Views on Childlessness*, transl. Kate Sotejeff-Wilson (London, 2022), 19–50; ET (of second half): eadem, *Negotiating Childlessness in the Middle Ages: Stories of Desired, Refused, and Regretted Parenthood*, transl. Kate Sotejeff-Wilson (York, 2025).

[14] Pierre André Sigal, 'La Grossesse, l'accouchement et l'attitude envers l'enfant mort-né à la fin du moyen âge d'après les récits de miracles', in *Santé, médecine et assistance au moyen âge (Actes du 110e congrès national des sociétés savantes)* (Paris, 1987), 23–41; Ronald C. Finucane, *The Rescue of the Innocents: Endangered Children in Medieval Miracles* (Basingstoke, 1997); Hilary Powell, 'The "Miracle of Childbirth": The Portrayal of Parturient Women in Medieval Miracle Narratives', *Social History of Medicine* 25 (2012), 795–811; Ben Nilson and Ruth Frost, 'Attitudes to Pregnancy, Childbirth and Postnatal Complications in Medieval English Miracula', *Gender & History*, early view, online at: <https://onlinelibrary.wiley.com/doi/10.1111/1468-0424.12735>, accessed 7 March 2024.

unexplored, we do not have a clear sense of how far medieval religious views of infertility varied, geographically or over time. Nor is it clear how far individual authors reimagined their source materials or reflected on infertile people's experiences.

This article will explore these questions by focusing on how stories about the miraculous conception of the Virgin Mary were retold in late medieval England. The first part will explore some of the general comments made by medieval religious writers about infertility, and the ways in which historians have approached them. The second and third sections will then move on to discuss a series of saints' lives and sermons for the feasts of the conception and nativity of the Virgin Mary (8 December and 8 September), as well as a *Life of St Anne*. The story of Mary's miraculous conception was an old one, which first appeared in an apocryphal infancy gospel, the *Protevangelium of James*, probably written in the late second or early third century.[15] The *Protevangelium* was widely copied and translated into numerous languages, and for Latin audiences it was incorporated into two later works, *The Gospel of Pseudo-Matthew* (written between *c.*550 and 800, likely seventh-century) and *The Gospel of the Nativity of Mary* (*c.*1000): two versions which gave different emphases to the story, as we will see.[16] Thanks to these two retellings, the *Protevangelium's* account had a profound influence on medieval and, later, Catholic ideas about Mary, despite its non-canonical status.[17] The story was retold many times in the later Middle Ages and offers one of the most detailed religious narratives about infertility and miraculous, delayed conception.

MEDIEVAL SOURCES AND APPROACHES TO INFERTILITY AND MARGINALIZATION

Several historians have highlighted sources that suggest infertility could lead to stigma and isolation in the Middle Ages. For example, Sylvie Laurent discussed how infertility was viewed as a divine

---

[15] Paul Foster, 'The *Protevangelium of James*', in Paul Foster, ed., *The Non-Canonical Gospels* (London, 2008), 110–25, at 113; Ronald F. Hock, *The Infancy Gospels of James and Thomas* (Santa Rosa, CA, 1995), 11–12.

[16] For dates see Brandon W. Hawk, *The Gospel of Pseudo-Matthew and the Nativity of Mary* (Cambridge, 2019), 26, 113.

[17] Foster, '*Protevangelium of James*', 112, 124–5; Hawk, *Gospel of Pseudo-Matthew and the Nativity of Mary*, 1.

punishment for the couple's sins.[18] In support of this, she quoted an early- to mid-fourteenth-century preaching handbook by John Bromyard, a Dominican friar based in Herefordshire. Bromyard described at length how God had created marriage for the purpose of having children, but he went on to ask why 'many' (*multi*) married couples remained childless. His answer was that many people married not primarily in order to have children, but for other reasons, such as money or lust.[19] He argued that these people did not use the sacrament of marriage as God intended, and so God withheld the blessing of children from them. For 'if married people intended the same goal as God intends, and used this sacrament ordained by Him reverently, it would seem to be amazing, in fact almost irrational and almost impossible, that they would be denied [marriage's] lawful goal and the blessing of children.'[20]

Because of the way it links infertility with sin and lust, this passage has been discussed by scholars interested in the history of contraception, even though Bromyard does not explicitly mention birth control as one of the sins he had in mind. His argument is hard to follow in places, and the various possible interpretations in relation to birth control have been discussed helpfully by Peter Biller.[21] The thrust, though, is to link childlessness within marriage with God's displeasure and with sinful behaviour. Bromyard's remarks thus suggest that couples experiencing infertility might find clergy (and perhaps laypeople too) viewing them negatively, as having done something to forfeit God's blessing of children.

Another scholar who emphasized the social stigma and marginalization that could result from infertility was Ronald Finucane, in his 1997 study of children in medieval miracle narratives. In a short discussion of fertility miracles, he commented that, in cases of infertility, 'the couple well knew what to expect from kin and neighbours:

---

[18] Laurent, *Naître au moyen âge*, 46–7.

[19] '[A]d finem libidinis vel diuitiarum quem intendunt, quem deus nec intendit nec ordinat.' John Bromyard, *Summa Praedicantium* (Nuremberg, 1518), 'Matrimonium', art. 4, fol. 202ᵛ.

[20] '[S]i coniuges eundem quem deus intendit intenderent finem, et modo ab ipso ordinato hoc sacramento reuerenter uterentur, mirabile - immo quasi irrationabile - et quasi impossibile videretur quod fine debito et prolis frustrarentur mercede.' Ibid.

[21] P. P. A. Biller, 'Birth-Control in the West in the Thirteenth and Early Fourteenth Centuries', *P&P* 94 (1982), 3–26, at 15 n. 50, and references cited there.

sterility brought shame and disappointment.'[22] Finucane cites as an example of this a miracle recorded at the shrine of St Thomas Cantilupe, bishop of Hereford, in around 1300, as part of his canonization process. A woman came to Cantilupe's shrine, asking for a child: many people thought she was infertile and she held this 'as if it were a reproach' (*quasi pro opprobrio*). After visiting the shrine, she had twins.[23]

Regina Toepfer has recently argued that this type of marginalization is embedded in one narrative strand of the Bible, which told of a series of infertile women who went on to conceive special children miraculously, including Sarah, the wife of Abraham; Rachel, the wife of Jacob; Hannah, the mother of Samuel; and Elizabeth, the mother of John the Baptist.[24] The stories of Rachel (Genesis 29–30) and Hannah (1 Samuel 1) include the most detail about the women's emotional responses to their situation. Both women's husbands had children by another wife, and the Bible talks about the women's sadness at their infertility, as well as how Hannah was mocked by her husband's fertile wife, Peninnah. Eventually, of course, both women went on to conceive special children, and Rachel is recorded as saying: 'God has taken away my reproach [in the Latin Vulgate text, *opprobrium*]' (Genesis 30: 23; NRSV).

There are, therefore, medieval sources that place infertile people on the margins of the Christian community, depicting them as feeling reproached (in the Cantilupe miracle) or (in Bromyard's case) as being potentially sinful, and there were biblical models for presenting things this way. However, these instances do not tell the full story. From Finucane's account, we have a relatively brief account of one miracle. The story may or may not be representative of wider experiences: other accounts of fertility miracles often do not mention this type of shame or marginalization. There are also signs that the anonymous author of the Cantilupe miracle modelled his reference to the woman's reproach on the biblical text: the phrase *quasi pro opprobrio* recalls the word used by Rachel in Genesis 30: 23. This does not necessarily mean the reproach was not real, but it suggests that the author was echoing the Bible text to present the experience of infertility in this way. Moreover,

---

[22] Finucane, *Rescue of the Innocents*, 18.

[23] Ibid. 17–18; *ActaSS*, Oct. 2, col. 686.

[24] Toepfer, *Infertility in Medieval and Early Modern Europe*, 22–3.

his emphasis on the woman's shame and sadness served to make the eventual birth of twins even more miraculous.

Similarly, John Bromyard's is only one voice. I have not found other treatises on preaching that suggest infertility was a punishment for acting against God's purpose for marriage. I have argued elsewhere, in relation to magic, that Bromyard's views were often stricter than those found in other works on preaching and confession.[25] There is as yet no detailed study of his thought on sexuality or marriage which can confirm whether his views on these topics were equally severe, but it is at least possible that with infertility, too, he took a harsher view, and expressed it more forcefully, than many of his clerical contemporaries.[26]

In fact, as other scholars have pointed out, attitudes to infertility are likely to have been complex. Jean-Claude Bologne, in one of the earliest studies to look at medieval infertility in detail, pointed to sources and genres where stigma and marginalization were prominent themes, notably in romance literature. Nonetheless, he argued for a diversity of views, pointing to the narratives of the birth of the Virgin Mary among other sources.[27] This diversity of views should not be surprising since, as the work of Moss and Baden and Toepfer highlights, the Bible, which provided many models for thinking about infertility in religious terms, did not speak with a single voice on the matter.[28]

Even within marriage, messages about the value of having children might be qualified. On the one hand, there was an expectation that marriage would result in children, and contemporaries expressed anxiety about royal and elite marriages which did not produce male heirs.[29] On the other hand, marriage theology and law, drawing on St Augustine, but much developed in the twelfth and thirteenth centuries, viewed reproduction as an important justification for marriage, and for sex within marriage, but not the only justification. Marriage was also a way of giving men and women a legitimate outlet for their sexual desire, and a sacrament that represented the love between Christ

---

[25] Catherine Rider, *Magic and Religion in Medieval England* (London, 2012), 64–7.

[26] On the manuscripts and date of the *Summa*, see Alexander Holland, 'John Bromyard's *Summa Praedicantium*: an Exploration of Late Medieval Falsity through a Fourteenth-Century Preaching Handbook' (PhD thesis, University of Kent, 2018), 59–80, 118–23.

[27] Bologne, *Naissance interdite*, 213–18.

[28] Moss and Baden, *Reconceiving Infertility*, 104–5; Toepfer, *Kinderlosigkeit*, 30–1.

[29] Robert Bartlett, *Blood Royal: Dynastic Politics in Medieval Europe* (Cambridge, 2020), 62–8.

and the Church.[30] Therefore, even people who knew themselves to be infertile could still legitimately marry and have sexual intercourse. For example, Peter Lombard, in a hugely influential textbook on theology, noted that some couples 'because of defect of age or some other cause, are not able to engender children,' but this did not invalidate their marriages.[31] Thus, despite the existence of sources that spoke of marginalization, from a legal and theological point of view, the marriages of couples experiencing infertility were still valid and indissoluble.

These voices are disparate, because they think about childlessness and infertility in the context of larger discussions of other issues, such as marriage law and practice, or as one among many miracle narratives. They do not add up to a consistent view: for example, the fact that infertility did not invalidate a marriage does not mean that childlessness within marriage was regarded as a positive thing for – or by – most people. Nor can we assume that biblical narratives of miraculous conception offered comfort to people who never went on to have the children they prayed for. However, this inconsistency is itself important. There were different strands to medieval churchmen's writing on infertility, drawing on earlier texts which themselves offered different models. These models might prompt later medieval writers to present the experience of infertility differently, depending on their audiences and interests. We can see this in late medieval English retellings of the conception and birth of the Virgin Mary.

The Birth of the Virgin: Marginalization in the Pre-Christian Past?

The story of Mary's birth to her parents, Anne and Joachim, is modelled on the Old and New Testament stories about special children like Isaac, Jacob, Joseph, Samuel and John the Baptist, all of whom were born after their parents had been infertile for long periods. The *Golden Legend* of Jacobus de Voragine, a hugely popular collection of saints' lives compiled in the mid- to late thirteenth century which survives in hundreds of manuscripts, formed the source for many later medieval versions. It was written to provide material for

---

[30] Pierre J. Payer, *The Bridling of Desire: Views of Sex in the Later Middle Ages* (Toronto, 1993), 75–6.
[31] Peter Lombard, *The Sentences* 4.31.2, transl. Giulio Silano (Toronto, 2010), 179.

preachers, but by the end of the thirteenth century, it was also being read by elite laypeople, so its message could reach lay audiences both directly (through reading) and indirectly (through preaching).[32] Jacobus's account of the nativity of the Virgin Mary told how Anne and Joachim, who were virtuous and charitable, had been married for twenty years without having a child. One day, Joachim went to make an offering at the Temple in Jerusalem, but the priest publicly humiliated and excluded him because of his childlessness:

> When the priest saw him, he angrily ordered him away and upbraided him for presuming to approach the altar of God, declaring that it was not proper for one who was subject to the Law's curse to offer sacrifice to the Lord of the Law, nor for a sterile man, who made no increase to the people of God, to stand among men who begot sons. Joachim, seeing himself thus rejected, was ashamed to go home and face the contempt of his kinsmen, who had heard the priest's denunciation.[33]

Instead of going home, Joachim went to live with his shepherds, and his disappearance caused Anne to assume he was dead. Later, an angel appeared to Joachim and told him that he and Anne would have a child. The angel also said the priest had been wrong to denounce Joachim, and offered a very different perspective on the couple's infertility: 'I have seen how you were put to shame, and heard the reproach of childlessness wrongly put upon you. God punishes not nature but sin, and therefore, when he closes a woman's womb, he does this in order to open it miraculously later on.'[34] The angel went on to list as examples several infertile women in the Bible who later had special children: Sarah, Rachel, the anonymous mother of Samson, and Hannah.

Here it was the man, not the woman, who was depicted as being excluded and humiliated because of infertility. Jacobus later described Anne weeping, but in his version of the story, she was said to be weeping because her husband had disappeared, 'not knowing where her husband had gone,' rather than explicitly because she was

---

[32] Giovanni Paolo Maggioni, 'Thirteenth-Century *Legendae Novae* and the Preaching Orders: A Communication System', in Samantha Kahn, ed., *Hagiography and the History of Latin Christendom 500-1500* (Leiden, 2019), 101–4, 117.
[33] Jacobus de Voragine, *The Golden Legend: Readings on the Saints*, transl. William Granger Ryan, 2nd edn (Princeton, NJ, 2012; first publ. 1993), 537–8.
[34] Ibid. 538.

childless.[35] Here the *Golden Legend*'s retelling differed from the original account in the *Protevangelium of James*, and also from the Latin version in the *Pseudo-Gospel of Matthew*, both of which described how Anne quarrelled with her slave, who told her that God had made her infertile. Then, upset, Anne lamented her situation, comparing herself to the birds and other creatures in the natural world that had offspring. She was then visited by an angel who told her she would conceive.[36] Instead, Jacobus's version is closer to another popular Latin version, the *Nativity of Mary*, which omitted the scenes featuring Anne and instead included the angel's speech to Joachim.[37]

Jacobus's version may simply reflect his sources, but it may also represent a choice to tell the story in this way: he drew on a wide range of hagiographical texts when compiling the *Golden Legend*, so he may well have known of the alternative episodes featuring Anne and chosen to omit them.[38] If so, it is difficult to know why. He often abbreviated his sources, boiling a story down to its essentials and focusing on episodes that would provide engaging material for sermons.[39] Perhaps he felt that Anne's reaction was not necessary to the story. Perhaps he also preferred the clear message the angel delivered to Joachim that infertility was not the result of sin. Whatever the reason, the story, as it was transmitted influentially by the *Golden Legend*, focused on the exclusion of a man.

This is revealing for what it suggests about the gendering of infertility. It is often assumed that infertility in the Middle Ages was viewed as a problem that lay in the woman. This assumption fits much of our evidence, but it obscures substantial differences between different situations and types of source material. For example, male infertility was recognized by medical writers as a possibility, although most of the time it was probably not the first explanation suggested by either doctors or their clients.[40] Treatment could be a different issue from causation: Joan Cadden, working on learned Latin medical texts, has argued that these works often presented women as the focus of

---

[35] Ibid. 538.

[36] Hock, *Infancy Gospels of James and Thomas*, 35–7; Hawk, *Gospel of Pseudo-Matthew and the Nativity of Mary*, 48–9.

[37] Hawk, *Gospel of Pseudo-Matthew and the Nativity of Mary*, 128–32.

[38] Steven A. Epstein, *The Talents of Jacopo da Varagine: A Genoese Mind in Medieval Europe* (Ithaca, NY, 2015), 68.

[39] Maggioni, 'Thirteenth-Century *Legendae Novae*', 102.

[40] Rider, 'Men and Infertility', 266.

treatment, but recipes for medicines did sometimes expect men to play a role in the treatment alongside their wives.[41] The *Golden Legend* reminds us that marginalization is a separate issue again from causation or treatment, and so experiences of infertility might be complex and gendered in different ways.

How might this story relate to the actual experiences of men and women in the Middle Ages? On the one hand, the story of Anne and Joachim was set in the distant, pre-Christian past, and the Jewish priest was shown to be wrong to have excluded Joachim. The story also described a case of miraculous fertility which led to the birth of a unique child. It did not necessarily mean God would act like this in all cases, and so offer reassurance to lay audiences. On the other hand, in Jacobus de Voragine's version, the angel speaks in universal terms. He says that when God closes a woman's womb, he does this in order that he may later open it miraculously. He does not say this is what God is doing in Joachim's case; he says this is what God does. The angel's message is also clear: Joachim and Anne are not being punished by God, and other virtuous people have experienced infertility. The priest was wrong to exclude Joachim.

We can explore some of the possible ways this story related to experience in one context – late-fourteenth- and fifteenth-century England – by looking at some of the retellings in Middle English vernacular sermons and saints' lives. These often drew on the *Golden Legend*, but they also edited the text, cutting sections, adding extra details, and incorporating information from other sources; although the exact transmission of this material is often hard to trace. They were written at a time when increasing numbers of laypeople were reading devotional works in the vernacular, and when the cult of St Anne was growing in popularity. Gail McMurray Gibson and Elizabeth L'Estrange have argued that Anne was sometimes used as a role model for late medieval men and women who were expected to produce children (appearing in books of hours, for example), and have shown how those who were seeking to have a child sometimes appealed to Anne for help.[42]

---

[41] Cadden, *Meanings of Sex Difference in the Middle Ages*, 249; Rider, 'Men's Responses to Infertility', 273–90.

[42] Gail McMurray Gibson, 'Saint Anne and the Religion of Childbed: Some East Anglian Texts and Talismans', in Kathleen Ashley and Pamela Sheingorn, eds, *Interpreting Cultural Symbols: Saint Anne in Medieval Society* (Athens, GA, 1990), 95–110; Elizabeth L'Estrange, *Holy Motherhood: Gender, Dynasty and Visual Culture in the Later Middle Ages* (Manchester, 2008), 13, 44–6.

The later fourteenth and fifteenth centuries were also a time when fertility and childlessness within marriage are likely to have been a prominent concern. The immediate context for the Middle English retellings was the period after the Black Death, which had led to a catastrophic fall in population. Demographic studies of England have shown that population growth remained low until at least the mid-fifteenth century, due to high mortality rates caused by repeated outbreaks of plague. This had consequences for the fertility of families: in the second half of the fourteenth century, around twenty-nine per cent of landowners had no child to succeed them and, even after the 1450s, when the population began to recover, around eighteen per cent of landowners left no child.[43] These figures do not just include those left childless by infertility, but also high rates of infant and child mortality, but anxiety about being left childless must have been real. At the same time, there were prominent cases of royal childlessness: Richard II and his wife Anne of Bohemia had no children, while Henry VI and his wife Margaret of Anjou had been married for eight years before a son was born.[44] In this context, the many vernacular retellings of Anne and Joachim's story might tell us something about the concerns of their lay readers and listeners, as well as the clergy who wrote them.

One of the most widely copied and influential sermon collections from late medieval England was the *Festial* of John Mirk, a collection of sermons for saints' feast days probably written in the 1380s. Mirk was a priest and Augustinian canon, who wrote to provide sermons for parish priests to use with their congregations.[45] The *Festial* was widely copied, surviving in twenty-two complete manuscripts, plus an additional later revised version in four manuscripts, and further manuscripts containing one or more individual sermons. It was also printed several times in the late fifteenth and early sixteenth centuries.[46]

[43] S. J. Payling, 'Social Mobility, Demographic Change, and Landed Society in Late Medieval England', *Economic History Review* 45 (1992), 51–73, at 54.

[44] On these cases, see Kristen Lee Geaman, 'Childless Queens and Child-like Kings: Negotiating Royal Infertility in England, 1382–1471' (PhD thesis, University of Southern California, 2013).

[45] John J. Thompson, 'Preaching with a Pen: Audience and Self-Regulation in the Writing and Reception of John Mirk and Nicholas Love', in Martha W. Driver and Veronica O'Mara, eds, *Preaching the Word in Manuscript and Print in Late Medieval England: Essays in Honour of Susan Powell* (Turnhout, 2013), 101–16, at 103.

[46] H. Leith Spencer, *English Preaching in the Late Middle Ages* (Oxford, 1993), 277–8; Thompson, 'Preaching with a Pen', 105.

Evidence suggests that some manuscripts of the *Festial* were owned by its target audience of parish priests, and so, indirectly, its content may have reached their lay congregations.[47] A few other manuscripts also contain Latin works for better-educated priests, while a few again might have had lay readers.[48]

Mirk includes two sermons on Mary's conception, one for the feast of the conception of the Virgin and one for the feast of her nativity. Both, like the rest of the *Festial*, draw heavily on the *Golden Legend*, but the *Golden Legend*'s material is divided between the two sermons, with the bulk of the account of Mary's conception falling into Mirk's sermon on the conception of Mary.[49] However, Mirk's editing of his source material produced some interesting differences between the *Festial* and the *Golden Legend*. Joachim's response to the priest's rebuke changes slightly. The encounter with the priest – Mirk calls him a 'bishop' – follows the *Golden Legend* quite closely, but after being excluded, Joachim is ashamed, and weeps.[50] The detail of his weeping is not mentioned in the *Golden Legend*, but it gives a little more emphasis to Joachim's emotional response.

There are other differences. Unlike in the *Golden Legend*, but as in earlier versions of the story, including the *Protevangelium*, Anne laments her childlessness, saying: 'Lord, woe is me for I am barren and may have no fruit, and now, moreover, my husband is gone from me'.[51] Later, after being told by the angel that she will have a child, Anne thanks God for curing her infertility: 'for I was a widow [thinking Joachim was dead] and now I am a wife; I was barren and now I shall have a child; I was in woe and weeping and now I shall be in joy and pleasure'.[52] However, Mirk omits the angel's speech to Joachim, so there is no statement that infertility is not, in fact, God's punishment. In this version, then, there is more emphasis on the sadness of both Anne and Joachim. Meanwhile, the 'bishop' is still

---

[47] Thompson, 'Preaching with a Pen', 105–7; *John Mirk's Festial*, ed. Susan Powell, EETS o.s. 334–5, 2 vols (Oxford, 2009–11), 1: xix.

[48] *John Mirk's Festial*, ed. Powell, 1: xlvi.

[49] Ibid. 1: xxxii.

[50] Ibid. 1: 17.

[51] 'Lord me ys woo for y am bareyn and may have no fryt, and now, more, myn hosbond ys gon fro me.' Ibid. 1: 18.

[52] '[F]or Y was a wydewe and now Y am a wyf; Y was baren and now Y shal haue a chyld; Y was in woo and wepyng and now Y schal ben in ioye and lykyng.' Ibid.

shown to be wrong to exclude Joachim, but this is less strongly emphasized. In this way, Mirk places a subtly greater emphasis on the ways in which infertility leads to marginalization (and the emotional responses to that), without the corresponding reassurance that it can happen to virtuous people as part of God's plan.

This emphasis on marginalization also appears in the much shorter account in Mirk's sermon for the nativity of the Virgin. There Mirk highlighted 'the joy and the gladness' Anne and Joachim felt when Mary was born, but also mentions their previous marginalization: 'by her birth, the great reproofs that they had suffered for such a long time because of *hur* [=her/their] barrenness were then put away, and from that time they went forth boldly among others of their lineage with worship and honour.'[53] The manuscript used as a base text for the modern edition uses 'hure' for both 'her' and 'their', so it is unclear whether Mirk was referring to 'her (i.e. Anne's) barrenness' or 'their (i.e. Anne and Joachim's) barrenness'.[54] Given that Mirk's Anne laments in his sermon for the conception of the Virgin that she is infertile, 'her' is perhaps more likely, but either reading is possible. Whoever was deemed to be the source of the infertility, however, the exclusion and emotional responses are presented as shared by Anne and Joachim.

Mirk's text was not stable, and a revised version of the *Festial* from the early fifteenth century tells a slightly different story. This version reinserted material from the *Golden Legend* and other works. Susan Powell and Helen Leith Spencer have argued that the anonymous redactor was likely to have been based in a university and was probably trying to add more scholarly material to the text for an academic audience.[55] Here, in the sermon for the conception of the Virgin, Joachim is described as 'confused and ashamed', but – as in the *Golden Legend* – he does not weep. Also following the *Golden Legend*, Anne does not lament her infertility, but the angel's speech to Joachim is reinstated: God 'sees the shame that you have because your wife Anne is barren. But I, the angel of God, am sent to comfort you. I tell you

---

[53] '[B]e þe burth of huer þe grete repreues þat þei haddon sufred so long tyme for hur barennesse þanne was putte away, and fro þat tyme þei went forth boldely among othur of hur lynage with worschep and honure.' Ibid. 2: 222.

[54] Ibid. 2: 660. I am grateful to Eddie Jones for pointers on how to approach translating *hur*.

[55] Ibid. 1: liii–liv; Spencer, *English Preaching*, 313–4.

God punishes sin, but not nature.'[56] A version of Mirk's sermon that was less closely tied to a parish context, and to a lay audience who might encounter or experience reproductive disorders, seems to have placed fidelity to the *Golden Legend* above discussing the marginalization and sadness that couples might experience.

By contrast, the *Speculum Sacerdotale*, another set of sermons from the early fifteenth century, written (like the *Festial*) for parish priests, but seemingly less popular and surviving in only one manuscript, pays more attention to Anne's feelings of exclusion.[57] The *Speculum*'s sermon for the nativity of Mary includes the speech Anne makes in the *Protevangelium of James* and in the *Gospel of Pseudo-Matthew*, in which she compares herself to the birds and animals who have offspring.[58] When Joachim goes missing, Anne prays:

> And as she prayed, she saw above her head a nest of birds in the tree, and she set then to prayer, lamentation and sorrow, and said: 'Lord,' she said, 'To whom shall I be likened? I am not like the birds of the sky, for they have young, and fruit of their bodies; nor to the beasts of the earth, for they engender and bring forth fruit; nor yet to the waters, for they bring forth fishes; nor yet to the trees, for they bring forth branches and fruits in their time. And each one of them blesses you and loves you according to their nature.'[59]

Here, infertility is something that marginalizes people not just in the human world, but also in comparison to the natural world, where everything produces offspring and praises God for it: everything, that is, except Anne.

[56] '[S]ees þe shame þt þu haste bicause þi wife Anne is bareyn. But I þe aungell of god am sent to þi confort I tell þe god takith vengeance for syn, but not of nature.' London, BL, MS Harley 2247, fol. 138ʳ.

[57] Spencer, *English Preaching*, 75, 277.

[58] There is also a short sermon for the Conception of the Virgin in this collection, which focuses on the later adoption of the feast: *Speculum Sacerdotale*, ed. Edward H. Weatherly, EETS o.s. 200 (London, 1936), 250–1.

[59] 'And as sche prayede, sche seeþ a-boue here hed a neste of breddes in the tre, and sche put then to hire prayere lementacion and sorowe and sayde: 'Lorde,' sche sayde, 'To whome schal I be lickened? I am noȝt like to bryddes of heuene, for they haue pulles and fruyte of hem, ne to bestes of þe erþe, for they engendreþ and bryngeþ forþ fruyte, ne ȝit to watres, for they brynge forþe fysshes, ne ȝet to trees, for they brynge forþe braunches and fruytis in here tymes. And ychone of hem blesseþ the and loueþ the in here kynde.' *Speculum Sacerdotale*, ed. Weatherly, 199.

Finally, the *Life of St Anne*, written in verse form by Osbern Bokenham, an Augustinian friar based at Clare Priory in Suffolk, speaks most clearly to the possible experience of infertility. Bokenham wrote a series of lives of female saints in English verse for several East Anglian noble and gentry women between 1443 and 1447, later copied together under the title *Legends of Holy Women*. These were based on the *Golden Legend*, but with some adaptations, as we will see. The *Life of St Anne* was commissioned by Katherine Denston, the wife of a wealthy Suffolk merchant named John Denston, and it speaks directly to the Denstons' own fertility concerns. As Gail McMurray Gibson and more recently Mary Beth Long have pointed out, at the end of the poem, Bokenham asks Anne to help Katherine and John have a son (they already had a daughter, named Anne).[60] Perhaps linked to this, as both Long and Alice Spencer have noted, Bokenham places particular emphasis on Anne's and Joachim's emotional responses to their infertility, following Joachim's exclusion from the Temple.[61] He discusses Anne's feelings first. She prays 'with great sadness, oppressed and prostrate'.[62] As in the *Protevangelium of James* and in the *Speculum Sacerdotale*, she sees the birds feeding their young and laments her childlessness but, unlike in the *Speculum*, she accepts God's will: 'I thank you, lord, that you have done what pleases you with me, excluding me from the gift of your benignity: such is my lot.'[63] Then the angel comes to Anne, with the news that she will conceive. However, after this, she quarrels with her maid, the maid mocks her for being childless and she weeps.[64] This order of events is the same as in the popular *Gospel of the Nativity of Mary*, but Bokenham's decision to reproduce the maid's rebuke (not found in the *Speculum Sacerdotale*) underlines the stigma Anne faces, as well as her changing feelings, as they move from grief, to acceptance, to joy, and back to sadness.

---

[60] Gibson, 'Saint Anne and the Religion of Childbed', 107; Mary Beth Long, *Marian Maternity in Late Medieval England* (Manchester, 2023), 169.

[61] Alice Spencer, *Language, Lineage and Location in the Works of Osbern Bokenham* (Cambridge, 2013), 75–6; Long, *Marian Maternity*, 170–3.

[62] *Legendys of Hooly Wummen by Osbern Bokenham*, ed. Mary S. Serjeantson, EETS o.s. 206 (Oxford, 1938), 47; ET: *A Legend of Holy Women: A Translation of Osbern Bokenham's Legends of Holy Women*, transl. Sheila Delany (Notre Dame, IN, 1992), 35.

[63] *Legendys of Hooly Wummen*, ed. Serjeantson, 48–9 (*A Legend of Holy Women*, transl. Delany, 36).

[64] *Legendys of Hooly Wummen*, ed. Serjeantson, 50.

In Bokenham's retelling, Joachim also articulates his sadness and feelings of exclusion in detail.[65] In a speech whose source I have not identified, Joachim ascribes the couple's infertility to Anne, describing how he has 'laboured in vain for twenty years' and his seed has been 'lost'.[66] He also reflects on the shame of public exclusion and his feelings of being less of a man: 'I lack the proof of manhood, and when men are counted I am left behind … when I think of the shame I felt when the bishop ordered me out of the temple and despised my offering, I want to mourn.'[67] Mary Beth Long has suggested that Joachim's shame results more from his public humiliation than from the infertility itself, and if so, this may reflect a fear of the public stigma surrounding infertility, as well as private sadness.[68] The range of emotions and models offered in Bokenham's retelling is thus more varied than in most other versions, talking at some length, and prominently, about both Anne and Joachim's sadness and feelings of exclusion. This set of varied, and changing, emotions may well have been intended to resonate with a patron who was experiencing fertility challenges, and so may reflect what Bokenham perceived the experience of infertility and exclusion to be.

Within Middle English retellings of this single story, then, we find subtly different perspectives on infertility and margins. The basic message is the same: Joachim and Anne were saintly people, and God had a plan to give them a special child, but the description of their experience differs. These versions vary in how far Joachim's treatment by the priest is criticized by the angel, and how clearly the angel states that infertility is not a divine punishment. They also vary in how far they discuss the couple's emotional responses, with some authors giving more space to this than others. As Kristen Geaman and Mary Beth Long have noted, different authors also placed different emphasis on how far Joachim, as well as Anne, was held responsible for the couple's infertility.[69] Beyond the question of responsibility, however, the emotional response is also gendered in a variety of ways. In many versions of the story, it is Joachim who is described as

[65] A point also made by Long, *Marian Maternity*, 169.

[66] *Legendys of Hooly Wummen*, ed. Serjeantson, 50–1 (*A Legend of Holy Women*, transl. Delany, 37).

[67] *Legendys of Hooly Wummen*, ed. Serjeantson, 51 (*A Legend of Holy Women*, transl. Delany, 37).

[68] Long, *Marian Maternity*, 171–2.

[69] Geaman, 'Childless Queens and Child-like Kings', 54–8; Long, *Marian Maternity*, 170.

marginalized and saddened following his public humiliation at the Temple, but only Bokenham links this to a sense that his manhood is threatened. There is more variation in how far Anne's emotions are discussed. Bokenham – writing for a woman who was herself struggling with infertility – gives Anne's emotions the most space. It seems likely that other versions, with a less clearly female audience in mind, regarded female responses as less important to discuss than Bokenham did.

In some cases, these changes to the narrative reflect wider changes in the text, for example in the case of the revised version of the *Festial*, where the redactor includes more material from the *Golden Legend* throughout. Here, it is not clear that there was a conscious intention to change the text's depiction of infertility. Nonetheless, these different retellings show different authors presenting different experiences of marginalization and infertility to their audiences, and making choices among the versions of the story circulating in late medieval England. These might reflect variations not just in the sources available to them, but also in how far they wanted to acknowledge the sadness of infertile couples, and how strongly they wanted to argue that they should not be excluded. In the case of Bokenham, we can perhaps go further and suggest that acknowledging the sadness and marginalization caused by infertility might have provided comfort and reassurance to specific patrons who were experiencing reproductive difficulties.

Conclusion

Many of the ideas about infertility, margins and peripheries expressed in the religious texts of the central and later Middle Ages were not new, based as they were on biblical and apocryphal models. They would also have a long future and remain relevant to Christians thinking about infertility in the twenty-first century. This article follows the studies by Moss and Baden and by Toepfer in highlighting the diversity of religious views of infertility that existed in the medieval period. Different sources had different perspectives, probably reflecting diverse attitudes and experiences at the time, as well as the fact that they were drawing on a range of earlier texts and writing in different genres for a variety of purposes. However, I have sought to go beyond simply highlighting diversity to reflect on what these variations might tell us about the variety of possible experiences of infertility – or, at least, about how clerical writers imagined these experiences.

There is indeed some evidence for infertility being a source of stigma and marginalization, putting people at the periphery of the Christian community; or at least evidence that this was feared. We should take seriously John Bromyard's remarks, and the hints of 'reproach' in Thomas Cantilupe's miracle. However, it seems likely that the more inclusive message of the Birth of the Virgin stories had a wider reach. They were copied more often, and increasingly in the vernacular, for educated lay audiences as well as clergy. The story of Anne and Joachim therefore offered a religious model of infertility with the potential to counter negative views which probably did exist in society at large. It may even have reflected the more mainstream view; or, through repetition, it may have become the more mainstream view. It may have offered reassurance to couples experiencing fertility challenges, although this reassurance would have been muted for couples who never went on to have children. It may also have prompted empathy on the part of those who had children.

There is much scope to explore these ideas in other texts, from medieval England and from other parts of the premodern world. We still do not know how far there were regional variations in religious ideas or differences over time, prompted by demographic change, notably the Black Death, or other factors. There is also a need for more comparative work. For example, Daphna Oren-Magidor has shown how St Anne's story lost prominence among English Protestant women after the Reformation, in favour of the biblical role models of Sarah, Rachel, Hannah and Elizabeth. Alongside this change, came a greater emphasis on how infertile women should pray directly to God rather than appealing to the saints. However, the messages may have remained similar: these biblical stories could still work against stigma by emphasizing that infertility was part of a larger divine plan.[70] There is therefore much to investigate in terms of both continuity and change.

This work could involve seeking out references to shame, marginalization and isolation in other texts that discuss infertility, as well as finding more inclusive messages to put alongside them. It is challenging to place these often brief comments into their wider contexts, but

[70] Oren-Magidor, 'From Anne to Hannah', 101.

variations in the retellings from different regions, and over time, have the potential to tell us more about how religious writers and their clerical and lay audiences thought about infertility. They can also highlight the range of possible views, along with the powerful voices that spoke against placing infertile people on the margins of the Christian community.

Papal Indulgences and the Conversion of Schismatics in Late Medieval Transylvania (*c.*1350–*c.*1450)

Teodora Popovici ⓘ
University of Bucharest

This article explores the self-representations of marginality found in the indulgence petitions addressed by Transylvanian supplicants to the papal chancery during the fourteenth and fifteenth centuries. As one of Hungary's border provinces, Transylvania was located on the eastern frontier of late medieval Latin Christendom. Although Transylvanian Catholics often expressed a sense of marginality in their petitions to the pope, this sentiment was not primarily defined by the petitioners' distance to the Apostolic see; rather, it was described in relation to the Greek Orthodox Christians in Transylvania and, later, to the approaching Ottoman Turks. To illustrate this point, the article presents three case studies of indulgence petitions submitted by Transylvanian supplicants between 1350 and 1450, highlighting how the petitioners' discourse about marginality changed over the course of this period. In addition, this article emphasizes the role attributed by petitioners to papal indulgences in converting the 'schismatics' in Transylvania to the Latin faith.

INTRODUCTION

As the easternmost province of the kingdom of Hungary, Transylvania was positioned at the edge of late medieval Latin Christendom. The official Transylvanian ecclesiastical hierarchy was part of the Catholic Church, but the region also encompassed many Greek Orthodox

I would like to thank Professors Radu Nedici and Marius Diaconescu from the University of Bucharest for their guidance and support. My gratitude also extends to Professor Robert Swanson for his kind comments and questions during the Society's conference, which have greatly contributed to the development of my ideas. Finally, I am indebted to the editorial team of SCH, my anonymous reviewers and my colleague Mihail-George Hâncu from the Institute for South-East European Studies in Bucharest for suggesting revisions that have enhanced the presentation of this article. E-mail: teodora.popovici@s.unibuc.ro.

Studies in Church History 61 (2025), 208–229 © The Author(s), 2025. Published by Cambridge University Press on behalf of the Ecclesiastical History Society. This is an Open Access article, distributed under the terms of the Creative Commons Attribution licence (http://creativecommons.org/licenses/by/4.0), which permits unrestricted re-use, distribution and reproduction, provided the original article is properly cited.
doi:10.1017/stc.2024.35

communities, referred to by Latin sources as the 'schismatics' (*scismatici*). They were subject to conversion attempts led by the papacy and the Hungarian royal authorities, particularly during the second half of the fourteenth century. This article explores the issue of self-perceived marginality among Transylvanian Catholics during the fourteenth and fifteenth centuries, based on their indulgence requests addressed to the papal chancery and on the indulgence letters issued by the papacy in response. These types of petitions were one of the most common forms of communication between centre and periphery within the late medieval Catholic Church; they thus provide interesting insights into the ways in which petitioners portrayed and perceived themselves in relation to the central authority of the church.[1]

Although Transylvanian Catholics belonged to the official church of their realm, a sense of marginality was often expressed in their petitions to the pope. However, this sentiment was not primarily defined in spatial terms, emphasizing the petitioners' distance from the Holy See; rather, it was linked to the presence of Greek Orthodox communities in Transylvania. Prior to the 1420s, Transylvanian supplicants almost always described their marginality as proximity to the 'schismatics', whom they depicted as stubborn and violent. Over the first half of the fifteenth century, a gradual shift in discourse can be noticed, as Transylvanian Catholics increasingly started to represent their marginality in relation to the Ottoman Turks. Their requests to the pope highlight the struggles faced by Transylvanian churches; the relationship between marginality, indulgences and devotion; and the perceived role of papal indulgences in the conversion of Greek Orthodox Christians to Catholicism.

The Mixed Confessional Landscape of Medieval Transylvania

Medieval Transylvania was organized as a voivodeship whose governor, the voivode, was directly appointed by the king of Hungary. The Catholic diocese of Transylvania was one of the largest in the kingdom and consisted of thirteen archdeaconries. The local episcopal

---

[1] This idea has been brilliantly illustrated by the collection of papers in Gerhard Jaritz, Torstein Jørgensen and Kirsi Salonen, eds, *The Long Arm of Papal Authority: Late Medieval Christian Peripheries and their Communication with the Holy See*, CEU Medievalia 8 (Budapest, 2005).

Teodora Popovici

see was in Gyulafehérvár (Alba Iulia), and its bishop was under the jurisdiction of the archbishop of Kalocsa.[2] The political organization of the area did not fully coincide with the ecclesiastical one, and although the jurisdiction of the bishopric mostly overlapped with the territory of the voivodate, it also included several other territories in northern Hungary, such as the archdeaconries of Szatmár (Satu Mare) and Ugocsa.[3] Moreover, certain parts of southern Transylvania, which were inhabited by Saxon colonists, had a special ecclesiastical status and were exempt from the authority of the Transylvanian bishop. The provostship (chapter) of Hermannstadt (Sibiu) and the chapter of Burzenland (Țara Bârsei) were placed directly under the jurisdiction of the archbishop of Esztergom, whose see was located north-west of Buda. Given the great distance to their bishop, the deans of these chapters were granted quasi-episcopal powers.[4] For the purposes of this article, I will take into consideration examples from both the diocese of Transylvania and from the exempt territories of the Transylvanian Saxons.

While the Latin church had a well-documented presence in Transylvania, the religious life of the Greek Orthodox communities is less understood. Several churches, monasteries and parochial networks are known, but the existence of a stable episcopal see in the area is uncertain for this period.[5] The confessional differences in the region were linked to its ethnic diversity: the Greek Orthodox Christians in Transylvania and eastern Hungary were mostly Vlachs (Romanians), Ruthenians and Serbs; while the Catholic population mainly comprised Hungarians, Saxons and Székelys. However, there are many notable examples of Greek Orthodox Christians converting to

[2] The most recent monograph about the ecclesiastical organization of the diocese of Transylvania is Adinel-Ciprian Dincă, *Instituția episcopală latină în Transilvania medievală (sec. XI/XII–XIV)* (Cluj-Napoca, 2017).
[3] In the late thirteenth century and during most of the fourteenth, the northern part of the diocese was subject to jurisdictional disputes between the bishop of Transylvania and the bishop of Eger: ibid. 51, 211–12.
[4] Although published more than a century ago, the most comprehensive work on the ecclesiastical organization of the Transylvanian Saxons remains Friedrich Teutsch, *Geschichte der evangelischen Kirche in Siebenbürgen*, 2 vols (Hermannstadt, 1921).
[5] For a brief English-language introduction to the church life of the Romanian Greek Orthodox communities in Transylvania, see László Makkai, 'Transylvania in the Medieval Hungarian Kingdom (896–1526)', in idem and András Mócsy, eds, *History of Transylvania*, 1: *From the Beginnings to 1606*, transl. Péter Szaffkó et al., East European Monographs 581 (New York, 2001), 347–606, at 567–87.

Catholicism, especially among the lay elites,[6] and some sources also allude to possible instances of Catholic conversions to Eastern Christianity, although these cases remain poorly documented.[7] Hungarian and Romanian historians have sometimes had divergent views about the proportion each confession represented in the overall population of medieval Transylvania, and the debate has been fuelled not only by the scarcity of statistical sources, but also by the different geographical definitions used by scholars who have made population estimates.[8]

Nevertheless, Greek Orthodox Christians remained the largest religious minority in late medieval Hungary, and converting them to Catholicism was an important challenge for both the papacy and the royal authorities.[9] This concern reached its peak during the reign of Louis I (1342–82). Some coercive measures were taken against the Greek Orthodox clergy in parts of Hungary,[10] while ordinary individuals were usually promised various concessions in exchange for converting, such as tithe exemptions and new church

---

[6] A useful review of several examples involving Romanian nobles from Transylvania, Banat and Maramureș can be found in Marius Diaconescu, 'Les implications confessionnelles du Concile de Florence en Hongrie', *Mediaevalia Transilvanica* 1 (1997), 29–62, at 57–61.

[7] Adrian Andrei Rusu, 'Preoți români ortodocși din districtul Hațegului în secolul al XV-lea', *Mitropolia Banatului* 32 (1982), 644–53, at 646.

[8] For example, the estimates given by the two major English-language syntheses of Transylvanian history might be contrasted. On the one hand, the Hungarian historian László Makkai suggested that roughly fifty per cent of Transylvania's population consisted of Hungarians and Székelys, while Vlachs formed about twenty-five per cent, and the remaining twenty-five per cent were Saxons, Serbs and Ruthenians. In this estimate, the author included only the territory of the voivodate of Transylvania: Makkai, 'Transylvania', 577. On the other hand, the Romanian historian Ioan-Aurel Pop concluded that between sixty and sixty-five per cent of Transylvania's inhabitants were Greek Orthodox Christians (Vlachs, Serbs and Ruthenians), while the remaining thirty-five to forty per cent were Catholics (Hungarians, Saxons and Székelys). However, he took into account both the territory of the voivodate and 'the neighbouring regions to the west and north': Ioan-Aurel Pop, 'Transylvania in the 14th Century and the First Half of the 15th Century (1300–1456)', in idem and Thomas Nägler, eds, *The History of Transylvania*, 1: *Until 1541*, transl. Bogdan Aldea and Richard Proctor, 2nd edn (Cluj-Napoca, 2018; first publ. 2003), 247–98, at 268–9.

[9] Pál Engel, *The Realm of St Stephen: A History of Medieval Hungary, 895–1526*, transl. Tamás Pálosfalvi (London, 2001), 172. For an interesting insight into the policy of the Avignon papacy regarding missionary work, see also James Muldoon, 'The Avignon Papacy and the Frontiers of Christendom: The Evidence of Vatican Register 62', *Archivum Historiae Pontificiae* 17 (1979), 125–95.

[10] Engel, *Realm of St Stephen*, 172; Ioan-Aurel Pop, *Din mâinile valahilor schismatici: românii și puterea în Regatul Ungariei medievale (secolele XIII–XIV)*, 2nd edn (Cluj-Napoca, 2017; first publ. 2011), 422.

buildings.[11] In this effort, Louis employed the support of the Franciscans, who undertook missionary work from several of their monasteries established across eastern Hungary.[12] The conversion campaigns have drawn the attention of several historians and theologians, although their interpretations of them have varied. Some scholars have viewed these measures as the systematic persecution of the Greek Orthodox Christians in Hungary,[13] while others have adopted a more nuanced position, highlighting the limited and uncertain application of the coercive measures, the benefices enjoyed by the newly converted, or the religious tolerance of Catholic landowners towards their Greek Orthodox serfs, who were allowed to observe their faith provided they fulfilled their economic obligations.[14] Apart from a few cases of mass conversions,[15] the missionary campaigns overall were ineffective, and they were eventually abandoned during the reign of King Sigismund of Luxembourg (1387–1437), who was a supporter of the reconciliation between the Latin and Greek churches.[16] Individual conversions were more common among the lay elites, for whom the new faith

---

[11] Viorel Achim, 'Considerații asupra politicii față de ortodocși a regelui Ludovic I de Anjou, cu referire specială la chestiunea dijmelor', in Ovidiu Cristea and Gheorghe Lazăr, eds, *Vocația istoriei: prinos profesorului Șerban Papacostea* (Brăila, 2008), 69–79, at 72–8.

[12] Viorel Achim, 'Les unités territoriales de l'ordre franciscain dans l'espace roumain aux XIVe–XVe siècles', in Maria Crăciun and Ovidiu Ghitta, eds, *Ethnicity and Religion in Central and Eastern Europe* (Cluj-Napoca, 1995), 24–30, at 25–7.

[13] Ioan Lupaș, *Viața religioasă a românilor ardeleni* (Sibiu, 1918), 22, 47; Ștefan Lupșa, *Catolicismul și românii din Ardeal și Ungaria până la anul 1556* (Cernăuți, 1929), 64–82; Zenovie Pâclișanu, 'Ungaria și acțiunea catolică în Orient', *Revista Istorică Română* 14 (1944), 180–97, at 183–5, 192; Ioan-Aurel Pop, 'Ethnie and confession. Genèse médiévale de la nation roumaine moderne', in Nicolae Bocșan, Ioan Lumperdean and idem, eds, *Ethnie et confession en Transylvanie (du XIIIe au XIXe siècles)* (Cluj-Napoca, 1996), 5–60, at 27–8; Pop, *Din mâinile valahilor schismatici*, 422–3.

[14] István Juhász, 'A középkori nyugati misszió és a románság', *Az Erdélyi Tudományos Intézet évkönyve* (1942), 171–99, at 179–80, 184–5; Adrian Andrei Rusu, 'Nobilimea românească și Biserica în secolul al XV-lea: exemplul hațegan', in Marius Diaconescu, ed., *Nobilimea românească din Transilvania/Az erdélyi román nemesség* (Satu Mare, 1997), 131–51, at 133; Makkai, 'Transylvania', 584–7; Achim, 'Considerații', 70–1.

[15] For example, see the mass conversions in the region of Medgyes (Medieș): Francisc Pall, 'Românii din părțile sătmărene (ținutul Medieș) în lumina unor documente din 1377', *Anuarul Institutului de Istorie din Cluj* 12 (1969), 7–35, at 28–32.

[16] The only notable exception would be the mission of Jacob de Marchia, which took place between 1435 and 1439. As one might expect, no conversion campaigns are attested in the first decade following the Florentine Union: Diaconescu, 'Les implications confessionnelles', 32.

brought the prospect of social ascent.[17] In some areas of Transylvania, the conversions gave birth to unique forms of devotion, which incorporated elements of both Latin and Slavonic rite.[18] While previous contributions have largely debated the political and religious marginality of the Greek Orthodox Christians in the kingdom, this article will examine the idea of marginality as experienced by the Catholic communities in Transylvania, analysing the language of indulgence petitions from the fourteenth and fifteenth centuries.

Papal Indulgences in Medieval Transylvania

An indulgence was a partial or total reduction of penance granted by a bishop for performing various pious acts. The remission might be expressed in days, years or quadragenes (units of forty days), or a combination of these. Papal indulgences were typically considered the most valuable, as they provided more days of pardon. Starting with the classic works of Henry Charles Lea and Nikolaus Paulus,[19] medieval indulgences have sparked the interest of church historians in relation to various research problems, such as devotional practices, the concept of crusade, and the causes of the Reformation. Although the local particularities of the phenomenon in Transylvania and eastern Hungary have not yet been fully clarified, a number of studies have made significant contributions in this direction. Katalin Erős has recently completed a valuable PhD dissertation analysing the various types of indulgence grants and their relation to piety in medieval Hungary.[20] Other notable contributions include Jan Hrdina's studies discussing the papal indulgences received by Central European churches during the Great Western Schism (1378–1417), which also

---

[17] Viorel Achim, 'Catolicismul la românii din Banat în Evul Mediu', *Revista istorică* 7 (1996), 41–55, at 44; Rusu, 'Nobilimea românească', 144; Ioan Drăgan, *Nobilimea românească din Transilvania între anii 1440–1514* (Bucharest, 2000), 259.

[18] Rusu, 'Nobilimea românească', 144–5.

[19] Henry Charles Lea, *A History of Auricular Confession and Indulgences in the Latin Church*, 3: *Indulgences* (Philadelphia, PA, 1896); Nikolaus Paulus, *Geschichte des Ablasses im Mittelalter*, 3 vols (Paderborn, 1922–3).

[20] Katalin Erős, 'Búcsúk és búcsúlevelek a késő középkori Magyarországon' (PhD thesis, Pázmány Péter Catholic University, Budapest, 2019).

contain a review of Transylvanian examples.[21] Most recently, the indulgences of the Marian churches in Hungary have been analysed by Karen L. Stark, who notes their significance for practices of Marian devotion.[22]

In a paper published at the turn of the twenty-first century, Viorel Achim identified an interesting problem regarding the relation between indulgence petitions and missionary work in eastern Hungary.[23] Achim examined an indulgence request addressed in 1421 to the papal chancery by petitioners from Belényes (Beiuș), a Hungarian town in the diocese of Várad (Oradea), which bordered the diocese of Transylvania to the west. Belényes formed the centre of a domain owned by the bishop of Várad, and the town's inhabitants were mainly Hungarian, but the surrounding estate included eighty-three villages of Greek Orthodox Vlachs. In their petition, the townspeople of Belényes depicted themselves as a Catholic enclave surrounded by Vlachs, whom they labelled as 'pagan', an equivocal description which might have equally hinted at their rustic life and their lax ecclesiastical organization.[24] The supplicants pointed to their recent efforts at converting the Vlachs to Catholicism, which, in their view, made the local church worthy to receive an indulgence of eight years and eight quadragenes at the feast of Corpus Christi.[25] The indulgence was depicted as a means to support the Catholics in their missionary endeavour, so that the Vlachs would be converted more quickly.[26]

Viorel Achim asked whether the supposed conversion accomplishments were real, or just a persuasive strategy used by the petitioners to

---

[21] Jan Hrdina, 'Pe drumul mântuirii: indulgențe papale în Ungaria și Transilvania în vremea Marii Schisme Apusene (1378–1417)', *Revista Ecumenică Sibiu* 1 (2009), 47–70; idem, 'Papal Indulgences During the Era of the Great Western Schism (1378–1417) and the Cultural Foundation of Their Reception in Central Europe', in Veronika Čapská, ed., *Processes of Cultural Exchange in Central Europe, 1200–1800* (Opava, 2014), 345–87, at 382–5.

[22] Karen L. Stark, 'The Garden Watered by the Virgin Mary: The Marian Landscape of Medieval Hungary (1301–1437)' (PhD thesis, Central European University, Vienna, 2022), 203–11, esp. 207–8.

[23] Viorel Achim, 'Convertirea la catolicism a românilor din zona Beiușului în două documente din anul 1421', *Mediaevalia Transilvanica* 5–6 (2001–2), 83–95.

[24] '[I]nter eos sunt octuaginta tres villae de paganis sive Valachis': Aloysius L. Tăutu, ed., *Acta Martini PP. V (1417–1431)*, 2 vols (Rome, 1980), 1: 446 (no. 181). The text of the document has also been reproduced in Achim, 'Convertirea', 94.

[25] Tăutu, ed., *Acta Martini PP. V*, 1: 446 (no. 181).

[26] '[U]t praedicti pagani eo citius convertantur ad fidem catholicam': ibid. See also the comments in Achim, 'Convertirea', 88.

gain indulgences from the pope. By surveying complementary sources, he concluded that systematic missionary work had not taken place in the area and that any alleged conversions were, at most, isolated cases.[27] Although the townspeople of Belényes only received two years and two quadragenes of pardon,[28] the example still raises interesting questions about the self-representations of marginality among Catholics in eastern Hungary. Viorel Achim focused on the petitioners' exaggeration of their own merits, but their sense of being surrounded appears as an equally striking element of discourse. As illustrated below, this idea is also present in petitions from the diocese of Transylvania and from the exempt ecclesiastical jurisdiction of the Transylvanian Saxons. The narrative devices used by petitioners to construct this image will be further explored in the next sections, by discussing similar examples.

Before moving forward, however, an additional question might be addressed: did Transylvania's marginal position within the Catholic Church and its confessional particularities make any difference to the reception of indulgences by Transylvanian Catholics? I would argue that, in the mixed confessional landscape of late medieval Transylvania, papal indulgences had a twofold role. On the one hand, they supported churches in areas with large numbers of Greek Orthodox Christians by encouraging donations from parishioners and prompting collective forms of devotion. On the other hand, papal indulgences could be used to reward Greek Orthodox Christians who agreed to convert to Catholicism, while also stimulating church attendance among them. Since many rural settlements lacked parish churches,[29] rewarding attendance was important in areas where a clerical hierarchy had not been previously well-established. Although the effectiveness of indulgence grants as incentives for conversion and church participation is questionable, they were nevertheless seen as tools for accomplishing these goals, both by the central and the local actors involved in these missionary efforts.

Across the late medieval period, Transylvanians obtained various types of papal indulgences. Most commonly, these were indulgences for visiting and financially supporting those churches close to Greek

---

[27] Achim, 'Convertirea', 88–93.

[28] Ibid. 94; compare also Tăutu, ed., *Acta Martini PP. V*, 1: 447 (no. 181a).

[29] László Makkai estimates that only one in three or one in four Transylvanian villages had its own church: Makkai, 'Transylvania', 576–7.

Orthodox communities, whose violence Transylvanian petitioners sometimes complained about. As in other parts of Europe, alms collected from distributing papal indulgences helped fund the construction of and repairs to church buildings.[30] One might assign equal importance to the indulgences issued for the churches of the newly converted, which served as a sign of a thriving religious life. Catholics could also occasionally obtain individual remission of penance if they were involved in local conversion actions. Other indulgences, issued at the request of the king, encouraged particular forms of devotion in the area, such as public prayers for the king's victory against the neighbouring Greek Orthodox states and for the successful conversion of the 'schismatics'.[31]

Signalling Marginality in Indulgence Petitions

Papal indulgences could be obtained by addressing a written request to the pontifical chancery and by paying a fee. Approved petitions were recorded in a series of registers known as *Registra Supplicationum*, the earliest of which is dated 1342.[32] The oldest Transylvanian indulgence petitions included in the *Registra* date from the middle of the fourteenth century. Most of them are known only by their register copies, with very few examples surviving in original form or as notarial confirmations. For the kingdom of Hungary, the earliest surviving originals date from the 1480s, and several notarial confirmations issued for Transylvanian petitioners are known from the beginning of the sixteenth century.[33] In most cases, the individuals petitioning the pope were prominent members of their community, such as the parish priest or the landowner who acted as the patron of the local church. The papal

---

[30] Nikolaus Paulus, *Indulgences as a Social Factor in the Middle Ages*, transl. John Elliot Ross (New York, 1922), 23.

[31] A notable example from the reign of Louis I can be found in Augustin Theiner, ed., *Vetera monumenta historica Hungariam sacram illustrantia*, 2: *Ab Innocentio Papa VI usque ad Clementem Papam VII, 1352–1526* (Rome, 1860), 27 (no. 44). The other types of indulgences are exemplified over the next sections.

[32] Leonard E. Boyle, *A Survey of the Vatican Archives and of its Medieval Holdings* (Toronto, 1972), 151–2. For an overview of the editions of the supplications addressed by Hungarian petitioners, see Bálint Lakatos, ed., *Regesta supplicationum, 1522–1523*, A VI: *Adorján pápa uralkodása alatt elfogadott magyar vonatkozású kérvények*, Collectanea Vaticana Hungariae 16 (Budapest, 2018), 269–71.

[33] For the list of surviving originals and notarial confirmations, see Lakatos, ed., *Regesta supplicationum*, 30–1.

letters issued as a result would sometimes recycle narrative elements of the initial petitions, which can prove useful in reconstructing the text of the supplications in cases where the register copies have been lost.

Transylvanians would often invoke their marginal position within the church as an argument for obtaining indulgences from the pope, sometimes requesting more days and years of remission than normally granted. Nevertheless, the borders of Latin Christendom were not usually described by petitioners in direct relation to the papal Curia, in terms of their geographical distance to the Apostolic see. Instead, they appeared as a mixed religious space, a grey area where Catholicism was not fully prevalent, and Christians 'lived among the schismatics'. Marginality was in that sense mainly linked to the idea of disunity. References to Transylvania's geographical remoteness to the Apostolic see are more frequent in requests for *confessionalia*,[34] whenever the supplication was made by someone else on the beneficiary's behalf, to justify why he or she could not come to the papal Curia personally.

The representations of marginality also had a social component. Greek Orthodox communities were often portrayed as violent, and petitions alluded to social tensions with the Catholics. This stereotypical portrayal often appeared in relation to the Vlachs and has been noted in other sources of the period as well.[35] As a result, missionary work served not only the salvation of souls, but was also a factor of social disciplining. During the fourteenth and early fifteenth centuries, whenever the 'schismatics' were mentioned in indulgence petitions, references to conversion efforts were generally made as well, although additional details were seldom given. It is worth stressing that the descriptions mostly addressed local realities, such as the Greek Orthodox Christians residing close to the petitioner's town or village; references to the Orthodox states bordering Transylvania are less frequent.

The tone of the supplications started to change during the first half of the fifteenth century, as Transylvanian Catholics began to describe their marginality in relation to the growing presence of the Ottoman

---

[34] *Confessionalia* were privileges which allowed the beneficiary to choose his or her confessor freely, instead of having their confessions heard by the local parish priest. These privileges would sometimes authorize the chosen confessor to grant the beneficiary a plenary indulgence: Paulus, *Geschichte des Ablasses*, 2: 124.

[35] See, for example, Adrian Magina, 'Răufăcători sau ... schismatici? Statutul ortodocşilor bănăţeni în jurul anului 1400', in Dumitru Ţeicu and Ionel Cândea, eds, *Românii în Europa medievală: între Orientul bizantin şi Occidentul latin* (Brăila, 2008), 283–91.

Turks.[36] In comparison to the cruelty of the Turks, the descriptions of Transylvanian Vlachs and other 'schismatics' began to soften. The focus of the petitions was placed on the foreigners' intrusion into the Christian universe, and while the 'schismatics' did not completely disappear from view, they were no longer the main cause of complaint. This observation is consistent with the fact that religious proselytism towards the Greek Orthodox Christians in Hungary saw a decline in the late fourteenth and early fifteenth century, during the reign of Sigismund of Luxembourg, when the stern conversion policy adopted by his predecessor, Louis I, was abandoned. Sigismund's support for reuniting the Latin and Greek churches was also closely tied to his vision for strengthening defences against the Ottomans.[37] Moreover, the status of the Greek Orthodox clergy in Hungary improved following the settlement of many Serbs in the kingdom after the advances of the Ottomans in the Balkans.[38] Naturally, the decree of union between the two churches adopted by the Council of Florence in 1439 also played a role in changing the discourse noticeable in the petitions.

The image of Hungary as the gateway of Christendom in relation to the pagans,[39] and later as the bulwark of Christendom in relation to the Ottoman Turks, was also present in other Hungarian diplomatic sources of the Middle Ages,[40] so it is not surprising to find it in indulgence petitions as well. In comparison to this, however, the discourse on the Greek Orthodox Christians living within the borders of the kingdom was more nuanced. Transylvanian Catholics were forced to live together with the 'schismatics', while the Ottoman Turks were seen as an outside danger; therefore, the 'schismatics' had to be

---

[36] On the image of the Turks in Hungarian petitions, see also Kornél Szovák, 'Partes Ungarie … satis occupate cum Turcis: A magyarországi török-kérdés a 15. századi pápai kérvénykönyvekben', in Péter Tusor, idem and Tamás Fedeles, eds, *Magyarország és a római Szentszék II. Vatikáni magyar kutatások a 21. században*, Collectanea Vaticana Hungariae 15 (Budapest, 2017), 89–105.

[37] Liviu Pilat and Ovidiu Cristea, *The Ottoman Threat and Crusading on the Eastern Border of Christendom during the 15th Century*, East Central and Eastern Europe in the Middle Ages, 450–1450 48 (Leiden, 2018), 80.

[38] Magina, 'Răufăcători', 291; Sima M. Ćirković, *The Serbs*, transl. Vuk Tošić (Malden, 2004), 115.

[39] Nora Berend, 'Hungary, "the gate of Christendom"', in David Abulafia and Nora Berend, eds, *Medieval Frontiers: Concepts and Practices* (Abington, 2016), 195–215.

[40] On the use of this concept in medieval Hungary, see Paul Srodecki, *Antemurale Christianitatis: Zur Genese der Bollwerksrhetorik im östlichen Mitteleuropa an der Schwelle vom Mittelalter zur Frühen Neuzeit*, Historische Studien 508 (Husum, 2015), esp. 88–103, 163–216.

converted, while the Turks were hopefully to be defeated. To illustrate all this, the sections that follow will present three case studies of Transylvanian indulgence requests that communicate marginality in relation to the Greek Orthodox Christians. These were selected because more information is known about the petitioners, and because their language reflects how patterns of representing marginality changed between the 1350s and the 1450s.

THE CASE OF NICOLAUS LACKFI'S TRANSYLVANIAN CHURCHES

The first example features Nicolaus (Miklós) Lackfi, a Hungarian noble serving as count of Zemplén, who participated in several military campaigns during the reign of Louis I.[41] The Lackfis were one of the wealthiest and most influential noble families in Hungary during the Angevin period.[42] Although the family had Transylvanian origins and owned several properties in the area, they had settled outside the voivodate by the middle of the fourteenth century, as they ascended into the political hierarchy of the kingdom and obtained more central estates, either by royal donation or by purchase.[43] Nicolaus was the son of Lack (László) and had seven brothers.[44] His father had gained prominence at the royal court as count of the Székelys between 1328 and 1344, and his brothers occupied various military and administrative offices in the kingdom.[45] Most notably, Nicolaus Lackfi's elder brothers, Stephanus (István) and Andreas (András), served as voivodes of Transylvania and held other high dignities throughout their careers.[46] One of Nicolaus's younger brothers, Dionysus (Dénes), became a

---

[41] János Karácsonyi, *A magyar nemzetségek a XIV. század közepéig*, 3 vols (Budapest, 1900–1), 2: 173–4. He should not be confused with his nephew, Nicolaus Lackfi the Younger, who served as voivode of Transylvania for a short time (1367–8), until his death in a military campaign in Wallachia: András Kovács, 'Voievozii Transilvaniei în perioada 1344–1359', in Dumitru Țeicu and Rudolf Gräf, eds, *Itinerarii istoriografice: studii în onoarea istoricului Costin Feneșan* (Cluj-Napoca, 2011), 37–65, at 51.

[42] Engel, *Realm of St Stephen*, 182.

[43] Marius Diaconescu, *Structura nobilimii din Transilvania în epoca angevină* (Cluj-Napoca, 2013), 291–3.

[44] See the family tree in Karácsonyi, *A magyar nemzetségek*, 2: 171.

[45] Diaconescu, *Structura nobilimii*, 293.

[46] Stephanus was voivode between 1344 and 1350, and Andreas held the office between 1356 and 1359: Karácsonyi, *A magyar nemzetségek*, 2: 173; Kovács, 'Voievozii Transilvaniei', 46–7, 60–1.

Franciscan friar and rose to the rank of archbishop of Kalocsa, which he held from 1350 to 1355.[47]

Although Nicolaus's career was not as outstanding as those of his brothers, he had gained the trust of Louis I as a military leader. He probably started his service as a knight at the royal court during the 1330s or 1340s, and became count of Zemplén around 1347.[48] He was present in the Hungarian campaigns in Naples (1350) and Lithuania (1351–2).[49] In 1356, Nicolaus was sent by the king to help Pope Innocent VI regain control over the Papal States, and he spent about two years leading the Hungarian troops in that campaign.[50] The proximity to the papal Curia provided Lackfi with an opportunity to make several requests to the pope, which the pontifical chancery in Avignon recorded in February 1358. Lackfi was mainly concerned with his family's estates in eastern Hungary and the condition of their churches. One of their domains, largely inhabited by Vlach serfs, was located in the county of Arad, at the border between the dioceses of Transylvania and Csanád (Cenad), in a region that might be considered marginal, not only in relation to the Apostolic see, but also in connection to the local ecclesiastical geography.

Among other privileges, Lackfi requested two sets of indulgences from the pope: one set for the parochial churches he had recently built for his converted Vlach serfs,[51] and a second one for several other churches under his patronage across Hungary.[52] The first group consisted of four churches: All Saints' Church in Szádvár, St Mary's Church in Aruahigh, and St Michael's and St Nicholas's churches in Szentmiklós.[53] Lackfi had built and endowed them with his own resources, which, along with his successful conversion efforts, must have been regarded as a great act of piety at the papal court.[54] The need

---

[47] Karácsonyi, *A magyar nemzetségek*, 2: 174.

[48] Ibid. 173–4.

[49] Ibid. 174.

[50] Antal Pór, *Nagy Lajos, 1326–1382* (Budapest, 1892), 338–41.

[51] Ştefan Pascu, ed., *Documenta Romaniae Historica*, C: *Transilvania* [hereafter: DRH C], 11: 1356–1360 (Bucharest, 1981), 235 (no. 226); Aloysius L. Tăutu, ed., *Acta Innocentii PP. VI (1352–1362)* (Roma, 1961), 206–7 (no. 112a).

[52] DRH C, 11: 237 (no. 227).

[53] All three settlements are now extinct. Szentmiklós may have been divided split into two parts, explaining the need for two separate parish churches: see DRH C, 11: 236 (no. 226) and nn. 5–7.

[54] '[D]e bonis a Deo sibi collatis edificari fecerit et bonis propriis dotaverit easdem': DRH C, 11: 235 (no. 226).

for a new foundation suggests that the villages had probably lacked their own devotional spaces previously. Although the churches had presumably been founded before Lackfi departed Hungary, they were yet to be assigned a bishop. Since they stood on the border between the dioceses of Transylvania and Csanád, Lackfi solicited permission to choose which diocese each church would belong to, but the pope passed the decision on to the archbishop of Kalocsa, whose final verdict is unknown.[55]

In his petition, Lackfi described the four churches as 'situated on his land, in the middle of the Vlachs, among violent people, some of whom have been recently converted to the Catholic faith' [author's translation].[56] The papal indulgences were meant to stimulate devotion among the new Catholics (*ad plebis devocionem augmentandam*), so that they would not return to their old ways. Accordingly, religious conversion was seen as an instrument of social disciplining, and the new faith created communal order where previously it had been absent. It is worth mentioning that Lackfi alluded to the idea of marginality only when referring to the churches of the converted Vlachs, while the other group of churches, for which he had formulated a separate indulgence request, did not enjoy any special description, although some of them were also situated in eastern Hungary.

For each church, Lackfi requested five years and five quadragenes of remission, which were meant to reward visits during the major Christian feasts of the year. However, his request was only partially fulfilled due to prevailing chancery practices, which limited the typical value of papal indulgences at that time.[57] The pope issued the two sets of indulgences, but their value was only one year and one quadragene for the churches of the converted Vlachs, and one hundred days for Lackfi's other churches.[58] Lackfi did not, therefore, receive anything more than petitioners from other parts of Latin Christendom would normally have received. The difference in value between the two indulgences suggests the importance the papal chancery accorded to the recently converted communities. At the same time, it was usual for bishops to issue more days of remission at the consecration of a new

---

[55] DRH C, 11: 237–8 (no. 228).
[56] '[I]n terra sua, in medio Olachorum, inter naciones protervas, quarum alique de novo sunt ad fidem catholicam conversi': DRH C, 11: 235 (no. 226).
[57] Paulus, *Geschichte des Ablasses*, 3: 150.
[58] DRH C, 11: 235-7 (nos 226 and 227).

church, compared to the number of days typically offered on other occasions.[59] The papal indulgences might have also been a way of instilling into the new Catholics basic teachings about sin and penance. Annually, there were fifteen feast days when the indulgence could be obtained, which made it a possible tool to encourage church attendance among villagers.

THE CASE OF ST MARY'S CHURCH IN KRONSTADT

The second example involves the Saxon town of Kronstadt (Brașov), a key economic centre of Transylvania. Kronstadt was a free royal town on the south-eastern border of Transylvania, part of the chapter of Burzenland, which fell under the direct jurisdiction of the archbishop of Esztergom. The local church, today known as 'The Black Church' (*Die Schwarze Kirche*; *Biserica Neagră*), was devoted to St Mary and received several papal indulgences in the fourteenth and fifteenth centuries. Most of these were obtained by the local parish priests. At that time, the main church building was still under construction, and alms collected from indulgences were one of the funding sources of the project. Construction started in the second half of the fourteenth century, possibly during the 1380s, and lasted for about a century.[60] The church is now considered the largest Gothic church in south-eastern Europe.[61]

In December 1399, the urban community of Kronstadt obtained two indulgence letters from Boniface IX. Unfortunately, both the original petitions and the register copies are lost, as only one supplication register is known for the pontificate of Boniface IX, dated 1394. However, the overall tone of the petitions can be inferred from the text of the final papal letters, which contain references to the religious conversions happening in Transylvania. The first letter, issued on 15 December 1399, granted four years and four quadragenes of remission to individuals involved in converting the local Greek

---

[59] Paulus, *Geschichte des Ablasses*, 3: 226.

[60] Irina Băldescu, *Transilvania medievală: topografie și norme juridice ale cetăților Sibiu, Bistrița, Brașov, Cluj* (Bucharest, 2012), 260; Daniela Marcu-Istrate, *Church Archaeology in Transylvania (c. 950 to c. 1450)*, East Central and Eastern Europe in the Middle Ages, 450–1450 84 (Leiden, 2022), 20.

[61] Marcu-Istrate, *Church Archaeology*, 20.

Orthodox Christians to Catholicism.[62] The beneficiaries of the indulgence were supposed to provide support to those wishing to convert, in the form of teachings, good words and their own pious example.[63] The second letter, dated 29 December 1399, rewarded visits and alms to the town's parochial church, granting an indulgence *ad instar* whose value was equivalent to the indulgence received by visiting St Mary's Church in Aachen.[64] It was one of the numerous indulgences of this type issued by Boniface IX, presumed to be plenary.[65] Since Aachen was a popular pilgrimage site among Catholics in Hungary, it is not surprising to see the community of Kronstadt choosing it as a reference point for their own indulgence. Hungarian royalty also favoured this pilgrimage destination, and King Louis I had even built a royal chapel there.[66]

Both letters referred to the coexistence between the Catholics and the 'schismatics', describing the city of Kronstadt as being 'situated at the borders of Christianity (*in confinibus christianitatis*), where large numbers of Greeks, Vlachs, Bulgarians, Armenians and other infidels, having a certain church for their use and cult, live together and coexist with the faithful who reside there'.[67] The wording is similar in both

---

[62] Franz Zimmermann, Carl Werner and Georg Müller, eds, *Urkundenbuch zur Geschichte der Deutschen in Siebenbürgen* [hereafter: UB Siebenbürgen], 3: *1391 bis 1415* (Hermannstadt, 1902), 246-7 (no. 1445).

[63] '[I]nfideles ipsos in huiusmodi eorum proposito et desiderio assiduis informationibus bonorumque verborum exemplis conservare et quotidie confortare eisque subveniendo vestrumque ad hoc pium et fructuosum praestando auxilium et favorem studeatis, ut per hoc infideles ipsi valeant et debeant huiusmodi eorum desiderium et propositum feliciter adimplere vosque per haec et alia bona quae domino inspirante feceritis possitis ad aeternae felicitatis gaudia pervenire': UB Siebenbürgen 3: 247 (no. 1445).

[64] Vilmos Fraknói, ed., *Monumenta Vaticana Historiam Regni Hungariae illustrantia*, series 1 [hereafter: MVH/1], 4: *Bullae Bonifacii IX. P. M., pars altera: 1396–1404* (Budapest, 1889), 163 (no. 208).

[65] Diana Webb, 'Pardons and Pilgrims', in Robert N. Swanson, ed., *Promissory Notes on the Treasury of Merits: Indulgences in Late Medieval Europe*, Brill's Companions to the Christian Tradition 5 (Leiden, 2006), 241–75, at 257.

[66] Enikő Csukovits, 'Cum capsa … cum bacillo. Középkori magyar zarándokok', *Aetas* 9 (1994), 5–27, at 7.

[67] '[I]n oppido de Corona seu vulgariter Brascho nuncupato, Strigoniensis diocesis, in confinibus christianitatis situato, in quo tam Grecorum, Walachorum, Bulgarorum, Armenorum quam aliorum infidelium multitudo quandam ecclesiam in oppido praedicto pro eorum usu et cultu eorum habentium una cum Christi fidelibus inibi degentibus habitat et moratur': UB Siebenbürgen 3: 247 (no. 1445), 15 December 1399. Author's translation.

letters, with only slight differences.[68] The unnamed church mentioned in the pope's letters was most likely a late fourteenth-century Greek Orthodox church on the site where St Nicholas's Church now stands in Șcheii Brașovului.[69] It was a wooden church devoted to St Mary, and its existence has been documented archaeologically.[70] Although the letters suggest that the Greek Orthodox church was located within the perimeter of the town, it was in reality serving the inhabitants of 'Bulgaria' (Belgerei, Șchei), a nearby village located in the western suburbs of Kronstadt (now part of the town), which is thought to have had a mixed population of Romanians and Slavs.[71]

The four groups acknowledged in Boniface's letters – Greeks, Vlachs, Bulgarians and Armenians – were broadly defined as 'infidels', but not every term necessarily had an ethnic meaning attached to it. A 'Greek' could be any Orthodox Christian in Transylvania or in the neighbouring states, regardless of his or her ethnicity. The 'Bulgarians' probably referred to the South Slavic immigrants in Belgerei, who lived together with the Vlachs, but the term might also allude to the presence of Bogomilism among them. The Armenian communities in Transylvania were largely involved in trade, and local fourteenth-century sources even mention the existence of an Armenian bishop in southern Transylvania, placed under the authority of the archbishop of Esztergom, but little is known about the diocese, its parishes or its relation to the other ecclesiastical structures in Hungary.[72]

Overall, Boniface's letters evinced an optimistic tone about the alleged religious conversions taking place in the region, describing

[68] 'Cupientes igitur, ut ecclesia Marie Virginis opidi de Corona, vulgariter Brascho nuncupati, Strigoniensis diocesis, in confinibus christianitatis situati, ubi tam Grecorum, Walachorum, Bulgarorum, Armenorum, quam aliorum infidelium multitudo, quondam ecclesiam in eodem opido pro eorum usu et cultu eorum habentium, unacum Christifidelibus in eodem opido degentibus habitat et moratur ... congruis honoribus frequentetur': MVH/1 4: 163 (no. 208), 29 December 1399.

[69] Candid Mușlea, *Biserica Sf. Nicolae din Șcheii Brașovului, 1: 1292–1742* (Brașov, 1943), 48–9.

[70] Luminița Munteanu and Mariana Beldie Dumitrache, 'Rezultatele cercetărilor arheologice la Biserica Sf. Nicolae din Șcheii Brașovului – etapa 1975', *Revista Muzeelor și Monumentelor: Monumente Istorice și de Artă* 45 (1976), 52–6, at 53–4.

[71] Latin sources refer to the village as 'Bulgaria', German sources use the name 'Belgerei', while 'Șchei' is the Romanian variant: Băldescu, *Transilvania*, 223. These toponyms suggest the presence of South Slavic immigrants from the Balkans, but the origins of the village's inhabitants have been widely debated by historians for more than a century: see Mușlea, *Biserica*, 15–29.

[72] Miklós Gazdovits, *Az erdélyi örmények története* (Cluj-Napoca, 2006), 290–5.

them as voluntary acts, in which the Catholics' role was only support-ive, as opposed to actively missionary. The indulgence issued on 15 December 1399 mentioned the infidels' desire to convert to Catholicism and the necessity to prevent any changes of mind among them;[73] while the second letter appears to suggest that some conver-sions had already happened.[74] The letters pointed to rebaptizing the converted, an idea promoted by Franciscan missionaries in Hungary, who saw any baptism performed by the Greek Orthodox clergy as null.[75] It should be borne in mind, however, that a convent of Franciscan friars would only be founded in Brașov at the beginning of the sixteenth century.[76]

This type of discourse started to change in the first half of the fifteenth century, as the town gained an increasingly significant stra-tegic position in defending the southern border of the kingdom against the Ottoman Turks. In 1422, following the Turkish invasion of Burzenland in the previous year, the parish priest of Kronstadt com-plained in a petition to the pope about the destructions caused by the Turks in Burzenland, but still kept the reference to the 'schismatics'.[77] At that time, the political and military context in south-eastern Europe had reached a difficult point, and the Turkish raid of 1421 caused long-lasting effects on the town's population and its hinterland, as many individuals were either killed or captured, and their houses destroyed.[78]

---

[73] '[Q]uamplures de huiusmodi et aliis infidelibus pro tempore advenientibus gratia divina inspirati se ad fidem praedictam convertere et veteri sorde et macula in sacro fonte baptismatis mundari desiderant et proponunt laudabiliter permanere et, nisi in huiusmodi eorum pio proposito et desiderio laudabili conserventur et assiduis instructionibus, auxiliis et favoribus confortentur, de totali huiusmodi desiderii et propositi omnium ipsorum collapsu verisimiliter formidetur': UB Siebenbürgen 3: 247 (no. 1445).

[74] '[I]n quaquidem ecclesia quamplures de infidelibus huiusmodi se ad sanctam fidem catholicam convertentes, veteri sorde et macula lavari cupientes, sacro lavantur baptismate': MVH/1 4: 163 (no. 208).

[75] Șerban Papacostea, 'La fondation de la Valachie et de la Moldavie et les Roumains de Transylvanie. Une nouvelle source', *Revue Roumaine d'Histoire* 17 (1978), 389–407, at 404–5.

[76] Adrian Andrei Rusu et al., *Dicționarul mănăstirilor din Transilvania, Banat, Crișana și Maramureș* (Cluj-Napoca, 2000), 81.

[77] Pál Lukcsics, ed., *XV. századi pápák oklevelei* [hereafter: Lukcsics], 1: *V. Márton Pápa (1417–1431)* (Budapest, 1931), 134 (no. 532).

[78] Gustav Gündisch, 'Siebenbürgen in der Türkenabwehr', *Revue roumaine d'histoire* 13 (1974), 415–43, at 419–21; Tamás Pálosfalvi, *From Nicopolis to Mohács: A History of Ottoman-Hungarian Warfare, 1389–1526*, The Ottoman Empire and Its Heritage: Polit-ics, Society and Economy 63 (Leiden, 2018), 68–70.

In the priest's petition, Kronstadt was described as 'barely a day away from the parts of the infidels', a position which made it vulnerable to foreign attacks.[79] The term 'infidels' referred to the Turks that had just attacked in 1421, while the one-day distance hinted at the town's position in relation to Wallachia, through which the Ottoman troops had invaded Transylvania. Once again, the large numbers of Vlachs, Armenians, Bulgarians and Greeks in the region were mentioned, but their presence appeared rather peripheral among the complaints of the priest.[80]

By 1450, when the southern border of Transylvania had suffered even more as a result of the Turkish raids, their violence had become the central element of discourse in the petitions, and the 'schismatics' were no longer mentioned.[81] In that timeframe, Burzenland had experienced two more Turkish invasions (1432, 1438) and possibly other small-scale raids, although, in the meantime, the town's fortifications had been visibly improved to better withstand the Ottoman pressure.[82] The 'schismatics' would make a reappearance in a papal indulgence letter received in 1474, but they were once again mentioned alongside the Turks, who were portrayed as the main enemy.[83] In comparison to them, the presence of the 'schismatics' appeared rather innocuous. The re-emergence of the Greek Orthodox Christians in the language of the petitions might, however, be linked to the revival of Catholic proselytism in Hungary during the reign of King Matthias Corvinus (1458–90).[84]

---

[79] '[A] partibus infidelium per unam vix dietam distat et nuper omnibus tam ecclesiis quam etiam habitationibus ipsius opidi per infideles desolatum fuit': Lukcsics 1: 134 (no. 532).

[80] '[I]n quo quidem opido tam Walachorum, Armenorum, Bulgarorum et Grecorum, quam aliarum infidelium copia unacum Christianis in eo degentibus morari solebat': Lukcsics 1: 134 (no. 532).

[81] Lukcsics 2: 275 (no. 1097).

[82] Markus Peter Beham, 'Kronstadt in der "Türkenabwehr" (1438–1479)', *Zeitschrift für Siebenbürgische Landeskunde* 32 (2009), 46–61, at 48–50.

[83] '[I]n confinibus christianitatis et in metis infidelium terrae Valachie situatum est, in quo quidem opido tam Valachorum, Armenorum, Bulgarorum et Grecorum, quam aliorum infidelium copia una cum ipsis christianis in ipso oppido degentibus morari solet ... etiam ab ipsis saevissimis Turchis crucis Christi inimicis totaliter combustum, desolatum et annichilatum': UB Siebenbürgen 7: 33-4 (no. 4029).

[84] Drăgan, *Nobilimea românească*, 102.

THE CASE OF KLEINENYED

The final example involves an indulgence petition addressed on behalf of the Catholic community in Kleinenyed (Sângătin),[85] a village in the chapter of Mühlbach (Sebeş), under the ecclesiastical jurisdiction of the bishop of Transylvania.[86] In one petition recorded on 13 July 1433, an indulgence letter was requested for those who would visit the local hospital and its nearby church, dedicated to the Holy Cross and to saints Cosmas and Damian, respectively.[87] The petitioner was only identified as 'Johannes, son of Balthasar', but a different register record from the same month revealed that he was serving King Sigismund of Luxembourg as secretary (*notarius*).[88]

The supplicant was a Transylvanian Saxon from Kleinenyed, later ennobled by King Sigismund in 1435.[89] According to the royal charter he received on that occasion, Johannes was part of the king's itinerant court and had served him over the years in Germany, Lombardy and Italy.[90] It was in this context that he reached the papal chancery with his indulgence request in 1433, as King Sigismund was present in Rome that year to be crowned emperor.[91] When Johannes became a noble, the king bestowed upon him and his family the estate of Szentjánoshegy (Nucet) in the county of Alba, and later sources identify him as 'Johannes Zaaz of Szentjánoshegy' or 'Johannes Zaaz of Enyed'.[92] 'Zaaz' was a Hungarian sobriquet meaning 'the Saxon', hinting at

---

[85] In Latin sources, the village was simply identified as 'Enyed'; for this reason, it has sometimes been confounded with the present-day town of Aiud (Enyed, Grossenyed): see Géza Antal Entz, 'Erdélyi', in Ernő Marosi, ed., *Magyarországi művészet, 1300–1470 körül*, 2 vols (Budapest, 1987), 1: 683–93, at 692; Ileana Burnichioiu, 'Biserica mică a cetăţii Aiudului în surse din secolul al XIX-lea', *Annales Universitatis Apulensis, Series Historica* 10/1 (2006), 7–23, at 17–18.

[86] Georg Müller, *Die deutschen Landkapitel in Siebenbürgen und ihre Dechanten, 1192–1848*, Archiv des Vereins für Siebenbürgische Landeskunde 48 (Hermannstadt, 1934), 49.

[87] Lukcsics 2: 87 (no. 203); Giorgio Fedalto, ed., *Acta Eugenii Papae IV (1431–1447)* (Rome, 1990), 127 (no. 206).

[88] Lukcsics 2: 113 (no. 284).

[89] For his diploma of nobility, see UB Siebenbürgen 4: 567–8 (no. 2227). For a brief biography of the petitioner, in the context of his church patronage in Mühlbach, see Gustav Gündisch and Theobald Streitfeld, 'Der Umbau der Mühlbacher Marienkirche im 15. Jahrhundert und seine geschichtlichen Voraussetzungen', in Gustav Gündisch et al., eds, *Studien zur Siebenbürgischen Kunstgeschichte* (Bucharest, 1976), 60–80, at 75–8.

[90] UB Siebenbürgen 4: 567 (no. 2227).

[91] Gündisch and Streitfeld, 'Umbau der Mühlbacher Marienkirche', 75.

[92] For example, see UB Siebenbürgen 5: 21–2, 44–6, 363 (nos 2329, 2358, 2359 and 2802).

the bearer's ethnic background.[93] Later in his career, he became the royal judge of Mühlbach and Hermannstadt.[94] One of his younger brothers, Georgius, studied canon law at Bologna, and became parish priest in Mühlbach.[95]

The wording of Johannes's petition is interesting, as it differentiates between the two elements defining Transylvanian marginality. According to it, the inhabitants of Kleinenyed lived 'amid the schismatics and close to the border of the Turks'.[96] The distinction is similar to the one found in the petition made by the parish priest of Kronstadt in 1422. Thus, while Transylvanian Catholics lived *among* the schismatics (*in medio Scismaticorum*), they were sharply separated from the Turks by a border (*meta*). Transylvania's border with Wallachia was understood as a border with the Turks, because the political events in the neighbouring voivodate were influenced by the intrusions of the Ottomans, who would promote their favourable voivode to the throne and proceed to invade Transylvania through Wallachia.[97] At this point, there was no mention of religious conversions anymore, which likewise illustrates the shift in discourse taking place in the 1420s and 1430s, against the troubled political and military background of those years.

Conclusion

The cases outlined above suggest that Transylvanian supplicants viewed receiving papal indulgences as a form of devotion to the same extent that other Christians in the Latin church did. However, apart from their traditional devotional significance, the grants acquired additional meaning within the regional context marked by confessional differences. Some petitioners regarded papal indulgences as a way of rewarding Catholics engaged in conversion attempts directed at the local Greek Orthodox Christians, even though the extent and success of these initiatives were sometimes exaggerated. The indulgence grants were also described as a potential means to encourage church attendance among the new converts, or finance the reparation of churches

[93] Victor V. Vizauer, 'Ethnic Nicknames (Sobriquets) in Transylvania during the 13th–14th Centuries', *Acta Musei Napocensis* 54 (2017), 17–39, at 25.
[94] Gündisch and Streitfeld, 'Umbau der Mühlbacher Marienkirche', 76.
[95] Ibid. 77.
[96] '[I]n medio Scismaticorum et prope Turcorum metas': Lukcsics 2: 87 (no. 203).
[97] Pálosfalvi, *From Nicopolis to Mohács*, 77–8.

that were struggling in the border regions affected by Ottoman raids. Requesting indulgences at the papal chancery was an occasion for interaction with the central authority of the church, and the supplications illustrate how marginality was articulated and used as an argumentative strategy in relation to the papacy. Most petitions were addressed by supplicants far from socially marginal in their own worlds, such as powerful barons and prosperous urban communities. In their accounts, the borders of Christianity were described as an area where Catholics were forced to coexist with the 'schismatics' or endure the cruelty of the Turks. The function of these descriptions as rhetorical devices does not, however, diminish their authenticity, as the representations of marginality were undoubtedly shaped by the various challenges faced by Transylvanian churches. Thus, they provide valuable insight into how Transylvanian petitioners represented and understood themselves as part of Latin Christendom.

Illuminating Faith: Marginalized Stained-Glass Fragments and Lost Schemes in the Pre-Reformation Parish Church

Lydia Fisher

University of Exeter

Stained-glass windows were a dominant focal feature within the pre-Reformation parish church building, where they were invested with multiple layers of spiritual meaning. A large and rich variety of stained-glass fragments survive in parish churches today, alongside textual evidence of lost glass, providing valuable insight into parochial religious experience. However, these sources have traditionally been marginalized in the art-historical canon in favour of fuller, sequential stained-glass programmes located in 'greater' ecclesiastical sites, such as cathedrals and minsters. This article places fragments and lost schemes at the centre of discussion. It traces and contextualizes three iconographic patterns that emerge from a closer study of fragments and textual accounts from the South-West of England. In doing so, it demonstrates the potential of such piecemeal evidence to illuminate the nature and function of the decorative arts in pre-Reformation worship.

INTRODUCTION

Difficult though it might be to comprehend from the fragmentary remains, we have to imagine a world in which prior to the Reformation, virtually every one of the more than ten thousand parish churches in England was filled with stained glass.[1]

Stained-glass windows were integral to the late medieval parish church building and its décor. As Richard Marks explains, they were once a universal feature. Yet it is due to the presence of fragmentary remains

History and Archaeology, University of Exeter, Exeter, UK. E-mail: l.j.fisher@exeter.ac.uk.

[1] Richard Marks, 'Medieval Stained Glass: Recent and Future Trends in Scholarship', in idem, *Studies in the Art and Imagery of the Middle Ages* (London, 2013), 33–63, at 38.

Studies in Church History 61 (2025), 230–257 © The Author(s), 2025. Published by Cambridge University Press on behalf of the Ecclesiastical History Society. This is an Open Access article, distributed under the terms of the Creative Commons Attribution licence (http://creativecommons.org/licenses/by/4.0), which permits unrestricted re-use, distribution and reproduction, provided the original article is properly cited.
doi:10.1017/stc.2024.38

and historical records of lost medieval glass, and not in spite of their existence, that it is possible to imagine a world in which this was the case. In the south-west region of England alone, here encompassing the counties of Cornwall, Devon and Somerset (pre-1974), medieval glass survives and is documented in over two hundred parish churches to date.[2] It is clear from this and wider regional surveys on the medium that glazing was not reserved for the largest churches, or even the wealthiest and most populous settlements. Instead, it was a prominent part of everyday parochial visual culture. Together, the cobbled pieces and descriptions of ancient glass that survive afford the researcher insightful glimpses into a lost religious tradition practised in the locality, one centred on liturgical performance, vivid sensory engagement and devotional experience. They constitute a vital source of information on medieval worship that has yet to be interrogated to its fullest potential.

This article addresses the theme of margins and peripheries through the lens of stained glass in three methodological senses. Firstly, discussion deliberately focusses on stray pieces of glass and accounts of lost windows traditionally marginalized by the canon. Until recently, this privileged extant, innovative and coherent programmes of stained-glass windows that could more readily be studied in relation to conventional art historical lines of enquiry, such as the significance of style, the identification of workshops and the skill of individual craftsmen.[3] Within the English context, a significant proportion of the literature on stained glass has been dedicated to the collections of 'great churches', such as the cathedrals at Wells and Canterbury, and York Minster, or the exceptionally well-preserved sequences remaining in smaller churches, such as St Peter Mancroft in Norwich and St Mary's Fairford (Gloucestershire).[4] Whilst the summary catalogues produced by the

---

[2] Lydia Fisher, 'Visualising Faith: Stained Glass Windows, Belief and the Parish in the South-West of England (*c.*1400–1700)' (PhD thesis, University of Exeter, 2023).

[3] Michael W. Cothren, 'Some Personal Reflections on American Modern and Postmodern Historiographies of Gothic Stained Glass', in Colum Hourihane, ed., *From Minor to Major: The Minor Arts in Medieval Art History*, The Index of Christian Art Occasional Papers 14 (Princeton, NJ, 2012), 255–70, at 255–9.

[4] Madeline H. Caviness, *The Windows of Christ Church Cathedral, Canterbury* (London, 1981); Tim Ayers, *The Medieval Stained Glass of Wells Cathedral*, 2 vols (Oxford, 2004); David King, *The Medieval Stained Glass of St Peter Mancroft, Norwich* (Oxford, 2006); Sarah Brown, 'Patronage and Piety in a Late Medieval English Parish: Reading Fairford Church and its Windows', *Journal of Glass Studies* 56 (2014), 287–301; Sarah Brown, *Stained Glass at York Minster* (London, 2017).

Corpus Vitrearum Medii Aevi have greatly enriched knowledge of smaller and displaced manifestations of glass situated within a wide range of ecclesiastic and domestic settings, the emphasis of their analysis remains on the documentation, provenance and classification of iconographic types, as opposed to the interpretation of meaning in light of late medieval spirituality.[5] Fragments need to be integrated into the conversation currently taking place in cathedral contexts around the role stained glass played in wider religious themes, such as the liturgy, devotional trends and the spiritual topography of the church building.[6]

Secondly, this article pulls the parish church from the periphery to the heart of study. Despite the wave of revisionist interest in the medieval parish as a socio-spiritual body in the 1990s and 2000s, research into the architecture and materiality of the parish church building has considerably lagged behind that generated on cathedral, monastic and collegiate sites which stand as grander monuments with greater institutional status.[7] This neglect caused Paul Binski to argue in 1999 for the urgent need to focus scholarly attention on the English parish church and its furnishings, 'rather than seeing it as some unfathomable, and perhaps embarrassing, epiphenomenon of something that

---

[5] Madeline H. Caviness et al., eds, *Stained Glass Before 1700 in American Collections: Mid-Atlantic and Southeastern Seaboard States*, Studies in the History of Art Monograph Series 1.23 (Washington, 1987); Richard Marks, *The Medieval Stained Glass of Northamptonshire* (London, 1998); Brian Sprakes, *The Medieval Stained Glass of South Yorkshire* (Oxford, 2003); Penny Hebgin-Barnes, *The Medieval Stained Glass of Lancashire* (Oxford, 2009); eadem, *The Medieval Stained Glass of Cheshire* (Oxford, 2010).

[6] Richard Marks's examination of Sir William Horne's glazing bequest to the church of Snailwell is a notable exception in a volume largely devoted to European cathedrals: Richard Marks, 'Sir William Horne and His "Scowred" Window at Snailwell, Cambridgeshire', in Evelyn Staudiger Lane, Elizabeth Carson Pastan and Ellen M. Shortell, eds, *The Four Modes of Seeing: Approaches to Medieval Imagery in Honor of Madeline Harrison Caviness* (Aldershot, 2009), 99–110. See also Elizabeth Carson Pastan and Brigitte Kurmann-Schwarz, eds, *Investigations in Medieval Stained Glass: Materials, Methods, and Expressions*, Reading Medieval Sources 3 (Leiden, 2019).

[7] For a selection, see Nicola Coldstream and Peter Draper, eds, *Medieval Art and Architecture at Wells and Glastonbury*, British Archaeological Association Conference Transactions 4 (Leeds, 1981); Laurence Draper and Nicola Coldstream, eds, *Medieval Art and Architecture at Canterbury before 1220*, British Archaeological Association Conference Transactions 5 (Leeds, 1982); Tim Tatton-Brown and Richard Mortimer, eds, *Westminster Abbey: The Lady Chapel of Henry VII* (Woodbridge, 2003); Roberta Gilchrist, *Norwich Cathedral Close: The Evolution of the English Cathedral Landscape* (Woodbridge, 2005); Julian M. Luxford, *The Art and Architecture of English Benedictine Monasteries, 1300–1540: A Patronage History* (Woodbridge, 2005); David Brown, ed., *Durham Cathedral: History, Fabric and Culture* (New Haven, CT, 2015).

was "really" going on elsewhere'.[8] Since the publication of this article, the roots of the parish church as an academic and popular object of study have been steadily growing, which has led to an appreciation that the structure and contents of these buildings were deeply embedded within the socio-religious life of their community.[9] However, there is much progress still to be made due to the sheer bulk of material to process in relation to questions of context, function and reception, within an architecturally diverse category of buildings numbering well into the thousands.[10]

Finally, this article adopts the South-West as a regional case study as it occupies the geographic periphery of the country and is often popularly perceived as a cultural backwater. Aside from a handful of studies and individual scholars invested in the subject, the South-West is often sidelined in mainstream studies on pre-Reformation religious practice in favour of urbanized or populous centres with better records.[11] More specifically, research into the glazing of south-western England is particularly lacking, despite it hosting a diverse body of evidence from the recognizable windows of St Neot (Cornwall) to the lesser known collections of glass at Bampton (Devon) or Langport (Somerset).[12] Even the substantially complete survivals housed at

---

[8] Paul Binski, 'The English Parish Church and its Art in the Later Middle Ages: A Review of the Problem', *Studies in Iconography* 20 (1999), 1–25, at 2.

[9] Most recently, see John Goodall, *Parish Church Treasures: The Nation's Greatest Art Collection* (London, 2015); Gabriel Byng, *Church Building and Society in the Later Middle Ages* (Cambridge, 2017); Helen E. Lunnon, *East Anglian Church Porches and their Medieval Contexts* (Woodbridge, 2020); Meg Bernstein, ed., *Towards an Art History of the Parish Church, 1200–1399*, Courtauld Books Online (London, 2021), at: <https://courtauld.ac.uk/research/research-resources/publications/courtauld-books-online/parish-church/>, accessed 8 March 2024.

[10] Peter Draper, *The Formation of English Gothic: Architecture and Identity* (New Haven, CT, 2006), 175–96.

[11] For a selection of literature published on the region see Robert Whiting, *Local Responses to the English Reformation* (London, 1998); Eamon Duffy, *The Voices of Morebath: Reformation and Rebellion in an English Village* (New Haven, CT, 2001); Nicholas Orme, 'Popular Religion and the Reformation in England: A View from Cornwall', in James D. Tracy and Marguerite Ragnow, eds, *Religion and the Early Modern State: Views from China, Russia and, the West* (Cambridge, 2004), 351–76; Joanna Mattingly, ed., *Stratton Churchwardens' Accounts, 1512–1578*, Devon and Cornwall Record Society n.s. 60 *(Woodbridge, 2018)*.

[12] Christopher Woodforde, *Stained Glass in Somerset, 1250–1830* (Oxford, 1946); Chris Brooks and David Evans, *The Great East Window of Exeter Cathedral: A Glazing History* (Exeter, 1988); Joanna Mattingly, 'Stories in the Glass: Reconstructing the St Neot Pre-Reformation Glazing Scheme', *Journal of the Royal Institution of Cornwall* 2nd n.s. 3 (2000), 9–55.

Doddiscombsleigh (Devon) and St Kew (Cornwall) have yet to receive sustained scholarly study. The oldest extant glass to be found outside of a cathedral in the region dates to the early fourteenth century at Bere Ferrers (Devon), coinciding with the foundation of a collegiate community there.[13] Elsewhere, the majority of surviving material dates from the late fourteenth to early sixteenth centuries, corresponding with the late medieval drive to expand, redevelop and embellish the parish church building.[14] Unlike the dominant glazing centres of York and Norwich, the names and dates of glaziers operating in the area is not well documented.[15] However, the South-West is well-served with the written evidence of eighteenth- and nineteenth-century antiquarians that account for the subject matter and composition of stained-glass windows that have since been lost or altered due to modern restoration.[16] Thus, it is high time that the spotlight was turned upon the glazing of south-western England.

This article argues that an integration of marginalized stained-glass fragments and lost glass into the mainstream of academic debates on the tenor of pre-Reformation parochial spirituality not only substantially augments the body of evidence we have as an entry point into the subject, but also generates a better understanding of the multifaceted role the medium played in quotidian religious life. There are methodological and interpretive challenges when encountering isolated remains or decontextualized pieces, but there are also benefits. A glass fragment often refers to its totality, conveying ideas beyond itself and testifying to a missing tradition of glazing. The sheer variety of these pieces correct any assumptions of homogeneity or perfection created by the unique programmes of large churches. Combined with the written evidence of absent schemes, this idea of variety encourages the researcher to view the parish church on a continuum more broadly, as an active, evolving building.

The discussion of this article draws out and contextualizes three striking iconographic patterns that arise from a closer study of these

[13] Nicholas Orme, *The Church in Devon 400–1560* (Exeter, 2013), 91, 109.

[14] Byng, *Church Building*, 1–50.

[15] Richard Marks, *Stained Glass in England during the Middle Ages* (London, 1993), 40–51.

[16] For example, John Collinson, *History and Antiquities of the County of Somerset*, 3 vols (Bath, 1791); Richard Polwhele, *The History of Devonshire*, 3 vols (London, 1793–1806); Joseph Polsue, *A Complete Parochial History of the County of Cornwall*, 4 vols (London, 1867–72).

sources. In doing so, this article does not intend to provide a comprehensive account of south-western glazing, but rather to provide an introduction to the available material and to pull at some of the interpretative threads that appear. It opens with the identification of Crucifixion scenes, exploring the significance of their proximity to altars and symbolic resonance with the mass. It proceeds with a consideration of scenes from the seven sacraments and their doctrinal value to the parish community. Finally, the article moves to examine evidence of narrative cycles and reflects upon their connection to devotional impulses.

CRUCIFIXION SCENES

The Crucifixion was a popular subject to depict in stained glass, either as an isolated scene or as a component of the wider Passion story. It famously adorns the fifteenth-century and sixteenth-century east windows of Great Malvern Priory (Worcestershire) and St Mary's Fairford, as well as having been intended for the chapel at Hampton Court Palace in London.[17] These pictorial imaginations of Christ's life and death intersected with a growing devotional intensity towards the figure of Christ and the mass in the two centuries preceding the break with Rome.[18] The medieval liturgy was mediated through the senses, as it was an elaborate ceremony focussed on movement, song and recitation, giving life to the written word.[19] Above all, however, there was a special emphasis on sight. The spiritual and salvific potency of seeing the elevation of the consecrated host was such that it led the fourteenth-century Dominican friar John Bromyard to comment that if Christ himself were to walk into the church during the height of the canon he would have been missed.[20] For large ecclesiastic sites, such as the cathedrals of Beauvais and Chartres in France, as well as Wells in England, it has been observed that glazing formed a vital part of a

[17] Marks, *Stained Glass*, 25.

[18] Eamon Duffy, *The Stripping of the Altars: Traditional Religion in England 1400–1580* (New Haven, CT, 1992), 91–107; Robert N. Swanson, *Religion and Devotion in Europe, c.1215–c.1515* (Cambridge, 1995), 137–41.

[19] Eric Palazzo, 'Art, Liturgy, and the Five Senses in the Early Middle Ages', *Viator* 41 (2010), 25–56.

[20] Dallas G. Denery II, 'From Sacred Mystery to Divine Deception: Robert Holkot, John Wyclif and the Transformation of Fourteenth-Century Eucharistic Discourse', *JRH* 29 (2005), 129–44, at 129.

Figure 1. Crucifixion window, St Winnow's parish church, St Winnow, Cornwall. © The author.

sophisticated physical infrastructure designed to support the perform-ance of the liturgy and reinforce visions of the elevated eucharist during the mass.[21] The evidence of fragments and lost schemes indicate that these observations are applicable to the stained-glass configurations of smaller churches.

The tradition of visualizing the Crucifixion in glass extended into the parish churches of the South-West of England. Christ is com-monly depicted nailed to the cross in a central light flanked by figures of the weeping Virgin Mary and St John the Evangelist in neighbour-ing lights. Fuller or complete examples of this can be seen in the churches of St Catherine's near Bath (Somerset), Kelly (Devon), St Winnow (Cornwall) and Winscombe (Somerset). These schemes are often both richly detailed and theologically sophisticated. For instance, at St Winnow, the Crucifixion is now set against plain glass (Figure 1). A skull and collection of bones appear in the ground beneath both the cross and the feet of the figures. Whilst accentuating the theme of death and sacrifice, these bones refer to Golgotha, or the place of a skull, as recounted in the canonical gospels, thereby setting the image in historical, biblical terms. The use of dark and dull colours further

[21] Ayers, *Stained Glass of Wells*, lxxv–lxxxviii; Cothren, 'Personal Reflections', 266–70; Gerald B. Guest, 'Stained Glass and Liturgy: The Uses and Limits of an Analogy', *Journal of Glass Studies* 56 (2014), 271–85.

Figure 2. Crucifixion window, St James' parish church, Winscombe, Somerset. © The author.

alludes to the eclipse which engulfed the land at the Son of God's death. At Winscombe, two trees grow beside Jesus' bleeding feet, an artistic motif denoting the tree of life and tree of knowledge of good and evil described in Genesis 2: 9 (Figure 2). The glass thus visualizes the restoration of Eden and salvation of humanity achieved through Christ's redemptive act on the cross, a lifegiving tree.[22] In the tracery

---

[22] Pippa Salonius, 'The Tree of Life in Medieval Iconography', in Douglas Estes, ed., *The Tree of Life* (Leiden, 2020), 280–343, at 295–7.

Figure 3. Crucifixion fragments, St Crida's parish church, Creed, Cornwall. © The author.

lights above, a collection of angels upholds shields exhibiting the instruments of Christ's torture. Reading from left to right, these emblems are: a crown of thorns, a robe and dice, three nails, a ladder with a hammer and pincers, a pillar with two whips, and the cross. The shields refer to pivotal moments in Christ's torment, such as the flagellation, thus symbolically guiding the viewer through the journey which led to Calvary.

The testimony of fragments strengthens this pattern of survival and reveals the widespread nature of this iconography. Fragments denoting this lost subject matter are easier to identify due to the highly recognizable set of motifs and symbolism often deployed. For instance, the scant shards of glass remaining in the east window at Creed display the side of Christ's head with faint traces of the crown of thorns alongside a pierced hand shedding blood (Figure 3). Christ's nailed hand is repeated in the east window's tracery of St Tudy (Cornwall). Meanwhile, in the south transept at Lamorran (Cornwall) a collection of glass contains the images of two skulls and some bones, reminiscent of those described at St Winnow. Sometimes, larger sections of the cross or of Christ's dying figure upon it survive, as at Laneast (Cornwall) (Figure 4). At Dinder (Somerset), the upper half of the cross inscribed with the letters *INRI* can be identified amongst a collection of

Figure 4. Fragment of Christ crucified, St Sidwell and Gulvat's parish church, Laneast, Cornwall. © The author.

fragments situated in a window over the pulpit which also showcases remains of the Holy Trinity. *INRI* stands for the mock title *Iesus Nazarenus Rex Iudaeorum*, or 'Jesus the Nazarene, King of the Jews', bestowed upon Jesus by Pontius Pilate (John 19: 19). In other locations, all that remains are the mournful outlines of the Virgin Mary and St John, as at Altarnun (Cornwall), Gidleigh (Devon) and Pitcombe (Somerset) (Figure 5). At Trull (Somerset), a nineteenth-

Figure 5. Fragment depicting St John the Evangelist, St Nonna's parish church, Altarnun, Cornwall. © The author.

century reconstruction of the crucified Christ was inserted into a fifteenth-century Crucifixion window which retained the by-standing Mother of God and favoured disciple because, 'a small piece of glass shewing a portion of a head crowned with thorns' confirmed its original presence.[23] Therefore, this assembly of glass remnants adds representational weight to the iconographic theme, a rare impression of which is given by the whole examples that can still be seen today.

Furthermore, it is possible to recover lost Crucifixion scenes from the documentary record. For instance, the scene once decorated the

[23] 'Trull', *Taunton Courier and Western Advertiser*, 11 February 1863, 7.

east window of the church at Clyst St George (Devon) alongside the representations of a clerical donor figure, identified in an inscription as the late fourteenth-century rector of the church John Allar, St George holding a shield and the crowned Virgin Mary carrying the Christ child in one arm and a rod in the other.[24] Having survived restoration work conducted on the chancel in 1854, this glass was unfortunately later destroyed when the church building was bombed during the Second World War.[25]

The frequency of this iconography in stained glass points to a dynamic relationship between windows, altars and the ritual of the mass, illuminated in one respect spatially. The Crucifixion theme was often incorporated into the east window positioned directly behind the high altar in the chancel or above a subsidiary altar in a side chapel, where a significant proportion of the aforementioned fragments and assemblages are found. The east window of the chancel or chapel was typically larger in scale than other windows in the space, as it physically occupied and defined the boundaries of the holy ground surrounding the altar. Its amplified imagery materially framed the altar, thus demonstrating that stained-glass windows were informed by an awareness of spatial setting and could operate as a backdrop to an altar in a similar vein to an altarpiece or reredos.[26] This has been acknowledged in higher status churches, such as in the case of the great east window at Gloucester Cathedral which was described by Richard Marks as a 'gigantic triptych'.[27] Yet, the pervasiveness of Crucifixion glazing in parish churches indicates that this also happened on a smaller scale.

Stained glass visualized the intrinsic meaning of the mass and renewed the events memorialized in the holy sacrament. As a memorial to the scriptural events, the glass underpins the purpose of the mass as an act of remembrance and solemn reflection, as immortalized in Christ's words repeated by the priest in the canon: 'As oft as ye shall

---

[24] Exeter, Devon Heritage Centre, MS West Country Studies Library, MATCH DAV-CHU1843, James Davidson's Church Notes on Devon, 1: 317; George Oliver, *Ecclesiastical Antiquities in Devon: Being Observations on Several Churches in Devonshire*, 2 vols (Exeter, 1840), 1: 152.

[25] Henry Thomas Ellacombe, *The History and Antiquities of the Parish of Clyst St. George* (Exeter, 1865), 20; Bridget Cherry and Nikolaus Pevsner, *The Buildings of England: Devon*, 2nd edn (Harmondsworth, 1989; first publ. 1952), 271.

[26] Allan B. Barton, 'The Ornaments of the Altar and the Ministers in Late-Medieval England', in Paul S. Barnwell, Claire Cross and Ann Rycraft, eds, *Mass and Parish in Late Medieval England: The Use of York* (Reading, 2005), 27–40, at 30.

[27] Marks, *Stained Glass*, 165.

do these things, ye shall do them in remembrance of me'.[28] The words and acts of Christ's final days were continuously renewed in the daily performance of the mass, which encouraged the laity to experience Christ's Passion and death as a present reality.[29] For instance, the *Lay Folks' Mass Book* was a widely circulated treatise translated around the twelfth century, which guided lay involvement in the mass. During the Gospel reading, it directed the laity to stand in respect and 'speke þou night, / bot þenk on him þat dere þe boght'.[30] The presence of the Crucifixion scene strengthened this contemplative experience and created the impression that the event was taking place in real time. It served as a reminder of humanity's salvation at Calvary and, by association, the perpetual, redemptive power of the mass daily enacted in the church.

Stained-glass windows also interpreted the intimate connection between Christ's body and the host consecrated by the priest. This is most apparent in the physical proximity of the glass to an altar where the bread was blessed, making the visual link inescapable. As the priest officiated over the ceremony with his back to the congregation, his gaze was directed towards Jesus' death upon the cross depicted in glass. At the point of elevation enacted directly in front of the window, the host would have been seen on a level visual plane as Christ's image. The identification was further enhanced pictorially by Christ's naked-ness, with his flesh laid bare before the viewer. The bond between the eucharist and the Crucifixion was stressed in contemporary didactic literature. For example, John Mirk's fifteenth-century *Instructions for Parish Priests* clearly relates the crucifix to the Eucharist by advising priests to teach the laity to 'be-leue on that sacrament; / That þey receyue in forme of bred, / Hyt ys goddess body þat soffered ded / Vp on the holy rode tre'.[31]

Therefore, to summarize, stained-glass windows added weight and significance to the physical setting and performance of the mass. Their

---

[28] *The Sarum Missal in English*, transl. and ed. Frederick E. Warren, 2 vols (London, 1913), 1: 46.

[29] Duffy, *Stripping of the Altars*, 91; Ellen M. Ross, *The Grief of God: Images of the Suffering Jesus in Late Medieval England* (New York, 1997), 13.

[30] '[S]peak thou nought, / but think on him that dear thee bought': *The Lay Folks' Mass Book*, ed. Thomas F. Simmons, EETS o.s. 71 (London, 1879), 18.

[31] '[B]elieve on that sacrament; / That they receive in form of bread, / It is God's body that suffered dead / Up on the holy rood tree': John Mirk, *Instructions for Parish Priests*, ed. Edward Peacock, EETS o.s. 31 (London, 1902), 8.

vivid imagery underscored both the doctrinal and scriptural meaning of the sacrament by connecting the priest's acts at the altar with the soteriological power of Christ's death on the cross. Fragments and textual evidence indicate that the presence of Crucifixion imagery above altars was far more pervasive than the surviving, cohesive programmes of cathedrals or larger churches suggest. The vibrant interaction between art, space and liturgy evident in these greater monuments also took place within the parish church setting.

THE SEVEN SACRAMENTS

Turning to another iconographic theme, several parish churches in south-west England illustrate remnants of the seven sacraments, one of the basic tenets of late medieval Christian faith.[32] At St Mary's Bishops Lydeard (Somerset), a collection of fifteenth-century fragments survives in a vestry window. Amongst them, a cleric in red vestments gathers around a font with a lay couple and a headless figure dressed in a blue tunic. An open rubric lies in the midst of the group and traces of a label identify the scene as a baptism (Figure 6). At Burrington (Somerset), pieces of glass in a north aisle window display the blessing at holy orders and the pinnacle of the eucharist ceremony where the priest elevates the host.[33] The documentary record of lost glass strengthens this pattern. For example, in 1434, Thomas Marshall, vicar of All Saints' Bristol, paid for two windows to be placed in the south aisle of the church, known as the Rood or Cross aisle, with one depicting the seven sacraments and the other the seven works of mercy.[34] Elsewhere in the late eighteenth century, the antiquarian Rev. John Collinson visited St Mary's Meare (Somerset) and commented: 'The east window of the north aile [*sic*] contains very fine old painted glass, in which are several historical groups of fine figures; but much obscured by dirt. The principal are the administration of Baptism, the Lord's Supper, and Extreme Unction.'[35] Some time after

---

[32] The seven sacraments encompassed baptism, the eucharist, confirmation, penance, extreme unction, matrimony and holy orders.

[33] Christopher Woodforde, *Stained Glass in Somerset 1250–1830* (London, 1946; repr. Bath, 1970), 168–9.

[34] Clive Burgess, ed., *The Pre-Reformation Records of All Saints', Bristol*, part 1, Bristol Record Society 46 (Bristol, 1995), 8.

[35] John Collinson, *History and Antiquities of the County of Somerset*, 3 vols (Bath, 1791), 2: 274.

Figure 6. Fragments depicting a baptism, St Mary's parish church, Bishop's Lydeard, Somerset. © The author.

Collinson's visit, the stained glass was removed and replaced with clear glass because it was believed to have made the interior too dark.[36]

The north aisle's east window at St Michael's Doddiscombsleigh (Devon) possesses the most famous and best-preserved example of a seven sacraments window in the country, enabling the researcher to contextualize these fragments and descriptions (Figure 7). The fifteenth-century window displays groups of figures enacting the sacraments and surrounding a modern depiction of Christ seated in majesty, created by the stained-glass workshop Clayton and Bell upon the window's

[36] William Phelps, *The History and Antiquities of Somersetshire*, 2 vols (London, 1836), 1: 575.

Figure 7. Seven sacraments window, St Michael's parish church, Doddiscombleigh, Devon. © The author.

restoration in the nineteenth century.[37] The sacraments are connected to Christ by red lines flowing from his five wounds. It is likely that the original image of Christ once resembled the solitary figure that now survives at Cadbury (Devon), where red lines stem from Jesus' bleeding hands, feet and side (Figure 8). This practice of connecting the sacraments to the figure of Christ can be witnessed in other examples across the south-western counties as the sacraments radiate from Christ showcasing the Passion wounds at Melbury Bubb (Dorset) and Crudwell (Wiltshire). Meanwhile, at Llandyrnog (Denbighshire), the sacraments

---

[37] John Stabb, *Some Old Devon Churches: Their Rood Screens, Pulpits, Fonts, etc.*, 3 vols (London, 1908–16), 2: 85.

Figure 8. Christ showcasing his wounds, St Michael's parish church, Cadbury, Devon. © The author.

are linked by red lines to a central crucifix. On occasion, sacrament windows formed part of a larger programme portraying central articles of the late medieval Christian faith, as at All Saints' Bristol cited above. For example, Thomas Habington, surveying the county of Worcestershire in the seventeenth century, recalled seeing the north aisle of Great Malvern Priory adorned with 'the Pater Noster, Ave Maria, the Creede, the Commandments, the Masse, the Sacraments issuing out from the wounds of our Saviour; my memory fainteth. But to conclude all in one, there is the whole Christian doctrine'.[38] Fragmented scenes of three

[38] Thomas Habington, *A Survey of Worcestershire*, ed. John Amphlett, 2 vols (Oxford, 1899), 2: 177.

sacraments – ordination, marriage and baptism – now reside in the east window of the church.

Therefore, whilst the sacrament window at Doddiscombsleigh is rare in its condition and completeness, the witness of fragments and lost glass indicates that the subject matter was not uncommon. This elucidates the complex, multifaceted role that stained-glass windows assumed within the parish church setting. For instance, in their full composition, these windows executed a form of doctrinal exegesis, as they interpreted and relayed the sacraments' value to the viewer. The programmes make a profound theological statement regarding the origins and virtue of the seven sacraments, as derived from Christ's blood and sacrifice.[39] As the twelfth-century French theologian and bishop Peter Lombard explained, 'before the advent of Christ, who brought grace, the sacraments of grace could not be granted, for they have derived their virtue from his death and passion.'[40] These stained-glass windows thus demonstrate how sophisticated theological ideas filtered down into the popular experience and imagination.

Moreover, these stained-glass assemblages imprinted the church's interior with the main purpose of the building: the performance of the sacraments. The sacraments held a central place in quotidian religious life. For instance, the laity were expected to attend the eucharist regularly and to partake of holy communion annually, at Easter. They were also expected to make their confession at least once a year during the season of Lent. Meanwhile, baptism, confirmation and marriage were rites of passage or life-cycle events conferred in a church which aimed to integrate an individual into the local Christian community.[41] This is reflected in the corporate character of these images. For instance, at Doddiscombsleigh, the individual's act of penance is set within the public space of the church where

---

[39] Gordon McNeil Rushforth, 'Seven Sacraments Compositions in English Medieval Art', *The Antiquaries Journal* 9 (1929), 83–100, at 84.

[40] Elizabeth Frances Rogers, *Peter Lombard and the Sacramental System* (New York, 1917), 85. Original Latin quoted in Rushforth, 'Seven Sacraments', 100: 'dicimus non ante adventum Christi, qui gratiam attulit, gratiae sacramenta fuisse danda; quae ex ipsius morte et passione virtutem sortita sunt.'

[41] Robert N. Swanson, 'Recording Liturgical and Sacramental Rites of Passage in Pre-Reformation English Parishes', in Frances Knight, Charlotte Methuen and Andrew Spicer, eds, *The Churches and Rites of Passage*, SCH 59 (2023), 142–63.

additional penitents wait in the background.[42] This sets the individual within a context of regular collective confession. By illustrating central aspects of sacramental performance, the windows prepared the congregation for the rites they regularly witnessed in the church, even visualizing what may not have been entirely visible from their position in the nave. These windows thus grant unique insight into the daily reality of religious practice and communal worship in the parish.

Furthermore, seven sacrament windows also formed a key part of the late medieval church's pastoral and educational drive, to ensure both the parochial clergy and laity understood and accepted key principles of the orthodox faith. The constitutions of the 1281 Council of Lambeth stipulated that the laity were to be instructed on the seven sacraments regularly in English, alongside other central articles of religious belief and practice, such as the Ten Commandments and the seven works of mercy.[43] This was subsequently expanded upon in the production of vernacular instructional manuals, such as the 1357 *Lay Folk's Catechism* and John Mirk's *Instructions for Parish Priests*.[44] Stained-glass sacrament schemes enshrined catechetical teaching, illustrating important stages in a Christian's life and spiritual development, thereby reinforcing verbalizations of their significance.

Therefore, an analysis of fragments and descriptions of lost glass indicates that a decorative feature which might have been assumed to be 'specialized', confined to a handful of churches, was actually quite commonplace. Illustrations of the seven sacraments were found in numerous parish churches across the South-West of England. Their existence demonstrates the manifold ways in which stained-glass windows communicated. On one level, they interpreted intricate theological beliefs surrounding the origins of the sacraments and delivered a powerful exposition of orthodox teaching. On another level, they reflected the enactment of the sacraments central to the routine religious life of the parish community.

---

[42] Tom Elich, 'Communal Reconciliation in Pre-Reformation England: Lessons from the Seven-Sacrament Fonts of East Anglia', *Studia Liturgica* 36 (2006), 138–65, at 156–65.

[43] Duffy, *Stripping of the Altars*, 54–5; Swanson, *Religion and Devotion*, 59–60.

[44] Thomas Frederick Simmons and Henry Edward Nolloth, eds, *The Lay Folks' Catechism; Or, The English and Latin Versions of Archbishop Thoresby's Instruction for the People*, EETS o.s. 118 (London, 1901), 60–8; Mirk, *Instructions for Parish Priests*, 16–63.

Passion Cycles

Finally, the testimony of surviving fragments, in combination with evidence from the written record, points to the widespread display of narrative Passion cycles. The Passion theme has not loomed large in accounts of English stained glass from this period except in recognition of a few select cases. Today, it finds expression in the well-preserved sequence which adorns the chapel at St Mary Magdalene's Newark (Nottinghamshire), spans the chancel and Corpus Christi chapel at Fairford, as well as in the remaining episodes that decorate the east window of St Peter Mancroft, including the entombment and resurrection. With regard to the South-West, the fifteenth-century series in the north chapel at St Kew (Cornwall) provides one of the best examples of a Passion window in the country, despite receiving little academic study (Figure 9). The window is divided into four main lights with ten labelled panels depicting individual events from Holy Week. It opens with Christ's triumphant entry into the city of Jerusalem on Palm Sunday and concludes with the harrowing of hell. However, two panels are missing and two out-of-place Nativity scenes have been inserted at the bottom of the window, which strongly suggests that it originally concluded with scenes of Christ's resurrection.

The coherency and preservation of St Kew's window may give the impression that such subject matter was rare, but the study of fragments draws the existence of further Passion windows into sharper focus. To take one example, the church of St Michael's Bampton (Devon) houses an important collection of fifteenth-century stained glass in a south aisle window that on first glance appears to be substantially complete (Figure 10). However, upon closer inspection, the glass is arranged in a kaleidoscopic manner, with pieces of glass cobbled together, proving to be illegible in many places. Only four subjects can be immediately deciphered, including depictions of the Holy Trinity, the Virgin Mary at the Annunciation and St George (originally St Michael) piercing a dragon beneath his feet.[45] One panel in the upper register presents the twelve apostles huddled around Christ's disappearing feet and floating figure with two trees in the background, thus representing Christ's Ascension at the Mount of

---

[45] Maurice and Wilfred Drake, *Saints and their Emblems* (London, 1916), 9.

Figure 9. Passion window, St James' parish church, St Kew, Cornwall. © The author.

Olives (Figure 11). It is possible to confirm the originality of this scene when tracing the restoration history of the window.[46]

[46] An inscription at the bottom of the window records how the glass was repositioned by local glass painter Maurice Drake in 1921 as a memorial to those parishioners who fought and died in the First World War. Before this move, the glass was located in the east window of the north chapel now obscured by an organ. Here, George Oliver observed 'a considerable collection of stained glass: it is easy to trace amongst the fragments, the subject of Christ's resurrection': Oliver, *Ecclesiastical Antiquities*, 1: 170; 'Bampton Church: Stained Glass', *Exeter and Plymouth Gazette*, 26 February 1921, 3.

Figure 10. South aisle window, St Michael's parish church, Bampton, Devon. © The author.

As a requisite component of the biblical narrative, it is unlikely that the Ascension scene initially stood as an isolated frame. It probably constituted a key part of a wider programme visualizing Christ's death and resurrection. The details preserved in a combination of fragments support this interpretation, from the repeated figure of Christ, whose head can be seen adorned with a crown of thorns, to instruments of Christ's torture, such as a ladder and whips. A scroll bearing the words 'Resurrec[tio] d[o]m̄[ini]' appears among the shards in the top left panel, and the letters 'dm̄' for *domini* are visible twice more, indicative that labels once accompanied the imagery, guiding the viewer through the narrative. The Passion window at St Kew confirms that this was a

Figure 11. Panel depicting the Ascension, St Michael's parish church, Bampton, Devon. © The author.

feature of such cycles and suggests a structure that the glass may have once followed.

Witness accounts from the nineteenth century identify the remains of further stained-glass Passion programmes in the region that no longer exist today. For example, all that remains in St Michael's Michaelstow (Cornwall) are traces of coloured glass. However, in the late nineteenth century, Sir John Maclean wrote about the south aisle's east window:

> The former contained remains of painted glass. The subject was prob-ably the last scenes in the life of Our Lord, as the fragments contained

several heads with the legend 'Hic ductus est ante Pilatum.' In the tracery of this window were two angels bearing shields, with the monograms of Our Lord and the Blessed Virgin. The window has been re-glased, and the ancient glass is gone.[47]

Elsewhere, in the east window of the south aisle at St Gorran's (Cornwall), the head of a male figure is all that survives in the tracery. However, in his topographical study of Cornwall published in 1820, Charles Gilbert noted: 'Some remains of stained glass are preserved in one of the windows, in which is represented the fixing of Christ to the cross, and the taking of him down from the same, after being crucified.'[48] This was corroborated by the writer Joseph Polsue, who saw 'scanty remains … [of] the principle [*sic*] scenes at the Crucifixion' in the window.[49] In 1824, at Mullion (Cornwall), Fortiscue Hitchins recorded seeing 'the ascension of Christ, with the apostles gazing on him with apparent wonder and amazement.'[50] It is also possible that the reclining figure seen in the south chapel window at Creed represents a sleeping disciple in the garden of Gethsemane or a soldier at the tomb (Figure 12). Thus, the combination of these sources indicates that the practice of depicting the climactic events of Christ's death and resurrection in the medium of stained glass was adopted by many parish churches.

Passion windows contributed to the liturgical rites and devotional practices performed in the parish church in diverse ways. The programme itself takes the viewer on a journey with Christ and His followers through His trial and persecution to the foot of the cross and beyond to His resurrection. This was a journey recreated in celebrated ecclesiastical processions in the church, from bearing palms and flowers around the churchyard and into the church via the west door to echo Christ's entry into Jerusalem on Palm Sunday; to 'creeping to the cross' in ritualistic mourning on Good Friday.[51] By

[47] Sir John MacClean, *The Parochial and Family History of the Deanery of Trigg Minor, in the County of Cornwall*, 2 vols (London, 1876), 2: 564.
[48] Charles Gilbert, *An Historical Survey of the County of Cornwall: To which is Added a Complete Heraldry of the Same with Numerous Engravings*, 2 vols (London, 1820), 2: 847.
[49] Polsue, *Complete Parochial History*, 2: 103.
[50] Fortiscue Hitchins, *The History of Cornwall: From the Earliest Records and Traditions, to the Present Time*, 2 vols (Helston, 1824), 2: 506.
[51] Duffy, *Stripping of the Altars*, 23–9; Ronald Hutton, *The Rise and Fall of Merry England: The Ritual Year 1400–1700* (Oxford, 1994), 21–3.

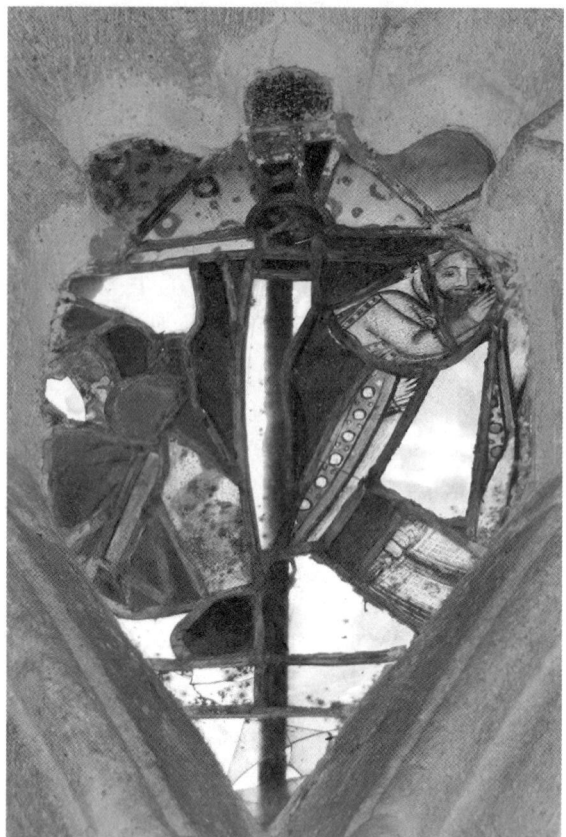

Figure 12. Fragments depicting a sleeping apostle or soldier, St Crida's parish church, Creed, Cornwall. © The author.

the fifteenth century, an expansive discourse had developed in the publication of vernacular literature, such as the widely disseminated *Speculum Sacerdotale* and John Mirk's *Festial*, which vigorously encouraged the laity to visualize and re-enact these pivotal moments in Christian history.[52] In ritually replicating these events, believers

[52] Edward H. Weatherly, ed., *Speculum Sacerdotale* (London, 1936), 128–9; John Mirk, *Mirk's Festial: A Collection of Homilies by Johannes Mirkus*, ed. Theodor Erbe, EETS extra series 96 (London, 1902), 115.

were transported. The laity sought to relive these experiences as Margery Kempe, a fifteenth-century laywoman who recorded her visions and experiences, described that whilst on procession on Maundy Thursday:

> Þe sayd creatur went procession with oþer pepil, sche saw in hir sowle owr Lady, Seynt Mary Mawdelyn, & þe xij apostelys. And þan sche be-held with hir gostly eye how owr Lady toke hir leue of hir blysful Son, Crist Ihesu ... Sche sey hyr Lord steyn vp in-to Heuyn.[53]

These visions were emotively manifested in the religious imagery of the window, which suggests that glass supported and inspired the devotional purpose of processions.

The glass also intersects with a growing affective trend in late medieval spirituality which focussed on the humanity and suffering of Christ. Parish clergy and their congregations were absorbing textual representations of Christ-the-Man and these fragments indicate how these ideas were given visual expression. These provided images of graphic accounts of the Passion, viscerally exposing the viewer to Jesus' humiliation, physical pain and anguish. These themes were elaborated upon in sermons, drama and devotional literature which were all designed to ignite the audience's imagination, as well as their compassion and empathy. As Richard Rolle meditated on Christ's cries, tears and anguish, he bade 'Loue, writ with þi blod so ofte Min harde herte tyl it be softe'.[54] This tradition was also geared towards inspiring the devotee to moral reform, as John Mirk's Passion sermon exhorted Christian men and women to 'kneliþ now adon, prayng to Crist þat he forȝeue you þat ȝe haue trespassyd aȝeyns hym by recheles sweryng'.[55] In this sense, glass harnessed the emotive power of images to move, direct and guide the individual in their daily interactions with the divine.

---

[53] 'The said creature went [on] procession with other people, she saw in her soul our Lady, saint Mary Magdalene, and the 12 apostles. And then she beheld with her ghostly eye how our Lady took her leave of her blissful Son, Christ Jesus ... She see her Lord ascend up into Heaven': Margery Kempe, *The Book of Margery Kempe*, ed. Sanford B. Meech and Hope E. Allen, EETS o.s. 212 (London, 1940), 174.

[54] 'Love, write with thy blood so oft Mine hard heart till it be soft': Richard Rolle, *Meditations on the Life and Passion of Christ*, ed. Charotte D'Evelyn, EETS o.s. 158 (Bungay, 1921), 39.

[55] '[K]neel now down, praying to Christ that he forgive you that ye have trespassed against him by reckless swearing': Mirk, *Festial*, 114.

In summary, fragments and textual sources suggest that the 'explosion' of narrative glass cycles observed in the great cathedrals of the Continent in the later medieval period was also experienced in smaller, parochial churches.[56] The proliferation of Passion windows demonstrate that stained glass both embodied and reinforced the performance of religious activities in the church, such as festive processions. Emotive stained-glass renderings of Christ and His suffering simultaneously cultivated an affective, inward-looking piety in the viewer that was popular in wider devotional traditions.

CONCLUSION

By drawing fragments and accounts of lost glazing from the periphery into the centre of research, this study has highlighted the potential for such piecemeal evidence to enrich and nuance understanding of the interaction between late medieval worship and the decorative arts within the parish church setting. These sources offer fresh perspectives on the agency of stained glass as a devotional medium, which both augmented collective forms of spirituality and directed individual piety. Here, the glazing of ordinary parish churches acted as a microcosm of the grander sequential programmes of large ecclesiastical sites which pushes the parish church building and its furnishing into sharper focus. In many cases where documentary records from this era no longer exist, as at Laneast and Creed, these remains comprise the only form of evidence that survives testifying to the daily reality of religious experience in a specific place which makes them an invaluable resource for study, in addition to showcasing the richness of material available in the South-West of England. Furthermore, this approach connects with a burgeoning trend in the wider academic field as scholars are increasingly turning towards fragments and decontextualized pieces. The growing study of fragmentology is not only spread across different fields of textual and visual art studies, from literature to music to textiles, but it is also rising with intensity, with a succession of volumes and essays

---

[56] Alyce A. Jordan, 'Stories in Windows: The Architectonics of Narrative', in Carson Pastan and Kurmann-Schwarz, eds, *Investigations in Medieval Stained Glass*, 189–201, at 189.

published in the past five years.[57] The implications of such research leads to a necessary re-evaluation of the canon or established corpus in any specific medium.

---

[57] See, for example, Heather Bamford, *Cultures of the Fragment: Uses of the Iberian Manuscript, 1100–1600* (Toronto, 2018); Mary M. Brooks et al., 'Fragments of Faith: Unpicking Archbishop John Morton's Vestments', *Antiquaries Journal* 100 (2020), 274–303; Giovanni Varelli, ed., Disiecta Membra Musicae: *Studies in Musical Fragmentology* (Berlin, 2020); Julian Luxford and Lucy Wrapson, 'Two Fragments of a Painted Screen from Hamstall Ridware, Staffordshire, with Passion Imagery Including the Seven Effusions of Christ's Blood', *Journal of the British Archaeological Association* 174 (2021), 130–53; Julia Boffey, 'Chaucer in Small Parcels: Odd Texts of Chaucer's Short Poems, and their Manuscript Contexts', in Corinne Saunders et al., eds, *Middle English Manuscripts and Their Legacies. A Volume in Honour of Ian Doyle* (Leiden, 2022), 55–68.

Reformations in Britain's Islands

Peter Marshall

University of Warwick

Historians of the Reformations have increasingly explored a comparative 'British' dimension, seeking to transcend the separate national historiographies of England, Scotland and Ireland. To date, however, little attempt has been made to survey patterns of religious change across the multiplicity of islands that came to form part of the composite British monarchy: in particular, the Channel Islands, Isles of Scilly, Isle of Man, Western Isles, Orkney and Shetland. This article argues that attention to the collective experience of islands enhances our understanding of the implementation and reception of religious change, requiring us to think more carefully about questions of environment, law, language and culture, and about the aims and achievements of confessional state-formation. The 'frontier' status of islands also underlines the interconnectedness of British Reformations with developments elsewhere in Europe.

In October 1604, the recently enthroned King James I, in a proclamation announcing his preferred regnal style, set out the terms of a new political geography. He intended to 'discontinue the divided names of England and Scotland' and adopt 'the name and style of King of Great Britain'. 'Palpable signs' indicated God's will for England and Scotland to be one: 'the Isle within itself hath almost none but imaginarie bounds of separation; without, but one common limit or rather Gard of the Ocean Sea, making the whole a little world'. There was, moreover, 'a communitie of language, the principall meanes of Civil societie', and 'an unitie of Religion, the chiefest band of heartie Union'.[1] It was a stirring adjuration, but James's contentions, on all these counts, were at best questionable. Particularly disingenuous

Department of History, University of Warwick. E-mail: p.marshall@warwick.ac.uk.

[1] James F. Larkin and Paul L. Hughes, eds, *Stuart Royal Proclamations*, 2 vols (Oxford, 1973–83), 1: 95–7.

Studies in Church History 61 (2025), 258–283 © The Author(s), 2025. Published by Cambridge University Press on behalf of the Ecclesiastical History Society. This is an Open Access article, distributed under the terms of the Creative Commons Attribution licence (http://creativecommons.org/licenses/by/4.0), which permits unrestricted re-use, distribution and reproduction, provided the original article is properly cited.
doi:10.1017/stc.2024.39

was the equation of his newly conjoined realms with a single contiguous land mass, 'the isle'.

In 1603, of course, James acquired kingship over another significant isle. But Ireland (with whose much-discussed history this article will not concern itself) accounted for only part of the composite Stewart monarchy's geographically fragmented character. By some calculations, more than six thousand islands surround the coasts of 'Great Britain', the great majority of them in offshore Scotland. When we include the Channel Islands, about 130 British isles are permanently inhabited today, though the figure was probably closer to 200 at the turn of the seventeenth century, a not inconsiderable augmentation of James's 'little world'.[2]

It is the contention of this article that an alertness to the experience of Britain's offshore islands brings into clearer focus some of the characteristic features, and intrinsic challenges, of the polity inherited by the early Stuart monarchy. More particularly, it seeks to offer a new perspective on the Reformations underway in that polity for more than two generations when James acquired the English throne. Applying an 'island lens' or 'island frame', I will argue, enhances our understanding of patterns of religious change in Britain in at least two key and complementary ways. In the first place, the reformation of religion in a wide variety of islands – James VI and I's rhetorical obliviousness notwithstanding – was a matter of real significance for ecclesiastical and secular authority. Islands were occasionally forgotten or neglected, but they were often seen to possess considerable symbolic and practical importance, representing both 'problem' and 'prize' in schemes of political and religious imperium. The ways in which centrally sanctioned authority sought to incorporate them, and the compromises it was sometimes prepared to make in doing so, shed light on what 'religious uniformity' actually meant, as an ideal and an attainment, in the British Reformation context.

In the second place, islands invite – demand even – a 'decentred' assessment of the Reformation, in ways that other types of local society, frequently dragooned into service as historiographical 'case studies', usually do not. Islands, then as now, are self-evidently different,

---

[2] David W. Moore, *The Other British Isles: A History of Shetland, Orkney, the Hebrides, Isle of Man, Anglesey, Scilly, Isle of Wight and the Channel Islands* (Jefferson, NC, 2005), 1. For a 'List of islands of the British Isles', see online at: <https://en.wikipedia.org/wiki/List_of_islands_of_the_British_Isles>, accessed 4 July 2024.

distinctive places, with clearly defined boundaries and their own unique histories and culture. They resist easy assimilation into grand narratives of historical development, a reason, perhaps, why they are often omitted from them. And yet islands were never simply places apart, separate and self-contained. The very category of 'island' implies a geographical and conceptual relationship to some other, larger entity. Early modern islanders had their own identities and priorities, but were usually acutely aware of the wider world, and the risks and opportunities it offered them. Foregrounding their experience encourages us to move beyond simplistic binaries of 'success' and 'failure' in studying the Reformation, and to appreciate better how the local conditions of its reception produced a variety of distinct yet 'entangled' outcomes across the British Isles.[3] Placing islands at the centre rather than the margins of analysis involves a close attentiveness to issues of environment, law, language and culture; to negotiations and accommodations, spoken and unspoken, of central authority with local communities and regional powerbrokers; to gaps between the ideological claims and practical achievements of confessional state-formation; and to the inextricable enmeshment of the Reformation in Britain with developments elsewhere.

A comprehensive analytical survey of the Reformation and Counter-Reformation in the islands of Britain has not hitherto been attempted, and this article can offer only a preliminary sketch of how it might look. Certainly, an aspiration among early modern historians to write conjoined histories of the British Isles is well-established. For a generation and more, scholars have sought to transcend separate English, Scottish, Irish and Welsh historiographies with the aim of producing holistic and inter-connected 'British History'. An initial driver was the so-called 'British Problem' as a cause of the mid-seventeenth-century crisis of the Stuart monarchy, but after a slew of important publications around the turn of the current century, the historiographical momentum appears to have slowed. Historians of religion in a broader frame have followed

---

[3] The historiographical shift away from comparative history, and towards methodologies known variously as 'transfer history', 'histoire croisée' and 'entangled history', typically has a global and transnational emphasis. For an overview, see Sönke Bauck and Thomas Maier, 'Entangled History', *InterAmerican Wiki: Terms – Concepts – Critical Perspectives* (2015), online at: <https://uni-bielefeld.de/einrichtungen/cias/wiki/e/entangled-history.xml>, accessed 4 July 2024. Islands, however, serve as a reminder that national polities, particularly the emergent ones of the early modern era, have their own histories of entanglement.

this lead, however, and we now possess several valuable studies of 'British' Reformation culture and politics.[4]

The principal aim of such research, however, has been to bring into dialogue the national histories of the three kingdoms. Despite adoption by numerous historians of the phrase 'Atlantic archipelago', islands as such have played relatively little role in this scholarship. The sole synoptic early modern overview is David Cressy's *England's Islands in a Sea of Troubles*, which, as its title suggests, deals only with the two dozen or so inhabited English islands (including the Channel Islands), along with Anglesey in Wales.[5] John Pocock, intellectual godfather of the new British history, titled his collected essays *The Discovery of Islands*.[6] But the only islands about which he has much to say are Great Britain and Ireland. Recent work by Alison Cathcart is more genuinely 'archipelagic' in its attentiveness to the significance of offshore islands for the state-building agenda of the Stewart monarchy, before and after 1603.[7] But the Reformation as such has not been a central focus of Cathcart's research, while the Atlantic archipelago's smaller islands feature only to a limited extent in three generally excellent volumes arising from a Trinity College, Dublin, project on 'Insular Christianity, 1530–1750'.[8]

---

[4] Seminal contributions include Conrad Russell, *The Causes of the English Civil War* (Oxford, 1990), 109–30; Steven G. Ellis and Sarah Barber, eds, *Conquest and Union: Fashioning a British State, 1485–1725* (London and New York, 1995); Brendan Bradshaw and John Morrill, eds, *The British Problem, c.1534–1707: State Formation in the Atlantic Archipelago* (Basingstoke, 1996); Brendan Bradshaw and Peter Roberts, eds, *British Consciousness and Identity: The Making of Britain* (Cambridge, 1998); Glenn Burgess, ed., *The New British History: Founding a Modern State 1603–1715* (London, 1999). On British Reformations, see Felicity Heal, *Reformation in Britain and Ireland* (Oxford, 2003); Ian Hazlett, *The Reformation in Britain and Ireland* (Edinburgh, 2003); Clare Kellar, *Scotland, England and the Reformation, 1534–1561* (Oxford, 2003); Alec Ryrie, *The Age of Reformation: The Tudor and Stewart Realms*, 3rd edn (London, 2024; first publ. 2009).

[5] David Cressy, *England's Islands in a Sea of Troubles* (Oxford, 2020).

[6] J. G. A. Pocock, *The Discovery of Islands: Essays in British History* (Cambridge, 2005).

[7] Alison Cathcart, 'The Maritime Dimension to Plantation in Ulster, *c.*1550–*c.*1600', *Journal of the North Atlantic*, special volume 12 (2019), 95–111; eadem, 'Island Empire: James VI and I and the Isle of Man in an Archipelagic Context', in Neil McIntyre and Alison Cathcart, eds, *Scotland and the Wider World: Essays in Honour of Allan I. Macinnes* (Woodbridge, 2022), 34–48; eadem, '"O Wretched King!": Ireland, Denmark-Norway, and Kingship in the Reign of James V', in Steven J. Reid, ed., *Rethinking the Renaissance and Reformation in Scotland: Essays in Honour of Roger A. Mason* (Woodbridge, 2024), 118–39.

[8] Robert Armstrong and Tadhg Ó hAnnracháin, eds, *Insular Christianity: Alternative Models of the Church in Britain and Ireland, c.1570–c.1700* (Manchester, 2013); Tadhg Ó hAnnracháin and Robert Armstrong, eds, *Christianities in the Early Modern Celtic World*

Scholarly treatment of religion and religious change in individual islands and island groups has been productive, but patchy. The Western Isles of Scotland are best served, usually in the context of Gaelic culture's broader confrontation with the priorities of the Stewart monarchy.[9] For the Channel Islands, there are fine individual studies of the Reformation and its aftermath in Guernsey and Jersey.[10] An unpublished Edinburgh thesis of 1940 remains the fullest account of religious change in Shetland, though a pair of illuminating essays by Charlotte Methuen suggest possibilities for future research. For Orkney, a 1959 article by Gordon Donaldson was long the only significant point of reference, now supplemented, and in part superseded, by my own recent reassessment.[11] A fuller understanding of the Reformation in the Isle of Man awaits a forthcoming study by Tim Grass, some first fruits of which appear in this volume.[12]

(Basingstoke, 2014); Robert Armstrong and Tadhg Ó hAnnracháin, eds, *The English Bible in the Early Modern World* (Leiden, 2018).

[9] See, in particular, Jane Dawson, 'Calvinism and the Gaidhealtachd in Scotland', in Andrew Pettegree, Alastair Duke and Gillian Lewis, eds, *Calvinism in Europe, 1540–1620* (Cambridge, 1994), 231–53; Wilson McLeod, *Divided Gaels: Gaelic Cultural Identities in Ireland and Scotland, c.1200–c.1650* (Oxford, 2004); Fiona A. Macdonald, *Missions to the Gaels: Reformation and Counter-Reformation in Ulster and the Highlands and Islands of Scotland, 1560–1760* (Edinburgh, 2006); Martin MacGregor, 'Civilising Gaelic Scotland: The Scottish Isles and the Stewart Empire', in Micheál Ó Siochrú and Éamonn Ó Ciadhra, eds, *The Plantation of Ulster: Ideology and Practice* (Manchester, 2012), 33–54; William Ian P. Hazlett, 'Reformation Entry into Gaelic Scotland, 1567–1630', in idem, ed., *A Companion to the Reformation in Scotland, c.1525–1638: Frameworks of Change and Development* (Leiden, 2021), 542–77.

[10] Darryl M. Ogier, *Reformation and Society in Guernsey* (Woodbridge, 1996); Helen M. Evans, 'The Religious History of Jersey, 1558–1640' (PhD thesis, University of Cambridge, 2001). See also Tim Thornton, *The Channel Islands, 1370–1640: Between England and Normandy* (Woodbridge, 2012).

[11] Ernest W. Wallis, 'The Church in Shetland During the Sixteenth and Seventeenth Centuries' (PhD thesis, University of Edinburgh, 1940); Charlotte Methuen, 'Orkney, Shetland and the Networks of the Northern Reformation', *Nordlit* 43 (2019), 25–53; eadem, '"Islands Not Far from Norway, Denmark and Germany": Shetland, Orkney and the Spread of the Reformation in the North', in James Kelly, Henning Laugerud and Salvador Ryan, eds, *Northern European Reformations: Transnational Perspectives* (London, 2020), 191–211; Gordon Donaldson, 'Bishop Adam Bothwell and the Reformation in Orkney', *RSCHS* 13 (1959), 85–100; Peter Marshall, 'Reformation on Scotland's Northern Frontier: The Orkney Islands, 1560–c.1700', in Kelly, Laugerud and Ryan, eds, *Northern European Reformations*, 21–48; idem, *Storm's Edge: Life, Death and Magic in the Islands of Orkney* (London, 2024), 101–34.

[12] Tim Grass, 'Language and the Manx Reformation, 1570–1698', in this volume.

Whether islands, collectively, do in fact represent a useful category for the study of the Reformation is by no means self-evident. The multitudinous islands dotted around the coastline of Great Britain were, and are, extremely diverse. Typologies are only ever crude and inexact, but it is nonetheless possible to discern some broad patterns. A few islands were large, close to the mainland, and relatively well-integrated with it. They included Anglesey and the Isle of Wight, and, in Scotland, Arran and Bute in the Firth of Clyde. The Isle of Man was comparable to Arran and Anglesey in size, but further from the mainland, and belongs in a category of its own.

Other islands clustered in archipelagos characterized by institutional and economic co-dependence, and a strong sense of collective identity not incompatible with inter-island rivalry: here we can count Orkney, Shetland, the Channel Islands, and the Isles of Scilly. The hundred and fifty-odd islands of the Hebrides, strung out along 200 miles of Scotland's ragged west coast from the southern point of Islay to the Butt of Lewis in the north, were scarcely an archipelago in the same sense, though there was a powerful cultural affinity – damaged but not destroyed by the Reformation – among the isles forming the arc of the Outer Hebrides, sometimes collectively referred to as *An t-Eilean Fada*, the Long Island.

Finally, there was a scattering of small, isolated island communities, with populations sometimes only in double-digits, such as Lundy in the mouth of the Bristol Channel, or the tiny Atlantic grouping fifty miles west of Harris, known, thanks to a cartographic error, as St Kilda, but more properly Hiort or Hirta.[13] More isolated still was the tiny community on North Rona, north-east of Lewis, whose entire population starved to death in the mid-1680s after rats from a shipwreck decimated its supplies of food.[14] The religious culture of these micro-communities represents a fascinating study in itself. Lundy lay outside formal diocesan structures, and had no resident priest before or after the Reformation. Prior to the beginning of the eighteenth century, the same was true of St Kilda. The clergyman Donald Munro, who travelled through the Hebrides in 1549, reported that a chaplain came out once a year with the landlord's steward, and at other times the islanders 'baptise ther barnes themselves'. There was an ancient chapel

---

[13] Roger Hutchison, *St Kilda: A People's History* (Edinburgh, 2014), 39–41.
[14] Martin Martin, *A Description of the Western Isles of Scotland* (London, 1703), 25.

on North Rona, but the inhabitants were, Munro claimed, 'simple people scant of any religion'.[15]

Perhaps islands were simply not very socially, politically or religiously significant. That was the impression received by the government of Venice from a long 'relation of England' despatched in 1622 by its ambassador in London, Girolamo Lando. He reported that the ruler of the kingdoms of England and Scotland, cut off from mainland Europe, 'has hardly any adjacent members except islands'. Of these, the Isle of Wight lay in an important situation, while Anglesey, separated by a small 'river', was considered part of the mainland. The other English islands were 'rather nests for birds than habitations for men'. 'Two little islands', Jersey and Guernsey, with 'scanty inhabitants', were all that remained from the patrimony of William the Conqueror. Lando ignored the Isle of Man. As for Scotland, the Hebrides and Orkneys were 'stones rather than rocks, and rocks rather than islands'. Their

> handful of people ... scarcely know of God, are rarely visited and resemble beasts more than men. They do not know the meaning of obedience to the king, who has not troubled to put restraint upon them ... and one may call them simply the hairs on the body of that kingdom.[16]

It is an arresting metaphor, appropriate in ways its author did not perhaps intend. Hair is both extraneous and integral to the body, seemingly dispensable, but performing crucial physiological functions. It also matters to external appearance and reputation, and, to varying degrees, demands to be tamed and controlled.

Scotland, unlike England, had an established concept of 'the isles', a geographical and cultural zone far from the usual seat of government in Edinburgh. A perception that the islands were not really part of the kingdom was widespread in late medieval and early modern Scotland.

---

[15] Cressy, *England's Islands*, 28; Donald Munro, 'A Description of the Western Iles of Scotland', in Arthur Mitchell and James Toshach Clark, eds, *Geographical Collections Relating to Scotland Made by Walter Macfarlane*, 3 vols (Edinburgh, 1906–8), 3: 291, 201. Munro's account provided the basis for George Buchanan's treatment of the Western Isles in his influential *Rerum Scoticarum Historia* of 1582: Roger A. Mason, 'From Buchanan to Blaeu: The Politics of Scottish Chorography, 1582–1654', in idem and Caroline Erskine, eds, *George Buchanan: Political Thought in Early Modern Britain and Europe* (London, 2012), 13–47, at 26–8.

[16] Allen B. Hinds, ed., *Calendar of State Papers Relating to English Affairs in the Archives of Venice*, 17: *1621–1623* (London, 1911), 424 (no. 603).

Chroniclers regularly referred to both the Western Isles and Orkney as places *beyond* Scotland, an attitude which likewise seemed to permeate the workings of government. A servant of James IV, travelling to Orkney in 1500, carried a warrant offering him protection 'from the day of the passing of him forth of our realm … until his return'. At a time of famine in 1555, the Scottish parliament banned export of foodstuffs 'forth of this realm', but made exception for trade with the Western Isles.[17]

Parallel assumptions inform a key text of Protestant national identity, John Speed's famous atlas of 1612. The work carries an instructive title: *The Theatre of the Empire of Great Britaine, presenting an Exact Geography of the Kingdomes of England, Scotland, Ireland, and the Iles Adioyning.* Speed was scrupulous in his coverage of the latter, providing maps and corresponding accounts of Jersey, Guernsey, the Isle of Wight, Anglesey, and the Isle of Man. There was commentary on the Northern and Western Isles in his short section on Scotland, though a description of Shetland as 'ever covered with ice and snow' suggests a limited awareness of actual conditions there.

If the islands were not fully part of the kingdoms, Speed was nonetheless eager to fold them into Jacobean imperial dominion. Orkney, Shetland and the Hebrides were places 'yielding both beauty and subjection to this Scottish kingdome'. Guernsey and Jersey were 'compassed … with the British Sea', along with 'all other ilands and ilets, which doe scatteredly environ it, and shelter themselves (as it were) under the shadow of great Albion'.[18] Speed's work was published as James VI and I was forcefully asserting the principle of *mare clausum*, sole imperium over the 'closed' territorial waters encompassing his kingdom. The islands enlarged but also created diplomatic complications for this claim to exclusive maritime jurisdiction, and, in practice, Speed and nearly all other cartographers restricted the potentially capacious descriptor 'British Sea' to what we now call the English Channel.[19] The title given to Speed's most iconic map, 'The British Islands, proposed in one view', was also something of a misnomer.

[17] Julian Goodare, *The Government of Scotland 1560–1625* (Oxford, 2004), 235–6; Marshall, *Storm's Edge*, 12; Thomas Thomson and Cosmo Innes, eds, *Acts of the Parliament of Scotland*, 12 vols (Edinburgh, 1814–75), 2: 495.

[18] John Speed, *The Theatre of the Empire of Great Britaine, presenting an Exact Geography of the Kingdomes of England, Scotland, Ireland, and the Iles Adioyning* (London, 1612), 1, 91, 94, 125, 132.

[19] David Armitage, *The Ideological Origins of the British Empire* (Cambridge, 2000), 100–24; Carl Moreland and David Bannister, *Antique Maps* (Oxford, 1986), 213–23.

Shetland does not appear at all, and Orkney is dislocated into a marginal box. Nor could Speed find room for Guernsey and Jersey, though they do appear skirting the rim of a map of the Commonwealth of England, engraved by Thomas Simon for a new great seal in 1648.[20]

In such representations, the marginality of islands is self-evident; they are positioned and defined by a peripheral relationship to mainlands. Such 'peripherality' is, however, constructed rather than natural, a reflection of the ideological functions of cartography. The Channel Islands indeed lie at the edge of 'the British Sea', but they are located just off the coast of Normandy, and Jersey is as close to Paris as to London. A map of the North Atlantic world deciding to place Orkney and Shetland at its centre would look far different.[21] Supposedly marginal, fringe locations are revealed as points of connection and confluence, roughly equidistant between Bergen and Edinburgh, Oslo and Dublin, and Reykjavik and London. The Isle of Man is often portrayed as a backwater, but similar cartographic reorientation reveals it to be the true geographical centre of Britain, ringed by the four nations of Scotland, England, Wales and Ireland. The Western Isles' proximity to Ireland, moreover, was a crucial cultural, economic and military fact of the era.

Peripheries, then, can turn out to be frontiers, zones of encounter rather than lonely termini. It is tempting for historians to follow the lead of some contemporary reformers, and regard island communities as 'dark corners' of the land. John Foxe, for example, portrayed Guernsey as 'an obscure Ieland ... in such an out-corner of the realme'.[22] But metaphors of angular enclosure are ill-chosen. Islands, particularly in an age when sea travel was generally easier than overland alternatives, were often remarkably open and accessible places.[23] This made them more

---

[20] Alfred Benjamin Wyon and Allan Wyon, *The Great Seals of England: From the Earliest Period to the Present Time* (London, 1887), 90–4 (plates 30–1).

[21] See the Kirkwall-centred map in Ronald Miller, *Orkney* (London, 1976), 10.

[22] John Foxe, *Actes and Monuments* (London, 1583), book 11, p. 1971. Compare Christopher Hill, 'Puritans and "The Dark Corners of the Land"', *TRHS* 13 (1963), 77–102. James Sharpe, 'Witchcraft in the Early Modern Isle of Man', *Cultural and Social History* 4 (2007), 11–28, at 22, contends 'there can be little doubt that the island was one of the "dark corners" of Europe'.

[23] For some conceptual and comparative perspectives on 'islandness', see, among a now voluminous body of literature, Pete Hay, 'A Phenomenology of Islands', *Island Studies Journal* 1 (2006), 19–42; Louis Sicking, 'The Dichotomy of Insularity: Islands between Isolation and Connectivity in Medieval and Early Modern Europe, and Beyond', *International Journal of Maritime History* 26 (2014), 494–511; Douglas Hamilton and John

significant, and more of a focus of anxiety, than Ambassador Lando or Cartographer Speed seemed willing to recognize.

Britain's islands were individually unique, and typologically diverse, but some common features conditioned their reception and negotiation of religious change. One was a tendency to manifest jurisdictional anomalies. Starting in the south, Jersey and Guernsey were possessions of the English Crown but not technically part of the kingdom of England. The Channel Islands were a remnant of the lost duchy of Normandy, controlled by royal governors, co-operating, or not, with local bailiffs and jurats, who administered in their courts a legal system derived from the customary law of Normandy.

Ecclesiastically, the islands belonged to the diocese of Coutances, an arrangement out of step with geopolitical realities at the end of the fifteenth century. Pope Alexander VI issued a bull in 1496 transferring them to the diocese of Salisbury, and a second in 1499 to Winchester. But curial forgetfulness and practicalities on the ground meant the instruction was effectively ignored, and bishops of Coutances carried on with routine administrative business. Remarkably, the break with Rome did not foreclose the arrangement. In 1542, Henry VIII sought to inhibit the bishop of Coutances from exercising papal jurisdiction, but was willing enough for him to exercise it in the king's name. Even in Edward VI's reign, the governor of Jersey, Sir Hugh Paulet, received orders 'to use the sayd bisshop as our Dyocesyan in all things not repugnante or contrary to the lawes and ordonnances of the realm.' Not until 1569 were the islands unambiguously brought within Winchester's ambit.[24]

Ecclesio-politics in the Isle of Man were no less convoluted. In the High Middle Ages, Man was a Hiberno-Norse territory nominally subject to the king of Norway, though, in reality, an independent lordship ruled by self-styled kings. In 1266, as a result of the Treaty of Perth, it came, along with the Hebrides, into the possession of the king of Scots. In the fourteenth century, the island was conquered by English adventurers, and at the start of the fifteenth, Henry IV bestowed

---

McAleer, eds, *Islands and the British Empire in The Age of Sail* (Oxford, 2021); Aideen Foley et al., 'Understanding "Islandness"', *Annals of the American Association of Geographers* 113 (2023), 1800–17.
[24] Evans, 'Religious History of Jersey', 3–5, 30; Thornton, *Channel Islands*, 75, 79. They remained under the jurisdiction of Winchester until November 2022 when they were returned to the diocese of Salisbury.

it on Sir John Stanley, whose grandson became earl of Derby. The Stanleys at first called themselves kings, but in 1504 settled for the more modest title of 'Lords of Man'. The island's own laws were (and are) promulgated by its parliament, the Tynwald.[25]

Church jurisdiction followed a similarly corkscrew course. Man belonged to the straggling medieval diocese of the *Suðreyjar*, the southern isles, later to be quaintly anglicized, via Latin, as 'Sodor'. The bishopric was in the mid-twelfth century confirmed by the papacy as part of the province of Nidaros (that is, Trondheim), though rival claims were advanced by archbishops of York. The church in Man became detached from the rest of the isles in the decades after English conquest, though its relationship to English episcopal structures was not fully clarified until 1542, when an act of the English parliament annexed it to the province of York.[26] For practical purposes, however, the Manx church remained largely autonomous; or rather, it fell under the authority of the Stanleys, who nominated episcopal candidates to the bishopric, and exercised their own de facto royal supremacy. The island's religious houses – a Franciscan friary, and Cistercian monastery and nunnery – were dissolved in 1540, but reform was otherwise slow to take root, despite the Protestant sympathies of the fourth earl of Derby, lord of Man from 1572 to 1593. The island lay outside the scope of the York Ecclesiastical Commission, and only in 1594 were the Elizabethan Injunctions imposed, the Tynwald ordering inquiry into superstitious practices at funerals, and absences from divine service.[27]

Further north, the threads of political and ecclesiastical power were equally tangled. Annexation of the Hebrides in 1266 did not lead to their integration into the Scottish state, but to the consolidation of a semi-independent lordship of the Isles, in the hands of Clan Donald. In 1493, James IV suppressed the lordship, but the result was a fragmentation of authority among successor MacDonalds and other

---

[25] Robert H. Kinvig, *The Isle of Man: A Social, Cultural and Political History* (Liverpool, 1975), 86–97; Tim Thornton, 'Scotland and the Isle of Man, *c.*1400–1625: Noble Power and Royal Presumption in the Northern Irish Sea Province', *ScHR* 77 (1998), 1–30.

[26] Alex Woolf, 'The Diocese of the Sudreyar', in Steinar Imsen, ed., *Ecclesia Nidrosiensis 1153–1537* (Trondheim, 2003), 171–81; Anne Ashley, 'The Spiritual Courts of the Isle of Man, especially in the Seventeenth and Eighteenth Centuries', *EHR* 72 (1957), 31–59, at 35–6.

[27] Tim Grass, 'The Reformation and the Isle of Man', *Isle of Man Studies* 17 (2021), 89–93; and compare 'Language and the Manx Reformation'. See also Ashley, 'Spiritual Courts', 36; William Sacheverell, *An Account of the Isle of Man*, ed. Joseph G. Cumming (Douglas, 1859), 182.

clan chiefs, rather than any tangible extension of royal authority. Scholars are divided on the extent to which in the sixteenth century a culturally unified and politically potent Gaeldom straddled the Irish Sea. There were certainly strong ties of kinship between the Western Isles and Ulster, along with regular political intrigues and much movement of mercenary Gallowglasses and Redshanks. Writing in the late 1590s, an English officer complained of how 'the Irish and the Scottish Ilanders are sprong out of one nation and people, ther bringing up hath benne alike, ther language one, and ther alyance and blood is dayly renued by matches and mariages'.[28] The portion of the diocese of the Isles severed from Man, with an episcopal seat now at Snizeort in northern Skye, continued under Nidaros's nominal authority until 1472, when the papacy transferred it to St Andrews, newly elevated to the status of archbishopric. We know little about Hebridean religious culture on the eve of the Reformation, but the diocese was certainly impoverished, its revenues syphoned into the hands of local elites.[29]

The diocese of Orkney, of which Shetland constituted an archdeaconry, was likewise transferred from Trondheim to St Andrews in 1472. Orkney's earlier position in the province of Nidaros had been more secure than that of the southern isles; indeed, it occupied a geographically central location within the archdiocese. Four of the ten bishops under the jurisdiction of Nidaros were in Norway, but from Orkney the province extended north-west to the diocese of the Faroes, to the two bishoprics in Iceland, and to Latin Christianity's westernmost outpost: the cathedral at Garðar on the southern tip of Greenland.[30] The Northern Isles remained Norwegian after the Treaty of Perth, though were increasingly open to Scottish immigration and influence. They came under Danish control with the Union of Kalmar

---

[28] For a broadly unitary 'Gaelic world', see Steven G. Ellis, *Ireland in the Age of the Tudors, 1447–1603*, 2nd edn (London, 2014; first publ. 1998). For a critique, see McLeod, *Divided Gaels*. Hiram Morgan, ed., 'A Booke of Questions and Answers Concerning the Warrs or Rebellions of the Kingdome of Irelande', *Analecta Hibernica* 36 (1995), 79–132, at 125.

[29] See Iain G. MacDonald, 'The Church in Gaelic Scotland before the Reformation', and Martin MacGregor, 'Gaelic Christianity? The Church in the Western Highlands and Islands of Scotland before and after the Reformation', in Ó hAnnracháin and Armstrong, eds, *Celtic World*, 17–28 and 55–70, respectively.

[30] Barbara E. Crawford, 'The Bishopric of Orkney', in Imsen, ed., *Ecclesia Nidrosiensis*, 143–58.

(1397), which conjoined the Norwegian and Danish Crowns. In 1468, Orkney, and in 1469, Shetland, were pledged to Scotland, after Christian I failed to come up with a cash dowry for the marriage of his daughter Margaret to James III of Scotland. Considerable controversy and uncertainty, then and subsequently, surrounded this development. James III acted swiftly to strengthen his control, in 1472 annexing the Orkney earldom to the Crown. But Christian I's successors insisted it was a temporary mortgaging, and repeatedly swore to recover the islands. In part, this was an effort to appease the Norwegian nobility, not consulted about the original alienation. But successive Danish sovereigns were, periodically at least, serious about reclaiming Orkney and Shetland, proffering the redemption money on various occasions through to 1667.[31]

Like Man and the Channel Islands, Orkney and Shetland exhibited hybrid models of law and governance. Scottish rule at first involved little more than a renaming of existing courts and officials, and the islands' own legal system, based on earlier Norwegian codes, operated alongside Scottish law until 1611. The church in Orkney, and to a lesser extent Shetland, was from the fourteenth century increasingly 'Scotticized'; indeed, Scottish-born bishops were useful diplomatic conduits between the courts in Copenhagen and Edinburgh.[32] The transfer to St Andrews was, however, resented in Norway, and apparently forgotten about in Rome. In 1520, Leo X ordered the bishop of Orkney to send to Trondheim money raised in the islands by his notorious plenary indulgence. Nidaros's archbishop in the 1520s, Olaf Engelbrektsson, commissioned a search of the curial archives for documents relating to the transfer, with a view to overturning it. He also sponsored a provocative ecclesiastical visitation of Shetland by a newly consecrated bishop of Skálholt in Iceland. Engelbrektsson was tenacious, but his campaign to recover the lost diocese

---

[31] Barbara E. Crawford, 'The Pawning of Orkney and Shetland: A Reconsideration of the Events of 1460-1469', *SchR* 48 (1969), 35–53; Brian Smith, 'When Did Orkney and Shetland Become Part of Scotland? A Contribution to the Debate', *New Orkney Antiquarian Journal* 5 (2010), 1–18; Ian Peter Grohse, 'The Lost Cause: Kings, the Council, and the Question of Orkney and Shetland, 1468–1536', *Scandinavian Journal of History* 45 (2020), 286–308.

[32] Gordon Donaldson, 'Problems of Sovereignty and Law in Orkney and Shetland', in David Sellar, ed., *The Stair Society: Miscellany Two* (Edinburgh, 1984), 24–34; Ian Peter Grohse, *Frontiers for Peace in the Medieval North: The Norwegian-Scottish Frontier, c. 1260–1470* (Leiden, 2017), 134–53.

was derailed by the Danish Reformation, whose imposition in Norway he sought energetically, but unsuccessfully, to impede.[33]

The Scandinavian Reformation ran in parallel to the English one and preceded by a generation Protestantism's political triumph in Scotland. It occasioned the creation of another remarkable map: a *Carta marina et descriptio septentrionalium terrarum* (maritime map and description of the northern lands), the work of an exiled Swedish churchman, Olaus Magnus, later to be appointed by the pope as titular archbishop of Uppsala. Printed in Venice in 1539, the map celebrates the wonders of the Baltic world, as well as exhibiting Swedish patriotism and offering fraternal support for Norwegian freedom from Denmark.[34] Islands are prominent in the *Carta marina*, particularly a majestic Iceland, which dwarfs in scale a shrivelled and cowering Denmark at the bottom of the frame.[35] Orkney and Shetland feature, not as marginal locations, but as key elements of an extended Scandinavian world, alongside the Faroes and the imagined island of Tile or Thule. Defiantly emblazoned with the lion of Norway, Orkney is of equivalent size to the whole of mainland Scotland. In a set of accompanying notes, Magnus explained that in Orkney 'they speak Norwegian, as a token that they belong to that kingdom, as do many other surrounding islands'.[36]

Language, and the challenges of effecting or resisting religious reform in non-anglophone or bilingual societies, has long been on the radar of historians of the British and Irish Reformations.[37] An island perspective underlines the importance of this issue, as well as the need to avoid blanket conclusions concerning it. In the sixteenth and seventeenth centuries, at least nine indigenous languages were spoken in British island communities. The people of the Channel Islands used related but distinct vernaculars derived from Norman-French:

---

[33] Marshall, *Storm's Edge*, 71–2; Henning Laugerud, *Reformasjon uten folk: det katolske Norge i før- og etterrefomatorisk tid* (Oslo, 2018), 89–133.

[34] Kurt Johannesson, *The Renaissance of the Goths in Sixteenth-Century Sweden*, transl. James Larson (Berkeley, CA, 1991), 175–83.

[35] Olaus Magnus, *Carta marina et descriptio septentrionalium terrarum* (1539), online at: <https://en.wikipedia.org/wiki/File:Carta_Marina.jpeg>, accessed 22 February 2024.

[36] Olaus Magnus, *Ain kurze Auslegung und Verklerung der neuuen Mappen von den alten Goettenreich und andern Nordlenden* (Venice, 1539), A4ᵛ. For further discussion of the *Carta marina* in its contemporary political and diplomatic context, see Alison Cathcart, '"O Wretched King!"', 132–7.

[37] See, in particular, Felicity Heal, 'Mediating the Word: Language and Dialects in the British and Irish Reformations', *JEH* 56 (2005), 261–86.

Jèrriais in Jersey and Guernésiais in Guernsey. The population of Scilly spoke Cornish. The Isle of Wight was anglophone and Anglesey, Ynys Môn, was Welsh-speaking. In the Isle of Man, the gentry used English, but many common people only understood Manx Gaelic. Some Scots was spoken in the Western Isles, but Gaelic was the dominant vernacular throughout the Hebrides and West Highland littoral. Olaus Magnus was partially correct to claim that Orcadians spoke Norwegian. Orkney and Shetland's medieval vernacular was Norn, a variant of old Norse, derived from the west Norwegian dialects of early Viking settlers. But in Orkney, and to a lesser extent Shetland, Norn was increasingly challenged by Scots, which, even before 1468, became the medium of earldom and episcopal administration, and predominant in the trading port of Kirkwall.[38]

The Reformations arrived in Britain at a moment when multiple native languages were at various stages of historical development, but when a privileged vernacular – English for England and Wales; Scots for Scotland – had already become associated with political loyalty and imperatives of state-formation. Different cultural meanings and value were nonetheless ascribed to insular languages. Prior to the reign of Charles I, for example, there does not seem to have been much hostility on the part of English governors to the French vernaculars of the Channel Islands.[39] It was otherwise in Scotland, where 'the isles' were firmly identified as the heartland of Gaelic language and culture, and of Catholic resistance to promulgation of the 'Word'. Here, a rhetoric of disparagement developed in parallel with the Reformation and with Anglo-Scottish efforts to 'civilize' Ireland.[40] Over the course of the sixteenth century, Scottish Gaelic was increasingly referred to by Lowlanders as 'Erse' (Irish), a means of denigrating the language and portraying its speakers as alien.[41] In 1529, James V was happy to tell the pope how 'the Isles formed the greatest part of the Scottish kingdom at

---

[38] Ragnhild Ljosland, 'The Establishment of the Scots Language in Orkney', *New Orkney Antiquarian Journal* 6 (2012), 65–80.

[39] Evans, 'Religious History of Jersey', 139–40; Thornton, *Channel Islands*, 147

[40] Jane H. Ohlmeyer, '"Civilizing of those Rude Partes": Colonization within Britain and Ireland, 1580s–1640s', in Nicholas Canny, ed., *The Oxford History of the British Empire*, 1: *British Overseas Enterprise to the Close of the Seventeenth Century* (Oxford, 1998), 124–45; Allan I. Macinnes, 'Making the Plantations British, 1603–1638: A Problematic Historiography', in Steven G. Ellis and Raingard Eßer, eds, *Frontiers and the Writing of History, 1500–1850* (Hanover-Laatzen, 2006), 95–125.

[41] Colin Kidd, *British Identities Before Nationalism: Ethnicity and Nationhood in the Atlantic World, 1600–1800* (Cambridge, 1999), 125–7.

the first: they received the faith with alacrity, and have maintained it consistently.'[42] Seventy years later, James VI, in his *Basilikon Doron*, observed how Highland Gaelic-speakers comprised 'two sorts of people; the one, that dwelleth in our maine land, that are barbarous and yet mixed with some shewe of civilitie; the other, that dwelleth in the Iles and are alluterlie barbares, without any sorte or shewe of civilitie.'[43] A few years later, James's secretary of state, Sir Alexander Hay, wrote in reference to the Hebrides about 'these unhallowed people with that unchristiane language'.[44]

The introduction, implementation and routinization of Protestant religion in the various islands of Britain involved complex calibrations between the language of the people, the language of the clergy, and the language of liturgy and other textual instruments. Historians have largely moved away from a paradigm privileging the translation of Scripture into the vernacular above all else, for all that this might seem to account for the Reformation's comparative success in Wales and near-total failure in Ireland. More important was the ability of reforming clergy to ingratiate themselves with local elites, and to craft a compelling, or at least socially useful, message in a language that ordinary people could understand.[45] The Isle of Man was unusual among Britain's larger island communities in the early modern period in sustaining an almost entirely indigenous parish ministry. In the early seventeenth century, an outsider, the Welsh-born bishop of Sodor and Man, John Phillips, translated the Book of Common Prayer into Manx, but it was never printed, and Manx clergy reportedly found Phillips's Welsh-based orthography effectively incomprehensible. Instead, ministers in Man's seventeen parishes used the English Prayer Book, but in a linguistically amphibian manner translated sections off-the-cuff to their congregations.[46] The effectiveness of this as an evangelization method must be considered moot.

In the Channel Islands, by contrast, parishioners had access to a government-sponsored French translation of the 1552 Prayer Book. After the middle of the sixteenth century, parish clergymen in both

---

[42] MacGregor, 'Gaelic Christianity?', 68.
[43] James VI, *Basilikon Doron* (Edinburgh, 1599), 42.
[44] James R. N. MacPhail, ed., *Highland Papers*, 4 vols (Edinburgh, 1914–34), 3: 302.
[45] On this theme, see Dawson, 'Calvinism in the Gaidhealtachd', 233–9; Donald Meek, 'The Reformation and Gaelic Culture', in James Kirk, ed., *The Church in the Highlands* (Edinburgh, 1998), 37–62.
[46] See Grass, 'Language and the Manx Reformation'.

Jersey and Guernsey were increasingly non-indigenous, but did not speak an entirely different language, as, from the early 1560s, there was an influx of refugee Huguenot clergy from Normandy. In 1563, churches in the French Reformed manner, with consistories, were established at Saint Helier in Jersey and Saint Peter Port in Guernsey, and thence rolled out to other parishes. The situation was formalized in 1576 with the drawing up of a church order for the two islands, the *discipline ecclésiastique*, and the establishment of two synods meeting together in an inter-island colloquy. In effect, a 'Stranger church', like the ones catering to Protestant refugees in London, was contracted to supply religious services and theological instruction to the population as a whole.[47]

In this context, the lack of a French translation of the 1559 Prayer Book hardly mattered. The Channel Islands represented a remarkable exception to the usual Elizabethan insistence on religious uniformity, one that two successive conformist bishops of Winchester, John Watson and Thomas Cooper, were required to stomach. It reflected an official willingness to accept the sometimes anomalous status of islands, linked to concerns over national security and a desire to promote the Protestant cause in France. The islands could also serve as a kind of homeland safety-valve: in 1595, the disruptive puritans Thomas Cartwright and Edmund Snape were permitted to go into exile in Guernsey and Jersey, and assume pastoral positions there.[48]

At the other end of Britain, too, island parishes were served by immigrant clergy. Even before the Reformation, priests in Orkney were largely, though not entirely, recruited from mainland Scotland, but the pattern became more marked in both Orkney and Shetland after *c*.1600. The fate of Norn has not to date registered much in the scholarship on bilingual societies and the Reformation, and the precise relationship is hard to fathom. Norn was probably used or understood by a majority of Orcadians in 1600, but by the end of the century was spoken only in pockets, and by 1750 was effectively extinct. In Shetland, the timescale of decline lagged a couple of generations behind.[49] For neither of the northern archipelagos is there evidence of

[47] Evans, 'Religious History of Jersey', 27–8, 37; Ogier, *Reformation and Society*, 94–112.
[48] Peter Heylyn, *A Full Relation of Two Journeys, the One into the Main-land of France, the Other into some of the Adjacent Ilands* (London, 1656), 326, 337.
[49] Of the twenty-five ministers appointed to Orkney parishes in 1600–40, twenty-two were born elsewhere, as were at least thirteen of eighteen in Shetland: Hew Scott, ed., *Fasti Ecclesiae Scoticanae* ... 7: *Synods of Ross, Sutherland and Caithness, Glenelg, Orkney and of Shetland*

Protestant attempts to evangelize in Norn, or use it in church services. The Reformation aligned itself with the socially ascendant language and accelerated the demise of the other. In the early 1640s, one minister commented patronisingly on how rural Orcadians 'either express, or try to express, the humanity and civility which they have taken from Scots who live among them'. However, there are reasons to suspect that a legacy of Norn seeped into layers of folklore and custom, to whose meanings the immigrant ministers had little or no access.[50]

In the Hebrides, nervousness about the incivility of Gaelic gave way to a pragmatic recognition on the part of the Kirk that ministers needed to be competent in the language if they were to stand any chance of making converts among often monoglot islanders. We know little about conditions on the ground in the decades following the Reformation parliament of 1560. It seems clear that in the diocese of the Isles the institutional structure of the old church collapsed fairly quickly, though there is debate among scholars as to whether this left a vacuum the Reformed Kirk failed to fill for a generation and more, or whether substantial foundations were laid, particularly by co-opting the talents of the Gaelic 'learned orders', families of poets and genealogists with established traditions of clerical service.[51]

No full translation of the Bible into Scots Gaelic appeared before the beginning of the nineteenth century, making the Highlands and Western Isles a case study in Calvinism's ability to proceed through oral forms of communication. The first Gaelic printed book, however, dates to 1567, the same year William Salesbury published his version of the New Testament in Welsh. John Carswell, a clerical convert who enjoyed the patronage of Archibald Campbell, fifth earl of Argyll, produced the *Foirm na n-Urrnuidheadh*, a translation of the Book of Common Order, along with parts of Calvin's Little Catechism and a variety of prayers. As superintendent of Argyll, and from 1565 bishop of the Isles, Carswell made strenuous efforts to promote the Reformation in his apparently unpromising territory.[52] Among the prayers

(Edinburgh, 1928), 210–78; Michael P. Barnes, *The Norn Language of Orkney and Shetland* (Lerwick, 1998), 21–8.

[50] Marshall, *Storm's Edge*, 179–80 (quotation at 179), 193–4, 198–9, 355–414.

[51] McLeod, *Divided Gaels*, 196–7; Macdonald, *Missions to the Gaels*, 11–21; Jane Dawson, *Scotland Reformed 1488–1587* (Edinburgh, 2007), 228–9.

[52] Tadhg Ó hAnnracháin, 'Introduction: Religious Acculturation and Affiliation in Early Modern Gaelic Scotland, Gaelic Ireland, Wales and Cornwall', in idem and Armstrong, eds, *Celtic World*, 1–13, at 5–6.

Carswell appended to the work was a form of blessing for a ship, for captain and crew to recite together before putting to sea. There is evidence of the prayer being used in the isles throughout the seventeenth century,[53] although, to Calvinists elsewhere, this manner of petitionary blessing probably seemed superstitious. Certainly, in 1602 the Channel Islands Colloquy denounced the 'detestable practice' of conducting quasi-baptismal ceremonies for boats.[54]

If islands complicate the relationship between Reformation and language, they do the same for policies of church governance. James VI and I's eagerness to bring greater ecclesiastical uniformity to his kingdoms had a significant island dimension. Orkney, for example, became a test-case for efforts to strengthen the place of episcopacy in the Kirk of Scotland. In 1605, after a lapse of episcopal oversight for a quarter century and more, James appointed as bishop of Orkney an able and ambitious royal chaplain, James Law, who shared the king's Erastian instincts in matters of ecclesiastical polity. Law travelled north in 1611 to impose religious and political order in the islands after the arrest and imprisonment of the unreliable regional ruler, Earl Patrick Stewart. The Norse law of Orkney and Shetland was abolished, and all ministers were reappointed to their benefices by the bishop. An unsuccessful rebellion led by Earl Patrick's illegitimate son Robert in 1614 provided an occasion for the imposition of still firmer episcopal control. Shortly afterwards, Law was transferred to the archbishopric of Glasgow, where, in the words of the Lord Advocate, there would be further opportunities to 'reduce the Church government to that happy estate which his Majesty has long wished'.[55]

At the same time, royal and privy council attention was increasingly focused on the Western Isles, not least because the political and religious situation there was seen to be destabilizing government authority in Ireland at the time of the Nine Years War (1593–1603). In 1607, the privy council authorized the earl of Argyll to take

---

[53] Thomas McLauchlan, ed., *The Book of Common Order Commonly Called John Knox's Liturgy. Translated into Gaelic anno domini 1567, by Mr. John Carswell, Bishop of the Isles* (Edinburgh, 1873), 240; 'A Collection of Highland Rites and Customs', in Michael Hunter, ed., *The Occult Laboratory: Magic, Science and Second Sight in Late Seventeenth-Century Scotland* (Woodbridge, 2001), 66; Martin, *A Description of the Western Isles of Scotland*, 127–30.

[54] Evans, 'Religious History of Jersey', 89.

[55] Marshall, *Storm's Edge*, 161, 164–5, 177–8. Adam Bothwell, nominally bishop from 1559 until 1593, had effectively resigned his office in 1568.

military action against Clan Donald for its long record of abetting rebellion in Ireland. Until there was an 'utter suppressing' and dispossession of the clan, 'uncivilitie and barbarities all continew, nocht only thair bot in the Iles'.[56]

Much controversy surrounds the promulgation of the 1609 Statutes of Iona, when nine Hebridean chiefs were summoned to the ancient seat of Scottish Christianity to be presented with articles by the bishop of Argyll and the Isles, Andrew Knox. The first of these required 'a regular parochial ministry to be established and maintained, with the same discipline as in other parts of the realm'. Other statutes attacked Hebridean customs of hospitality, arms-bearing and military quartering, and ordered every chief owning at least sixty cattle to send his eldest son to school in the Lowlands.[57] Historians disagree over whether the statutes were an attempt to suppress the traditional Gaelic social order, or simply aimed to delegate royal authority to existing social elites. The extent to which they were enforced is also disputed, though they were reiterated by a privy council order of 1616, which also decreed that lairds should not be allowed to inherit land in the isles unless they could speak, read and write English, and thus be 'better preparit to reforme thair countreis and to reduce the same to godlines, obedience, and civilitie'.[58]

A Jacobean policy of pan-British religious order extended to the Channel Islands, heralded by a conciliar letter of 1613 declaring the king's intention to conform the islands to 'uniformity of government in other partes of his domynions', and lauding his success in achieving this in Scotland. Over the following decade, in the face of local opposition, a dean was appointed for Jersey, use of a new French translation of the Prayer Book was enjoined, reformed discipline laid aside, and a set of ecclesiastical canons issued. Despite the apparent heavy hand, the reforms were in some ways cautious and gradualist, however. Initially, only Jersey was targeted; the Presbyterian polity in Guernsey remained intact until Charles I sought to dismantle

---

[56] Scott R. Spurlock, 'Confessionalization and Clan Cohesion: Ireland's Contribution to Scottish Catholic Renewal in the Seventeenth Century', *RH* 31 (2012), 171–94, at 175.
[57] David Masson, ed., *The Register of the Privy Council of Scotland*, 9: *1610–1613* (Edinburgh, 1889), xxvii–xxviii.
[58] Julian Goodare, 'The Statutes of Iona in Context', *ScHR* 77 (1998), 31–57; Martin MacGregor, 'The Statutes of Iona: Text and Context', *InR* 57 (2006), 111–81; Alison Cathcart, 'The Statutes of Iona: The Archipelagic Context', *JBS* 49 (2010), 4–27; Goodare, *Government of Scotland*, 234–5.

it. Jacobean Jersey ministers were not required to submit to episcopal ordination, use the surplice, or deliver readings from the Apocrypha. Unlike in Orkney, there was no move to abolish local customary law, and unlike the concurrent policy in the Western Isles, no attempt to promote the status of English at the expense of the local vernacular.[59]

The Channel Islands' proximity to Catholic France was a powerful argument against measures likely to produce instability. All around Britain, in fact, islands were a potential front-line in confrontation with the forces of the Counter-Reformation. In the immediate aftermath of the Armada of 1588, to the intense annoyance of Elizabeth's government, a Spanish privateer, under the protection of Earl Robert Stewart, used Orkney as a base to prey on English shipping.[60] British Catholics themselves regularly identified islands as weak points in the nation's military and spiritual defences. In 1575, the Welsh exile Morris Clynnog sought to persuade Gregory XIII to send an expedition of 10,000 men to Anglesey, and use it as a launch-pad for attacking the mainland. Reports of a Catholic conspiracy to seize the Isle of Man reached the English government in early 1593.[61] In 1591, and again in 1619, William Semphill, a Scots soldier in Habsburg service, sent detailed plans to the Spanish government for seizing the Northern Isles as a prelude to an invasion of Scotland. During the Anglo-Spanish War of Charles I's reign (1625–30), Philip IV dusted off these proposals for serious discussion.[62] Other plans, laid but not hatched, involved the Isles of Scilly. The renegade Englishman Thomas Stukeley proposed an expedition to seize them in 1575, as in 1642 did the Irish Franciscan Hugh Bourke. It would, he wrote to a compatriot in Rome, 'give a startling lesson to the English'.[63]

An actual Catholic presence, in many of the islands, was limited. There was a scattering of recusants in Anglesey and the Isle of Wight, but not markedly more so than in adjacent mainland counties. A stray Lazarist missionary undertook a short visit to Orkney in the 1650s, but

---

[59] Evans, 'Religious History of Jersey', 131–43; Thornton, *Channel Islands*, 139–42.

[60] Peter D. Anderson, *Robert Stewart, Earl of Orkney, Lord of Shetland, 1533–1593* (Edinburgh, 1982), 122–5.

[61] Glanmor Williams, *Wales and the Reformation* (Cardiff, 1997), 262; Cathcart, 'Island Empire', 40.

[62] Marshall, *Storm's Edge*, 149, 245–6.

[63] Richard Simpson, *The School of Shakespeare*, 2 vols (London, 1878), 1: 75; HMC, *Report on Franciscan Manuscripts Preserved at the Convent, Merchants' Quay, Dublin* (Dublin, 1906), 220.

none made it to Shetland, and post-Reformation Catholic communities would not take shape in the Northern Isles until well into the nineteenth century. Missionary engagement with the Isle of Man was similarly limited, though there is a revealing comment in a letter from a late-seventeenth-century bishop of Sodor about an islander reported to be in a Jesuit college abroad: 'this person having our language [Manx] is the man I most fear'.[64]

The exception is the sustained missionary campaign in the Western Isles undertaken in the second quarter of the seventeenth century by Irish Franciscans based at Louvain. In the Franciscans' Latin letters to *Propaganda Fide* in Rome, describing efforts in Barra, the Uists, Skye, Jura, Mull and other islands, we possess the record of an entirely non-anglophone campaign of evangelism. Indeed, at one stage, the missionaries, fearful their correspondence might be interrupted, took to writing in Gaelic, and having their letters translated into Latin in Louvain. In 1626, the missionaries established a base at the disused friary at Bonamargy on the coast of Antrim in north-east Ireland. Through the 1630s, Catholics from the Hebrides were reported to be flocking there to receive the sacraments, particularly confirmation. The Catholic bishop of Down and Connor was said to have confirmed 700 Scots on one occasion in 1639.[65] Whether the Franciscan mission to the Western Isles should be regarded as a resounding success or a disappointing failure is a judgement on whether the glass looks half-full or half-empty. The friars themselves produced astonishing accounts of their achievements: thousands of souls gained, in a pattern more redolent of missionary endeavour in the New World than of the piecemeal underground advances in England and Lowland Scotland. The authorities in Rome were sceptical, but the missionaries responded with detailed lists of converts, island by island.[66]

What seems likeliest is that the Franciscans were not so much making Catholics of people who had hitherto been convinced Protestants, as meeting the pressing religious needs of communities starved of regular and reliable pastoral provision of any kind over the preceding two generations. Catholic belief persisted across

---

[64] Cressy, *England's Islands*, 100–2; Marshall, *Storm's Edge*, 290; Grass, 'Reformation and the Isle of Man', 96.

[65] Cathaldus Giblin, ed., *Irish Franciscan Mission to Scotland 1619–1646: Documents from Roman Archives* (Dublin, 1964), vii–xvi, 198; Macdonald, *Missions to the Gaels*, 55–96; Spurlock, 'Scottish Catholic Renewal', 178–9.

[66] Giblin, ed., *Franciscan Mission*, 129–38.

swathes of the Western Isles after 1560, but without institutional structures or much, if any, clerical instruction; a leading historian of Scottish Catholicism writes of a 'religious vacuum' in the lands of Clan Donald around the turn of the seventeenth century.[67] In August 1625, on Eigg, where no Catholic priest had visited since about 1556, Fr Cornelius Ward preached and said mass before a large crowd. Afterwards, he was confronted by an eighty-year-old woman who complained it was not like the masses she attended in her youth, when the custom was to give the pax to the people to be kissed. Ward had to explain how the ritual did not pertain to the substance of the mass and could safely be omitted. This little face-off between the catechetical priorities of the Counter-Reformation and the social functions of late medieval Christianity is one the late John Bossy would surely have appreciated.[68]

The Franciscan mission petered out in the late 1640s, chronically underfunded and hampered by lack of understanding of conditions on the ground from the Roman authorities, who expected widely dispersed priests to be able to convene every three days to discuss progress. A recurrent complaint of the missionaries was their lack of 'faculties' to bless chapels and liturgical objects, and, crucially, to issue dispensations for marriages contracted within canonically prohibited degrees.[69] Some places where the missionaries scored considerable successes – Lewis, Skye, Arran, Islay – were to be almost wholly lost to Protestantism in the coming decades. But where the resources of the Scottish Kirk were stretched particularly thin, and where Catholic missionaries operated under the protection of sympathetic MacDonald and MacNeill chiefs, lasting results ensued. The islands of Barra, Eriskay, South Uist and Benbecula are to this day some of the most Catholic parts of the United Kingdom.

To ask, however, whether the Reformation – or the Counter-Reformation – succeeded or failed in Britain's islands may be the

---

[67] Scott Spurlock, 'The Laity and the Structure of the Catholic Church in Early Modern Scotland', in Armstrong and Ó hAnnracháin, eds, *Insular Christianity*, 231–51, at 246. See also idem, 'Catholicism in Scotland to 1603', in James Kelly and John McCafferty, eds, *The Oxford History of British and Irish Catholicism*, 1: *Endings and New Beginnings, 1530–1640* (Oxford, 2023), 68–88, at 75–6.

[68] Giblin, ed., *Franciscan Mission*, 66. For John Bossy's influential argument about the Catholic Reformation reshaping a predominantly social religious system in doctrinal and hierarchical ways, see his *Christianity in the West, 1400–1700* (Oxford, 1985).

[69] Giblin, ed., *Franciscan Mission*, 24, 35, 57, 92–3, 98, 118–19.

wrong question. Julian Goodare, in his study of Scottish government under James VI, astutely notes how:

> it is all too easy, immersed in government papers, to adopt the government's own value system … and say: These were the problems facing Scotland. We ought rather to say: These were the problems facing Scotland's rulers. Many histories … have assumed that the problem of early modern Scotland was 'lawlessness', 'disorder', 'lack of effective control', or some such phrase. James VI and his councillors thought they had a problem of 'disorder' when people would not obey them; the people themselves may have perceived a problem of unreasonable royal demands and interference.[70]

Islands encapsulate this conundrum in a particularly focused way. They were never 'remote' or 'peripheral' to those who actually lived there, people whose priorities in religion, as in much else, were seldom precisely the same as those of the central authorities, or of the clergymen sent to instruct them. Much more could be said about the challenges the topography and environment of islands routinely presented to externally imposed institutional structures: the difficulties of integrating and aligning them to dioceses, synods, presbyteries, or even parishes. This was not a uniquely insular problem: geographically large parishes, with attendant difficulties for parishioners' access to services, were found in moorland northern England, and across the Scottish Highlands. However, the challenge posed to theology by geography was particularly evident in island settings, and much commented on. In Orkney, Shetland and across much of the Hebrides, for example, there were usually far fewer available ministers than there were inhabited islands or functioning kirks, and in consequence, weekly attendance at divine worship was for many people simply not the norm.[71] The extent to which this was in any way a 'problem' depends on one's perspective.

The voices and beliefs of ordinary islanders are usually silent, muted or refracted in our sources. A fair amount is said about them, secondhand, in a spate of books about islands – topographies, histories and

---

[70] Goodare, *Government of Scotland*, 17.
[71] Marshall, 'Northern Frontier', 28–30; Wallis, 'Church in Shetland', 55–7, 62–3, 65–7, 77, 174–5. Logistical, transport and attendance problems are recurrent complaints in Duncan C. Mactavish, ed., *Minutes of the Synod of Argyll, 1639–1661*, 2 vols (Edinburgh, 1943–4).

travelogues – published around the turn of the eighteenth century. They included works by Philippe Falle on Jersey, James Wallace and John Brand on Orkney and Shetland, William Sacheverell and George Waldron on the Isle of Man, and on the Western Isles by the Skye gentleman Martin Martin, who also published an account of a voyage to St Kilda.[72] Often, in these sources, the authorial emphasis is on 'ignorance' and 'superstition'. Yet, in spite of themselves, the accounts paint a picture of remarkably dynamic religious cultures, in which Christianity coexisted with older structures of belief, and outwardly conforming Protestantism with habits of pilgrimage to ancient chapels and wells.

'Remote', 'marginal', 'peripheral', islands were nonetheless continuous objects of interest and attention in the early modern period. As was well understood by numerous writers, from Thomas More to Francis Bacon, William Shakespeare and Daniel Defoe, fictional islands could be invaluable devices for framing and focusing social, moral and political issues.[73] For historians of the Reformation, islands are similarly useful framing instruments. By virtue of their characteristic placement on boundaries, and their tendency to operate as zones of encounter and competition, islands discourage the stubbornly residual tendency to conceptualize the Reformation in exclusively national settings. By virtue of their usually self-evident distinctiveness – from each other, and from an imagined (and often imaginary) mainland norm – islands allow us to observe with enhanced clarity processes that may have been taking place less perceptibly elsewhere. An island perspective necessarily steers us away from diffusionist models of religious change, which prioritize the concerns of central authority. Islands were, at times, conspicuous targets for externally driven campaigns of incorporation and 'civilization', but not infrequently they exposed the limitations of such ambitions, and revealed

---

[72] Philippe Falle, *An Account of the Isle of Jersey* (London, 1694); James Wallace, *A Description of the Isles of Orkney* (Edinburgh, 1693); John Brand, *A Brief Description of Orkney, Zetland, Pightland-Firth and Caithness* (Edinburgh, 1701); Sacheverell, *Account of the Isle of Man*; George Waldron, 'A Description of the Isle of Man', in *Compleat Works, in Verse and Prose, of George Waldron*, ed. Theodosia Waldron (London, 1731); Martin, *Description of the Western Isles*; idem, *A Late Voyage to St. Kilda, The Remotest of all the Hebrides* (London, 1698).

[73] For an insightful discussion, see Roland Greene, 'Island Logic', in Peter Hulme and William H. Sherman, eds, *The Tempest and its Travels* (London, 2000), 138–45.

the necessity for reform, if it were to be by any measure successful, to indigenize and evolve.

Islands, then, matter for the history of the Reformation, and they mattered to reformers too. The last words can go to a reformer who was also the first major historian of the British Reformations: the martyrologist John Foxe. In a tract published at the start of 1559, Foxe wrote excitedly from exile in Basel that the light of the gospel had now 'finally reached the furthest bounds of the Ocean, and the Orkneys themselves, so that with the circle of its journey completed so to speak, it has no further spaces to which it might spread'.[74] His claim illustrates nicely how the very marginality of islands could invest them with symbolic and cultural significance: for Foxe, the Reformation's ability to reach Orkney was the final and irrevocable proof of its triumph. The assessment was wide of the mark, but the effusions of an Englishman in Switzerland about a Scottish archipelago claimed by Denmark provide us with a satisfactorily paradoxical conclusion. For historians of the Reformation in Britain, an attentiveness to islands is an antidote to insularity.

---

[74] John Foxe, *Germaniae ad Angliam de Restituta Evangelii Luce Gratulatio* (Basel, 1559), 46–7.

Language and the Manx Reformation, 1570–1698

Tim Grass

Ramsey, Isle of Man

This article explores how the language barrier reinforced the Manx church's peripheral position by its effect on the course of Protestant reform on the Isle of Man. It considers the nature of this barrier, focusing on the lack of published Manx translations of the Bible and the Book of Common Prayer, and outlines how this affected the course taken by reform. Lack of access to Manx texts and education militated against the emergence of a body of theologically aware laity, while the necessity for parish clergy to be bilingual restricted the pool of potential candidates, hindering the infusion of new personnel and ideas from elsewhere. Educational and economic factors combined with language to exacerbate these problems and retard the impact of new patterns of clergy recruitment and training. The consequence was to limit the Manx church's participation in developments shaping the Church of England, and to complicate attempts by later seventeenth-century bishops to overcome this.

According to James Sharpe, the Isle of Man in the seventeenth century was 'geographically marginal, culturally isolated, and economically backward',[1] amply justifying for many the perception of it as a periphery. To a significant extent, this was due to the language barrier: for the majority of people, their first language was Manx rather than English. In spite of recent scholarly interest in the way Protestant reform deployed Celtic languages,[2] Manx has attracted relatively little comment, probably because of its limited geographical range;

I wish to thank Alan Ford and Crawford Gribben for their comments on an earlier draft of this article, as well as the peer reviewers and the audience at the EHS Summer Conference in 2023. 26 Fairway Drive, Ramsey, Isle of Man, IM8 2BB. E-mail: tgrass. work@gmail.com.

[1] James Sharpe, 'Towards a Legal Anthropology of the Early Modern Isle of Man', in Richard McMahon, ed., *Crime, Law and Popular Culture in Europe, 1500–1900* (Abingdon, 2013), 118–37, at 120.

[2] See, for example, Toby C. Barnard, 'Protestants and the Irish Language, *c.*1675–1725', *JEH* 44 (1993), 243–72; Glanmor Williams, 'Unity of Religion or Unity of Language? Protestants and Catholics and the Welsh Language 1536–1660', in Geraint Jenkins, ed., *The Welsh Language before the Industrial Revolution* (Cardiff, 1997), 207–33; Karl S. Bottigheimer and Ute Lotz-Heumann, 'The Irish Reformation in European Perspective',

Studies in Church History 61 (2025), 284–303 © The Author(s), 2025. Published by Cambridge University Press on behalf of the Ecclesiastical History Society.
doi:10.1017/stc.2024.41

thus, the language has also been peripheral in terms of scholarly attention.[3]

This article draws on research for my forthcoming book on the course of Protestant reform on the Isle of Man. It argues that the language barrier did much to shape that course by limiting the Manx church's participation in developments which defined the reforming Church of England, and hindering attempts by later seventeenth-century bishops, especially Isaac Barrow (1663–71), to foster such participation.[4] Language difference thus ensured the Manx church's continuing peripheral status within the Church of England. This worked in three ways. First, the lack of printed editions of the Bible and the Prayer Book in Manx hindered the formation on the island of Christian laity from whom might be drawn candidates for ordination. Second, the need for Manx-speakers, coupled with the poverty of almost all the seventeen parish livings,[5] severely limited the possibility of attracting parochial clergy from elsewhere, or, if non-Manx speakers took up positions on the island, rendered their ministry less effective. Third, the limited education available to local ordinands and the consequent persistence of traditional localized patterns of recruitment meant that they were insufficiently equipped to engage with wider ecclesiastical issues and trends.

ARG 89 (1998), 268–308, esp. 284–5; David N. Griffiths, *The Bibliography of the Book of Common Prayer 1549–1999* (London, 2002), 498, 510, 575; Felicity Heal, 'Mediating the Word: Language and Dialects in the British and Irish Reformations', *JEH* 56 (2005), 261–86; J. Robert Wright, 'Early Translations', in Charles Hefling and Cynthia Shattuck, eds, *The Oxford Guide to the Book of Common Prayer: A Worldwide Survey* (Oxford, 2006), 56–60. These offer comments on the case of Manx but no sustained consideration.

[3] For a rare example of an article devoted to this topic, see David Craine, 'The Bible in Manx', *Proceedings of the Isle of Man Natural History & Antiquarian Society* [hereafter: *PIMNHAS*] 5/5 (1954–6), 540–54.

[4] The most recent overviews are all dated: A. W. Moore, *Diocesan Histories: Sodor and Man* (London, 1893), 97–185; idem, *A History of the Isle of Man*, 2 vols (Douglas, 1900), 1: 341–72; W. S. Dempsey, *A History of the Catholic Church in the Isle of Man* (Billinge, 1958), 117–36 (ch. 12, 'The So-Called Reformation'). The fourth volume of the *New History of the Isle of Man* will offer somewhat more up-to-date coverage, although it has been some years in preparation.

[5] J. Roger Dickinson, *The Lordship of Man under the Stanleys: Government and Economy in the Isle of Man, 1580–1704*, Chetham Society 3rd series 41 (Manchester, 1996), 345–6.

The Island's Political and Ecclesiastical Status

By way of background, some comment on the Isle of Man's distinctive political and ecclesiastical status will be helpful. Since 1406, it had been ruled by the Stanley family of Lancashire. Whilst they owed allegiance to the English crown, and had found it politic to gradually abandon the title 'King of Man' in favour of 'Lord of Man', the change made no practical difference and for the most part they continued to rule autonomously.[6] Many civil appointments were made from Lancashire families in the service of the Stanleys, including most of the governors, who effectively ruled the island in the absence of the lord.

The island tended to be of interest to London only when strategic defence considerations (or later, economic ones) were in view. This explains why, when a succession dispute broke out within the Stanley family after the death of the fifth earl in 1594, Elizabeth I took the charge of the island into her own hands, lest there be no chain of command to deal with enemy threats.[7] Indeed, there had been fears in the 1570s that it could serve as a staging post to spirit away Mary Queen of Scots and, in the 1580s and 1590s, that it could be used either to get priests away from Lancashire or into England, or by Spaniards against England, or as a base for 'piracy'. The island was seen as 'infected' with papists, and there was a recurrent fear of its invasion from Ireland or the Western Isles of Scotland.[8] Direct rule

---

[6] See ibid. 15–18.

[7] See *Calendar of State Papers Domestic: Elizabeth, 1595–97*, ed. Mary Anne Everett Green (London, 1869), 82 (Elizabeth to the bailiffs of the Isle of Man, 1 August 1595), *British History Online* [hereafter: *BHO*], at: <http://www.british-history.ac.uk/cal-state-papers/domestic/edw-eliz/1595-7/pp82-98>, accessed 1 November 2018.

[8] See, for example, *Calendar of State Papers Domestic: Elizabeth, Addenda, 1566–79*, ed. Mary Anne Everett Green (London, 1871), 362 (examination of Henry Simpson, 8 October 1571), *BHO*, at: <http://www.british-history.ac.uk/cal-state-papers/domestic/edw-eliz/addenda/1566-79/>, accessed 5 April 2018; *Calendar of State Papers, Scotland*, 5: *1574–81*, ed. William K Boyd (London, 1907), 70–1 (Advertisements to the Earl of Leicester, 1574), *BHO*, at: <http://www.british-history.ac.uk/cal-state-papers/scotland/vol5/pp68-83>, accessed 1 November 2018; *Calendar of State Papers Domestic: Elizabeth, 1581–90*, ed. Robert Lemon (London, 1865), 633 (information from John Waren, 11 December 1589), *BHO*, at: <http://www.british-history.ac.uk/cal-state-papers/domestic/edw-eliz/1581-90/pp631-637>, accessed 1 November 2018; *Calendar of State Papers, Scotland*, 10: *1589–1593*, ed. William K. Boyd and Henry W. Meikle (Edinburgh, 1936), 688–93, at 690 (no. 694), *BHO*, at: <http://www.british-history.ac.uk/cal-state-papers/scotland/vol10/pp681-711>, accessed 6 April 2018; ibid. 828–9 (no. 783, Robert Bowes to [Burghley], 1 January 1593), *BHO*, at: <http://www.british-history.ac.uk/cal-state-

therefore lasted until the resolution of the succession dispute in 1609.

Political peripherality was reflected in ecclesiastical matters. In the twelfth century, the diocese of Sodor had included most of the Western Isles of Scotland,[9] but by the sixteenth, the Western Isles had come under Scottish jurisdiction and the diocese had shrunk to comprise only the Isle of Man. It had been neglected by a succession of jurisdictions, partly because of its remoteness. The diocese appears to have been placed under York in 1458, but the lack of clarity in official sources regarding who occupied the see during the first half of the sixteenth century indicates how tenuous the link with the wider church actually was. The see was formally incorporated into the province of Canterbury in 1541, as an afterthought in the act incorporating the diocese of Chester, before being returned the following year to the jurisdiction of York.[10] But successive archbishops took very little interest, and 'any attempt to treat Sodor and Man as comprised in the province of York for any effective purpose other than the consecration of the bishops seems quickly to have lapsed'.[11] The diocese appears only in one or two references in provincial act books and intermittent records of attendance at convocation (when Manx delegates were usually represented by proctors). York's jurisdiction in appeals from the Manx church courts was acknowledged only vaguely, and such appeals were very rare indeed, in part because they were discouraged by the Stanleys.[12]

---

papers/scotland/vol10/pp820-833>, accessed 6 April 2018; *Calendar of State Papers, Scotland*, 11: *1593–1595*, ed. Annie I. Cameron (Edinburgh, 1936), 116–18, at 117 (no. 85, Robert Bowes to Burghley, 7 July 1593), *BHO*, at: <http://www.british-history.ac.uk/cal-state-papers/scotland/vol11/pp114-136>, accessed 6 April 2018; *Calendar of State Papers, Ireland, 1592–1596*, ed. Hans Claude Hamilton (London, 1890), 126, *BHO*, at: <http://www.british-history.ac.uk/cal-state-papers/ireland/1592-6/pp120-136>, accessed 1 November 2018.

[9] On the later medieval diocese, see Alex Woolf, 'The Early History of the Diocese of Sodor', and P. J. Davey, 'Medieval Monasticism and the Isle of Man *c.*1130–1540', in Seán Duffy and Harold Mytum, eds, *A New History of the Isle of Man*, 3: *The Medieval Period, 1000–1406* (Liverpool, 2015), 329–48 and 349–76, respectively.

[10] 'An Act for disseevering the Bishoprick of Chester and of the Isle of Man from the Jurisdiction of Canterbury to the Jurisdiction of York', 1541 (33 Henry VIII, c. 31).

[11] Anne Ashley, 'The Spiritual Courts of the Isle of Man, especially in the 17th and 18th Centuries', *EHR* 72 (1957), 31–59, at 36. The name of the diocese changed gradually during the seventeenth century.

[12] J. A. Sharpe and J. R. Dickinson, 'Courts, Crime and Litigation in the Isle of Man, 1580–1700', *HR* 72 (1999), 140–59, at 145, 146 n. 17. For historical surveys of the status

In effect, the Manx church was ruled by the lord of Man. A ruling of 1541 had confirmed his status as 'Metropolitan and & Chiefe of holy church'.[13] This was directed against the bishop and clergy, who were seen as infringing on the lord's ecclesiastical prerogatives, but it may also have had in view any potential claim from Henry VIII. The ruling was confirmed in 1610.[14] Except during the period of direct rule by the English crown (which saw one significant appointment in 1605, of John Phillips as bishop), the Stanleys as lords of Man possessed the power of nominating candidates for the episcopal see, and thirteen of the island's seventeen livings were also in their gift. Reflecting the situation with civil appointments, the body of domestic chaplains and incumbents of livings in the family's gift provided a number of personnel for higher clergy appointments, including at least five of the nine archdeacons appointed during this period and five of the eleven bishops.

As governors of the Manx church, the Stanleys walked a tightrope, needing to keep on the right side of the English monarchy, but (mostly) being reluctant to adopt new religious opinions. The third earl, Edward (r. 1521–72) went no further in reform than acceding to the dissolution of the island's monastic establishments in 1540. In 1549, he voted against the Act of Uniformity which enforced the use in England of the new Book of Common Prayer. By 1559, he was willing to accept the Elizabethan revision and to assist in its enforcement in the diocese of Chester, although he turned a blind eye to many traditional practices, and, in 1570, as well as sheltering two Roman Catholic priests, he forbade his chaplains in Lancashire to use the English book.[15]

---

of the Manx church, see Augur Pearce, 'The Offshore Establishment of Religion: Church and Nation on the Isle of Man', *Ecclesiastical Law Journal* 7 (2003), 62–74; Peter W. Edge and C. Augur Pearce, 'The Development of the Lord Bishop's Role in the Manx Tynwald', *JEH* 57 (2006), 494–514.

[13] Douglas, Manx National Heritage Library [hereafter: MNHL], MS 00510C, John Quayle, 'A Collection of several Law-Cases or Precedents taken out of the Antient and Modern Records of the Isle of Mann, setting forth the Constitution and Course of Proceedings used in the several Courts of Judicature within the said Isle, and the nature of our antient Customary Laws' (mid-eighteenth century), 31.

[14] A. W. Moore, ed., *Notes and Documents from the Records of the Isle of Man* (Douglas, n. d.), 26 (citing the *Liber Scaccarii* for 1610, but reference not traced); K. F. W. Gumbley, 'Church Legislation in the Isle of Man', *Ecclesiastical Law Journal* 3 (1994), 240–6, online at: <http://www.gumbley.net/article.htm#return6>, accessed 1 December 2021.

[15] J. J. Bagley, *The Earls of Derby 1485–1985* (London, 1985), 42, 46–7, 48.

The last bishop to appear in Catholic succession lists was Thomas Stanley, who belonged to another branch of the family. He had been appointed in 1555 (that is, under Mary I, when the English church once again came under Roman jurisdiction) and held office until his death in 1569.[16] Only from the 1570s do the first parish clergy with Protestant sympathies appear; this may be due to the lack of extant records before that point, but it is worth noting that one John Stephenson, vicar of Maughold for a few years after the death of his father (also John) in 1576, was said to have been the last Roman Catholic priest in the parish.[17]

THE LACK OF PRINTED MANX TEXTS

The importance of the preached and written word to Protestant thinking, reflecting belief in the supreme authority of Scripture in matters of faith and practice, makes it appropriate to consider the absence of printed Manx texts and its impact on the course of reform. According to Erkki Kouri, writing on Protestant reform in Scandinavia, 'The principle that the Word of God had to be preached to people in their mother tongue, and that they should be given the opportunity to read it in the vernacular, helped to create and nourish new written languages in remote and obscure parts of Europe.'[18] Moreover, the easiest way of making vernacular texts widely available was through printing. Even where the majority of the population could not read, Bob Scribner has suggested, printing was able to create a group of opinion-formers who could spread new ideas by oral means, notably through preaching and the discussion of what was preached or of texts read aloud in group settings.[19]

However, Felicity Heal argues that the Isle of Man offers a counter-example to the theory that print culture was central in disseminating

---

[16] Conrad Eubel, ed., *Hierarchia catholica medii aevi sive summorum pontificum, S. R. E. cardinalium, ecclesiarum antistitum series*, 3: *Saeculum XVI ab anno 1503 complectens* (Regensburg, 1910), 302, 321.

[17] J. W. and C. K. Radcliffe, *A History of Kirk Maughold* (Douglas, 1979), 88.

[18] E. I. Kouri, 'The Early Reformation in Sweden and Finland, *c.*1520–1560', in Ole Peter Grell, ed., *The Scandinavian Reformation: From Evangelical Movement to Institutionalisation of Reform* (Cambridge, 1995), 42–69, at 57. Kouri demonstrates this with reference to Swedish and Finnish, although the impact was less significant for Icelandic and Norwegian.

[19] R. W. Scribner, 'Oral Culture and the Diffusion of Reformation Ideas', *History of European Ideas* 5 (1984), 237–56, at 241–4; idem, *The German Reformation* (Basingstoke, 1986), 20.

Protestantism: here, she writes, change was achieved entirely orally.[20] This needs nuancing, as we shall see, but holds true in terms of the lack of printed texts. Reform on the Isle of Man was carried out in the absence of published vernacular religious material and did not result in the production of such material until the eighteenth century. Only then did agencies exist with the funds to sponsor the publication of works for which the market was extremely limited; only then, too, had education resulted in a growth in popular literacy. It has been estimated that the island's population in 1600 was about 7,000,[21] and, on the basis of surviving parish registers, Dickinson calculates the figure during the decade 1665–74 at 10,464.[22] Most had Manx as their first language, and many outside the commercial centres were monoglot. Until the Prayer Book was translated in 1610, there were no documents of any kind in Manx; all we have are brief quotations in the proceedings of church courts, often of insults or slanders for which the speakers had been presented. The earliest oral composition is the 'Manx Traditionary Ballad', which may have been composed early in the sixteenth century, although no manuscripts of it are known before the eighteenth.[23] Unlike Irish and Scots Gaelic (to which Manx is closely related), there was thus no literary form of the language; in consequence, Manx did not share in the common literary register of the other two languages.[24]

By 1570, the English Bible and the Book of Common Prayer had become fixtures in the worship of the established church in England, but the lack of records for preceding decades means that we do not know whether they had been introduced on the Isle of Man. The legislation mandating them applied to the island, but the royal

---

[20] Felicity Heal, *Reformation in Britain and Ireland* (Oxford, 2003), 283 n. 124; compare eadem, 'Mediating the Word', 280.

[21] Sharpe and Dickinson, 'Courts, Crime and Litigation', 158.

[22] Dickinson, *Lordship of Man*, 10. In the 1690s, William Sacheverell calculated it at about 16,000, which was probably an over-estimate: Preston, Lancashire Archives, Kenyon of Peel Hall Papers, DDKE/Box 84/79, 'Mr Sacheverell's Computation about the Isle of Man'.

[23] R. L. Thomson, 'The Manx Traditionary Ballad', 2 parts, *Études celtiques* 9 (1961), 521–48; 10 (1962), 60–87, part 1 at 522.

[24] Christopher Lewin, e-mail to the author, 7 August 2023. A variation of this argument is offered by Steven G. Ellis, 'A View of the Irish Language: Language and History in Ireland from the Middle Ages to the Present', in Ann K. Isaacs, ed., *Languages and Identities in Historical Perspective* (Pisa, 2005), 67–78, at 70–1, who asserts that the Protestant Reformation contributed to a decline in the mutual comprehensibility of Scottish, Irish and Manx Gaelic. Welsh was related most closely to Cornish and Breton; there were thus two 'families' of Celtic languages.

visitation of 1559 which imposed use of the English Prayer Book does not appear to have extended to the Isle of Man,[25] perhaps because it was ruled by the earls of Derby. In any case, it would have been characteristic of Earl Edward to stall on, or even attempt to obstruct, its application. Given his religious outlook, along with the fact that the last bishop whose appointment was recognized by Rome remained in office until 1569, it may be surmised that worship had continued to be conducted according to traditional Latin rites. Clergy, who were mostly Manx-speakers, presumably offered extempore translation of appropriate parts of the liturgy into Manx and, in a few locations, English – primarily those connected with island government: the parish church of Malew and the garrison chapels at Castle Rushen in Castletown, and Peel. This was certainly the practice by the middle third of the seventeenth century, but we lack evidence to confirm what happened before then. It is possible that, as sometimes happened in Ireland, individual clergy might continue to celebrate Catholic rites alongside occasional use of the Book of Common Prayer in English or Latin, with translation into Manx.[26]

When translation was undertaken, it was of the Prayer Book rather than, as in Wales and Scotland, the Bible.[27] The 1604 edition of the Prayer Book was translated by Bishop Phillips in 1610, with the help of Hugh Cannell (d. 1670), vicar of Kirk Michael. Phillips had been appointed by James VI/I in 1605, and was the third successive Welsh bishop in the diocese after John Meyrick (1576–99) and George Lloyd (1600–5). These three bishops would have brought with them an approach which stressed the importance of vernacular religious provision: the leaders of the Elizabethan church in Wales were convinced that if reform was to take root and the nation be united in religious matters, it was necessary to use Welsh, even if the crown's long-term aim might be its replacement by English.[28] Phillips is said to have

---

[25] Glanmor Williams, *Renewal and Reformation: Wales, c.1415–1642* (Oxford, 1993), 305; compare C. J. Kitching, ed., *The Royal Visitation of 1559: Act Book for the Northern Province*, Surtees Society 187 (Woodbridge, 1972).

[26] Steven G. Ellis, 'The Irish Reformation Debate in Retrospect', in Mark Empey, Alan Ford and Miriam Moffitt, eds, *The Church of Ireland and its Past: History, Interpretation, and Identity* (Dublin, 2017), 255–65, at 262.

[27] Heal, *Reformation*, 282.

[28] Geraint Jenkins, 'From Reformation to Methodism 1536–*c*.1750', in Prys Morgan, ed., *Wales: An Illustrated History* (Stroud, 2001), 167–209, at 193; W. Ian P. Hazlett, *The Reformation in Britain and Ireland* (London, 2003), 79–80.

learned Manx sufficiently well to preach in it, and the records portray him as a bishop who was strongly committed to fulfilling his ministry, if not always as diplomatic or as thick-skinned as the post called for.[29] Nevertheless, his translation was not too well received. One of the two vicars-general, William Norris, could only read the odd word; his colleague William Crowe could read part of it, but thought that few other clergy would be able to do so because it was 'spelled with vowels wherewith none of them are acquainted'. They also denied having been consulted about the possibility of printing it, which Phillips said had been his intention, although the limited market would have made it an unattractive economic proposition to any printer.[30]

Why did the translation meet such a cool reception? The Manx historian A. W. Moore (1853–1909) suggested that it was due to jealousy of Phillips as an incomer,[31] but jealousy does not appear to have been a characteristic reaction of locally born clergy to the appointment of outsiders to higher office during this period. Another possibility might have been clerical reluctance to change the way they conducted worship.[32] However, clergy were unlikely to be rejecting the principle of translation, since they already practised this extempore. Neither is it likely that Manx-born clergy were basing their opposition on a belief that Manx was not a fitting language for divine worship. Moreover, since much of the content of the Prayer Book would have been familiar, it is unlikely that lack of familiarity with Protestant understandings of key theological concepts was a major issue. Part of the problem may have been that, naturally enough in an oral culture, clergy were used to a verbal approach rather than a written one: traditional Catholic practice involved providing basic instruction in the vernacular, including the Lord's Prayer, the Ten

---

[29] The lack of any study of Phillips is a significant lacuna in the historiography of the Manx church.

[30] Phillips to the Earl of Salisbury, 1 February 1611, in MNHL, MS 00559C, 'A Booke containing the Answers of the Officers, Deemsters, Vicars General and 24 Keys to certaine Articles objected by John now Bishop of this Isle against John Ireland Esquire Lieutenant and Captain of the Isle of Man', 1610 (early eighteenth-century copy); quoted in A. W. Moore, assisted by John Rhŷs, eds, *The* Book of Common Prayer *in Manx Gaelic: Being Translations made by Bishop Phillips in 1610, and by the Manx Clergy in 1765*, 2 vols, Manx Society 32, 33 (Douglas, 1893), 1: xii.

[31] Moore, *Sodor and Man*, 136.

[32] Michael John Hoy, '*Isaac Barrow: Builder of Foundations for a Modern Nation: The Church, Education and Society in the Isle of Man, 1660–1800*' (PhD thesis, University of Liverpool, 2015), 76.

Commandments and the Creed, as well as translating the epistles and gospels of the liturgy.[33] On this reading, they may have seen little need for the constraint imposed by a written translation. More recently, and more cogently, it has been argued that the problem was the orthography, as implied by the comments of the vicars-general above. Since Manx did not yet have a systematized orthography, Phillips appears to have devised his own orthographical system; for those who had learnt to read and write through the medium of English (as local clergy would have done), rather than his native Welsh, the result may have been too different for them to recognize.[34] For a partial parallel, we may cite the Salesbury translation of the New Testament into Welsh (1567), which was criticized by contemporaries for its idiosyncratic orthography (closer to English and French) that made it impossible for the great majority of readers to understand it.[35] This said, whilst it is usually considered that Phillips's orthography was influenced by Welsh, it should be noted that he had held appointments in Yorkshire from 1579 onwards, and so it is possible that other linguistic influences were at work.[36]

In spite of the cool reception accorded to the translated Prayer Book, copies appear to have been made and used in worship. The Manx National Heritage Library has a well-used manuscript dating to the late 1620s, with subsequent emendations, possibly from the parish of Malew, in which the seat of government at Castle Rushen was located.[37] I have also discovered a fragment from the rubric for the visitation of the sick, which survived because someone had used it to record a debt; the rubric does not appear in the extant copy of the whole Prayer Book, and this fragment may have come from a different document or possibly a different copy of the book.[38] Regular use of the

---

[33] Heal, 'Mediating the Word', 280; compare Peter Marshall, *The Catholic Priesthood and the English Reformation* (Oxford, 1994), 29–30.

[34] Robert Leith Thomson, '*Early Manx: A Contribution to the Historical Study of Manx Gaelic Arranged as a Supplementary Volume to the Moore-Rhys Edition of the Phillips Prayer Book (1610)*' (BLitt dissertation, University of Glasgow, 1953), 9–10.

[35] Williams, 'Unity of Religion or Unity of Language?', 215–16; Heal, 'Mediating the Word', 274. Hazlett describes it as Latinized: Hazlett, *Reformation in Britain and Ireland*, 81.

[36] Joseph Foster, ed., *Alumni Oxonienses 1500–1714* (Oxford, 1891), *s.n.* 'Phillips, John', *BHO*, at: <http://www.british-history.ac.uk/alumni-oxon/1500-1714>, accessed 7 February 2018. I owe this suggestion to Professor Max Wheeler.

[37] MNHL, MSS 00003, 00004 (2 vols). For the dating, see Thomson, 'Early Manx', 4.

[38] Another fragment, from the *Benedicite*, was at one time in Moore's possession: Paul Rogers, 'Padjer Moghrey' (2023), unpublished document, in private hands.

Prayer Book would have ceased after regime change late in 1651 brought the island more into line with English policies. Nevertheless, clandestine use appears to have continued: according to Moore, one clergyman, John Cosnahan (1580–1656) at Santan, had people coming 'from all parts of the Island to have their children baptised during the period 1650–6 as he is said to have been the only clergyman who dared to baptise in accordance with the rites of the Established Church'.[39] If nothing else, this indicates that there was widespread conformity to Church of England rites by this period, although whether Protestant teaching had been internalized cannot be determined.

By 1663, the newly installed Bishop Barrow displayed no awareness of the translation's existence; he did, however, express disapproval of the practice of translating the liturgy extempore on the grounds that the clergy understood neither the English language nor the text of Scripture.[40] This would seem to confirm that the Phillips translation had fallen out of regular use and not been restored after 1660; after a new edition of the Prayer Book appeared in 1662, it was also out of date. By the end of the seventeenth century, William Sacheverell, governor of the island from 1693 to 1696, described the Phillips translation as 'scarce intelligible by the Clergy themselves, who Translate it off of hand more to the Understanding of the People', an apparent instance of a translation itself needing to be translated.[41] All the same, parts of it would appear in print subsequently. Bishop Wilson may have drawn on Phillips's translation of the catechism in his bilingual *Coyrle Sodjey* (literally, 'Further Instruction'; English title, *Principles and Duties of Christianity*), which was the first book to be published in Manx, in 1707. Phillips's translation of the Psalms, lightly revised, was incorporated into the Manx translation of the Bible published between 1767 and 1772.[42]

---

[39] MNHL, MS 00220A, A. W. Moore, 'Old Manx Families' (1889), 41. The parish's register of baptisms from this period has not survived.

[40] MNHL, MS 09782, Castle Rushen Papers, Ecclesiastical Courts, Box 2, Bishop Barrow, report on the condition of the diocese (1663). See also Craine, 'Bible in Manx', 542.

[41] William Sacheverell, *An Account of the Isle of Man, its Inhabitants, Language, Soil, remarkable Curiosities, the Succession of its Kings and Bishops, down to the present Time* (London, 1702), 8.

[42] MNHL, MS 13047, Robert Leith Thomson, 'The Clergy and their Writings in Manx' (typescript, n.d.), 3.

It has been asserted that Phillips also translated the Bible into Manx with Cannell's help. The first to claim this was James Chaloner, writing in 1653, although his work was not published until 1656. Chaloner also stated that the translation was not printed because of Phillips's death.[43] In an order increasing the now elderly Cannell's stipend in 1658, Chaloner (by then the island's governor) referred to him as one of the island's first preachers, who had taught the Manx to read the Scriptures in their own tongue, and who assisted Phillips in translating the Bible.[44] Yet in spite of these contemporary references, such a translation has never come to light. The portions of Scripture appointed to be read in worship – that is, the Sunday Epistles and Gospels, and those biblical verses that were integrated into the liturgy – were translated as part of the Prayer Book, as was the Psalter,[45] and it is possible that this was what was being referred to. In the absence of further evidence, the possibility that the claim is true cannot be ruled out, but there are no references to such a work's existence in extant diocesan records.

Publication of both texts came much later. The Manx Prayer Book was not published until 1765, in a new translation reflecting the 1662 Book of Common Prayer; this was two centuries later than the appearance of the Book of Common Order in Scottish Gaelic (1567)[46] or the Book of Common Prayer in Welsh (1567),[47] and over 150 years later than for the Book of Common Prayer in Irish (by 1608).[48] The complete Manx Bible was only published as one volume in 1775.[49]

---

[43] James Chaloner, *A Short Treatise of the Isle of Man*, ed. and intro. J. G. Cumming, Manx Society 10 (Douglas, 1864), 9. For the date of Chaloner's work, see John Callow, '"In so shifting a Scene": Thomas Fairfax as Lord of the Isle of Man, 1651–60', in Andrew Hopper and Philip Major, eds, *England's Fortress: New Perspectives on Thomas, 3rd Lord Fairfax* (Abingdon and New York, 2016), 21–52, at 31.

[44] MNHL, MS 10071/3/9, Liber Scaccarii, 1658, fol. 101ᵛ (28 August 1658).

[45] The readings appointed for morning and evening prayer, however, were not translated; this would have entailed an almost complete translation of the Bible.

[46] The Book of Common Order was the first book published in Gaelic: Diarmaid MacCulloch, *Reformation: Europe's House Divided, 1490–1700* (London, 2004), 381. However, the Book of Common Prayer did not appear until 1794: Griffiths, *Bibliography*, 498.

[47] Alec Ryrie, *The Age of Reformation: The Tudor and Stewart Realms 1485–1603*, 2nd edn (Abingdon, 2017; first publ. 2009), 278.

[48] Wright, 'Early Translations', 58; 'Leabhar na hUrnaí Coitinne: The Book of Common Prayer in Irish Gaelic', online at: <http://justus.anglican.org/resources/bcp/Ireland/Gaelic.htm>, accessed 9 August 2023. An Irish translation had been authorized as early as 1550 but not produced: Ryrie, *Age of Reformation*, 275.

[49] The New Testament in Irish appeared in 1603: Heal, 'Mediating the Word', 263.

The timeline was similar in Scotland: although a version in classical Scottish Gaelic had appeared as early as 1603, the New Testament in a more popular register of the language was not published until 1767, with the whole Bible following in 1801.[50] This contrasts with the appearance in English during the sixteenth and seventeenth centuries of several editions of the Prayer Book, as well as various translations of the Bible and a number of authoritative doctrinal statements.[51] Clearly, the English authorities in church and state did not see a Manx Bible and Prayer Book as priorities, although since the island's strategic military position was recognized, and there were recurring fears that it could be used as a staging post by Catholic missionaries, one would have expected encouragement for anything which might contribute to making the populace more tractable.

Other factors retarding translation and publication may have included belief in the superiority of English. Archbishop Neile, reporting on the state of the diocese in 1634, commented that 'the late Bp [Phillips] translated our Comon Prayer Booke; but how faithfully, I know not', and opined that it would be better for the local populace to learn English.[52] Bishop Barrow, who in the 1660s did much to shape the development of the island's religious and educational institutions, expressed the same view.[53] Soon after becoming bishop, he produced a report on the state of his diocese, concluding that the people were loose living because they were 'without any true sense of religion'. Their ministers were 'very ignorant, and wholly illiterate'. Believing that the state of the people was down to the lack of means for Christian instruction, and the clergy ill-equipped, Barrow concluded that the problems could only be resolved through education, in English rather than Manx, so that the laity could be fortified against ungodliness and sectarianism by reading the Bible, the Prayer Book and other devotional works. However, to educate the people, it was necessary to begin with the clergy. As there was nothing printed or written in Manx, the clergy officiated 'by an extempor[ar]y translation of the English Liturgye into the Manks language, and soe allsoe of the holy Scriptures'. Barrow

[50] Bottigheimer and Lotz-Heumann, 'Irish Reformation', 284.

[51] Anthony Milton, 'Introduction', to idem, ed., *The Oxford History of Anglicanism*, 1: *Reformation and Identity, c.1520–1662* (Oxford, 2017), 1–27, at 2–3.

[52] Kew, TNA, SP16/259/78e, Archbishop Neile's report on the state of his jurisdiction, January 1634.

[53] Moore, *Sodor and Man*, 158; Michael Hoy, 'Political or Pastoral: Isaac Barrow's English Schools', *PIMNHAS* 12/4 (2011–13), 762–8, at 762, 765; Hoy, 'Barrow', 81.

disapproved of this practice, as we have seen.[54] All this would have fitted with the eighth earl's conviction that Manx was the language of rebellion, which needed to be replaced through re-education.[55] Barrow worked to establish a system of English-medium petty schools in the parishes, supplemented by restoring the grammar schools in the towns. He also laid much of the groundwork for the establishment of an academic institution in the Isle of Man for the training of clergy.[56]

Where clergy did not use the Phillips translation (and there is very little evidence regarding the extent of its dissemination or use), their practice of extempore translation meant that oral transmission remained primary. There is some limited evidence of the importation of English Bibles, Testaments and primers from the late seventeenth century,[57] but their readership must have been limited, perhaps being found primarily among the merchant community and the growing number of schools. In the parish of Malew (which included the island's capital, Castletown), merchants were bequeathing copies of the (English) Bible and Prayer Book in their wills from the beginning of the seventeenth century; this may indicate that they were among the early adopters of reform, but there is no evidence that they engaged in any kind of propagation of these ideas.

For the majority who were unable to understand English, then, Scripture continued to be accessible only as clergy offered extempore translations of the service and the Scripture readings, or preached in Manx. In most parishes, sermons were probably infrequent, certainly before the changes which ensued from 1651 onwards, since only a minority of clergy were considered sufficiently educated to be licensed to preach. Non-preaching clergy in the Church of England were supposed to read one of the sermons in the two *Books of Homilies*, but it is not clear how widely this rule was observed on the island: Moore asserts that these were not introduced until the time of Bishop

---

[54] MNHL, MS 09782, Castle Rushen Papers, Ecclesiastical Courts, Box 2, Barrow's report. See also Moore, *Sodor and Man*, 158; Craine, 'Bible in Manx', 542; Hoy, 'Political or Pastoral', 762, 765; idem, 'Barrow', 81.

[55] Hoy, 'Political or Pastoral', 764, following Peter G. Clamp, 'English Schooling in the Isle of Man, 1660–1700: The Barrovian Design', *Journal of Educational Administration and History* 20 (1988), 10–21, at 11.

[56] For Barrow's educational achievements, see Hinton Bird, *An Island that Led: The History of Manx Education*, 2 vols (Port St Mary, [*c*.1990]), 1: 9–15.

[57] See the records of imports in MNHL, MS 10058, Ingates, Outgates, Licences etc., Ramsey, 4 April 1648, 13 January 1693, 8 March 1694, 7 March 1695, 11 October 1695.

Parr (1635–44), and none appeared in printed translation until after 1820.[58] Even where clergy were licensed to preach, there were a fair number of complaints that they did not.[59] The Reformation expectation of being able to profit by hearing the word penetrated local minds,[60] but often went unfulfilled until the end of the seventeenth century. The earliest extant documents in Manx apart from the Prayer Book are sermons from 1696 onwards,[61] but the limited number and range of items published in Manx during the following half-century (which were all religious in nature) contrasts with the volume of liturgical texts, sermons, and works of theology and church practice available in English by that point.[62]

For many, English was in any case no substitute for Manx in worship. Growing antagonism was shown towards the use of English, and some laity refused to attend English services, especially when these began to increase in frequency from the late seventeenth century. William Gill, presented in 1678 for non-attendance in Lezayre, asserted that 'he would not stay in the church whilst Mr ffox read in English, for he would as soon sitt upon ye side of Skyhill as be in ye church when he did not und'stand w[ha]t was spoken'.[63] A number of people were presented in the adjoining parishes of German and Patrick in 1685 for creating a disturbance while Samuel Wattleworth was preaching in English, even though he 'also did preach in Manks & read both lessons yt day in Manks besides ye prayers of ye Church with ye

---

[58] Moore, *History*, 1: 361.

[59] For example, MNHL, MS 10194, Diocesan presentments, Arbory, 13 April 1673 and 7 June 1674 (Samuel Robinson for only reading an English homily); ibid., Ballaugh, 18 November 1685 (Henry Lowcay for not preaching in either Manx or English).

[60] See, for example, MNHL, MS 09756, 'Bishop Foster's Visitation 1634', response from the parish of German; and the presentments of Samuel Robinson in the 1670s (see previous note).

[61] Christopher Lewin, 'A Manx Sermon from 1696', *Zeitschrift für celtische Philologie* 62 (2015), 45–96, online at: <https://doi.org/10.1515/zcph.2015.004>, accessed 5 November 2024. There is a considerable corpus of early Manx manuscript sermons, mostly held by MNHL.

[62] Such published (and some unpublished) material as there was, can be found online at: <http://corpus.gaelg.im>, accessed 5 November 2024.

[63] MNHL, MS 10194, Diocesan Presentments 1678. It would be incautious to read developed Protestant sentiments into this utterance: more probably it was expressing opposition to the increasing use of English as the language of incomers. The case was recorded in English, but we do not know the extent to which Manx was used in proceedings.

Epistle & Gospell' and 'every other Sunday preacheth in Manks with much satisfaction'.[64]

The lack of written and preached vernacular material must also have hindered the formation of a critical mass of laity who could share in creating a climate in which religious change received informed consideration. This is similar to Wales, for which Glanmor Williams has contended that '[t]he Reformation as a body of doctrine and belief could not come of age for most people until the eighteenth century had made many of them literate'.[65] Whilst the educated middling merchant classes in urban areas formed the demographic group which in many parts of Europe was usually first to accept and spread the new Protestant convictions, it is likely that such a class only began to appear on the island during the late seventeenth century, and its emergence may well be connected with the growing use of English as well as the beginnings of a degree of urbanization. An increase from the 1670s in bequests of personal copies of the Bible may be related to Barrow's efforts to extend educational provision.[66]

The slowness of the seventeenth-century church to produce standard editions of the Bible and the Prayer Book in Manx may have weakened the church's position in the minds of the populace. Baptist Levinz, bishop from 1684 to 1693, was apprehensive about the impact of one Roman Catholic missionary who was Manx and spoke the language:

> one of ye Jesuits yt is to come heer is a native of this place, of a good family & interest heer, tho hee has been out of his country ever since his youth & bred up in one of ye Jesuits Colleges abroad, this person having our language is ye man I most fear.[67]

We do not know who this was, but whether Levinz's fears were justified or not, he recognized that language was an issue which affected the church's hold on the people. Had there been a mission by Manx-speaking Roman Catholics, they might have seen

---

[64] MNHL, MS 14425, Archidiaconal Wills 1684–8 (transcription by Joyce M. Oates, 2017), 70.

[65] Williams, *Renewal and Reformation*, iv.

[66] For the similar case of Orkney and Shetland, see Charlotte Methuen, 'Orkney, Shetland and the Networks of the Northern Reformation', *Nordlit* 43 (2019), 25–53, at 46, online at: <https://septentrio.uit.no/index.php/nordlit/issue/view/398>, accessed 8 February 2024.

[67] Oxford, Bodl., MS Tanner 28, fol. 175, Levinz to Archbishop Sancroft, 12 September 1688.

considerable success, given the attachment of many local people to traditional customs and practices.[68]

The Language Barrier and Clerical Recruitment

It was not only the case that the lack of material in Manx impoverished the formation of local candidates for ordination. The need for Manx-speakers, coupled with the poverty of local livings, hindered clerical recruitment from off the island. Incumbents were expected to be bilingual and, as we have seen, there were complaints when they did not preach or conduct worship in Manx. Yet it was rare for incoming clergy to learn Manx well enough to preach in it; Phillips was an exception, and unusual among the bishops of this period in recognizing the importance of using Manx.

The difficulty of attracting educated clergy from elsewhere meant that during the period under review, up to three-quarters of clergy may have been born on the island, and about a sixth were sons of clergy serving there.[69] Formal training for ministry, however, was largely unknown on the island until after the Restoration. From 1580, clergy in England were expected to be graduates of one of the universities, and by 1640, three-quarters of clergy in most areas of England met this requirement.[70] In contrast, on the Isle of Man, the proportion was about a tenth: the bishops and archdeacons, as well as a few other clergy from elsewhere, some of whom had held previous appointments in the gift of the Stanleys. None of the island's university-educated clergy during this period was Manx-born.

Clerical education was restricted by the lack of local provision and by the lack of fluency of many in English. Manx candidates for ordination could not afford to go to England or Ireland for education,

---

[68] On the continued popularity of practices which may represent an attempt to fill the gap left by the loss of the supernatural in worship, see Ronald Hutton, 'The English Reformation and the Evidence of Folklore', *P&P* 148 (1995), 89–116; idem, 'The Changing Faces of Manx Witchcraft', *Cultural & Social History* 7 (2010), 153–69; Jim Sharpe, 'Witchcraft in the Early Modern Isle of Man', *Cultural & Social History* 4 (2007), 11–28.

[69] These figures are based on my research, which includes the compilation of a prosopography of all those known to have ministered on the island between 1540 and 1698; approximately one hundred and seventy individuals have been identified. This has now been deposited as MNHL, MS 15879, 'Clergy on the Isle of Man, 1540–1698', typescript, 2024.

[70] I. M. Green, 'Teaching the Reformation: The Clergy as Preachers, Catechists, Authors and Teachers', in C. Scott Dixon and Luise Schorn-Schütte, eds, *The Protestant Clergy of Early Modern Europe* (Basingstoke, 2003), 156–75, at 160.

and no real attempt was made to give them access to theological reading matter until Thomas Fairfax as lord of Man had a library sent over in 1659.[71] By and large, new priests learned on the job, as they had done for centuries. As noted above, around a sixth were sons of priests; others had been parish clerks or schoolmasters. My research has identified at least eleven who appear to have served as parish clerks before ordination, all between 1577 and 1665; between 1593 and 1685, about fourteen served as schoolmasters prior to ordination; two of these held both offices.

There is a further dimension to be taken into account: whilst it was rare for parochial clergy to be appointed from outside the diocese, it was even rarer for bishops or archdeacons to be appointed from within it, arguably because the Stanleys were looking elsewhere for appointees. There had been no Manx-born bishop since William Russell in the mid-fourteenth century, and in 1703 Samuel Wattleworth became the first Manx archdeacon since the fifteenth century.[72] Moreover, the poverty of the diocese forced bishops to hold it in conjunction with other church offices, and they and the archdeacons were frequently non-resident, for geographical and economic as well as cultural reasons. Indeed, Tynwald concerns led to attempts to legislate against non-residence (not restricted to clergy) in 1541 and 1696.[73] Non-residence was the subject of complaint at other points also. The result was a lack of strong bonds between the local, non-graduate parochial clergy, unable for economic reasons to benefit from the training and publications available in English, and non-local, often non-resident, graduate higher officials (although local clergy were appointed to middle-ranking ecclesiastical offices, such as registrar or vicar-general).

There appear to have been two consequences of this division. First was the lack of stable mechanisms for making and communicating decisions and ensuring that due action was taken, because key figures were absent. Decisions were often put off until the bishop or archdeacon should visit the island, or were made conditional upon the

---

[71] For the catalogue, which ran to over two hundred titles, see MNHL, MS 09782, Castle Rushen Papers, Castle Accounts I, Box 7, 'A Catalogue of ye books sent from my lord ffayrefax for ye library in ye Isle of Mann' (1659).

[72] Ashley, 'Spiritual Courts', 42.

[73] For 1541, see Quayle, 'Precedent Book', 32 (regarding the archdeacon and the other two rectors). For 1696, see MNHL, MS 09864, GR1/21, Statute book, reproduced in Gerald Bray, ed., *Records of Convocation*, 1: *Sodor and Man 1229–1877* (Woodbridge, 2005), 114; Dickinson, *Lordship of Man*, 345.

ordinary's pleasure.[74] Second was arguably a tension between the new ideals voiced by higher clergy from elsewhere, especially after 1660, which advocated a measure of distancing between the priest and his flock as a professional set apart by education and calling,[75] and the realities of a body of parochial clergy who were drawn from the local populace and still mostly formed in the traditional mould. Change in this respect was some decades behind England and Wales.

The impact of new English patterns of recruitment and training was thus unavoidably hindered.[76] Few of the parochial clergy were able exponents of Protestant doctrine. The earliest clergy to do that in England were usually well educated, and we have seen that there were very few of those on the island. Clergy probably did hold increasingly 'Protestant' views, but the great majority lacked the ability or the intellectual training to do much beyond rehash what they had received, and they had no printed Manx texts to which they could direct the attention of their hearers. We saw earlier that it was Barrow who, in the late 1660s, first made a systematic attempt to improve clerical education, as part of a package which addressed the problems of clerical poverty, ignorance and contemptibility in the eyes of the populace, and lay ignorance. Apart from sending a few promising students to Trinity College, Dublin, he engaged in financial dealing and political lobbying to secure funding for an academic institution on the island, which by the end of the century had begun to feed ordinands into the church.[77]

CONCLUSION

We have seen how the language barrier meant that there could be only a limited amount of the cross-fertilization provided in the Church of England more generally by the spread of new ideas and new

---

[74] For example, in a dispute about the fruits of Michael vicarage, see MNHL, MS 10071/5/2, Liber Cancellarii, 1604–5. For the case of a cleric accused of conducting a marriage in Malew without banns or licence, see MNHL, MS 10194, Diocesan Presentments, 1690.

[75] Most notably by Barrow: see MNHL, MS 09782, Castle Rushen Papers, Ecclesiastical Courts, Box 2, Barrow's report.

[76] For these patterns, see Rosemary O'Day, *The Clerical Profession: The Emergence and Consolidation of a Profession 1558–1642* (Leicester, 1979), 6, 159–60.

[77] By this period, Trinity's early puritan orientation had given way to a more high-church outlook, which would have been congenial to Barrow: see John Victor Luce, *Trinity College Dublin: The First 400 Years* (Dublin, 1992), 28.

approaches to the conduct of worship. This was exacerbated by the non-residence of key drivers of change, notably most of the bishops. Again, the failure of new approaches to make headway was compounded by poverty. Even when parishes wanted to introduce the latest 'ornaments' in worship, they could not afford to do so; out of thousands of wills from this period, I have found no bequests for such purposes.

This article demonstrates that the use of Manx combined with poverty, political status and remoteness reinforced the island's peripheral status by hindering its participation in the intellectual life of the Church of England and the mediation of the fruits of that life to the local populace. It also places the history of the island's church during this period into the wider setting of the history of the Church of England as a whole, but also relates it to developments in the life of the churches of the other surrounding nations. Further research might usefully continue tracing into the eighteenth and nineteenth centuries the use of Manx in religious life, and compare what happened on the Isle of Man with the course of Protestant reform in other island communities, especially other societies whose first language was not that of their rulers in church and state.

St Patrick's Purgatory: Theology and History in the Reformation and Counter-Reformation

Alan Ford ⓘ

University of Nottingham

Patrick's purgatory in Lough Derg, Donegal, is one of the great medieval pilgrimage sites. On the extreme edge of Europe, it physically embodied the theological idea of purgatory, offering pilgrims a this-worldly encounter with its horrors. Despite Protestant efforts to destroy it, it survived the Reformation and posed a classic challenge for Protestant and Roman Catholic historians. For the latter, it exemplified the continuity of Catholicism in Ireland from Patrick to the present, a living embodiment of the unchanging loyalty of the Irish people to their national saint. For Protestant historians, it was, like purgatory, a twelfth-century invention, revealing both the medieval corruption of the Roman Catholic Church as it added non-scriptural embellishments to the Christian faith, and the superstition of Irish Catholicism. The interaction, and tension, between theological belief and historical objectivity was to prove a persistent challenge for both sides, right down to the twentieth century.

St Patrick's purgatory in Lough Derg, County Donegal, is one of the great Irish pilgrimage sites. First coming to prominence in the twelfth century, it gained a Europe-wide reputation, and, despite Protestant efforts to destroy it, survived the Reformation and continues to attract

My thanks to Dáibhí Ó Cróinín who generously gave me his collection of texts relating to the purgatory and drew my attention to the early history of the idea of purgatory in Ireland; to Ian d'Alton, Phelim Dolan, Patrick Little, John McCafferty, Thomas O'Connor, Jane Stevenson, and the anonymous readers for their comments on earlier drafts of the article; and to Stuart Kinsella and Jason Harris for help with references. All translations are my own. E-mail: Alan.Ford@nottingham.ac.uk

Studies in Church History 61 (2025), 304–324 © The Author(s), 2025. Published by Cambridge University Press on behalf of the Ecclesiastical History Society. This is an Open Access article, distributed under the terms of the Creative Commons Attribution licence (http://creativecommons.org/licenses/by/4.0), which permits unrestricted re-use, distribution and reproduction, provided the original article is properly cited.
doi:10.1017/stc.2024.42

pilgrims to the present day.[1] Its history is a classic example of the competing religious and scholarly imperatives of Protestant and Roman Catholic scholars. For Roman Catholics, it offered an example of the continuity of the Catholic tradition in Ireland from Patrick to the present, a living embodiment of the unswerving loyalty of the Irish people to their national saint despite hardship and persecution. For Protestants, it was, like purgatory, a twelfth-century invention, revealing the medieval corruption of the Catholic Church as it added non-scriptural embellishments to the original purity of the Christian faith.

The first we hear of Patrick's purgatory is in the later-twelfth century. Henry of Saltrey, a Cistercian monk in England, records a story he had heard about an Irish knight, Owein, or Owen.[2] Owen had gone to visit a cave in Ireland, where he experienced the horrors and agonies of purgatory, but, thanks to his faith in Christ, he had, after gaining a glimpse of the gates of paradise itself, emerged unscathed and cleansed of his sins.[3] Henry also provided a backstory for the origin of the Irish purgatory: Christ had appeared to St Patrick and led him to a cave, promising that anyone who entered it and stayed for a day and night truly penitent would be purged of the sins of his whole life. He then recounts how Patrick built a church on that spot and made the Augustinian canons its guardians. Giraldus Cambrensis, who visited Ireland in the later-twelfth century, confirms in his *Topographia* that the purgatory was in Lough Derg in the remote north-west of Ireland.[4]

With its echoes of both pagan and Christian tales of descents into the underworld, and the crucial promise of freeing oneself from the consequences of sin and avoiding purgatory after death, Henry's

[1] The best modern introduction remains Michael Haren and Yolande de Pontfarcy, *The Medieval Pilgrimage to St Patrick's Purgatory, Lough Derg, and the European Tradition* (Enniskillen, 1988). For a further collection of texts, see Giovanni Maggioni, Roberto Tinti and Paolo Taviani, eds, *Il Purgatorio di San Patrizio: Documenti Letterari e Testimonianze di Pellegrinaggio (secc. XII–XVI)* (Florence, 2018). The literature on the purgatory is substantial: see the 'Hell-on-line' bibliography, online at: <http://www.hell-on-line.org/BibPatrick.html, accessed 27 July 2023.
[2] Yolande de Pontfarcy, 'H. [Henry] of Saltrey (*fl. c.*1184), *ODNB*, online edn (2004), at: <https://doi.org/10.1093/ref:odnb/12973>, accessed 11 December 2023.
[3] Robert Easting, ed., *St Patrick's Purgatory: Two Versions of Owayne Miles and the Vision of William of Stranton; Together with the Long Text of the Tractatus De Purgatorio Sancti Patricii* (Oxford, 1991); Eileen Gardiner, Visions of Heaven & Hell *Before Dante* (New York, 1989), 135–48.
[4] Gerald of Wales, *The History and Topography of Ireland*, transl. John O'Meara (London, 1982), 29, §38.

account proved to be immensely appealing.[5] The fame of St Patrick's purgatory spread rapidly across Europe, attracting pilgrims from as far away as Hungary, with retellings, not to mention embellishments, in English, Anglo-Norman, French, Catalan and Italian. The thirteenth-century English Benedictine cartographer, Matthew of Paris, knew of it; Ranulph Higden described it in his world history, the *Polychronicon*; it even entered into that standard preachers' *vade mecum*, the *Legenda Aurea*; and it became a part of mainstream European literature, mentioned by Shakespeare, Rabelais and Ariosto, as well as the subject of a play by the seventeenth-century Spanish dramatist, Calderon.[6] The very idea that an entrance to purgatory could be located in the most marginal part of the most western country of the known world had, of course, an instinctive appeal – it represented a 'pilgrimage to the edge' poised between this world and the next.[7] The idea that you entered the underworld through a cave was equally resonant for those versed in classical literature. St Patrick's purgatory became, for much of the later Middle Ages, the ultimate destination for European pilgrims, the longest possible journey for the greatest possible reward. Indeed, as St Patrick himself had put it in his Confession, to travel to Ireland was to go to 'the furthest land, where there was no one beyond'.[8]

The sixteenth-century Reformation, however, problematized the question of purgatory. Put simply, Protestant denial of its existence stimulated determined Catholic defence. The Protestant rejection was, of course, part of the very beginnings of the Reformation. Luther's attack on indulgences eventually led him to the conclusion that purgatory was unbiblical, thus separating the living from the dead,

---

[5] For the 'pre-history' of purgatory, see Jacques Le Goff, *La Naissance du Purgatoire* (Paris, 1981); ET: *The Birth of Purgatory*, transl. Arthur Goldhammer (London, 1984), 17–51.

[6] Fernando Gómez, 'Religion, Heritage, and Politics: Literary Representations of St. Patrick's Purgatory in Spain during the 1620s and the Agenda of the Irish Émigrés Behind Them', *Symposium: A Quarterly Journal in Modern Literatures* 66 (2012), 16–30; Haren and de Pontfarcy, *St Patrick's Purgatory*, 168–74; C. G. Zaleski, 'St. Patrick's Purgatory: Pilgrimage Motifs in a Medieval Otherworld Vision', *Journal of the History of Ideas* 46 (1985), 467–85, at 472.

[7] Lawrence J. Taylor and Maeve Hickey, 'Pilgrimage to the Edge: Lough Derg and the Moral Geography of Europe and Ireland', in Nieves Herrero and Sharon R. Roseman, eds, *Tourism Imaginary and Pilgrimages to the Edges of the World* (Bristol, 2015), 92–119; Le Goff, *Birth of Purgatory*, 201.

[8] '[A]d exteras partes, ubi nemo ultra erat': 'St Patrick's Confessio', §51, Royal Irish Academy, online at: <https://www.confessio.ie/#>, accessed 11 March 2024.

spiritually and physically.[9] It was also part of a wider Protestant suspicion of 'Popish superstition', the nexus of Catholic belief centred on shrines, pilgrimages, saints and relics, which saw miracles as proof of God's continuing validation of their church as the true church. Protestants rejected the idea that miracles still occurred: they had ceased with the end of the apostolic era.[10] They were, as a result, instinctively critical of Catholic saints' lives with their extraordinary wonders and marvels.[11]

The Protestant distrust of purgatory also slotted neatly into the Reformation approach to ecclesiastical history. The template for Protestant church history was laid down by Matthias Flacius Illyricus (1520–75) and the Magdeburg Centuriators in Germany.[12] Convinced that the early church was pure and biblical, they explored the ways in which the papal church had corrupted that purity by adding false beliefs and abuses.[13] Their overarching apocalyptic framework linked the growth in abuses to the rise of Antichrist, who had been unleashed in the papacy around the year 1000, after which the Roman church had begun to introduce unbiblical ideas and practices such as transubstantiation, indulgences, prayer for the dead and, of course, purgatory. This Protestant interest in change over time was facilitated by their appropriation of the tools of humanist scholarship with its desire to return *ad fontes* and its use of historical-critical methodology to expose forgeries and later additions. In short, Protestant scholars developed a 'hermeneutic of suspicion' as they sought to distinguish between early-pure and later-corrupt doctrines and practices.[14]

---

[9] Scott Hendrix, 'Luther', in David Bagchi and David Steinmetz, eds, *The Cambridge Companion to Reformation Theology* (Cambridge, 2004), 39–56, at 43; Craig Koslofsky, *The Reformation of the Dead: Death and Ritual in Early Modern Germany, c.1450–1700* (London, 2000), 19–39.

[10] Robert B. Mullin, *Miracles and the Modern Religious Imagination* (New Haven, CT, 1996), 12–15.

[11] Robert Bartlett, *Why Can the Dead Do Such Great Things? Saints and Worshippers from the Martyrs to the Reformation* (Princeton, NJ, 2013), 85–91.

[12] Matthias Flacius Illyricus et al., *Ecclesiastica Historia*, 12 vols (Basel, 1559–74).

[13] Harald Bollbuck, 'Searching for the True Religion: The Church History of the Magdeburg Centuries between Critical Methods and Confessional Polemics', *Renaissance Studies* 35 (2021), 100–117; Charlotte Methuen, 'History and Heresy in the Lutheran Reformation', *Reformation & Renaissance Review* 24 (2022), 3–22.

[14] John M. Headley, *Luther's View of Church History* (New Haven, CT, 1963); Robin B. Barnes, *Prophecy and Gnosis: Apocalypticism in the Wake of the Lutheran Reformation* (Stanford, CA, 1988); Mark Thompson, 'Luther on God and History', in Robert Kolb and Irene Dingel, eds, *Oxford Handbook of Martin Luther's Theology* (Oxford,

The Roman Catholic response to Protestant history was provided by the Italian oratorian, Caesare Baronio (1538–1607), in his massive *Annales Ecclesiastici*, covering the first twelve centuries of the church.[15] If Protestant religious history was about change, Baronio was most definitely concerned with continuity. The popes had faithfully handed on the word of Christ, contained, as the Council of Trent stipulated, both in the scriptures and in tradition, which was little changed from that of the early church.[16] Against the hermeneutic of suspicion, Baronio offered the 'hermeneutic of trust'. The church, as the eternal defender of orthodoxy, could be relied upon to preserve the Christian truth down the ages against the threats of heretics, whether in the sixth or the sixteenth century.[17]

This determination to trace continuity over time greatly stimulated Roman Catholic scholarship, and indeed some of the best history of this period comes from Jean Bolland (1596–1665) and his fellow Flemish Jesuit hagiographers – the Bollandists – who sought to use source criticism to sort out the true from the false in the complex mass of medieval saints' lives and miracles.[18] In the case of Protestant scholars, theological imperatives tended to drive them towards historical questioning. For those on the other side of the religious divide, however, such reappraisals were a source of tension: the Bollandists sailed perilously close to the Index and the Spanish Inquisition when they questioned the historical basis of popular piety, or the Carmelites'

2014), 127–42; Bollbuck, 'Church History of the Magdeburg Centuries'; Jerry H. Bentley, *Humanists and Holy Writ: New Testament Scholarship in the Renaissance* (Princeton, NJ, 1983).

[15] Caesare Baronio, *Annales Ecclesiastici*, 12 vols (Rome, 1588–1607); Cyriac K. Pullapilly, *Caesar Baronius, Counter-Reformation Historian* (Notre Dame, IN, 1975).

[16] Wim François, 'Scripture and Traditions at the Council of Trent: The Fourth and Fifth Sessions 1546', in Nelson H. Minnich, ed., *The Cambridge Companion to the Council of Trent* (Cambridge, 2023), 72–96.

[17] Stephano Zen, *Baronio storico. Controriforma e crisi del metodo umanistico* (Naples, 1994); Giuseppe Antonio Guazzelli, 'Cesare Baronio and the Roman Catholic Vision of the Early Church', in Katherine Van Liere, Simon Ditchfield and Howard Louthan, eds, *Sacred History: Uses of the Christian Past in the Renaissance World* (Oxford, 2012), 52–71; Stefania Tutino, *Shadows of Doubt: Language and Truth in Post-Reformation Catholic Culture* (New York, 2014), 74–112.

[18] Hippolyte Delehaye, *Legends of the Saints*, ed. Thomas O'Loughlin (Dublin, 1998), v–xvi; David Knowles, 'Great Historical Enterprises, 1: The Bollandists', *Transactions of the Royal Historical Society* (1958), 147–66.

claim to be the oldest religious order, founded by Elijah.[19] The reluctance to allow for change or development, the prioritizing of theology and faith over history, the timeless, unchanging nature of Christian truth as it were, created obvious problems for Roman Catholic historians who wished to explore change and development, right down to the twentieth century.[20]

These battles were fought at length across the various sixteenth-century European national reformations, as writers such as Jean Crespin (1520–72) in France and John Foxe (*c.*1516–87) in England applied Protestant methodology to the history of their churches, and were in turn responded to by Catholic scholars.[21] However, the slow pace of reform in Ireland, and the constant warfare and instability of the sixteenth century – one account of late-sixteenth century Ireland is aptly entitled *The Age of Atrocity* – together with political weakness, ethnic and cultural divisions, and the lack of a university or printing press, limited the possibility of intellectual debate.[22] As a result, in Ireland, formal conformity to the established church was not slowly transformed into commitment to Protestantism; rather, it was replaced, by the beginning of the seventeenth century, with a firm adherence to Counter-Reformation Catholicism. Irish pilgrimages to Lough Derg continued uninterrupted during the sixteenth century. Indeed, for the last three decades of that century, the see in which the

---

[19] Knowles, 'The Bollandists', 156; Andrew Jotischky, *The Carmelites and Antiquity: Mendicants and their Pasts in the Middle Ages* (Oxford, 2002), 5–6.

[20] Gregor Klapczynski, *Katholischer Historismus? Zum historischen Denken in der deutsch-sprachigen Kirchengeschichte um 1900* (Stuttgart, 2013); Eric Cochrane, 'What Is Catholic Historiography?', *CathHR* 61 (1975), 169–90; Kenneth L. Parker, 'Re-Visioning the Past and Re-Sourcing the Future: The Unresolved Historiographical Struggle in Roman Catholic Scholarship and Authoritative Teaching', in Peter D. Clarke and Charlotte Methuen, eds, *The Church on its Past*, SCH 49 (Woodbridge, 2013), 389–416.

[21] Jean Crespin, *Le Livre des martyrs* (Geneva, 1554); John Foxe, *The Unabridged Acts and Monuments Online*, The Digital Humanities Institute (Sheffield, 2011), at: <http://www.dhi.ac.uk/foxe>, accessed 24 October 2024; Thomas Freeman, 'The Power of Polemic: Catholic Responses to the Calendar in Foxe's "Book of Martyrs"', *JEH* 61 (2010), 475–95.

[22] David Edwards, Pádraig Lenihan and Clodagh Tait, eds, *Age of Atrocity: Violence and Political Conflict in Early Modern Ireland* (Dublin, 2007). For the debate on the Irish reformation, see Nicholas Canny, Karl S. Bottigheimer and Steven G. Ellis, 'The Debate about the Irish Reformation: Some Reflections on Twentieth-Century Historiography', in Mark Empey, Alan Ford and Miriam Moffitt, eds, *The Church of Ireland and its Past: History, Interpretation and Identity* (Dublin, 2017), 237–64.

purgatory was located, Clogher, was outside the influence of the Dublin government and left unfilled by the crown.[23]

It was not until the early decades of the seventeenth century that Irish Protestantism was in a position to challenge Roman Catholic theology and piety, as the power of the established church and state was extended to every county and diocese in Ireland (including Clogher). The foundation of Trinity College Dublin in 1592 provided the church with a Protestant seminary, which set about Hibernicizing European anti-Catholicism.[24] The first Protestant writer to raise the issue of St Patrick's purgatory was the Welsh-English historian, Meredith Hanmer, writing around 1600, who took up the suggestion, originally made by Higden in his *Polychronicon*, that the Patrick associated with the purgatory might not have been the saint, but a later abbot of the monastery there who, Hanmer surmised, 'was given to superstition'.[25] But the figure who laid down what would become the standard Irish Protestant theological and historical objections to purgatory in general, and Lough Derg in particular, was the leading scholar in the early seventeenth-century Church of Ireland, James Ussher (1581–1656), who, after serving as Professor of Theology at Trinity College, Dublin, from 1607, became bishop of Meath in 1621 and, in 1625, was made archbishop of Armagh.[26]

Ussher's 1624 *Answer to a challenge made by a Jesuit in Ireland* was a response to an Irish Jesuit, William Malone (1586–1656), who had challenged Protestants:

> Your doctors and masters grant that the Church of Rome, for four or five hundred years after Christ, did hold the true religion. First, then I would

---

[23] Katherine Walsh, '… *in Finibus Mundi*: Late Medieval Pilgrims to St Patrick's Purgatory, Lough Derg, and the European Dimension of the Diocese of Clogher', in Henry Jefferies, ed., *History of the Diocese of Clogher* (Dublin, 2005), 41–69. For the early modern practice of the pilgrimage, see Bernadette Cunningham and Raymond Gillespie, 'The Lough Derg Pilgrimage in the Age of the Counter-Reformation', *Éire-Ireland* 39 (2004), 167–79.

[24] Alan Ford, 'Protestant Attitudes to Catholicism in Ireland', in James E. Kelly and John McCafferty, eds, *The Oxford History of British and Irish Catholicism*, 1: *Endings and New Beginnings, 1530–1640* (Oxford, 2023), 310–18, at 314–15.

[25] Hanmer's history was not published until 1633: James Ware, ed., *The Historie of Ireland, Collected by Three Learned Authors Viz. M. Hanmer … E. Campion … and E. Spenser* (Dublin, 1633), 86.

[26] Alan Ford, *James Ussher: Theology, History, and Politics in Early-Modern Ireland and England* (Oxford, 2007).

fain know, what Bishop of Rome did first alter that religion … ? In what pope his days was the true religion overthrown in Rome?[27]

In other words, this was an Irish version of the more famous dispute between John Jewel and Thomas Harding which had laid down the template for Protestant-Catholic controversy in Elizabethan England.[28] The result was a lengthy treatise, with separate chapters on different Roman Catholic 'inventions': the real presence and transubstantiation, prayers for the dead, the invocation of saints, image-worship and purgatory.

Ussher's primary objection to purgatory was that it was unscriptural:

> For extinguishing the imaginary flames of Popish purgatory, we need not go far to fetch water: seeing the whole current of God's word runneth mainly upon this, that 'the blood of Jesus Christ cleanseth us from all sin' … And if we need the assistance of the ancient fathers in this business: behold they be here ready, with full buckets in their hands.[29]

Having cited the patristic authorities supporting the binary fate after death of heaven or hell, he then went on to explore when the idea of an intermediary purgatory arose, beginning with the late sixth-century pope, Gregory I, and tracing its development through to St Thomas Aquinas in the thirteenth century.[30] Since Ussher was especially concerned with when these doctrines and practices developed over time, he sought 'both to understand the times wherein the authors lived, and likewise what books be truly or falsely ascribed to each of them'. He thus appended to the book a 'chronological catalogue' dating when his authors wrote.[31]

All this was, of course, standard European reformed historical theology. More innovative was the way in which Ussher applied this to Ireland, in his *Discourse of the Religion Anciently Professed by the Irish.*

---

[27] James Ussher, *An Answer to a Challenge Made by a Jesuite in Ireland. Wherein, the Judgement of Antiquity in the Points Questioned is Truly Delivered* (London, 1631), sig. B1ʳ; idem, *The Whole Works of the Most Rev. James Ussher*, 17 vols (Dublin and London, 1829–64), 3: 3.
[28] Peter Milward, 'The Jewel-Harding Controversy', *Albion* 6 (1974), 320–41; Angela Ranson, 'The Jewel–Harding Controversy: Defending the Champion', in eadem, André Gazal and Sarah Bastow, eds, *Defending the Faith* (University Park, PA, 2018), 119–38.
[29] Ussher, *Answer to a Challenge*, 173–4; idem, *Whole Works*, 3: 177.
[30] Ussher, *Answer to a Challenge*, 173–94; idem, *Whole Works*, 3: 177–97.
[31] Ussher, *Answer to a Challenge*, 'To the Reader'; idem, *Whole Works*, 3: xiii.

This first appeared in 1622 as an addendum to an anti-Catholic work by an Irish judge, and was enlarged for its second edition in 1631.[32] Here, Ussher sought to show that the early Irish church created by Patrick – the 'island of saints and scholars' – was pure and uncorrupted and, indeed, largely free from direction from Rome. Antichrist's rise to power in the papacy after the millennium was linked by Ussher to the subsequent extension of papal authority to Ireland during the early twelfth century, as *pallia* were for the first time sent from Rome as marks of authority for Irish bishops.[33] Into this tale of papal corruption and deceit – what he termed 'the time of Satan's loosing' – he slotted the 'invention' of St Patrick's purgatory.[34]

Ussher's treatment was relatively brief: he explained that the first reference he had been able to find to the link between Lough Derg and Patrick was Henry of Saltrey's late-twelfth-century account. None of the reliably early Patrician sources made any mention of the saint founding Lough Derg; nor did Patrick himself ever mention purgatory. In other words, just as the idea of purgatory was a late innovation, so too was its link to Patrick. Rather than believing tales of visions and dreams, Ussher suggested that all one needed to do was to make a visit to Lough Derg, go into the cave, and see for oneself that there was no physical evidence for an entry to purgatory.[35]

There were a number of early-seventeenth-century Roman Catholic responses to Protestant attacks on St Patrick's purgatory.[36] The most comprehensive was a long account published in Thomas

---

[32] Christopher Sibthorp, *A Friendly Advertisement to the Pretended Catholics of Ireland ... in the end whereof, is added an Epistle Written to the Author, by the Reverend Father in God, James Ussher Bishop of Meath: Wherein it is further Manifested, That the Religion Anciently Professed in Ireland is, for Substance, the same with that, which at this Day is by Publick Authority Established Therein* (Dublin, 1622); James Ussher, *A Discourse of the Religion Anciently Professed by the Irish and British* (London, 1631); idem, *Whole Works*, 4: 235–381.

[33] Ussher, *Discourse*, 76–7; idem, *Whole Works*, 4: 320–1.

[34] Ussher, *Discourse*, 27; idem, *Whole Works*, 4: 269. The reference is to Rev. 20: 7: 'And when the thousand years are expired, Satan shall be loosed out of his prison' [AV].

[35] Ussher, *Discourse*, 21–2; idem, *Whole Works*, 4: 263–4. Ussher returned to the subject in his later history of the British churches: James Ussher, *Britannicarum Ecclesiarum Antiquitates* (Dublin, 1639), 897–8.

[36] Philip O'Sullivan Beare, *Patritiana Decas* (Madrid, 1629), 89–133; Denis C. O'Sullivan, ed., *The Natural History of Ireland: Included in Book One of the Zoilomastix of Don Philip O'Sullivan Beare* (Cork, 2009), 252–9; William Thirry, *De Nominibus, Tribulationibus, et Miraculis S. Patricii Ibernorum Apostoli* (Douai, 1617).

Messingham's pioneering work of hagiography, his 1624 *Florilegium*.[37] The *Florilegium* contained a series of saints' lives, mostly from previously printed editions, including those of Brigid, Columba and Patrick.[38] It was part of the wider resurgence of interest in Irish saints in the early seventeenth century that culminated in the massive *Acta Sanctorum Hiberniae* of John Colgan, which appeared at Louvain in 1645.[39] Messingham clearly saw these saintly *vitae* as having both a pastoral and polemical purpose: they gave life to Scripture, providing the faithful with examples of heroism, virtue and piety, which they could follow in their everyday lives. He also stressed their importance in an Irish context, where Protestants openly rejected purgatory, penance and praying to saints. Miracles, clear evidence of God's power and glory, provided a source of strength and resilience for the Irish people at risk of being seduced by heretical preachers. More than that, the fact that the Irish church was blessed with so many saints with such a rich heritage of miracles was further proof of the rectitude of Roman Catholicism.[40]

The Patrician text which Messingham chose to edit – the *vita* written around the end of the twelfth century by the Cistercian monk Jocelin of Furness – fitted his purpose precisely. It was syncretic, bringing together a wide range of sources relating to the saint, early and late, and it unapologetically celebrated all the miracles associated with him.[41] Immediately following Jocelin's life, Messingham added a further twenty-four page account of St Patrick's purgatory. This was mainly the work of the leading resident Roman Catholic Irish prelate, David Rothe (1573–1650), the bishop of Ossory, a noted writer on

---

[37] Thomas Messingham, *Florilegium Insulae Sanctorum seu Vitae et Acta Sanctorum Hiberniae* (Paris, 1624).

[38] Thomas O'Connor, 'Towards the Invention of the Irish Catholic *Natio*: Thomas Messingham's *Florilegium* (1624)', *Irish Theological Quarterly* 64 (1999), 157–77; Salvador Ryan, 'Steadfast Saints or Malleable Models? Seventeenth Century Irish Hagiography revisited', *CathHR* 91 (2005), 251–77.

[39] John Colgan, *Acta Sanctorum Veteris et Majoris Scotiae seu Hiberniae* (Louvain, 1645); Canice Mooney, 'Father John Colgan O.F.M.: His Work, Times and Literary Milieu', in Terence O'Donnell, ed., *Father John Colgan O.F.M. 1592–1658* (Dublin,1959), 7–40.

[40] Messingham, *Florilegium*, 'Praefatio ad lectorem', unpaginated.

[41] Ibid. 1–85; Bernadette Cunningham and Raymond Gillespie, '"The Most Adaptable of Saints": The Cult of St Patrick in the Seventeenth Century', *Archivium Hibernicum* 49 (1995), 82–104.

Irish religious history.[42] Though he had never himself visited the shrine, Rothe collected contemporary accounts and combined them with the relations of medieval visitors to give a detailed description of the workings of the pilgrimage.[43]

More importantly from our point of view, he also brought together three different kinds of authority to support his firm contention that the purgatory had been founded by St Patrick himself. First, he cited a number of historical sources, ranging from Henry of Saltrey and Giraldus Cambrensis in the twelfth century, through to Jacobus de Voragine (*c*.1160/70–1240), Caesarius of Heisterbach (*c*.1180–*c*.1249), Matthew of Paris (1200–59), Ranulph Higden (*c*.1280–1364), Denis the Carthusian (1402–71), Boninus Mombritius (1424–*c*.1500), and Joannes Camers (1447–1546), down to Franciscus Maurolycus, who died in 1575.[44] Rothe dealt with the suggestion made by Higden that there were two Patricks, and that it was the second, Abbot Patrick, who had founded the purgatory, by showing that early writers had also called the saint by the title abbot, and that this had led to the confusion.[45] The obvious difficulty here was the lack of pre-twelfth-century support: his only earlier reference, which Rothe somewhat tentatively proposed, as it would pre-date St Patrick, came from the fourth-century pagan poet, Claudian, who recounted that Ulysses in his wanderings was washed up on a shore in Gaul, where 'is heard the mournful weeping of the spirits of the dead as they flit by with faint sound of wings'.[46] Another source of authority for Rothe was the church's worship: he cited liturgical references celebrating St Patrick as the founder of the purgatory which appear in early printed breviaries and ancient manuscripts. Though vague about dating, he was confident of their authority, and deeply averse to the Protestant hermeneutic of suspicion: 'Who would dare to

---

[42] Messingham, *Florilegium*, 86–109. Rothe's contributions are marked by an 'A' in the margin: ibid. 87.

[43] Ibid.

[44] Ibid. 92, §8.

[45] Ibid. 93, §14.

[46] Ibid.; Claudian, *In Rufinum*, book 1, poem 2; ET: *Claudian with an English Translation by Maurice Platnauer*, 2 vols (Cambridge, MA, 1963), 1: 35. See also the unsuccessful attempt by Geoffrey Keating to bridge the gap between Patrick and Henry of Saltrey: Salvador Ryan, 'Reconstructing Irish Catholic Origins after the Reformation', in van Liere, Ditchfield and Louthian, eds, *Sacred History*, 186–205, at 192–3.

complain of a custom so accepted, so ancient, so well-proven, which is the most repeated, the most celebrated in sermons and in the hearts of the faithful; unless he was greedy for new things, and a despiser of both antiquity and piety?'[47]

Rothe gave pride of place not to history or liturgy, but to tradition. The primary basis for the identification of the purgatory with Patrick was 'its constant and consistent reception by every age, and the memory of people throughout this whole nation. For it is not without reason that everyone says this, especially when it is agreed almost without contradiction by pious, learned and wise men.'[48] Similarly, Messingham, in his prefatory note to the discussion of the purgatory, drove home the key Roman Catholic theological point. He quoted the ending of St John's Gospel: 'There are also many other things that Jesus did, which if they were all written down, I think even the world itself would not be able to contain the books that would be written.'[49] This, he argued, blew out of the water the rejection by the 'Philistine Luther and his heterodox camp' of apostolic and church traditions as 'human invention'.[50]

Religious arguments in the early modern period were not just intellectual. As government power extended to the whole country, reformed theological scepticism was backed by Protestant state power. In 1632, during a period when the Irish government was following a firmly anti-Catholic policy, the Protestant bishop of Clogher, James Spottiswood, along with the sheriffs of Donegal and Fermanagh, was ordered by the Lords Justices in Dublin to suppress the 'abusive and superstitious … ceremonies, pilgrimages, and offerings' that took place on the island. Spottiswood, together with twenty armed men, rowed out to the island in Lough Derg and destroyed the cave, reporting that it was 'a poor beggarly hole, made with some stones,

---

[47] 'Reclamare autem usui tam recepto, tam vetusto, tam probato, qui creberrimus erat, et celeberrimus in sermonibus et cordibus fidelium, quis ausit: nisi novitatis avidus, et vetustatis pariter ac pietas aspernator.' Messingham, *Florilegium*, 92, §11.
[48] 'Primum igitur firmamentum receptae traditionis, sit ipsa tam constans et consona receptio eius ab omni aevo, et memoria hominum per universam hanc nationem. Neque enim sine causa dicitur, quod omnium fertur ore, praesertim quando id ore piorum, eruditorum, prudentium, nemine poenae [= paene] refragante constituitur.' Messingham, *Florilegium*, 91–2, §7.
[49] 'Sunt autem et alia multa, quae fecit Jesus, quae, si scribantur persingula, nec ipsum mundum arbitror capere eos, qui scribendi sunt libros.' Ibid. 86.
[50] Ibid.

laid together with mens hands without any great art: and after covered with earth, such as husbandmen make to keep a few hogs from the rain.'[51] As so often with official efforts to impose conformity in Ireland, Roman Catholic resilience ensured that the effect was only temporary, and the pilgrimage subsequently resumed.[52]

Fifteen years later, Henry Jones (1605–82) renewed the scholarly assault, publishing a lengthy response to Rothe.[53] Ussher's nephew and his pupil at Trinity, Jones used his access to his uncle's library to research the history of the shrine.[54] By the 1640s, he was one of the leading Irish resident Protestant churchmen, helping to bring together the depositions produced in the wake of the 1641 rebellion and frame the rising as part of an international antichristian Roman Catholic conspiracy.[55] His treatment of the purgatory was much more extensive than Ussher's relatively brief mention in the *Discourse of the Religion Anciently Professed*. Like Rothe, he gave a detailed description of its location and the practices of the pilgrims there, but with, of course, a sceptical Protestant tone.[56]

Jones went on to explore the purgatory's history, using the medieval pilgrims' stories to expose inconsistencies in the accounts of the shrine and its access to purgatory, and hammering home the basic point that there was no reliable reference to St Patrick's having founded it before the later twelfth century: no author 'for more than 700 years after S. Patrick, doth write one word of this purgatory'.[57] He then made four additional points. First, he dismissed Rothe's reliance upon tradition, which he saw as a means of 'imposing for undeniable verities,

[51] The relevant documents are given in Henry Jones, *Saint Patricks Purgatory Containing the Description, Originall, Progresse, and Demolition of that Superstitious Place* (London, 1647), 129–32.

[52] Cunningham and Gillespie, 'Lough Derg Pilgrimage', 175–6.

[53] Jones, *Patricks Purgatory*.

[54] Ibid. 24; Patrick Little, 'Politics of Preferment: The Marquess of Ormond, Archbishop Ussher and the Appointment of Irish Bishops, 1643–47', in idem, ed., *Ireland in Crisis: War, Politics and Religion, 1641–50* (Manchester, 2020), 138–54, at 144–7; Dublin, Trinity College Dublin, College Muniments, P/1/144.

[55] Henry Jones, *A Remonstrance of Divers Remarkeable Passages concerning the Church and | Kingdome of Ireland* (London, 1642); idem, *A Perfect Relation of the Beginning and Continuation of the Irish-Rebellion* (London, 1642); Joseph Cope, 'Fashioning Victims: Dr Henry Jones and the Plight of Irish Protestants, 1642', *HR* 74 (2001), 370–91.

[56] Jones, *Patricks Purgatory*, 2–3.

[57] Ibid. 21, 27.

matters doubtful and most uncertain'.[58] Stories about the lake and the purgatory, and its association with Patrick, were mere 'fables', undocumented and unprovable folk tales.[59] Second, he argued for a purely psychological explanation for the visions and vivid experiences of the pilgrims. They were a product of their lengthy fast, 'causing a crazed brain … to make fancies real'.[60] Third, it was manipulated by the Roman Catholic Church to exploit lay superstition, and 'a mere imposture and fraud'.[61] And finally, like Ussher, he emphasized the cave's this-worldly ordinariness: water, grass, rock, and no entrance to purgatory.[62]

Jones's determined reductionism and Rothe's robust defence of Roman Catholic piety reflected not only their contrasting theological approaches to purgatory, but also their differing hermeneutics, for Jones's suspicion and Rothe's trust used exactly the same sources to produce startlingly different conclusions. As we have noted, this tension between humanist source criticism and piety was not solely a product of the sectarian divide; it was also evident within the Roman Catholic camp. It was thus significant when, in 1668, the Bollandists, embarking on their apparently endless journey through the saints' calendar, reached 17 March and tackled Ireland's national saint. Jean Bolland, laying down his basic hagiographical principles in 1643, had expressed some doubts about the propensity of the Irish *vitae* to exaggerate, warning that they were 'clearly full of marvels, interwoven with almost unbelievable miracles'.[63] Though aware of the importance of tradition, Bolland also insisted that sources had to be judged in terms of historical accuracy and the authors' closeness to the events being recorded. Quoting St Augustine, he observed: 'History sometimes lies, but tradition much more frequently.'[64] In particular, he made a distinction between apostolic traditions which, though passed down orally, were faithfully preserved within the church, and popular

---

[58] Ibid. 19.

[59] Ibid. 45, 97, 115.

[60] Ibid. 16.

[61] Ibid. 17.

[62] Ibid. 5.

[63] 'Plane portentosæ sunt Sanctorum Vitæ, atque ex miraculis, fere incredibilibus, contextæ': *ActaSS*, Jan. 1, xxxiv. Bernard Joassart, 'Érudition et hagiographie aux XVIIe et XVIIIe siècles', Annuaire de l'École pratique des hautes études. *Section des sciences historiques et philologiques* 141 (2010), 202–6, at 202–3.

[64] 'Nonnumquam & historia, & multo magis fama mentitur': *ActaSS*, Jan. 1, xxxiv. See Augustine, *In Iohannis Evangelium Tractatus*, PL 35, col. 1859.

traditions, handed down by the people. The latter must not, he warned, be equated with the former, for rather than truthfully relaying what had happened, they tended, over time, to get more and more unreliable, especially 'in the case of wild and ignorant people'.[65] Bolland was dismissive of the allegation that his meticulous scholarship would aid Protestant heretics who scoffed at Roman Catholic superstition: 'We do not write for them.' He did, however, align his efforts with those reformed scholars on the other side of the Reformation divide who are 'lovers of antiquity, and nearer to the kingdom of God', such as William Camden and Gerard Vossius, and also Ussher.[66]

These critical principles were applied to St Patrick in 1668 by two Bollandist scholars, Daniel Papebroch (1628–1714) and Godfrey Henschen (1601–81).[67] They took a cautiously sceptical approach to his miracles, lamenting the 'easy credulity' of those who wrote them down and wishing, anachronistically, that those authors could have had the benefit of first reading Bolland's guiding principles of hagiography.[68] As part of their treatment of Patrick's life, they also provided a five-page study of his purgatory.[69] When introducing the shrine, though they related the story that it had been divinely revealed to St Patrick as a way to win over the stiff-necked Irish, they noted that this was according to the tradition of the inhabitants, rather than to any historical record. They then moved on to the chief historical source, the story of Owen, as told by Henry of Saltrey. This they accepted as authentic. But they neatly sidestepped the theologically difficult question of the reality of his experience in an earthly purgatory, by stressing that his account was based on a vision. One had, they suggested, to distinguish between seeing things with physical eyes, *oculis corporeis*, and seeing them through our imagination, as in this

---

[65] *ActaSS*, Jan. 1, xxxiv.

[66] 'Illis non scribimus ... Sunt inter eos quidam amatores antiquitatis, eoque propius distantes a regno Dei, qui gaudebunt in lucem proferri multa quocumque etiam squallore obsita, quibus ipsi ad eas quas moliuntur humanæ litteraturæ lucubrationes vtantur. Vsus est sane in Italia illustranda Philippus Cluuerius, in Britannia Guilielmus Cambdenus: neque istiusmodi scripta omnia respuent Iacobus Vsserius, Gerardus Ioannes Vossius, Ioannes Meursius, aliique.' *ActaSS*, Jan. 1, xxxviii.

[67] On Papebroch's clashes with curial censors, see Andreea Badea, 'Credibility of the Past: Writing and Censoring History within Seventeenth-Century Catholicism', in eadem et al., eds, *Making Truth in Early Modern Catholicism* (Amsterdam, 2021), 191–210, at 195–6.

[68] *ActaSS*, Mar. 2, 584, §19.

[69] Ibid. 587–92.

case. While accepting that visions could be inspired by evil spirits, in the case of Owen's account, they argued that it was possible to see from the effect – his repentance of his sins – that it was genuine.[70] In other words, we have left behind the medieval purgatory and are already on the way to the Counter-Reformation and modern reconstruction of Lough Derg as a penitential pilgrimage, a spiritual or devotional exercise, rather than a this-worldly physical entrance into purgatory.[71]

Though their knowledge of Irish history was limited, the Bolland-ists' approach to their sources was clearly more analytical and sceptical than that of Rothe. Take the liturgical evidence for Patrick's connec-tion with the purgatory. Where Rothe simply gathered together all the evidence he could find and asserted that the fact that it was included in the liturgy confirmed its truth, for the Bollandists, 'the insertion of a legend in the breviary, or the missal, or the martyrology, was not a reason for inferring that their historical content was accurate … Documents are to be valued according to their sources.'[72] That said, the Bollandists were still deeply respectful of tradition. Thus, after raising the issue of the two Patricks, and noting Ussher's point that the earliest biographies make no mention of this important matter, they nevertheless opted to follow 'the tradition of the Irish' and come down on the side of the saint as the founder of the purgatory.[73] Similarly, they chose to explain away the anachronism of Patrick's handing over the site to the Augustinians by arguing that the name of the order was often projected back onto an earlier foundation that had later become Augustinian.[74]

The argument between the Roman Catholic and Protestant churches over St Patrick's purgatory thus neatly reflects their hermen-eutical assumptions. On the Roman Catholic side, the value accorded to tradition, the irrepressible power of demotic piety, and the accept-ance of the consensus of Roman Catholic churchmen, all pointed to continuity between St Patrick as founder of the purgatory and the first historical accounts which appear in the twelfth century. On the

---

[70] Ibid. 587, §34.

[71] On this, see Cunningham and Gillespie, 'The Lough Derg Pilgrimage', 175–9 (part 3).

[72] Aurelio Palmieri, 'The Bollandists: The Period of Trial', *CathHR* 9 (1924), 517–29, at 524.

[73] '[N]on tamen sine scrupulo, propter antiquorum omnium Biographorum hac de re silentium, quos par erat Reformation em adeo illustrem non reticuisse.' *ActaSS* Mar. 2, 588–9, §41.

[74] Ibid. 588, §36.

Protestant side, the distrust of tradition, a more critical attitude towards sources and their dating, and an awareness of anachronism, led them towards an historical scepticism and reductionism which was perfectly in tune with their theological suspicion of Roman Catholic 'superstition'.

For Protestants, there was here, then, a coincidence between their theological principles and their historical judgement. It is as if they were led to question the Catholic sources, and subject them to close historical analysis by the theological need to prove them wrong. The result is some pioneering history, which, especially when one detaches the historical analysis from its apocalyptic structure, comes to conclusions which are in line with modern historians: Ussher anticipated by precisely 350 years the conclusion of Jacques Le Goff, that purgatory as a single place in which souls were purged was a late-twelfth-century invention.[75]

It may therefore be no coincidence that the Protestant seventeenth-century historian whose approach to Patrick was the least sectarian and the most 'modern', was that decidedly unapocalyptic scholar, James Ware (1594–1666).[76] It was he who chose to publish in 1658 Patrick's Confession and his letter to Coroticus, the only two works which are now thought to be by the saint.[77] Ware's 1654 account of the purgatory was for the most part straightforward and neutral, providing a description of the pilgrimage and a valuable map of the island, and avoiding the polemics and mockery of Jones.[78] He was also open to the idea that the purgatory had a pre-twelfth-century existence. He noted the presence of an early saint, Dobheóg, with a monastery in Lough Derg. The discoverer of the purgatory could thus be either St Patrick himself or the ninth-century Abbot Patrick. The only hints of scepticism come when Ware refers to the grounds of the papal suppression in 1497 as being because it was essentially spurious – 'utpote

---

[75] Le Goff, *Birth of Purgatory*, 193–201. Le Goff sees Henry of Saltrey's account as crucial in the twelfth century development of the idea of purgatory. He argues that the Lough Derg pilgrimage was first initiated by English (that is, Anglo-Norman) monks in the twelfth century: ibid. 199.

[76] William O'Sullivan, 'Sir James Ware', *DIB*, online edn (2009), at: <https://doi.org/10.3318/dib.008928.v1>, accessed 24 October 2024; Mark Empey, 'Value-Free History? The Scholarly Network of Sir James Ware', *History Ireland* 20 (2012), 20–3.

[77] James Ware, ed., *S. Patricio, qui Hibernos as Fidem Christi Convertit, a Adscripta Opuscula* (London, 1656).

[78] James Ware, *De Hibernia et Antiquitatibus eius, Disquisitiones* (London, 1654), 191.

supposititium' – and when he remarks briefly: 'Wonders beyond belief are told about this cave'.[79]

On the Roman Catholic side, on the other hand, there was a tension between historical method and orthodox belief, evident in the work of the Bollandists as they trod the difficult path between their strict historical criteria and the instinctive reverence for the sacred past which was such a feature of Catholic popular piety. The actual practice of the pilgrimage in the seventeenth century is not easy to trace, so it is difficult to be ascertain the extent to which the new Counter-Reformation emphasis upon internal spirituality reshaped the experience of pilgrims to the lake, and brought the marginal medieval pilgrimage back into the European Catholic mainstream.[80] Roman Catholic determination to stick with medieval legends about Patrician origins could only have been reinforced by the mockery of Protestant controversialists such as Jones, and by the exercise of state power to proscribe attendance and destroy the shrine.

Let us draw these threads together. The Reformation and Counter-Reformation unleashed a torrent of ecclesiastical history writing, which greatly enlarged knowledge of the church's past, subjecting it to critical investigation using the tools of humanist scholarship. But history was part of a broader intellectual enterprise. In particular, it was closely linked to theology which provided an overarching framework for the work of historians: presentist apocalyptic and the corruption of early purity on the Protestant side; and a theology which insisted on the authority of tradition and the unchanging verities of the faith on the Roman Catholic side. What we have here, of course, is that universal combination which is the fate of humanities scholars in every era: the interpenetration of their subjective assumptions and objective research. The hermeneutics which were a part of Reformation and Counter-Reformation history writing thus both helped and hindered interpretation. That tension remained, on both sides, right down to the twentieth century and even into the twenty-first.

The locally-born parish priest, Daniel O'Connor, in the standard and much-reprinted late-nineteenth-century account of the pilgrimage, like Rothe, simply accepted all the medieval accounts as true and

---

[79] 'De hoc antro, mira fidem superantia narrantur': ibid. 191.
[80] Cunningham and Gillespie, 'Lough Derg Pilgrimage', 169–70.

castigated those who rejected the authority of tradition.[81] In the entry for the purgatory in the *Catholic Encyclopedia* of 1913, the Roman Catholic scholar William Henry Grattan Flood claimed that: 'St. Patrick's connection with the purgatory which bears his name is not only a constant tradition, but is supported by historical evidence, and admitted by the Bollandists.'[82] The great Jesuit medievalist, Aubrey Gwynn, recognized in 1944 the absence of historical sources linking it to Patrick prior to the twelfth century, but opted instead to trust the authority of local tradition.[83] Indeed, as late as 1970, Gwynn, in the entry for the Augustinian monastery on Saints' Island in Lough Derg, stated that it was originally founded by St Patrick or St Dabheóg, and quoted Grattan Flood as an authoritative source.[84] On the other side, Irish Protestant evangelicals continued well into the twentieth century to denounce the pilgrimage as 'Catholic superstition' without any real connection to the Irish national saint.[85]

It is by now abundantly apparent that this 'pilgrimage to the edge' posed, in concrete form, a standing challenge for religious historians: how to deal with the complicated interpenetration of fact, story, vision, memory and myth. To modern post-Enlightenment scholars, instinctively empiricist, one of the purposes of their discipline is to distinguish between history and myth. To those attuned to more postmodern sensibilities, the binary division is, of course, itself a myth. For the believing Christian scholar, moreover, there is the additional

---

[81] Daniel O'Connor, *St. Patrick's Purgatory, Lough Derg: Its History, Traditions, Legends, Antiquities, Topography, and Scenic Surroundings* (Dublin, 1895), 11. This work was reprinted in 1903, 1910 and 1931.

[82] William Henry Grattan Flood, 'St. Patrick's Purgatory', *Catholic Encyclopedia* (1913), Wikisource, online at: <https://en.wikisource.org/wiki/Catholic_Encyclopedia_(1913)/St._Patrick%27s_Purgatory>, accessed 11 December 2023.

[83] Aubrey Gwynn, 'Review of Alice Curtayne, *St Patrick's Purgatory* (London, 1944)', *Studies* 33 (1944), 553–4, at 554. For the traditionalist Roman Catholic reaction against the post-Vatican II re-evaluation of purgatory, see Diana Walsh Pasulka, *Heaven Can Wait: Purgatory in Catholic Devotional and Popular Culture* (New York, 2014).

[84] Aubrey Gwynn and R. Neville Hadcock, *Medieval Religious Houses Ireland* (London, 1970), 193.

[85] See, for example, William E. Kenny, *Purgatory*, 1st edn (Dublin, 1939), 2nd edn (Dublin, 1951), and *Church of Ireland Gazette*, 29 May 1931, 309; though note the pioneering early example of a non-sectarian Protestant approach to the topic, heavily influenced by the Bollandists: St John D. Seymour, *St. Patrick's Purgatory: A Mediaeval Pilgrimage in Ireland* (Dundalk, 1918).

tension between historical reductionism and belief in miracles.[86] Whichever approach one takes, sorting out what the sources may be telling us and how they might be misleading us is a complex process, dealing as it does with issues of belief and faith, judgement and discernment, credence and credulity, memory and forgetting.

But sort out we must. In this process of discrimination, a broader comparative context might help. The trajectory of historical argument about the Lough Derg purgatory over the centuries can be seen as a subset of the wider interpretative journey taken by Patrician studies. Ussher, Colgan, Messingham and Rothe all struggled to make sense of the records associated with Ireland's patron saint. Though they were even prepared to set aside religious differences in order to cooperate in tracking down manuscripts and essential texts, they still found it very difficult to sort out early from late sources, and to distinguish between the genuine writings of Patrick and subsequent works attributed to him.[87] Generally speaking, they tended to conflate sources from across the centuries, resulting in complicated, syncretic lives of Patrick which mixed fact, legend and hagiography, often to suit sectarian polemic. It was not until the nineteenth century that the study of Patrick began to be put on a firm footing, and a progressive process of winnowing down began, led by Protestant scholars such as James Henthorn Todd and William Reeves, and Roman Catholic writers adhering to Bollandist principles, such as John Lanigan and Hippolyte Delehaye.[88] This process culminated – to cut a long story short – in the seminal and decisive 1962 article by Daniel A. Binchy, 'Patrick and his

---

[86] O'Connor, 'Thomas Messingham's *Florilegium*', 167 n. 72; Brad S. Gregory, 'Historians' Metaphysical Beliefs and the Writing of Confessional Histories', *Fides et Historia* 43 (2011), 9–17. More generally, on the danger of what they term the secular dogmatic rejection of the supernatural, see Kyle Jackson et al., 'The Unbelieved and Historians, Part I: A Challenge', *History Compass* 14 (2016), 594–602. For another historian's approach to the supernatural, see Carlos M. N. Eire, *They Flew: A History of the Impossible* (New Haven, CT, 2023).

[87] William O'Sullivan, 'Correspondence of David Rothe and James Ussher 1619–23', *Collectanea Hibernica* 36/37 (1994), 7–49; Bernadette Cunningham and Raymond Gillespie, 'James Ussher and his Irish Manuscripts', *Studia Hibernica* 33 (2004–5), 81–99.

[88] Dáibhí Ó Cróinín, 'J. H. Todd and the *Life of St Patrick*', and Thomas O'Loughlin, 'Bishop William Reeves, Adomnán, and the Begining of Historical Theology in Ireland', in Empey, Ford and Moffitt, eds, *The Church of Ireland and its Past*, 108–23 and 124–43, respectively; Hippolyte Delehaye, 'Le Pèlerinage de Laurent de Pászthó au Purgatoire de S. Patrice', *AnBoll* 27 (1908), 35–60.

Biographers'.[89] Binchy rigorously distinguished between the two sources Patrick wrote himself – the Confession and the letter to Coroticus – and those which were a product of subsequent centuries, too far removed from Patrick to be reliable. The sources claiming that Patrick founded the purgatory fall into this second category: later and of little value.

It is possible to construct a plausible but unprovable pre-history for a shrine or religious centre in Lough Derg before the first appearance of St Patrick's purgatory in the historical record in the twelfth century. There was an earlier monastic settlement in the lake, linked to the local saint, Dobheóg, whose possible association with a shrine may have later 'made way' for the more famous Patrick at the instigation of the Augustinian canons when they arrived in the twelfth century.[90] Nor is it clear that purgatory in Ireland was a purely twelfth-century invention: despite the nominalism of Ussher and Le Goff, Irish interest in a purgatory-like concept with an earthly location can be found as early as the eighth century.[91]

None of this brings the purgatory in Lough Derg back to St Patrick. It remains firmly anchored in the twelfth century, just when the remote Irish church was opening itself to European religious orders and new theological ideas.[92] Attempts to trace the purgatory's earlier origins only lead us away from the realm of history into the more shadowy borderlands of legend and belief, and the complex interplay between historical fact and religious faith. As with the story of Patrician studies, so too with St Patrick's purgatory in Lough Derg: history and hagiography, history and piety, indeed history and theology, can be uneasy bedfellows.

---

[89] Daniel A. Binchy, 'Patrick and his Biographers: Ancient and Modern', *Studia Hibernica* 2 (1962), 7–173.

[90] Pádraig Ó Riain, *Dictionary of Irish Saints* (Dublin, 2011), 268, 529–30; Yolande de Pontfarcy, 'The Historical Background to the Pilgrimage to Lough Derg', in Haren and eadem, eds, *St Patrick's Purgatory*, 9–14.

[91] Marina Smyth, 'The Origins of Purgatory through the Lens of Seventh-Century Irish Eschatology', *Traditio* 58 (2003), 91–132, at 131 n. 170, notes that Le Goff paid no attention to the insular evidence for a pre-twelfth century interest in purgatory. Compare also Tom Sjöblom, 'The Irish Origins of Purgatory', *Studia Celtica Fennica* 2 (2005), 152–65.

[92] Marie Therese Flanagan, *The Transformation of the Irish Church in the Twelfth and Thirteenth Centuries* (Woodbridge, 2010).

The Margins are in our Minds: The Earliest Capuchin Missions to the Ottoman Empire

John-Paul Ghobrial

University of Oxford

This article offers a close reading of a collection of letters written by Capuchin missionaries in the Ottoman empire in the early seventeenth century. It does so with a view towards understanding how the early Capuchins reflected on their position in both local and global contexts. Rather than see these early Capuchin missions as operating 'in the margins' – whether by virtue of their presence in the world of Eastern Christianity, or by virtue of their distance from Rome or their own countries of origin – this article starts from a different perspective, that is, by situating these individuals at the heart of the Ottoman communities in which they established themselves. To this end, the article shows how Capuchin missionaries envisioned themselves as participating in a global religious order based in Brittany whilst they sought in their everyday lives to achieve proximity to Ottoman Christians and Muslims. In its attention to questions of distance, mobility and the specificity of place, the article contributes to recent attempts to reimagine the field of 'global Catholicism': where is the centre; where are the margins; and who decides which is which?

In April 1632, Michel-Ange de Nantes received the news that he was to be sent to the Levant. From Brittany, he was to travel to Marseille and then onwards to Aleppo, where he would join the few Capuchin

Balliol College, University of Oxford, Oxford, OX1 3BJ. E-mail: john-paul.ghobrial@ history.ox.ac.uk.

This article started life as a lecture given at the Ecclesiastical History Society's conference on 'Margins and Peripheries' in July 2023. I am grateful to Peter Marshall for the invitation, and to all those present for their insights and stimulating questions. In revising the lecture for publication, I benefitted enormously from the excellent comments provided to me by Bernard Heyberger, Fred Smith, and the two anonymous reviewers for Studies in Church History, and to Aurélien Girard for his assistance with a few specific queries in the final stages of publication. Finally, I am grateful to Peter Marshall and the editors of the journal for their kindness and support throughout this process.

Studies in Church History 61 (2025), 325–359 © The Author(s), 2025. Published by Cambridge University Press on behalf of the Ecclesiastical History Society. This is an Open Access article, distributed under the terms of the Creative Commons Attribution licence (http://creativecommons.org/licenses/by/4.0), which permits unrestricted re-use, distribution and reproduction, provided the original article is properly cited.
doi:10.1017/stc.2024.40

fathers who had already been living there for several years. Stopping in Paris, Michel-Ange de Nantes encountered rumours circulating about other Capuchins who had gone before him: it was said that some had failed to learn the local languages and had no choice but to return to France, while others in Rome had claimed that Capuchin missionaries had been unable to live in 'good conscience' abroad. Even the *Propaganda Fide*, the recently established office of the papacy tasked with responsibility for missions, had written to Père Joseph de Paris, director of the order, about news it had received that some Capuchins had allegedly converted to Islam. As he travelled, he continued to encounter other, different reports about the mission abroad, which some in Marseille described as being well-regarded by local communities in Aleppo, both Christian and Muslim. In this way, Michel-Ange de Nantes spent a hot, uncertain summer in Marseille, waiting three months for a ship, and finally departing on 8 September 1632, which happened to be the feast of the birth of the Virgin Mary.

If he felt trepidation during his journey, his concerns seem to have disappeared by the time of his arrival in Aleppo. In his first letter from Aleppo – written to Raphael de Nantes, the provincial, or head, of the order in Brittany – he described how impressed he was by what the Capuchins had already accomplished there. The rumours he had heard of the hardships faced by missionaries was wrong. Instead, he described the close, personal relations he had quickly developed himself with both local Christians and Muslims. He spent some three years studying Arabic and Armenian before deciding, in 1636, to leave Aleppo in hopes of establishing a Capuchin presence further east in Baghdad and Mosul. From 1637 to 1641, Michel-Ange focused his energies among the local communities in Baghdad, even becoming superior of the Capuchin household there. This too was a period of great success: in 1638, he wrote that he had received more alms from Ottoman subjects than he could ever obtain in France. During the day, he conversed with local notables and higher clergy, joined the laity in their daily devotions, and sometimes even offered medical advice to Christian and Muslim families. At night, he wrote letters that would make their way to France, inspiring and energizing other Capuchins, even Père Joseph, the head of the order, who passed his time reading stories of the conquests of Godefroy de Bouillon, leader of the First Crusade and the first ruler of the Latin Kingdom of Jerusalem. It is unclear how much of his life Michel-Ange de Nantes spent in this way, before he travelled back at some point to Brittany, where he died in Auray in 1664.

Almost all that we can know about Michel-Ange de Nantes relies on information taken from twenty-six letters he wrote over a period of some nine years spent in the Ottoman empire.[1] That these letters survive at all is down to some measure of luck. It was at some point after 1641 that Michel-Ange de Nantes's letters were recovered, copied and assembled into a single manuscript as part of a larger collection of letters written by Capuchins in the Ottoman empire. Little is known about the identity of the compiler, but what is clear is that the manuscript itself was sent, probably in 1648, to Marcellinus de Pise, a Capuchin of the province of Lyon, who had been collecting materials to use for his continuation of a history of the order that had been started earlier in the century. While Marcellinus's history was published in Lyon only in 1675, the letter book itself has somehow survived and is preserved today at the Bibliothèque nationale de France.[2] Comprising a total of 116 letters written by twenty-six Capuchins over a period stretching from 1626 to 1641, the collection offers an idiosyncratic window into the earliest Capuchin missions to the Ottoman empire. Some missionaries are much better represented than others. In contrast to the twenty-six letters written by Michel-Ange de Nantes, for example, we learn almost nothing from the collection about one of his companions, Charles-François d'Angers, whose presence can only be gleaned from occasional references to him made by Michel-Ange de Nantes. For others, such as Agathange de Vendôme, we do not possess a single letter in the collection, despite its being clear from other sources that Agathange de Vendôme had studied Arabic and conversed with locals for nearly a decade as he travelled from Jerusalem to Aleppo to Cairo, before his death in

---

[1] My account of the career of Michel-Ange de Nantes draws on the letters held in the manuscript under study in this article, namely MS NAF 10220, in the Bibliothèque nationale de France, Paris (full discussion below). On the reading of Godefroy de Bouillon, see Guillaume de Vaumas, 'L'activité missionnaire du Père Joseph de Paris', *Revue d'histoire des missions* 15 (1938), 336–59; his death in Auray is noted in Joseph Michel, 'Essai de répertoire des bretons partis dans les missions étrangères avant 1800' (PhD thesis, University of Rennes, 1946), which is an unpublished dissertation that I have been unable to consult directly. However, Marc-Antoine Alix drew on Michel's study for his MA dissertation, 'Missionnaires bretons dans les Nouvelles Mondes (XVIe – XVIIIe siècles)' (MA thesis, University of Rennes, 2017), see 166–7 for the relevant entry. I am very grateful to Aurélien Girard for drawing my attention to Alix's MA thesis.
[2] The manuscript is part of the Nouvelles acquisitions françaises (NAF) MS 10220, under the title 'Relations des missions des Capucins au Levant (1607–1641). XVIIe siècle', hereafter NAF 10220.

Ethiopia in 1638.[3] Despite the echoes of his movements in the archives, Agathange's voice is absolutely silent in this letter book. This is a reminder of how little can ever be known about a category of individuals who spent much of their lives far from home, in oral conversations with the local societies in which they lived, and who rarely, if ever, published any works in print. In search of past lives spanning great distances, historians must depend on the haphazard survival of letters and other scraps of paper, all of them witnesses to the desires of the dead for connection to distant family, friends and others in the worlds they left behind.

I. INTRODUCTION: MARGINS AND PERIPHERIES

Did these missionaries think of themselves as living 'on the margins' or 'at the peripheries'? This is an important question in as much as the everyday lives of missionaries play a central role in debates about the nature, global or otherwise, of early modern Catholicism. These debates have tended to revolve around rival ways of conceptualizing 'the making of Roman Catholicism as this planet's first world religion': Europe and the world, converters and the converted, or in the apt formulation by Simon Ditchfield, the 'papacy and the peoples'.[4] Whereas an earlier generation of scholarship took for granted a centre-periphery model in which Catholicism spread outwards from Rome to Africa, Asia and the Americas, recent approaches have sought to decentre our focus away from assumptions about the centrality of Rome in the making of global Catholicism. This work of 'decentering' has transformed our understanding of early modern Catholicism in important ways. Some scholars have emphasized the importance of new relationships that developed directly between different regions in this period and without any reference to Rome.[5] Others have challenged Eurocentric ideas of Christianity, emphasizing instead the dynamism of the Christian world beyond Latin Christendom, especially in the

---

[3] See, for example, Ladislas de Vannes, *Deux martyrs capucins, les bienheureux Agathange de Vendôme et Cassien de Nantes* (Paris, 1905).

[4] Simon Ditchfield, 'Decentering the Catholic Reformation: Papacy and Peoples in the Early Modern World', *Archiv für Reformationsgeschichte* 101 (2010), 186–208, at 207.

[5] See, for example, Luke Clossey, *Salvation and Globalization in the Jesuit Missions* (Cambridge, 2010); Gauvin A. Bailey, *Art on the Jesuit Missions in Asia and Latin America, 1542–1773* (Toronto, 1999).

Christian East.[6] In the most recent and transformative example of this approach, Simon Ditchfield has emphasized 'reciprocity' and the creativity that underlay the ways in which European forms of Catholicism 'were owned and adapted to local needs by the indigenous peoples of Asia, America, Africa, and parts of Europe itself'.[7] In place of traditional ideas of a 'global Catholicism' with its notional headquarters in Rome, therefore, scholars have proposed the importance of frameworks such as 'local religion', 'polycentric' Christianity, and even 'composite Catholicism' as ways of rethinking the place of geography in our understanding of early modern Catholicism.[8]

These approaches have coincided with a second set of transformations in the ways in which scholars have studied the history of the missions themselves. Where missionary orders, and their archives, were traditionally sifted for documentary sources about the societies they encountered, a more recent wave of scholarship has made missionaries themselves the subject of critical study. These approaches offer alternative ways of imagining the experience of missionaries. Christian Windler, for example, has shown how the work of missionaries in Persia was subject to competition between multiple Catholic actors, whether papal, national, or the orders themselves.[9] Similarly, Megan Armstrong's study of the 'reinvention of Catholicism' in the Holy Land demonstrates how competition between different religious orders defies any simplistic ways of thinking about 'Catholic mission'

[6] Bernard Heyberger, *Les chrétiens du Proche-Orient au temps de la réforme catholique (Syrie, Liban, Palestine, XVIIe–XVIIIe siècles)* (Rome, 1994); idem, *Middle Eastern and European Christianity, 16th–20th Century: Connected Histories. Essays by Bernard Heyberger*, ed. Aurélien Girard et al. (Edinburgh, 2023); Dorothea Weltecke, 'Space, Entanglement and Decentralisation: On How to Narrate the Transcultural History of Christianity (550 to 1350 CE)', in Nikolas Jaspert and Reinhold F. Glei, eds, *Locating Religions* (Leiden, 2016), 315–44; Samantha Kelly, *Translating Faith: Ethiopian Pilgrims in Renaissance Rome* (Cambridge, MA, 2024); John-Paul A. Ghobrial, 'Connected Histories and Eastern Christianities', in Bruno Boute, Birgit Emich and Andreea Badea, eds, *Pathways through Early Modern Christianities* (Paderborn, 2023), 187–210.
[7] Ditchfield, 'Decentering the Catholic Reformation', 207; compare idem, 'Rome calling? Rewriting the Catholic Reformation for the 21st Century', in Matteo Al Kalak, Lorenzo Ferrari and Elena Fumagalli, eds, *La crisi della modernità. Storie riletture e revisioni per Gianvittorio Signorotto* (Rome, 2023), 305–28, at 306.
[8] These are some of the frameworks identified as 'pathways' to early modern Christianity in Boute, Emich and Badea, eds, *Pathways through Early Modern Christianities*.
[9] Christian Windler, *Missionaries in Persia: Cultural Diversity and Competing Norms in Global Catholicism* (London, 2024).

as a unified, coherent set of aspirations.[10] In another recent approach to missions in Asia, one group of historians has focused on 'patterns of localization' as a way of recovering a sense of the place of missionaries in a defined set of contexts, for example in courts, cities, the country-side, and in their own households.[11] Taken together, these approaches have emphasized the importance of situating the analysis of mission-aries firmly within the context of the local societies in which they were rooted, in some cases disconnected entirely from Rome.

Underlying both these fields – 'global Catholicism' and 'early modern missions' – are a set of assumptions rooted in how historians think about issues of distance in the early modern world. On the one hand, these works have shown how the circulation of information created a sense of simultaneity between communities dispersed around the world.[12] They have shown us how Europeans conflated geography, sometimes seeing in the missions to the Americas models for how to approach the 'other Indies' at home.[13] They have also challenged contemporary ideas about the expansion of Catholicism, emphasizing the spread of Catholicism as a granular process that took place at the level of individuals.[14] All of this is a testament to the fruitful ways in which scholars of early modern Catholicism have increasingly adapted the language of global history, especially the way global historians have engaged critically with the study of space, mobility and circulation.[15]

---

[10] Megan Armstrong, *The Holy Land and the Early Modern Reinvention of Catholicism* (Cambridge, 2021).

[11] See, most recently, Nadine Amsler et al., eds, *Catholic Missionaries in Early Modern Asia: Patterns of Localization* (London and New York, 2020); R. Po-Chia Hsia, *A Companion to Early Modern Catholic Global Missions* (Leiden, 2018), especially the introduction (1–14), at 8.

[12] Clossey, *Salvation and Globalization;* Markus Friedrich, *The Jesuits: A History* (Princeton, NJ, 2022). On communication and community in other contexts, see Francesca Trivellato, *The Familiarity of Strangers: The Sephardic Diaspora, Livorno, and Cross-Cultural Trade in the Early Modern Period* (New Haven, CT, 2009); Sebouh Aslanian, *From the Indian Ocean to the Mediterranean: The Global Trade Networks of Armenian Merchants from New Julfa* (Berkeley, CA, 2014); John-Paul A. Ghobrial, *The Whispers of Cities: Information Flows in Istanbul, London and Paris in the Age of William Trumbull* (Oxford, 2013).

[13] Adriano Prosperi, '"Otras Indias": Missionari della Controriforma tra contadini e selvaggi', in *Scienze, credenze occulte, livelli di cultura: Convegno internazionale di studi (Firenze, 26–30 giugno 1980)* (Florence, 1982), 205–34.

[14] Karin Vélez, *The Miraculous Flying House of Loreto* (Princeton, NJ, 2018).

[15] See, for example, Sebastian Conrad, *What is Global History?* (Princeton, NJ, 2016), 16. More generally, see John-Paul A. Ghobrial, 'Introduction: Seeing the World like a

Yet, as Jeremy Adelman has argued, even global historians still have a good deal of work to do when it comes to thinking about the problem of distance in a critical and reflexive way.[16]

For missionaries far from home, being 'on the margins' was as much a state of mind as a lived reality. To this end, this article applies the insights of global history to help us rethink how global Catholicism was lived and experienced by missionaries, particularly in relation to this volume's focus on margins and peripheries. It does so through the close study of a collection of letters written by Capuchins during the order's earliest presence in the Ottoman empire. The focus on this book of letters allows us to recover a sense of the different ways in which a single missionary order reflected on its position in local, Ottoman and global contexts. In what follows, I emphasize the significance of these reflections as windows into both individual and collective forms of belonging as they intersected within a single community: the Capuchins of the province of Brittany. Members of a global religious order, but also individuals resident in local Ottoman societies, their reflections on distance do not map easily onto the frameworks generally used to understand early modern Catholicism, whether centre-periphery or local-global. Instead, this article argues that an emphasis on geography distracts us from more important aspects of the missionary experience, namely the specificity with which Catholic orders regarded particular societies and places in the early modern world. Within the global theatre of Catholic missions, the Ottoman empire offered a unique stage.

In emphasizing the specificity of the Capuchin experience in the Ottoman empire, I build here on a generation of scholarship that has transformed our understanding of the ways in which the work of Catholic missions in the Christian East was distinct from that of missions in Africa, Asia and the Americas. This was implicit in the earliest handbooks written for the instruction of missionaries such as that of the Discalced Carmelite Thomas á Jesu (1564–1627), which contained a special chapter for missionaries travelling to the East that circulated widely among the Capuchins.[17] The distinctiveness of the

Microhistorian', in idem, ed., *Global History and Microhistory*, issue supplement 14, *P&P* 242 (2019), 1–22, as well as the other contributions in that volume.
[16] Jeremy Adelman, 'The Problem of Distance', in Stefanie Gänger and Jürgen Osterhammel, eds, *Rethinking Global History* (Cambridge, 2024), 210–34.
[17] Thomas á Jesu, *De procuranda salute omnium gentium* (Antwerp, 1613), 346–512 (ch. 7, on the 'oriental' churches).

Ottoman empire was also present in the basic, but vexing, question about how to 'convert' Eastern Christians, a problem that would generate much debate in later decades.[18] At the same time, it has long been clear that generic categories like 'Eastern Christianity' are deeply problematic: in 2003, Bernard Heyberger was already cautioning against the dangers of treating Eastern Christian confessions as fixed and stable, emphasizing instead the dynamic and connected histories of different communities of Christians across the Ottoman empire.[19] All of this should serve as a warning against too easily incorporating the Ottoman empire into debates about 'global Catholic missions', at least not without giving sufficient attention to the ways in which contemporaries regarded it as being distinct in space and time from other societies where Catholic missionaries travelled in this period.

What follows in this article, therefore, is the study of a group of Capuchins from Brittany who were dispersed across a constellation of places, all of them different from one another even as they shared the status of being part of the political world of the Ottoman empire. Rather than see these early Capuchin missions as operating 'on the margins' – whether by virtue of their presence in the world of Eastern Christianity, or by virtue of their distance from Rome or their own countries of origin – this article starts from a different perspective, that is, by situating these individuals at the heart of the Ottoman communities in which they established themselves. Neither 'local' nor 'global', the early Capuchin missionaries thought about their own position in the Ottoman empire in three main ways. First, I show how the circulation of letters between Capuchins facilitated their participation in a global order organized around the Capuchin province of Brittany. Next, I argue that, within this order, the Capuchins developed a distinct sense of the specificity of their presence within the Ottoman empire. This specificity was not defined in a geographic sense, or as a function of distance, but rather by the unique circumstances of religious diversity they faced in the Ottoman empire and, in particular, in terms of their aspirations to achieve proximity to Ottoman Christian communities. Finally, in the last section of this article, I explore

---

[18] For an excellent study of this process, see Cesare Santus, *Trasgressioni necessarie. Communicatio in sacris, coesistenza e conflitti tra le comunità Cristiane orientali* (Rome, 2021).

[19] Bernard Heyberger, 'Pour une "histoire croisée" de l'occidentalisation et de la confessionnalisation chez les chrétiens du Proche-Orient', *The MIT Electronic Journal of Middle Eastern Studies* 2 (2003), 36–49; Ghobrial, 'Connected Histories and Eastern Christianities', 187–8.

how the specificity of their work in the Ottoman empire played itself out in everyday life as the Capuchins sought to become closer to the societies in which they lived. Seeing global Catholicism through the eyes of someone like Michel-Ange de Nantes, we can understand how the everyday work of 'global Catholicism' could enable a missionary in the Ottoman empire to feel as though they were at the centre of Christianity despite the great distance – thousands of kilometres, between Brittany and Aleppo – that separated them from home.

II. BRITTANY IN ALEPPO: A GLOBAL CAPUCHIN ORDER

The main materials for this study survive today in a single manuscript located at the Bibliothèque nationale de France under the shelfmark NAF 10220.[20] There is no indication of who copied and compiled these letters into a single manuscript. A note scribbled onto the first folio of the manuscript indicates only that the 'book of letters and relations' had been sent from the 'superior of the province of Brittany to R. P. Marcellin' for the purpose of the 'composition of his annals of the mission'.[21] Other annotations in the manuscript include reference to the dispatch of specific copies of letters that had been 'sent to R. P. Marcellin de Pise in 1648', all of which suggests that the letter book had come into the possession of Marcellinus de Pise, a Capuchin of the province of Lyon, at some point in the 1640s.[22] Little more can be known about the larger context surrounding Marcellinus's writing of a history of the order. Given the focus of the manuscript on letters written by Capuchins from Brittany – almost all the letters are addressed to Raphael de Nantes, Capuchin provincial of Brittany in the 1630s – it may be that his history was intended to celebrate the contributions of the province to the order's success in the Ottoman empire. At any rate, it appears that Marcellinus de Pise's history was only published decades after the manuscript itself had been returned to Brittany.[23]

---

[20]   The original letters on which Marcellinus de Pise's copy is based may or may not survive today, but this article refers only to NAF 10220 itself. It appears that a later copy of the letters was completed in the nineteenth century: this is MS 1533, which can be found today in the Bibliothèque franciscaine des Capucins, Paris. A cursory review of the contents of MS 1533 suggests it to be a faithful copy of NAF MS 10220.

[21]   Paris, BN, NAF 10220, inside cover.

[22]   BN, NAF 10220, fols 350, 461.

[23]   BN, NAF 10220, inside cover, suggests the manuscript was returned at some point to the provincial of Brittany. For the earlier history of the order, see Giovanni Boveri,

Representing a foundational moment in the Capuchin mission to the Ottoman empire, the manuscript includes some 116 letters by twenty-six individual missionaries written from fifteen different locations in the Ottoman empire including, in order of frequency: Aleppo, Sidon, Satalie (Antalya), Cairo, Tripoli, Beirut, Mosul, Constantinople, and Baghdad. Table 1 details the names of all the missionaries represented in the collection as well as the number of surviving letters and general dates covered by the letters. Table 2 contains information of all the locations of the letters. In addition, the manuscript contains copies of several important documents related to the Capuchin missions in the East, for example, early charters and instructions related to the founding of the mission in the Levant in 1625 under the leadership of Père Joseph (François Leclerc du Tremblay, 1577–1638).[24] Moreover, a 'table des lettres et relations' at the beginning of the manuscript flags twenty-four letters as being of particular importance ('les plus notables'); however, further study would be needed to establish whether there is any relationship between these letters – they were written by different authors and from different locations – or why the compiler thought they deserved to be singled out in this way in the table of contents. Whilst all the letters appear to be written in the same hand, there are also a number of marginal annotations that are written in Arabic, which correspond to Arabic terms transcribed in the letters; and in one case there is also a copy of an entire letter in Arabic.[25] All of this suggests that whoever compiled the manuscript had access to the original letters as sent from the Ottoman empire, and they must have possessed at least rudimentary abilities in writing Arabic or had help from someone who did.

While the presence of Catholic missions in the Middle East dated back to the medieval Franciscan presence in the Holy Land, the beginning of the seventeenth century witnessed the arrival of new orders in the wake of the establishment of the Sacred Congregation of the *Propaganda Fide* in 1622. In addition to the reinvigoration of

---

Annalium seu Sacrarum historiarum ordinis Minorum S. Francisci qui Capucini nuncupantur, 2 vols (Lyons, 1632–9); the continuation by Marcellinus de Pise was published in *Annalium seu Sacrarum historiarum ordinis Minorum S. Francisci, qui Capucini nuncupantur* (Lyon, 1676), later translated into Italian as *Annali de' Frati Minori Capuccini composti dal padre Marcellino da Mascon e tradotti in volgare dal P.F. Antonio Olgiati da Como*, 3 vols (Trent, 1708–14).

[24] Benoist Pierre, *Le père Joseph. L'Éminence grise de Richelieu* (Paris, 2007).

[25] See, for example, BN, NAF 10220, 596–7.

Table 1. The Capuchin Letters in NAF 10220

Name of Capuchin	Number of letters	Locations	Period covered
Adrien de La Brosse	4	Beirut	August 1628 – February 1629
Agathange de Morlaix	4	Cairo, Jerusalem	January 1640 – November 1640
Albert de Nantes	1	Aleppo	November 1629
Alexis de Lamballe	14	Sidon, Satalie	December 1626 – May 1641
Blaise de Nantes	2	Isfahan	February – July 1640
Bonaventure du Lude	2	Aleppo	January 1634 – December 1639
Brice de Rennes	9	Tripoli, Beirut	February 1637 – August 1641
Cassien de Nantes	2	Cairo	March – November 1634
Cesarée de Roscoff	4	Cairo, Rennes	November 1630 – March 1632
Charles de Nantes	3	Aleppo	November 1638 – January 1639
Ephrem de Nevers	1	Basra	September 1639
Etienne de Châtellerault	2	Babylon	December 1637 – October 1638
Felicien de Rennes	9	Satalie, Constantinople	March 1638 – February 1640
Gabriel d'Alençon	3	Tripoli, Beirut	March 1630 – October 1639
Gilles de Loches	4	Sidon, Cairo	March 1628 – December 1630
Guillaume de Beaufort	3	Sidon	December 1638 – September 1640
Jean-Chrysostome d'Angers	1	Aleppo	June 1631
Martial de Thorigny	2	Aleppo	September 1639 – January 1641
Michel-Ange de Nantes	26	Paris, Marseille, Aleppo, Baghdad, Mosul	April 1632 – August 1641
Michel de Rennes	11	Aleppo, Sidon, Damascus, Satalie, Beirut, Tripoli, Rome	January 1634 – June 1641

(Continued)

Table 1 *Continued*

Name of Capuchin	Number of letters	Locations	Period covered
Philémon de Saint-Benoît	2	Sidon	August 1633 – December 1634
Pierre de Guingamp	2	Nicosia	October 1637 – March 1640
Pierre de Morlaix	3	Cairo	May 1639 – December 1640
René de Nantes	1	Sidon	November 1641
Thomas de Saint-Calais	1	Sidon	November 1626
Toussaint de Landerneau	1	Isfahan	April 1634

Catholicism in the Holy Land, the seventeenth century also witnessed increased competition between different religious orders over who would have jurisdiction over specific locations in the Ottoman empire.[26] In the early 1620s, a handful of Jesuits could already be found in Constantinople, Syria and Mediterranean islands including Cyprus, whilst Discalced Carmelites and Augustinians had been dispatched mainly to Isfahan and other locations in Safavid Iran.[27] In the Arab provinces of the Ottoman empire, the Capuchins became more present from the early seventeenth century, especially in the period that followed the mission of the Friar Minor Tommaso Obicini di Novara, who served as a papal emissary to a synod with the Church of the East held in Diyarbakir in 1616.[28]

---

[26] See, for instance, Armstrong, *The Holy Land and the Early Modern Reinvention of Catholicism*; Heyberger, *Les chrétiens du Proche-Orient*; Windler, *Missionaries in Persia*.

[27] Charles A. Frazee, *Catholics and Sultans: The Church and the Ottoman Empire, 1453–1923* (Cambridge, 1983); H. Chick, *A Chronicle of the Carmelites in Persia: The Safavids and the Papal Mission of the 17th and 18th Centuries*, 2nd edn (London, 2011; first publ. 1939); John M. Flannery, *The Mission of the Portuguese Augustinians to Persia and Beyond (1602–1747)* (Leiden, 2013).

[28] The synod is described in Pietro Strozzi, *Synodalia Chaldaeorum, videlicet Epistola synodica Eliae patriarchae Babylonis, archiepiscoporum eius obedientiae, …* (Rome, 1617). For a bio-bibliographical sketch of Tommaso Obicini, see Claudio Balzaretti, 'Un importante ma dimenticato orientalista del sec. XVII: Tommaso Obicini da Novara o.f.m.', *Novarien* 19 (1989), 49–70; idem, 'Padre Tommaso Obicini: Un mediatore nel vicino Oriente all'inizio del Seicento', *Novarien* 32 (2003), 183–90.

Table 2. The Composition of Letters in NAF 10220

Location	Number of letters composed	Period covered
Aleppo	18	June 1631 – January 1641
Babylon	2	December 1637 – October 1638
Baghdad	4	August 1637 – August 1641
Basra	1	September 1639
Beirut	9	August 1628 – January 1641
Cairo	12	November 1630 – December 1640
Constantinople	4	August 1638 – January 1640
Damascus	1	December 1637
Isfahan	2	April 1634 – February 1640
Jerusalem	1	June 1640
Marseille	2	June – July 1632
Mosul	9	March 1638 – July 1640
Nicosia	2	October 1637
Paris	1	April 1632
Rennes	1	March 1640
Rome	1	June 1641
Satalie (Antalya)	13	March 1638 – October 1640
Sidon	18	November 1626 – November 1641
Tripoli	10	March 1630 – August 1641
Unidentified	5	January 1639 – June 1641

Seen within this larger context, the letters collected in NAF 10220 provide only a small window into a much longer history of Catholic missions in the Ottoman empire. They are not witnesses to the earliest presence of Capuchins.[29] Nor should they be seen as offering a complete account even of the short period during which the letters were composed, since they were assembled, and therefore curated, by the anonymous compiler in Brittany. Moreover, the letters provide a distorting impression if we try to read them as signs of any 'permanent' Capuchin presence in a given location. With the exception of a couple of Capuchin households established in key centres like Aleppo and Sidon, the presence of a missionary in any given location was not necessarily sustained over a long

---

[29] The earliest letters from Sidon, Aleppo and Beirut date to 1627, 1627 and 1629, whereas Heyberger has identified the first presence of Capuchins at earlier dates: 1625, 1623 and 1626 respectively: see Heyberger, *Les chrétiens du Proche-Orient*, 275.

period of time. This was the case for example with Mosul: the town witnessed the arrival of the first Capuchins in 1638, but they had left by 1641, after which the order ceased to maintain a permanent presence in the city again until the 1660s.[30] The impression of ubiquity painted by the list of locations in Table 2 is also misleading in that the actual number of missionaries at any one place in time rarely exceeded a couple of individuals; sometimes there may have been more if we take into account the possibility of missionaries travelling through a location. Individual Capuchins were themselves sometimes ignorant of the presence nearby of other members of their order, and in some cases they seem unaware even of previous Capuchin missions in the places where they were.[31] Unlike modern historians who can build a complete picture of the missions retrospectively through the gathering of archival sources, individual missionaries could be entirely in the dark when it came to their position relative to other missionaries in both space and time. This is a reminder that episodes of exchange between Catholicism and Eastern Christianity were never sequential and cumulative in the tidy way often imagined by twentieth-century church historians.

NAF 10220 quickly complicates any ideas of the triumphant spread of global Catholic missions. Instead, we find a tentative process through which a very small number of individuals – dispersed across a vast, changing set of locations – managed to establish permanent missionary households in only a few locations. This may explain the acute sense of solitude, loneliness and isolation we find repeatedly in the earliest letters of the Capuchins: not only the quiet solitude of living by oneself, or the unpredictability of travelling alone, but also the all-consuming worry and fear about the fate of friends who were themselves living and travelling on their own. Writing from Tripoli in 1640, Brice de Rennes noted that he 'was alone most of the time, on account of the small number of clerics we are here'.[32] On the same day,

---

[30] Michel-Ange de Nantes writes about these challenges in his letters from Mosul from May to July 1640: BN, NAF 10220, with letters starting on 474, 483, 501.

[31] In the letters describing a Capuchin visit to the patriarch of the Church of the East in 1640, no reference was made to the earlier synod that had been held between the Capuchin Tommaso Obicini and the Church of the East in Diyarbakir in 1616: BN, NAF 10220, 22 May 1640, 474.

[32] BN, NAF 10220, Brice de Rennes, 14 March 1640 (Tripoli), 441. References to specific quotations include an indication of the author, date, location of writing (where known), and relevant page number of the letter as contained in the manuscript's modern pagination.

less than fifty miles away in Beirut, another missionary confessed that he was contemplating leaving the mission and returning to France. He did not want to do so, but felt that he could not persevere any longer without the company of others: 'It is a pity to be all on one's own as a cleric in such situations of great risk.'[33] Frequent news of the deaths of other missionaries would only reinforce these feelings of isolation. After describing a sickness from which he was slowly recovering, Brice de Rennes wrote in 1640:

> It displeases me that being alone here as I am without any companions, I am unable to carry out my work. Father Gabriel has left me here alone so that he can travel to assist Father Pierre de Guingamp, who is himself alone in Cyprus. I have received news that Father Felicien de Rennes has died at Satalie [Antalya] three days after his return from Constantinople, thereby leaving Father Alexis de Lamballe alone now at Satalie, and this after he had spent six months on his own without being able to confess to anyone while Father Felicien was away in Constantinople. Your Reverence can see from this the sadness and chagrin that remains for a poor cleric who is all alone.[34]

Rather than seeing this automatically as a sign of their being on the margins, we should also consider other reasons that explain the frequency of such comments by missionaries, for example the way in which everyday life in the mission must have challenged individuals who had chosen to live life under a rule, that is, within a community. How could they remain faithful to this vow when isolated in conditions that were so far from the communal modes around which the order was organized in western France? However, not all individuals felt the same way. Writing from Beirut in February 1629, Adrien de La Brosse wrote that if he ever felt he was living as a Friar Minor, 'it is here and now', and he claimed never to have thought, even once, of returning to France.[35]

Reflections on isolation must also be seen as part of a larger missionary rhetoric aimed at recruiting more missionaries to assist with the work required in the Ottoman empire. Writing from Sidon in December 1638, Guillaume de Beaufort requested the dispatch of more missionaries: 'Above all, take care to choose healthy men,

---

[33] BN, NAF 10220, Michel de Rennes, 13 March 1640 (Beirut), 438.
[34] BN, NAF 10220, Brice de Rennes, 20 April 1640 (Tripoli), 457.
[35] BN, NAF 10220, Adrien de La Brosse, 8 February 1629 (Beirut), 90.

because even with those who have only ordinary illnesses in the province, when they arrive in this country, these illnesses will increase, especially the headaches'.[36] Another missionary, writing from Tripoli in 1640, was more specific:

> It seems to me that it would be preferable either to leave our [current] locations in order to be together in groups of at least two, or to abandon the missions entirely, because being here alone means we cannot travel to preach neither to the countryside nor to the city. Instead, one acts as a sort of chaplain to two or three Franks [European Christians], something which I think is better suited to the Observants than ourselves. They tell us continually that they are chaplains for the French, and I respond to them that I did not come here to preach to anyone other than local [Ottoman] Christians.[37]

Beyond the question of numbers, the letters also expressed a preference for the skills and talents needed for the work of mission. Apart from obvious considerations like the need for people who could learn languages effectively, there was an acute demand for more manual labour and technical skills. Writing from Mosul in 1638, Michel de Rennes reiterated a previous request for more friars:

> We ask for help in the form of four missionaries and two lay friars … . The friars should be young clerics, fervent and humble, who will live in poverty. You would do us a great deed if they could be taught bloodletting, and if they could be introduced to some carpenters to teach them how to work. Over here they have no idea what a door or window is. The friars will also need to bring tools with them from France, because they do not have [good ones here] and they only use axes for all of their projects.[38]

The assumption was that the presence of more friars would contribute to the making of a well-functioning household, thereby freeing up the missionaries to focus entirely on engaging with local communities. Not only does such rhetoric reflect the genuine practical needs of everyday life, but it is an important reminder of the extent to which

---

[36] BN, NAF 10220, Guillaume de Beaufort, 10 December 1638 (Sidon), 333.

[37] BN, NAF 10220, Brice de Rennes, 20 April 1640 (Tripoli), 457–8.

[38] BN, NAF 10220, Michel-Ange de Nantes, 8 April 1638 (Mosul), 209; for similar comments on the need for skills and manual labour, see BN, NAF 10220, 446.

these letters were also intended to contribute to fundraising efforts among patrons and donors in France.[39]

Far from communicating a sense of being on the margins, the letters suggest the extent to which individual missionaries imagined themselves as participating in a much wider global order of Capuchins, one that had its heart in Brittany. On the most basic level, this is because the great majority of Capuchins studied in this article actually came from one of two provinces of the order, namely Brittany and Touraine, both of which in 1641 were still under the supervision of a single provincial, Raphael de Nantes.[40] The shared origins of the missionaries are also clear in the epithets used in the naming practices of those who joined the order, for example, the appellation of 'de Nantes' for six of them: Albert de Nantes, Blaise de Nantes, Cassien de Nantes, Charles de Nantes, Michel-Ange de Nantes and René de Nantes. In some cases, they even came from the same families. By the late seventeenth century, specific locations in the Ottoman empire had effectively been 'twinned' with one or another of the two provinces. Writing in 1684, a Capuchin publishing under the pseudonym Michel Febvre explained that missionaries originally from Touraine tended to be dispatched to Cyprus, Aleppo, Cairo, Diyarbakir, Mosul and Baghdad, while those from Brittany were based mainly in Damascus, Tripoli, Beirut, Sidon and Mount Lebanon.[41] Moreover, a close reading of the letters makes clear that in addition to maintaining a correspondence between Brittany and the Ottoman empire, Capuchins living in the Ottoman empire also regularly exchanged letters with one another.

If they retained a close link to Brittany, and to one another, the early Capuchins also envisioned themselves as part of a global Capuchin network extending across North Africa, the Caribbean and the

---

[39] See, for example, the general circulars composed by Michel-Ange de Nantes addressed to 'the Capuchins of Brittany': in French, 9 January 1634 (Aleppo), 153; in Italian, 9 January 1634 (Aleppo), 659.

[40] Raphael de Nantes served as the first provincial of Brittany for over a decade, elected several times in succession from as early as 1629, in which capacity he received letters from the province's missionaries from around the world. He was also the author of *L'Exaltation de la sacré couronne de nostre seigneur et les SS. Practiques des serviteurs de Jesus par le P. Raphael de Nantes Capucin* (Rennes, 1638).

[41] Michel Febvre, *Théâtre de la Turquie: ou sont représentées les choses les plus remarquables qui sy passent aujourd'huy touchant les mœurs, le gouvernement, les coûtumes & la religion des Turces, & de treize autres sortews de nations qui habitent dans l'Empire Ottoman* (Paris, 1682), 515.

Americas. The letters show Capuchins in the Ottoman empire occasionally comparing their own experiences with those of friends based in Morocco, Canada and Guinea. Writing from Sidon in 1626, for example, Gilles de Loches thanked God that he was being treated better by the locals than his counterparts who had gone to Morocco in 1624.[42] In 1636, another missionary wrote from Aleppo to ask Raphael de Nantes whether he could send him any news of whether 'there are Capuchins of our province in Canada' and of those who had travelled to Guinea 'what good have they accomplished, have they returned, and if so from which Guinea (because there are two)'.[43] In return for this news, he reassured Raphael de Nantes that 'all our missionaries in Persia, Egypt, and Palestine are well.' In this way, the early Capuchin missions were constituted by a group of individuals who shared a common origin in as much as they came from the same region in western France, and in some cases, even from the same families.[44] A more refined prosopography could help better understand the proximity of individual Capuchins to one another, but what is clear here is the sense that through the work of the Capuchins, Brittany had itself been transplanted into the Ottoman empire.

III. A 'Babylon of Confusion': The Specificity of the Ottoman World

Across the great distance that separated Brittany and Aleppo, a global order of epistolary communication worked against any sense of being on the margins of Christendom. Yet this impression of simultaneity should not be confused with the idea that the experience of Capuchins in the Ottoman empire resembled that of Capuchins living in other parts of the world. Instead, the Capuchins themselves quickly developed a sense of the specificity of their circumstances in the Ottoman empire. Unlike in Morocco, for example, where their counterparts lived among Muslim communities, the Capuchins in the Ottoman empire focused their missionary work mainly on local Christian

---

[42] BN, NAF 10220, Gilles de Loches, 1 December 1626 (Sidon), 69. On the Capuchin mission in Morocco, see Apollinaire de Valence, ed., *L'histoire de la mission des pères capucins de la province de Touraine à Maroc par le P. François d'Angers (1624–1636)* (Rome, 1888).
[43] BN, NAF 10220, Michel-Ange de Nantes, 2 October 1634 (Aleppo), 202.
[44] This was the case, for example, with Albert de Nantes and Raphael de Nantes who were brothers.

communities. Ottoman Christians constituted a patchwork of communities of different languages, theologies and liturgical traditions, in which one of the few characteristics they shared in common was their legal status as *dhimmīs*, or non-Muslim subjects, of the Ottoman sultan. Some of these Christian communities, such as the Copts, traced their origins back to the apostolic missions of the early Christian church; others celebrated their distinctiveness, for example, the Maronites who wrote with pride of their history of close ties to Rome going back to earlier centuries.[45] In specific locations, missionaries encountered these 'Eastern Christianities' alongside the other communities with which they lived: Muslims, both Sunni and Shi'i, but also Yazidis, Druze and Jewish communities. Beyond their distinct confessional identities, Christian and non-Christian communities alike inhabited a complex linguistic world in which Turkish, Persian, Arabic, Greek, Armenian, Kurdish and Aramaic were spoken across the collective locations of the Capuchins.

Even in their earliest despatches, therefore, the Capuchins invoked the twin themes of 'disorder' and 'Babylon' as a way of characterizing the religious diversity they encountered in the Ottoman empire. When Michel Febvre described the Ottoman empire as a 'true Babylon of confusion', for example, he identified some fourteen different sects he had encountered: six Muslim (Turks, Arabs, Kurds, Turcoman, Yezidis and the Druze), six Christian (Greeks, Armenians, Syrians, Nestorians, Maronites and Copts), Jews, and a final sect that he designated as 'sunworshippers' ('solaires ou chamsi', for Arabic *shamsi*).[46] Febvre's categories conflate linguistic and confessional identity, but Capuchins also saw these differences expressed in physical ways. As Gilles de Loches described in 1628 in Sidon, 'some people are completely white, others are entirely black, and some are olive-coloured'.[47] The impression of disorder was also rooted in the observations the Capuchins made of everyday devotions and practices, especially the blurring of confessional boundaries that they witnessed in the use of shared rituals and sacred spaces. Writing from Beirut in 1628, Adrien de La Brosse admitted that he found it difficult to

---

[45] Sam Kennerley, *Rome and the Maronites in the Renaissance and Reformation: The Formation of Religious Identity in the Early Modern Mediterranean* (London, 2022).
[46] Febvre, *Théâtre de la Turquie*, 345.
[47] BN, NAF 10220, Gilles de Loches, 20 March 1628 (Saida), 77; see also his wider comments in the same letter on different species of animals and plants.

'distinguish between different sorts [of people] here, because of the great familiarity that exists between Christians and Turks.'[48] There are various ways of understanding these comments. On the one hand, such reactions might reflect the simple fact that missionaries could not always understand local customs. On the other hand, it also reveals something of the genuine mixing of different confessions and religions that took place in the Ottoman empire, especially in the 'everyday religion' that James Grehan has identified in agrarian societies far from the imperial capital of Istanbul.[49] Whatever the case, it is clear that the Capuchins used these observations to construct ideas of the religious and cultural specificity of individual locations within the wider Babylon in which they found themselves. An example of this can be seen in the way in which Gilles de Loches described several locations in the region around Beirut in 1628:

> There are the Raphadins who are of the religion of the Persians … . They are a very superstitious people who do not want either to drink or to dine with anyone who is not of their faith. These people comprise some seven or eight hundred villages in this country, and they are very difficult to convert despite the fact that they have more affection for the French than any other nation … . We also have Turkmen … in the mountains and the plains. These people are docile and speak the Turkish language … . Moreover, there are the Arabs who have their own law and who live always in the countryside. These groups of infidels, or Muslims, are separate from the Jews and the Christians, of whom only the Maronites are Catholic. In Sidon, there are mostly Greeks, small numbers of Armenians, and a handful of Maronites. But in Damascus, Tripoli, and Jerusalem, you will find Abyssinians, Copts, Jacobites, and Nestorians.[50]

Moreover, distinctions made about specific localities developed in tandem with the crystallization of ideas about specific communities. By 1627, the Druze were assumed to have 'no religion'; by 1634, the Mandeans were regarded simply as Christians who preserved a particular devotion for John the Baptist; and in 1640, Michel-Ange de

---

[48] BN, NAF 10220, Adrien de La Brosse, 25 August 1628 (Beirut), 79.
[49] James Grehan, *Twilight of the Saints: Everyday Religion in Ottoman Syria and Palestine* (Oxford, 2016); for an older tradition of such work, see F. W. Hasluck, *Christianity and Islam under the Sultans* (Oxford, 1929).
[50] BN, NAF 10220, Gilles de Loches, 20 March 1628 (Beirut), 75–7.

Nantes could write that the Nestorians, one of the Christian communities in the region around Baghdad, were the 'least liked' by other Ottoman Christians.[51] In some cases, it is very striking how quickly an individual might develop such views. Only four months after his arrival in Sidon in 1627, Thomas de Saint-Calais could write optimistically that 'Having arrived in this country, I find a completely new world, which I have never seen before … nowhere near as diabolical as [I] thought. If liberty is given [to us], we will convert the whole country in no time'.[52] These views also contributed to strategic assessments about which locations were better suited for the presence of Capuchin missions. In 1637, Etienne de Châtellerault criticized the focus of the Capuchins on Ottoman cities like Aleppo, arguing instead that smaller towns like Mardin, Diyarbakir and Urfa were a better destination for new missions. Not only were there more Christians residing in such towns, but the people living there were 'very docile' and open to evangelism.[53]

It is striking that the letters exchanged between Capuchins differs in tone from the writings that Capuchin writers composed for audiences outside the order. Where NAF 10220 suggests an attention to the specificity of the Ottoman empire, letters composed for non-Capuchin audiences, at least in this letter book, fold Ottoman distinctiveness into a more generic rhetoric about disputation between Christianity and Islam. In the few letters in the collection that were sent to the *Propaganda Fide*, for example, Capuchins made much of the time they spent engaged in theological disputations with Ottoman Christians and Muslims. Consider one account sent by Michel de Rennes to Rome in June 1641, which described the conversations he had held with a Muslim *qadi*, or judge, visiting from Cyprus. As Michel de Rennes told the story, the *qadi* had been so moved by their conversations that before returning to Cyprus he had asked him for a copy of an Arabic Gospel because he had 'lived as a Christian in his

---

[51] On the Druze having 'no religion', see BN, NAF 10220, Gilles de Loches, 3 November 1627 (Sidon), 70; on the Mandeans, see Bonaventure du Lude, 23 December 1639 (Aleppo), 389; and on the Nestorians, see the reference to their being prohibited from entering the Holy Sepulchre in Jerusalem in Michel-Ange de Nantes, 8 July 1640 (Mosul), 483. Compare, on the Druze, Bernard Heyberger, 'Peuples "sans loi, sans foi, ni prêtre": druzes et nusayrîs de Syrie découverts par les missionnaires catholiques (XVIIe–XVIIIe siècles)', in idem and Rémy Madinier, eds, *L'Islam des marges. Mission chrétienne et espaces périphériques du monde musulman XVIe–XXe siècles* (Paris, 2011), 45–80.
[52] BN, NAF 10220, Thomas de Saint-Calais, 3 November 1627 (Sidon), 70.
[53] BN, NAF 10220, Etienne de Châtellerault, 1 December 1637 (Babylon), 228, and more generally his account of his journey to Mardin in the same letter.

heart' ('il demeura chrestien en son coeur'). After returning to Cyprus, the *qadi* began to preach publicly about the superiority of the Gospels, at which point he was imprisoned under the trumped-up charge of having gone mad. Given a chance to redeem himself eight days later, the *qadi* was released, only to be later found proclaiming in front of an assembled crowd that Christianity was superior to Islam. The crowd set upon and killed him. The message of Michel de Rennes's letter was clear enough to readers in Rome: the efforts of the Capuchins had inspired a Muslim convert to sacrifice his life for Christianity in a way that recalled a much longer tradition of Christian polemics about Islam.[54]

This polemical interest in disputation was also suggested in works that were printed and published by Capuchin authors. An example from a later period is a book first published in Latin by the *Propaganda Fide*, entitled *The Book comprising Answers of the People of the Holy Catholic Universal Apostolic Church to the Objections of the Muslims, Jews and Heretics who oppose the Catholics.*[55] Written by Michele Febvre, the author who, as discussed above, had invoked the imagery of a 'Babylon of confusion', the book was subsequently translated into Arabic and Armenian. The topics in the book were aimed to assist in the refutation of Muslims, Jews and especially Eastern Christians. Judging from the small size of the book, some have suggested it was intended to support the everyday work of the Capuchins; however, as Feras Krimsti has argued, it would have been unthinkable to travel around the Ottoman empire carrying such a potentially inflammatory work written in Arabic.[56]

---

[54] The anecdote is taken from chapter 3 of 'Une breve relation faicte par F. Michel de Rennes … contenant les choses remarquables … qu'il a presenté aux SCPF', in BN, NAF 10220, Michel de Rennes, 13 June 1641 (n.pl., but probably Tripoli), 548–56, with reference to the *qadi*'s conversion 'in his heart' on 548–9. For a similar example, published in 1589 in Italian and German, see Charlotte Methuen, '"And our Muḥammad goes with the Archangel Gabriel to Choir": Sixteenth-Century German Accounts of Life under the Turks', in eadem, Andrew Spicer and John Wolffe, eds, *Christianity and Religious Plurality*, SCH 51 (Woodbridge, 2015), 166–80, at 166–88.

[55] Michel Febvre, *Praecipuae Objectiones quad virgo solent fieri per modum interrogationis a Mahumeticae legos sectoribus, Judaeis, et haereticis Orientalibus adversus catholicos earumque solutiones* (Rome, 1679). On the author, see Bernard Heyberger, 'Justinien de Neuvy, dit Michel Febvre', in David Thomas and John Chesworth, eds, *Christian-Muslim Relations: A Bibliographical History*, 9: *Western and Southern Europe (1600–1700)* (Leiden, 2017), 579–88; and idem, 'Polemic Dialogues between Christians and Muslims in the Seventeenth Century', *Journal of the Economic and Social History of the Orient* 55 (2012), 495–516.

[56] The Arabic translation of the book appears to survive in only two printed copies, neither of which are held in any library or archive in the Middle East. Feras Krimsti, 'A Refutation of Muslims, Jews, and "Heretical" Christians, printed in

Tales of martyrdom and refutations of Islam: these sorts of works appear at first to reinforce a sense of the Capuchins occupying an ambiguous and timeless space on the frontiers between Christendom and the Islamic world. However, one must be cautious not to use such sources as a window into the experience of Capuchin missionaries in this period. Unlike the letters under study, these sources were not written by and for the Capuchins. Instead, they offer a glimpse into what wider Catholic audiences wanted to hear from the Capuchins, and they cannot provide a useful indication of their actual undertakings on the ground. To understand the Capuchins' attitudes to the specificity of the Ottoman empire, we need to turn instead to the critical work of reading the letters for what they reveal about how the Capuchins viewed their own positions within local Ottoman societies.

IV. Proximity and Distance in Everyday Life

NAF 10220 is a testament to the main activities that the early Capuchins focused on in the Ottoman empire. Most individuals spent their time in three main ways: the study of local languages, chief among them Arabic; the translation of devotional works into local languages and, to a lesser extent, the composition of new, original works; and the daily participation in the everyday lives and religious devotions of Eastern Christian communities. Taken together, these three activities all shared a common goal, namely to reduce the distance between Capuchins and the societies in which they lived.

Most missionaries began to study local languages only after their arrival in the Ottoman empire.[57] Decades later, this would become a point of derision among later writers, most notably Eusèbe Renaudot, the French theologian and orientalist who, in 1701, wrote a fierce critique of the Capuchins as part of a treatise submitted to the papacy on the limited progress made in the spread of Catholicism in the Ottoman empire.[58] Nonetheless, there is already in these early

---

Arabic', *Blog der Forschungsbibliothek Gotha*, University of Erfurt (5 October 2022), online at: <https://blog-fbg.uni-erfurt.de/2022/10/a-refutation-of-muslims-jews-and-heretical-christians-printed-in-arabic-a-catholic-missionary-at-work-in-17th-century-aleppo/>, accessed 5 December 2024.

[57] BN, NAF 10220, Michel-Ange de Nantes, 19 April 1632 (Paris), 113.

[58] The treatise is part of a manuscript containing a wide selection of Renaudot's writings: 'Collection de mémoires sur les liturgies des églises orientales et de documents relatifs aux

missions clear evidence of an engagement with the study of Ottoman languages, especially Arabic.[59] As Adrien de La Brosse wrote in 1629, knowledge of Arabic, in particular, was highly valued among Ottoman Christians and also important from a practical perspective: 'It is necessary to learn it, and speak it, because we are most of the time without any interpreters.'[60] Written Arabic also offered a way of bypassing the patchwork of colloquial languages spoken in the region, which La Brosse had described in the same letter as 'extremely difficult Moorish languages, different from both Turkish and Arabic'.[61] Less clear are the methods the Capuchins used for studying Arabic. Requests were occasionally made for the dispatch of grammars and lexica that had been published in Europe, although it is unclear whether any of these requests were ever fulfilled.[62] However, surviving evidence suggests that, very early on, the Capuchins began to develop their own study materials such as the 'dictionary of vulgar [that is, colloquial spoken] Arabic' that Albert de Nantes was reported to have completed in Beirut as early as 1629.[63] Moreover, there was a cumulative and collaborative aspect to language study: a missionary who knew a language could teach it to one who had just arrived, an approach that was effective in the case of Arabic, but less so for languages studied by only one or two individuals, for example Syriac and Armenian.[64]

---

affaires diplomatiques et religieuses de la seconde moitié du règne de Louis XIV, formée par l'abbe Eusèbe Renaudot', in BN, NAF 7468, 368–98.

[59] For some examples of reference to the study of Arabic, see BN, NAF 10220, letters starting at 90, 184, 305.

[60] BN, NAF 10220, Adrien de La Brosse, 25 August 1628 (Beirut), 78–9; see also the reference to the study of Arabic by Agathange de Vendôme in: BN, NAF 10220, Adrien de La Brosse, 25 November 1629 (Beirut), 93.

[61] BN, NAF 10220, Adrien de La Brosse, 25 August 1628 (Beirut), 78–9.

[62] BN, NAF 10220, Michel-Ange de Nantes, 12 May 1633 (Aleppo), 133. In the same letter, reference is also made to an Armenian grammar and dictionary printed in Milan. For an Ethiopic New Testament, see BN, NAF 10220, Gilles de Loches, 1 March 1629 (Sidon), 91. For other requests for books, see BN, NAF 10220, Brice de Rennes, 15 January 1641 (Beirut), 521; for the specific request for the dispatch of 'Arabic, Latin, or Italian books of Christian doctrine that are to be found in Paris' to be used 'for the instruction of children', see BN, NAF 10220, Brice de Rennes, 25 April 1641 (Tripoli), 527.

[63] BN, NAF 10220, Adrien de La Brosse, 25 November 1629 (Beirut), 93. Many such works known by the authors of earlier studies are difficult to locate today, for example, those referenced in Louis de Gonzague, *Les anciens missionnaires Capucins de Syrie et leurs écrits apostoliques de langue arabe* (Assisi, 1932).

[64] BN, NAF 10220, Michel-Ange de Nantes, 12 May 1633 (Aleppo), 133.

The emphasis on language study in the letters should not distract us from the fact that, then as now, some people simply picked up languages more easily than others. Shortly after his arrival in Tripoli in July 1636, Brice de Rennes described how he had impressed Ottoman Christians by the progress he had already made in both Arabic and Turkish. By his account, he had learned enough Arabic in five months to be able to give as good a sermon in Arabic as in French. That was because, in his words, 'I've received a God-given grace for languages, which is why I am not at all surprised [by my progress].'[65] Others were apparently less blessed: in 1632, Jean-Chrysostome d'Angers was forced to return to France after having spent three years in Aleppo trying to learn Arabic, but with no success.[66]

Most importantly, the study of Arabic provided Capuchins with an opportunity to become closer to local communities by receiving language instruction directly from Ottoman Christians. It is difficult to know much about these local teachers, most of whom are not identified by name in the correspondence. However, in those cases where it is possible to identify them, it becomes clear that the Capuchins often studied Arabic with individuals whom other sources show to have had reputations in their own communities as celebrated scholars and prolific copyists. This was the case even for the gifted Brice de Rennes who, it appears, studied Arabic with Yuhanna al-Ghurayr, a Syrian Orthodox priest and later bishop of Damascus, who was responsible for composing over fifty manuscript works.[67] While scholars such as Aurélien Girard and Giovanni Pizzorusso have transformed our understanding of the consolidation of a linguistic register of missionary and Catholic Arabic, further work still remains to understand the place of language study in cultivating personal ties between Capuchins and Ottoman Christians and Muslims.[68]

[65] BN, NAF 10220, Brice de Rennes, 13 February 1637 (Tripoli), 259.

[66] BN, NAF 10220, Michel-Ange de Nantes, 19 April 1632 (Paris), 113; the study of Karshuni is described in BN, NAF 10220, Etienne de Châtellerault, 8 October 1638 (Babylon), 305; on the printing of Armenian, see BN, NAF 10220, Blaise de Nantes, 25 February 1640 (Isfahan), 432.

[67] Jean Fathi, 'Ibn al-Ghurayr', in David Thomas and John A. Chesworth, eds, *Christian-Muslim Relations: A Bibliographical History*, 10: *Ottoman and Safavid Empires (1600–1700)* (Leiden, 2017), 299–307; and idem, 'Yūḥannā ibn al-Ghurayr, passeur de la tradition syriaque et arabe chrétienne au XVIIe siècle', *Journal of Eastern Christian Studies* 68 (2016), 81–209.

[68] Aurélien Girard, 'Teaching and Learning Arabic in Early Modern Rome: Shaping a Missionary Language', in Jan Loop, Alastair Hamilton and Charles Burnett, eds, *The*

A second main focus of the daily lives of Capuchins involved the copying, translation and composition of Arabic texts, again often in collaboration with local Ottoman Christians. These unique works tend to survive today, if at all, only in small numbers of manuscript copies in church libraries and monastic collections in the Middle East, many of which are not easily accessible to scholars. However, a recent series of ground-breaking digitization projects has unearthed an entire corpus of manuscripts still in need of systematic study. In NAF 10220, it is possible to identify several categories of works that caught the attention of the earliest Capuchins. These included: sacred texts, for example the Gospels, the New Testament, and in time, the Psalter; spiritual works, normally translations of European Catholic Reformation writers; pastoral works, including catechisms; polemical works; and linguistic works, including grammars and dictionaries. Although these activities gained real momentum only in the second half of the seventeenth century, it is clear that by 1640, Capuchins were already occupied with the translation and composition of texts, and that these activities were being carried out at several different locations across the Ottoman empire.[69] One reason for this was that translation was an activity that could be carried out virtually anywhere. While travelling on the caravan from Aleppo to Baghdad, for example, Juste de Beauvais was reported to have completed an Arabic translation of Richelieu's catechism. Such efforts also reflected the usefulness of having manuscripts to offer as gifts to local notables. On the same journey, Juste de Beauvais presented some Armenian priests in Urfa with a copy of a translation of Bellarmine's catechism into Arabic that he had completed while travelling.[70]

As with other mobile communities of Catholics in this period, the work of translation afforded Capuchins a way of reducing the distance between themselves and the worlds they had left behind.[71] In some cases, missionaries selected works for translation that reflected

---

Teaching and Learning of Arabic in Early Modern Europe (Leiden, 2017), 189–212; Giovanni Pizzorusso, *Propaganda Fide*, 1: *La congregazione pontificia e la giurisdizione sulle missioni* (Rome, 2022).

[69] For references to translation, see BN, NAF 10220, letters starting at 78, 217, 437, 474, 483, among others.

[70] BN, NAF 10220, Etienne de Châtellerault, 1 December 1637 (Babylon), 232; the Armenian priests in Urfa are on 225.

[71] See, for example, Frederick E. Smith, *Transnational Catholicism in Tudor England: Mobility, Exile, and Counter-Reformation, 1530–1580* (Oxford, 2022); Liesbeth Corens, *Confessional Mobility and English Catholics in Counter-Reformation Europe* (Oxford, 2019).

perfectly the reforming spirit of early modern Catholicism in Rome. This was the case, for example, with a three-volume abridgement of the *Annales Ecclesiastici*, the triumphant history of the church written in the sixteenth century by Cesare Baronio. The *Annales* offered a history of the church from the establishment of Christianity at the start of the first millennium until the present. Brice de Rennes had started working on an Arabic translation while living in Damascus in 1644, and he completed the work with the help of local scribes, including a man whom he identifies only as a deacon named Yusuf ('Yusuf Shammās').[72] Brice spent six years working on the translation before he travelled to Rome in 1650, where he published the first two volumes of the work. He returned to Syria in 1655, where he continued his work on a third and final volume.[73] Originally written in Rome in the sixteenth century, rendered a hundred years later into Arabic in Damascus, printed on the *Propaganda Fide* press in Rome, and circulated in physical copies back to the Ottoman empire, the three volumes comprise over 1,000 pages in total, yet Brice de Rennes's Arabic translation still lacks any systematic, critical study.[74]

The act of translating Baronius into Arabic captures something important about the ambitions of the early Capuchins, but it would be misleading to characterize the significance of such works as being primarily scholarly or even evangelical. Rather, the act of collaborative translation afforded Capuchins with an opportunity for daily conversations and personal interactions with Ottoman Christians. The correspondence provides us with countless examples of how capacious these forms of participation could be, from attempts to treat the medical needs of Ottoman subjects, to engaging in local business transactions, to education of the local youth. Chief among these was an activity referred to throughout the letters by the term 'preaching' (*prêcher*). The term is used to describe those situations in which the

---

[72] The reference to Yusuf can be found in the preface to volume 1 of *Analu. Ecclesiasticor. Caesaris Baronii S.R.E. Card. Arabic Epitome* (Rome, 1653).

[73] On the popularity of the work among Eastern Christians in later decades, see John-Paul A. Ghobrial, 'Catholic Confessional Literature in the Christian East? A View from Rome, Diyarbakir, and Mount Lebanon, ca. 1674', in Tijana Krstić and Derin Terzioğlu, eds, *Entangled Confessionalizations? Dialogic Perspectives on the Politics of Piety and Community Building in the Ottoman Empire, 15th–18th Centuries* (Piscataway, NJ, 2022), 383–99.

[74] The only modern study is Andrea Trentini, 'Baronio arabo: vicende e tematiche dell'*Annalium Ecclesiasticorum Arabica Epitome*', in Luigi Gulia, ed., *Baronio e le sue fonti (Atti del convegno internazionale di Studi Sora 10–13 ottobre 2007)* (Sora, 2009), 719–42.

Capuchins sought to evangelize Ottoman Christians through sermons, lessons and participation in liturgical services. Writing from Tripoli in February 1637, for example, Brice de Rennes offered a moving account of the first time he 'preached' in the presence of some three hundred Christians. This appears to have involved him reciting the Our Father in Arabic, which incited the tears of those around him: 'They came to me afterwards and kissed my hand, saying what I had preached was like a pearl'.[75] Some months later, further east near Mardin, Juste de Beauvais preached to a village of Syrian Orthodox Christians. Etienne de Châtellerault described the experience in the following way:

> Father Juste preached in Arabic, and after he had finished, the entire crowd came to him to kiss his hands. Whether he liked it or not, he accepted it, which is why I permitted it as well. They called him 'Abona Emoutran' [Arabic, *abūna* and *mutrān*, a combination of the titles used to address priests and bishops, respectively], which in our language means 'Our Father the Bishop'. As for me, they called me 'Abona Elcacia' [Arabic, *qasīs*, meaning priest], which in our language signifies 'Our Father the Priest'. We spent our entire visit to this village in possession of these marks of distinction ('avec ces qualités').[76]

Clearly, this reference to preaching refers to an official permission obtained from higher clergy which allowed the Capuchins to preach in the churches of Eastern Christian communities. In 1637, Michel-Ange de Nantes provided a fascinating account of how his companion, Juste de Beauvais, had used one such permission to insinuate himself into the local Maronite community in Aleppo. This was how one missionary described Juste de Beauvais's entrance into the church:

> Having received the letter from the Patriarch giving him permission to preach, Father Juste went one Sunday to the Maronite church and had the Patriarch's letter read out loud. After it was read, he told the assembled crowd in a loud voice in Arabic that if there was anyone from among their priests or deacons who did not agree to our Fathers preaching in their church, in contravention to what had been expressed by their Patriarch, then he would not do anything contrary to their wishes. He went even further, saying that if there was anyone at all in

---

[75] BN, NAF 10220, Brice de Rennes, 13 February 1637 (Tripoli), 259.
[76] BN, NAF 10220, Etienne de Châtellerault, 1 December 1637 (Babylon), 224.

their community – if even just one woman – who did not want them to preach in their church, he would not do so … . There were four priests present of whom two had been persuaded by other clerics to try and prevent our Fathers from preaching, but they did not dare to oppose us publicly and formally [in such circumstances]. All the common people declared loudly that they wanted us to preach, so Father Juste left, having agreed all of these arrangements.[77]

On this basis, the Capuchins continued to preach at weekly services for the Maronites in Aleppo. One can only speculate what local priests made of this brazen behaviour, but as Michel-Ange de Nantes noted with glee in another letter, 'no one dared challenge the authority of their patriarch in this regard'.[78]

At the same time, references to preaching should be understood as a sort of shorthand for a wide spectrum of forms of participation that the Capuchins used to make themselves omnipresent in the devotional lives of Ottoman Christians. They attended local liturgies; they were present at local funerals; they even sought opportunities to live in the residences of the higher clergy.[79] Writing from Aleppo in January 1634, Michel de Rennes described how he had gradually established himself as the confessor to one of the bishops of Aleppo whilst he continued to study Arabic: he hoped, thereby, to give 'some of the first rudiments of our faith to many people, both the notables and the lowly'.[80] This strategy also applied to the laity, with whom marks of 'good affection' were frequently reported.[81] Michel-Ange de Nantes summed up the situation well when he wrote from Mosul in 1638 that 'These people hold us in such high affection that they want us to bless their houses and they stop us on the road to take us into their houses. … We move with much ease among them'.[82]

---

[77] BN, NAF 10220, Etienne de Châtellerault, 1 December 1637 (Babylon), 231.

[78] BN, NAF 10220, Michel-Ange de Nantes and Charles François d'Angers, 28 March 1638 (Mosul), 281.

[79] See, for example, Michel-Ange de Nantes's description of the 'good affection' he had developed with them in his letter dated 24 January 1633 (Aleppo), 123. Some months later, Michel-Ange de Nantes wrote of his desire to travel and 'reside' with the Armenian patriarch in Mesopotamia: BN, NAF 10220, 12 May 1633 (Aleppo), 133.

[80] BN, NAF 10220, Michel de Rennes, 15 January 1634 (Aleppo), 185.

[81] BN, NAF 10220, Michel-Ange de Nantes, 24 January 1633 (Mosul), 123.

[82] BN, NAF 10220, Michel-Ange de Nantes and Charles François d'Angers, 28 March 1638 (Mosul), 290.

In the areas of language study, the production of manuscripts, and everyday devotions, therefore, the Capuchins' efforts were aimed at achieving a single goal: the cultivation of personal relationships with and above all proximity to Ottoman Christians. This desire for proximity was also a function of the fact that the missionaries relied – in a material sense – on local communities for financial resources, political support, access to markets, and even for the provision of buildings and accommodation in which to live. Christian Windler has shown, for a different context, the extent to which Carmelites relied on local economies for a good portion of their livelihood.[83] Although we lack the sort of account books that would provide such a level of detail for the early Capuchins, the theme of their reliance on charity is an oft-repeated topic in the correspondence. Writing from Babylon in 1638, for example, Etienne de Châtellerault shared with Raphael de Nantes in Brittany the stories that were circulating about Juste de Beauvais, one of the earliest missionaries to establish himself in Baghdad in 1628. He was reputed to have spent an entire year living with the poor, begging for alms, and relying on the charity of Ottoman Christians and even the local Ottoman pasha.[84] Ten years later, another missionary, Gabriel d'Alençon in Beirut, would still write, with admiration, that the mission in Baghdad continued to depend entirely on alms.[85] Not only a reflection of local realities, these claims also made for effective rhetoric in the circulars that were regularly sent across Europe to raise funds for the Capuchins from Catholic patrons.

The dependence on local communities extended even to a reliance on political support from Ottoman officials and local elites. Because the political fortunes of such notables could change rapidly, the early Capuchins experienced a distinct form of precarity that exposed them to local intrigues, factionalism, and the complicated relations that linked provinces back to the imperial capital in Istanbul. The earliest Capuchins to arrive in Beirut, for example, had quickly endeared themselves with Fakhr al-Din al-Maani, the local Druze emir of Mount Lebanon. However, all this changed in 1633 when Fakhr al-Din was arrested under suspicion of planning a rebellion against

---

[83] Windler, *Missionaries in Persia*, 235–51.
[84] BN, NAF 10220, Etienne de Châtellerault, 8 October 1638 (Babylon), 306–8, for a fascinating biographical sketch of Juste de Beauvais's arrival in Baghdad.
[85] BN, NAF 10220, Gabriel d'Alençon, 2 October 1639 (Beirut), 377.

the Ottoman state.[86] It would take years for those seen as allies of Fakhr al-Din to recover from his fall from grace, including the Capuchins, some of whom had also been arrested and transferred with him to Istanbul. Likewise, the correspondence is full of countless stories of the complicated challenges that faced the early Capuchins when it came to navigating local politics. Importantly, these political circumstances differed from one location to another, meaning that accumulating local knowledge in one place did not necessarily translate into progress in another. Far from the courtly rhythms of the imperial capital in Istanbul, the learning curve for Capuchins in this period was very steep indeed.

This precarity may explain why so little reference to the topic of conversion is made in NAF 10220. The word itself is rarely used by any of the letter-writers; nor do the letters contain the regular reports of numbers of converts that one finds, for example, among the writings of Carmelites in this period.[87] In some ways, this silence may reflect the extent to which the early Capuchins struggled to make sense of what exactly it meant to convert people who were, ostensibly, already Christians. Here the correspondence suggests a mix of the facile and the confused, at any rate certainly nothing that can be identified as a coherent Capuchin 'approach' to conversion. Some missionaries in this period imagined a sort of top-down conversion of Ottoman Christians. Michel-Ange de Nantes wrote in 1635 that:

> if we win a Patriarch, and his clerics, then we win all the people who are submitted to him, because each church having its own bishop in this country, new bishops are only made from their clergy [who are already submitted to them]. If we win the youth, we win everything.[88]

Others reported initial success in developing good relationships with local Christians, but they wondered where to go from there. Writing from Tripoli in 1640, Gabriel d'Alençon reflected on these challenges: having described the 'good affection' he had developed with the Syrian Orthodox community in Tripoli, many of whom affirmed that they

---

[86] See, for example, the references to the Druze emir in BN, NAF 10220, letters at 109, 111, 139, 142, 197 and 437. Several biographies of Fakhr al-Din are available in Arabic; for an introduction in French, see Michel Chebli, *Fakhreddine II Maan, prince du Liban (1572–1635)* (Beirut, 1984).

[87] Bernard Heyberger, 'Les chrétiens d'Alep (Syrie) à travers les récits des conversions des missionaires Carmes Déchaux (1657–1681)', *Mélanges de l'école française de Rome* 100–1 (1988), 461–99.

[88] BN, NAF 10220, Michel-Ange de Nantes, 10 March 1635 (Aleppo), 203–4.

accepted the supremacy of the pope, he wrote to Raphael de Nantes for further advice on what he should do next.

> I want to know your advice on the matter. Are they obliged to leave their sect, or can they receive the sacraments of their priests while acknowledging nonetheless the sovereignty of the Roman Pontiff and all that is believed and taught by the Roman Church? And must we absolve as heretics those who come to us and say that they have never had any differences between us and them?[89]

These anxieties point to the early signs of a set of doubts and questions that would develop decades later into what Cesare Santus has demonstrated to be full-fledged debates about *communicatio in sacris*, that is, the participation of Catholic converts in the rituals and ceremonies of their traditionalist communities.[90]

Beyond conversion, very little attention was given to the subject of church union, which would become an important priority in later Catholic missions to Eastern Christianity. In some ways, this is unsurprising given that the Capuchins, unlike the Jesuits, were not known for their contributions to theological debate or their knowledge of church history. Instead, the correspondence shows that Capuchins focused their efforts mainly on persuading the higher clergy to accept the authority of the pope in Rome.[91] Writing from Tripoli in 1640, Gabriel d'Alençon reported that he had met with the Greeks and Syrian Orthodox who had agreed to recognize the pope as 'the sovereign pontiff', even if there were some who, although accepting the pope, wished to remain 'in their own sect'.[92] Likewise, the few accounts of meetings between Capuchins and the patriarchs of specific Christian communities tend to focus either on local matters – for example, obtaining permission to preach – or on the authority of the pope, but rarely on securing 'professions of faith' that would confirm the patriarch's conformity with Roman doctrine.[93] Above all, the reluctance to

---

[89] BN, NAF 10220, Gabriel d'Alençon, 11 March 1640 (Tripoli), 434.

[90] Santus, *Trasgressioni necessarie*; Christian Windler, 'Ambiguous Belongings: How Catholic Missionaries in Persia and the Roman Curia dealt with *Communicatio in Sacris*', in R. Po-chia Hsia, ed., *A Companion to the Early Modern Catholic Global Missions* (Leiden, 2020), 205–34.

[91] BN, NAF 10220, Brice de Rennes, 14 March 1640 (Tripoli), 441.

[92] BN, NAF 10220, Gabriel d'Alençon, 11 March 1640 (Tripoli), 434.

[93] Marie-Hélène Blanchet and Frédéric Gabriel, *L'union à l'épreuve du formulaire. Professions de foi entre églises d'Orient et d'Occident (XIIIe–XVIIIe siècle)* (Leuven, 2016).

engage with issues of union reflected the reality that doing so risked alienating the Capuchins from the very communities to which they were trying to gain access. This awareness created the possibility for disagreements to emerge between the activities of the early Capuchins and expectations placed on them by the *Propaganda Fide*. In March 1638, the Capuchins in Mosul received instructions from Rome encouraging Juste de Beauvais to travel to Rabban Hormizd, the seat of the patriarchate of the Church of the East, in order to persuade the Nestorians to agree to a union with Rome.[94] Juste de Beauvais preferred instead to remain in Baghdad as his companions tried to explain to *Propaganda* officials in Rome:

> We have taken the view that to effect a union, it is more important to know them [the Nestorians], to win their friendship and thereby to render them more open ['plus facile'] to the idea [of union]. Otherwise, if those who have never met us and who do not know us well find that we speak immediately about union, we will be pushed away rather than advanced [in our work].[95]

In other words, the very act of bringing Eastern Christians closer to Rome risked being counter-productive: it could result in the Capuchins' being pushed to the margins of the local societies in which they lived. This may be why some missionaries in this period looked for less explicit ways to facilitate the conformity of Eastern Christians with Roman doctrine, for example through the translation of Roman canon law into Arabic.[96]

V. Conclusion

Standing in Europe, it is rather easy to be taken in by the story of a global, triumphant Catholicism that drew the margins of the world into a centre of gravity based around Rome. However, listening to the voices of Capuchins in the letters they sent to one another, one is forced to wonder: where is the centre; where are the margins; and

---

[94] BN, NAF 10220, Michel-Ange de Nantes and Charles François d'Angers, 28 March 1638 (Mosul), 282.

[95] Ibid.

[96] For the example of the Discalced Carmelite Johannes Petrus a Matre Dei, see Herman G. B. Teule, 'The Shining Lamp: An Arabic Florilegium of Conciliar Texts', in Emiliano Fiori and Bishara Ebeid, eds, *Florilegia Syriaca: Mapping a Knowledge-Organizing Practice in the Syriac World* (Leiden, 2023), 365–80.

indeed, who decides which is which? This article has suggested that traditional models of centres and peripheries – constructed around as yet unrefined ideas of geography and distance – are not suitable for recovering the actual experience of mobility as lived by Capuchins in the earliest years of their mission to the Ottoman empire. Through epistolary communication, individual Capuchins felt themselves part of a global order based in Brittany even whilst they focused their daily lives on finding a place at the centre of Ottoman Christian communities. No matter where they were in the Ottoman empire, they developed a distinct sense of the specificity of place. This was also, we must remember, only one of several competing views of what mission should look like in the Ottoman empire, nor is it a foregone conclusion that other orders would act in the same way, be they Franciscans, Jesuits or Carmelites. Whatever the case, modern historians need to incorporate ideas of specificity more effectively into our understandings of the shape, scale and places of 'global Catholicism'. When we do so, we may well find that the margins are in our minds, if they are there at all.

Perhaps the greatest sign of the confidence the early Capuchins felt in their place in the world comes from some of the last letters in the collection. Writing from Mosul in 1640, Michel-Ange de Nantes reports an encounter with a local priest whom he had met on the road. The priest asked him:

> To what end do you seek to persuade our Patriarch of your lies? .... Why are you trying to seduce us away from our religion and obedience to our patriarch in order to impose on us the law and religion of the Franks? Truly, you act in this way as if we do not already have our own shepherds and bishops to look after our salvation.[97]

Months later, Michel-Ange de Nantes reported another encounter with a man who spoke even more directly when he asked him in the presence of the patriarch: 'When will you leave this city?'. To this question, the Capuchin's response was deceivingly straightforward: 'If we ever do leave, there will be others who come in our place.'[98] This reply betrays little sense of a man who felt himself to be on the margins, far from the centre of Christianity. Instead, Michel-Ange de Nantes seems convicted of his rootedness and permanence, if not for himself

---

[97] BN, NAF 10220, Michel-Ange de Nantes to the *Propaganda Fide*, 22 May 1640 (Mosul), 479.
[98] BN, NAF 10220, Michel-Ange de Nantes to the *Propaganda Fide*, 8 July 1640 (Mosul), 483.

than certainly on behalf of his order. His was a community that had its centre not in Rome, but in the neighbourhoods of Brittany, where he and his compatriots shared childhoods, memories, and sometimes even families, long before they ever arrived in the Ottoman empire.

In so much as this article is based only on the voices of Capuchins, further research remains to incorporate alongside these voices the perspectives of Ottoman Christians themselves. When we do so, we come into direct contact with communities of Eastern Christians who regarded themselves, if not as the centre of Christianity, then at least as autonomous Christians, each with their own independent visions of their place in the world. Here at the level of everyday life in communities scattered across different localities in the Ottoman empire, we begin to glimpse the possibility of a third way of imagining the 'missionary theatre' of the Ottoman empire: not a world of Eastern Christianity suspended in time on the margins of Western Christendom, nor simply another stage for the performance of global Catholic ambitions, but rather what Peter Brown has called, in a different context, a series of 'little Romes', that is, an archipelago of communities, each with its own particular set of priorities, worldviews and aspirations.[99] For some of these 'little Romes', friendship and proximity with Roman Catholicism was a path they were willing to explore so long as they could do so on their own terms. This was something that was well understood by the earliest Capuchins who lived in their midst, trying day after day to carve out for themselves a secure place in these other worlds.

---

[99] Peter Brown, *The Rise of Western Christendom: Triumph and Diversity, A.D. 200–1000*, 10th edn (London, 2013; first publ. 1996), xxvii.

'We are at the furthest part of the inhabited world': Venetian Greeks and the English Reformations

Anastasia Stylianou ⓘ

University of Oxford

This article examines encounters between Venetian Greeks and English reformers, c.1545–c.1700, focusing on two figures, Andronikos Noukios alias Nikandros (c.1500–c.1556) and Kyrillos Loukaris (1572–1638), and their textual afterlives. It is the first study to examine the role the Venetian empire played in Greek Orthodox contacts with the Church of England during the early modern period. In doing so, it takes an under-utilized approach to studying early modern encounters between Eastern and Western Christianities, bringing the field of religious history into direct dialogue with that of bibliographical history to extend our understanding of the long-term intellectual and religious impact of specific episodes of encounter. It argues that Anglo-Hellenic religious contacts were shaped by a shared sense of operating on the peripheries of power, but also limited by the mutual perception of the other as intriguing but inferior, or of marginal importance.

Venetian Greeks and English Protestants represent two religious and ethnic groups who could be seen, in different ways, as operating on the margins of early modern European history. Yet an examination of interactions between these two communities has potential to shed new light on the unfolding of the Reformations. Relatively little work exists exploring Anglo-Greek religious encounters in this period,[1] and no

Department for Continuing Education, University of Oxford, Oxford, UK. E-mail: anastasia.stylianou@conted.ox.ac.uk.

I am grateful to Cambridge University Library for the award of the Munby Fellowship in Global Bibliography, St John's College, Cambridge, for a Visiting Fellowship, and the Leverhulme Trust for an Early Career Fellowship. These awards enabled me to conduct the research presented in this article.

[1] The main recent studies are Judith Pinnington, *Anglicans and Orthodox: Unity and Subversion, 1559–1725* (Leominster, 2003); Peter M. Doll, ed., *Anglicanism and Orthodoxy: 300 Years after the 'Greek College' in Oxford* (Oxford, 2006); Anastasia Stylianou, 'Textual Representations of Greek Christianity during the English Reformations', *Journal*

Studies in Church History 61 (2025), 360–383 © The Author(s), 2025. Published by Cambridge University Press on behalf of the Ecclesiastical History Society. This is an Open Access article, distributed under the terms of the Creative Commons Attribution licence (http://creativecommons.org/licenses/by/4.0), which permits unrestricted re-use, distribution and reproduction, provided the original article is properly cited.
doi:10.1017/stc.2024.43

study focuses specifically on the impact of the Venetian empire on the nature and direction of Greek Orthodox relations with the English church. This is a significant lacuna. The Venetian empire was home to the second largest population of Greek Christians after the Ottoman empire, which in this period included Greece. Moreover, Venice – occupying a liminal position between 'East' and 'West' – played a critical role in mediating Greek contacts with Western Christianity, and English dialogue with Eastern Christianity.

This article has three main objectives. First, it seeks to rebalance early modern historiography on Anglo-Greek religious encounters by highlighting the role of the Venetian Greek community. Secondly, in response to the wider subject of this volume, the article examines the concept of marginality, asking how far the course of Anglo-Hellenic religious relations was shaped by Greek and English Christians' experiences of – and fears about – being marginalized. Thirdly, it approaches the study of early modern encounters between Eastern and Western Christianities by bringing the field of religious history into direct dialogue with that of bibliographical history. While there has been excellent work on Greek involvement in manuscript and book production in Venice,[2] and there is increasing scholarly interest in Eastern Christian contacts with the West,[3] there are surprisingly few studies examining Greek books as a site for cross-confessional encounters.[4] This

---

of Medieval and Early Modern Studies 53 (2023), 25–54; Colin Davey, *Pioneer for Unity: Metrophanes Kritopoulos (1589–1639) and Relations Between the Orthodox, Roman Catholic and Reformed Churches* (London, 1987); John Penrose Barron, *From Samos to Soho: The Unorthodox Life of Joseph Georgirenes, a Greek Archbishop* (Oxford, 2017).

[2] See, *inter alia*, Rosa Maria Piccione, ed., *Greeks, Books, and Libraries in Renaissance Venice* (Berlin, 2021); Evro Layton, *The Sixteenth-Century Greek Book in Italy: Printers and Publishers for the Greek World* (Venice, 1994); Deno J. Geanakoplos, *Greek Scholars in Venice: Studies in the Dissemination of Greek Learning from Byzantium to Western Europe* (Cambridge, MA, 1962).

[3] See, *inter alia*, the work of John-Paul Ghobrial, such as 'Migration from Within and Without: The Problem of Eastern Christians in Early Modern Europe', *TRHS* 27 (2017), 153–73; that of Sam Kennerley, such as *Rome and the Maronites in the Renaissance and Reformation: The Formation of Religious Identity in the Early Modern Mediterranean* (Abingdon, 2022); and that of Richard Calis, such as 'The Impossible Reformation: Protestant Europe and the Greek Orthodox Church', *P&P* 259 (2023), 43–76.

[4] Nil Palabiyik, 'The First Greek Printing Press in Constantinople (1625–1628)' (PhD thesis, Royal Holloway, University of London, 2014), and see also her series of articles on Nikodemos Metaxas' printing venture, such as 'Redundant Presses and Recycled Woodcuts: The Journey of Printing Materials from London to Constantinople in the Seventeenth Century', *Papers of the Bibliographical Society of America* 110 (2016), 273–98. Palabiyik's work has been pioneering in drawing together these two historiographies.

article argues that examining textual afterlives (in terms of evidence of both ownership and usage) extends our understanding of early modern contacts between Eastern and Western Christianities. In this particular case, without considering such textual afterlives, one might conclude that Anglo-Hellenic religious contacts in the Reformation era comprised, essentially, a series of interesting encounters between individuals with little lasting impact. However, looking at how these encounters were memorialized in manuscripts and published books, and considering who collected these texts, demonstrates that these episodes of direct contact had longer-lasting and unexpected repercussions.

The article focuses on case studies of two individuals: Andronikos Noukios, alias Nikandros (c. 1500–c. 1556), and Kyrillos Loukaris (1572–1638). Both were unusual among their Greek contemporaries in the extent of their contacts with England and in the degree of their appreciation of English Christianity, which was probably shaped by their cosmopolitan experiences in Venice. More documentary evidence survives concerning Nikandros's and Loukaris's contacts with England than for most other Venetian Greeks of the period, and yet both remain enigmatic and contradictory figures. Scholars have struggled to discern exactly what the two men really thought of the English church, or of Protestantism more generally. Nikandros and Loukaris are also significant because of their textual legacy, which resulted in a long afterlife in Anglo-Greek religious relations. The two figures have not hitherto been directly compared. There is a wealth of scholarship on Loukaris, the most prominent figure in Anglophone scholarship on the early modern Greek church.[5] In contrast, Nikandros has received more limited scholarly attention, generally within the field of Venetian bibliographical history,[6] although John Muir's recent translation of Nikandros's autobiography into English will doubtless introduce him to a wider scholarly audience.[7] A direct comparison between the two figures, standing respectively at the beginning and end of the Reformation period, highlights the impact of the Reformations and of Northern European proto-imperialism upon Greek individuals' religious

---

[5] See the historiographical survey in Calis, 'Impossible Reformation', 45–7.

[6] Layton, *The Sixteenth-Century Greek Book*, 421–3; Piccione, ed., *Greeks, Books, and Libraries*, 18, 179, 314. There are also some older works on Nikandros as a Greek visitor to England, such as David E. Eichholz, 'A Greek Traveller in Tudor England', *Greece and Rome* 16/47 (1947), 76–84.

[7] John Muir, *Greek Eyes on Europe: The Travels of Nikandros Noukios of Corfu* (Abingdon, 2022).

identity, textual outputs and – above all – the nature of their contacts with the West.

BEGINNING WITH BOUNDARIES

An analysis of Greek Christianity calls into question many unconscious assumptions in early modern studies about boundaries, identities and peripheries. While scholarship has recognized the importance of the protracted Venetian-Ottoman conflict over Mediterranean territory in defining the shifting boundaries of Europe and 'the East' from the fifteenth to seventeenth centuries, the experiences of the inhabitants of the Greek islands and mainland coastal settlements, who suffered extended periods of violence, and the protracted refugee and migrant crisis across Europe have largely been overlooked. Similarly, although there are many works on English relations with the Ottoman empire,[8] no full-length study has explored English contacts with one of the empire's largest ethno-religious minority groups, the Ottoman Greek population. Similarly, among the many Anglophone works on Venice, only a handful focus on the Venetian empire's largest ethno-religious minority,[9] and none specifically on English contacts with the Venetian Greek community.

We need to recognize at the outset that Greek individuals' religious identity could be nuanced, and historians must be wary of drawing too firm a line between Catholic and Orthodox: intermarriage and even inter-communion were not uncommon, and confessional identity could be mutable.[10] The Greek population in the Ottoman empire was nominally almost entirely Orthodox, but Catholic missionaries sought – and sometimes found – opportunities to persuade Greek

---

[8] See, for example, Gerald MacLean, *Looking East: English Writing and the Ottoman Empire before 1800* (Basingstoke, 2007); Nabil Matar, *Turks, Moors & Englishmen in the Age of Discovery* (New York, 1999).

[9] The most significant recent work being Ersie C. Burke, *The Greeks of Venice, 1498–1600: Immigration, Settlement and Integration* (Turnhout, 2016).

[10] Consider, for example, Joseph Georgirenes: see Barron, *From Samos to Soho*, esp. 1–4. For further analysis of the complexity of Eastern Christians' confessional identities, see Cesare Santus, *Trasgressioni necessarie: Communicatio in sacris, coesistenza e conflitti tra la comunità cristiane orientali (Levante e Impero ottomano, XVII–XVIII secolo)* (Rome, 2019), particularly chapter five examining the case of the Ionian islands, 241–302; Bernard Heyberger, 'The Westernisation and Confessionalisation of Christians in the Middle East: An "Entangled History"', in Aurélien Girard et al., eds, *Middle Eastern and European Christianity, 16th–20th Century: Connected Histories. Essays by Bernard Heyberger* (Edinburgh, 2023), 163–81.

individuals and communities to enter into some degree of union with Rome, and many Ottoman Greek clergy benefitted from a Catholic education in Italy.[11] The confessional status of the Greek community in the Venetian empire was complex and contentious throughout the early modern period. Contemporaries and historians alike have disagreed over where to place the emphasis.[12] Were the Venetian Greeks essentially Eastern-rite Roman Catholics, or (sometimes-Nicodemite) Greek Orthodox? The answer depends on the region, period and individual in question.

In Venice itself, in the early sixteenth century, the state gave the city's Greek population permission to construct their own church in which they would worship according to the Greek rite; in accordance with the terms of the union of the Council of Florence (1439), this was under the pope's direct jurisdiction.[13] In the later sixteenth century, growing tensions between the papacy and Venice (including its Greek population) led to the state's creation of the Greek Metropolitanate of Venice: the Metropolitan of Philadelphia was responsible for most Greek Orthodox Christians in the Venetian empire and was ordained by the ecumenical patriarch. This gave the Greek population in the Venetian empire a greater degree of independence from the Roman Catholic Church, though close cooperation with the Venetian Catholic and state authorities remained necessary.[14] The Interdict crisis of 1606–7 raised the fleeting possibility of some form of union between a Venetian Catholic church separated from the papacy and the Venetian Greek church; indeed, reformist theologian Paolo Sarpi opened discussions with the Greek archbishop, Gabriel Severos, to that end. With the resolution of the Interdict crisis, however, such hopes largely faded away.[15]

---

[11] Molly Greene, *The Edinburgh History of the Greeks, 1453 to 1768: The Ottoman Empire* (Edinburgh, 2015), 139–45.

[12] For differing perspectives see, for example, Burke, *Greeks of Venice*, 113–42; Molly Greene, *Catholic Pirates and Greek Merchants: A Maritime History of the Mediterranean* (Princeton, NJ, 2010), 67–73; Caterina Carpinato, 'Venice in the Time of Gavrill Seviros (before 1540–1616): People, Books, Languages and Images. Dialogue with Greeks (and with Greek)', in Piccione, ed., *Greeks, Books, and Libraries*, 15–32.

[13] Burke, *Greeks of Venice*, 120–34.

[14] Ibid. 134–42; Greene, *Catholic Pirates*, 70–2.

[15] Vittorio Frajese, 'La via greca allo stato moderno: Seviros e la politica ecclesia di Sarpi', in Dimitris G. Apostolopulos, ed., *Gavriil Seviros arcivescovo di Filadelfia a Venezia e la sua epoca* (Venice, 2004), 145–59. For the English reaction to this situation, see Stefano Villani, *Making Italy Anglican: Why the Book of Common Prayer was Translated into Italian* (Oxford, 2022), 25.

Venetian Greek Christians, uniquely located on the boundary between East and West, possessed a particular ability to navigate confessional divides and to forge transcultural and even diplomatic networks. Their political marginality made them seem relatively unthreatening, and their tales of sufferings at the hands of both Muslim and Catholic states engendered Protestant sympathies; meanwhile, their extensive mercantile networks meant that they operated within a vast web of Greek trading relationships stretching from the Ottoman empire to Britain. Diego Pirillo has argued that religious refugees 'functioned as …[an] alternative diplomatic network outside of formal channels';[16] as we shall see, this is particularly true of Venetian Greek relations with Protestant Europe. In the case of Greek travellers to early modern Britain, many came as refugees and émigrés in search of patronage from the English state and church, and most left Britain within a few years to seek further opportunities elsewhere. This might lead to the assumption that these Greek figures played only a passive role in domestic affairs and were fairly marginal to international religio-political currents; in fact, Venetian Greek travellers to Britain had a significant, long-term impact upon the religio-political history of the English and Greek-Orthodox churches, and upon intellectual life in Britain and the Ottoman empire.

NIKANDROS

While recent scholarship has highlighted the relative marginality of the Henrician Reformation to religious and intellectual currents on the European continent,[17] works on the English Reformations remain more numerous and better known than those on Eastern Christianity in the sixteenth century, creating in the minds of students and scholars alike an enduringly skewed impression of the English Reformations as central to early modern religious history, and of Eastern Christianity as an obscure and peripheral topic. Given this fact, consideration of Nikandros's autobiographical account of his visit to Britain is important, as it undercuts Anglophone assumptions about the 'marginal', highlighting how concepts of 'peripheries' are inevitably subjective.

---

[16] Diego Pirillo, *The Refugee Diplomat: Venice, England, and the Reformation* (Ithaca, NY, 2018), 4.
[17] Peter Marshall, 'Britain's Reformations', in idem, ed., *The Oxford Illustrated History of the Reformation*, 2nd edn (Oxford, 2017; first publ. 2015), 186–226, at 186–7.

John Muir's recent translation of Nikandros's work is engagingly, and aptly, titled *Greek Eyes on Europe*. This article goes further in asking how Nikandros's particular identity as a Venetian Greek might have shaped his view of the Reformations, especially with regards to England.

Some information about Nikandros's life as a Venetian Greek is essential for understanding his worldview, and for assessing his portrayal of England and its Reformation, and how this was both shaped and limited by mutual perceptions of the other ethnicity and religion as peripheral and alien. Andronikos Noukios, alias Nikandros, was born on Corfu (in the Venetian empire), around the turn of the sixteenth century. He emigrated to Venice in 1537, during the Turkish siege of Corfu, and remained there working as a copyist and in the printing trade.[18] Situated as it was on the cusp between East and West, Venice was not only central to the European trade in Greek manuscripts[19] but was itself 'the European capital of Greek printing'.[20] From 1542 until 1545, Nikandros was the leading editor and proof-reader for the Greek publishing house of Damiano di Santa Maria, whose works were printed by the Nicolini da Sabbio printers.[21] The works he produced included two Greek Orthodox liturgical books – an *Apostolos* in 1542, and a *Typikon* in 1545 – and the first translation of Aesop's fables into modern Greek, in 1543.[22] By 1541, Nikandros was also working in the scriptorium of the Spanish ambassador, Don Diego Hurtado de Mendoza.[23] Don Diego employed around eight Greek scribes, but had a particularly close relationship with Nikandros, whom he housed in the Spanish imperial embassy.[24] Within the city's Greek community, Nikandros played an active role. He was a member of Venice's Greek Brotherhood (*Scuola di San Nicolò*

---

[18] Layton, *The Sixteenth-Century Greek Book*, 421.

[19] Anthony Hobson, *Renaissance Book Collecting: Jean Grolier and Diego Hurtado de Mendoza, their Books and Bindings* (Cambridge, 1999), 72.

[20] Rosa Maria Piccione, 'Greek Books in Renaissance Venice: Methodological Approaches and Research Perspectives', in eadem, ed., *Greeks, Books and Libraries*, 1–12, at 1–2.

[21] For the Greek printing house of Damiano di Santa Maria, see Layton, *The Sixteenth-Century Greek Book*, 421–3, 337; Maria Kostaridou, 'Nikandros Noukios, a Greek Traveller in Mid-Sixteenth Century Europe,' *Journeys* 6 (2005), 3–23, at 6. For the Nicolini da Sabbio printers, see Layton, *The Sixteenth-Century Greek Book*, 28–30, 62–5, 184–7, 402–20.

[22] Layton, *The Sixteenth-Century Greek Book*, 198, 344–5.

[23] Ibid. 421.

[24] Hobson, *Renaissance Book Collecting*, 73.

dei Greci) from 1541 to 1547, serving as its secretary in 1543 and 1547.[25] By 1541, Nikandros had also received the lowest rank of ecclesiastical ordination as a reader for San Giorgio dei Greci.[26]

In 1545, Nikandros encountered an old acquaintance, Gerhard Veltwyck of Revenstein, ambassador to Emperor Charles V, who was on his way to the Ottoman empire to negotiate a truce.[27] Nikandros offered his services to Veltwyck, and, as part of the embassy, travelled first from Venice to Constantinople, and then to the Netherlands, via Germany. Nikandros then joined Veltwyck's embassy to England. When the rest of the embassy left England in 1546, Nikandros remained for a short while, entering into service in a civilian capacity under Thomas of Argos, the commander of a unit of four-hundred Greek mercenaries fighting in Henry VIII's wars against Scotland and France, before travelling back to Italy in 1547. Nikandros subsequently produced a three-volume account of his journey, written in Neo-Greek, which included an account of the Henrician Reformation.[28]

Nikandros's choice of subject matter underlines that, to a Venetian audience of the earlier sixteenth century, England was an intriguingly peripheral place. Nikandros does not describe his travels in the Ottoman empire, claiming that the country is 'known to practically everyone and it is easy to find out about'.[29] In contrast, he promises his friend Cornelius (the dedicatee of Book II) 'a taste of the north and of what lies on the shores of Ocean' (46). For Nikandros, coming from one of Europe's Renaissance capitals, England was intriguingly alien and rather backward. The English are 'barbarians' (50), governed by irrational passions rather than civilised rationality, being greedy and 'given to silly impulses which they cannot restrain and full of suspicion' (51). Even the geography of Britain is strange, the sea surrounding the islands having 'no bounds' and being 'barely known', while the night 'is not as dark as it is with us' (54, 52).

Much of Nikandros' description of Britain, which comprises Book II of his autobiography, is taken up with the Henrician Reformation.

[25] Layton, *The Sixteenth-Century Greek Book*, 421.
[26] Muir, *Greek Eyes on Europe*, 1.
[27] Ibid. 18.
[28] See Nikandros Noukios, *Voyages*, ed. Julius A. de Foucault (Paris, 1962); for an English translation, see Muir, *Greek Eyes on Europe*.
[29] Muir, *Greek Eyes on Europe*, 18. References to Nikandros's autobiography (ibid. 18–120) will hereafter be given in parentheses in the text using Muir's pagination.

This includes an extended, rather sensationalist account of Henry's marriages, exaggerated tales of monastic corruption prior to the dissolution of the monasteries, and the report of the suppression of the cult of the 'rebel' Thomas Becket, all of which suggest that he received his information second-hand from highly partisan sources, and in a rather garbled fashion. Since Nikandros probably spoke no English, and would have spent his time at court with Gerard Veltwyck's embassy, the likely sources for his material would have been educated, Italian-speaking, evangelical-leaning courtiers. These probably included former protégés of Thomas Cromwell, given the number of propaganda tales about England's monasteries and the similarities between Nikandros's justification of the Henrician Reformation and those found in apologetic literature of the 1530s (55–8, 61–6).[30] Nikandros's sympathies clearly lie with the English king: he portrays the pope as unreasonable (57), while Henry – 'an energetic man of noble birth' (57) – is given two lyrical speeches, the first defending the break with Rome (57–8), and the second dissolving the monasteries in the light of their shocking corruption (65–7).

Nikandros's autobiography reveals a broad knowledge of Western Christian confessions, distinguishing between Lutheranism and Anabaptism – and disapproving of both (24, 29) – and noting how they differ from the Henrician Reformation. He also shows an interest in other cultures and faiths, including Judaism (24, 27–8). His worldview was probably influenced by the religiously diverse and highly intellectual circles in which he moved in the Venetian empire. It has been suggested that Nikandros's father, Menandros Noukios, had been the financial patron of an edition of the Orthodox Divine Liturgy directed at Western Christian humanists and intellectuals.[31] Moreover, Nikandros's Venetian employer, Don Diego, was a man of extensive interreligious and intercultural contacts, having excellent Arabic and amassing 153 Arabic manuscripts during his time in Venice, as well as collecting Lutheran books.[32]

While Nikandros's cosmopolitan Venetian background may have made him more interested in other faiths and cultures, his lifelong experience of living as a member of a religious minority within a Catholic empire no doubt shaped his cautious treatment of Catholicism

---

[30] I am grateful to Diarmaid MacCulloch for this insight.
[31] Muir, *Greek Eyes on Europe*, 1; Layton, *The Sixteenth-Century Greek Book*, 547.
[32] Hobson, *Renaissance Book Collecting*, 71, 77, 86–7.

in his writing. Despite the admiration he expressed for Henry VIII's religious reforms, his text is not, overall, anti-papal or anti-Catholic; for example he shows a certain sympathy for the papacy when discussing the sack of Rome (1527), and he describes the Greeks and Italians as sharing the same religion and faith.[33] Nikandros would have been well aware that the Venetian Greek church depended on the papacy. Moreover, Muir argues that Nikandros's formal dedications of his books to particular people suggests that 'he intended publication at some point and was looking for financial backing and support'.[34] If Nikandros did originally aim to publish his work, this would have necessitated particular care in what he said about the Catholic Church. He would probably have been aware, both through his father and his own work with the da Sabbio printing firm that, in 1527, Stefano da Sabbio had been summoned before the Catholic authorities of Venice for printing a *Horologion*, an Orthodox liturgical text, which allegedly contained verses criticizing the Catholic Church. Stefano had, in turn, blamed the work's editor, the Greek Demetrios Zenos.[35] Those involved seem to have escaped lightly, but the episode showed that, although Venice permitted its citizens a remarkable degree of religious liberty compared to most other European states of the period, Greek Orthodox printing in Venice was nonetheless under surveillance from the Catholic Church and that producing material criticizing Catholicism was dangerous.

While Nikandros's visit to England is an unusual episode in sixteenth-century Anglo-Hellenic relations, can it be said to be anything more than a curiosity? It left no apparent impression on English religious life, despite the interest in Greek Christian history and religion displayed by the Henrician apologists of the late 1520s and early 1530s. The Henrician reformers' interest was in the glorious precedent of Byzantium, a caesaropapist empire that had stood in opposition to Rome;[36] contemporary Greek Venetians served no apologetical purpose, seeming in almost every way Italian, and often having sad tales to tell of living out their lives as refugees or émigrés (36), in awkward cooperation with the Venetian Catholic regime.

Equally, Nikandros's visit to England seems to have had limited direct impact on his own religious beliefs, and no obvious impact on

---

[33] Stylianou, 'Textual Representations', 36.
[34] Muir, *Greek Eyes on Europe*, 8.
[35] Layton, *The Sixteenth-Century Greek Book*, 404.
[36] Stylianou, 'Textual Representations', 27–9.

the Venetian Greek community more widely. In 1547, the Greek brotherhood sent Nikandros as their representative to intercede with Pope Paul III in an attempt to lift the bull of 6 March 1543 that restricted the religious freedoms granted to the Venetian Greeks. Nikandros, for all his praise of England's break with Rome, was highly successful in his mission to restore a peaceable relationship between the papacy and the Venetian Greek church.[37] His final literary effort, Τραγωδία εἰς τήν τοῦ Αὐτεξουσίου ἀναίρεσιν (*Tragōdia eis tēn tou Autexousiou anairesin*), in 1551,[38] was a Greek translation and adaptation of a 1546 anti-papal satire, *A Tragedy on the Refutation of Free Will*, by the Italian Protestant Francesco Negri of Bassano.[39] This contrasts strangely with his 1547 mission to Rome, but it may be that he was primarily interested in the topic of free will. It perhaps suggests that his time in England sparked an interest in Reformation thought. His translation seems, however, to have remained unpublished.[40]

It is through the textual afterlives of his (also unpublished) autobiographical account of his European travels that Nikandros's encounter with proto-Protestantism had longer-lasting cross-confessional influence. One copy belonged to Don Diego.[41] Given that it contains only Books I and II, it may have been copied before Nikandros had finished writing Book III. This suggests the intriguing possibility that Nikandros gave the manuscript to Don Diego during his 1547 embassy to Rome. If so, the manuscript's up-to-date survey of the Reformations in Germany and England, and the reasons for England's break with Rome, may have been of particular interest to Don Diego, who had become Spanish ambassador to Rome that year.[42] The work, perhaps because of its carefully ambiguous treatment of Roman Catholicism, subsequently survived the Spanish Inquisition's censorship of Don Diego's library in the 1570s, and was later bequeathed – along with the bulk of Don Diego's books – to Philip II's library at the El Escorial.[43] Thus, one copy of the only work by a sixteenth-century Greek Orthodox author to describe the early Reformations in Germany

---

[37] Layton, *The Sixteenth-Century Greek Book*, 421.
[38] Ibid. 422; Muir, *Greek Eyes on Europe*, 3.
[39] Francesco Negri of Bassano, *Della tragedia intitolata libero arbitrio* (Basel, 1546).
[40] Layton, *The Sixteenth-Century Greek Book*, 422.
[41] Madrid, Escorial, MS Scorialensis Ψ.iv.16, fols 42–119; Muir, *Greek Eyes on Europe*, 13.
[42] Hobson, *Renaissance Book Collecting*, 80–2.
[43] Ibid. 86–7.

and England found its way into the library of 'the Most Catholic King of Spain'.

Meanwhile, another copy of Books I and II found its way into very different hands, belonging by 1637 to Archbishop William Laud.[44] We know that Laud had a strong interest in Greek Christianity, collecting Greek manuscripts, dispensing patronage for the printing of Greek texts, and engaging in correspondence with leading figures in the Greek Orthodox Church.[45] However, paradoxically, Laud's marginal notes in Nikandros's text are suggestive of the limits of English interest in Greek Christianity. Laud seems to have read Nikandros simply as an eyewitness source for sixteenth-century British and German religious history, rather than engaging with the text as a Greek Orthodox perspective on the events of the Reformation. Laud's marginal notes are limited, either functioning as place-markers or taking Nikandros's narrative at face value.[46]

LOUKARIS

While Nikandros's role in Reformation history has been largely overlooked, his Venetian-Greek compatriot Kyrillos Loukaris has received rather more scholarly attention. Yet, as with the case of Nikandros, examining Loukaris's life and legacy through the analytical lenses of marginality and bibliographical history sheds important new light on early modern Anglo-Hellenic religious contacts. Scholarship on Kyrillos Loukaris has long been dominated by two related questions: first, did Loukaris actually write 'his' confession; secondly, was he a 'Protestant patriarch'?[47] Contemporaries in both East and West

---

[44] Oxford, Bodl., MS Laud Gr. 19. Nothing is known of the manuscript's provenance prior to Laud's ownership: Muir, *Greek Eyes on Europe*, 13.

[45] Hugh Trevor-Roper, 'The Church of England and the Greek Church in the Time of Charles I', in Derek Baker, ed., *Religious Motivation: Biographical and Sociological Problems for the Church Historian*, SCH 15 (Oxford, 1978), 213–40.

[46] For example, when Nikandros tells a tale of a monastery of English Franciscans performing a pretend miracle with a mechanical crucifix, Laud writes in the margin, 'A dramaturgical device conceived by one of the Franciscans in England for the sake of gain': Muir, *Greek Eyes on Europe*, 147.

[47] For an overview, see Paschalis M. Kitromilides, 'Orthodoxy and the West: Reformation to Enlightenment', in Michael Angold, ed., *The Cambridge History of Christianity*, 5: *Eastern Christianity* (Cambridge, 2006), 193–202. For a classic proposition, see Hadjiantoniou, *Protestant Patriarch*. For a convincing refutation, see Calis, 'Impossible Reformation'.

hotly debated these questions during Loukaris's lifetime and after his death. This article takes a different approach, assessing the broader impact of Loukaris's contacts with the English church, and asking how far this episode of closer collaboration between the Greek and English churches had a lasting impact on the religious history of either or both nations. It argues that the attempted co-operation stemmed partly from shared fears of being marginalized, yet foundered precisely because the two confessions were, in different sense, operating on the peripheries of power.

The relationship which developed between Loukaris and the Church of England was shaped both by Loukaris's own Venetian background and by the fact that many of his protégés were Venetian Greeks. Although Loukaris spent his ecclesiastical career in the Ottoman empire, he was by birth and upbringing a Venetian Greek: born on Crete in 1572, at the age of twelve he travelled to Italy, where he studied for four years in Venice under the famous Greek scholar and cleric Maximos Margounios, and from 1589 for six years at the University of Padua. Loukaris's Venetian education had a lifelong impact on him. Most obviously, it equipped him with the languages to forge collaborative networks with the Western Protestant powers and to read both Protestant and Catholic texts. Under Margounios's tuition, Loukaris improved not only his Greek but also his Italian and Latin.[48] Additionally, the young Loukaris was probably influenced in his theological worldview by Margounios, who was a leading apologist for Orthodoxy against Catholicism.[49] Loukaris's time at the ethnically diverse University of Padua also would have brought him into direct contact with northern European Protestants, possibly even English students.[50]

Loukaris's eventual election, first to the see of Alexandria and then to that of Constantinople, strengthened ties between the Venetian and Ottoman Greek worlds.[51] Loukaris patronized fellow Venetian Greeks and those with whom he had forged ties while in the Venetian empire. For example, in order to revitalize the Patriarchal Academy of Constantinople, he invited his former classmate at the University of

---

[48] Hadjiantoniou, *Protestant Patriarch*, 9–10, 22.
[49] Kitromilides, 'Orthodoxy and the West', 193.
[50] Hadjiantoniou, *Protestant Patriarch*, 23. See also Jonathan Woolfson, *Padua and the Tudors: English Students in Italy, 1485–1603* (Toronto, 1998).
[51] Greene, *Catholic Pirates*, 71–2.

Padua, the leading neo-Aristotelian thinker Theophilos Korydalleus, to take charge of the school.[52] Similarly, his protégé Nikodemos Metaxas, who attempted to establish a Greek printing press in Constantinople, was from the Venetian-ruled island of Cephalonia, while the second student whom Loukaris sent to study at Oxford – Nathaniel Konopios – was a fellow Cretan.

Loukaris was elected patriarch of Alexandria in 1601,[53] and ecumenical patriarch in 1621,[54] occupying the ecumenical throne until his execution in 1638, nearly seventeen years later. The Ottoman Greek Church faced political, economic and educational limitations and challenges, particularly in comparison both to the status of Islam in the Ottoman empire and to the global power of Roman Catholicism, and Loukaris's chief concern during his patriarchate was the recent arrival among his flock of well-funded and highly-educated Catholic missionaries. In attempting to remedy the risk of religious marginalization, Loukaris looked to Protestant northern Europe for support.[55] By the early 1610s, Loukaris was in correspondence with George Abbot, archbishop of Canterbury from 1611 to 1633.[56]

Through Abbot, King James I communicated an offer to fund four scholarships for the education of Greek students in England. However, this attempted Anglo-Hellenic educational collaboration bore limited fruit: Loukaris seems to have sent just two students, the first, Metrophanes Kritopoulos, studying in Oxford from 1617 until 1622 and then spending a further two years in London under the patronage of Archbishop Abbot; and the second, Nathaniel Konopios, only arriving in England after Loukaris's death.[57] The educational initiative was undermined by differing English and Greek aims. Abbot wished Kritopoulos to socialize almost exclusively with English scholars and clerics to their mutual benefit, and then to return promptly to the Ottoman empire, benefitting the Ottoman Greek Church by his enhanced education and furthering Anglo-Greek relations. Instead,

---

[52] Kitromilides, 'Orthodoxy and the West', 196.

[53] The second-ranking Patriarchal See in the Orthodox Church.

[54] The spiritual leader, as 'first among equals', of the Orthodox Church worldwide, and direct head of the Orthodox Church throughout the Ottoman Empire.

[55] Hadjiantoniou, *Protestant Patriarch*, 51–6.

[56] Davey, *Pioneer for Unity*, 67–8.

[57] Davey, *Pioneer for Unity*, 71–145; William B. Patterson, 'Cyril Lukaris, George Abbot, James VI and I, and the Beginning of Orthodox Anglican Relations', in Doll, ed., *Anglicanism and Orthodoxy*, 39–56, at 51.

to Abbot's disappointment, Kritopoulos spent considerable time and money on helping fellow Greek émigrés in London, including Metaxas's printing ventures.[58] Moreover, Kritopoulos clearly felt that an alliance with the Church of England alone would be insufficient: with Loukaris's support, he travelled home overland through Europe in order to forge connections with other European Protestant churches and with the Greek community in Venice.[59] Kritopoulos's actions led Abbot to conclude that the Greeks were a 'base' nation, and he would 'entreat so well no more of his [Kritopoulos'] fashion'.[60] The educational alliance was hindered by an English belief in the sufficiency of their support, a Greek awareness of the actual limits to English power, and English stereotyping of Greek national character.

Loukaris also tried to use the Anglo-Hellenic alliance to have Greek Orthodox apologetic works printed in London and to establish a Greek printing press in Constantinople. His pro-Catholic Greek opponents had access to printing by exporting texts to Catholic Italy and then importing the printed books, and in 1626 the papacy's global missionary arm, the *Congregatio Propaganda Fide*, also founded a printing press in Rome to publish material for the proselytizing of Eastern Christians.[61] In 1623, under Loukaris's patronage, the Venetian-Greek monk Nikodemos Metaxas travelled to London to learn the art of printing, and Loukaris sent him (via Kritopoulos) various manuscripts to publish.[62] In 1627, Metaxas took back to Constantinople the printing press that he had purchased, along with copies of his published books. Metaxas profited from the protection of the English, travelling to Constantinople on a vessel belonging to the Levant Company, unloading his cargo under the privileges of the English ambassador Sir Thomas Roe,[63] and living in the English ambassador's household.[64] Metaxas's printing press was, however, short lived. In 1628, it was closed by the Ottoman authorities at the

---

[58] Davey, *Pioneer for Unity*, 111–45.

[59] Ibid. 147–228.

[60] Ibid. 131. See also, in this volume, Alex Beeton, '"A true object of Charity": Greek Clergymen in Interregnum Oxford and Cambridge', esp. 386, for a discussion of English generosity and suspicion towards Greek travellers seeking financial aid during the Interregnum.

[61] Hadjiantoniou, *Protestant Patriarch*, 80.

[62] Palabiyik, 'The First Greek Printing Press', 36, 39, 59.

[63] Ibid. 24.

[64] Davey, *Pioneer for Unity*, 272; Michael Strachan, *Sir Thomas Roe, 1581–1644: A Life* (Salisbury, 1989), 172–3.

instigation of the French Jesuits, who alleged that Metaxas was printing material that contained blasphemy against Islam. Although this accusation was found to be false, Metaxas (a Venetian subject) was encouraged by Venice to stop his printing activities and leave Constantinople in order to calm relations between the Orthodox and Catholics there.[65] This was a significant blow to the anti-Catholic faction in the Greek church: once again, no material could be printed by Greeks in the Ottoman empire, while Venetian Greeks were subject to Venetian censorship, meaning that they could not print anti-Catholic apologetics.[66] The fate of Metaxas's printing press highlights the increased religio-political agency available to the Greek Orthodox Church in Constantinople through collaboration with the English, but also the limits of English power in the Ottoman empire.

In 1629, a Latin 'Confession of Christian Faith' was published in Geneva, purportedly authored by Loukaris. The work was heavily Calvinist.[67] In the very same year, an English translation was printed in London by the printer and bookseller Nicholas Bourne.[68] Whether or not Loukaris actually wrote it, the work was certainly a triumph for Loukaris's Protestant supporters. It seemed that the Orthodox Church had finally responded decisively to the Reformations, coming down on the side of the Protestants. However, publication of the confession (whoever its author) backfired: in the short term, it isolated Loukaris from many of his previous supporters, and increased Catholic opposition to him; in the longer term, it pushed the wider Orthodox Church into careful examination of Reformation theology and towards an emphatic rejection of Calvinism in particular, and much Protestant theology more generally.[69]

In 1638, Loukaris's rivals accused him of plotting treason; he was imprisoned by the Ottoman authorities, secretly executed, and replaced

---

[65] Palabiyik, 'The First Greek Printing Press', 26. Venice may have feared that such heated antagonism would spill over to its own territories.

[66] Ibid. 48; Davey, *Pioneer for Unity*, 279.

[67] Kitromilides, 'Orthodoxy and the West', 197.

[68] Cyril Lucaris, *The Confession of Faith of ... Cyrill ... Written at Constantinople, 1629* (London, 1629).

[69] Kitromilides, 'Orthodoxy and the West', 197–202. For discussion of earlier Greek Orthodox engagement with Protestant theology, see Dorothea Wendebourg's study of the dialogue between Constantinople and Tübingen in the late sixteenth century: *Reformation und Orthodoxie: der ökumenische Briefwechsel zwischen der Leitung der Württembergischen Kirche und Patriarch Jeremias II. von Konstantinopel in den Jahren 1573–1581* (Göttingen, 1986).

by his Catholic-backed rival, Kyrillos Kontaris.[70] The English ambassador was outraged, but found himself powerless.[71] The demise of Loukaris highlights the limits of English power and of the Anglo-Hellenic alliance. His death marked the end of a period of unprecedently close relations between the Greek Orthodox Church and the English church. A synod of the Greek church in Constantinople in 1638 deemed the confession heretical and Loukaris a heretic. Subsequent synods of the Orthodox Church in Constantinople (1638, 1642, 1672, 1691), Iaşi (1642), and Jerusalem (1672) did not proclaim Loukaris a heretic, as they did not believe him to have been the confession's true author, but they all condemned the confession itself as heretical. Moreover, two widely accepted Orthodox confessions were produced by Peter Moghila (1640) and Dosietheos, patriarch of Jerusalem (1672), both of which favoured Catholicism in their evaluation of the Western Reformation debates.[72] The English – and Dutch – efforts of the earlier seventeenth century had failed to secure a Protestant-leaning Greek church. The later seventeenth century saw a short-lived rapprochement between the Orthodox and Catholic churches, and a cooler relationship between the English and the Greek Orthodox ones.[73]

A consideration of bibliographical history, however, suggests that the closer religious contacts forged between the Greek Orthodox Church and the Church of England during Loukaris's patriarchate were not entirely transitory. While the high hopes of an enduringly warm relationship between the two confessions were not realized, the period of collaboration had an impact on both churches for the remainder of the seventeenth century, and each kept an increased interest in and knowledge of the other's history and theology. This is revealed by close analysis of the bibliographical impact of the mutual patronage relationships forged between Loukaris and leading English ecclesiastical and diplomatic figures.

The most obvious sustained benefit which the Church of England derived from the close relationship between Loukaris and the English embassy in Constantinople was intellectual. The Stuart period saw a new-found English interest in collecting Ottoman-Greek texts and

[70] Ibid. 199.
[71] Davey, *Pioneer for Unity*, 300–1.
[72] Kitromilides, 'Orthodoxy and the West', 199–201.
[73] Ibid. 201–2.

antiquities. While not generally to the benefit of the Ottoman Greek population, it transformed English libraries, and is an important theme in early modern bibliographical history. During his time in Constantinople, the English ambassador Thomas Roe acquired manuscripts and antiquities for the duke of Buckingham, the earl of Arundel, the archbishop of Canterbury, and for his own private collection.[74] Loukaris proved a particularly useful source of items and information. Roe aimed to export as many rare patristic Greek manuscripts as possible, for publication in England and for the use of English Protestant scholars in their anti-Catholic apologetics. This aim was in line with Loukaris's own goals, and he advised Roe on the choice of manuscripts to send to Archbishop Abbot.[75] Many, such as the now famous Codex Alexandrinus, were given by Loukaris as gifts to the English Crown and church.[76]

To show his gratitude to Oxford, his alma mater, in 1628, Roe donated to the Bodleian Library a collection of twenty-seven Greek manuscripts that he had acquired during his time in Constantinople.[77] Marking a turning point in the library's curation of Greek manuscripts, this was the first collection to be kept separately and numbered as a collection.[78] It includes a wide range of religious texts by both early church and later Byzantine writers, and provided English scholars with rare source material by lesser-known authors such as the twelfth-century theologian Euthymius Zigabenus[79] and the fourteenth-century ecclesiastical historian Nikephoros Kallistos Xanthopooulos.[80] Roe's collection also reveals the close link between the early modern Venetian and Ottoman Greek worlds, and the overlapping nature of English encounters with the two; for example, the Venetian-Greek scribe Georgios Kontis of Cephalonia was commissioned by Roe to produce two compilations of patristic texts.[81]

---

[74] Strachan, *Sir Thomas Roe*, 167–72.

[75] Ibid. 168, 170, 172.

[76] Ibid. 172.

[77] These are Bodl., MSS Roe 1–25 and 27–9. See Henry O. Coxe, *Bodleian Library Quarto Catalogues*, 1: *Greek Manuscripts*, 2nd edn (Oxford, 1969; first publ. 1853), 458–90.

[78] 'Roe Manuscripts', *Bodleian Archives & Manuscripts*, online at: <https://archives.bodleian.ox.ac.uk/repositories/2/resources/9575>, accessed 10 February 2024.

[79] Bodl., MS Roe 7, fols 1–314.

[80] Bodl., MS Roe 3, fols 131–55.

[81] Bodl., MSS Roe 5 and 8. See Coxe, *Greek Manuscripts*, 461, 463. Kontis had also previously owned Bodl., MS. Roe 4, and presumably sold or gifted it to Roe: Coxe, 460–1.

Just as Roe's close relations with Loukaris and the wider Ottoman Greek Church had a significant impact upon the development of English libraries, so too English royal and ecclesiastical patronage of Loukaris's protégé Metrophanes Kritopoulos transformed the library of the patriarchate of Alexandria. Kritopoulos had explained to Abbot that 'in poor, suffering Greece, books are rare'; thus, in the period when their relationship was cordial, Abbot bought him 'out of the shop many of the best Greek authors, and among them Chrysostom's eight tomes … [and] furnished him also with other books of worth, in Latin and in English.'[82] Other friends also gifted printed books: for example, the Royal Librarian Patrick Young presented Kritopoulos with the works of John of Damascus and John Cassian as a mark of friendship.[83] By the end of his time in England, Kritopoulos had amassed enough books to fill four large crates, shipped first from London to Venice, and later to the Ottoman empire.[84] Given the lack of access to printing in the Ottoman empire, these books would have been highly valued. While Kritopoulos collected many further books on his travels home through Western Europe, the impact of the Anglo-Hellenic alliance cannot be overstated, as English royal sponsorship had enabled Kritopoulos to travel to the West to study at Oxford, and his large collection of Western printed works had its origins in his time in England. Kritopoulos's collection equipped the Patriarchal Library of Alexandria and the scholars who used it to evaluate and respond to Reformation controversies and contemporary Western theology. To this day, 265 volumes bearing Kritopoulos's name remain in the library; of these fifty-eight relate to Protestant theology and seventeen to Roman Catholic theology.[85]

The English printing ventures of another of Loukaris's protégés, the Venetian monk Nikodemos Metaxas, also had important consequences for libraries in both England and the Ottoman empire. Metaxas published at least three works during his time in England.[86] These were compendia of writings by later Byzantine and contemporary Greek Orthodox theologians and apologists. His primary aim was to make these texts available to Greeks in the Ottoman empire and he

---

[82] Davey, *Pioneer for Unity*, 114.
[83] Ibid. 131, 137.
[84] Ibid. 140–1.
[85] Ibid, 287.
[86] For discussion of these, see Palabiyik, 'Redundant Presses and Recycled Woodcuts'; idem, 'The First Greek Printing Press'.

exported many copies to Constantinople when he travelled there in 1627.[87] However, my analysis of the ownership marks in copies that can be found today in the libraries of the University of Cambridge highlights that some copies were sold in England, perhaps to cover publishing costs and fund the purchase of the second-hand printing press that Metaxas then took to Constantinople. My research also provides new insights into the circulation of these works in seventeenth-century England, suggesting that Loukaris and Metaxas's printing venture had a long-term impact on English intellectual and religious life, albeit probably an unintended one.

The second work which Metaxas published comprises a collection of tracts by three Orthodox apologists famed for their critical evaluation of Catholicism, namely the fourteenth-century Byzantine theologian Gregory Palamas; the fifteenth-century Ecumenical Patriarch Gennadius Scholarios; and the Venetian Greek humanist (and former teacher of Loukaris) Maximos Margounios.[88] All the tracts in this volume were written in vernacular Greek, and formed part of Loukaris's attempt to improve the religious education of a broader swathe of the Ottoman Greek population. The tracts have separate title pages and pagination, but were intended to be bound together as a single volume.[89] A copy of this printed volume survives in the library of St John's College, Cambridge.[90] The note inside the front cover states that the book was part of the bequest of Thomas Morton. Morton, an alumnus of St John's who went on to hold the bishoprics of Chester, Coventry and Lichfield, and Durham, donated £100 to St John's for the purchase of books in 1628, 1634, 1637 and 1639, along with books from his own library. He was a moderate Calvinist and the author of anti-papal polemic pamphlets, and is it is tempting to wonder whether this Metaxas volume either came from his own library or whether he had a direct hand in its selection. Certainly, by

---

[87] Palabiyik, 'The First Greek Printing Press', 86–124.

[88] Gregory Palamas, Λόγοι ἀποδεικτικοί δύο [*Logoi apodeiktikoi dyo; Two apodeictic orations*]; George Scholarios, Τὸ Σύνταγμα: Ἐπιγραφόμενον, Ὀρθοδόξου Καταφύγιον, [*To Suntagma: Epigraphomenon, Orthodoxou Kataphygion; A treatise called the Orthodox refuge*]; and Maximos Margounios, Διάλογος. Τὰ πρόσωπα, Γραικός κ(αὶ) Λατῖνος, (ἤτοι) Ὀρθόδοξος κ(αὶ) Λατῖνος [*Dialogos. Ta prosōpa, Graikos k[ai] Latinos, [ētoi] Orthodoxos k[ai] Latinos; A dialogue between a Greek and a Latin, or an Orthodox and a Latin*] (London, 1526).

[89] Palabiyik, 'The First Greek Printing Press', 52.

[90] Cambridge, St John's College Library, Ss.5.1(1–2).

the end of the 1630s at the latest, through the printing ventures of Metaxas and Loukaris, the academics and students of a leading Cambridge college had access to a collection of tracts by key Greek Orthodox apologists.

By the early eighteenth century, another of Metaxas's works had also entered into the possession of the University of Cambridge.[91] The work was primarily one of anti-papal apologetics, and contained texts by the Byzantine mystic, Neilos Cabasilas; the fourteenth-century Italian-Greek theologian, Barlaam of Calabria; the sixteenth-century Venetian-Greek theologian, Giorgios Koressios; the recently-deceased patriarch of Alexandria and relative of Loukaris, Meletios Pegas; and the recently-deceased Greek metropolitan of Venice, Gabriel Severos.[92] The copy in question had originally been part of the library of John Moore (1646–1714), bishop of Norwich, the most prolific English book collector of his age. As commemorated in the bookplate at the bottom of the title page, upon Moore's death, together with the rest of his library, it passed to King George I, who bequeathed it to Cambridge University Library in 1715.[93]

Finally, texts relating to Loukaris himself found a ready audience in England for the remainder of the seventeenth century. In northern Europe, he was the best-known Orthodox primate of the early modern period. He also quickly became seen as a martyr and proto-Protestant reformer. In 1680, Thomas Smith, fellow of Magdalen College, Oxford, published *An Account of the Greek Church ... To Which is Added an Account of the State of the Greek Church under Cyrillus Lucaris ... with a Relation of his Sufferings and Death*. This work coincided with an important, but again short-lived, Anglo-Hellenic initiative, in which

---

[91] Cambridge, University Library, Syn.6.62.16.

[92] Meletios Pegas, Περὶ τῆς ἀρχῆς τοῦ Πάπα ... [*Peri tēs arches tou Papa*; *Concerning the primacy of the Pope*]; George Koressios, Διάλεξεις μετά τινος τῶν Φράρων ... [*Dialeksis meta tinos tōn Frarōn*; *A dialogue with a certain Friar*]; Gabriel Severos, Εκθεσις κατὰ τῶν ἀμαθῶς λεγόντων καὶ παρανόμως διδασκόντων ... [*Ekthesis kata tōn amathōs legontōn kai paranomōs didaskontōn*; *Exposition against those who speak ignorantly and teach without permission*]; idem, Περὶ τῆς διαφορᾶς ... [*Peri tēs diaphoras*; *On the difference*]; Neilos Cabasilas, Βιβλία δύο ... [*Biblio dyo*; *Two books*]; Barlaam of Calabria, Λόγος περὶ τῆς τοῦ Πάπα ἀρχῆς ... [*Logos peri tēs tou Papa arhēs*; *A treatise concerning the primacy of the Pope*] (London, 1627?). For further details of these texts, see Palabiyik, 'The First Greek Printing Press', 80–2.

[93] 'The Books that built the Library', *Cambridge University Library*, online at: <https://exhibitions.lib.cam.ac.uk/royal/case/the-books-that-built-the-library/>, accessed 10 February 2024.

a Greek church was established in London between *c.*1676 and 1681, under the patronage of the bishop of London, Dr Henry Compton.[94] By the time Smith's text was completed, the project was foundering, and Smith's preface awkwardly tries to commend the bishop for his pious initiative, while lamenting the likely failure of the project due to the Greeks' ingratitude.[95] The work is interesting as an English revisionist history of Loukaris's reign as ecumenical patriarch, and in revealing a strong deprecating strain in English sentiments towards Greek Orthodoxy by the later seventeenth century. Smith depicts the Greeks as sadly beset not only by Ottoman persecution, but also by 'corruptions and errours … to the great … dishonour of our Holy Religion', in that these 'superstitious rites' have exposed Ottoman Christians to the 'censure and contempt' of their Muslim neighbours.[96] He describes Loukaris as a 'great man' who tried to bring a about 'a Reformation';[97] however, since Loukaris's death, he sees little hope of the Greeks themselves initiating one: the recent synods in the Greek church and their condemnation of Loukaris's confession show that the Greeks 'have of late more than ever been wrought upon by the sly artifices … of the subtile Emissaries of Rome.'[98] The project to found a Greek church in London under Anglican patronage is presented by Smith as an alternative means by which to bring the Greeks closer to the doctrine and worship of the Church of England,[99] which Smith clearly sees as in harmony with the original objectives of the ultimately unsuccessful alliance between Loukaris and the English church in the earlier seventeenth century.

Meanwhile, St John's College, Cambridge, acquired in the mid-seventeenth century a copy of the Swiss theologian Johannes Heinrich Hottinger's *Analecta historico-theologica* (Zurich, 1652).[100] This vast tome of Protestant apologetics includes a very lengthy appendix concerning 'Cyril, celebrated Patriarch of Constantinople, and martyr'. The appendix reproduces Loukaris's confession, and rebuts Orthodox and Catholic criticism of it by including after each chapter of the confession a substantial analysis of supporting

---

[94] See Barron, *From Samos to Soho*, 153–217.
[95] Thomas Smith, *An Account of the Greek Church…* (London, 1680), A4^r.
[96] Ibid. A3^v.
[97] Ibid. A4^v.
[98] Ibid. A4^v.
[99] Ibid. A3^v.
[100] St John's College Library, U.10.19.

evidence found in the patristic Greek Fathers. The text is in Greek and Latin and – given the editor's inclusion of abundant supporting references to scriptural and patristic sources, as well as an account of the life, death and posthumous reception of Loukaris – would have been highly informative for students and academics studying Protestant apologetics, Calvinist theology, or Greek Christian history and theology from the Protestant perspective. In 1653, Robert Metcalfe, an alumnus of St John's and former regius professor of Hebrew at Trinity College, Cambridge, left in his will £100 per year for the purchase of divinity texts by St John's library.[101] A bookplate on the inside of the front cover of St John's copy of the *Analecta* states that it was bought with Metcalfe's bequest, while the handwritten '1653' under the bookplate suggests that the book was bought in the year that Metcalfe's fund was established, and only a year after the book had been published in Zurich. The copy is very well-thumbed and ink-spattered throughout, suggesting that this account of Loukaris's life and martyrdom was well read in subsequent decades.

St John's neighbour, Trinity College, acquired in 1679 a copy of a 1645 edition of Loukaris's confession, possibly printed at Amsterdam.[102] It had come from the private library of one of the college's fellows, James Duport, an eminent Greek scholar and a bibliophile, who left his collection of 2,144 books to the college library upon his death. Duport was more Laudian than Calvinist by inclination and had preached against puritanism throughout the Interregnum; his ownership of the Confession suggests a cross-confessional interest in the text among English clerics and scholars.[103] This is, likewise, indicated by the bequest in 1691 of a copy of Thomas Smith's *An Account of the Greek Church* (1680) to Trinity by former Royalist army officer Sir Henry Puckering, who had a strong dislike for Protestant dissenters and was suspected of Catholic sympathies.[104]

---

[101] 'Robert Metcalfe (1579–1652/3)', *Library & Archives: St John's College*, online at: <https://www.joh.cam.ac.uk/library/special_collections/early_books/metcalfe.htm>, accessed 10 February 2024.

[102] Cambridge, Trinity College, E.79.79[4].

[103] Rosemary O'Day, 'Duport, James (1606–1679)', *ODNB*, online edn (2004), rev. 3 January 2008, at: <https://doi.org/10.1093/ref:odnb/8301>, accessed 10 February 2024.

[104] Cambridge, Trinity College, L.12.76; Jan Broadway, 'Puckering [*formerly* Newton], Sir Henry, third baronet (*bap.* 1618, d. 1701)', *ODNB*, online edn (2004), at: <https://doi.org/10.1093/ref:odnb/20057>, accessed 10 February 2024.

CONCLUSION

'We are here today at the furthest parts of the inhabited world':[105] Nikandros depicts the Greek commander Thomas of Argos as saying these words to his unit of mercenaries fighting for Henry VIII. For Venetian Greeks and the English, each was the 'Other': an intriguing but alien Christian people, inhabiting territories on the peripheries of their known worlds. In a turbulent and changing international landscape, each felt an enduring sense of their own unique ethno-religious importance, and yet also faced issues of political and geographical marginalization. A shared curiosity about each other, and a shared fear of being pushed to the peripheries, were motivating factors in attempts at Anglo-Hellenic religious contact and collaboration. Yet, partly because of a sense on each side that the other's confessional or cultural identity was of secondary importance to their own, such attempts quickly broke down.

This does not mean, however, that such encounters are unimportant to early modern religious and intellectual history. Using bibliographical methodology can unearth new evidence that Anglo-Greek religious contacts in this period had often unexpected but enduring textual legacies. Nikandros's visit to England led to the only Greek eyewitness description of the Henrician Reformation; this account entered into the libraries of Don Diego, the Spanish ambassador to Rome; of Philip II at the Escorial; and of Archbishop William Laud. Meanwhile, English patronage enabled Loukaris to send Kritopoulos to collect books in England, and Metaxas to print several volumes of Greek Orthodox apologetics, while Thomas Roe's warm relationship with Loukaris facilitated English acquisition of precious and rare Greek texts for English libraries such as the Bodleian. Moreover, while English backing of Loukaris ended in disappointment, the patriarch was commemorated as a martyr and proto-Greek-reformer. He lived on in English libraries, private and institutional, and of all confessional stripes: his patriarchate was remembered as unusual, and perhaps unhappily peripheral to the ultimate course of Greek Orthodox history, but it was not forgotten.

---

[105] Muir, *Greek Eyes on Europe*, 75.

'A true object of Charity': Greek Clergymen in Interregnum Oxford and Cambridge

Alex Beeton

The History of Parliament Trust

This article uses the case studies of two Greek clergymen, Anastasius Comnenus and Hierotheos Abbatios, to explore Anglo-Greek interactions and perceptions in early modern England. Both men visited the universities of Oxford and Cambridge in the mid-seventeenth century on fund-raising trips. This article details their time in the universities and in England more widely. It focuses on the issue of charity: who gave them money and why. This approach, making extensive use of new archival material, offers a fruitful perspective on English attitudes to Greek travellers. Suspicion was balanced by philhellenism and a desire to reference the Greek Orthodox Church in confessional or ecclesiastical disputes. These were common trends in early modern Europe, but they were inflected by specific contextual concerns in England. This article also demonstrates that analysing questions of charity can help to recover insights into the decision-making and agency of the early modern Greek traveller.

During the time of the English Commonwealth (1649–53), two Greeks named Hierotheos Abbatios and Anastasius Comnenus visited the new republic.[1] Both were Orthodox priests; both visited the universities of Oxford and Cambridge; and both wanted money, though for different purposes. Abbatios wanted to raise funds for a scheme to promote closer relations between the Protestant and Greek Orthodox churches. Comnenus was attempting to pay the ransom for

The History of Parliament Trust, 18 Bloomsbury Square, London, WC1A 2NS. E-mail: abeeton@histparl.ac.uk.

I am grateful to Eloise Davies, Sarah Mortimer, Anastasia Stylianou, and Studies in Church History's anonymous readers for their comments on various drafts of this piece. I am also very grateful to Alasdair Grant for drawing my attention to Philippus Cyprius's *Chronicon Ecclesiae Graecae*.

[1] The transliteration of their names meant that there was variation in the English spelling of Abbatios and Comnenus. I have followed Keetja Rozemond in using 'Hierotheos Abbatios': Keetja Rozemond, *Archimandrite Hierotheos Abbatios: 1599-1664* (Leiden, 1966). For Comnenus, I have preferred the more common 'Anastasius' to the 'Anastatius' which was occasionally used in English sources.

Studies in Church History 61 (2025), 384–404 © The Author(s), 2025. Published by Cambridge University Press on behalf of the Ecclesiastical History Society.
doi:10.1017/stc.2024.44

several friends who had been kidnapped by pirates from Algiers. Abbatios would leave England after a few months; Comnenus would stay for well over a decade. Although, as is discussed below, both men are known to historians, little has previously been written about their visits to England. This article explores their time in England using a wealth of new archival materials. It focuses on the issue of charity and the questions of who helped the Greek travellers, why, and how the two men presented themselves to an English audience. The fact that they had come from the peripheries of Christian Europe and from Greece specifically shaped English interest in the travellers and their treatment, showing how marginality could influence charitable giving.

This article contributes to a growing body of literature investigating Greek travellers to western Europe. Recent studies of such journeys to the British Isles, mainland Europe and beyond have complemented Jonathan Harris's study from the 1990s on the fifteenth- and sixteenth-century movement of Greeks to the west.[2] The work of John-Paul Ghobrial and Richard Calis in particular has brought to the fore the difficulty of recovering the motivation and identity of the historical traveller who moved through a multiplicity of contexts, often having to assimilate in order to please the particular locality in which they had landed.[3] Such an obscuring of the traveller is unfortunately apparent in any study of the two subjects of this article. The secondary literature on Abbatios and Comnenus is very small; similarly sparse are references to them in primary printed sources or archival collections. A reconstruction of their time in England is therefore comparable to a mosaic formed from numerous tesserae and is reliant on fragments, such as mentions in the account books of educational institutions. Very little can be recovered of their actual motivations.

---

[2] Jonathan Harris, *Greek Emigres in the West, 1400–1520* (Camberley, 1995).

[3] Richard Calis, 'The Impossible Reformation: Protestant Europe and the Greek Orthodox Church', *P&P* 259 (2023), 43–76; John-Paul A. Ghobrial, 'Migration from Within and Without: The Problem of Eastern Christians in Early Modern Europe', *TRHS* 27 (2017), 153–73; idem, 'Moving Stories and What They Tell Us: Early Modern Mobility between Microhistory and Global History', issue supplement 14, *P&P* 242 (2019), 243–80; Alasdair C. Grant, 'Scotland's "Vagabonding Greekes", 1453–1688', *Byzantine and Modern Greek Studies* 46 (2022), 81–97; Sundar Henny, 'Nathanael of Leukas and the Hottinger Circle: The Wanderings of a Seventeenth-Century Greek Archbishop', *International Journal of the Classical Tradition* 27 (2020), 449–72; Efterpi Mitsi, *Greece in Early English Travel Writing, 1596–1682* (Cham, 2017), 17–41. See also, in this volume, Anastasia Stylianou, '"We are at the furthest part of the inhabited world": Venetian Greeks and the English Reformations'.

However, this article suggests that investigating why and how Comnenus and Abbatios came to be seen as worthy recipients of English charity offers a useful new perspective on Greek travellers to England and Anglo-Greek interactions more widely. As the experiences of these two men suggest, Greek travellers were treated with unusual generosity, largely because of English interest in Hellenic studies and in using information about Greek Orthodoxy in confessional or ecclesiastical debates. However, the same sources also suggest underlying suspicion in England about the possibility of deception. As well as revealing English attitudes, this article recovers insights into how Greek travellers, far from their homes, negotiated interactions in unfamiliar settings. As will be shown, Comnenus and Abbatios assuaged English doubts by emphasizing their personal distress, their written credentials, and their position in the Greek Orthodox Church. More generally, charitable records lead to the suggestion that the two men were aware of what their audiences wanted to hear, especially in the context of places of learning, and acted on this knowledge to secure aid and patronage.

This article also makes an important contribution to understandings of Anglo-Greek relations during the seventeenth century. Historians have traditionally focussed their attentions on the early decades of the century when, under the patriarch of Constantinople, Kyrillos Loukaris (1572–1638), the English and Greek Orthodox churches enjoyed warm relations, most evident in the establishing, in 1617, of a scholarship program for young Greek clergymen to be trained in English universities. Scholars have uncovered the motivations and concerns which drove these interactions and emphasized the deep interest of the Church of England in its Greek peer.[4] John Barron's important study on the peripatetic career of a Greek archbishop, Joseph Georgirenes, brilliantly reconstructed the eventful life of his

---

[4] Colin Davey, *Pioneer for Unity: Metrophanes Kritopoulos (1589–1639) and Relations Between the Orthodox, Roman Catholic and Reformed Churches* (London, 1987); W. B. Patterson, 'Cyril Lukaris, George Abbot, James VI and I, and the Beginning of Orthodox-Anglican Relations', in Peter M. Doll, ed., *Anglicanism and Orthodoxy 300 Years after the 'Greek College' in Oxford* (Oxford, 2006), 39–55; idem, *King James VI and I and the Reunion of Christendom* (Cambridge, 1998), 196–219; Hugh Trevor-Roper, 'The Church of England and the Greek Church in the Time of Charles I', in Derek Baker, ed., *Religious Motivation: Biographical and Sociological Problems for the Church Historian*, SCH 15 (1978), 213–40. See also Anastasia Stylianou, 'Textual Representations of Greek Christianity During the English Reformations', *Journal of Medieval and Early Modern Studies* 53 (2023), 25–54.

subject in 1670s England as he successfully fundraised for the foundation of England's first Greek Orthodox church.[5] However, the middle decades of the seventeenth century, during which the British Civil Wars occurred and England became a republic, have been relatively underexplored by historians. As this piece argues, analysing these years reveals that the experiences of Comnenus and Abbatios were comparable to those of other Greek travellers to western Europe, but were inflected by the concerns of mid-century England, including a particularly fervent wave of interest in the propagation of the gospel under the English Commonwealth and later the settlement of the Restoration church.

The first of the two Greeks to reach England was Hierotheos Abbatios (1599–1664). Abbatios arrived in Oxford in July 1649, preceded by a letter of recommendation from the university's chancellor, the earl of Pembroke.[6] As Pembroke explained, Abbatios had 'spent much time and travaile in translating the Confessions of Faith, Catechismes, and the like of the forraigne parts into the Vulgar Greeke, for the benefitt of the Easterne Churches'.[7] He came to England accompanied by 'sundry ample Testimonies from forrayne Universities, professing the Protestant Reformed Religion' and with a wish to visit Oxford 'to see if anything there may be had to the improvement of so pious & glorious a worke'.[8] The work to which Pembroke was referring was Abbatios's translation of the *Ecclesiarum Belgicarum Confessio* (1627) into the Greek vernacular. This was a bilingual Greek-Latin text, which included the *Belgic Confession* (1561), the *Heidelberg Catechism* (1563), and some canons of the Synod of Dordrecht (1618–19).[9] It had been conceived as part of the

---

[5] John Penrose Barron, *From Samos to Soho: The Unorthodox Life of Joseph Georgirenes, a Greek Archbishop* (Bern, 2017), esp. 153–205.
[6] For references to Abbatios in Oxford college account books, all of which are held in archives in Oxford, see Brasenose College Archives, SB Accounts, No. 2, A 2.44, 1650–1, 'Dona et Regarda'; Christ Church College Archives, D&C i.b.3, fols 4, 7; Corpus Christi Oxford College Archives, C/1/1/10, fol. 59ᵛ; Exeter College Archives, RA2/02, July 1649–November 1649; Jesus College Archives, BU:AC:Gen:1, fol. 184; Magdalen College Archives, LCE/29, 1649, expenses inside and outside college; Queen's College Archives, LR C, 1649-1650, 'Custos Forinsecorum'; University College Archives, UC:BU2/F1/1, fol. 236; St John's College Archives, ACC I.A.33, 18 August [1649].
[7] Oxford, Oxford University Archives [hereafter: OUA], NEP/Supra/Reg T, fol. 55.
[8] Ibid.
[9] Vasileios Tsakiris, 'The "Ecclesiarum Belgicarum Confessio" and the Attempted "Calvinisation" of the Orthodox Church under Patriarch Cyril Loukaris', *JEH* 63 (2012), 475–87, at 480–1.

efforts by Kyrillos Loukaris to initiate closer relations between the Reformed and Orthodox churches, and its significance is discussed below.[10] After a short period in Oxford, Abbatios continued to Cambridge and then appears to have left England, reaching Geneva two years later, in 1651, and the Greek island of Cephalonia by 1658.[11]

Abbatios's journey to England was thus one stop in an extended peripatetic period. He had come from Cephalonia, where he had been a monk and abbot. In 1636, he had left the island following an earthquake and begun travelling in order to raise funds to repair damage wrought by the disaster.[12] By 1644, Abbatios had reached the Netherlands, where the States General decided that both he and the sometime metropolitan of Ephesus, Meletios Pantogalos, ought to stay for the winter at the university of Leiden to become acquainted with the Reformed faith before travelling back east.[13] However, the States General subsequently decided that Abbatios should remain in Leiden for another purpose: to translate the *Ecclesiarum Belgicarum Confessio* into vernacular Greek, a work which would be printed at the expense of the States General and could then be distributed throughout the Greek-speaking east.[14] By 1648, Abbatios had finished his project and 1,000 copies had been printed. His hope was to acquire the position of metropolitan in the synod of the churches under the patriarchate of Constantinople so that his translation might be widely circulated. Because ecclesiastical positions were often determined by who could pay the Ottoman authorities the highest amount, such a plan required money which Abbatios failed to raise in the Netherlands.[15] He therefore decided to go on a fundraising tour, equipped with travelling expenses and an honorarium from the States General.[16]

---

[10] Ibid. 475–87.

[11] Rozemond, *Hierotheos Abbatios*, 48. For Abbatios in Cambridge, see the following, which are all held in archives in Cambridge: Christ's College Archives, B.1.10, fol. 129; Clare College Archives, CCAD 2/1/1/3, Michaelmas 1649–Annunciation 1650, general expenses; CUL, GBR/0265/UA/U.Ac.2/1, fol. 752; QC 15, 1648–9; Emmanuel College Archives, Bur.8.2, expenses since the accounts of 19 October 1649; St Catharine's College Archives, L/26, fol. 188^v; St John's College Archives, SJAR/3/2/4/6, fol. 406^v; Trinity College Archives, Senior Bursar's Audit Book, 1637–1659, 1649, fol. 12^r.

[12] For Abbatios's life, see Rozemond, *Hierotheos Abbatios*, esp. 17–49.

[13] Ibid. 23–5.

[14] Ibid. 31–2.

[15] Ibid. 45.

[16] Ibid. 45–8.

It was this fundraising impetus which took Abbatios to Oxford in 1649.[17]

Similarly, seeking funds was the aim of the second Greek clergyman, Anastasius Comnenus (*fl.* 1649–63), described as the 'Governour of the Monastery of Mount Sinai' (that is, St Catherine's Monastery) and also the archbishop of Laodicea.[18] The self-declared cause of his journey was a kidnapping: he and several other Greek priests had been captured and robbed by pirates. Comnenus had been freed, but needed to raise a substantial sum to pay off his ransom and that of those who were still held as hostages 'in Algeers'.[19] By the time he reached England, his mission had taken him across north-western Europe, his testimonials and a brief mention in a near-contemporary work on the Greek church by Philippus Cyprius showing that he had passed through Germany, Sweden and the Netherlands.[20] In England, academic financial records show that he was in Cambridge in October 1651, Oxford in December 1651, London in March 1653, and Winchester College in southern Hampshire later the same year.[21]

There was nothing unusual about requests to university colleges for charity or financial support, but, in the context of collegiate charity, the treatment of Comnenus and Abbatios – both of whom benefited from financial collections at Oxford and Cambridge – is

---

[17] For his preparations, see London, BL, Add. MS 22953, fol. 73ʳ; Oxford, Bodl., Selden Supra 108, fol. 219ʳ.

[18] Gloucester, Gloucestershire Archives, D1086/R23.

[19] Winchester, Winchester College Archives, Bursars' Book, 1644–1671, 1652–3, 'Custus Necessariorum cum Donis'.

[20] *Ecclesiae Londino-Batavae Archivum*, ed. John Henry Hessels, 3 vols (Cambridge, 1887–97), 3: 2213; Philippus Cyprius, *Chronicon Ecclesiae Graecae* (Leipzig, 1687), 489.

[21] For Cambridge (NB all the following archives are in Cambridge), see Clare College Archives, CCAD 2/1/1/3, Michaelmas 1651–Annunciation 1652, general expenses. Clare potentially paid him twice as in September 1651 they made a payment to another 'poor Grecian': ibid., Annunciation 1651–Michaelmas 1651, general expenses. Emmanuel College Archives, Bur.8.2, expenses since the accounts of 2 October 1651; St John's College Archives, SJAR/3/2/4/6, 1650, fol. 25ᵛ. For Oxford (NB all the following archives are in Oxford), see Corpus Christi College Archives, C/1/1/10, fol. 84ʳ; Exeter College Archives, RA2/02, 1651–2; Magdalen College Archives, LCE/29, 1651, expenses inside and outside college; Merton College Archives, SC/MCR/F/1/4/2, fol. 120ᵛ; New College Archives, 988, 18 December 1651; Pembroke College Archives, PMB/D/1/1/1, fol. 4ᵛ; St John's College Archives, ACC I.A.35, fol. 69ᵛ. For London, see Grant, 'Vagabonding Greekes', 90. For Winchester College, see Winchester College Archives, Bursars' Book, 1644–1671, 1652–3, 'Custus Necessariorum cum Donis'.

notable.[22] Abbatios was treated as a distinguished guest, donating a copy of his translation of the *Ecclesiarum Belgicarum Confessio* to the Bodleian Library at Oxford and receiving an impressive £50 from the university.[23] Such a sum easily dwarfed that given to the numerous others who sought charity from the colleges.[24] Irish Protestants, for example, displaced by the bitter fighting begun by the 1641 rebellion of Irish Catholics, came to England in such large numbers during the 1640s and 1650s that the frequent references to them in collegiate account books were usually anonymous, while the amounts they received rarely exceeded a few shillings and pence.[25] The university donations to the two Greeks easily surpassed not only such small contributions, but also the funds offered in more comparable cases such as that of Jan Sictor. Sictor was a Bohemian poet forced into exile after the victory of Catholic forces at the Battle of the White Mountain in 1620. A learned man, Sictor gravitated towards the English universities in search of patronage and charity and was still capable of attracting generous one-off gifts, such as £1 from Merton, in the mid-seventeenth century.[26] Like the Greeks,

---

[22] The collections were raised via colleges, for which see above, nn. 6, 11, 21. I have been unable to find the original orders for the collections in Cambridge, though the fact that such orders were made is mentioned in some of the account book references: see, for example, St John's College Archives, SJAR/3/2/4/6, fols 406ᵛ, (1650) 25ᵛ. The order by Oxford for Comnenus's collection does not survive, for which see Alex Beeton, '"Not Infected with the Venime of the Times": The Rump Parliament and Places of Learning, 1649–53' (DPhil. thesis, University of Oxford, 2022), 299 n. 89.

[23] OUA, NEP/Supra/Reg T, fols 61, 63. Abbatios's donation was not recorded in the Bodleian's book of benefactors: Bodl., MS Lib. recs b. 903. See also, Anthony Wood, *The Life and Times of Anthony Wood*, ed. Andrew Clark, 5 vols (Oxford, 1891–1900), 1: 154–5.

[24] For charity-giving in Interregnum England, and religious refugees in the early modern period more widely, see Jeremy Fradkin, 'Christian Hospitality and the Case for Religious Refuge in Interregnum England', *P&P* 254 (2022), 51–85; Anthony Milton, *England's Second Reformation: The Battle for the Church of England, 1625–1662* (Cambridge, 2021), 339–44; Nicholas Terpstra, *Religious Refugees in the Early Modern World* (Cambridge, 2015).

[25] For example, Exeter College in summer and autumn 1649 recorded giving 2s. 6d. to 'a distressed minister from Ireland' and 1s. 6d. to '2 poore Irish': Exeter College Archives, RA2/02, Expenses for 20 July–2 November 1649. For Irish refugees in England during the 1640s and 1650s, and the often-conflicting emotions they engendered in the English, see Bethany March, '"Lodging the Irish": An Examination of Parochial Charity Dispensed in Nottinghamshire to Refugees from Ireland, 1641–1651', *Midland History* 42 (2017), 194–216.

[26] For donations to Sictor, see Emmanuel College Archives, Bur.8.2, Expenses since the accounts of 17 April 1651; Merton College Archives, SC/MCR/F/1/4/2, fol. 111ʳ; SC/MCR/F/1/4/3, fol. 11ʳ. For Sictor more widely, see William Poole, 'Down and Out

Sictor's prominence, learning and extraordinary origins seem to have led to him receiving financial aid from the universities.[27] However, the collections for the Greeks far exceeded what Sictor and those like him could hope to receive. It seems that many agreed with one of the testimonials to Comnenus, which affirmed that the Greeks were 'true object[s] of Charity'.[28]

The entries in college account books suggest that both were received warmly in the universities. Although it is unclear where either stayed when in the university towns, hospitality may have been provided by well-wishers in the colleges or even by the university authorities. For example, Cambridge University's governing body reimbursed an official £2 'for his carefull attendance upon a Grecian' in 1651.[29] Given the date, this almost certainly refers to Comnenus, suggesting that the university had taken upon itself the duties of providing hospitality for Comnenus during his stay. There are no hints about where Abbatios stayed while in Oxford, but he clearly had links to some well-connected scholars since Christ Church decided 'That the Gretian have 20s: more added to the 10l: formerly given him by this Colledge [presumably as part of the university's collection]'.[30] He also may have been allowed to use Oxford's academic resources and interact with the university community more generally, since the registers of the Bodleian Library for the time Abbatios was in Oxford seem to record a 'Graec[ian]' using library materials.[31] As all this suggests that, in addition to unusually generous collections on their behalf, both Abbatios and Comnenus made friendships while in Oxford and

---

in Leiden and London: The Later Careers of Venceslaus Clemes (1589–1637), and Jan Sictor (1593–1652), Bohemian Exiles and Failing Poets', *The Seventeenth Century* 28 (2013), 163–85; Robert Fitzgibbon Young, *A Czech Humanist in London in the 17th Century* (London, [1925]).

[27] However, see Anthony Milton's discussion of how fundraising efforts in the 1620s for the Palatinate in the Universities of Oxford and Cambridge were affected by the Calvinism and Arminianism of the respective universities: Anthony Milton, *Catholic and Reformed: The Roman and Protestant Churches in English Protestant Thought, 1600–1640* (Cambridge, 1995), 511.

[28] *Ecclesiae Londino-Batavae Archivum*, 3: 2213–14.

[29] CUL, GBR/0265/UA/U.Ac.2/1, fol. 767.

[30] Christ Church College Archives, D&C i.b.3, fol. 7.

[31] Bodl., MS Lib. recs e. 544, fols. 84^v. Subsequent entries in the register record a 'Gr' using records for the period roughly corresponding with Abbatios's time in Oxford: ibid., fols. 85^v-8^v. However, this evidence is far from certain, especially as he is not recorded in the lists of foreign visitors to the university: Bodl., MS Lib. recs e. 533; Bodl., MS Wood E.5.

Cambridge, were given access to university resources, and were treated well by both university and collegiate authorities.

Why did they receive special treatment? In part, their reception in the universities exemplifies interest in Hellenic studies among English academic communities in the early modern period. Curiosity about Greek travellers among western Europeans had a long lineage. Jonathan Harris has suggested that Greek émigrés in the fifteenth and sixteenth centuries were often treated with sympathy and curiosity by western elites due to the latter's growing enthusiasm for their language and culture.[32] Such pro-Greek sentiments remained in force in the seventeenth century, especially its first half when, as Mordechai Feingold has demonstrated, the teaching of Greek boomed at institutions such as Oxford.[33] As Colin Davey's work has demonstrated, the future patriarch of Alexandria, Metrophanes Kritopoulos, attended Balliol College for five years from 1617, and attracted widespread interest and friendship from members of the university, especially those involved in the teaching or learning of Greek.[34] The chance for Englishmen to deepen their knowledge of the Greek language, history or culture stimulated such encounters. Although there is no evidence that Abbatios and Comnenus acted as teachers, it is certain that English scholars were keen to extract information from them (more on which below) and this potential utility influenced the hospitality with which they were met.

As well as benefitting from such attitudes, it might also be suggested that Greek travellers such as Abbatios and Comnenus were aware that they were likely to receive a favourable reaction from scholarly institutions and therefore deliberately visited them. This point might be shown with the example of Comnenus, who, after visiting the universities, travelled to Winchester College and was given £2. The warden of the school was John Harris, 'so admirable a Grecian, and so noted a preacher, that sir Hen. Savile [the eminent scholar and one of the translators of the King James' Version of the Bible] used frequently to say that he was second [only] to St. Chrysostome'.[35] Harris's fame as a teacher and scholar of Greek was well-earned. Before

[32] Harris, *Greek Emigres*, 62–84.

[33] Mordechai Feingold, 'The Humanities', in Nicholas Tyacke, ed., *The History of the University of Oxford*, 4: *Seventeenth-Century Oxford* (Oxford, 1997), 211–357, at 256–61.

[34] Davey, *Metrophanes Kritopoulos*, 88–111.

[35] For Harris's reputation as a Greek scholar, see Anthony Wood, *Athenae Oxonienses*, ed. Philip Bliss, 4 vols (London, 1813–20), 3: 455.

becoming warden, he had held the prestigious position of regius professor of Greek at Oxford, during which period Kritopoulos had studied at the university. As detailed in the autograph album of the future patriarch, the two had enjoyed a 'long friendship and acquaintance'.[36] Bearing in mind Harris's reputation as an eminent 'Grecian', it is very possible that Comnenus went to Hampshire expecting a friendly reception. Indeed, it seems likely that Comnenus would have been aware of Harris, and Harris of Comnenus, given the Greek's stay in the universities and the links between Winchester College and its sister foundation of New College, Oxford. However, even if Comnenus was unfamiliar with Harris, his trip to Winchester College and the donation made there show the interest in learned Greeks which was prevalent among English academics. That there was an awareness of this interest on the part of the travellers is suggested by the fact that places of learning played such a prominent part in the itineraries of both Abbatios and Comnenus.

However, alongside curiosity there are unmistakeable hints of a struggle by Abbatios and especially by Comnenus to be considered 'true object[s] of Charity' in the face of English suspicion. As John Paul-Ghobrial, among others, has argued, a Greek clergyman travelling to raise funds was so frequent a phenomenon in the early modern world as to be something of a trope and to lead to suspicions of fraudulent behaviour.[37] In the words of the early modern Scottish traveller William Lithgow, one should be wary of 'vagabonding *Greekes*' with 'their counterfeit Testimonials'.[38] To overcome doubts, it was useful to have convincing credentials and letters of recommendation. A sense of the importance the English placed on this can be seen occasionally in account books, such as that of Jesus College, Cambridge, which described the expenditure as 'Our Coll: Proportion of 50l given by Convocation to Hierotheus Cephalonius

---

[36] Davey, *Metrophanes Kritopoulos*, 93.

[37] Ghobrial, 'Migration from Within and Without', 160–6; Grant, 'Vagabonding Greekes', 94; Henny, 'Nathanael of Leukas', 454–5.

[38] The quotation is in Misti, *Greece in Early English Travel Writing*, 31. Italics original. See also Ghobrial, 'Migration from Within and Without', 162; Grant, 'Vagabonding Greekes', 94; Henny, 'Nathanael of Leukas', 454–5. Although it is beyond the scope or aim of this article to determine whether Comnenus was what he claimed to be, it is interesting to note that certain elements of his story – such as the familial link to the Byzantine imperial family of the same name, the supposed robbery by pirates, and his role at the renowned monastery of St Catherine – are consistent with some of the claims associated with fraudulent Greek travellers.

Constantinopolitanus on my Lo: our Chancellors l[ett]re to the universitie'.[39] Revealingly, the ruling body of Jesus College deemed a reference to the letter written by Pembroke, the chancellor, necessary in order to justify why Abbatios was receiving their money, not the Greek's project. It was Pembroke's word which lent validity to Abbatios's claims and settled any doubts.

Comnenus arrived in England in a far weaker position than Abbatios. His story was far less easy to prove and, initially, his testimonials were from non-English authorities. His case is therefore indicative of the means by which some Greek travellers attempted to overcome the suspicions of their hosts. A later seventeenth-century work on the Greek church by Philippus Cyprius discussed Comnenus's time travelling through Germany, and described him as truly 'è gente Imperatoriâ Comnenâ' ('from the imperial Comnenus family').[40] This would seem to imply that Comnenus had either declared himself to be descended from the Byzantine ruling dynasty of the eleventh and twelfth centuries when he was in Germany, or that he had allowed the idea to circulate. However, such claims are notably absent from any of the English sources. Why Comnenus, seeking to impress his hosts, would make no mention of this royal connection is unclear, but it may perhaps reveal an aspect of English suspicion. As Jonathan Harris has pointed out, Greeks seeking western interest had claimed kinship with the imperial families of Constantinople since the fall of the city in 1453.[41] Although it is dangerous to make inferences based on an absence of evidence, it is possible that the English had notions about what constituted a false claim by a journeying Greek, with one of these being an alleged imperial genealogy. For this, or some other reason, Comnenus does not seem to have invoked his ancestry to impress the English.

Instead, descriptions of Comnenus in financial sources suggest that he heavily emphasized the humanitarian plight underlying his mission. Winchester College's accounts indicate that he summarized his cause as being to redeem captives from Algiers, while a glimpse of the emotive appeal he made, and the sympathy he engendered, is captured in an entry from St John's College, Cambridge, that £1 was to given

---

[39] Jesus College Archives, BU:AC:Gen:1, fol. 184.
[40] Cyprius, *Chronicon*, 487.
[41] Harris, *Greek Emigres*, 81–4.

towards the 'releife of a poore captive Grecian'.[42] It is also clear that Comnenus emphasized his status in the Greek Orthodox Church, perhaps in order to support the veracity of his claims. It was certainly something noted by many college bursars, including those of Clare College, Cambridge, who described the donation as going to a 'Grecian Archimandrite upon mount Sinai'.[43] Finally, it appears that Comnenus tried to ensure that, like Abbatios, he had strong English testimonials. As mentioned above, he gained one such accreditation in 1652 signed by a number of leading English ministers. This document was important for Comnenus's hopes of receiving charity, since the signatories specified that they had carefully scrutinized his non-English testimonials.[44] The implication of this wording was that certificates held by a traveller decreased in value the further away they were from the locale in which they had been issued. At least one other English certificate for Comnenus survives and is discussed below.[45] The collection of such documents by Comnenus suggests that he was cognisant of the need to impress potential donors with regionally specific certificates.

The stories of Abbatios and Comnenus also help us to gauge the extent to which the English were interested in Greek travellers for confessional reasons. Dorothea Wendebourg's seminal work on the later sixteenth-century dialogue between Lutheran theologians in Tübingen and Patriarch Jeremiah II on the subject of the *Confessio Augustana Graeca* (the Greek version of the 1530 Augsburg Confession produced by Philipp Melanchthon and the Greek deacon Demetrios Myros in 1559) highlighted the extent to which early modern Protestant communities were fascinated by the Greek Orthodox Church and interested in finding a confessional ally against Roman Catholicism.[46]

---

[42] Cambridge, St John's College Archives, SJAR/3/2/4/6, 1650, fol. 25ᵛ. For Winchester College, see Winchester College Archives, Bursars' Book, 1644–1671, 1652–3, 'Custus Necessariorum cum Donis'.

[43] Clare College Archives, CCAD 2/1/1/3, Michaelmas 1651–Annunciation 1652, general expenses.

[44] *Ecclesiae Londino-Batavae Archivum*, 3: 2213–14.

[45] Gloucestershire Archives, D1086/R23.

[46] Dorothea Wendebourg, *Reformation und Orthodoxie: Der okumenische Briefwechsel zwischen der Leitung der württembergischen Kirche und Patriarch Jeremias II. von Konstantinopel in den Jahren 1573–1581* (Göttingen, 1986). For a recent discussion which extensively analyzes Wendebourg's book, considering the motivation for these encounters, see Colton Moore, 'Wittenberg and Byzantium: Lutheran Incentives to Correspond with the Patriarch of Constantinople (1573–1581)', *Journal of Religious History* 46 (2022), 3–23. See also Calis, 'Impossible Reformation', 43–76.

The Greek church was an important reference point in Protestant-Catholic rivalry but also more widely, owing to its historic links to patristic authorities and to the primitive church.[47] In the words of Sundar Henny, eastern Christianity was 'a window through which one could look (even if just through a glass darkly) at how things were done in the early church'.[48] As Jean-Louis Quantin has recently explored, interest in the Greek Orthodox Church, and especially the early Church Fathers, burgeoned in seventeenth-century England for a variety of reasons, with the 'Church of England claim[ing] to be the most faithful to antiquity'.[49] One reason why Abbatios and Comnenus were received with interest, therefore, was because of their association with the Greek Orthodox Church and the possibility that two Greek clergymen could provide advice or aid to Englishmen pursuing their own ecclesiastical or confessional ends.

Comnenus, in particular, seems to have attracted English interest because of his religious standing. It is clear that during Comnenus's stay in Oxford he was mined for anti-Catholic information by one of the leading religious figures of the Interregnum, the Independent minister, dean of Christ Church, and vice-chancellor of the university, John Owen. In his *Vindication of the Animadversions on Fiat Lux*, published in 1664, Owen quoted conversations with two Greeks when attacking the Roman Catholic claim to agreement with the Greek church. The Franciscan friar Vincent Canes's *Fiat Lux* (1662), which Owen was criticizing, praised the unity of Roman Catholicism in contrast to the discord of the Protestant sects.[50] Owen utilized his conversations with Greeks to challenge this argument. As he wrote, he had personally known some 'eminent members of that Church'.[51] One had been '*Conopius*'; that is, Nathaniel Konopios, who was a Greek scholar in Oxford in the late 1630s and 1640s, and would go on to be an important figure in the seventeenth-century Greek Orthodox Church, serving as metropolitan of Smyrna.[52]

---

[47] Grant, 'Vagabonding Greekes', 87.

[48] Henny, 'Nathanael of Leukas', 457.

[49] Jean-Louis Quantin, *The Church of England and Christian Antiquity: The Construction of a Confessional Identity in the 17th Century* (Oxford, 2009), 12. See also, Milton, *Catholic and Reformed*, 379–81.

[50] Patricia C. Brückmann, 'Vincent Canes [*alias* Thomas Bodwill; *name in religion* John Baptist] (1608–1672)', *ODNB*, online edn (2004), at: <https://doi.org/10.1093/ref:odnb/4549>, accessed 4 November 2024.

[51] John Owen, *A Vindication of the Animadversions on Fiat Lux* (London, 1664), 551.

[52] Ibid. For Konopios, see Patterson, 'The Beginning of Orthodox-Anglican Relations', 39–55.

Owen went on to write that the other man whom he met 'not many years ago, [was] called *Anastatius Comnenus Archimandrite* as his Testimonials bespake him, of a *Monastry* on *Mount Sinai.*'[53] These conversations probably took place when Comnenus visited the university in late 1651, though they may have occurred later. Given he had been one of the signatories of Comnenus's 1652 English testimonial, Owen was almost certainly instrumental in the charitable reception Comnenus received at Oxford.[54] Now, years after their meeting, Owen made use of their discussions in attacking Roman Catholicism, writing that: 'Both these [Greeks] I am sure made it their business to inveigh against *your Church* & practices, having the Arguments of *Nilus* against your Supremacy at their fingers ends.'[55] A fourteenth-century bishop of Thessalonika, Nilus Cabasilas, had attacked the papal claims to primacy and by citing his opinions, via Konopios and Comnenus, Owen was buttressing his own argument by associating it with a historical strand of the Greek Orthodox Church antipathetical to Roman Catholicism.[56] Owen's point was to challenge *Fiat Lux*'s claim that the Roman Catholic and Greek churches 'are so well agreed', and in the process to suggest that it was actually the Greek and Reformed churches which were compatible and in agreement.[57]

Comnenus seems to have been aware of his value to English churchmen, and either attracted or pursued the attention of patrons very dissimilar to Owen. In 1658, a certificate on his behalf was produced by two episcopalian clergymen, Peter Gunning and William Chamberline.[58] The testimonial outlined Comnenus's reason for coming to England and that he now was seeking sufficient funds to 'discharge of his debt' accrued during his stay in England.[59] The certificate also implied that Comnenus had expressed pro-episcopalian sympathies to Gunning and Chamberline, who wrote that they thought it fit to recommend him:

---

[53] Owen, *Vindication*, 552. Italics original.

[54] *Ecclesiae Londino-Batavae Archivum*, 3: 2213–14.

[55] Ibid. Italics original.

[56] George A. Hadjiantoniou, *Protestant Patriarch: The Life of Cyril Lucaris (1572–1638) Patriarch of Constantinople* (Richmond, VA, 1961), 81.

[57] Owen, *Vindication*, 552.

[58] Several years before receiving this certificate, Comnenus had travelled to Scotland: Grant, 'Vagabonding Greekes', 90.

[59] The same year, Comnenus petitioned the Council of State for funds: London, TNA, SP, 25/78, fol. 522.

to the charity of all our friend[s] of the church of England, to which he hath chosen to joine himselfe, by professing his communion with us (which he thinks he hath cause to deny to papists & others) in receiving the H[oly]. Eucharist with us for the most part every Lords day.'[60]

After the Restoration, Comnenus publicly demonstrated his episcopalian sympathies. In 1663, a gout-ridden Comnenus was drawing a pension from John Cosin, bishop of Durham and, at some point after 1660, he produced a poem in praise of 'Gods sacred guift the Prelacy', in which he decried the recent times when 'Sordid Mechanicks boldly did invade' the hierarchy of the church.[61] Today, this poem is part of MS 688 in Lambeth Palace Library, a collection of miscellaneous documents dating from the sixteenth to the early eighteenth centuries. The manuscript was bound when Thomas Tenison was archbishop of Canterbury (1694–1715) and was recorded amongst Tenison's manuscripts in a 1720 library catalogue.[62] The poem appears to be a fair copy, written out in a neat hand, in English. It is entitled, 'Doron Ekklesiasikon' followed by the English description: 'A poemme written by a Grecian, the Bishop of Mount Sinai, nam'd, Anasstatius Comnenus'.[63]

The poem's content and its custodial history suggest that it was written after the Restoration and designed to impress Comnenus's episcopalian patrons; perhaps it was written at their instigation. As William White and Anthony Milton have recently argued, there were significant concerns within the episcopalian community after 1660 that Charles II would implement a broad-based church settlement designed to appease many of his new subjects, rather than a hardline episcopalian one.[64] Just as Owen had been keen to have the support of

---

[60] Gloucestershire Archives, D1086/R23.

[61] *The Correspondence of John Cosin, D.D. Lord Bishop of Durham: Together with Other Papers Illustrative of His Life and Times*, ed. George Ornsby, Surtees Society 52 and 55, 2 vols (Durham, 1869–72), 2: 102–3 and n.[†]. London, LPL, MS 688, vol. 2, fols 526[r–v]. See also a poem written in Greek by Constantine Rhodocanaces, a member of London's Greek community, to celebrate the Restoration discussed by Barron, *Samos to Soho*, 154–5.

[62] See the manuscript description on the library's online catalogue: 'Overview', *CalmView*, online at: <lambethpalacelibrary.org.uk>, accessed 22 June 2024.

[63] LPL, MS 688, vol. 2, fol. 523[r].

[64] Milton, *England's Second Reformation*, 481–91; William White, *The Lord's Battle: Preaching, Print and Royalism During the English Revolution* (Manchester, 2023), 199–205.

a learned Greek priest for his arguments, so it is probable that Cosin, Gunning and Chamberline would have welcomed the appearance of Comnenus's polemical poem, which insisted that the 'Fair'st English Church' with its episcopalian government possessed such an 'Aposto-like frame of Discipline; / That our Greeke Church, in thy faire face doth see, / Her selfe, when in her primitive purity'.[65] Were the new king to read the poem, lines such as 'Witnes Gods Hand! then Scisme cease dispute, / Gods hand writes BISHOPS, his owne Institute' would leave no doubt that episcopacy was the divinely sanctioned and historically correct form of church government.[66] Not only was rule by prelacy justified, but Comnenus drew a link between a robust church hierarchy and a secure English monarchy: the former was, he said, 'The strong foundation, on w[hi]ch safely stands / The strength of Thrones, and golden peace of lands'.[67] That the poem was part of Tenison's collection and was written in, or translated into, English suggests that it circulated in episcopalian networks and may have been disseminated more widely to influence those deciding the ecclesiastical future of England. If, as seems likely, the work was a consequence of Comnenus's association with episcopalian circles following the Restoration, then his standing as a learned Greek was being utilized in the same way as it had been by Owen, but to very different ends.

Comnenus's case highlights how deep-rooted European attitudes to Greek Orthodoxy could be inflected by particular contextual issues; the same might be seen with Abbatios and the intersection of his project with mid-century English concerns with the propagation of the gospel, especially inside the universities. English interest in the propagation of the gospel in Britain and the wider world had long preceded the creation of the Republic, but was especially fervent during its rule.[68] As has recently been argued by Jeremy Fradkin, 'the early years of the English Commonwealth constituted an extraordinary evangelical moment' when there was notable enthusiasm in the British Isles and New England for the promulgation of the gospel via education

---

[65] LPL, MS 688, vol. 2, fol. 523ʳ.

[66] Ibid., fol. 528ʳ.

[67] Ibid., fol. 524ᵛ.

[68] The seminal work on the 'Puritan' interest in propagation is Christopher Hill, 'Puritans and "the Dark Corners of the Land"', *TRHS* 5th series 13 (1963), 77–102. See also Patrick Seamus McGhee, '"Heathenism" in the Protestant Atlantic World, *c.*1558–*c.*1700' (PhD thesis, University of Cambridge, 2019), esp. 113–56.

and preaching.[69] This interest was not fully matched by government action, but, even so, a spate of acts was passed by the Rump Parliament for propagating the gospel pertaining to Wales, parts of northern England, Ireland and New England, through means such as education or the widespread employment of a financially supported preaching ministry.[70] These schemes were very relevant to places of higher education, since they required an educated preaching ministry. As Charles Chauncey, the president of Harvard College in Massachusetts, explained: 'if there should not be some supply by schools of learning, Gods people would soon be left without a teaching ministry.'[71]

The leading figures of the English universities were fervent supporters of evangelism during the Commonwealth. Their zeal was exemplified by the certificates both Oxford and Cambridge produced in support of the propagation act for New England.[72] As these testimonials indicated, substantial parts of both universities' governing bodies saw evangelism as part of Protestantism's global fight against Roman Catholicism. This international attitude was evident in a 1649 certificate of Cambridge college heads encouraging contributions to the New England propagation scheme. Drawing on historical precedent and quoting Matthew 23: 15, they argued that the Pharisees had historically spared no pains in gathering converts for Judaism while the Jesuits *at this day refuse not to compasse Sea and Land for spreading of* Popery'. Compared to these opponents, '*Shall* Christianity, *shall* Protestantisme *finde fewer Zelots set on worke for their propagation? God forbid*'.[73] Such phrasing tapped into the tradition of anti-Catholicism which was a prominent presence in early modern English universities.[74]

[69] Jeremy Fradkin, 'Religious Toleration and Protestant Expansion in Revolutionary England, 1642–1658' (DPhil thesis, Johns Hopkins University, 2019), 121–68, quotation at 145. For the issue of propagation during the Commonwealth more generally, see Christopher Hill, 'Propagating the Gospel', in H. E. Bell and R. L. Ollard, eds, *Historical Essays 1600–1750, presented to David Ogg* (London, 1963), 35–59.

[70] For a summary of all the propagation legislation passed by the Commonwealth, see William Bradford Bidwell, '*The Committees and Legislation of the Rump Parliament, 1648–1653: A Quantitative Study*' (PhD thesis, University of Rochester, 1977), 200–8.

[71] Charles Chauncy, *Gods Mercy Shewed to his People* (Cambridge, MA, 1655), 29.

[72] [University of Oxford], *To Our Reverend Brethren the Ministers of the Gospel in England and Wales* (n.pl., 1649); Bodl., MS Wood 423, fol. 30^{r-v}.

[73] Ibid., fol. 30^v. Italics original.

[74] See Eloise Davies, 'Beyond the Jesuit College: The Role of Cambridge's "Puritan" Colleges in European Politics and Diplomacy, 1603–1625', in Alex Beeton et al., eds, *The Mind is its Own Place? Early Modern Intellectual History in an Institutional Context*, History of Universities 36 (Oxford, 2023), 25–43.

Abbatios's project was relevant to these English concerns for several reasons, including Roman Catholic missionary efforts in the Greek-speaking east. In 1573, the Roman Catholic Church founded the Congregation for the Dissemination of the Faith and began strenuous missionary work to the east as well as to the west.[75] Roman Catholic evangelism in the Greek Orthodox world through education and proselytizing became one of the most pressing worries in the Orthodox Church of the late-sixteenth and seventeenth centuries.[76] In 1581, the Greek College of St Athanasius had been founded in Rome by Pope Gregory XIII. The College was established in order to train young men from the Orthodox east as Roman Catholic clergy before returning them to minister in their birthplaces.[77] In Istanbul, a permanent Jesuit school giving free education in the vernacular was founded in 1609, greatly to the concern of the patriarch at the time, Kyrillos Loukaris. Loukaris noted the success of such schemes and the sophisticated arguments made by the Roman Catholic missionaries, processes aided by *Propaganda Fide*'s polyglot printing press at Rome, which, from 1628, began publishing books in Greek targeting the Greek Orthodox community.[78]

Abbatios's translation of the *Ecclesiarum Belgicarum Confessio* was part of a reaction by a segment of the Orthodox Church against these Roman Catholic activities. This Orthodox response was closely associated with Patriarch Loukaris, a significant but complicated figure in the history of the Greek Orthodox Church, known for his efforts to promote closer connections with the Reformed communities of Europe.[79] As highlighted by Vassa Kontouma's important work on Patriarch Dositheus II (1641–1707), a figure known 'pour combattre les avatars du calvinisme

---

[75] Trevor-Roper, 'The Church of England and the Greek Church', 217.

[76] Davey, *Metrophanes Kritopoulos*, 41–51; Paschalis M. Kitromilides, 'Orthodoxy and the West: Reformation to Enlightenment', in Michael Angold, ed., *The Cambridge History of Christianity*, 5: *Eastern Christianity* (Cambridge, 2006), 187–209, at 193–202; Rozemond, *Hierotheos Abbatios*, 8–15.

[77] Kitromilides, 'Orthodoxy and the West', 188.

[78] Calis, 'Impossible Reformation', 62.

[79] For the classic studies of Loukaris, see especially Hadjiantoniou, *Protestant Patriarch*; Gunnar Hering, *Ökumenisches Patriarchat und europäische Politik, 1620–1638* (Wiesbaden, 1968); Trevor-Roper, 'The Church of England and the Greek Church', 213–40; Steven Runciman, *The Great Church in Captivity: A Study of the Patriarchate of Constantinople From the Eve of the Turkish Conquest to the Greek War of Independence* (Cambridge, 1968), 259–88; Stylianou, '"We are at the furthest part of the inhabited world"'.

dans la théologie grecque de son époque' ('to combat the avatars of Calvinism in the Greek theology of his age') but equally determined to avoid Roman Catholic encroachment in the east, Loukaris's legacy was enormously controversial, and synods held in Constantinople (1642) and in Jerusalem (1672) issued anathemas against the supposedly pro-Calvinist 1629 *Confession of Faith* attributed to him.[80] However, recent scholarship, especially by Ovidiu Olar and Richard Calis, has pushed back against former understandings of Loukaris as a pro-Protestant patriarch.[81] As Olar has pointed out, the purported Calvinism of Loukaris 'présente beaucoup de traits particuliers' ('presents many particular traits').[82] They have instead reinterpreted Loukaris, and documents such as his *Confession of Faith*, particularly by drawing attention to the geopolitical context of the Ottoman world. Their re-evaluation has introduced a more subtle understanding of the patriarch as an anti-Catholic leader, fiercely committed to administrative and pastoral work, who 'wanted a reformation of his church and believed that Calvinism could provide a model, but he understood this reformation as a "renovation" and "restitution", not as a conversion'.[83]

The dissemination of key texts in vernacular Greek was an important part of Loukaris's plans for the revitalization of the Greek Orthodox Church in the face of Roman Catholic proselytization. During his various tenures of the patriarchate throne, he oversaw the introduction

---

[80] Vassa Kontouma, 'La *Confession de Foi* de Dosithée de Jérusalem: Les versions de 1672 et de 1690', in Marie-Hélène Blanchet and Frédéric Gabriel, eds, *L'Union à l'épreuve du formulaire. Professions de foi entre églises d'Orient et d'Occident (XIIIe–XVIIIe siècle)* (Leuven, 2016), 341–72, at 343. See also Vassa Kontouma and Sébastien Garnier, 'Concilium Hierosolymitanum 1672', in Alberto Melloni, ed., *The Great Councils of the Orthodox Churches: From Constantinople 861 to Constantinople 1872*, Conciliorum Oecumenicorum Generaliumque Decreta 4 (Turnhout, 2016), 267–327; Ovidiu Olar, '"Un temps pour parler": Dosithée de Jérusalem et le synode de Jassy (1642)', *Analele Putnei* 10 (2014), 215–25. On the 1629 *Confession of Faith*, see Ovidiu Olar, 'Les confessions de foi de Cyrille Loukaris (†1638)', in Blanchet and Gabriel, *L'Union à l'épreuve du formulaire*, 270–310, at 281.

[81] See Calis, 'Impossible Reformation', 43–76; Ovidiu Olar, *La boutique de Théophile. Les relations du Patriarche de Constantinople Kyrillos Loukaris (1570–1638) avec la Réforme* (Paris, 2019); Eleni Gara and Ovidiu Olar, 'Confession-Building and Authority: The Great Church and the Ottoman State in the First Half of the Seventeenth Century', in Tijana Krstić and Derin Terzioğlu, eds, *Entangled Confessionalizations? Dialogic Perspectives on the Politics of Piety and Community-Building in the Ottoman Empire, 15th–18th Centuries* (Piscataway, NJ, 2022), 159–214.

[82] Olar, 'Les confessions de foi de Cyrille Loukaris', 281.

[83] Gara and Olar, 'Confession-Building and Authority', 175.

of a Greek printing press in Istanbul to publish religious works, and the production of an edition of the New Testament in Greek which was published in Geneva in 1638. Neither of these schemes proved successful: the press in Istanbul lasted less than two years before effectively ceasing operations in January 1628, while the vast majority of the Greek New Testaments remained in Geneva for a century due to a pay dispute with the printers.[84] However, the notion of disseminating printed vernacular material in order to defend the Greek Orthodox Church against Roman Catholic encroachment survived amongst Loukaris's faction, even after his death. Abbatios's translation of the *Ecclesiarum Belgicarum Confessio* was part of this endeavour. As mentioned above, this important text had been printed in a bilingual Latin-Greek edition in 1627 and contained the *Belgic Confession*, the *Heidelberg Catechism*, and some of the canons of the Synod of Dordrecht. It was intended to present a unified picture of the Reformed communities of western Europe to the Greek-speaking east and, by being translated into Greek vernacular, was intended to have a wide readership.

To the English university-men who were interested in Protestant propagation and wary of Roman Catholic expansion, Abbatios and his mission were of great interest. The translation of the *Ecclesiarum Belgicarum Confessio* was perceived by the Protestant powers as a way of disseminating Reformed doctrine in a readily accessible form.[85] For these reasons, the Dutch had sponsored Abbatios and printed about 1,000 copies of his work for distribution.[86] Many in England shared these attitudes, as shown by the generous welcome Abbatios enjoyed. While staying in Oxford, Abbatios attracted enough interest that a motion was made in the House of Commons for a public collection to be raised on his behalf.[87] Perhaps significantly, the proposer of the motion was James Chaloner, a leading figure of Parliament's Committee for Regulating the Universities, the pre-eminent committee for educational institutions of the Republic, suggesting that the motion may have originated in Oxford or Cambridge.[88] In the end, nothing appears to have been done about the establishment of a national

---

[84] Calis, 'Impossible Reformation', 67–8; Hadjiantoniou, *Protestant Patriarch*, 77–88, 93–4.

[85] Rozemond, *Hierotheos Abbatios*, 34–5.

[86] Ibid. 35.

[87] *JHC* 6, 282 (21 August 1649).

[88] For the Committee for Regulating the Universities and Chaloner's role, see Beeton, 'Rump Parliament and Places of Learning', esp. 39–80 and appendix 1.

collection for Abbatios. However, its proposal reflects how intriguing Abbatios's project was to his English hosts. This interest indicates how broader European attitudes to Orthodoxy, particularly its anti-Catholic potential, could be influenced by specific contextual concerns, in this case the propagation-moment during the English Republic.

The case studies of Abbatios and Comnenus offer evidence as to what it took for Greeks to be considered worthy recipients of charity. In particular, new archival materials, such as college financial records, have provided a valuable perspective on English attitudes to figures travelling from what they perceived to be the periphery of Christian Europe to its English centre. This article has argued that Greek travellers were treated with suspicion as potential fraudsters, but also with a curiosity which reflected a deep interest in Hellenic studies and the Greek Orthodox Church. The cases of both Abbatios and Comnenus also remind historians that the deep-rooted attitudes to Greeks in Protestant Europe could be inflected by the issues of a particular historical moment. Interest in the Greek Orthodox Church as an important reference point in confessional or ecclesiastical disputes was common across early modern Europe and Comnenus's experience shows that England was no different. After being mined for information by John Owen for a polemical dispute with the Franciscan friar Vincent Canes, Comnenus seems to have become part of episcopalian efforts to shape the Restoration Church of England. Abbatios's translation of the *Ecclesiarum Belgicarum Confessio* reflected a related, but different, type of interest in Greek Orthodoxy. Namely, the desire of Europe's Reformed communities to pursue closer ties with their Greek peers and battle the common threat of global Catholicism. This was of particular relevance to the England of 1649 with the new regime investing much time and effort in schemes for the propagation of the gospel. Because Abbatios and Comnenus came from outside the mainstream of English life, they were of unusual interest and value to their English hosts, and it is apparent that Comnenus especially knew how to play to an audience. In many ways, it might be concluded that it was thanks to their marginality that the two men came to be seen as 'true object[s] of Charity' in seventeenth-century England.

Body, Filial Piety and Rites: Xia Dachang as a Chinese Perspective on the Rites Controversy

Manning Chan ⓘ

University of California, Santa Cruz

*The Chinese Rites Controversy (c.1643–1724) marked the most signifi-
cant rupture in seventeenth- to eighteenth-century Sino-European relations. Fourteen Chinese Roman Catholics on the fringes of political and
cultural circles, neither a part of the state authorities nor influential literati,
defended the legitimacy of Chinese rites. Among them, Xia Dachang
grounded his analysis on an exhaustive study of the Confucian 'Book of
Rites' (*Liji*). This article, focusing on Xia's treatises, proposes a novel
approach to reassessing the Controversy by analysing the role of the human
body in Neo-Confucianism. It aims to reveal previously overlooked yet
essential aspects of the debates: the Neo-Confucian conception of the human
'being' and the interconnectivity between external physical presence and
actions, and internal moral values.*

The Qing empire under Kangxi (r. 1661–1722) saw the peak of the
Chinese Rites Controversy (*c.*1643–1724), a dispute centred on the
practices of Chinese Roman Catholics regarding Confucian offering
rites and the proper translation of 'God'. Remarkably, it was not the
political or cultural elites who first spoke out to defend the practice of
Chinese ancestral offering rites. Instead, fourteen Chinese Roman
Catholic laypeople, despite their marginal political and social status,
emerged as the earliest Chinese individuals committed to writing in
defence of these rites. Among them, Xia Dachang (d. 1698) drew
exhaustively upon the Confucian 'Book of Rites' (*Liji*) to argue that
the rites of ancestral offerings were compatible with Roman Catholic
beliefs.[1]

University of California, Santa Cruz, California. E-mail: mchan37@ucsc.edu.

[1] Xia Dachang: Chinese name, 夏大常; Christian name, Mathias. He contributed three
treatises to the defence of ancestral offering rites: '禮記祭禮泡製' ['Liji jili paozhi';
'Sacrificial Rites in the Book of Rites']; '禮記祭制撮言' ['Liji jizhi cuoyan'; 'Summary
of the Book of Rites concerning Sacrificial Rites']; and '禮儀問答' ['Liyi wenda'; 'Catechism of Rites'], in Nicolas Standaert and Adrian Dukink, eds, 耶穌會羅馬檔案館明清天
主教文獻 [*Yesuhui luoma danganguan mingqing tianzhujiao wenxian; Chinese Christian*

Studies in Church History 61 (2025), 405–418 © The Author(s), 2025. Published by Cambridge
University Press on behalf of the Ecclesiastical History Society.
doi:10.1017/stc.2024.45

This article aims to offer a new perspective on the Chinese Rites Controversy. Scholars such as Li Tiangang, Huang Yi-nong and Wu Liwei have pioneered the study of Chinese perspectives during the Controversy, while Po-chia Hsia's observations on ethnographic authority have highlighted the competition among missionaries during the Controversy for expertise in matters of Chinese religion and culture. Nicolas Standaert, meanwhile, has made groundbreaking contributions by examining multi-level interactions within early modern Christian communities and the exchange of knowledge about Chinese rites between China and Europe.[2] In building on their work, this article draws attention to some previously overlooked facets. It reconsiders Xia Dachang's views on ancestral offering rites by introducing a new approach that investigates the role of the human body in the Neo-Confucian framework, uncovering differing perceptions of human existence in the Western and Chinese traditions, and the inseparability of internal morality (filial piety) from external materiality (bodily presence and actions).

FILIAL PIETY, THE QING EMPIRE AND THE CHINESE RITES CONTROVERSY

During the last four decades of the seventeenth century, Emperor Kangxi navigated a period of significant political uncertainty, eventually solidifying his rule over China proper where Han Chinese predominated. In the late seventeenth century, Kangxi faced a dual

---

Texts from the Roman Archives of the Society of Jesus], 12 vols (Taipei, 2002), 10: 79–104, 105–14, 115–44, respectively.

[2] 李天綱 [Li Tiangang], 中國禮儀之爭—歷史. 文獻和意義 [Zhonguo liyi zhi zheng: lishi, wenxian and yiyi; The Chinese Rites Controversy: History, Documents and Meaning] (Shanghai, 1998), 1–389; 黃一農 [Huang, Yi-nong], 兩頭蛇: 明末清初的第一代天主教徒 [Liangtou she: Mingmo Qingchu de diyidai Tianzhujiaotu; Two-headed Snakes: The First Generation of Chinese Catholics in the Late Ming and Early Qing] (Xinzhu, 2005), 1–545; 吳莉葦 [Wu Liwei], 中國禮儀之爭—文明的張力與權力的較量 [Zhongguo Liyi Zhi Zheng: wenming de zhangli yu quanli de jiaoliang; The Chinese Rites Controversy: Tension in Culture and Struggle in Power] (Shanghai, 2007), 1–135; Nicolas Standaert, Chinese Voices in the Rites Controversy: Travelling Books, Community Networks, Intercultural Arguments, ed. Paul Oberholzer (Rome, 2012), 1–473; R. Po-chia Hsia, 'Chinese Voices in the Rites Controversy: From China to Rome', and Nicolas Standaert, 'Chinese Voices in the Rites Controversy: The Role of Christian Communities', in Ines G. Županov, ed., The Rites Controversies in the Early Modern World (Leiden, 2018), 29–49 and 50–67, respectively.

challenge: resistance from Manchu elites who vehemently opposed the sinicized political reforms introduced by his father, Emperor Shunzhi, and a series of uprisings in southern China, where the Manchu occupation had been met with strong opposition from the Chinese populace. In response, after ascending to the throne in 1667 and neutralizing Oboi (1610–69), a significant threat to his rule, Kangxi distanced himself from those Manchu elites who opposed the integration of Chinese elements into Manchu traditions. Instead, he strategically adopted a Confucian persona to mitigate the Chinese elites' antipathy toward their Manchu rulers. He authorized the commentary of Zhu Xi (1126–1271) and his school of Neo-Confucianism as state orthodoxy, writing that 'Master Zhu epitomised the study of Confucian Classics, carried on the lost knowledge of Confucianism, enlightened us, and established the norm for the next billions of generations.'[3] In 1670, Kangxi's Sacred Edict, emphasizing Confucian principles, notably placed the maxim that 'Highly esteemed filial piety and brotherly submission to give due weight to social relations' at the forefront of its sixteen state policy directives.[4]

Emperor Kangxi initially welcomed the growing number of European Roman Catholic missionaries in China, expressing his acceptance of them in the 1692 Edict of Toleration, which commended the Roman Catholic missionaries for not causing disturbances in the provinces. Furthermore, Kangxi commended Matteo Ricci (1552–1610), who arrived in China in the early 1580s, for his strategy of cultural accommodation. This approach, aimed at adapting Roman Catholicism to fit with Confucianism, became known as 'the rules of Matteo Ricci'.[5] However, a century later this attempt at a reconciliation of traditions faced a decisive setback in 1693, when Charles Maigrot

---

[3] '朱夫子集大成, 而緒千百年絕傳之學, 開愚蒙而立億萬世一定之規.' 康熙 [Kang Xi], 御纂朱子全書 [*Yuzhuan Zhuzi quanshu; The Imperial Edition of the Complete Writings of Master Zhu Xi*], in Ji Xiaolan, ed., 景印文淵閣四庫全書 [*Jingyin wenyuange siku quanshu; The Siku Imperial Library*] 720–1 (Taipei, 1986), 720: 2.

[4] '敦孝悌以重人倫': '聖諭十六條' ['Sheng yu shi liu tiao'; 'Emperor's Moral Instructions, in Sixteen Articles'], 5; from Paris, BN, Department of Manuscripts, online at: <https://gallica.bnf.fr/ark:/12148/btv1b9006137j/f11.item>, accessed 26 November 2024; ET: 'Asia for Educators', Columbia University, online at: <http://afe.easia.colum bia.edu/ps/cup/qing_sacred_edict.pdf#page=1&zoom=auto,0,511>, accessed 28 January 2024.

[5] '利瑪竇規矩': 王伯多祿 [Wangbo Duolu], '京都總會長王伯多祿等十八人致外省各堂會長書' ['Jingdu Zonghuizhang Wangbo duo lu deng shiba ren zhi waisheng ge tanghuizhang shu'; 'A Letter to the Fathers in Other Provinces written by Father Provincial

(1652–1730), the head of Chinese missions and vicar apostolic in Fujian province, issued the *Interdict*, which banned Chinese Christians from practising Confucian ancestral rites, including rituals such as offering sacrifices to express reverence and love for the deceased. This ban was further reinforced in 1704 by Pope Clement XI (1649–1721), who condemned these rites and prohibited further debate on the matter. In reaction, Kangxi, in 1721, outlawed any missionary work that did not adhere to Ricci's approach and openly criticized Pope Clement XI's decree, stating that: 'It is impossible to reason with them [Western missionaries] because they do not understand larger issues as we understand them in China. There is no single Westerner versed in Chinese works, and their remarks are often incredible and ridiculous'.[6] In 1724, Kangxi's successor, Yongzheng, formally proscribed Roman Catholicism in China, and missionary work was significantly restricted there until 1858.[7]

Given the prioritization of Confucian teachings in Qing statecraft and the emperors' close surveillance of Roman Catholic missions in China, one might expect significant defences of ancestral offering rites from the Chinese political or cultural elite. However, Qing officials and the Chinese cultural elite were largely absent from these discussions. Instead, the debate was taken up by fourteen Chinese Roman Catholic laymen on the fringes of political and social power.[8] Among them, Xia Dachang, the most academically qualified, who had passed the basic civil service examination but lacked the credentials for an official position.

Wangbo Duolu'], in Standaert and Dukink, eds, *Chinese Christian Texts*, 10: 508; ET: Don Alvin Pittman, *Toward a Modern Chinese Buddhism: Taixu's Reforms* (Honolulu, 2001), 35.

[6] '只可說得西洋等小人如何言得中國之大理。況西洋等人無一通漢書者，說言議論，令人可笑者多': Yuan Chen, ed., 康熙與羅馬使節關係文書影印本 [*Kangxi yu Luoma shijie quanxi wenshu*; *Facsimile of Documents on the Relationship Between Kangxi and Roman Envoys*] (Beijing, 1932), 41–2. The English translation is cited from Dun Jen Li's *China in Transition, 1517–1911* (New York, 1969), 22.

[7] Thomas H. Reilly, *The Taiping Heavenly Kingdom: Rebellion and the Blasphemy of Empire* (Seattle, 2004), 43.

[8] Nicolas Standaert, 'Chinese Voices in the Rites Controversy,' 64. Hsia claims that Qiu Sheng earned the highest *jinshi* degree in the civil service examination, with four others holding lower degrees, but he provides no evidence. This claim is further called into question by Qiu's unusual practice for an early-modern literatus: in his 述聞篇 ['Shuwen pian'; 'On Recounting Heard Knowledge'], Qiu only cites Confucian classics once, specifically *Mengzi*, while defending Confucian rites. See Hsia, 'Chinese Voices in the Rites Controversy,' 31. According to M. Courant, the librarian at the National Library of France, Xia Dachang in fact held only the title of *Xiucai*, reflecting his achievement of the basic degree in the civil service examination: see Li Tiangang, *The Chinese Rites Controversy*, 228.

Despite their lack of government roles or recognition as influential scholars, these individuals became the first Chinese voices in the dispute, authoring, in response to a request from the Jesuit missionaries, no fewer than twenty-eight treatises defending the practice of ancestral offering rites.[9]

The lack of involvement of the Chinese elite in the controversy surrounding ancestral offering rites is a complex issue that requires further exploration. One reason might be that the emperors had already provided an official, definitive position on the Confucian Rites Controversy, leading the elites, especially non-Catholics, to refrain from getting involved. Insights into this lack of elite participation can be found in the writings of the fourteen Chinese Roman Catholics, who faced dual pressures: local societal pressure to adhere to Confucian rites; and opposition from some European Roman Catholic missionaries, who viewed these Chinese religious practices as heterodox. In Fujian province, for example, Chinese Roman Catholics were even barred from confession due to the ongoing controversy, leading them to urgently request that Roman Catholic missionaries acknowledge the legitimacy of Chinese rites.[10]

WESTERN MISSIONARIES' INTERPRETATION OF CHINESE TRADITIONS

In the course of the Controversy, the Jesuits grappled with a significant dilemma: balancing cultural accommodation with doctrinal fidelity. Matteo Ricci viewed Confucianism as a beneficial moral system for governing the empire, with ancestral rites expressing love, gratitude and filial piety, rather than superstition.[11] He noted that the Chinese, according to Confucian classics, did not see the deceased as gods, nor did they pray to them or expect favours.[12] Indeed, he saw ancestral rites as originally civil ceremonies which had become tainted by superstitious beliefs from Buddhism and Daoism.[13] To counter

---

[9] These texts are reprinted in Standaert and Dukink, eds, *Chinese Christian Texts*, 9: 1–50, 63–528; 10: 35–42, 79–144, 163–478; 11: 1–268, 279–96.

[10] Yan Mo, '草稿' ['Caogao'; 'The Drafts'] and '草稿抄白' ['Caogao chaobai'; 'The Copy of the Draft'], in Standaert and Dukink, eds, *Chinese Christian Texts*, 10: 61–6 and 87–114, respectively, at 63–4 and 97.

[11] George Harold, *Generation of Giants: The Story of the Jesuits in China in the Last Decades of the Ming Dynasty* (Notre Dame, IN, 1962), 291.

[12] Matteo Ricci, 耶穌會與天主教進入中國史 [*Yesuhui yu Tianzhujiao jinru Zhongguo shi; The History of Jesuits and Catholicism in China*], transl. Wen Zheng (Beijing, 2014), 70.

[13] Harold, *Generation of Giants*, 295.

the materialist and atheist philosophy of Neo-Confucianism,[14] Ricci argued that if body and soul were extinguished at death, ancestral rites would be empty gestures.[15] Using the scholastic-Aristotelian distinction between vegetative, sensitive and rational souls (*shenghun*, *juehun* and *linghun*), he explained that while the first two cease to exist at death, the rational soul is immortal.[16] The soul cannot move freely between worlds, as 'the Lord of Heaven has created all things, each with its designated place', so any return of an ancestor's soul must be by divine will.[17] Ricci suggested that instead of traditional rites, it would be preferable for Chinese believers to transform these practices into acts of charity to the poor, thereby comforting the souls of their ancestors.[18]

Later Jesuit missionaries generally followed the framework established by Ricci.[19] Francesco Saviero Filippucci (1632–92) further emphasized that the reason for offering sacrifices was simply love. Out of love, offerings are arranged, kneeling occurs, incense is burned, wine is offered, candles are lit, and the family mourns together to demonstrate filial respect.[20] Another Jesuit missionary, Giulio Aleni (1582–1649), even suggested integrating Christian elements into these Confucian rites, such as placing a cross at the ritual site, dedicating offerings to God before the ancestors, praying to God during the rites,

[14] Jacques Gernet, *China and the Christian Impact: A Conflict of Culture* (New York, 1985), 147. See also Matteo Ricci, 天主實義今注 [*Tianzhu shiyi jinzhu; The True Meaning of the Lord of Heaven*] (Beijing, 2014), 125.

[15] Ricci, *The True Meaning of the Lord of Heaven*, 115.

[16] Gernet, *China and the Christian Impact*, 147.

[17] Ricci, *The True Meaning of the Lord of Heaven*, 123–4.

[18] Ricci, *The History of Jesuits and Catholicism in China*, 71.

[19] Ana Carolina Hosne, *The Jesuit Missions to China and Peru, 1570–1610: Expectations and Appraisals of Expansionism* (New York, 2013), 86. Examples include Juan Garcia (1605–65), '天主聖教入門問答' ['Tianzhu shengjiao rumen wen da'; 'Catechism of the Holy Catholic Church']; Francesco Saviero Filippucci (1632–92), '臨喪出殯儀式' ['Linsang chubin yishi'; 'Rituals for Funeral and Burial'], and '喪葬儀式' ['Sangzang yishi'; 'Funeral and Burial Rites']; Ferdinand Verbiest (1623–88), 天主教喪禮問答 ['Tianzhujiao sangli wenda'; 'Catechism of the Catholic Funeral Rites']; and Giulio Aleni (1582–1649), '口鐸日鈔' ['Kouduo richao'; 'Diary of Oral Admonitions'], and '性學觕述' ['Xingxue cushu'; 'A Brief Account of the Study of Human Nature'], in Standaert and Dukink, eds, *Chinese Christian Texts*, 2: 385–518; 5: 439–66, 467–92, 493–508; 6: 45–378; 7: 1–594, respectively.

[20] Filippucci, 'Funeral and Burial Rites', in Standaert and Dukink, eds, *Chinese Christian Texts*, 5: 473–4.

or giving the offerings to the needy instead of presenting them to ancestors.[21]

The Jesuits initially adopted a policy of accommodation, interpreting these rites as cultural rather than religious, thereby not conflicting with Roman Catholic teachings. However, this stance was not universally accepted within the Roman Catholic Church. Other missionary groups, notably the Dominicans and Franciscans, viewed these practices as idolatrous and in direct violation of Roman Catholic doctrine.

Dominican missionaries, in contrast to the Jesuits, rejected ancestral offering rites outright. In 1643, Juan Bautista Morales (1597–1664) reported to Pope Innocent X (1574–1655) his observations of these rites, detailing the sacrifices, timing, prayer content, decoration and arrangement of the sacrifice site, and the role of a ritual host akin to a priest.[22] While acknowledging the participants' expression of gratitude to their ancestors, Morales noted that they also prayed for blessings such as health, longevity and good harvests.[23] However, unlike the Jesuits, he did not differentiate between the original Confucian practices and those influenced by local religions. Crucially, Morales pointed out that participants believed the souls of their ancestors were present on the tablets to receive sacrifices, leading him to label the rites as blasphemous and 'illicit'.[24]

Francisco Varo (1627–87), another Dominican friar, conducted a more thorough study of Chinese ancestral offering rites based on Zhu Xi's commentary, which Emperor Kangxi had made an official civil service examination text. Varo also concluded that these rites were fundamentally flawed because they revered ancestors (seen as 'fake masters') with rituals intended for blessings and sacrifices.[25] Varo argued that these rites should be considered blasphemous, as all offerings should be reserved for the one true God.[26] More importantly, however, Varo referenced Zhu Xi (1130–1200), the prominent Neo-Confucian

[21] Aleni, 'Diary of Oral Admonitions', in Standaert and Dukink, eds, *Chinese Christian Texts*, 7: 469.
[22] Ray Robert Noll, ed., *100 Roman Documents Concerning the Chinese Rites Controversy (1645–1941)*, transl. Donald F. St Sure and Edward Malatesta (San Francisco, CA, 1992), 2.
[23] Ibid. 2–3.
[24] Ibid. 3–4.
[25] 李良爵 [Li Liangjue], '辨祭參評' ['Bianji canping'; 'A Commentary of the Debates of Sacrifices'], in Standaert and Dukink, eds, *Chinese Christian Texts*, 10: 363–438, at 369.
[26] Ibid. 376.

(*daoxue*) philosopher, who had stated that the ritual participants' *qi* (vital energy flow) could connect with the ancestor's *qi*. Therefore, if one could show reverence with all sincerity, as Varo interpreted the matter, the ancestor's soul would be present on the tablet on which their name was inscribed.[27] Thus, Varo proclaimed, while expressing filial piety through actions such as weeping or the cleaning and tidying of tombs was permissible, offering more elaborate rites was both unacceptable and unnecessary, as no one would perform such rituals for their living parents.[28] In making this critique, Varo equated the Chinese word *qi* with soul.

In the *Interdict*, Charles Maigrot, relying on Dominican works on Chinese rites during the Controversy, unequivocally declared Chinese ancestral offering rites to be idolatrous, branding any missionary acceptance of these practices as 'tolerance of evil'.[29] He criticized the Confucian 'Book of Rites' (*Liji*) in particular, cautioning missionaries against teaching it to avoid instilling 'atheism and various superstitions' in their students.[30] Maigrot's strong condemnation of both Confucian rites and teachings asserted their incompatibility with Christianity.[31] However, unlike Varo, he did not substantiate his claims with references from the Confucian classics or other scholarly studies. This approach was to be criticized in Emperor Kangxi's 1721 decree, which expressed frustration with Western missionaries for criticizing Chinese traditions without thoroughly understanding or investigating them.[32]

Xia Dachang: Bridging Confucianism and Roman Catholicism

Xia Dachang, a licentiate from Jiangxi province who held a basic degree from the civil service examination but had no prospect of office, served as a Chinese assistant to the French Jesuit missionary Adrien Greslon (1618–96). Xia authored three treatises offering a comprehensive discussion of the ancestral rites. His writings, along with those of contemporaries such as Li Jiugong and Yan Mo, responded to questions posed

[27] Ibid. 419–20.
[28] Ibid. 397, 404.
[29] Noll, ed., *100 Roman Documents*, 8.
[30] Ibid. 10.
[31] Ibid.
[32] Li, *China in Transition*, 22.

by Jesuit missionaries, thus creating dialogues between Chinese believers and Western missionaries.[33] These texts, particularly those written around the time of Maigrot's 1693 *Interdict*, suggest a period of active engagement and debate over cultural and religious practices.

On the basis of Zhu Xi's commentary, Varo dismissed ancestral offering rites and Maigrot condemned the rites and the Confucian classic *Liji*. In contrast, Xia Dachang's three treatises, authored in around 1698, sought to refute their views through an extensive study of *Liji*.[34] Xia's aim was to reconcile Chinese traditions with Roman Catholic beliefs, highlighting filial piety (*xiao*) as a common value in both. He insisted that the discussion on ancestral offering rites should be rooted in their original Confucian meaning. Xia's analysis of the *Liji* asserted that these rites were driven by humanity, morality and social order, rather than a desire to seek blessings from ancestors.[35] He explained that they originated from the profound grief experienced upon a parent's death, with the rites serving as a way to continue honouring parents posthumously.[36] Xia questioned the belief in ancestors' bestowing blessings or causing disasters, citing Zhu Xi – a state orthodoxy prevalent among intellectuals in his era – to support his argument that the rites were about serving and respecting ancestors, not seeking their protection.[37]

---

[33] Xia's 'Catechism of Rites' and another five of the twenty-eight treatises – 李九功 [Li Jiugong]'s '禮俗明辨' ['Lisu mingbian'; 'Difference between Rites and Secular Customs']; 嚴謨 [Yan Mo]'s '李師條問' ['Lishi tiaowen'; 'Questions from Father Li'] and '草稿抄白' ['Caogao chaobai'; 'Copy of the Draft']; and those by two unknown authors, '禮儀答問' ['Liyi dawen'; 'Catechism of Rites'] and '芻言' ['Chuyan'; 'The Humble Opinions'] – were written to respond to questions about ancestral offering rites. Among these six writings, twenty-three common questions have similar wording and contents. Scholars point out that, according to the handwritten Portuguese annotations, 'The Humble Opinions' was most probably written at the request of Giandomenico Gabiani (Jesuit missionary, 1623–94). See Li Tiangang, *The Chinese Rites Controversy*, 146–7. The person 'Lishi' indicated in the title of 'Lishi tiaowen' ['Questions from Father Li'] could be Simon Rodrigues (Jesuit missionary, 1645–1704): see ibid. 141; Liwei, *The Chinese Rites Controversy*, 74. In other words, it is reasonable to infer that Jesuit missionaries raised specific concerns about ancestral offering rites. Hence, Xia and other believers provided their responses in these six writings.

[34] The estimated date of Xia's writings is cited from Li Tiangang, *The Chinese Rites Controversy*, 228; Liwei, *The Chinese Rites Controversy*, 85.

[35] Xia, 'Sacrificial Rites in the Book of Rites', 84.

[36] Ibid. 88–9, 93–4, 100–1, 104.

[37] If he cannot say for sure whether the deceased ancestors would be present during the ritual, how 'could he believe that ancestors have the power to give blessings or disasters to their descendants?': ibid. 83; Xia, 'Catechism of Rites', 136.

Xia Dachang argued that while the *Liji* mentions blessing associated with practising ancestral offering rites, in Confucianism, these 'blessings' refer to a state of peace and harmony in all relationships achieved through cultivating filial piety.[38] Although the *Liji* states that 'The sacrifices of such men have their own blessing', Xia argued that one should not stop at this point but consider the following explanation:

> [This is] not indeed what the secular culture calls a blessing. The blessing here means perfection. It is the name given to the *bai shun* [fulfilment of duties]. When nothing is left incomplete or improperly discharged, this is what we call perfection. Perfection implies completing everything that should be done in one's internal self, and externally the performance of everything according to the proper way.[39]

Thus, the blessings mentioned are not granted by departed ancestors but are the result of the ritual participant's moral perfection and their fulfilling of internal (filial piety) and all necessary external (ritual performance) requirements.

Filial piety, as a key aspect of humanity, Xia went on, aligns with one's internal self and exerts a moral influence that encourages respect for elders and authorities.[40] These rites enable individuals to demonstrate love and reverence towards their parents, reinforcing the concept of filial piety throughout society. Xia Dachang argued that consistently showing love and reverence to one's ancestors teaches individuals how to maintain harmonious relationships with others.[41] He cited the *Liji*: 'Among all methods of ensuring good conduct, rites are paramount, with sacrificial rites being the most critical'.[42] Xia contended that since ancient rulers prioritized sacrificial rites over legal systems for governance, these ancestral offering rites held an indispensable place in Chinese society and should not be lightly discarded.[43]

---

[38] Xia, 'Sacrificial Rites in the Book of Rites', 97–9.

[39] '賢者之祭也, 必受其福' and '非世所謂福也。福者, 備也, 備者百順之名也。無所不順者之謂備, 言內盡于己, 外盡于道也': ibid. 97. My translation of 'Liji' ['Sacrificial Rites in the Book of Rites'] in this article is based on the translation made by James Legge and taken from Donald Sturgeon, 'Chinese Text Project: A Dynamic Digital Library of Premodern Chinese', online at: <https://ctext.org>, accessed 28 January 2024.

[40] Xia, 'Sacrificial Rites in the Book of Rites', 98–9.

[41] Ibid. 102.

[42] '凡治人之道, 莫急于禮。禮有五經, 莫重于祭': ibid. 94–5.

[43] Ibid.

Xia then pointed out how the purpose of these rites was to express and nurture filial piety, differentiating them from the Roman Catholic practice of offering sacrifices to God. He argued that these Confucian rites were essential not just for expressing humanity, but also for fostering morality, thus playing a key role in traditional Chinese ethical education and statecraft. The potential abolition of these rites could cause trouble, as it might be perceived as an attempt by Roman Catholics to undermine Chinese political and educational foundations.[44] He advised the Roman Catholic community to utilize this aspect of human nature to guide the Chinese people towards understanding the transcendent nature of God.[45] The purpose of ancestral rites in China, and the emphasis placed on them, lay in expressing and cultivating filial piety among descendants, a virtue that closely aligned with the ethical teachings of the Ten Commandments in the Bible.[46] The act of undertaking ancestor rites aimed to honour one's roots and origins. If one traced the source of one's ancestors, paying homage to and remembering them, then God would be recognized as the ultimate origin that humanity should honour and revere.[47]

While he referenced Zhu Xi to argue that ancestral rites focused on respecting ancestors rather than seeking blessing, Xia, following Ricci, criticized Zhu Xi's cosmology for denying a transcendent divine creator, and deemed this view most harmful to the Chinese.[48] Moreover, in order to claim that belief in the immortality of the soul could be found in the Confucian classics, Xia and other Chinese defenders of Confucian rites, along with the Jesuits, used the term *linghun* (rational soul) interchangeably with *hun* (a vital substance),[49] the original term found in the *Liji*, asserting that these ancestral souls were neither regarded as deities nor capable of freely traversing back to the human world without God's permission.[50]

---

[44] Ibid. 96.
[45] Ibid. 94.
[46] Ibid. 90.
[47] Ibid. 93.
[48] Xia, 'Sacrificial Rites in the Book of Rites', 85.
[49] However, Xia did not offer a definition of the concept of *po*.
[50] Xia, '贛州堂夏相公聖名瑪第亞回方老爺書' ['Ganzhoutang Xiaxianggong shengming Madiya hui fanglaoye shu'; 'Letter from Xia of the Ganzhou Church, Saint Name Matthias, to Mr. Fang'] and '禮儀問答' ['Catechism of Rites'], in Standaert and Dukink, eds, *Chinese Christian Texts*, 10: 35–42, at 39; and 130. See also 邱晟 [Qiu Sheng], '述聞篇' ['Shuwen pian'; 'On Recounting Heard Knowledge']; and 李九功 [Li Jiugong], '證禮蒭議 (早期抄本)' ['Zhengli chuyi (zaoqi chaoben)'; 'Treatise on Ancestral Rites (Early

However, like Varo, Xia and the pro-rites missionaries overlooked the fact that the Christian notion of the rational soul was absent from Zhu Xi's Neo-Confucianism, the state orthodoxy prevalent at the time. While they used Zhu Xi's interpretation to argue that Confucian rites were non-idolatrous, they paradoxically dismissed Zhu's understanding of *qi* as vital energy flow – the very rationale Zhu used to justify the rites as non-superstitious – in their attempt to prove the immortality of the soul in Confucianism.[51] They also neglected Zhu's explanation that *hun* – which drives mental functions – and *po* – which contributes to the body's physicality and senses – are vital substances generated by *qi* that together animate the human body and its faculties.[52] Despite this, Xia and the pro-rites missionaries still translated *hun*, derived from *qi*, as 'soul' and interchangeably employed the term *linghun* (rational soul). Yet, if *qi* and *hun* could be equated to the Christian rational soul, it became difficult to dismiss the anti-rites missionaries' belief that Confucianism contained elements of superstition, given that the accepted reading of the Confucian classics is that they do not, as the pro-rites group argued, explicitly state that *qi*, *hun* or *po* cannot traverse freely or are subject to the Christian God. Conversely, if they could not be equated, how could one convince the Chinese that the Confucian classics supported belief in the immortality of the rational soul?

Although Xia and the Jesuit missionaries recognized filial piety as a core value of ancestral offering rites that aligned with Roman Catholic beliefs, they overlooked the deeper understanding that, in the Neo-Confucian context of their time, filial piety (as an internal morality) was inseparable from external materiality, namely, bodily presence and actions. According to Zhu Xi, descendants expressed filial piety through rites that reassembled the deceased's *hun* and *po* by performing rituals with perceivable reverent love, *as though* the

---

[51] 朱熹 [Zhu Xi], '四書或問' ['Sishu huowen'; 'The Queries of the Four Books'], in Wang Yiliang, ed., 朱子全書 [*Zhuzi quan shu; Complete Writings of Master Zhu Xi*], 27 vols (Shanghai and Hefei, 2010), 6: 3; 朱熹 [Zhu Xi], '朱子語類' ['Zhuzi yulei'; 'Thematic Discourses of Master Zhu Xi'], in Yiliang, ed., *Complete Writings of Master Zhu Xi*, 14: 154.

Manuscript)'], in Standaert and Dukink, eds, *Chinese Christian Texts*, 9: 63–90 and 10: 177–362, at 9: 74 and 10: 289–90.

[52] Zhu Xi, 'The Queries of the Four Books' and 'Thematic Discourses of Master Zhu Xi', in Yiliang, ed., *Complete Writings of Master Zhu Xi*, 6: 3; Zhu Xi, 'Thematic Discourses of Master Zhu Xi', in Yiliang, ed., *Complete Writings of Master Zhu Xi*, 6: 3 and 14: 74, 163–4.

departed were still alive.[53] Zhu emphasized that while the existence of *hun* and *po* after death was a real aspect of the ritual process and not merely symbolic, they should not be considered 'gods' or 'ghosts,' as they are products of *qi*, the vital energy foundational to humans and the universe.[54] In short, physical participation in rites – through bodily presence and actions – was essential for embodying and cultivating intangible moral values such as love, reverence and filial piety.

To summarize, Xia Dachang and the pro-rites Jesuit missionaries argued for Confucian belief in the immortality of the soul, whereas anti-rites missionaries, including the Dominicans and the mission administrator Charles Maigrot, challenged Confucian belief in the soul's presence in ancestral rites. Both sides recognized the importance of filial piety and its parallels with Roman Catholicism, yet they disagreed over the necessity of maintaining traditional ancestral offering rites. While Maigrot and the Dominican missionaries called for a complete ban on these rites, the Jesuits, as noted earlier, suggested reforming them by integrating them with Roman Catholic rituals. This Jesuit proposal reflects a shared concern about superstition with the Dominicans and Maigrot. However, Xia and the missionaries arguably failed to recognize the difficulties of accommodating Zhu Xi's Neo-Confucianism to the Christian notion of the soul, nor did they fully acknowledge the interconnectivity between internal morality and external ritual in Confucian practices. The episode shows that, even when indigenous actors were fully involved in the process, accommodationist strategies on the peripheries of Christianity remained fraught with cultural difficulty.

Conclusion

The Chinese Rites Controversy was not only a pivotal moment in Sino-European relations but also offers important lessons for contemporary, twenty-first-century Confucian-Christian dialogue on cultural assimilation and religious tolerance. Re-evaluating the Controversy through the lens of the human body reveals a critical oversight by Xia Dachang and the Western missionaries: the differing perceptions of human existence in the two traditions and the inseparability of internal

---

[53] Zhu Xi, 'Thematic Discourses of Master Zhu Xi', in Yiliang, ed., *Complete Writings of Master Zhu Xi*, 14: 174, 894.
[54] Ibid. 155, 899.

morality (filial piety) from external materiality (bodily presence and actions). This disconnect led to an underestimation of the need to appreciate and respect cultural differences.

Historically, the Controversy created a rift between the Qing state and the papacy, and it remains an unresolved issue. The challenge of reconciling Chinese identity with Christian beliefs is becoming increasingly contentious in China, prompting Sinophone scholars to call for a deeper exploration of this topic, given its ongoing relevance in the contemporary Chinese context. However, current studies have not significantly advanced beyond the seventeenth-century debates between Xia and the European missionaries on how to interpret the nature of Confucian offering rites.

The modern scholar of comparative religion, Chen Ming, has critiqued a long tradition of studies comparing Confucianism and Christianity: 'Dialogues either became an abstract discussion of logic among texts or fell into the trap of finding and proving doctrinal similarities. While well-intentioned, these dialogues lost their foundation and have achieved little success'.[55] If progress is to be made, it is necessary to re-examine the historical script and seek to identify overlooked aspects in the centuries-long Confucian-Christian debate over ancestral rites. Such an approach could lead to a deeper and more nuanced understanding of the 'other'. In the seventeenth-century Neo-Confucian context, the Qing state viewed ancestral offering rites as reflecting the interdependence between visible ritual performance and invisible moral values. Removing the external aspect of the ritual equates to disregarding the distinctive Chinese perspective on the nature of human beings and the development of a moral society. Acknowledging this distinctiveness might prove crucial in contemporary Confucian-Christian dialogue.

---

[55] '對話被抽象為從文本到文本的邏輯研討或淪為互相確證的對教義間最大公約數的找尋。在各種善意得到展現的同時，對話也因失去根柢而收效甚微': 陳明 [Chen Ming], '儒耶對話 以何為本?—兼議利瑪竇、何光滬關於儒教的若干論述' ['Ruye Duihua Yihe Weiben: Jianlun Li Madou, He Guanghu Guanyu Rujiao de Ruogan Lunshu'; 'What is the Foundation of Confucian-Christian Dialogue? Remarks on Li Madou and He Guanghu's Studies on Confucianism'], in Luo Bingxiang and Xie Wenyu, eds, 耶儒對談: 問題在哪裡 [*Ruye duitan: wenti zai nali?*; *A Confucian-Christian Dialogue in Contemporary Context*] (Guilin, 2010), 1–700, at 435–6.

An Anglican 'Republic of Letters'? George Berkeley and the Early Enlightenment in Colonial New England, 1724–75

Daniel Inman
London

When George Berkeley was seeking funds to establish a college on Bermuda, he expressed the need to train a colonial clergy that he deemed 'meanly qualified in both learning and morals' who might yet become instrumental in a 'reformation of manners' and 'the propagation of the Gospel among the American savages' on Britain's imperial periphery. When Berkeley arrived in Rhode Island in 1724, however, he encountered instead Anglicans who were well read in the philosophy and theology of the early Enlightenment. Using the correspondence of Berkeley and the New England priest and theologian Samuel Johnson, this article explores how Anglican clergy and their institutions – operating in a religiously plural environment as members of a denominational minority – were actively developing an 'Anglican republic of letters' that was advancing early Enlightenment thought in the colonies in the decades prior to the Revolution.

INTRODUCTION

On 24 July 1730, the Connecticut Anglican minister and theologian Samuel Johnson (1696–1772) penned a letter of thanks to the philosopher George Berkeley, whose hospitality he had just enjoyed at his home in Newport, Rhode Island. He wrote of 'the vast pleasure and advantage I enjoyed in your most engaging conversation. I think myself very unhappy that I am so remote from it: I design, however,

St Luke's and Christ Church, Chelsea, London, UK. E-mail: danielinman@chelseaparish.org.

I am grateful to the reviewers for their comments on the original manuscript, as well as to Professor Andrew Chandler for his advice and encouragement.

Studies in Church History 61 (2025), 419–439 © The Author(s), 2025. Published by Cambridge University Press on behalf of the Ecclesiastical History Society.
 doi:10.1017/stc.2024.46

if I can pay my respects to you again before winter'.[1] He proceeded also to thank Berkeley for the gift of a sizeable number of books to be dispersed 'into these parts', including eight cases of books to the rector of Yale College, Elisha Williams (1694–1755); a copy of Hooker's *Polity* to Johnson's pupil Henry Caner (*c*.1699–1792); a book by William Chillingworth (1602–44, possibly his *The Religion of the Protestants*) and one of Berkeley's own *Dialogues* to a Mr Wilmore. 'All in these parts', wrote Johnson, 'who have any taste for learning and good sense are mightily enamoured with your philosophy. Twenty at least I know of who entirely fall in with it and many have got the booksellers of Boston to send for several sets of your books.'[2]

The gratitude expressed by Johnson for the Berkeleys' hospitality and books was, on one level, unremarkable: testimony to a happy meeting of two learned people who had discussed philosophy and theology on a summer's afternoon. On another, the meeting of Berkeley and Johnson was symbolic of a growing network of learning and education – an Anglican republic of letters, perhaps – that was no longer purely defined by correspondence across the Atlantic and written material dispatched from London or Oxford but, unusually, by face-to-face conversation.

The art of propagating the gospel to England's, and then Britain's, imperial peripheries in the early eighteenth century might be imagined as an exercise in the pure transmission of orthodox Christian theological principles: the conveyance of 'a serious Sense of Religion' to both colonists and natives. Indeed, it was evident in the original seal of the Society for the Propagation of the Gospel (SPG): a preacher aboard a ship, holding a Bible and looking out to a host of people running to the shore, above whom was written the text from Acts 16: 9: 'Transiens adiuva nos' ('Come over and help us').[3] Chartered by the Crown on 16 June 1701, the SPG sought to meet this objective, and its work was enthusiastically promoted by both church and Crown, with annual anniversary sermons used, not only to raise funds, but also to underline the Church of England's providential duty to minister to Britain's 'Plantations, Colonies and Factories beyond the Seas'

---

[1] New Haven, CT, Yale University Archives, Johnson Family Papers, MS 305, folder 175, Samuel Johnson to George Berkeley, 24 July 1730; quoted in *The Correspondence of George Berkeley*, ed. Marc A. Hight (Cambridge, 2013), 329–30.
[2] Ibid.
[3] A text also used on the original Massachusetts Bay Colony's seal, struck in 1629.

through the 'better Support and Maintenance of an Orthodox Clergy in Foreign Parts'.[4]

This article explores the way in which the Church of England's life on the imperial peripheries was more than simply the transmission of the gospel, but was also instrumental in the development of the early Enlightenment in New England. The role of missionaries in the 'scientific' study and interpretation of the frontier has already been considered by several scholars, noting the influence, in particular, of Samuel Purchas and White Kennett as English authors who sought 'to bridge intellectually and spiritually the Anglican community across the Atlantic'.[5] Similarly, those in the colonies could be equally interested in the geographical and ethnographical. The SPG missionary Francis Vernod, for example, wrote home to the SPG in the January of 1723/4 from South Carolina, offering a wealth of information to the Society, not just on the difficulty of converting enslaved peoples on plantations, but also on the rites and custom of the Cherokees, the quality of the harvest that year, the provision of other religious groups, and the condition of buildings.[6] This was information which clearly assisted the objectives of the SPG, but which could also be an important source of information for the imperial authorities more generally, not least through the secretary of the Society's presence on the Council of Trade and Plantations.[7]

However, Anglican clergy in the colonies were not only increasingly engaged in interpreting the New World to the metropolis, but were also themselves actively propagating and institutionalizing early Enlightenment philosophy and theology. Hitherto, attention has largely focussed on the Boston 'liberalism' of Congregationalists, particularly of Benjamin Colman and John Leverett at Harvard at

---

[4] Daniel O'Connor, *Three Centuries of Mission: The United Society for the Propagation of the Gospel 1701–2000* (London, 2000), 7.

[5] Louisiane Ferlier, 'Building Religious Communities with Books: The Quaker and Anglican Transatlantic Libraries, 1650–1710', in Mark Towsey and Robert B. Kyle, eds, *Before the Public Library: Reading, Community and Identity in the Atlantic World, 1650–1850'* (Leiden, 2018), 31–51. See White Kennett, *Bibliothecae Americanae Primordia* (London, 1713), ii.

[6] Oxford, Bodl., USPG MSS, A18, fols 69–75, Francis Vernod to the Secretary of the SPG, 13 January 1723/4.

[7] William Bulman has highlighted the significance of the colonial chaplain as an enlightened interpreter in his book, *Anglican Enlightenment* (Cambridge, 2015), illustrating the role of Lancelot Addison in seventeenth-century Tangier in describing Islam and Judaism in north Africa and its contribution to developing concepts of religion per se.

the turn of the eighteenth century. John Corrigan, in particular, has delineated how the 'catholick Congregationalists' at Harvard and Brattle Street Church combined their commitment to covenant theology with an enthusiasm for the latitudinarian writings of John Wilkins, Joseph Glanvill, John Locke, Edward Stillingfleet, John Tillotson and Simon Patrick, leading Anglican writers in the late seventeenth century who combined an interest in the new experimental philosophy with a plea for moderation in religion.[8] Through Berkeley's encounter with Johnson in Rhode Island, however, it is asserted in this article that local Anglican individuals and institutions were very much part of this transatlantic 'republic of letters'.

EDUCATION, EMPIRE AND GEORGE BERKELEY

The eighteenth-century Anglican Atlantic networks of the SPG and the Society for Promoting Christian Knowledge (the SPCK, also founded by Thomas Bray just before the SPG in 1698) were marked by their strongly educational instincts. After all, if the Restoration church's new baptism service for those of riper years were to be employed on English plantations in the Americas and Indies, then schooling and books were requisite preliminaries.[9] The ambitions of George Berkeley in the mid-1720s were in this vein. As a young Irish Anglican who had been a distinguished fellow of Trinity College, Dublin, Berkeley's instincts to serve the New World were in large part prompted by his anxieties about the old: 'We have made a jest of public spirit and cancelled all respect for whatever our laws and religion repute sacred'.[10] When he returned to England in 1720 after a continental tour as private tutor to St George Ashe, he encountered a society that he had come to believe was mired in sin. By the spring of 1724, he had secured preferment to the deanery of Derry, but its handsome income was no

---

[8] John Corrigan, *The Prism of Piety: Catholic Congregational Clergy at the Beginning of the Enlightenment* (New York, 1991), 9–31. Corrigan builds upon the earlier work of Norman Fiering ('The First American Enlightenment: Tillotson, Leverett, and Philosophical Anglicanism', *New England Quarterly* 54 [1981], 307–44) and Theodore Hornberger ('Benjamin Colman and the Enlightenment', *New England Quarterly* 12 [1939], 227–40) in elucidating the influence of Anglican writings on the Boston 'liberals'.

[9] Roman Catholic missions were generally less committed to educating those enslaved prior to their baptism.

[10] George Berkeley, *Essay towards Preventing the Ruin of Great Britain*, in *The Works of George Berkeley, Bishop of Cloyne*, ed. Thomas E. Jessop, 9 vols (London, 1948–57), 6: 84.

inducement to settle; rather, it spurred him to greater zeal in his desire to effect moral and religious reform. In the summer of 1722, he had already written to his great friend John Percival, an Irish nobleman, of his vision:

> I have determined with myself to spend the residue of my days in the island of Bermuda, where I trust in Providence I may be the mean instrument of doing good to mankind. Your Lordship is not to be told that the reformation of manners among the English in our western plantations, and the propagation of the Gospel among the American savages, are two points of high moment. The natural way of doing this is by founding a college or seminary in some convenient part of the West Indies, where the English youth of our plantations may be educated in such sort as to supply the churches with pastors of good morals and good learning, a thing (God knows!) much wanted. In the same seminary a number of young American savages may also be educated till they have taken their degree of Master of Arts. And being by that time well instructed in Christian religion, practical mathematics, and other liberal arts and sciences, and early endued with public spirited principles and inclinations, they may become the fittest missionaries for spreading, religion, morality, and civil life, among their countrymen.[11]

A few months later, Berkeley published a tract, *A Proposal For the better Supplying of Churches in our Foreign Plantations, and for Converting the Savage American to Christianity* (1725), which further outlined his reasoning. In common with earlier calls to missionary zeal, Berkeley presented his scheme as a means of renewing the faith at home as much as securing Protestant influence abroad, noting that 'the protestant religion hath of late years considerably lost ground, and America seems the likeliest of place, wherein to make up for what hath been lost in Europe, provided the proper methods are taken'.[12]

---

[11] George Berkeley to John Percival, 4 March 1722/3, in Hight, *The Correspondence of George Berkeley*, 185–6. See also the pamphlet, 'Proposals for Propagating the Gospel in All Countries', published in Gordon's *Geographical Grammar* in early 1701, which urged that new seminaries be established to train clergy in 'pagan languages' so that 'in process of time, [they might] extend the knowledge of the English Tongue over that large American Continent on the Western parts of our English Plantations; and together with it the knowledge of our most holy Religion: And so make at once a mighty accession of Members to the Christian Church, and add a vast Tract of Land to the English Empire.' London, LPL, SPG Papers, 7: 4–7, 6 January 1701.

[12] George Berkeley, *A Proposal For the better Supplying of Churches in our Foreign Plantations, and for Converting the Savage American to Christianity* (London, 1724), in *British Imperialism: Three Documents*, Research Library of Colonial America, ed. Richard C. Robey (New York, 1972), 17–18.

The choice of Bermuda was misguided. Berkeley believed the American mainland to have 'little sense of religion', with Anglican clergymen there being 'very meanly qualified both in learning and morals'. They have, he continued, 'quit their native country on no other motive, than that they are not able to procure a livelihood in it'.[13] Drawing on out-of-date travelers' reports, Berkeley thought Bermuda was a moral, climatic, geographical and economic idyll, the inhabitants having 'the greatest simplicity of manners, more innocence, honesty, and good nature.'[14] Berkeley's second edition of the *Proposal*, published several months later (having acquired a royal charter for the proposed college) was moderated only insomuch as it stressed that 'gospel liberty' did not require the emancipation of the enslaved (no doubt to placate commercial and mercantile anxiety); further, it asserted that the needs of the English settlers, 'themselves degenerated into Heathens', had not been forgotten.[15]

Berkeley paid no attention to the colleges already present on the mainland, having decided that Harvard and Yale 'subsisted to little or no purpose' and supplied evidence that 'where Ignorance or ill Manners once take place in a Seminary, they are sure to be handed down in a Succession of illiterate or worthless Men'.[16] Making no reference to the Codrington bequest or even to the College of William and Mary (a 1693 Church of England foundation in Williamsburg, Virginia), Berkeley pursued his project zealously, gaining funds and parliamentary support.[17] He seemed willfully ignorant of those who questioned it, not least Thomas Bray who published in 1727 a dossier on his societies' missionary activity across the Atlantic – his *Missionalia* – that was quietly devastating of Berkeley's casual assumptions about the usefulness of the American clergy (whom Bray robustly defended). Nor was Bray impressed by Berkeley's suggestion of transporting

<hr>

[13] Edwin Gaustad, *George Berkeley in America* (New Haven, CT, 1979), 32.

[14] George Berkeley to John Percival, 4 March 1722/3, in Hight, *The Correspondence of George Berkeley*, 186.

[15] Berkeley, *Works*, 7: 360–1; quoted in Gaustad, *George Berkeley in America*, 34. Gaustad suggests that Berkeley had probably been reliant on reports of Bermuda from Lewis Hughes, a clergyman who had written a century earlier in support of commercial investment: Lewis Hughes, *A Letter, Sent Into England from the Summer Ilands* (London, 1615); idem, *A Plaine and True Relation of the Goodnes of God towards the Sommer Ilands* (London, 1621).

[16] Berkeley, *Works*, 7: 354.

[17] The principal source of funds for the project was derived from Berkeley's being named as co-executor and joint residuary legatee of the estate of Esther Van Homrigh in June 1723.

native American children to Bermuda to be educated ('the most *Unchristian*, or rather the most *Anti-Christian* Method, to propagate the Gospel', he wrote).[18] Whether it was Berkeley's unwillingness to engage with those 'who would be more ready and Capable to Assist him' from 'our *Religious Societies*' (the SPG and SPCK, the latter to which Berkeley had been elected in 1725),[19] or just fury at what he considered sheer naivety, Bray was evidently anxious that Berkeley's highly publicized and well-funded scheme would undermine the endeavours of the church societies.

By the summer of 1728, however, considerable sums had been promised by Parliament (£20,000) despite the questions raised by both sceptical merchants and those who argued funds should be preserved for the founding of Georgia. Furthermore, it was unclear whether George II would sustain his father's financial commitment to the college.[20] In a bid to keep the project alive and encourage ministers to provide the promised money, Berkeley set out from Gravesend to Rhode Island via Williamsburg, Virginia, with his family and future tutors.

Arriving in January 1729, and expecting to stay for a period, Berkeley bought a farm in Middletown – staffed by enslaved Africans – just outside Newport, which he expanded in the Palladian style and renamed Whitehall. It was an architectural expression of the learned society that Berkeley hoped to bring to both Newport and, in due course, the wider colonies through his plans for St Paul's College.

Colonial Clergy and the 'New Learning'

However, far from discovering a clergy 'very meanly qualified both in learning and morals', Berkeley was soon visited by Samuel Johnson, the rector of Christ Church, Stratford, with whom he established a friendship. Johnson had read Berkeley already and, in him, Berkeley encountered the fruit of what, by the third decade of the eighteenth century, was a growing appetite among the New England clergy for

---

[18] Thomas Bray, *Missionalia: Or, A Collection of Missionary Pieces Relating to the Conversion of the Heathen; Both the African Negroes and the American Indians* (London, 1727), 73. Italics original.
[19] Ibid. 40.
[20] Funding for the college was also promised from the king, who offered £1,000 per annum from the revenues derived from the recently acquired island of St Kitts. The monies promised by Parliament would equate to roughly £2.3 m p.a. today.

what Johnson called the 'New Learning'. Johnson himself had been something of a prodigy. The son of a Congregationalist Connecticut farmer, able to read and write by the age of four and to understand Hebrew by the age of five, he went to the Collegiate School (the original name of Yale University) in 1714, there composing 'A Synopsis of Natural Philosophy', which he duly expanded into 'An Encyclopedia of Philosophy'. In 1716, he became a tutor at Yale, whereupon he lectured on Locke, Copernican astronomy, medicine and algebra.[21] Ordained as a Congregationalist pastor for West Haven in 1720, Johnson had been developing doubts about his ministry as he continued to digest the 800 or so books which had been donated to Yale by the American-born colonial agent for Connecticut and Massachusetts, Jeremiah Dummer, in 1714.

Dummer had been the first American to gain a European degree (at Utrecht) having proved himself at Harvard and – through his study of mathematics as a preliminary to his continental theology – he exhibited the growing influence of Newtonian rationality on American theology, much to the unhappiness of some Massachusetts Calvinists. Reflecting on the importance of Dummer's gift to Yale, Johnson in his *Autobiography* (1771) reflected that, in the early part of the century, 'there was no such thing as any books of learning to be had in those times under a 100 or 150 years old such as the first settlers ... brought with them' and the value of lighting upon Bacon's *Advancement of Learning*, in particular, reshaped Johnson's approach to intellectual endeavour. In his *Autobiography*, Johnson wrote how, aged eighteen:

> [He] had then all at once the vast pleasure of reading the works of our best English poets, philosophers and divines, Shakespeare and Milton etc. Locke and Norris etc., Boyle and Newton etc., Patrick and Whitby, Barrow, Tillotson, South, Sharp, Scot and Sherlock etc. All this was like a flood of day to this low state of mind ... he found himself like one at once emerging out of the glimmer of the twilight into the full sunshine of open day.[22]

---

[21] Joseph J. Ellis, *The New England Mind in Transition: Samuel Johnson of Connecticut, 1696–1772* (New Haven, CT, 1973), 44–6. It is suggested that Johnson had been introduced to Jonathan Edwards as a thirteen-year-old: see Claude M. Newlin, *Philosophy and Religion in Colonial America* (New York, 1962), 25. Newlin offers a helpful overview of the sea-change in American philosophy and the roles of Johnson and Edwards therein.

[22] Herbert and Carol Schneider, eds, *Samuel Johnson, President of King's College: His Career and Writings*, 4 vols (New York, 1929), 1: 7.

Johnson's 'enlightenment' was not limited to his exposure of late Stuart and Williamite logic and mathematics, but was also enabled through his reading of works by Richard Hooker, Thomas Ken, Robert Nelson, William Laud, John Pearson and Jeremy Taylor in Dummer's collection. Reading these in the company of some of his Yale colleagues, a small group that included the rector of Yale, Timothy Cutler, fellow tutors Daniel Browne, George Pigot and another Congregational minister James Wetmore, they became anxious about the validity of their own orders. With them, Johnson renounced his Congregationalist orders in 1722 – an event sometimes referred to in the denominational historiography as the 'great apostasy' – and travelled to England, whereupon they were ordained in the Church of England.[23]

While Johnson returned to America with clearly more defined views about the significance of the sacraments and episcopacy, his high churchmanship was nonetheless coupled with a theology shaped by his reading of John Tillotson, Benjamin Hoadly, William Beveridge and John Locke *inter alia* during 1719–22, that was increasingly anti-determinist in its understanding of salvation and practical in its focus on virtue and piety.[24] In this sense, he was emblematic of the SPG's mission, as articulated by Bray, to establish 'natural Religion' as the foundation to all theological engagement before proceeding to the necessity of revelation.[25]

While Anglicans were a religious minority in New England, Johnson's ethical and theological writings – many of which were irenic defences of Anglican doctrine and polity – were emblematic of a post-Newtonian philosophy that was finding a ready audience in Harvard and Yale, as John Corrigan and Norman Fiering have identified.[26] Henry Newman (who matriculated at Harvard in 1687) noted how tutors like John Leverett and the college treasurer Thomas Brattle had encouraged such engagement, and that there were twenty times more friends to the Church of England in America 'since these gentlemen governed the College'. Indeed, they recommended 'the reading of

---

[23] Sydney E. Ahlstrom, *A Religious History of the American People* (New Haven, CT, 1972), 224. Corrigan considers the 'Yale incident' briefly in his monograph but gives relatively little attention to Johnson.

[24] For Johnson's catalogue of reading between 1719 and 1755, see Schneider and Schneider, eds, *Samuel Johnson, President of King's College*, 1: 497–502.

[25] Robert Prichard, *A History of the Episcopal Church* (Harrisburg, PA, 1991), 34.

[26] Corrigan, *The Prism of Piety*, 58–64; Fiering, 'First American Enlightenment', 322–3.

episcopal authors as the best books to form our minds in religious matters, and preserve us from those narrow principles that kept us at a distance from the church of England'.[27]

As Harry Stout has explored in *The New England Soul*, for tutors like Leverett who had hitherto contended with a very restrictive Calvinist mindset, such writers were increasingly revered. The new century, informed by the different tenor of politics and religion that followed the accession of William and Mary, had, Stout asserts, inaugurated a process of 'anglicization' in New England in which ties with the mother country were increasingly valued, and English authors – theological and otherwise – treasured:

> No well-read provincial could escape the excitement these luminaries were generating in science, literature, epistemology, and ethics; nor could they resist English influence in dress, speech, literary style, or architecture. For New England elites, England supplied standards of urbanity, sophistication, and broad-mindedness to be emulated for both intellectual and social reasons.[28]

The transmission of books and missionaries by the Church of England, not least those that Johnson oversaw extending their reach into New England, were symptomatic of what Rusty Roberson (with a view to the Scottish missionary groups, in particular) describes as a broader 'Christian knowledge movement' that was traversing the Atlantic. Like the Society for the Reformation of Manners and other civic groups in the late seventeenth and early eighteenth centuries, the leading moral reformer Josiah Woodward viewed 'in our Northern plantations in America … a more remarkable Reformation' than was evident in 'either of Her Majesty's Kingdoms'. Pan-Protestant, valuing moderation and rejecting narrow principle, Woodward identified the efforts of the transatlantic societies as effecting a reformation just as significant for Christianity as that which had transpired in the sixteenth century, not least through its influence upon third-generation Congregationalists like

---

[27] Boston, Massachusetts Historical Society, Newman Papers, Henry Newman to Mr Taylor (of the SPG), 29 March 1714; quoted in Corrigan, *The Prism of Piety*, 19.

[28] Harry S. Stout, *The New England Soul: Preaching and Religious Culture in Colonial New England* (New York, 2012), 120–1. See also Richard L. Bushman, *The Refinement of America: Persons, Houses, Cities* (New York, 1992), 174.

Leverett.[29] This was echoed south of the Scottish border among those who supported the work of Bray's societies, with White Kennett writing to Colman of his hopes 'for the Union of all Protestants in some future Age, when Charity and Peace shall prevail above Interest and Passion', underlining to Colman that the SPG missionaries were sent to bring Christian knowledge, rather than 'only contending for Rites and Ceremonies, or for Powers and Privileges.'[30]

INSTITUTIONALIZING ENLIGHTENED ANGLICANISM

In effecting this 'reformation', the dispatch of books from Oxford or London by Anglicans, both by the missionary societies and by individuals, was a crucial element in the development of the eastern seaboard's intellectual stimulation. In their study of eighteen colonial libraries before 1750, entitled *The Enlightened Reader in America*, David Lundberg and Henry May identified John Locke as being by far the most popular author, whose *An Essay Concerning Human Understanding* (1690) was the most frequently held item and continued to be throughout the century, even as more radical voices entered the American sphere after 1760. Alongside Locke as popular items in libraries can be identified John Tillotson's *Sermons* (1682), Joseph Addison's *Evidences of the Christian Religion* (1721) and George Berkeley's *Alciphron* (written while he was in America, and published in 1732). As Stout has written,

> a new generation of more tolerant Anglican preachers and essayists came to be widely read and admired for their pleasing style. According to the new liberal spirit, these authors could no longer be ignored simply because

---

[29] Josiah Woodward, *An Account of the Progress of the Reformation of Manners, in England, Scotland, and Ireland, And other Parts of Europe and America. With Some Reasons and Plain Directions for our Hearty and Vigorous Prosecution of this Glorious Work*, 12th edn (London, 1704), 7–9; quoted in Rusty Roberson, 'Enlightened Piety during the Age of Benevolence: The Christian Knowledge Movement in the British Atlantic World', *ChH* 85 (2016), 246–74, at 259. Roberson's study of the Scottish SPCK (SSPCK) outlines how the surprisingly ecumenical efforts of Anglicans and Presbyterians through the Society to undermine Jacobite culture was part of its original work in providing educational opportunities in the Highlands: ibid. 255–62. See also Stout, *New England Soul*, 124.

[30] *Life of the Right Reverend Dr. White Kennett, Late Lord Bishop of Peterborough, with several Original Letters of the late Archbishop of Canterbury, Dr. Tennison, the Late Earl of Sunderland, Bishop Kennett, &c. And some curious Original Papers and Records, never before Published* (London, 1730), 122–4. Kennett's letter was dated 28 July 1716.

they endorsed a different polity. Truth and "elegance" (a new value) came from many sources and had to be taken wherever they appeared.[31]

Perhaps most emblematic of the new learning in the realm of epistemology was the reading of Locke. He had been the subject of censure in Oxford in 1703, but by the mid-eighteenth century, Locke and the other latitudinarian pragmatists were required reading at the university as the Aristotelian method and the Laudian curriculum were being questioned.[32] As Nathan Guy has observed, Locke was read in continuity with Hooker and the Great Tew circle and, as Brian Young has noted, this 'Anglophone new logic became the accepted means of intellectual engagement in eighteenth-century England' and endured in a manner unlike the more radical Newtonian physico-theology of Samuel Clarke.[33] Moreover, the likes of Locke and Tillotson were also influential in shaping institutional expression in the colonies: Locke's broad and inclusive form of political philosophy was well suited to a religiously plural environment (in which there was constant watchfulness for what was perceived as theocratic tyranny), and Tillotson's advocacy of practical charity found broad receptivity in those seeking to cultivate public virtue in the colonies as much as in London.[34]

---

[31] Stout, *New England Soul*, 132.

[32] Nicholas Amhurst, a fellow of St John's College until he was expelled in 1719, wrote scornfully of the curriculum in the 1720s, but admitted that there had been improvements in the public examinations, such 'that *Locke, Clarke* and *Sir Isaac Newton* begin to find countenance in the schools, and that *Aristotle* seems to totter on his antient throne.' Italics original; Nicholas Amhurst, *Terrae Filius, or The Secret History of the University of Oxford in Several Essays*, 2 vols (London, 1726), xviii–xix; quoted in Lucy S. Sutherland and Leslie G. Mitchell, *The History of the University of Oxford*, 5: *The Eighteenth Century* (Oxford, 1986), 610. For a good overview of the changing curriculum, see also Laurence W. B Brockliss, *The University of Oxford: A History* (Oxford, 2016), 242–9.

[33] See Nathan Guy, *Finding Locke's God: The Theological Basis of John Locke's Political Thought* (London, 2020), 51; Brian M. Young, *Religion and Enlightenment in Eighteenth-Century England* (Oxford, 1998), 7.

[34] Alongside Butler's *Analogy*, it was arguably Tillotson's sermons that shaped the Anglophone theological mind more than any other writer between 1690 and 1770 – establishing, as Caroline Winterer has argued, the premium of simple prose that would be so valued by the leading figures of the 'second Enlightenment' in America. Thomas Paine in *Common Sense* (1776), for example, wrote that Tillotson offered 'nothing more than simple facts, plain arguments, and common sense', and Benjamin Franklin also commended Tillotson for using 'the plainest Words': Thomas Paine, *Common Sense* (Philadelphia, PA, 1776), 17; Benjamin Franklin, 'On Literary Style', *Pennsylvania Gazette*, 2 August 1733, online at: <https://founders.archives.gov/documents/Franklin/01-01-02-0102>, accessed 31 October 2024; both quoted in Caroline Winterer, *American Enlightenments: Pursuing Happiness in the Age*

Gillian Brown argues that, apart from his political treatises, Locke's *Some Thoughts Concerning Education* (1693) was 'probably the most widely instituted pedagogical theory in eighteenth-century Anglo-American culture', with his notions of consent increasingly shaping conceptions of household authority; in particular, how children consenting to the authority of their parents was the means by which citizens were formed in their relationship to the state.[35] All of this was the cultural background that was informing the changing curriculum of America's education – both that which was established and seeking to break free of a rigid Calvinism and those, as with Berkeley's planned institution, that were being fostered in the imagination.

While Stout and Corrigan note the receptivity of Congregationalists and Presbyterians to Anglican learning, what they do not delineate to the same degree is how Anglicans in colonial England were themselves propagators of such theology and homiletics, or the significance of Anglican library deposits in shaping this 'ecumenical' embrace of the 'New Learning'. While Berkeley had been dismissive of Dissenters, he encountered in Johnson (who remained close to Yale) a pre-existing shared conception of education, and an absence of formal Church of England institutions in New England. This allowed for a readier collaboration between Protestants of various stripes in the early to mid-century than would have been encountered in England or Ireland. Not only was there a pan-Protestant commitment to outmanoeuvring 'popery' that shaped the American religious mind, as documented by Carla Gardina Pestana, but there was also a shared dissemination of what Roberson and Stout term a practical 'enlightened piety' which was shaped by a Lockean liberalism and around which a consensus was forming, not only among the younger faculty at Harvard or Yale, but through active propagation by a new generation of colonial Anglicans.[36]

Such intellectual collaboration was perhaps not surprising: in the context of Whig political dominance in England and anxiety about Roman Catholicism, Locke's epistemic minimalism ('everyone is

---

of Reason (New Haven, CT, 2016), 175.). Tillotson's upbringing as a nonconformist aided his broad acceptance, of course. See also Stout, *New England Soul*, 125–6.

[35] Gillian Brown, *The Consent of the Governed: The Lockean Legacy in Early American Culture* (Cambridge, MA, 2001), 34–6.

[36] See David Hempton, *Methodism: Empire of the Spirit* (New Haven, CT, 2006), 32–54; Carla Gardina Pestana, *Protestant Empire: Religion and the Making of the British Atlantic World* (Philadelphia, PA, 2011), 1–15.

orthodox to himself) chimed with the language of liberty in Hanoverian propaganda and a broader resistance to 'priestcraft' in a variety of colonies under threat from French and Indian enemies (the latter often equated with Roman Catholics for their 'superstitions'). In Locke's *Reasonableness of Christianity* (1695), as well as in *A Letter Concerning Toleration* (1689), both staples of colonial libraries, the inward persuasion of the mind took precedence over the 'creeds and profitable inventions', the 'lustrations' and 'expiations' of their 'pompous, fantastical, cumbersome ceremonies'; likewise, against their 'systems of divinity', 'vain philosophy', 'foolish metaphysics', and those 'speculations and niceties, obscure terms, and abstract notions' of the 'holy tribe' of the priests.[37] Building on the pragmatism of Hooker and the epistemic breadth of the latitudinarians, this not only chimed with the tenor of New England politics but, interestingly, also with Johnson's Anglicanism – episcopal yet learned, sacramental and enlightened – and consequently acted as a catalyst for the Church of England's cultural and political influence in New England society in a way that few might have expected in the late seventeenth century.[38]

Despite his initial dismissal of the colonial colleges, it is indicative of a shared philosophy of learning that, through his connection to Johnson, Berkeley decided to endow Yale with both books and property. He had already given books to the college via Johnson in September 1731, writing from Rhode Island of how he prayed 'God's blessing on you and your endeavours to promote religion and learning in this uncultivated part of the world'.[39] Having returned to London in the autumn of 1731, having accepted no further funds were going to be forthcoming from the metropolis, Berkeley wrote to Johnson in July 1732 offering his Rhode Island estate to Yale:

> It is my opinion that as human learning and the improvements of reason are of no small use in religion, so it would very much forward those ends, if some of your students were enabled to subsist longer at their studies, and if by a

---

[37] John Locke, *Reasonableness of Christianity* (London, 1695), 6, 147, 159, 169–70; quoted in Mark Goldie, 'Locke, the Early Lockeans, and Priestcraft', *Intellectual History Review* 28 (2018), 125–44, at 131.

[38] New England politics was also more hospitable to the English Crown and its institutions than it had been, looking to it for stability within its borders and defence from without; the 'King's Church' now found a presence in New England that would have been impossible a century earlier.

[39] Schneider and Schneider, eds, *Samuel Johnson, President of King's College*, 1: 81–2.

public trial and premium an emulation were inspired into all. This method of encouragement hath been found useful in other learned Societies, and I think it cannot fail of being so in one where a person so well qualified as yourself, has such influence, and will bear a share in the elections.[40]

Building upon the legacy of Dummer, it was a remarkable gift to a Dissenting college by the dean of Londonderry. As Johnson reflected to the bishop of London in 1732, while Berkeley's college would:

> especially if it had been executed on the Continent ... have been of great advantage to the interest of religion and learning in America, so it has, on the other hand, been happy since in the conversion (besides a number of other good people) of the worthy persons who have all had a public education in the neighboring College [Yale], and two of them have been dissenting teachers.[41]

Berkeley's donation did indeed energize Johnson's mission to spread the Church of England's influence in New England, and despite not having its own college, the church proved remarkably agile as a minority institution. Operating outside of a parochial system, without a local episcopate, and engaging in formal education largely in the Congregationalist colleges, greater emphasis was thus laid upon ideas and theological convictions as a means of influence. As has been noted of the SPCK in America by Brent Sirota, who views the Society as emblematic of an 'Anglican revival' that shaped the church after the Glorious Revolution, it was 'improvisational ... with its peculiar status as an unincorporated entity possessed of the favor but not the official mandate of episcopal superiors':

> It was the heir to the diversely articulated spirit of revivalism that had informed much of Anglican churchmanship throughout the last two decades of the seventeenth century; but despite its outsized deference to the episcopal hierarchy, the lower clerical initiative and lay collaboration that animated much of its programs were somewhat out of keeping with its Restoration bequest.[42]

---

[40] George Berkeley to Samuel Johnson, 25 July 1732; quoted in ibid. 1: 82. A further endowment of books was promised for Yale.

[41] George Berkeley to Edmund Gibson, 5 April 1732; quoted in ibid. 1: 81–2.

[42] Craig Rose, 'The Origins and Ideals of the SPCK, 1699–1716', in John Walsh, Colin Haydon and Stephen Taylor, eds, *The Church of England, c. 1689–c. 1833* (Cambridge, 1993), 172–90, at 179–80; Brent Sirota, *Christian Monitors: The Church of England and the Age of Benevolence, 1680–1730* (New Haven, CT, 2014), 111.

Indeed, when seeking the support of bishops and Parliament, it was perhaps inevitable that these extra-diocesan Anglican societies would soon be aligning themselves with the requisite sources of influence and power, namely the Whig establishment, rather than the agitators for the sacerdotal interest in Convocation. As Sirota has argued, far from being a monolithic instrument of the Crown and hierarchy, the church had its own 'blue-water policy' akin to the entrepreneurial instincts of Britain's maritime and commercial empire; institutions like the SPG or even Berkeley's Bermuda project were 'all manifestations of an established church struggling with its own insularity' and 'might be better understood as efforts at the *de-territorialization* of Anglicanism, a process of rendering the established church less dependent on the political, diocesan, and parochial structures that had proved difficult if not impossible to reproduce abroad.'[43]

INSTITUTIONALIZING THE NEW LEARNING

However, this is not to suggest that the failure of Berkeley to establish his college in either Bermuda or in New England diminished the appetite of Anglicans to set up their own institutions of learning, even while they bolstered the libraries of Yale and Harvard and catalyzed a pan-continental appetite for Anglican authors. Berkeley's vision of education was 'to ground these young *Americans* thoroughly in Religion and Morality, and to give them a good Tincture of other Learning; particularly of Eloquence, History and practical Mathematics; to which it may not be improper to add some skill in Physics.'[44] Such aspirations did not dissipate as he sailed back to London from Boston.

Following Francis Bacon, Berkeley would not be alone in rethinking the categories of knowledge and the structure of learning within the colonies, and he could do so with a freedom that was harder to procure through the collegiate structure of Oxford or Cambridge. This 'free and catholick air' was, as David Hall has shown, already being expressed in the organization of college libraries. The donations of Dummer and Berkeley to Yale, for example, indicate how early efforts to endow American libraries produced collections that contained contributions other than biblical commentaries and extensive discourses on

---

[43] Sirota, *Christian Monitors*, 224–5.
[44] Ibid. 225. Italics original.

predestination. Rather than the medieval divisions of the arts into the trivium and quadrivium, libraries now began to arrange their collections around Baconian schemes. Samuel Johnson himself would write *An Introduction to the Study of Philosophy* in 1743, which aimed to give to students 'a General Idea or Scheme of all the Arts and Sciences and the several things which are to be known and learnt', organizing knowledge in such a way as to stress its unity: a scheme that Thomas Clap would use to reorganize the library at Yale in the same year.[45]

Enlightened Anglican ideals would also be influential in the founding of new colleges from the 1740s onwards. When Johnson became instrumental in the foundation of King's College in New York, the first Anglican establishment in the northern colonies, he sought Berkeley's advice and established a college that aimed to embed the 'new learning'. Although Johnson, Berkeley and others referred to King's as a 'seminary', it was not a theological college in any real sense. Divinity was not the predominant discipline, and there was no prospect of there being a professorship in divinity (despite initial promises to the Dutch Reformed that they would have their own theological professorship). George Berkeley, offering Samuel Johnson advice in 1749, suggested that teachers be secured from the seminaries of New England, for 'none can be got in Old England (who are willing to go) worth sending'; that 'Greek and Latin classics be well taught' even if 'the principal care must be good life and morals'; that the terms should be the same as those of Oxford and Cambridge, so as to 'give credit to the College'; and that there was a need to recommend 'this nascent seminary to an English bishop'.[46]

Johnson had mirrored Oxford in insisting upon a four-year course of study, in the preponderance of classics in the education of undergraduates, but with moral philosophy rather than theology being the pinnacle of this liberal education. As David Humphrey has indicated, Johnson's curriculum 'reflected his debt to the ideal of gentlemanly education – 'polite learning' – which the Renaissance had added to the medieval curriculum.'[47] Humphrey suggested that Johnson's model of making moral philosophy, rather than theology, the final-year

---

[45] Hugh Amory and David Hall, eds, *A History of the Book in America*, 1: *The Colonial Book in the Atlantic World* (Chapel Hill, NC, 2007), 421.

[46] George Berkeley to Samuel Johnson, 23 August 1749; quoted in Schneider and Schneider, eds, *Samuel Johnson, President of King's College*, 1: 134–5. Berkeley's own college, Trinity College Dublin, was likewise originally organized according to such a model of provost and two fellows.

[47] David C. Humphrey, *From King's College to Columbia, 1746–1800* (New York, 1976), 174.

discipline was 'to synthesize and rationalize for seniors the intellectual experience of the previous three and a half years' and was emblematic of an educational program with 'more recent origins'. This was reflective of his own conversion in 1715 at Yale when, after having prepared in Latin the mandatory 'System of Arts' or 'Encyclopedia', he became 'wholly changed to the New Learning'.[48]

Young men at King's were expected to read the New Testament in Greek in their early years, as at Oxford and Cambridge, but Johnson also had the intention of providing courses in husbandry, commerce, surveying and navigation. Largely on account of its small staff and lack of resources, such courses were never offered after the college opened in 1754, with gentlemen largely remaining dedicated to the classics and moral philosophy.[49]

However, even if the college's aspirations to be a centre of the 'new learning' in New York had limited success in its actual teaching, its broadly latitudinarian instincts were to some degree achieved in its openness to those beyond the Church of England. When the terms of the charter of the college were sealed at the end of October 1754, Anglican influence had been carefully circumscribed, in part due to pressure from Presbyterians and others in the city, who were already resistant to the limited Anglican establishment within the colony and resented further encroachment. The bishop of London was denied authority over the college, and the composition of the board was relatively ecumenical. Ex officio membership was granted to only one of New York's Anglican 'established' rectors – the rector of Trinity Church, upon whose land the college was to be built – and his presence was neutralized by ex officio membership being granted also to the senior ministers of the Dutch Reformed, Lutheran, French and Presbyterian churches in the city.[50] The controversy over the college's governance had resulted in an institution that was in the end far less denominationally prescriptive than the newly established Presbyterian college in New Jersey (Princeton), Yale or Harvard. Moreover, despite Johnson's desire that the college should be a source of Anglican influence, he allowed students to worship at the church of their choice

[48] Schneider and Schneider, eds, *Samuel Johnson, President of King's College*, 2: 186; 1: 6.
[49] These practical courses were included in announcements of the beginning of tuition in the college, as outlined in 'An Advertisement', *New York Gazette*, 3 June 1754; quoted in Schneider and Schneider, eds, *Samuel Johnson, President of King's College*, 4: 223.
[50] Humphreys, *From King's College to Columbia*, 67–9.

on Sundays. Also, unlike Oxford, Cambridge or Dublin, there were no religious tests for tutors or governors.

Indeed, as the Great Awakening and Whitefield's 'enthusiasm' disturbed many across the northern colonies, Johnson continued to hope that people would be drawn to the Church of England through its reasoned and moderate approach to faith and morals, not least as expressed in his institution. In a letter from 1759 to the archbishop of Canterbury, Thomas Secker (several years after the charter had been secured), Johnson defended the work of the SPG in the northern colonies against those of other denominations who charged the Society and its missionaries with stealing their own congregants. This, Johnson argued, was the result of the migration of Anglicans to the northern colonies from England, and also those who 'in consequence of Mr. Whitefield's rambling once and again through the country' followed:

> a good many strolling teachers who propagated so many wild notions of God and the Gospel that a multitude of people were so bewildered that they could find no rest to the sole of their feet till they retired into the Church [of England] as the only ark of safety.[51]

Anglican commitment to such enlightened moderation would also be in evidence in institutions beyond New England. Philadelphia's local Philosophical Society, led by Benjamin Franklin, sought to establish a new college in the 1750s, and had already drafted plans for a college in which classical languages were abandoned and academic exchange was conducted in English; they hoped to employ the Scottish Episcopalian William Smith, who had written *A General Idea of the College of Mirania* in 1753, subtitled 'a sketch of the method of teaching science and religion', in the context of New York debates around collegiate education. Informed by the reform of teaching at Aberdeen, he proposed an institution that wished to move beyond the philological and Aristotelian emphases of the medieval curriculum. In his idealized college, students would learn, alongside classics, mathematics, ethics, oratory, chronology, history, 'the most plain and useful Parts of natural and mechanic Philosophy', husbandry, chemistry and

---

[51] Samuel Johnson to Thomas Secker, 1 March 1759; quoted in Schneider and Schneider, eds, *Samuel Johnson, President of King's College*, 1: 285. See also Claude M. Newlin, *Philosophy and Religion in Colonial America* (Westport, CT, 1962), 104–5.

agriculture.[52] As at King's, however, limited resources meant that the College of Philadelphia (later the University of Pennsylvania) under William Smith's aegis was a mixture of both old and new learning.

Even if ambitions for the new colleges in New York and Philadelphia were inevitably restrained by resources, there is strong evidence that it was Anglican clergy and those influenced by its clerical Enlightenment who were instrumental in the pursuit of new institutional schemes that integrated public virtue with public usefulness. Their aspirations for education were far more adventurous than any found in England beyond the Dissenting academies or institutions like the Royal Society (Oxford and Cambridge being largely resistant to any kind of professional education until the later nineteenth century) and would remain lively foundations of enquiry, albeit shorn of royal patronage, after the Revolution.

CONCLUSION

On 18 February 1731, in the church of St Mary-le-Bow, George Berkeley ascended the pulpit to deliver the anniversary sermon for the SPG, preaching on John 13: 3 ('This is Life Eternal, that they may know Thee the only true God, and Jesus Christ whom thou hast sent'; AV). Having a decade earlier urged his Bermuda proposal on Londoners on account of an American clergy 'very meanly qualified both in learning and morals', he now adopted, with some degree of experience, a more emollient tone towards the work of the clergy in New England:

> The Missionaries employed by this Venerable Society have done, and continue to do, good Service, in bringing those Planters to a serious Sense of Religion, which, it is hoped, will in time extend to others. I speak it knowingly, that the Ministers of the Gospel, in those Provinces which go by the Name of New-England, sent and supported at the Expence of this Society, have, by their Sobriety of Manners, discreet Behaviour, and a competent Degree of useful Knowledge, shewn themselves worthy the Choice of those who sent them; and particularly in living on a more friendly Foot with their Brethren of the Separation; who, on their Part, are also very much come off from that Narrowness of Spirit, which formerly kept them at such an unamicable Distance from

---

[52] William Smith, *A General Idea of the College of Mirania* (New York, 1753), 16.

us. And as there is reason to apprehend, that Part of America could not have been thus distinguished, and provided with such a Number of proper Persons, if one half of them had not been supplied out of the dissenting Seminaries of the Country, who, in Proportion as they attain to more liberal Improvements of Learning, are observed to quit their Prejudice towards an Episcopal Church.[53]

It is not unlikely, of course, that Berkeley had Samuel Johnson in mind when referring to those 'proper Persons ... supplied out of dissenting Seminaries'. Johnson, like many whom he would tutor at Yale, and such as were inspired by the 'more liberal Improvements of Learning', was emblematic of how Anglican clergy had, by the mid-eighteenth century, established a considerable network of learning across the Atlantic. This 'Anglican republic of letters' was the result of considerable benefactions, especially in relation to public and private libraries, and bearing fruit; as Bray had insisted, it was in evidence some time before Berkeley had ventured to the New World.

While the clergy of the northern colonies had a reverence for episcopacy and were eager to see a bishop sent to the American colonies, their emphasis in their writings upon virtue, charity and toleration bears witness to the influence of Locke and Tillotson, in particular. Such priorities were arguably the practical reality of a pluralist Protestant society, but it is also clear that, by the 1740s, there was considerable ambition on the part of Anglicans to establish institutions that were negotiating religious diversity, stressing 'useful' over 'classical' learning, and freely embracing the epistemic modes of Bacon, Locke and Newton. The reach of this 'republic of letters' extended far beyond the church (indeed, despite the establishment of King's, the majority of colonial clergy remained educated at Harvard and Yale), as Stout and Corrigan have noted. This article has sought to explore, however, how the Church of England had become by the mid-century a serious intellectual force in its own right, institutionally as much as philosophically. In conclusion, we might note that Samuel Johnson's King's College would be responsible for the education, among others, of Alexander Hamilton, John Jay, Governeur Morris and Robert Livingston, members of the Whig elite and, in due course, five of the 'founding fathers' of the United States.

---

[53] George Berkeley, *A Miscellany, Containing Several Tracts on Various Subjects. By the Bishop of Cloyne* (London, 1752), 215–16.

The Wesleyan Reform Crisis in Mid-Victorian Oxford

Martin Wellings
London

Between 1849 and 1856, the Reform controversy cost the Wesleyan Methodist denomination an estimated 100,000 members. Triggered by personality conflicts within the Wesleyan ministry, the Reform movement drew on long-standing grievances, including tensions between itinerant ministers and local lay leaders. This case study of Wesleyan Reform in the Oxford Circuit explores the interplay of local and national events, and considers how protagonists in the controversy saw themselves as central to the structure and flourishing of Methodism and their opponents as subsidiary or peripheral. Different standpoints, combined with the perception or fear of marginalization, fractured the Oxford Wesleyan Circuit, in a microcosm of the impact of Wesleyan Reform on the denomination as a whole.

On Sunday 19 August 1849, the Rev. John Wesley Button preached his farewell sermon as superintendent minister of the Oxford Wesleyan Circuit. Wesleyan ministers were stationed annually by the Wesleyan Conference and appointments were renewable for a maximum of three years by local agreement. Button had been in Oxford since 1846, thus achieving the maximum term permitted under the Wesleyans' rules, and for the past two years had also served as chairman of the Oxford District. As he prepared to move to the superintendency of the Bristol (South) Circuit, it might have been inferred that Button was concluding a successful and popular ministry in Oxford. Any such impression, however, was challenged by an anonymous article which appeared in the *Oxford Chronicle* the following weekend. According to 'A Looker-On', although Button was undoubtedly a gifted preacher, with 'a grasp of intellect and powers of mind beyond the ordinary class', his 'tyrannical conduct' and 'spirit of domination' had rendered him obnoxious to many, such that a sermon which would normally have been 'crowded

31 Long Lane, Finchley, London, N3 2PS. E-mail: martin.wellings@methodist.org.uk.

Studies in Church History 61 (2025), 440–458 © The Author(s), 2025. Published by Cambridge University Press on behalf of the Ecclesiastical History Society.
doi:10.1017/stc.2024.50

by an attentive congregation' was delivered to many empty seats.[1] A swift rebuttal of the allegation of a poorly attended service came from two of the trustees of the Wesleyans' New Inn Hall Street chapel, but they acknowledged that Button had been engaged in a dispute with some of the local preachers of the circuit, and that some might have stayed away 'out of a chivalrous feeling for an individual'.[2] That individual, not named in the initial correspondence, was the Oxford schoolmaster Josiah Munday Crapper, a longstanding local preacher, who resigned or was removed from the preaching plan in the summer of 1849, prompting the resignation or expulsion of a dozen other local preachers.[3] This local dispute, focussed on policy and personalities within the Oxford Circuit, was given added significance and impetus by the Reform controversy which gripped the Wesleyan Connexion from the late 1840s into the next decade.[4] The interplay of local and national events complicated and exacerbated the crisis at both levels, and the quarrel between Button and Crapper offers a case study of this intertwining. Margins and peripheries, moreover, supply a lens through which to examine events, perceptions and protagonists, as all the disputants saw themselves as central to the structure of Methodism and their opponents as peripheral. Before taking up the lens, however, it is necessary to give an account, first of the Reform controversy in mid-nineteenth-century Wesleyanism, and then of the manifestation of the crisis in Oxford.

Wesleyan Reform was the latest in a series of disputes which had racked the Wesleyan Connexion in the half-century following the death of John Wesley in 1791. Although differing in size and detail, all might plausibly be seen as outcomes of the extraordinary growth and evolving ecclesial independence of the Wesleyan movement in these years. Wesley left a Connexion of some 70,000 members and 400 preaching houses, served by 300 travelling preachers;[5] by 1851, at the time of the

---

[1] 'Wesleyans', *Oxford Chronicle and Berks and Bucks Gazette*, 25 August 1849, 2 [hereafter: *OC*].

[2] Edward Thurland and W. Wiseman (to the editor), 'A Reply to "Looker-On"', *OC*, 1 September 1849, 1.

[3] William Bartlett (to the editor), *OC*, 8 September 1849, 3, naming Josiah Crapper. Bartlett was one of the expelled preachers.

[4] For the Reform crisis, see Evelyn C. Urwin, *The Significance of 1849: Methodism's Greatest Upheaval* (London, 1949); W. R. Ward, *Religion and Society in England, 1790–1850* (London, 1972), 236–73.

[5] *Minutes of the Methodist Conferences*, 1: *1744–1803* (London, 1812), 243–4. The total of 72,476 members included 13,700 in Ireland.

National Religious Census undertaken by the government, the membership figure for England and Wales alone had increased to 358,000; the Wesleyans' claim of 1,544,528 attendances on Census Sunday supports the estimate of three to five adherents for every individual who had accepted the discipline of membership.[6] Wesley's 300 travelling preachers had increased to over a thousand ministers, serving 6,579 places of worship.[7] Expansion required effective governance: mechanisms to raise funds for buildings, stipends and pensions; protocols to ensure orthodoxy in preaching; and prudence to avoid incurring crippling chapel debts by over-extension. The energies of spontaneous evangelism needed to be harnessed, lest revival tip over into religious or political anarchy. Methodism remained a mass movement, but also a movement with upwardly mobile members, seeking to realize their social, educational and political aspirations.[8]

Numerical and institutional growth, moreover, was linked to Methodism's evolving ecclesiology. The Wesleys' Methodism had been a renewal movement uncomfortably contained within the Church of England, but expansion after 1791 both pushed and encouraged the Connexion along the road to independence, initially by permitting Methodist worship to take place at the same time as services in the parish church, then by allowing Methodist preachers to administer Holy Communion. Travelling preachers became 'ministers' in the 1820s and ordination by the laying on of hands, abandoned after Wesley's death, was resumed by the Conference in 1836. Although the Wesleyans remained coy about using the word 'church', preferring to refer to themselves as a 'Connexion', a society or a body, the

---

[6] David Hempton, *Methodism: Empire of the Spirit* (New Haven, CT, and London, 2005), 1–2. The 1851 Census recorded attendances, not attendees, and the relationship between those categories has been interrogated by historians. A figure of 924,000 Wesleyan attendees has been calculated from the attendances by Michael R. Watts, *The Dissenters*, 2: *The Expansion of Evangelical Nonconformity* (Oxford, 1995), 22–9, with table at 28.

[7] The Wesleys' itinerant or travelling preachers evolved into Wesleyan Methodist ministers in the early nineteenth century, but ministers might still be referred to as 'itinerants' or 'travelling preachers'.

[8] For an overview of this period, see John Kent, 'The Wesleyan Methodists to 1849', in Rupert Davies, A. Raymond George and Gordon Rupp, eds, *A History of the Methodist Church in Great Britain*, 4 vols (London, 1965–88), 2: 213–75; Ward, *Religion and Society in England*, 70–104, 135–76; Clive Murray Norris, '"A blessed and glorious work of God, … attended with some irregularity": Managing Methodist Revivals, c.1740–1800', in Charlotte Methuen, Alec Ryrie, and Andrew Spicer, eds, *Inspiration and Institution in Christian History*, SCH 57 (Cambridge, 2021), 210–32.

movement gradually clarified its relationship to the Church of England, becoming a separate denomination.[9]

Managing expansion and developing ecclesiology came together, institutionally and theologically, in the Wesleyan Conference. John Wesley called the first Conference in 1744, meeting with a small number of like-minded clergy and lay preachers to consolidate his movement. The Conference quickly became an annual gathering of Wesley's itinerant preachers, summoned to confer on policy, doctrines and discipline.[10] By his 1784 Deed of Declaration, Wesley bequeathed his authority over his Connexion to a named group of one hundred preachers, meeting in Conference, adding the proviso that this self-perpetuating 'Legal Hundred' should involve the other travelling preachers in its decisions. Wesley thus placed control of the movement – the interpretation of doctrine; the selection, training and deployment of personnel; the management of property; and the determination of policy – in the hands of a clerical oligarchy. In the early nineteenth century, this practical and legal authority was underpinned by the theology of a 'collective pastorate', asserting that the ministers assembled in Conference and appointed to their various stations were called by God to exercise control over the Connexion.[11] John Bowmer likened the Conference to the chapter-meeting of a religious order,[12] and its devotional framework, its tone of piety and its inquiries into ministerial character evoked the intimate and sometimes uncomfortable fellowship of the local Methodist class-meeting. However, the sheer size of the assembly offered plentiful scope for grandstanding oratory, political manoeuvring, personal rivalries, and elements of group-think. Managing Methodism therefore meant managing the Conference, and the

---

[9] Margaret Batty, 'The Contribution of Local Preachers to the Life of the Wesleyan Methodist Church until 1932, and to the Methodist Church after 1932, in England' (MA thesis, University of Leeds, 1969), 142, dates the change of nomenclature to 1818 and use of the word 'minister' to 1827. Ordination by the imposition of hands was considered in 1822, and introduced in 1836: William Peirce, *The Ecclesiastical Principles and Polity of the Wesleyan Methodists*, 3rd edn (London, 1873; first publ. 1854), 278–9.

[10] For the origins and development of the Conference, see Henry D. Rack, ed., *The Works of John Wesley*, 10: *The Methodist Societies. The Minutes of Conference* (Nashville, TN, 2011), 6–15.

[11] John Bowmer, *Pastor and People: A Study of Church and Ministry in Methodism from the Death of John Wesley (1791) to the Death of Jabez Bunting (1858)* (London, 1975), 202–18. The theory was classically expressed by John Beecham in *An Essay on the Constitution of Wesleyan Methodism* (1829) and by Alfred Barrett in *An Essay on the Pastoral Office* (1839).

[12] Bowmer, *Pastor and People*, 58.

consummate exponent of this art, from the 1810s until his retirement in 1851, was Jabez Bunting.[13] In alliance with other ministers and a group of wealthy lay Methodists, Bunting's achievement was to give structure, coherence and leadership to Wesleyanism. Methodism's visible success, moreover, meticulously tabulated in quarterly and annual membership statistics, seemed to validate the system and to refute the objections of critics and reformers.

The evolution of Wesleyanism did not go unchallenged. Between the 1790s and the 1830s, different elements of the polity and practice of Methodism were called into question, highlighting strands which came together in the Reform controversy.[14] A demand for lay representation in the Conference was voiced as early as the 1790s, leading to the expulsion of Alexander Kilham and the formation of the Methodist New Connexion in 1797. Revivalism, impatient of Connexional control, found expression in the Primitive Methodists, founded in 1808, and the Bible Christians, from 1815. The authoritarianism of the Conference, overruling local decision-making, provoked a secession in Leeds in 1826 and the creation of the Protestant Methodists. In 1834, opposition to the creation of a theological institution for the training of ministers coalesced around a senior preacher, Dr Samuel Warren. What may have been thwarted ambition on Warren's part – Bunting was named as President of the institution – joined with political and social grievances and personality conflicts in Liverpool, Manchester and Rochdale, to give birth to the Wesleyan Methodist Association in 1835.[15]

By the 1840s, then, the ingredients of Wesleyan Reform were in place: the assertion of lay rights, disputes over revivalism, disgruntlement over high-handed behaviour by the Conference, and quarrels within the ministerial elite, especially among those who felt marginalized by Bunting and his friends. These elements were combined in a

---

[13] Bunting was lauded by Wesleyan loyalists and vilified by reformers. For a critical appraisal, see Ward, *Religion and Society in England*, 256–9; idem, *Early Victorian Methodism: The Correspondence of Jabez Bunting, 1830–1858* (London, 1976), xvi–xxiii. A more positive account is given by David Hempton, 'Jabez Bunting: The Formative Years, 1794–1820', in idem, *The Religion of the People: Methodism and Popular Religion c.1750–1900* (London, 1996), 91–108.

[14] This is summarized in John T. Wilkinson, 'The Rise of other Methodist Traditions', in Davies, George and Rupp, eds, *History of the Methodist Church*, 276–329.

[15] See David A. Gowland, *Methodist Secessions: The Origins of Free Methodism in Three Lancashire Towns* (Manchester, 1979).

series of anonymous publications, entitled *Fly Sheets from the Private Correspondent*, published between 1844 and 1849, and sent by post to all Wesleyan ministers.

The *Fly Sheets* were unsparing in their denunciation of Bunting and his allies. The first number set the tone:

> Dr Bunting's whole system of government has been opposed to the advice and practice of Mr Wesley; his system being of EXCLUSIVENESS, FAVOURITISM, and SELFISHNESS, as exemplified in the formation and packings of his Committees, his opposition to open, free discussion in the general assembly ... and his invariable attempt to confine the knowledge, the power, and privileges of the body to his own chosen few.[16]

Beginning from an attack on 'location' (ministers ceasing to be itinerant and taking permanent posts in the Connexional bureaucracy, principally the Mission House), 'centralization' (concentrating offices and meetings in London), and 'secularization' (exchanging the spiritual work of preaching and pastoral care for administration), the *Fly Sheets* portrayed a metropolitan clique which was dominating the Connexion, manipulating appointments and committees to cling on to power, sidelining opponents, and ignoring the ethics and values of traditional Methodism. Bunting was described as 'the Dictator' and 'the great Ruler', and likened to Napoleon.[17] His allies in the Conference and at the Wesleyan Missionary Society were accused of extravagance and inefficiency, a love of fine living, and a desire for personal prestige: particular scorn was poured on the quest for American honorary degrees.[18] Critical comparisons were drawn between Bunting's ally Robert Newton and the American revivalist James Caughey, who had made a controversial tour of Britain in the early 1840s.[19] Persistent allegations of corruption and tyranny were levelled at 'the London clique' and their friends.[20]

The *Fly Sheets* were not the first anonymous publications to criticize the Wesleyan leadership, and nor were their authors the first itinerants to resent Bunting and his pre-eminence. What gave the *Fly Sheets*

---

[16] *The Fly Sheets ... carefully copied from ... the originals* (Birmingham and London, n.d. [1849]), 1–2.
[17] Ibid. 42, 91, 105.
[18] Ibid. 62–3, 112.
[19] Ibid. 68–74.
[20] For instance, ibid. 19 (tyranny) and 101–2 (London clique).

traction was the action of the Conference in response.[21] In 1847, it was agreed to issue a declaration repudiating any connection with the publications. Some seventy ministers resisted the pressure to sign the declaration and *Fly Sheet No. 4* mocked the failure of the 'Inquisition'.[22] Two years later, the Conference sought to identify the author or authors by questioning those suspected: James Everett, Samuel Dunn and William Griffith. Everett ignored the summons to attend the Conference; Dunn and Griffith declined to give the undertakings required; and all three were expelled, thus supplying a tailor-made example of tyranny by 'the Clique'. Widely reported in the religious and secular press, this became a catalyst for an explosion of protest in which ambitions for reform, long-standing grievances and local antagonisms merged. Whatever their specific grievances, disgruntled Wesleyans now had a clear goal: the reinstatement of the 'Three Expelled'. Supporters organized mass meetings, signed petitions and withheld contributions to Methodist funds. Superintendents responded with expulsions, and rival Reform societies were set up. Until 1856, the reformers continued to petition the Conference; in 1857, most of the reformers joined with the Association to form the United Methodist Free Churches, while the remainder constituted the Wesleyan Reform Union. It has been estimated that the controversy cost Wesleyan Methodism around 100,000 members.[23]

Oxford Wesleyanism escaped largely unscathed from the controversies which troubled the Connexion in the decades after Wesley's death. The New Connexion, the Bible Christians, the Protestant Methodists, and the Wesleyan Methodist Association made no showing in the Oxford Circuit, and when Primitive Methodism began tentatively to establish itself around Oxford in the 1830s, it did so through pioneer evangelism and not through secessions from the Old Connexion.[24] Extant records show only two indications of dissent or dissatisfaction within the Wesleyan community in this period. William Ray (1814–84), schoolmaster and local preacher, was questioned by the quarterly local preachers' meeting in summer 1846 because of

---

[21] This is described in detail in Benjamin Gregory, *Side Lights on the Conflicts of Methodism* (London, 1898), 405–75.

[22] *Fly Sheets*, 97.

[23] Urwin, *Significance of 1849*, 23.

[24] The first Primitive Methodist preachers arrived in Oxford in 1825 but were rebuffed; a second attempt in 1835 was short-lived: John Petty, *History of the Primitive Methodist Connexion from its Origin to the Conference of 1860* (London, 1864), 231, 320.

'peculiar views' on the doctrine of the Trinity. It became apparent that Ray had been drawn to the teaching of the New Jerusalem Church and, in March 1847, it was resolved that he should be dropped from the preaching plan; by 1851, Ray was leading a small New Jerusalem congregation in east Oxford.[25] Less dramatic at the time, but more serious for the future, in 1844, Henry Leake (1809–86) resigned from the Wesleyan Connexion 'on conscientious grounds.'[26] The grounds were not specified, but speeches at Reform meetings in 1850 and 1851 made it clear that Leake had become dubious of the claims made for the authority of Wesleyan itinerants, and that reading some of the works designed to buttress those claims had served only to increase his disquiet.[27] Leake had been a local preacher since 1834 and a trustee of the New Inn Hall Street chapel since 1836. He was one of Oxford's Wesleyan elite: the only local preacher to be styled 'esquire' and the only trustee to be designated 'gentleman'. Leake was affluent enough to build a new chapel at Rose Hill, on the outskirts of Iffley, in 1835 and to donate it to the Connexion.[28] The parting in December 1844 was amicable: the local preachers' meeting unanimously passed a resolution affirming 'undiminished esteem for his private and public character' and expressing 'earnest wishes for his prosperity & happiness in whatever sphere of Christian labor [sic] & usefulness he may feel himself called upon to move.'[29] That sphere was Congregationalism, where Leake was already helping to supply the pulpit at George Street during an interregnum in 1844–5,[30] while also developing new work in the villages of Frilford and Longworth, to the south-west of Oxford.

[25] Oxford, Oxfordshire History Centre, Oxford Methodist Circuit Archive [hereafter: OMCA], NM5/A/A4/1, Local Preachers' Minute Book 1830–66, September and December 1846, March 1847; Kate Tiller, ed., *Church and Chapel in Oxfordshire 1851* (Oxford, 1987), 76. The congregation in 1851 numbered 40.
[26] OMCA, NM5/A/A4/1, Local Preachers' Minute Book 1830–66, 27 December 1844.
[27] Henry Leake, *Speech of H. Leake, Esq., Chairman, at a Wesleyan Reform Meeting, held in Oxford on Friday Evening, July 5th 1850* (London, 1850), 1. The works which failed to convince Leake were Edmund Grindrod's *Compendium of the Laws and Regulations of Wesleyan Methodism* (1841) and Charles Welch's *The Wesleyan Polity Illustrated and Defended* (1829).
[28] OMCA, NM5/A/MS1/1, James Nix, 'Methodism in Oxford', 22, 30. Leake's father and brother were also Wesleyan trustees. For the Rose Hill chapel, see W. J. S. Bayliss, 'How Rose Hill Chapel began', *Oxford Methodist Circuit Magazine*, April 1935, 36–7.
[29] OMCA, NM5/A/A4/1, Local Preachers' Minute Book 1830–66, 27 December 1844.
[30] Oxfordshire History Centre, NC6/1/A1/1, George Street Congregational Church, Oxford: Church Book 1832, unpaginated, showing Leake preaching eight times over the interregnum.

Leake was 'set apart to the Christian ministry' at Frilford in February 1845, but whether he regarded this as Congregational ordination is unclear: he presided at a Wesleyan Reform meeting in Oxford in 1850 as 'Henry Leake, Esq.'[31]

Porous boundaries between some Wesleyans and other areas of evangelical Nonconformity may help to explain the difficulties which embroiled Button and Crapper in 1849. Crapper (1810–92) was a year younger than Henry Leake, and also part of an Oxford Wesleyan dynasty.[32] Less affluent than Leake, he built a career as a schoolmaster, running an independent school, first in Brewer Street and then in St John's Street. He matriculated as a member of the University in 1840, but did not proceed to a degree.[33] Crapper became a fully accredited local preacher in 1831, and in the mid-1840s served as superintendent and secretary of the New Inn Hall Street Sunday School.[34] Moreover, in December 1841, he married Charlotte Wilson, daughter of the Wesleyan superintendent minister, the Rev. Maximilian Wilson. Crapper, therefore, was well-connected in Oxford Wesleyanism, and it may well be asked how and why he came to be expelled in summer 1849.

The local preachers' meeting minutes record that in June 1849 Crapper was questioned by the preachers about his involvement with the Summertown Congregational chapel. It was alleged that Crapper had been supplying the pulpit for the Congregationalists, who were without a pastor from April 1847 until December 1851, and that he had administered Holy Communion there. The Wesleyan preachers resolved: 'That this meeting does not consider Brother Crapper's Present Position, in relation to Methodism, a proper one', and asked him 'respectfully … to discontinue his connection with the Independents at Summertown, and come among us as a Local Brother, or discontinue his connection as a Local Preacher.' Button, from the chair, proposed that: 'If, previous to the plan going to press, Brother Crapper promise to give up his connection with the Summertown Independent Church, his name shall be continued on the plan.' This

---

[31] *Evangelical Magazine and Missionary Chronicle*, May 1845, 259. I am indebted to Shirley Martin for this reference. See also Henry Leake, *Speech of H. Leake, Esq.*, 1.

[32] His father Shem was described as 'an old and respected member of the Wesleyan Connexion': 'City and County Intelligence', *OC*, 26 September 1846, 2.

[33] Joseph Foster, *Alumni Oxonienses*, 4 vols (Oxford, 1888), 1: 313.

[34] OMCA, NM5/25/A14/1, Oxford Wesleyan Sunday and Day Schools Committee, 1842–73, 12 October 1846 (superintendent), 6 October 1848 (secretary) and 16 April 1849 (pro secretary).

was carried unanimously.[35] By the next meeting, held at the end of September, however, Button had departed for Bristol, and Crapper and other local preachers had resigned or been expelled.

The picture painted by the minutes shows good cause for Button and the assembled Wesleyan Local Preachers to find fault with Josiah Crapper. Although it was not uncommon for Wesleyan preachers to preach occasionally for other denominations, effectively to take charge of a church and to administer the sacraments was a clear breach of Wesleyan discipline. The puzzle here is, first, that Crapper would surely have been well aware of this and, second, that the June resolutions, as recorded in the minutes, offered him a straightforward way out: by ending his connection with the Summertown Independents and resuming his position as a Wesleyan local preacher.

The only clues to resolve the puzzle are to be found in the local preachers' meeting minutes and in the press coverage of the subsequent dispute from the autumn of 1849. Discrepancies between these sources – particularly the absence from the minutes of any context for a dispute which seemed to erupt without explanation in summer 1849 and escalate thereafter – may be explained partly by the brevity of the minutes and partly by the fact that the minute-taker was William Hopewell, the junior itinerant and Button's loyal colleague.[36] Local evidence suggests that Josiah Crapper had a long-standing affinity with Summertown. It is possible that the Crapper family owned property in this growing village,[37] and it was certainly the case that Crapper was deputed by the Oxford Local Preachers in March 1847 to take the lead in providing afternoon and evening preaching there, and to look for a rented room as a base.[38] The departure of George Brown, the Independent minister, in April 1847, may have looked like an opportunity for the Wesleyans to realize a long-held ambition to establish a new cause in Summertown.

---

[35] OMCA, NM5/A/A4/1, Local Preachers' Minute Book 1830–66, 20 June 1849.

[36] Until September 1870, it was the practice for the minutes to be taken by the junior itinerant, so this was not unusual. It is striking, however, that there are no references to any difficulties with Crapper, or to the situation in Summertown, before June 1849.

[37] For the cottages built in 1822–3 and named Crapper's Row, see Ruth Fasnacht, *Summertown since 1820* (Oxford, 1977), 22.

[38] OMCA, NM5/A/A4/1, Local Preachers' Minute Book 1830–66, March 1847. Four of the committee of five appointed to arrange preaching in Summertown subsequently became reformers.

What, then, led Josiah Crapper from pioneering a new Wesleyan work in Summertown to an entanglement with the Congregationalists and a quarrel with the superintendent? It is possible that Crapper was already sufficiently disgruntled with Button to be considering leaving Wesleyanism for the Congregationalists, as Henry Leake had done several years earlier. It is also possible that Crapper wished to help the Congregationalists and saw no reason not to do so, and that Button saw an opportunity to assert his authority by rebuking an influential local preacher. William Bartlett's letter to the *Oxford Chronicle* in September 1849 claimed that Crapper had explained what he was doing in Summertown to the preachers the previous December; that the preachers' meeting raised no objections, but that Button then omitted Crapper from the preaching plan, declaring his intention of removing him from the list of local preachers, and brought false charges without notice at the June 1849 preachers' meeting. Another correspondent added that Button expelled Crapper when he declined to answer 'an insulting and inquisitorial question'.[39] Although the minutes claim that the assembled preachers supported Button in his actions, it seems that after the June 1849 preachers' meeting between ten and fifteen local preachers expressed opposition to the proceedings, and they too were summarily dropped from the plan. When Button left the Oxford Circuit in August 1849, half of the local preachers were effectively suspended and feelings were running high.

The case of Josiah Crapper was quickly subsumed into the wider question of Wesleyan Reform. The Oxford newspapers soon picked up and relayed the news from the Manchester Conference of the expulsion of Everett, Dunn and Griffith, and reported the response. Thus, the *Oxford University and City Herald* reprinted a critical article on 'The Wesleyan Despotism' from the *Church and State Gazette*,[40] while the conservative *Oxford Journal* and liberal *Oxford Chronicle* carried advertisements for the pamphlets on the Conference produced by the *Wesleyan Times* and verbatim accounts of the first protest meeting addressed by the 'three expelled' at Exeter Hall, London, on 31 August.[41] Letters about Crapper and the Oxford Local

[39] Bartlett (to the editor), *OC*, 8 September 1849, 3; 'An Office-bearer in the Wesleyan Society' (to the editor), *OC*, 29 September 1849, 2.
[40] *Oxford University and City Herald*, 8 September 1849, 3.
[41] 'Wesleyan Methodism', *Jackson's Oxford Journal*, 1 September 1849, 2; *OC*, 1 September 1849, 2.

Preachers evolved into discussions of 'arbitrary power' and 'priestly absolutism', extending the criticism from Button to Bunting and the dominant faction in the Wesleyan Conference. The coverage of the controversy was such that non-Methodist readers of the *Chronicle* began to object to the amount of space devoted to it.[42]

During the autumn of 1849 and through 1850, the Reform crisis continued and deepened. Meetings were held to express support for the 'three expelled', to call for their reinstatement, and to raise funds for their support. The Conference was urged to change its rules and to admit lay representatives. In addition to the weekly *Wesleyan Times*, a new monthly, the *Wesleyan Review and Evangelical Record*, was launched, to make the case for reform. Meanwhile, the Conference held firm. A declaration of support for 'Methodism as it is', issued by the president, was signed by almost every Wesleyan minister.[43] When the reformers organized a delegate meeting in London in March 1850, the president declined to receive a deputation.[44] The 1850 Conference refused to consider memorials from circuits, pleading for a change of heart, and the effect was to endorse a hard line in the localities.[45] Reformers withheld contributions to Connexional funds; superintendents expelled officeholders and members; and, in some places, meetings and services were disrupted by protests or tussles for control of property and pulpits.[46] Although presented as a stark conflict between Conference loyalists and reformers, the reality was far more nuanced. As Benjamin Gregory observed, the appearance of Conference unanimity was misleading: there were liberal-minded ministers in the Connexion, and their sensitivity and discretion did much to defuse tensions.[47] Many lay Methodists were not persuaded by the rhetoric of the *Wesleyan Times*; some who sympathized with the 'three expelled' disliked the tone of the *Fly Sheets*;[48] many were genuinely undecided and open to persuasion. As circuits sought to weather the 'ecclesiastical

---

[42] 'Wesleyan Methodism', *OC*, 1 September 1849, 2; 'Wesleyan Methodism', *OC*, 15 September 1849, 1; 'An Office-bearer in the Oxford Circuit' (to the editor), *OC*, 27 October 1849, 2; 'To Correspondents', *OC*, 10 November 1849, 2.
[43] 'Miscellaneous', *OC*, 9 February 1850, 4, reported that 1,160 of the 1,200 ministers had signed.
[44] 'Conference despotism', *OC*, 23 March 1850, 2.
[45] Gregory, *Side Lights*, 476–81.
[46] For example, 'Marriage in a Wesleyan Chapel – A Scene', *OC*, 20 July 1850, 3.
[47] Gregory, *Side Lights*, 481–90.
[48] Thus Henry Leake, *Speech of H. Leake, Esq.*, 1.

tornado',[49] much depended on local issues and local personalities, and not least on the approach taken by the superintendent.

The course of the controversy in the Oxford Circuit tracked developments nationally. Button's successor, the experienced and emollient Joseph Earnshaw, suffered from poor health, so in autumn 1849 the acting superintendent was the more abrasive Charles Westlake, who inflamed the situation by provocative interventions.[50] Letters and news items in the local press continued through the autumn of 1849 and into 1850. On 23 October 1849, a public meeting was held at the Adullam Chapel, affirming support for Everett, Dunn and Griffith, and calling for lay representation in the Conference.[51] By the beginning of 1850, there was a Reform committee in Oxford, making plans for a visit to the city by the 'three expelled' and arranging for delegates to be sent to the national 'Peoples' Conference' in London in March.[52] Local gatherings were held to make the case for Wesleyan Reform and to hear expelled preachers like William Bartlett; while in July 1850, Dunn and Griffith came to address a 'large meeting' of Wesleyans from Oxford and adjacent circuits.[53] With Robert Day, another hardliner, as superintendent from summer 1850, Oxford Wesleyans were forced to choose sides. Some made their peace with the Conference; others resigned or were expelled. William Leggatt, a local preacher, class leader and Woodstock ironmonger, had been kept in membership by Earnshaw, despite his attendance at the March 1850 Reform conference, and had engaged in negotiation with other reformers, but he was expelled by Day for 'stopping supplies and Agitation'.[54] G. G. Banbury, another local preacher and class leader, and Reform delegate in 1850, stayed on the preaching plan until spring 1851, when he was told by Day that he must promise not to attend any meetings of the expelled or lose his

---

[49] Gregory, *Side Lights*, 481.

[50] Nix, 'Methodism in Oxford', 30–1. For praise of Earnshaw, see James Goold, 'The Oxford Delegates', *OC*, 4 May 1850, 1.

[51] 'Meeting to sympathise with the expelled Wesleyan ministers', *OC*, 27 October 1849, 2.

[52] For the selection, see Goold, 'Oxford Delegates', responding to a critical letter, 'The Oxford Delegates', *Watchman and Wesleyan Advertiser*, 27 March 1850, 102.

[53] 'Woodstock', *OC*, 11 May 1850, 3; 'The Revs S. Dunn and W. Griffith at Oxford', *OC*, 13 July 1850, 2.

[54] For the negotiations, see OMCA, NM5/A/A4/1, Local Preachers' Minute Book 1830–66, 3 July 1850. For the expulsion, see OMCA, NM5/A/A4/1, Local Preachers' Minute Book 1830–66, 18 December 1850; and OMCA, NM5/A/A2/4, Circuit Schedule Book 1845–66, September 1850.

membership.[55] As attitudes hardened and options diminished, by the beginning of 1851, the Reform Committee was beginning to set up a parallel structure, with its own prayer meetings, class-meetings and preaching services.[56] Gradually a separate reformers' preaching plan developed, and by November 1851, the Oxford reformers reported to a district meeting that they had ninety members, twelve local preachers and seven chapels, and 'a majority of members on their side'.[57] By 1856, there were nine preaching places on the reformers' plan, including villages to the north and east of Oxford.[58] Numbers of places fluctuated, but during the 1860s, new chapels were built in Combe, Kidlington, Bicester and Woodstock; while Leake's chapel at Rose Hill, reduced to single-figure membership by Day's expulsions, was bought from the Wesleyans and presented to the reformers.[59] The Old Connexion held on, despite losses of members and societies, but when Benjamin Gregory arrived as Wesleyan superintendent in autumn 1857, 'he found Methodism in a truly pitiable condition ... reduced ... almost to ruin.'[60] For the next three-quarters of a century, until Methodist Union in 1932, reformers and Wesleyans maintained a separate existence in Oxford, with parallel and overlapping circuits.

How might the lens of margins and peripheries shed light on the Reform crisis in Oxford Methodism? First, as has already been noted, there was a complex interplay between the reality and perceptions of local and national events. Oxford was by no means unique in this respect: David Bebbington has shown, for example, how local issues were key to the emergence of Free Methodism in Louth in the 1850s.[61] Wesleyan itinerants, like Button, Charles Westlake and

---

[55] 'Mr G. G. Banbury, JP, Woodstock', *Methodist Monthly* 1898, October 1898, 294.

[56] OMCA, NM5/B/A2/1, Circuit Wesleyan Reform Committee Minute Book, 1850–4, entries for 9 and 16 December 1850, and 3 February 1851.

[57] OMCA, NM5/B/A1/1, District Wesleyan Reform Committee Minute Book, 1851–3, 11 November 1851.

[58] OMCA, NM5/A/A1/2, Plan for Wesleyan Methodist Society, Oxford Circuit, January to March 1856.

[59] G. G. Banbury, 'Oxford Circuit', *United Methodist Free Churches Magazine*, May 1863, 327–9.

[60] J. R. Gregory, ed., *Benjamin Gregory, DD. Autobiographical Recollections, edited with Memorials of His Later Life* (London, 1903), 407. However, the transformation, apparently achieved within a matter of months, suggests that the situation was not quite as hopeless as Gregory (or his biographer) suggests.

[61] David W. Bebbington, 'Secession and Revival: Louth Free Methodist Church in the 1850s', *Wesley and Methodist Studies* 7 (2015), 54–77.

Robert Day came to the troubles of the 1840s schooled by their experiences of the Leeds and Warrenite controversies of the 1820s and 1830s.[62] They were instinctively wary of 'agitators' and predisposed to cling to 'Methodism as it is' in the face of challenge and change. Committed to the authority of the 'pastoral office' and the ecclesiology of the 'collective pastorate', they deployed the disciplinary machinery of the Connexion to quell any suggestion of local irregularity or dissent. Local Wesleyans, on the other hand, brought their knowledge of specific grievances to the interpretation of national issues, so that the injustice apparently done to Josiah Crapper became a local example of the arrogance and tyranny of the Conference. Crapper was a surrogate for the 'three expelled', and Button an Oxford equivalent of Jabez Bunting. This may be seen in the description of the June 1849 local preachers' meeting in the letter from 'Office-bearer' to the *Oxford Chronicle* in the autumn: Crapper, like Everett, Dunn and Griffith, was confronted by unjust accusations and 'inquisitorial' questions; like the 'three expelled', he declined to answer.[63]

If national events offered a way of understanding local issues, grievances felt locally inspired an engagement with a national campaign for redress. Oxford reformers soon moved beyond sympathy for Josiah Crapper and other local preachers to organizing meetings in support of Everett, Dunn and Griffith, and to subscriptions for funds to help them. Oxford delegates attended the Reform meeting in London in March 1850, and gatherings of Oxford reformers endorsed the demand for the reinstatement of the 'expelled' and the rescinding of the 'laws of 1835' which codified the ability of the Conference and the district meetings to interfere in the circuits. This constitutional issue reinforces the point that the highly centralized polity of Wesleyan Methodism ensured that local disputes soon became national concerns: there was a rapid route from the periphery to the centre, because all appeals for resolution, redress or reform inevitably ended with the Conference.

---

[62] Button (1798–1879) and Day (1794–1864) both entered the ministry in 1820; Westlake (1805–58) entered the ministry in 1830. For their obituaries, see *Minutes of Conference* (London), 1859, 204; 1864, 15; 1879, 39–40. The *Minutes of Conference* were issued annually, published in London by the Wesleyan Methodist Book Room. Until 1875, several years' worth of the *Minutes* were subsequently issued in combined volumes, so there are different extant volume numbers and sets. The relevant obituaries can be found by referring to the year of the *Minutes* and the page.

[63] 'An Office-bearer in the Wesleyan Society' (to the editor), *OC*, 29 September 1849, 2.

It is worth noting that developments in communications in this period assisted the connection of centre and periphery. The first railway line between Oxford and London opened in 1844, with a second line opening in 1851.[64] Meanwhile, the *Oxford Chronicle*, launched in 1837, brought a liberal-leaning newspaper to the city.[65] Although the conservative *Oxford Journal* and *University and City Herald* paid some attention to Wesleyan Reform, it was the *Chronicle* that devoted most space to the controversy, regularly reprinting news and comment from the *Wesleyan Times* to keep Oxford's reading public abreast of national developments.

Secondly, it may be suggested that both sides in the Reform controversy saw themselves as central to the life and prosperity of Wesleyan Methodism and felt that their opponents were seeking to push them to the periphery. For the itinerants, the Conference was 'the living Wesley',[66] the embodiment of the whole Connexion. Stationed in their several circuits, they represented the 'body' of Methodism and its authority in each place, preaching 'our doctrines' and enforcing 'our discipline'. Pre-eminent in the polity of Methodism, they were physically located in close proximity to the main places of worship: in Oxford, the superintendent's house was on the same site as the New Inn Hall Street chapel. Their preaching, pastoral care and strategic leadership were crucial to the success of their circuits. Arguably, the itinerants were the epitome of Methodism. And yet, their Connexional identity placed the itinerants at a remove from the circuits. Unlike Baptist and Congregational ministers, their membership was not held locally. They were stationed by the Conference, not chosen by the circuits. They were answerable to the Conference, and not to the circuits. The strict three-year itinerancy made ministers and their families relative strangers in their circuits, certainly by comparison with trustees, class leaders and local preachers, who were rooted in the community. It was easy for an itinerant to feel isolated and vulnerable, vested with formal authority and yet treated with coolness or disrespect – marginalized – by local people.

Although the Reform crisis was sparked by a dispute among ministers, many of the leading advocates of Reform were local preachers, and

---

[64] C. J. Day, 'Communications', in Alan Crossley, ed., *A History of the County of Oxford*, 4: *The City of Oxford* (Oxford, 1979), 284–95, at 294–5.
[65] Nesta Selwyn, 'Social and Cultural Activities', in Crossley, ed., *The City of Oxford*, 425–41, at 441.
[66] Bowmer, *Pastor and People*, 52.

this was certainly the case in Oxford. The rhetoric of Reform, locally and nationally, emphasized Methodism's debt to its local preachers. 'A Wesleyan Methodist', deploring the refusal of the president to receive a deputation from the Reform meeting in March 1850, observed that many of the delegates were local preachers, 'men who have travelled some thousands of miles on foot, preached some thousands of sermons, met classes, and performed various other duties in the church, and that *gratuitously*'.[67] With two itinerants to cover a circuit of seventeen preaching places, Oxford depended on its local preachers for some twenty-three of its twenty-eight regular Sunday services. Moreover, many of the village societies seldom saw the itinerants: every service was conducted by a local preacher. When the same individual was also a trustee, a class leader, a Sunday school teacher, and perhaps also a freelance evangelist, it may be seen that men like Josiah Crapper, William Leggatt and Gabriel Banbury might well regard themselves as key to the flourishing of Methodism. Nearly half a century after the Reform crisis, Banbury still remembered being threatened because of his Reform sympathies by Robert Day, the itinerant 'sent by the Conference to Oxford'.[68] The *Oxford Chronicle* struck the same note in its description of the preachers expelled by Button as 'respectable tradesmen of this city ... beloved by the Wesleyan Methodist society.'[69] Time and again, itinerants were accused of treating solid citizens with scorn and contempt, marginalizing them in their own communities.

Both sides sought to use their power to overcome their opponents. Reformers boycotted services, such as Button's farewell sermon in August 1849, and withheld the voluntary contributions on which Wesleyan finances relied, hoping that 'stopping the supplies' would compel concessions by the Conference. Superintendents used their legal and constitutional powers to expel members, sometimes finding that the expelled refused to go quietly. Through the early 1850s, in the Circuit and in local Wesleyan societies and organizations, there was a struggle for control, as competing loyalties were gradually resolved and settled. The outcome was a Pyrrhic victory for the Conference, leaving a vigorous Reform denomination established alongside the Wesleyans.

---

[67] 'Conference Despotism', as highlighted by a letter from 'A Wesleyan Methodist' (to the editor), *OC*, 23 March 1850, 2. Italics original.
[68] 'Mr G. G. Banbury, JP, Woodstock', 294.
[69] 'Wesleyans', *OC*, 25 August 1849, 2.

Thirdly, it has already been noted that village societies were particularly dependent on local preachers, and it may be asked whether this translated into greater support for Wesleyan Reform on the geographical margins of the Circuit. This seems not to have been the case. Some villages took up the cause – Kirtlington and Rose Hill, in particular – but most did not. The influence of William Leggatt and Gabriel Banbury established a sturdy Reform society in the small market town of Woodstock. Most of the reformers, however, were Oxford-based, and the strongest Reform society was in the city centre. In this respect, Wesleyan Reform reflected the demographics of the Old Connexion. Likewise, the leading reformers were mostly master craftsmen and skilled artisans, as were the trustees, leaders and local preachers who eventually decided to stay with the Wesleyans.

Finally, the perspective of those observing the 'Wesleyan Disruption'[70] from the sidelines may be considered. The controversy attracted considerable comment from the press, both secular and religious. In Oxford, it was the *Chronicle* that devoted by far the most space to the issue, to the extent that by November 1849 non-Methodist readers began to object.[71] The *Chronicle* sided with the reformers, describing the behaviour of the Conference as a 'grief to all liberal-minded Christians.'[72] Although focussing mainly on questions of liberty and justice, the *Chronicle* also used 'the baneful results of a clerical convocation' to warn against Tractarianism, as Oxford high churchmen mobilized in opposition to the Gorham Judgement in summer 1850.[73] Meanwhile, *Jackson's Oxford Journal*, conservative in tone, confined its reporting to the major Reform meetings in October 1849 and July 1850, but did not fill its columns with news from the *Wesleyan Times*. Equally conservative, and even more devoted to the established church, the *University, City, and County Herald* also reported the visit of Dunn and Griffith, justifying its coverage as an opportunity to lament the feeble 'bond of cohesion' among 'sectarians' and 'dissenters' and encouraging Wesleyans to seek reconciliation with the Church of England.[74]

---

[70] Headline in the *University, City, and County Herald*, 13 July 1850, 3.
[71] 'To Correspondents', *OC*, 10 November 1849, 2.
[72] 'Literature', *OC*, 18 May 1850, 4.
[73] 'Much Ado About Nothing', *OC*, 27 July 1850, 2.
[74] 'The Contentions among the Wesleyans', *University, City, and County Herald*, 13 July 1850, 2. The *Herald* was careful to describe Dunn and Griffith as 'Mr' and not 'Rev.'.

Many Wesleyans in this period would have indignantly rejected the identification with Dissent, but a common evangelicalism did connect Methodists with Baptists and Congregationalists. Given this kinship, and given their commitment to religious liberty, Wesleyan Reform posed a dilemma for Oxford's Nonconformists. Although there was plenty of comment in the wider Nonconformist press, Nonconformists in the city trod carefully. The Summertown Congregationalists clarified that Crapper had not been called to their pastorate in 1849; nor had he been paid a salary, although an 'acknowledgment' was made for the services of 'occasional preachers'.[75] The deacons of the Adullam Chapel, the largest Nonconformist building in the city, made their premises available for Reform meetings, and eagle-eyed reporters at Dunn and Griffith's visit in July 1850 spotted two Congregationalist ministers on the platform and one Baptist minister in the audience.[76] There is no evidence, however, of pulpit references to Wesleyan Reform at New Road Baptist or George Street Congregational chapels, or of an accession of ex-Wesleyan members to either cause in the early 1850s.[77]

Wesleyan Reform began with an attack on a metropolitan clique, but the 'centre' resented by the reformers was essentially clerical, rather than geographical. London circuits were among the first to rally to the 'three expelled' and it was the pretensions of the Conference that antagonized lay Methodists, in city and countryside. Somehow, the absorbing interplay of personalities and power struggles within the Conference blinded many itinerants – at least while meeting together – to the wider life, concerns and grievances of the Connexion. Turning inwards, the Conference cut itself off from a significant part of the Wesleyan membership. The Reform crisis saw members and lay leaders reassert their centrality to the life of Methodism and reclaim the importance of the localities. In this context, the dispute between John Wesley Button and Josiah Crapper took on significance not only for the development of Methodism in Oxford, but as an emblem of the issues affecting the life of the whole denomination.

---

[75] 'One of the Deacons of Summertown Church' (to the editor), *OC*, 8 September 1849, 2.
[76] 'The Revs S. Dunn and W. Griffith at Oxford', *OC*, 13 July 1850, 2. The Congregationalists were William Fergusson (Bicester) and John Tyndal[e] (George Street); the Baptist was Edward Bryan (New Road).
[77] However, details of new members recorded in the respective church books as received 'by profession of faith' would not normally include comment on any previous denominational allegiance.

Financing the Rural Periphery: Stipend Cross Subsidy in the Free Church of Scotland, 1843–1900

John W. Sawkins [iD]

Heriot-Watt University

In May 1843, around two-fifths of the clergy of the Church of Scotland resigned in protest over the 'intrusion' of the state in matters relating to ecclesiastical governance. The greatest single challenge facing the newly established Free Church of Scotland was financial: how to pay the stipends of its ministers. The solution was the Sustentation Fund, the aim of which was to guarantee a minimum stipend for all ministers by redistributing funds raised. This article describes and analyses the development of the Sustentation Fund, highlighting its critical role in financially cross-subsidizing congregations in peripheral rural areas. In analysing the direction and scale of cross subsidy, the results throw new light on two questions. First, the extent to which, across geographical location and time, rural congregations were dependent on urban cross subsidies. Second, the geographical location and financial commitment across time, of the church's urban, net contributor, congregations.

INTRODUCTION

On 18 May 1843, a schism, or 'Disruption', of the Church of Scotland took place, when ministers supporting the long-running campaign against the intrusion of the state in matters relating to ecclesiastical governance dramatically walked out of the annual meeting of the church's General Assembly, held that year in St Andrew's Church, Edinburgh. Led by the charismatic Rev. Dr Thomas Chalmers, they convened at the nearby Tanfield Hall to sign an Act of Separation and Deed of Demission, by which they signalled their intention to quit the established church, voluntarily renouncing their rights to salary (stipend) and accommodation (church and manse). Of the 1,195

Edinburgh Business School, Heriot-Watt University, Edinburgh, EH14 4AS.
E-mail: j.w.sawkins@hw.ac.uk.

Studies in Church History 61 (2025), 459–499 © The Author(s), 2025. Published by Cambridge University Press on behalf of the Ecclesiastical History Society. This is an Open Access article, distributed under the terms of the Creative Commons Attribution licence (http://creativecommons.org/licenses/by/4.0/), which permits unrestricted re-use, distribution and reproduction, provided the original article is properly cited.
doi:10.1017/stc.2024.49

clergymen in the Church of Scotland, 454 or 38.1% joined the newly constituted Free Church of Scotland.[1]

From the outset, Chalmers maintained that the Disruption was not merely another denominational secession, but a severing of the historic relationship between church and state in Scotland. At the Free Church's first General Assembly meeting he declared: 'though we quit the Establishment, we go out on the Establishment principle; we quit a vitiated Establishment, but would rejoice in returning to a pure one. To express it otherwise – we are the advocates for a national recognition and national support of religion – and we are not Voluntaries.'[2]

The Free Church was thereby committed, from its inception, to offering the ordinances of religion nationally. That meant not only the rapid recruitment of a ministerial labour force sufficient to cover every parish in Scotland, but also the equally onerous task of duplicating the established church's physical infrastructure, its national network of church buildings and manses, to accommodate its new members and adherents. The immediate and most pressing challenge facing the newly created church was therefore financial.[3]

The economic context within which the nascent church met this challenge was extraordinarily difficult, with Highland Scotland in the mid-1840s suffering the disastrous effects of potato blight, poor harvests and famine. Yet by May 1847, the progress of the Free Church, measured in terms of money raised, stipends paid and buildings erected, had greatly exceeded the expectations of the sceptics. In total, over £312,000 had been contributed to the centrally managed Sustentation Fund for the support of the ministry. Through it, 590 ministers were in receipt of a minimum stipend (known as the 'Equal Dividend') of £120, with another 83 enjoying a lesser level of financial support (Table 1). In addition, the church claimed to have built or taken possession of a total of 730 churches,[4] and had a leadership which included amongst its number 'the most prominent, able and

[1] Stewart J. Brown, *Thomas Chalmers and the Godly Commonwealth in Scotland* (Oxford, 1982), 335.
[2] William Hanna, *Memoirs of the Life and Writings of Thomas Chalmers*, 4 vols (Edinburgh, 1849–52), 4: 348–9.
[3] 'The great challenge now confronting those who had left the Establishment was the financial one.' Brown, *Godly Commonwealth*, 336.
[4] Ibid. 339.

zealous members of the established church'.[5] Taken together, the Free Church of Scotland could fairly be judged to have met its core objective of establishing an organization supporting a territorial ministry across the whole of Scotland within just four years of the Disruption.

Yet, despite this early success, the Free Church's financial progress thereafter lost momentum, and, with it, faded the hope of dislodging the Church of Scotland from its position as the numerically largest national church. Indeed, over the following three decades, the latter not only survived, but enjoyed a remarkable recovery,[6] with a successful fundraising campaign enabling it to extend its reach amongst the general population, whilst embracing progressive theological debate and innovative liturgical practice.

In contrast, the Free Church found itself increasingly driven to rein in its church extension ambitions, as the perennial need to raise funds for its entire range of activities through voluntary giving weighed on it more and more heavily.[7] This was the enduring general financial challenge that it faced. Equally important, however, was the very specific need to develop and sustain a system for redistributing the funds it raised to support ministers and ministries in the poorest and most sparsely populated parts of Scotland – the peripheral rural areas – without which it would have been unable to fulfil its mission as a national church.

This article describes and analyses how the Free Church met the challenge of redistributing its funds for the support of its national ministry, from urban centres of population to the rural periphery, through the development and operation of its most important financial system, the Sustentation Fund. Throughout the nineteenth century, this was the primary means by which the church financed, and thereby maintained, its presence throughout Scotland, through the ingathering and redistribution of money raised by its local associations and

---

[5] Stewart J. Brown, 'After the Disruption: The Recovery of the National Church of Scotland, 1843–1874', *Scottish Church History* 48 (2019), 103–25.

[6] Ibid. 103–25.

[7] Articles exhorting members to increase their giving were regularly published in the Free Church of Scotland, *Home and Foreign Record*. Its August 1855 edition, for example, warned that failure to make adequate financial provision would mean that, 'Year by year our Free Church movement will contract itself within narrower limits. We shall get an ill-furnished, dwarfed, spiritless, successless minister. Congregations will decline in numbers, and will come to be made up of but the more illiterate, the less wealthy, and the least influential portion of the community.' Free Church of Scotland, *Home and Foreign Record*, August 1855, 3.

congregations. Characterizing the Sustentation Fund as an archetypal cross-subsidy scheme, this article draws on published financial information to analyse, for the first time, the direction, and calibrate the scale, of the extensive urban-rural cross subsidies, from the 1843 Disruption to the union of the Free and United Presbyterian churches in 1900.

To date, studies describing the development of the Free Church during this period, whilst rich in insights relating to politics, society and culture, have generally paid relatively little attention to the detail of the organization's finance and economics;[8] ironic in light of the prominence given to these matters by Chalmers and other early Free Church leaders.[9] This article's contribution to the existing literature rests therefore on its deployment of financial data to enrich and extend current narratives of the church's financial development, particularly in relation to the financial sustainability of its national mission. In particular, it throws new light on the question of why the Free Church took so long to secure the modest ministerial stipend payment of £150 agreed at its inception. This, it is argued, resulted from the church's inability to resolve incentive problems typical of cross-subsidy schemes and intrinsic to the design and operation of the Sustentation Fund.

---

[8] Amongst the many studies covering the 'Disruption', the following remain pre-eminent: George D. Henderson, *Heritage: A Study of the Disruption* (Edinburgh, 1943); Brown, *Godly Commonwealth*; Alexander C. Cheyne, *Studies in Scottish Church History* (Edinburgh, 1999), chs 4, 5 (79–122); Stewart J. Brown and Michael Fry, eds, *Scotland in the Age of the Disruption* (Edinburgh, 1993). Early apologetic accounts from different perspectives include Robert Buchanan, *The Ten Years' Conflict*, 2 vols (Glasgow, 1852); James Bryce, *Ten Years of the Church of Scotland*, 2 vols (Edinburgh, 1850); Alexander Turner, *The Scottish Secession of 1843* (Edinburgh, 1859). An important finance paper for the post-Disruption period is Robert Buchanan, 'Finance of the Free Church of Scotland', *Journal of the Statistical Society of London* 33 (1870), 74–110. Partisan accounts may be found in Norman L. Walker, *Chapters from the History of the Free Church of Scotland* (Edinburgh, 1895); Thomas Brown, *Annals of the disruption with extracts from the narratives of ministers who left the Scottish establishment in 1843* (Edinburgh, 1893). Recent PhD theses examining its various aspects include Keith A Campbell, 'The Free Church of Scotland and the Territorial Ideal, 1843–1900' (PhD thesis, University of Edinburgh, 1999); Kenneth R Ross, 'The Free Church Case 1900–04 and its Origins' (PhD thesis, University of Edinburgh, 1987). An outstanding recent study is Ryan Mallon, *Dissent after Disruption: Church and State in Scotland, 1843–1863* (Edinburgh, 2021).

[9] For example, Dr Robert S. Candlish, whose name, along with that of Chalmers, is associated with the early design of the Sustentation Fund: see Alexander Lee, 'The Sustentation Fund', *The Free Church of Scotland Monthly: August* (Edinburgh, 1900), 1. Amongst the most forthright tracts by Chalmers is Thomas Chalmers, *An Earnest Appeal to the Free Church of Scotland on the Subjects of its Economics* (Edinburgh, 1846 [Scottish edn]; Philadelphia, PA, 1847 [American edn]).

The findings also have wider relevance to the study of the mid-nineteenth-century recovery of the established Church of Scotland,[10] in that the challenges posed by the Sustentation Fund framed, and ultimately constrained, the Free Church's ability to respond energetically to the established church's revival.

Anticipating and Realizing a Disruption

The Disruption of 1843 was the culmination of a decade-long struggle between established church and state over the right of local patrons, typically wealthy landowners, to present a minister of their choice to vacant parish charges. It was played out, however, against a background of political, ecclesiastical and economic events, which were reshaping Scottish society in a quite fundamental way.[11]

Politically, the British parliament had, between 1828 and 1832, enacted three landmark reforms: first, in 1828, the repeal of the Test and Corporation Acts, granting Protestant Dissenters full civil and political rights; second, in 1829, the Catholic Emancipation Act, granting Roman Catholics the right to sit in Parliament and to hold most public offices; and third, in 1832, the Reform Act, which swept away old parliamentary boundaries, broadening the franchise and increasing parliamentary representation in the rapidly growing urban areas. Within this new political context, the existing ecclesiastical settlement, in particular the pecuniary privileges of the established churches across Britain and Ireland, came under pressure.

In Scotland, Protestant Dissenters, led by Andrew Marshall, a leading minister of the United Secession Church, launched a 'Voluntary' campaign to disestablish and disendow the established Church of Scotland. By the early 1830s, voluntary church associations had

---

[10] The mid-nineteenth-century revival of the established church received early scholarly attention in several nineteenth- and twentieth-century biographies of leading established church ministers; an approach taken up by Andrew L. Drummond and James Bulloch, *The Church in Victorian Scotland 1843–1874* (Edinburgh, 1975). Brown's (2019) seminal study of the phenomenon brings to bear new insights relating to matters including the revival of the parish ideal, the renewal of worship and the development of doctrine: Brown, 'After the Disruption', 103–25. Although the established church's relationship with the Free Church features clearly, greater focus is given to the initiatives taken by the Church of Scotland. However, an understanding of the financial constraints within which the rival Free Church operated during this period is clearly salient to the broader narrative.

[11] See Stewart J. Brown, 'The Ten Years' Conflict and the Disruption of 1843', in idem and Fry, eds, *Scotland in the Age of the Disruption*, 1–27.

sprung up in all of Scotland's major towns and cities, challenging and disrupting established church activities in the name of 'Voluntaryism'.[12] Within the Church of Scotland, the evangelical party, committed to the parish ministry, overseas mission and a concern for Christian discipline and formation, took control of the church's General Assembly from the moderate party in 1834, adopting a more robust approach to church defence and extension, whilst campaigning for the abolition of patronage.

Economically, the forces unleashed by the Industrial Revolution continued to incentivize agricultural labourers in rural areas to migrate to urban areas to work in rapidly growing industries, from those supporting the production of iron, to the spinning and weaving of cotton. Improving transport networks were, at the same time, creating national markets for goods, while overseas markets were gradually being opened up by entrepreneurial merchants commissioning shipping to export the products of industry. The benefits of economic growth were, however, unevenly spread; and a new wealthy mercantile middle class emerged, soon to deploy its power in the political arena. As the 1840s began, the country's political and ecclesiastical leaders could not foresee the extent of suffering soon to be visited on the country through the repeated failure of the potato crop.

Against this background, in the anticipatory planning for a break with the established church, the leaders of the Free Church were clear that substantial sources of finance had to be identified and exploited rapidly lest the entire project be stillborn. Denied access to the Church of Scotland's primary sources of income – parish teinds, government and church endowments – they also recognized the criticality of building an organizational structure to support fundraising mechanisms that would secure the ongoing sustainability of financing arrangements, thereby guaranteeing the church's survival.[13] Chalmers and the other church leaders reluctantly but pragmatically concluded, therefore, that voluntary giving would, perforce, be the financial bedrock on which the church was built.

---

[12] Stewart J. Brown, 'Religion and the Rise of Liberalism: The First Disestablishment Campaign in Scotland, 1829–1843', *JEH* 48 (1997), 682–704.

[13] 'The Free Church required not only high principles, but also brick, mortar, and above all money. The consolidation of the Disruption would in the final analysis be a financial achievement.' Brown, *Godly Commonwealth*, 337.

The scale of the voluntary fundraising task, unprecedented in Scotland's ecclesiastical history, had been outlined by Chalmers at a convocation of evangelical ministers held in Edinburgh in November 1842. Here, he promised not only to raise funds sufficient to build a national network of churches and manses, but also to provide at least £100,000 per annum for the support of clergy quitting the establishment. This was an extraordinarily ambitious objective and claim, greeted by some of those attending with incredulity.[14]

To achieve the ultimate goal of a national church funded sustainably through voluntary contributions, Chalmers drew on the experience from two key periods of his ministry. First, the period 1819 to 1823, when, as minister of St John's parish, Glasgow, he had sought to reinvigorate the traditional parochial system within the context of an impoverished urban area.[15] Second, the period 1834 to 1841, when he led the Church of Scotland's church extension campaign, adding over 200 churches to its stock in the face of a well-organized and increasingly vocal Voluntary campaign.[16]

Chalmers presented to the convocation the key features of a centralized arrangement for the ingathering and distribution of money: the Central or Sustentation Fund scheme. The scheme required local congregational associations to organize in order to collect and remit funds they had raised, on a quarterly basis, to the church's headquarters in Edinburgh. The pooled funds were then to be redistributed through an 'equal dividend' paid annually to every minister of the church, regardless of the contribution of his local congregation. In this way, ministers serving remote and economically poor rural areas – particularly the Highlands and Islands – would be guaranteed a basic minimum stipend. Chalmers was clear, however, that money remitted to the Fund should not be directed exclusively towards the stipends of existing clergy. Importantly, it was to fund church extension through the employment of new territorial missionaries and to organize congregations in districts lacking a Free Church presence. Nevertheless, having met their obligations under the scheme, local congregations

---

[14] Brown, *Godly Commonwealth*, 336–7; Buchanan, 'Finance of the Free Church', 86.

[15] Brown, *Godly Commonwealth*, 91–151.

[16] See ibid. 236–78. 'During the seven years of Chalmers's convenership, from May 1834 to May 1841, 222 new churches had been built increasing the total number of churches in the Scottish Establishment by over 20 per cent.' Brown, *Godly Commonwealth*, 278. Compare also Brown, 'Religion and the Rise of Liberalism', 682–704.

would be permitted to supplement their own minister's stipend, raising it above the level of the equal dividend.

At the close of the convocation, Chalmers energetically initiated the formation of local societies or associations, whose primary purposes were the organization of congregations and the collection of funds. The first of these, established in December 1842, was formed near his home in the parish of Morningside, Edinburgh. Under the auspices of a new Provisional Committee created in February 1843, travelling agents were sent around the country to organize new associations, often through the revival of dormant local societies of his church extension movement.[17] By the day of the Disruption, 687 local associations committed to financially supporting the Free Church were in existence throughout Scotland.[18] Within four years, just under 700 ministers had been employed to serve a network of 730 churches stretching across the entire country.[19]

EMERGING FINANCIAL CHALLENGES

Despite such rapid progress, there were early signs that support for the Sustentation Fund was waning, and a view emerged that failure to meet its ambitious financial targets posed an existential risk to the entire Free Church project. In presenting the annual report on the Sustentation Fund to the Free Church's 1848 General Assembly, Dr Robert Buchanan[20] noted that, because of inadequate fundraising, the equal dividend – i.e. base ministerial stipend – had fallen back from £122 in 1846, to £120 in 1847,[21] well short of the £150 target set at the Disruption. Several reasons for this were offered: the church's rapid expansion, whereby the number of new ministers admitted to the

---

[17] Brown, *Godly Commonwealth*, 333.
[18] Ibid. 338.
[19] Ibid. 339.
[20] The Rev. Robert Buchanan (1802–75) succeeded Thomas Chalmers as minister of the Tron Kirk, Glasgow, in 1833. He joined the Free Church in 1843, serving as minister of the Tron Free Church (1843–57), Convener of the Sustentation Fund Committee (1847–75), and Moderator of the Free Church General Assembly (1860). He was prominent in church union debates, actively promoting negotiations with the United Presbyterian Church, the Reformed Presbyterian Church and the Presbyterian Church of England. Hew Scott, Fasti ecclesiae scoticanae: *The Succession of Ministers in the Church of Scotland from the Reformation*, 2nd edn, 7 vols (Edinburgh, 1915–28), 3: 475–6.
[21] Free Church General Assembly, *Report and Speeches on the Sustentation Fund*, 23 May 1848, 1–9.

equal dividend 'platform' outstripped increases in funds raised to support their stipends; the energy diverted towards fundraising efforts for church, school and manse building projects; and the extraordinarily challenging external economic environment. In addition, Buchanan advanced the view that responsibility for the success or failure of the Sustentation Fund lay not with the church's Sustentation Committee, but with local churches, their ministers, elders and deacons, without whose active advocacy, he argued, any actions by the church's central bureaucracy, based in the capital, would be ineffective:

> In efforts of this kind we have no system of electric wires, to propagate from a single centre the influence that will reach in undiminished force the remotest extremities. A touch in Edinburgh, whether in the shape of a speech or a circular, tells very feebly by the time it reaches the Pentland or Solway First, and in truth is not felt at all in many places much nearer to hand. (Hear, and a laugh.)[22]

Furthermore, he argued, if the local courts of the church failed to take up their responsibilities to support the Fund the consequences would be catastrophic for the church:

> the Deacons' Courts that neglect this Fund are thereby doing what in them lies to destroy the Free Church of Scotland ... let Synods, Presbyteries, and Deacons' Courts undervalue and trifle with this fundamental interest, and there is no power or agency which the [Sustentation Fund] Committee can employ that will long avert the decline and fall of the Sustentation Fund, and with it our national Free Church.[23]

Aware of the growing precariousness of the church's financial position, Buchanan, on his appointment as convener of the Sustentation Fund Committee in 1847, led a programme of presbytery visits or 'conferences' to explore the reasons for shortfalls in financial contributions to the Sustentation Fund, and to encourage greater efforts in its promotion. From June 1847, accompanied by the superintendent of associations, Mr Handyside, he travelled to sixty presbyteries within a year, meeting with two office-bearers and the presbytery

[22] Ibid. 4.
[23] Ibid.

elder for every congregation within each presbytery's bounds. The purpose of these meetings was to establish and agree an amount of money which individual congregations would be 'recommended and urged to raise'.[24] Through this work, Buchanan became aware of an underlying problem, which simple exhortation was incapable of addressing. That problem was financial free-riding, or the propensity of some congregations to limit their contributions to the Fund, relying instead on the generosity of others to maintain the level of the equal dividend.

CROSS SUBSIDY

As originally conceived by Chalmers and Candlish, the Sustentation Fund was to be the mechanism by which contributions from individual church congregations for the support of the ministry would be pooled and reallocated on a common basis. Regardless of the level of contribution by any individual congregation, every minister was to receive the same equal dividend stipendiary payment. Thus, in design and operation, the Sustentation Fund was, in essence, a vast cross-subsidy scheme in which the link between the amount paid into the Fund by a congregation, and the amount paid out to that congregation's minister was severed.

The need for cross subsidy emerged from the conjunction of the Free Church's desire to offer the ordinances of religion nationally, and the vast difference in prosperity between the wealthy urban areas, such as the cities of Edinburgh, Glasgow, Dundee and Aberdeen, and the poorer, peripheral rural areas, particularly the Highlands and Islands.[25] Without some means of transferring resources between these areas, the church would be unable to provide sustainable staffing

---

[24] Ibid. 5.

[25] Within Scotland's largest towns and cities there were many areas of extreme poverty. The work of Thomas Chalmers in meeting the spiritual needs of those resident in one such area, the Cowgate of Edinburgh, is outlined in Stewart J. Brown, 'The Disruption and Urban Poverty: Thomas Chalmers and the West Port Operation in Edinburgh, 1844–47', *Records of the Scottish Church History Society* 20 (1978), 65–89. On the economic gap between urban and rural areas, see Thomas Christopher Smout, *A Century of the Scottish People 1830–1950* (Glasgow, 1986), 10–13. A fascinating complementary perspective on the cultural gap between Lowlands and Highlands is offered in James L MacLeod, *The Second Disruption: The Free Church in Victorian Scotland and the Origins of the Free Presbyterian Church* (East Linton, 2000), 125–78.

for sparsely populated rural parishes and would thereby fail to fulfil its national mission. Instead, it would be obliged to focus its work in the relatively affluent cities and provincial towns.

Cross-subsidy schemes in which participants are not, or cannot be, excluded from some or all of the benefits enjoyed by its members, are open to exploitation through self-interested strategic behaviour. Without exclusion, free-riding behaviours are incentivized.[26] If not arrested, these individual behaviours undermine the collective arrangement, risking the collapse of any cross-subsidy scheme.[27] This risk, and the necessary mitigations, was fully understood and clearly articulated by Chalmers in his 1846 *cri de coeur*, *An Earnest Appeal to the Free Church of Scotland on the Subjects of its Economics.*[28]

On the question of exclusion, which meant limiting the number of minsters admitted to the scheme, Chalmers took the view that the benefits of the equal dividend should be strictly restricted to those who had 'come out' of the Church of Scotland in 1843.[29] He further noted the problem of free-riding, with 'many congregations in certain parts of the Church, who, trusting to the more generous or wealthy congregations in other parts of it, fall miserably short in their contributions to the Central Fund.'[30] Furthermore, this brought the associated problems of cross-subsidy 'addiction' on the part of net beneficiaries, and 'aid fatigue' on the part of net contributors.[31]

Nevertheless, Chalmers was pragmatic enough to understand that permanent cross subsidy would be required for the poorest congregations of a national church. In characteristic style, he urged those in the most adverse situations to do all they could to reduce their dependence on financial subsidies.[32]

By 1848, Buchanan was able to offer the Free Church General Assembly a compelling narrative based on information gathered from

---

[26] That is, where net beneficiaries of a scheme 'free-ride' on the efforts of net contributors to the scheme.

[27] Seminal contributions to the economics literature on the question of cross-subsidy were made by Gerald R. Faulhaber. See, for example, Gerald R. Faulhaber, 'Cross-subsidization: Pricing in Public Enterprises', *American Economic Review* 65 (1975), 966–77.

[28] Chalmers, *An Earnest Appeal.*

[29] Ibid. 55.

[30] Ibid. 23.

[31] Ibid. 22, 26.

[32] Ibid. 25–6.

presbytery 'conferences' which corroborated Chalmers' earlier analysis. On the problem of free-riding he observed:

> It is to be feared there are congregations not a few that are taking their ease in this matter somewhat selfishly, and without much concerning themselves as to the burden they may be thereby imposing upon others. Nothing, indeed, can be more delightful than to see the abundance of one congregation supplying the want of another, where that want is real. But, on the other hand, nothing can be more offensive than to find the apathy, or indolence, or niggardliness of one congregation pillowing itself on the self-denying labours and sacrifices of another perhaps poorer than itself. (Applause.)[33]

Buchanan went on to calibrate the extent of the problem at that date:

> It is necessary, Sir, at this point, that I should present some statistics, from which it will sufficiently appear how very limited are the contributions which many of our congregations make to this Fund, and how reasonable it is both to ask and expect that increase which the Assembly has proposed.

Of the 698 ministerial charges of the Free Church, there are

31	that have contributed	£25 and under.	
158	"	"	50 and under.
450	"	"	100 and under.

The 31 have contributed	£523, 17s. 8d.	= £16, 17s.	each
158	"	"	5,443, 9s. 10d.	= 34, 9s.	"
450	"	"	27,034, 14s. 9d.	= 60, 1s.	"

It thus appears that considerably more than two-thirds of our whole income are contributed by one-third of our congregations; and these 450 congregations cost the Fund this year, beyond their own contributions, £30,728:5:3. (Hear). I just ask, without going into details, whether any man can credit the supposition that there are not among

---

[33] Free Church General Assembly, *Report and Speeches on the Sustentation Fund*, 23 May 1848, 8.

these 450 congregations many which ought to be independent of such assistance.[34]

Buchanan's presbytery 'conversations' were just one of several initiatives taken which, throughout the life of the scheme, sought to address its shortcomings as a means of supporting a national ministry. Modifications to the Sustentation Fund's rules and associated advocacy occurred repeatedly, as the church sought to increase the equal dividend and to extend it to a growing number of ministers.

Sustentation Fund: Initiatives and Innovations

Although committing itself, at the 1843 Disruption, to achieving a £150 equal dividend, the church first met this target a full quarter of a century later, in 1868. The failure to achieve this objective and suggestions as to how persistent financial shortfalls might be made good were, throughout this period, the leitmotif of annual reports of the Sustentation Fund Committee to the church's General Assembly.

Two general types of approach to the deficiency were taken by the Committee during this period. First, changes to the rules of the scheme itself. Second, centrally coordinated campaigns of visitation by Sustentation Committee representatives to presbyteries for exhortation and encouragement. The fortunes of each approach were mixed as the following examples illustrate.

In 1844, under the leadership of Chalmers, the 'Half-More System' was introduced.[35] The purpose was to limit the number of ministers being admitted as full beneficiaries of the equal dividend, and to incentivize the giving of congregations to the Fund. A rule change determined '[t]hat every minister admitted to a new charge shall receive from the Sustentation Fund the contribution of his Association, if up to or less than £100, and the half more.'[36] Thus, for example, the minister of a congregation contributing £80 to the Fund was entitled to receive back £120. Importantly, ministers ordained

---

[34] Ibid. 8.

[35] The principles of the arrangement were set out in detail by Chalmers in an appendix entitled 'On certain requisite Modifications by which our present System of an Equal Dividend might be Improved': 'Appendix V', in Chalmers, *Earnest Appeal* (American edn), 54.

[36] Free Church of Scotland, *Acts of the General Assembly of the Free Church of Scotland, VII Act anent the Future Arrangements of the Sustentation Fund* (1844), 17.

before Whitsunday 1844 were excluded from the change and continued to receive the full equal dividend.

The arrangement proved unpopular amongst the clergy from the beginning, with opposition amongst the recently ordained being particularly marked.[37] Therefore, at the May 1848 General Assembly, after the death of Chalmers in May 1847, the scheme was ended with the equal dividend principle offered as the justification:

> That the principle of an equal dividend in distributing the Central Fund, ordained by the General Assembly which met at Glasgow in 1843, ought to be maintained; and that the deviation from that principle introduced by the Resolutions of the Assembly of 1844, has been found inexpedient, and should be gradually terminated ... .[38]

The process of transferring ministers from the half-more scheme to the full equal dividend began in 1848; it continued until 1852, thereby placing further pressure on the Sustentation Fund, leading to falls in stipend. Buchanan's extensive national programme of visitations, entitled presbytery 'conferences', in 1847–8 mitigated the effect of this somewhat by giving a boost to Fund donations. However, the marked step up in the level of donations to the Fund did not endure the removal of the temporary stimulus of the presbytery conferences, and the equal dividend thereafter fell back as ministerial numbers continued to rise at a rate faster than the donations would support.[39]

In 1853, the Sustentation Fund Committee sought to arrest continuing falls in the equal dividend by introducing a new rating system. This had two elements. First:

> the particular sum which each congregation is to be expected to contribute to that fund shall henceforth be arranged by the Deacons' Courts, with the concurrence of the Committee on the Sustentation Fund ... That in every case in which the Deacons' Court and the Sustentation Fund Committee shall agree as to the

[37] The revised terms of the scheme meant that all those recently ordained were denied access to the full equal dividend.

[38] Free Church of Scotland, *Acts of the General Assembly of the Free Church of Scotland, IV Act anent the Appropriation of the Sustentation fund* (1848), 14.

[39] Ministerial numbers grew during this period as a consequence of the 1852 union with the Original Secession Synod.

amount of the stipulated contribution, the congregation shall take its place in the present scheme, and be entitled to participate in all its provisions.[40]

Second, a 'Supplementary Sustentation Fund' was established. This was a capital fund, designed to receive the amounts raised excess to that agreed, and entitling contributing congregations to draw a pound for every pound deposited to supplement their minister's stipend up to a limit of £150.

This rating system was regarded as highly interventionist, and quickly became deeply unpopular.[41] The May 1855 General Assembly brought it to an end,[42] again citing the equal dividend principle in rationalizing this action:

> that the plan of an Equal Dividend is better fitted than any other yet proposed to secure the ends for which the Sustentation fund was instituted and is maintained; and, while it is desirable to adopt measures for preventing the decline of the Equal Dividend, through the failure of congregations to discharge their duty, these measures ought to be such as tend to preserve the general principle of the plan.[43]

In ending this initiative, the same 1855 General Assembly praised another devised by Buchanan a year earlier, the 'One-Fourth-More movement'.

In August 1854, Buchanan presented to a meeting of the Commission of the General Assembly a visitation plan for the purpose of promoting giving to the Sustentation Fund. Modelled on his successful 1847–8 presbytery 'conferences', a series of deputies, appointed by the Sustentation Fund Committee, were delegated to visit

---

[40] Free Church of Scotland, *Acts of the General Assembly of the Free Church of Scotland, III Act anent the Sustentation Fund* (1853), 14–15.

[41] The scheme 'was denounced in certain quarters as an interference with the principle of a freewill offering, and was characterised as a rating scheme. In these circumstances, the success of it was rendered hopeless, and, after a short ineffectual struggle, the plan was abandoned.' Free Church of Scotland, *Proceedings of the General Assembly* (Edinburgh, 1875), 55.

[42] 'That the existing regulations for the distribution of the Sustentation Fund having proved unsatisfactory the Church, and having failed in securing the object for which they were enacted, be now rescinded.' Free Church of Scotland, *Acts of the General Assembly of the Free Church of Scotland* (Edinburgh, 1855), 205.

[43] Ibid. 189.

congregations and deacons' courts throughout the country. This time they were tasked with conveying a specific request in order:

> not merely to press upon them the necessity of vigorous and united action to obtain an increase in the fund, but to lay before each of them the definite proposal of endeavouring to realise an increase of one-fourth upon their previous rate of contribution. This proved to be the most successful appeal that had yet been made. It set before each congregation a specific thing to do – a thing that, unless in very exceptional cases, could without difficulty be done.[44]

This initiative proved extremely effective, and with a large uplift in income to the Fund, the equal dividend rose from £119 in 1854, to £132 in 1855.

For the next decade, only minor modifications to the operation of the Fund were adopted and the equal dividend remained stubbornly below the target of £150, despite Scotland's growing wealth and the rise in salaries paid in other professions. At the 1867 General Assembly, the inadequacy of the minimum stipend was again noted, and a resolution passed raising the target minimum from £150 to £200.[45] More significant in terms of the operation of the Fund was the creation of a Surplus Fund.

The Surplus Fund was to receive the surplus of the annual revenue of the Sustentation Fund once it had paid the £150 equal dividend to all entitled. However, the critical innovation was that distributions from this fund were to be made according to congregational giving per head, with thresholds set at 10s. and 7s. 6d. No congregation giving less than £60 per year was to be entitled to participate in the fund. Those congregations giving 10s. or more per head would receive a distribution from the Surplus Fund, and those giving between 7s. 6d. and 10s. would receive an amount half as large as that offered to the 10s. or more congregations. No minister was to receive more than £50 from the Surplus Fund; however, should support be forthcoming, the church would thereby secure stipends of £200 for all its ministers: £150 through the equal dividend, and £50 from the Surplus Fund.

---

[44] Free Church of Scotland, *Proceedings of the General Assembly* (Edinburgh, 1875), 55.
[45] Free Church of Scotland, *Proceedings of the General Assembly* (Edinburgh, 1867), 353.

Incentivized by this new initiative, the equal dividend finally achieved the £150 target the following year, advancing to £157 in 1875, and £160 in 1879. The arrangements were reviewed again in 1874, and two further targets were formally adopted by the church. These were the attainment of a £200 stipend for all ministers, and a minimum contribution rate of ten shillings per member per year. Further minor amendments to the Sustentation Fund's operations occurred in 1877, 1889 and 1895.

Although the various innovations did modify the way in which the Sustentation Fund operated, its essential character, as a means by which the ministerial stipends of those serving poorer congregations were cross subsidized by those serving richer congregations, remained intact from the time of the Disruption to the Free Church's union with the United Presbyterian Church in 1900. The Free Church ministry as a whole proved reluctant, throughout the whole of this period, to surrender the principle of the equal dividend, or to restrict admission to the equal dividend platform as of right to all inducted to serve a congregation. The warnings of Chalmers and the 'Half-More Scheme' designed to incentivize giving did not, through accident or design, fundamentally shape the operation of the scheme after his death.[46]

Calibrating Cross Subsidy

In order to assess and calibrate the quantum and direction of cross subsidy across time, data extracted from the Free Church's financial records – primarily the church's annual accounts and Sustentation Fund reports to the General Assembly – are deployed and analysed.

Table 1 records the annual amounts contributed to the Sustentation Fund; the number of ministers participating in the Fund; the equal dividend agreed at annual meetings of the Free Church General Assembly; and the number of full equal dividend payments made. The positive impact on overall giving of the One-Fourth-More movement (1854) and the creation of the Surplus Fund (1867) are clearly evident.

---

[46] 'And not only would the system of an equal dividend lessen the amount of Church Extension, we also fear that it would greatly vitiate its quality. The prospect of a sure hundred a year might bring an earthly element into play, and call forth the sordid appetencies of the ecclesiastical aspirant.' Chalmers, *An Earnest Appeal* (American edn), 33.

It may be further observed that relatively large rises in the number of ministers participating in the Fund, for example in 1849 and 1857, coincide with moderations in the progress of the equal dividend. However, this is generally only one of a number of causal factors in play at these points in time.

In Table 2, the national position with respect to financially self-sustaining congregations is set out. Using the church's own definition of a self-sustaining congregation – one in which contributions to the Sustentation Fund exceed the equal dividend in any one year – it is clear that, throughout the period, fewer than a third of congregations exceeded this threshold. For years in which data on the number of congregations were published, the proportion contributing more than the equal dividend ranged from 19.6% to 34.0%. For each advance in the equal dividend, it was generally the case that the number and percentage of congregations recorded as being self-sustaining temporarily fell back. It should further be noted that the overall position is flattered by the use of the equal dividend as the benchmark throughout, rather than the target stipend, which, from 1867 onwards, was £200.

In Table 3, a more detailed geographical analysis is offered with decennial observations of congregational contributions to the Sustentation Fund aggregated by synod. This clearly reveals the regional disparities in absolute and relative terms. Two synods – Glasgow and Ayr, and Lothian and Tweeddale – dominate all others in terms of total financial contributions, in contrast to Shetland and Orkney, whose funds raised were extremely modest throughout the period. More generally, the synods containing the largest urban conurbations made the largest absolute and relative contributions throughout the period of study, with those located at the greatest distance from the towns and cities, the geographical periphery, making the lowest contributions.

Thus, as a percentage of all giving, the proportions of the church's total contributions made by the synods covering Scotland's leading cities – Lothian and Tweeddale (including Edinburgh), Glasgow and Ayr (including Glasgow), Aberdeen (including Aberdeen), and Angus and Mearns (including Dundee) – were 68.8% in 1844, 63.0% in 1854, 63.6% in 1864, 65.6% in 1874, 64.9% in 1884 and 65.3% in 1894.

Analysing the data at the sub-synod, presbytery level, Table 4 presents the amounts given by the four city presbyteries alone. Despite the reduction in the range and number of congregations covered by this narrower definition, the percentage of contributions by city presbyteries to the Fund was substantial, ranging between 45.3% in 1844 and 35.4 in 1864, generally accounting for just under two-fifths of the total.

In Table 5, the largest contributions to the Sustentation Fund by congregation for every presbytery at decennial frequency are presented. Two results stand out. First, the consistency of the identity of the most generous congregations (in absolute terms) throughout the period. In just under four-fifths of the presbyteries, one or two congregations are listed as being the largest contributors. Second, evidence of a decrease in giving by the highest contributing congregations towards the end of the period, with fifty-one of the seventy-two most generous congregations by presbytery recording a reduction between 1884 and 1894; a result consistent with the hypothesis of aid fatigue.

Within this subset of congregations, the position of St George's Free, Edinburgh, is notable for the relative and absolute size of its contributions. To put this into context, in terms of total synod contributions (Table 3), St George's Free, by itself, would have ranked twelfth by contribution level in 1854, and tenth by contribution level in 1894. This represented 21.3% and 22.2% of the total contributions of the presbytery of Edinburgh in the respective years; indicative of the critical importance of, and increasing reliance on, the fundraising efforts of this leading urban congregation.

Focusing more closely on the question of the quantum of cross subsidy flowing to peripheral rural areas, Tables 6, 7 and 8 analyse the number and percentage of self-sustaining congregations on a decennial basis for rural synods in Lowland (Dumfries), Highland (Sutherland and Caithness) and Islands (Orkney) areas, recording the amounts paid to, and due from, the Sustentation Fund for the ministers employed within these areas.

For Dumfries, the pattern is of a decline in drawings from the Sustentation Fund, and greater financial self-sufficiency, in the first half of the century; followed by an increase in drawings, a reduction in financial self-sufficiency, and a growing reliance on the Fund during the final quarter century. For Sutherland and Caithness, with a similar number of congregations, the percentage self-sustaining is substantially lower, ranging from 20.0% in 1874 to just 5.5% in 1900. The net amount drawn down from the Sustentation Fund rises markedly in the later years reaching nearly £3,500 in 1900. In the case of Orkney, no congregation is recorded as self-sustaining in the sampled years. Whilst the number of churches in this synod is small, the net amount drawn from the Sustentation Fund rises across time to £1,505 in 1900, representing a doubling in the level of financial support between 1844 and 1900.

Looking at the quantum of cross subsidy flowing from urban areas, illustrative data relating to two urban presbyteries, one Lowland (Edinburgh) and one Highland (Inverness) are presented in Tables 9 and 10. For Edinburgh, the proportion of self-sustaining congregations is consistently between three-fifths and three-quarters, with net contributions to the Fund rising across time to reach £13,850 in 1900. In contrast, Inverness, a smaller and less prosperous urban area with a smaller number of congregations, has just one self-sustaining congregation (out of seven) in 1844, and three (out of fourteen) in 1900. In terms of the Sustentation Fund, the presbytery drew a modest amount in the early years, moving to a break-even position in 1864 and 1874, before falling back into modest deficit from 1884 onwards. The pre-eminence of the presbytery of Edinburgh in supporting the Sustentation Fund is clear.

A final piece of analysis, illustrating the relative contributions of urban and rural areas, and the geographical location of the church's leading net contributor congregations, is presented in Table 11. This summarizes the number of congregations in each presbytery contributing less than half, and more than double, the equal dividend set in the years 1854 and 1894. The data illustrate the geographical contours of cross subsidy, with the number of congregations donating less than half the equal dividend in both years being higher, in relative and absolute terms, in the rural areas; whilst those donating more than double the equal dividend being confined almost exclusively to those presbyteries within which was located a large urban conurbation or county town.[47] The table also illustrates the impact of urbanization and rising prosperity on giving in the case of the presbytery of Dumbarton, where rapid industrial growth across the period led to a sharp rise in the number of congregations contributing generously to the Fund.[48]

---

[47] An exception to this rule was Rothesay in the presbytery of Dunoon and Inverary, whose contributions to the Sustentation Fund in 1854 were £343 for Rothesay Free and £313 for Rothesay West Church.

[48] For example, in 1894, the following notable contributions were made: Alexandria (£408), Helensburgh Park (£420), Helensburgh West (£453).

CONCLUSION

The Free Church's Sustentation Fund, throughout the period of its operation, displayed all the characteristics of an archetypal cross-subsidy scheme. Designed as a means by which financial resources could be transferred across the church in order to support payment of a basic stipend (the 'Equal Dividend') for all ministers, it achieved its overall aim of redistributing money raised by congregations located in wealthier urban areas to the poorer congregations located in peripheral mainland rural and island locations, on a scale hitherto unmatched amongst ecclesiastical institutions. It thereby enabled the Free Church to sustain its ministry across the whole country. In its operation, however, it displayed an openness to 'free-riding' by less generous congregations, and, latterly, aid fatigue on the part of the largest net contributors, creating difficulty for those maintaining the system of transfer between churches located in prosperous urban centres and those in the poorer rural periphery.

Evidence from the church's financial records establishes that around two-thirds of congregations located in peripheral rural areas were cross subsidized by the Fund throughout the period of study; a proportion little changed by occasional adaptations to its rules of operation. Clerical support for the equal dividend principle thwarted both the early attempt by Chalmers to sharpen the economic incentives faced by the congregations of ministers newly admitted to the Fund, and successive attempts by the Sustentation Fund Committee to set binding fundraising targets for individual congregations.

Analyses of financial information relating to typical urban, rural and islands synods and presbyteries offer a preliminary calibration of the extent to which congregations in the peripheral rural areas remained dependent on the annual stipendiary cross subsidy received from the Sustentation Fund, with the poorer islands areas making the smallest contributions and securing the highest levels of support. However, disaggregating the results down to presbytery and congregational level reveals the extent which, within the overall aggregate flows, important counter-narratives are observed. Thus, whilst there was a general flow of funds from south to north, and urban to rural, there were large areas of rural Lowland Scotland, and large numbers of urban parishes in every city and town benefitting from the Sustentation Fund.

Had Chalmers not established the Sustentation Fund apparatus as a means of redirecting the surpluses generated in a relatively small number of its urban congregations, the national aspirations of the emergent Free Church would have been thwarted. This therefore offers a lens through which to observe the Free Church wrestling with its heritage and conscience throughout the nineteenth century. On the one hand, the church, committed by its founder to the establishment principle, set out to offer the ordinances of religion to the entire Scottish population, making good on this pledge by funding ministers and buildings across the country in short order. On the other hand, it found itself forced by circumstances to operate as a de facto voluntary, continuing to devote time, financial and human resources, into raising money sufficient to fund its activities from its wealthier members,[49] never raising enough to fully endow its activities in order to liberate it from the annual fundraising round.

The Sustentation Fund itself was an important part of the Free Church's financial legacy which it took into the United Free Church following merger with the United Presbyterian Church in 1900. It was, however, a legacy which left unresolved the incentive problems typical of cross-subsidy schemes. These problems, intrinsic to the design and operation of the Sustentation Fund, would first undermine, and ultimately inhibit, the attempts of the new church to increase the number and proportion of financially self-sustaining congregations,[50] with implications for its own development in the early twentieth century. The findings therefore give new insight into the financial development of both the Free and United Free churches, against which narratives relating to the established church's revival may be set.

With hindsight, the predictions of Chalmers on the dire consequences to the church of extending the benefits of the equal dividend beyond ministers who left the Church of Scotland in 1843 look overstated. However, his predictions relating to the long-run behaviour of aid-giving and aid-receiving congregations under a cross-subsidy arrangement were surely validated: 'The equal divided, carried out and persisted in, will not only operate, which it has already done, to

---

[49] Despite a downturn in giving by the wealthier congregations in Edinburgh, Glasgow, Dundee and Aberdeen towards the end of the period, consistent with the hypothesis of emerging 'aid fatigue', the leading contributors, such as St George's Free, Edinburgh, remained the reliable financial sheet anchor of the Fund throughout.
[50] John W. Sawkins and Em Bailey, 'Ministerial Stipend Cross Subsidy in the United Free Church of Scotland', *Scottish Church History* 50 (2021), 1–27.

a fearful extent, as a sedative on the efforts of the aid-receiving, but as a sedative too, and that right soon, on the liberalities of the aid-giving congregations.'[51]

APPENDIX

Table 1. Sustentation Fund: Contributions, Ministers Participating and Equal Dividend: 1843/4 to 1898/9

Year	Amount Contributed to Sustentation Fund £ s d	No. of Ministers Participating in the Fund each year	Amount of Dividend paid each year £ s d	No. of full equal Dividends paid
1844	68,704 14 8	583	105 0 0	470
1845	77,630 12 0	627	122 0 0	557
1846	82,681 17 4	672	122 0 0	580
1847	83,117 16 10	673	120 0 0	590
1848	88,996 9 5	684	128 0 0	596
1849	87,115 3 4	705	123 0 0	623
1850	89,764 3 6	720	123 0 0	680
1851	91,527 8 8	736	123 0 0	668
1852	90,794 10 5	745	122 0 0	675
1853	90,885 8 0	759	121 0 0	691
1854	94,635 10 6	765	119 0 0	696
1855	103,553 17 3	786	132 0 0	700
1856	108,972 12 5	790	140 0 0	712
1857	108,638 4 5	811	138 0 0	700
1858	108,920 7 0	825	138 0 0	703
1859	110,141 11 8	827	138 0 0	713
1860	109,259 17 11	846	135 0 0	723
1861	112,093 5 0	859	138 0 0	731
1862	112,616 6 5	872	137 0 0	724
1863	114,292 19 9	885	137 0 0	722
1864	115,784 19 6	894	138 0 0	715
1865	119,450 3 11	903	144 0 0	710
1866	120,296 11 5	902	143 0 0	741
1867	121,725 6 3	917	144 0 0	731
1868	131,312 10 5	923	150 0 0	728

(*Continued*)

[51] Chalmers, *An Earnest Appeal* (American edn), 58.

Table 1 *Continued*

Year	Amount Contributed to Sustentation Fund £ s d	No. of Ministers Participating in the Fund each year	Amount of Dividend paid each year £ s d	No. of full equal Dividends paid
1869	132,125 16 7	942	150 0 0	740
1870	131,262 19 1	947	150 0 0	757
1871	137,034 14 6	948	150 0 0	775
1872	137,677 15 5	957	150 0 0	778
1873	136,322 19 10	969	150 0 0	783
1874	152,112 8 4	975	150 0 0	770
1875	163,696 16 0	997	157 0 0	772
1876	166,427 9 3	1014	157 0 0	774
1877	172,641 18 3	1059	157 0 0	761
1878	179,092 12 1	1075	157 0 0	766
1879	175,990 0 5	1094	160 0 0	776
1880	171,719 10 9	1095	160 0 0	791
1881	171,976 9 0	1097	160 0 0	796
1882	172,892 3 10	1106	160 0 0	794
1883	174,607 14 2	1105	160 0 0	822
1884	171,156 14 7	1116	160 0 0	815
1885	171,358 2 0	1126	160 0 0	808
1886	171,800 2 11	1131	160 0 0	821
1887	172,125 4 1	1141	160 0 0	807
1888	168,657 19 2	1137	160 0 0	826
1889	170,346 19 3	1146	160 0 0	828
1890	171,799 3 0	1147	160 0 0	839
1891	175,719 17 5	1169	162 10 0	821
1892	175,672 17 8	1165	160 0 0	836
1893	176,297 12 4	1165	160 0 0	830
1894	169,943 7 9	1158	160 0 0	853
1895	171,690 10 5	1165	160 0 0	848
1896	172,629 9 3	1163	160 0 0	879
1897	172,441 1 8	1154	160 0 0	885
1898	173,526 11 1	1149	160 0 0	875
1899	184,028 6 0	1144	160 0 0	875
1900			160 0 0	

Source: Free Church of Scotland, *Financial Report of the Sustentation Fund Committee for the Year Ending 15th May 1900* (Edinburgh, 1900).
Notes: Year convention: 1844 relates to year May 1843 – May 1844 etc.
Census month May.

Table 2. Self-Sustaining Congregations: Scotland

Year	Number of Charges (Congregations)	Equal Dividend Paid £ s d	Number Self-Sustaining	% Self-Sustaining
1844		105 0 0		
1845		122 0 0	128	
1846	670	122 0 0	169	25.2
1847		120 0 0		
1848	750	128 0 0	147	19.6
1849	750	123 0 0	167	22.3
1850	753	123 0 0	163	21.6
1851	761	123 0 0	173	22.7
1852	740	122 0 0	167	22.6
1853	756	121 0 0	191	25.3
1854	759	119 0 0	206	27.1
1855	769	132 0 0	180	23.4
1856	773	140 0 0	177	22.9
1857	786	138 0 0	196	24.9
1858	792	138 0 0	203	25.6
1859	794	138 0 0	199	25.1
1860	804	135 0 0	216	26.7
1861	821	138 0 0	214	26.1
1862	826	137 0 0	215	26.0
1863	835	137 0 0	228	27.3
1864	842	138 0 0	229	27.2
1865	834	144 0 0	205	24.6
1866	849	143 0 0	228	26.8
1867	862	144 0 0	229	26.6
1868	864	150 0 0	248	28.7
1869	874	150 0 0	253	28.9
1870	880	150 0 0	262	29.8
1871	885	150 0 0	265	29.9
1872	892	150 0 0	272	30.1
1873	900	150 0 0	271	30.1
1874	906	150 0 0	308	34.0
1875	918	157 0 0	283	30.8
1876	933	157 0 0	293	31.4
1877	978	157 0 0	312	31.9
1878	988	157 0 0	320	32.4
1879	996	160 0 0	294	29.5

(Continued)

Table 2 *Continued*

Year	Number of Charges (Congregations)	Equal Dividend Paid £ s d	Number Self-Sustaining	% Self-Sustaining
1880	1000	160 0 0	292	29.2
1881	1006	160 0 0	290	28.8
1882	1008	160 0 0	291	28.9
1883	1011	160 0 0	291	28.8
1884	1014	160 0 0	298	29.4
1885	1018	160 0 0	296	29.1
1886	1018	160 0 0	294	28.9
1887	1022	160 0 0	283	27.7
1888	1026	160 0 0	294	28.7
1889	1030	160 0 0	298	28.9
1890	1036	160 0 0	295	28.5
1891	1045	162 10 0	304	29.1
1892	1047	160 0 0	312	29.8
1893	1047	160 0 0	319	30.5
1894	1047	160 0 0	313	29.9
1895	1050	160 0 0	299	28.5
1896	1047	160 0 0	321	30.7
1897	1046	160 0 0	323	30.9
1898	1047	160 0 0	328	31.3
1899	1053	160 0 0	337	32.0
1900	1062	160 0 0	348	32.8

Sources: Free Church of Scotland, *Abstract Shewing the State of the Associations for The Year Ending 15th May 1846 as Compared with The Year Ending 15th May 1845* (Edinburgh, 1846); Free Church of Scotland, *(Supplement to) The Home and Foreign Record, Extract from Public Accounts* (Annual); Free Church of Scotland, *Report on the Public Accounts of the Free Church of Scotland* (Annual); Free Church of Scotland, *(Financial) Report of the Sustentation Fund Committee* (Annual; 1867–1900).

Notes: Year convention: 1844 relates to year ending May 1844 etc.

'Self-Sustaining' is defined as remitting to the Sustentation Fund an amount greater than, or equal to, the equal dividend.

Number of charges excludes preaching stations.

Data reported annually on a consistent basis from 1867 to 1900.

Table 3. Ranked Contributions to the Sustentation Fund by Synod

Year	1844 £	1844 Rank	1854 £	1854 Rank	1864 £	1864 Rank	1874 £	1874 Rank	1884 £	1884 Rank	1894 £	1894 Rank
1. Lothian and Tweeddale	13,018	2	17,294	2	20,370	2	25,213	2	29,226	2	28,623	2
2. Merse and Teviotdale	1,135	9	2,883	8	3,569	9	4,611	9	5,015	9	4,834	9
3. Dumfries	814	13	2,221	11	2,939	10	3,605	10	4,230	10	3,987	10
4. Galloway	874	11	1,863	13	2,105	14	2,620	14	3,103	14	2,926	14
5. Glasgow and Ayr	14,063	1	24,681	1	29,669	1	41,009	1	46,459	1	46,433	1
6. Argyll	1,829	7	2,530	9	4,067	8	5,015	8	6,327	8	6,266	8
7. Perth and Stirling	4,152	3	8,838	3	8,145	5	8,934	5	10,041	5	10,230	5
8. Fife	2,255	6	4,269	6	5,831	6	6,825	6	7,839	6	7,638	6
9. Angus and Mearns	2,893	5	6,882	5	10,179	4	13,137	4	14,175	4	13,513	4
10. Aberdeen	3,758	4	8,394	4	10,895	3	13,501	3	14,893	3	14,307	3
11. Moray	1,665	8	3,971	7	5,263	7	6,154	7	6,895	7	6,569	7
12. Ross	857	12	2,081	12	2,665	12	3,135	12	3,501	13	3,428	13
13. Sutherland and Caithness	883	10	2,412	10	2,875	11	3,398	11	3,970	11	3,468	12
14. Glenelg	597	14	1,652	14	2,240	13	3,038	13	3,927	12	3,640	11
15. Orkney	200	15	712	15	860	15	1,020	15	1,311	15	1,288	15
16. Shetland	17	16	150	16	208	16	287	16	347	16	359	16
TOTAL	49,019		90,842		111,887		141,509		161,267		157,515	

Source: Free Church of Scotland, *Abstract (Report) of (on) the Public Accounts of the Free Church of Scotland* (Annual).

Notes: 1844 – year to 31st March 1844.

Census month March.

Expressed in full pounds (£).

Table 4. City Contributions

Year	Edinburgh Presbytery Contributions £	Glasgow Presbytery Contributions £	Aberdeen Presbytery Contributions £	Dundee Presbytery Contributions £	Total City Presbytery Contributions £	Total All Contributions £	% City Presbytery Contributions / All Contributions
1844	11,347	7,161	2,250	1,473	22,231	49,019	45.3
1854	13,545	11,959	4,331	2,879	32,714	90,842	36.0
1864	15,498	14,457	5,529	4,167	39,651	111,887	35.4
1874	19,323	20,369	6,932	6,186	52,810	141,509	37.3
1884	22,445	21,953	7,475	7,153	59,026	161,267	36.6
1894	21,498	21,820	7,350	7,089	57,757	157,515	36.7

Source: As Table 3.
Note: Four city presbyteries – Edinburgh, Glasgow, Dundee, Aberdeen.
Expressed in full pounds (£).

Table 5. Largest Congregational Contribution to the Sustentation Fund by Presbytery

Year	1844		1854		1864		1874		1884		1894	
	Congregation	Contribution to Sustentation Fund £	Congregation	Contribution to Sustentation Fund £	Congregation	Contribution to Sustentation Fund £	Congregation	Contribution to Sustentation Fund £	Congregation	Contribution to Sustentation Fund £	Congregation	Contribution to Sustentation Fund £
Edinburgh	High	2,339	St George's	2,888	St George's	3,283	St George's	3863	St George's	5184	St George's	4769
Linlithgow	Kirkliston	90	Kirkliston	180	Falkirk	197	Falkirk	343	Falkirk	261	Kirkliston	275
Biggar and Peebles	Broughton	64	Culter	107	Culter	112	Peebles	194	Innerleithen	179	Peebles	189
Dalkeith	Dalkeith	124	Musselburgh	258	Penicuik	339	Penicuik	421	Penicuik	413	Penicuik	335
Haddington and Dunbar	Haddington	221	Haddington St John's	158	Haddington St John's	195	Haddington St John's	253	Haddington St John's	305	Haddington St John's	296
Duns and Chirnside	Dunse	127	Dunse	147	Dunse	153	Dunse	190	Duns	199	Duns	170
Kelso	Kelso	146	Kelso	176	Kelso	179	Kelso	200	Kelso	222	Kelso	197
Jedburgh	Hawick	133	Hawick	206	Hawick	201	Hawick	270	Hawick	324	Hawick	363
Selkirk	Melrose	56	Melrose	130	Melrose	158	Galashiels	264	Galashiels	293	Galashiels	339
Lockerbie	Moffat	85	Moffat	137	Moffat	147	Langholm	190	Moffat	190	Moffat	219
Dumfries	Dumfries	112	Dumfries	166	Dumfries	202	Dumfries	224	Dumfries	349	Dumfries	299
Penpont	Glencairn	100	Glencairn	163	Penpont	198	Penpont	211	Glencairn	194	Penpont East	172
Stranraer	Stranraer	113	Stranraer	161	Stranraer	150	Stranraer	175	Stranraer	197	Stranraer	171
Wigtown	Whithorn	49	Newton Stewart	112	Newton Stewart	115	Newton Stewart	203	Isle of Whithorn	121	Newton Stewart	132
Kirkcudbright	Kirkcudbright	160	Kirkcudbright	180	Kirkcudbright	214	Kirkcudbright	239	Kirkcudbright	254	Kirkcudbright	299
Ayr	Newton-on-Ayr	148	Ayr	242	Ayr	347	Ayr	421	Ayr	454	Ayr	372

(Continued)

Table 5 *Continued*

Year	1844		1854		1864		1874		1884		1894	
	Congregation	Contribution to Sustentation Fund £	Congregation	Contribution to Sustentation Fund £	Congregation	Contribution to Sustentation Fund £	Congregation	Contribution to Sustentation Fund £	Congregation	Contribution to Sustentation Fund £	Congregation	Contribution to Sustentation Fund £
Irvine	Kilmarnock High	246	Kilmarnock High	283	Kilmarnock High	322	Kilmarnock High	433	Kilmarnock High	302	Kilmarnock High	252
Paisley	Paisley, High	265	Paisley, High	287	Paisley St George's	285	Paisley St George's	409	Paisley St George's	443	Paisley St George's	501
Greenock	Gourock	643	Greenock Middle	709	Greenock Middle	556	Greenock West	593	Greenock Middle	679	Greenock West	482
Hamilton	Hamilton	157	Hamilton	305	Hamilton	492	Hamilton	529	Hamilton, St John's	324	Hamilton West	335
Lanark	Lesmahagow	135	Lesmahagow	192	Lesmahagow	193	Lesmahagow	258	Lesmahagow	223	Lesmahagow	211
Dumbarton	Luss	158	Helensburgh	268	Helensburgh Park	248	Helensburgh West	602	Helensburgh West	603	Helensburgh West	453
Glasgow	Glasgow, St John's	986	Glasgow, St John's	1652	Glasgow, St John's	1369	Glasgow, St Matthew's	1545	Glasgow, College	1410	Westbourne	1334
Dunoon and Inveray	Rothesay First	382	Rothesay, First	343	Rothesay West	391	Rothesay Free Parish	477	Rothesay Free Parish	424	Rothesay Free Parish	361
Kintyre	Campbelton	227	Campbelton	244	Campbelton	338	Campbelton Lochend	279	Campbelton Lochend	341	Campbeltown Lochend	273
Islay	Kilmeny	35	Killarrow	64	Bowmore	80	Killarrow	133	Kildalton &c	137	Bowmore	82
Lorn	Oban	73	Oban	77	Oban	108	Appin	132	Appin &c	183	Appin &c	182
Mull	.		.		.		.		Tobermory	194	Tobermory	179
Stirling	Stirling North	314	Stirling North	338	Stirling North	490	Stirling North	508	Stirling North	666	Stirling North	629
Dunblane	Doune	95	Kilmadock	132	Callander	157	Callander	216	Callender	308	Bridge of Allan	262

(Continued)

Table 5 *Continued*

Year	1844		1854		1864		1874		1884		1894	
	Congregation	Contribution to Sustentation Fund £	Congregation	Contribution to Sustentation Fund £	Congregation	Contribution to Sustentation Fund £	Congregation	Contribution to Sustentation Fund £	Congregation	Contribution to Sustentation Fund £	Congregation	Contribution to Sustentation Fund £
Dunkeld	Dunkeld	50	Dunkeld	96	Blair Atholl	144	Moulin	122	Cargill	121	Moulin	175
Breadalbane	Ardeonaig	45	Aberfeldy	100	Aberfeldy	148	Aberfeldy	145	Killin	132	Aberfeldy	176
Perth	Perth St Leonard's	450	Perth St Leonard's	546	Perth St Leonard's	511	Perth St Leonard's	421	Perth, West	475	Perth West	482
Auchterarder	Crieff	152	Auchterarder	161	Auchterarder	210	Auchterarder	247	Crieff	278	Crieff	368
Dunfermline	Dunfermline, St Andrews	92	Dunfermline Abbey	126	Dunfermline Abbey	166	Dunfermline Abbey	266	Dunfermline Abbey	269	Dunfermline Abbey	284
Kinross	Milnathort	63	Orwell	109	Strathmiglo	106	Orwell	109	Orwell	116	Cowdenbeath	110
Kirkcaldy	Kirkcaldy	255	Leven	307	Kirkcaldy	380	Kirkcaldy	581	Kirkcaldy, St Brycedale	642	Kirkcaldy St Brycedale	527
Cupar	Cupar	295	Cupar	340	Cupar	384	Cupar	453	Cupar	390	Cupar	425
St Andrews	St Andrews	203	St Andrews	177	St Andrews	236	St Andrews	286	St Andrews	374	Newport	320
Meigle	Blairgowrie	85	Blairgowrie	400	Blairgowrie South	252	Blairgowrie South	295	Blairgowrie First	288	Blairgowrie First	280
Forfar	Kirriemuir South	74	Forfar	168	Forfar First	236	Forfar First	276	Forfar First	301	Forfar First	259
Dundee	Dundee St John's	318	Dundee St John's	508	Dundee St Paul's	620	Dundee St Paul's	873	Dundee St Paul's	904	Dundee St Paul's	764
Brechin	Montrose St John's	265	Montrose St John's	364	Montrose St John's	407	Montrose St John's	362	Brechin West	349	Brechin West	302
Arbroath	Arbroath Ladyloan	222	Arbroath Ladyloan	242	Arbroath Ladyloan	313	Arbroath Ladyloan	375	Arbroath Ladyloan	445	Arbroath Ladyloan	362

(Continued)

Table 5 *Continued*

Year	1844		1854		1864		1874		1884		1894	
	Congregation	Contribution to Sustentation Fund £	Congregation	Contribution to Sustentation Fund £	Congregation	Contribution to Sustentation Fund £	Congregation	Contribution to Sustentation Fund £	Congregation	Contribution to Sustentation Fund £	Congregation	Contribution to Sustentation Fund £
Fordoun	Fordoun	95	Fordoun	135	Fordoun	128	Stonehaven	135	Stonehaven	163	Stonehaven	206
Aberdeen	Aberdeen East	428	Aberdeen West	385	Aberdeen West	1084	Aberdeen West	887	Aberdeen West	791	Aberdeen South	699
Kincardine-O'Neil	Cluny	86	Banchory Ternan	142	Banchory Ternan	164	Banchory Ternan	230	Banchory Ternan	173	Banchory-Ternan	172
Alford	Kinnethmont	43	Kinnethmont	64	Kinnethmont	103	Kinnethmont	92	Alford	80	Auchindoir	70
Garioch	Old Meldrum	90	Inverury	129	Inverury	174	Inverurie	200	Inverurie	239	Inverurie	216
Ellon	Cruden	40	Old Meldrum	150	Old Meldrum	185	Old Meldrum	170	Old Meldrum	183	Old Meldrum	169
Deer	Peterhead	56	Fraserburgh	129	Peterhead	150	Fraserburgh	177	Fraserburgh	210	Fraserburgh	165
Turriff	Drumblade	52	Turriff	79	Fyvie	130	Gamrie	152	Monquhitter	211	Turriff	197
Fordyce	Banff	88	Banff	132	Banff	213	Banff	269	Banff	304	Banff	295
Strathbogie	Keith	88	Huntly	227	Huntly	274	Huntly	239	Huntly	250	Huntly	258
bernethy	Duthill	17	Laggan	59	Duthill	90	Cromdale	110	Cromdale	118	Kingussie	112
Aberlour	.		Rothes	74	Rothes	101	Rothes	108	Rothes	117	Rothes	110
Elgin	Elgin	132	Elgin High	250	Elgin South	171	Elgin High	278	Elgin High	283	Elgin High	290
Forres	Forres	90	Forres	130	Forres	145	Forres	189	Forres	210	Forres	177
Inverness	Kirkhill	111	Inverness High	220	Inverness High	306	Inverness High	468	Inverness High	421	Inverness High	480
Nairn	Auldearn	83	Nairn	231	Nairn	121	Nairn	206	Nairn	310	Nairn	283
Chanonry	Cromarty	100	Cromarty	164	Cromarty	225	Cromarty	287	Cromarty	215	Cromarty	214
Dingwall	Urquhart	57	Urquhart	152	Dingwall	214	Dingwall	251	Dingwall	288	Dingwall	244

(Continued)

Table 5 *Continued*

Year	1844		1854		1864		1874		1884		1894	
	Congregation	Contribution to Sustentation Fund £	Congregation	Contribution to Sustentation Fund £	Congregation	Contribution to Sustentation Fund £	Congregation	Contribution to Sustentation Fund £	Congregation	Contribution to Sustentation Fund £	Congregation	Contribution to Sustentation Fund £
Tain	Tain	160	Tain	204	Tain	221	Tain	265	Tain	292	Tain	265
Dornoch	Helmsdale	69	Dornoch	132	Dornoch	164	Dornoch	168	Dornoch	200	Helmsdale	170
Tongue	Eddrachillis	28	Tongue	80	Strathy &c	69	Strathy and Halladale	96	Strathy and Halladale	90	Strathy and Halladale	79
Caithness	Wick	150	Wick	168	Thurso First	204	Thurso First	245	Thurso First	313	Thurso First	224
Lochcarron	Lochalsh	38	Plockton	91	Gairloch	95	Lochbroom	155	Lochbroom	185	Lochbroom	140
Abertarff	Fort Augustus and Glengarry	21	Glen Urquhart	106	Glen Urquhart	167	Glen Urquhart	152	Glen Urquhart	163	Glen Urquhart	166
Skye and Uist	Kilmuir	50	Snizort	102	Duirinish	113	Harris	150	South Uist &c	130	Snizort	117
Lewis	Knock	79	Stornoway	122	Stornoway	139	Stornoway	173	Stornoway English	217	Stornoway English	213
Orkney	Stromness	56	Stromness	111	Kirkwall	136	Stromness	106	Kirkwall	117	Kirkwall	157
Shetland	Unst	13	Lerwick	50	Lerwick	59	Lerwick	57	Lerwick	71	Lerwick	43

Sources: Free Church of Scotland, *Abstract of the Public Accounts of the Free Church of Scotland for the Period from May 18, 1843 to March 30, 1844* (Edinburgh, 1844); Free Church of Scotland, *Eleventh Report on the Public Accounts of the Free Church of Scotland for the Year Ended 30th March 1854* (Edinburgh, 1854); Free Church of Scotland, *Twenty-First Report on the Public Accounts of the Free Church of Scotland for the Year Ended 30th March 1864* (Edinburgh, 1864); Free Church of Scotland, *Thirty-First Report on The Public Accounts of the Free Church of Scotland for the Year Ended 31st March 1874* (Edinburgh, 1874); Free Church of Scotland, *Forty-First Report on the Public Accounts of the Free Church of Scotland for the Year Ended 31st March 1884* (Edinburgh, 1884); Free Church of Scotland, *Fifty-First Report on The Public Accounts of the Free Church of Scotland for the Year Ended 31st March 1894* (Edinburgh, 1894).
Note: Census month March.

491

Table 6. Self Sustaining Congregations: Lowland Rural Synod of Dumfries

Year	Number of Charges (Congregations)	Equal Dividend £	Number Self-Sustaining	% Self Sustaining	Amount paid to Sustentation Fund £	Amount due from Sustentation Fund £	Net Amount Paid To (Due From) Sustentation Fund £
1844	22	105	1	4.5%	814	2,310	(1,496)
1854	24	119	6	25.0%	2,221	2,856	(635)
1864	26	138	8	30.8%	2,939	3,588	(649)
1874	30	150	8	26.7%	3,605	4,500	(895)
1884	35	160	9	25.7%	4,230	5,600	(1,370)
1894	34	160	7	20.6%	3,987	5,440	(1,453)
1900	34	160	7	20.6%	4,033	5,440	(1,407)

Sources: Free Church of Scotland, *Report on the Public Accounts of the Free Church of Scotland* (Annual).
Notes: The southern synod of Dumfries comprised three presbyteries: Dumfries, Lockerbie and Penpont.
Preaching stations excluded from total number of charges.
Expressed in full pounds (£).
Figures for 1844 exclude those congregations which made no contribution to the Sustentation Fund.
Amount due from Sustentation Fund calculated as (number of congregations) x (equal dividend).

Table 7. Self-Sustaining Congregations: Highland Rural Synod of Sutherland and Caithness

Year	Number of Charges (Congregations)	Equal Dividend £	Number Self-Sustaining	% Self Sustaining	Amount paid to Sustentation Fund £	Amount due from Sustentation Fund £	Net Amount Paid To (Due From) Sustentation Fund £
1844	19	105	2	10.2%	883	1,995	(1,112)
1854	34	119	4	11.8%	2,412	4,046	(1,634)
1864	34	138	4	11.8%	2,875	4,692	(1,817)
1874	35	150	7	20.0%	3,398	5,250	(1,852)
1884	36	160	5	13.9%	3,970	5,760	(1,790)
1894	36	160	5	13.9%	3,468	5,760	(2,292)
1900	36	160	2	5.5%	2,276	5,760	(3,484)

Sources: As Table 6.

Notes: The northern synod of Sutherland and Caithness comprised three presbyteries: Caithness, Dornoch, Tongue. Other notes as Table 6.

Table 8. Self-Sustaining Congregations: Islands Rural Synod of Orkney

Year	Number of Charges (Congregations)	Equal Dividend £	Number Self-Sustaining	% Self Sustaining	Amount paid to Sustentation Fund £	Amount due from Sustentation Fund £	Net Amount Paid To (Due From) Sustentation Fund £
1844	9	105	0	0	200	945	(745)
1854	14	119	0	0	712	1,666	(954)
1864	14	138	0	0	860	1,932	(1,072)
1874	14	150	0	0	1,020	2,100	(1,080)
1884	15	160	0	0	1,311	2,400	(1,089)
1894	15	160	0	0	1,288	2,400	(1,112)
1900	15	160	0	0	895	2,400	(1,505)

Sources: As Table 6.
Notes: The island synod of Orkney.
Other notes as Table 6.

Table 9. Self-Sustaining Congregations: Lowland Urban Presbytery of Edinburgh

Year	Number of Charges (Congregations)	Equal Dividend £	Number Self-Sustaining	% Self Sustaining	Amount paid to Sustentation Fund £	Amount due from Sustentation Fund £	Net Amount Paid To (Due From) Sustentation Fund £
1844	34	105	20	58.8%	11,347	3,570	7,777
1854	39	119	26	66.7%	13,545	4,641	8,904
1864	44	138	28	63.6%	15,498	6,072	9,426
1874	48	150	37	77.1%	19,323	7,200	12,123
1884	54	160	37	68.5%	22,445	8,640	13,805
1894	56	160	38	67.9%	21,498	8,960	12,538
1900	55	160	39	70.1%	22,650	8,800	13,850

Sources: As Table 6.
Notes: Notes as Table 6.

Table 10. Self-Sustaining Congregations: Highland Urban Presbytery of Inverness

Year	Number of Charges (Congregations)	Equal Dividend £	Number Self-Sustaining	% Self Sustaining	Amount paid to Sustentation Fund £	Amount due from Sustentation Fund £	Net Amount Paid To (Due From) Sustentation Fund £
1844	7	105	1	14.3%	371	735	(364)
1854	9	119	4	44.4%	1,069	1,071	(2)
1864	10	138	4	40.0%	1,399	1,380	19
1874	11	150	4	36.4%	1,651	1,650	1
1884	13	160	3	23.1%	1,737	2,080	(343)
1894	13	160	3	23.1%	1,724	2,080	(356)
1900	14	160	3	21.4%	1,955	2,240	(285)

Sources: As per Table 6.
Notes: Notes as Table 6.

Table 11. Number of Congregations by Presbytery Contributing Less Than Half, and More Than Double the Equal Dividend in 1854

	1854		1894	
Presbytery	No. of Cong's. Donating < £60	No of Cong's Donating > £238	No. of Cong's. Donating < £80	No of Cong's Donating > £320
Edinburgh	3	15	0	17
Linlithgow	5	0	3	0
Biggar and Peebles	3	0	1	0
Dalkeith	4	1	2	1
Haddington and Dunbar	4	0	7	0
Duns and Chirnside	1	0	3	0
Kelso	5	0	4	0
Jedburgh	1	0	2	1
Selkirk	1	0	5	1
Lockerbie	3	0	3	0
Dumfries	2	0	5	0
Penpont	1	0	2	0
Stranraer	3	0	1	0
Wigtown	1	0	3	0
Kirkcudbright	2	0	2	0
Ayr	6	1	13	1
Irvine	5	1	3	0
Paisley	0	2	1	1
Greenock	0	5	1	3
Hamilton	1	1	3	1
Lanark	1	0	3	0
Dumbarton	1	1	4	5
Glasgow	1	12	9	13
Dunoon and Inverary	6	2	8	1
Kintyre	4	1	2	0
Islay	2	0	5	0
Lorn & Mull	9	0	11	0
Stirling	3	1	1	1
Dunblane	5	0	5	0
Dunkeld	3	0	4	0
Breadalbane	5	0	7	0
Perth	4	3	7	3

(Continued)

Table 11 *Continued*

Presbytery	1854		1894	
	No. of Cong's. Donating < £60	No of Cong's Donating > £238	No. of Cong's. Donating < £80	No of Cong's Donating > £320
Auchterarder	0	0	1	1
Dunfermline	2	0	3	0
Kinross	2	0	2	0
Kirkcaldy	1	2	3	1
Cupar	4	1	5	1
St Andrews	1	0	4	1
Meigle	3	1	4	0
Forfar	3	0	2	0
Dundee	4	4	2	7
Brechin	2	1	2	0
Arbroath	2	1	1	1
Fordoun	5	0	5	0
Aberdeen	6	4	9	6
Kincardine-O'Neil	7	0	11	0
Alford	2	0	7	0
Garioch	5	0	5	0
Ellon	3	0	2	0
Deer	4	0	3	0
Turriff	3	0	4	0
Fordyce	4	0	3	0
Strathbogie	6	0	5	0
Abernethy	5	0	4	0
Aberlour	3	0	4	0
Elgin	2	1	1	0
Forres	3	0	5	0
Inverness	0	0	6	1
Nairn	1	0	2	0
Chanonry	1	0	4	0
Dingwall	2	0	3	0
Tain	5	0	2	0
Dornoch	4	0	3	0
Tongue	7	0	8	0
Caithness	4	0	2	0
Lochcarron	2	0	7	0

(*Continued*)

Table 11 *Continued*

Presbytery	1854		1894	
	No. of Cong's. Donating < £60	No of Cong's Donating > £238	No. of Cong's. Donating < £80	No of Cong's Donating > £320
Abertarff	5	0	6	0
Skye and Uist	5	0	9	0
Lewis	5	0	7	0
Orkney	12	0	6	0
Shetland	5	0	10	0

Sources: Free Church of Scotland, *Eleventh Report on the Public Accounts of the Free Church of Scotland for the Year Ended 30th March 1854* (Edinburgh, 1854); Free Church of Scotland, *Fifty-First Report on The Public Accounts of the Free Church of Scotland for the Year Ended 31st March 1894* (Edinburgh, 1894).

Notes: Excludes Preaching Stations

1854 Equal Dividend = £119

Thresholds: Half <£60 : Double > £238

1894 Equal Dividend = £160

Thresholds: Half <£80 : Double > £320.

The Fanaticisms of Hannah Whitall Smith

Emily J. Bailey

Towson University

This article investigates personal and public facets of the life and work of Hannah Whitall Smith (1832–1911) as a lens through which to explore the complexities of marginalization and belonging within the late nineteenth-century Holiness movement. Despite her significant contributions as a lay Christian leader, prolific author and social activist, Smith's legacy remains largely understudied. Examining selections from her extensive collected works, including correspondence and Smith's file of 'fanaticisms', this article investigates how supposed margins and peripheries are not places of obscurity or insignificance, but fertile contexts of religious dialogue and innovation.

INTRODUCTION

What does it mean to occupy the liminal space of a religious margin? Who has the authority to define and enforce religious boundaries? While sometimes relegated to the obscure, or insignificant, the marginalized often come into focus when their intersections with the mainstream are explored, revealing a fertile context for understanding religious dialogue, authority, innovation and acceptance. Although this may be said of many religious contexts and spaces, this article examines the intersections of the marginalized and mainstream in the microcosm of the life of one individual: Hannah Whitall Smith (1832–1911), a prominent and well-connected figure in the Holiness movement in the USA and Great Britain, and a vital force in women's suffrage and temperance causes.[1] Despite a lasting wealth of

E-mail: ebailey@towson.edu.

[1] See Edward H. Milligan, 'Smith [*née* Whitall], Hannah [known as Mrs Pearsall Smith] (1832–1911)', *ODNB*, online edn (2004), rev. 22 September 2011, at: <https://doi.org/10.1093/ref:odnb/47062>, accessed 18 September 2024.

Studies in Church History 61 (2025), 500–519 © The Author(s), 2025. Published by Cambridge University Press on behalf of the Ecclesiastical History Society.
doi:10.1017/stc.2024.48

correspondence, diaries and other publications, Smith's legacy remains conspicuously understudied and undervalued, possibly a lingering consequence of a life-long balancing act at the margins.[2] Like many prominent nineteenth-century women, Smith's life and perspective can be reconstructed in surprising detail by a rich textual legacy. Smith was a prolific writer, publishing several major works about Holiness theology, which sold millions of copies during her lifetime.[3] In addition to her books, she provided countless contributions to newspapers, magazines and religious journals, while maintaining a staggering pace of correspondence. This abundant output of writing raises the question of how she had time to do anything but write. However, her historical record reveals that her life's work extended far beyond the written page. As the wife of another prominent religious reformer, the mother of seven children (only three of whom survived into adulthood), and an active speaker and preacher, Smith left a remarkable legacy of both private and public accomplishments.

The margins of Smith's private and public lives have yet to be examined, particularly with regard to her role as a Holiness reformer well-known in her own time. Although referring to Smith's relationship with Quakerism, Carole Dale Spencer's characterization of her as an 'orthodox heretic' is apt.[4] As evidenced by her private correspondence and public activities, she was at once accepted and repudiated; applauded and questioned.[5] This study seeks to examine Smith's work as a critical lens through which the complex and often contradictory relationship between marginalization and belonging played out at the end of the nineteenth and beginning of the twentieth centuries. As a

[2] The author is grateful to the Lilly Library at Indiana University, Bloomington, for assistance with the Papers of Hannah Whitall Smith 1817–1987 (this collection also includes later family papers and bound volumes relating to descendants of Hannah Whitall Smith in addition to her own papers), and to the B. L. Fisher Library Archives at Asbury Theological Seminary for assistance with the Hannah Whitall Smith Collection in their archive.

[3] Smith's most famous work, *The Christian's Secret of a Happy Life*, was published in 1875 (New York); this was followed by monographs including *Every-day Religion, or, The Common-sense Teaching of the Bible* (New York, 1893); *The Unselfishness of God and How I Discovered It* (New York, 1903); and *The God of All Comfort* (London, 1906), all of which were well-known at the time.

[4] Carole Dale Spencer, 'Hannah Whitall Smith and the Evolution of Quakerism: An Orthodox Heretic in an Age of Controversy', *Quaker Studies* 18 (2013), 7–22.

[5] A 2020 doctoral dissertation offers the first scholarly exploration of Smith's private correspondence: Meg Ann Meneghel McDonald, 'Becoming a "heretic": Hannah Whitall Smith, Quakerism, and the Nineteenth-Century Holiness Movement' (PhD thesis, Indiana University, 2000).

female religious pioneer who defied convention, within her own religious circles, Smith was perceived as a model of piety by some, while being branded a fanatic by others who rejected her unique brand of Christianity and methods of practising it.

As someone who occupied peripheries, it is perhaps not surprising that Smith regularly played the concurrent roles of dissenter and conformist, with strong opinions about the unconventional religious movements of her era and her positionality in relation to them. As part of her legacy, Smith left a personal archive. Although she was labelled as radical in her own right, her papers include files of newspaper and periodical clippings about what she perceived as 'fanaticisms' and her encounters with them. What these artefacts illustrate is that she was herself marginalized while she attempted to define the margins, offering a reminder that peripheral religious boundaries are rarely tidy. Rather, they are contentious, blurred, changing and subjective.

PRIDE IN THE 'PECULIAR'

In 1892, Hannah clipped and saved a short article from *Housekeepers Weekly*, which lauded her for the extent of her influence on Christian women around the globe, while noting that 'curiously enough, a large proportion of her hearers' were clergymen, 'despite the stress which the pulpit generally lays on the Pauline prohibition of "the sex" from public speaking.'[6] To navigate the trajectory that brought public opinion to this conclusion by the 1890s, it is critical to situate Smith in her religious context. As both a product and innovator, first in the nineteenth-century religious landscape in the United States and then in Great Britain, Smith's spiritual journey reflected the dynamic religious marketplaces of her time.[7]

In Christian circles during Hannah's formative years, mainstream and sectarian ideas collided as religious innovations tempted converts with new and renewed avenues to the promise of salvation. The convergence of these paths with popular political and social movements contributed to a widely varied religious landscape, in which

[6] Wilmore, KY, Asbury Theological Seminary, B. L. Fisher Library Archives, Papers of Hannah Whitall Smith, Box 4, Anon., 'Hannah Whitall Smith', *Housekeepers Weekly*, 4 June 1892.
[7] See R. Laurence Moore, *Selling God: American Religion in the Marketplace of Culture* (Oxford, 1994), for a study of the competitive American religious marketplace.

experimentation was sometimes applauded, and at other times con-demned.[8] Smith's personal route to the Holiness tradition was shaped by her work as a lay preacher, prolific author, and vocal champion of social causes including temperance, abolition and women's suffrage. The composite result of these causes was unsettling to Smith's detract-ors, but deeply appealing to her intimate circle of American friends, and later to her supporters in the Higher Life Movement in the United Kingdom.

Hannah Tatum Whitall's unique brand of theology was moulded by her upbringing and marriage. Her religious life began as a 'birth-right' Quaker – an adherent 'born to one or more parents in the Society of Friends' – in Pennsylvania in 1832.[9] By Hannah's own account, she did not encounter other faiths during a strict, but loving and contented childhood.[10] Her family embraced Quakerism to the extent that 'every word and thought and action of [their] lives was steeped' in it.[11] In diaries from her teenage years – a time in which she could have perhaps rebelled against the simplicity and order estab-lished by her parents and community – she instead embraced their Quakerism to the fullest.

By the 1850s, when young Hannah was writing with effusive affection and praise for her given faith, American Quakerism was diverse and evolving. Internal schisms and social change contributed to Quaker branches, such as the Gurneyite tradition in which Hannah grew up, that varied from traditional Friends. Deeply leaning toward evangelical Christianity and the authority of Scripture, the Gurneyites embraced social reform and individual spiritual freedom, both of which would undoubtedly influence Hannah's later theology.[12]

When reflecting on her early Quaker ideals in her spiritual auto-biography, *The Unselfishness of God and How I Discovered It* (1904), Smith confessed that her understanding of faith was affective rather than doctrinal at that stage of her life.[13] This feeling was especially

---

[8] Lydia Willsky-Ciollo, 'New Religious Movements in the Long Nineteenth Century', *Nova Religio: The Journal of Alternative and Emergent Religions* 23 (2019), 5–17.
[9] See 'Birthright/convinced Friend', Quaker.org (January 2009), online at: <https://quaker.org/glossary/>, accessed 15 September 2024.
[10] Smith, *The Unselfishness of God* (New York, 1903; repr. Wilmore, KY, 2018), 20–1.
[11] Ibid. 37.
[12] Thomas Hamm, *The Transformation of American Quakerism: Orthodox Friends, 1800–1907* (Bloomington, IN, 1992), 36–7.
[13] Smith, *The Unselfishness of God* (reprint), 47.

grounded in a sense of pride of being among those who were 'peculiar', that is, set apart and chosen by God, and as such criticized and ostracized. The Pennsylvania Quakers with whom the young Hannah lived and worshipped led lives of nonconformity, forgoing worldly influences such as extravagant nineteenth-century fashion trends. They also advocated for moral principles such as abolition and pacifism, which would starkly differ from the pro-slavery and wartime realities of Hannah's early adulthood.[14]

Although the peak of the Second Great Awakening – a period of intense religious revivalism and experimentation – had occurred in the early nineteenth century, its effects were still being felt in America in the 1850s. In contrast to the emphasis on human sinfulness and depravity that characterised the First Great Awakening (1720 to 1740s) of the previous century, nineteenth-century revivalists such as Charles Grandison Finney and Francis Asbury emphasized emotional expressions of faith and social reform akin to those towards which Hannah had gravitated in her Quakerism. The Protestant Christian climate in America was highly denominational, with mainline Methodists, Baptists and Presbyterians vying for converts alongside sectarian movements like Seventh-day Adventism and the Church of Latter-day Saints. It was also a context in which female leaders, including Adventist prophetess Ellen G. White and Christian Science foundress Mary Baker Eddy, carved out a place for women's religious innovation.

It was within this religious atmosphere that Hannah met and married Robert Pearsall Smith (1827–98) in 1851. Robert's Quaker pedigree rivalled Hannah's, with a family tree that traced a steady line of Quakers to the time of William Penn, the seventeenth-century founder of the province of Pennsylvania. Together, these ardent Quakers gravitated to new religious ideas, taking a circuitous route to Wesleyan Holiness by way of Methodism, the Plymouth Brethren (an Irish offshoot of evangelical Anglicanism) and the Baptist tradition. For Hannah, this resulted in a unique theological position that reconciled mainstream beliefs with elements of mysticism, revelation and individual religious experience.

In 1857, the death of their five-year-old daughter Nellie from an infection pushed Hannah into what she identified as a new era in her personal faith, one in which emotions were set aside to make room for

---

[14] Thomas Hamm, *The Quakers in America* (New York, 2003), 187.

scriptural pragmatism.[15] A move to New Jersey in 1864 for Robert to manage his retired father-in-law's successful glass factories at Whitall, Tatum & Company also marked a pivotal point in the Smiths' spiritual lives. It was there that they had their first encounter with the Wesleyan Holiness tradition, being exposed to the work of William Boardman and his *The Higher Christian Life*, published in 1859.[16] The Smiths seem to have been particularly drawn to Boardman's emphasis on achieving holiness through God's grace, which deeply resonated with Hannah's developing theology of spiritual achievement, particularly after Nellie's death. As they became more deeply involved with the Methodist revivalists, Robert began writing and preaching, quickly attracting interest in both the USA and Great Britain, and once again shifting the course of the Smiths' lives.

Negotiating Margins

The rapid growth and institutionalization of the American Methodist movement made it one of the largest and most influential denominations by the middle of the nineteenth century. However, it had not always enjoyed this position. When the Wesley brothers brought their nascent sect across the Atlantic in the eighteenth century, their emphasis on personal piety and revivalism, driven by camp meetings and preaching circuit riders, felt anything but mainline. By Smith's time, this had shifted. The establishment of Methodist seminaries and publishing houses bolstered the movement's perceived respectability. While an internal schism in 1845 led to a split between the northern church and its southern counterpart, many mainstream Methodists were anti-slavery, pro-temperance and, in some cases, pro-women's suffrage, bringing them into tension with societal norms.[17]

However, the strain of Wesleyanism to which the Smiths turned with renewed interest was far from the mainline. As a revivalist movement, the Holiness tradition more closely paralleled Wesley's early sect than what Methodism had become by the second half of the nineteenth century. The new community emphasized evangelism, personal holiness and lay leadership, with itinerant preachers traveling

---

[15] Smith, *The Unselfishness of God* (reprint), 172.
[16] William Edwin Boardman, *The Higher Christian Life* (Boston, MA, 1859).
[17] Kenneth E. Rowe, Russell E. Richey and Jean Miller Schmidt, *American Methodism: A Compact History* (Nashville, TN, 2012), 81–5.

to spread their message, as had Wesley's circuit riders of the prior century. The pragmatic Smith found herself in intensely emotional gatherings of fellow believers, moved to tears that seemed to surprise her. Rather than rejecting this renewed depth of heartfelt faith, she attempted to embrace it, confessing, on the first occasion of attending such a meeting, to having wept so much that she 'was obliged surreptitiously to lift up my dress and use my white under-skirt to dry my tears.'[18]

Despite this moment of religious emotion, Smith longed for the sanctifying experiences of her fellow believers, who in advancing to the camp meeting altars claimed to have tangible moments of divine blessing and consecration. While Robert experienced such a moment at a camp meeting, taking on the mantle of a 'divine glow', Hannah lamented that her lack of an emotional nature precluded her from such a blessing.[19] Her testimony of Robert's experience reveals the potency of these moments for believers:

> He said they had had one day a special meeting to pray for the 'Baptism of the Spirit,' and that after the meeting he had gone alone into a retired spot in the woods, to continue the prayer by himself. Suddenly, from head to foot he had been shaken with what seemed like a magnetic thrill of heavenly delight, and floods of glory seemed to pour through him, soul and body, with the inward assurance that this was the longed-for Baptism of the Holy Spirit. The whole world seemed transformed to him, every leaf and blade of grass quivered with exquisite colour, and heaven seemed to open out before him as a present blissful possession.[20]

In a nineteenth-century milieu in which women were perceived as being emotional and domestic, and men intellectual and worldly, the Smiths flipped the narrative. The 'domestic religion' of influential mainline Christian women like Catharine Beecher (1800–78), Harriet Beecher Stowe (1811–96) and Sara Josepha Hale (1788–1879) undoubtedly contributed to the ways in which Protestant women and the home were viewed as being sanctified and associated with morality at this point in American history, yet Smith was by all accounts praised for her intellect alongside her domesticity.[21] Perhaps

[18] Smith, *The Unselfishness of God* (reprint), 286.
[19] Ibid. 288.
[20] Ibid. 288–9.
[21] Stuart M. Blumin, *The Emergence of the Middle-Class: Social Experience in the American City, 1730–1900* (Cambridge, 1989), 182, 184. The Beechers were Congregationalists, while Hale was a devout Presbyterian.

a hallmark of her ability to bridge divides, Smith retained and came to appreciate her sense of pragmatism for the remainder of her life, though sometimes admitting to being jealous that her husband was able to access the emotions that she often could not.

Hannah's followers appear to have appreciated her less emotional nature. An obituary for her from 1911 in the *British Friend* suggested that in all things:

> she trod an even pathway. Her logical mind and strong common sense preserved her from the dangers that beset more ardent temperaments. A certain familiarity of language on sacred topics hindered her acceptance with some, but a long and consistent life, drawn out in widowhood to her eightieth year, had sealed her witness to the reality of an overcoming faith.[22]

From this perspective, as from Smith's own, it was possible to be a rational mystic: deeply rooted in faith and prophecy, while approaching such topics with reason and logic.

Despite the Smiths' gravitation toward other beacons of spiritual promise, the Quaker underpinning of their confession remained. Tendencies toward congregational egalitarianism, inner reflection, female religious agency, and mysticism, all rooted in her Quaker upbringing, persisted in Hannah's writing and later lay ministry. Despite adopting the Holiness movement, she at the same time maintained a firm connection to her Quaker heritage by continuing to attend and speak at Society of Friends meetings until the end of her life, suggesting that she did not think of her drift away from the movement as a complete severing of ties.[23] Where other Christians maintained that theological distinctions and doctrinal purity required converts to have a singular denominational adherence, Smith's perspective from the boundaries was one in which a believer had a

---

[22] Bloomington, IN, Indiana University Bloomington, Lilly Library, Smith, H.W. mss., 1817–1987, Box 17, R. Hingston Fox, 'Hannah Whitall Smith and the Holiness Movement', *Reprint from the British Friend* (1911), 1–7.

[23] For further discussion of Hannah and the Holiness tradition, see Debra Campbell, 'Hannah Whitall Smith (1832–1911): Theology of the Mother-hearted God', *Signs: Journal of Women in Culture and Society* 15 (1989), 79–101; Carole Dale Spencer, 'Hannah Whitall Smith's Highway of Holiness', in Jon R. Kershner, ed., *Quakers and Mysticism: Comparative and Syncretic Approaches to Spirituality* (London, 2019), 141–59; eadem, 'Hannah Whitall Smith: Nineteenth-Century Free-lance Quaker Heretic', in C. Wess Daniels and Rhiannon Grant, eds, *The Quaker World* (New York, 2022), 185–94.

flexibility of personal practice that allowed for a degree of spiritual syncretism: always Christian in Smith's case, but decidedly interdenominational and exploratory.

By no means an apostate, by her own account Smith looked for something more interesting to spark her religious curiosity, but wished for it to come from her familiar Society of Friends. While Robert travelled for his religious work, Smith remained at home with their children, maintaining a pattern of normal life to the greatest extent possible. Her letters indicate that this included regular attendance at Friends meetings, despite having experimented with other traditions, but she was not content with the state of them. In a letter to Robert in 1873, Smith vented her frustration, indicating that Methodism had earned her attention once again:

> if the Friends do not hurry up and get more lively, soon I shall have to take the children somewhere else, and I must say that the Methodists do look very inviting. There is so much in their church to interest young Christians, and there is such a grand scope for religious work among them. If ever I give up my hold on Friends it will be to go to the Methodists, so prepare thyself, darling.[24]

In this same year, Robert persuaded Hannah to bring their family to join him in England, which they did in early 1874. There, too, Smith found herself at the margins of the Quaker tradition to which she had dedicated so much of her spiritual energy over the course of her life. Writing to her sister Mary just a month after settling into her new English home, Smith confessed to being:

> astonished at the *insignificance* of the Society here. No other word can express it. They have neither energy nor weight in the religious world, as far as I can discover. American Friends may certainly stop bowing down to the English any more, for the shoe is altogether on the other foot.[25]

As she gravitated toward a more complex and individualized definition of religious experience, Smith's social and political stances did not always align with orthodox Quakerism. For instance, she sidestepped Quaker pacifism following the death of the Grand Duke Sergei Alexandrovich of

[24] Indiana University Bloomington, Lilly Library, Box 9, Hannah Whitall Smith to Robert Pearsall Smith, 24 March 1875.
[25] Indiana University Bloomington, Lilly Library, Box 20, Hannah Whitall Smith to her sister Mary, 10 February 1874. Emphasis original.

Russia during a period of political unrest in 1905, applauding the violence that led to the Duke's demise: 'Yes, we did rejoice in the assassination of the Grand Duke, and we only hope there will be some more! I have always said that Quaker or no Quaker, if I had lived in Russia, I should have been a Nihilist! It is the only voice the people have.'[26]

For Smith, the reconciliation of disparate religious ideas seems to have been grounded in a belief that incongruent theologies and praxes could inform one another, but only when Smith detected compatibility. For instance, Meg Ann Meneghel-McDonald finds that although her religious posture 'was transformed by evangelical Protestantism, from a quiet, reflective tradition to a more active, yet structured approach to worship',[27] her embrace of Holiness sanctification still resonated with her Quaker foundation in the teaching of perfectionism.

For Quakers, perfectionism is not about achieving flawless behaviour. Instead, the tradition posits that through a spiritual rebirth guided by the Holy Spirit, individuals can embark on a continuous journey of purification. As one perfects the spirit, they progressively emerge out of the mire of sinfulness and away from further acts of wrongdoing.[28] Similarly, in the Holiness tradition, sanctification is identified as a deliverance from sin through the intervention of the Holy Spirit in this lifetime. Although there are dogmatic differences between Quaker and Holiness traditions, and strict practitioners would reject these equivalencies, Smith was not concerned with theological precision.

It is also significant that, from the Smiths' perspectives, these traditions were neither theologically nor practically mutually exclusive. Indeed, a strain of Quaker Holiness tradition emerged in America in the 1860s, which the Smiths welcomed as an interdenominational experiment. Like the Holiness movement for which the Smiths also became key evangelists, this community embraced personal holiness and promised the forgiveness of sins through sanctification.[29] Intertwined with the broader Holiness movement of the time, direct spiritual experiences were central for the Quaker Holiness believers, as for Wesleyan

---

[26] Hannah Whitall Smith to Mary Berenson, 22 February 1905, in *Philadelphia Quaker: The Letters of Hannah Whitall Smith*, ed. Logan Pearsall Smith (New York, 1905), 167–8.

[27] McDonald, 'Becoming a "heretic"', 2.

[28] Carole D. Spencer, 'Holiness: The Quaker Way of Perfection', *Quaker History* 93 (2004), 123–47.

[29] Carole Dale Spencer, *Holiness: The Soul of Quakerism. An Historical Analysis of the Theology of Holiness in the Quaker Tradition* (Milton Keynes, 2007), 183–6.

followers. This unique marriage of views was relatively short-lived, challenged by the rise of Pentecostalism and by further shifts in American Quakerism, but it offers an important glimpse into diverse expressions of the faith into the beginning of the twentieth century.[30]

Operating at the borders of tradition – and claiming insider knowledge and familiarity, while simultaneously challenging normative practices – made it possible for the Smiths to carve out spaces between established religious constructs. In what often comes across as a conscious embracing of this liminality, Hannah Smith's later work reveals a confidence in her personal theological position, and pride in her role as a popular 'heretic'. In a not untypical letter to friends in February 1901, Smith revealed that she was writing her autobiography, which she posited as a history of her soul starting in her early Quaker days. She confided:

> I am putting all my heresies into my story, and am trying to show the steps that have led to them; and I flatter myself that it is going to be very convincing! So if you feel afraid of becoming heretics, I advise you not to read it. For my part, I always did love being a heretic as some of you know. What fun it was in those old days when our little flock of 'Mystic Birds' used to be taking our mystic flights higher and higher into the unexplored regions of God's love, and how restful it is now, in our old age, to have folded our wings in the blessed haven of absolute certainty that God is enough! All religion is enfolded for me now in these three words. God is enough for me, and for everybody, and for all the needs of all the limitless universe He has created![31]

Robert Smith, too, seemed to revel in his nonconformity. In a letter to one of her daughters in 1873, Hannah wrote that: 'The Square Friend is out this week in a very severe piece against father, but he is not fazed by it in the least. In fact, I think he likes it because it will give publicity to his tract. He has distributed about 800.'[32] Cloaking her

---

[30] Ibid.

[31] Smith references five 'mystic birds' in several of her letters, denoting a close circle of friends who supported her unconventional religious tendencies: Hannah Whitall Smith, circular letter to friends and family, including her cousin Carrie Lawrence, 18 February 1901, in *Philadelphia Quaker*, 139.

[32] Indiana University Bloomington, Lilly Library, Box 9, Hannah Whitall Smith to one of her children, 20 April 1873. Smith had two daughters, Mary and Alys, and one son, Logan, who survived into adulthood; when she addresses letters 'Dear Daughter' or 'Dear Darling', it is not always apparent to which of her children she is writing.

own 'radicalism' in calm logic, Smith was entering a phase as an 'eminent preacher' and well-known author in her own right.[33]

In her best-known work, Smith's *The Christian's Secret of a Happy Life* (1875), Hannah began by modestly (and misleadingly) claiming that she knew little about theology.[34] While this modesty may have been a strategy, like Robert's radicalism, to draw in more readers, Hannah's work offered a significant exegetical framework for fellow Christians to follow in their own spiritual journeys. The book was not only popular – selling more than two million copies globally during Hannah's lifetime – but also made clear that her desire to reject tradition in favour of personal spiritual experiences was not merely a product of a lifetime spent on the margins. Rather, it was a deliberate choice to challenge established norms and offer a new path for spiritual fulfilment. This was a path that moved beyond 'goody sermons' in which nothing clear or useful was preached, instead challenging believers to grapple with their convictions.[35]

Hannah was also adamant that her work was not merely an appendage to her husband's, even before a scandal nudged him out of the public eye. In a letter to Robert in 1873, she voiced her frustrations that some of Robert's circle had challenged her views, fearing that she was tainting her husband's theology:

> If the brethren really convince thee that such a heretic as I am will hinder thy work, I can very easily keep clear of thy work and do my own in different places. I do not intend to be 'endorsed' by anybody. I *must* have freedom to hold my own views; and as I have not the least desire to preach unless the Lord wants me to, He shall be my only backer.[36]

The challenger in this instance was Sir Stevenson Arthur Blackwood (1832–93), who sponsored Robert's work in England, and promoted the Keswick Convention.[37]

---

[33] Indiana University Bloomington, Lilly Library, Box 17, Poster, 'Religious Meetings', Bessbrook, Northern Ireland, 1874.

[34] Hannah Whitall Smith, *The Christian's secret of a happy life* (Grand Rapids, MI, 1875; repr. Wilmore, KY, 2017), iii, vi.

[35] Indiana University Bloomington, Lilly Library, Box 9, Hannah Whitall Smith to Robert Pearsall Smith, 26 April 1873.

[36] Indiana University Bloomington, Lilly Library, Box 9, Hannah Whitall Smith to Robert Pearsall Smith, 7 March 1875. Emphasis original.

[37] Ibid.

In 1875, however, the couple's power dynamic shifted within their religious circles when Robert was accused of sexual misconduct by a female American journalist. The nature and validity of his actions were hotly debated, but they ultimately led him to withdraw from public ministry and strained many of his personal and professional relationships. This unsettling episode, and the sudden bout of stress-induced illness that it caused Robert, prompted the Smiths to return home to Pennsylvania.[38] While her husband re-established his business ties, Hannah rekindled her Quakerism, and was accepted back into the fold despite her 'continuing commitment to the explicit universalism of her "Restitution" heresy.'[39] Smith by now was arguing for the ultimate salvation of all souls, a view that was seen as heretical not only by fellow Quakers, but across those Christian denominations which had teachings about eternal punishment for the wicked. In contrast, Smith argued that God's grace was so complete that all of creation would eventually be redeemed and restored, prompting some publishers to censor the chapters of her spiritual autobiography that addressed the topic.[40]

IDENTIFYING FANATICISMS

As evidenced by scrapbooks filled with newspaper clippings about her work, by the 1870s, Hannah had taken on leadership roles in a myriad of religious and social activities. However, as a nineteenth-century woman, her movements were constrained by social conventions, and Hannah was unable to transcend some of the boundaries placed on women's public engagement. Her initial deference to Robert's religious work after their move to England meant that Hannah first gained acceptance within her local community of women, then through other prominent female social circles. Following the Smiths' return to America after Robert's scandal, she aligned herself with movements such as the Women's Christian Temperance Union (WCTU).

Such marginalization did not come without discouragement. On more than one occasion in her correspondence, Hannah vented

[38] Indiana University Bloomington, Lilly Library, Box 9, Hannah Whitall Smith to an unnamed friend, 7 July 1875.
[39] Melvin E. Dieter, 'The Smiths: A Biographical Sketch with Selected Items From the Collection', *The Asbury Seminarian* 28 (1983), 7–42, at 24.
[40] Smith, *The Unselfishness of God* (reprint), 210–27 (chs 23–4).

annoyance at the obstacles placed in her way, such as being denied access to the pulpit when invited to speak in churches where ministers were uncomfortable with recognizing female exegetes as public preachers, and her own peculiar theology that challenged religious formalism and emphasized individual surrender to God. Smith was particularly frustrated that this was not simply a matter of denominational difference, but depended on the views of individual ministers and congregations. She shared the scenario about a fellow female Quaker preacher with her son Frank, a student at Princeton, who would die later that year of typhoid fever:

> what does thee suppose the Presbyterians will do with me? … I am a woman, and I am preaching? Thee knows the time they are having about Sarah Smiley in Brooklyn now, I suppose. Dr. Cuyler, a Presbyterian minister had her to preach in his pulpit, and his Presbytery took him up, and he made a splendid defence, and there was a great time. They first passed a vote of census, and then withdrew that, and referred the matter back to an old decision of a General Assembly forty years ago, which amounts, they say, to nothing.[41]

Hannah believed that popular opinion among her fellow Christians, at least the female ones, favoured woman preachers. However, as her letter to Frank demonstrates, without formal recognition and ordination of women, religious congregations were uncertain about how, or whether, to move forward with welcoming women into their pulpits.[42]

Smith also intimated that as her popularity increased, so too did her intermittent fatigue at being in the public eye. In a letter to her sister Mary dated 1875, the same year that her popular *The Christian's Secret*

---

[41] Indiana University Bloomington, Lilly Library, Box 8, Hannah Whitall Smith to Frank Whitall Smith, 10 February 1872.

[42] While mainline churches struggled with the question of female preaching, Quaker and Holiness communities were often more flexible. Quakers had long held a more egalitarian view when it came to the 'inner light' guiding believers, and it was relatively common in many Quaker communities for women to speak in meetings, though with more limitations by the nineteenth century as social conventions shifted: see Carole D. Spencer, 'Evangelism, Feminism and Social Reform: The Quaker Woman Minister and the Holiness Revival', *Quaker History* 80 (1991), 24–48, at 24. The Wesleyan Holiness tradition was more conservative in its approach, but also contended that the Holy Spirit could move through women just as it did through men, opening the door to female prophecy and, eventually, preaching: see Michelle Sanchez, 'Your Daughters Shall Prophesy: The Rise of Women's Ordination in the Holiness Tradition', *Priscilla Papers* 24 (2010), 17–22.

of a Happy Life was published, putting Smith in high demand, she lamented the discomforts of nineteenth-century transatlantic travel, and the pressure to maintain a punishing writing and speaking schedule while juggling the roles of wife (of a convalescent husband), mother, activist and religious reformer:

> once on shore, my life of weary wandering must begin. I can not tell thee how dreary the show-life I have to live this summer looks to me in prospect. I feel just as if the children and I were a sort of traveling Barnum's Hippodrome, with a 'woman preacher' on show instead of a tight rope walker.[43]

This was the same year that Robert was accused of sexual misconduct, pushing him out of the spotlight, just as Hannah was stepping into it. Suddenly, she was the religious expert, sought after on her own account, but increasingly exhausted by what her newfound fame entailed.

As the Smiths settled back into life in the USA, Hannah questioned the efficacy of their work in England. Shortly after returning to America, she confided to a friend: 'I have no doubt they [the English people] will be better off without us than they would have been with us, and I quite think we had ceased to be the least necessary in the work.'[44] This air of finality, however, was temporary, with the Smiths maintaining close ties with their English friends, and returning to England in 1888. As she entered these later years during her final 'epoch' of faith, Smith seems to have comfortably settled into her role as a public religious figure who could influence those around her through her unique theology.[45]

The widespread circulation of Hannah's publications, and substantial documentation in her scrapbooks detailing an overwhelming schedule, point to a religious figure who was well-liked and respected. Yet Smith never fully entered the mainstream. What kept Hannah on the margins? While many factors may have presented hurdles as she attempted to navigate her religious context, the perception of her teachings as heresies seems to have bolstered rather than hindered

---

[43] Indiana University Bloomington, Lilly Library, Box 9, Hannah Whitall Smith to her sister Mary, 23 May 1875.

[44] Indiana University Bloomington, Lilly Library, Box 9, Hannah Whitall Smith to her friend Mrs. Shipley, 7 August 1875.

[45] Smith, *The Unselfishness of God* (reprint), 305.

her efforts. Like other religious 'fanatics', Smith's later works reflect a zeal for an uncompromising and unorthodox view of faith when compared with her contemporaries. Yet Hannah did not believe that her own work crossed a line. When exploring the idea of the heretical through fanaticism in Smith's writing, the concept of fanaticism was as nuanced for its author as was her broader approach to faith. Later in life, Hannah reflected on this by curating a small archive of periodical clippings under the category of 'fanaticisms.' As her granddaughter Ray Strachey highlighted in her compilation of Smith's complete papers about fanaticism, which she edited for publication after Hannah's death in 1911, Smith believed that the fanatics that she had encountered in her life were not lost causes, but in fact 'acting in good faith'; this is to say that they were not wicked or ill intentioned, but erroneous.[46] She consistently used the term to describe movements which she believed to have at least some elements of sound doctrine and practice, but which fell short in some aspects, such as emphasizing emotion over her pragmatic brand of religious criticism.

From Smith's position of pragmatism, fanatics were misguided interpreters of faith, being drawn even further toward the margins than Smith and her supporters. As she read about different movements, particularly in periodicals, and saved clippings relating to those that most concerned her, Smith analysed them to uncover their heresies. Pantheists, Harmonists, Seventh-day Adventists and Christian Scientists all appear in her file, belonging to the category of traditions that she believed were incompatible with authentic religious convictions and risked engendering disillusionment among followers.

To share her position about these errant zealots, Hannah prepared a manuscript of her findings, which further delved into her reservations about emotional excess, spiritual hubris, and the dangers of misplaced emphases on outward expressions versus inward experiences of faith. These extracts from her papers include references to the religious mania of celibate communities like the Shakers, accusations about the ignorance of pseudo-perfectionists such as Noyes's followers at Oneida, and the false prophethood of millenarian communities like

---

[46] Ray Strachey, *Religious Fanaticism: Extracts from the Papers of Hannah Whitall Smith* (London, 1928), 19. This author was fortunate to encounter Hannah's compilation of fanaticisms through Strachey's text, but also as part of the Hannah Whitall Smith Collection at the B. L. Fisher Library Archives at Asbury Theological Seminary, where a collection of Smith's clippings about movements that she considered to be fanatical is kept.

the Millerites. Regarding the latter, although labelled a prophet herself, it is worth noting that many of the movements that Hannah regarded as fanatical had proclaimed prophets for their leaders. This was a feature of her religious climate about which Smith was wary. She found it a 'curious fact in connection with many of these prophecies' that when foretold events failed to occur, adherents retained their beliefs instead of walking away from their refuted prophets.[47] When considered alongside fellow female reformers in her time, such as Adventist prophetess Ellen G. White, Smith claimed superiority. Although both came from offshoots of Methodism, White's role as a proclaimed prophet received an unequivocal rejection by Smith.

For Smith, the boundary between fanaticism and moderation was a space in which individuals could evaluate and try to overcome spiritual shortfalls, to which she admitted personal susceptibility. The common thread setting fanatics apart from legitimate religious practitioners was a default to 'emotional nature', a problematic consequence of the era of heart-driven reforms with which Hannah struggled so deeply:

> After careful study of the subject of fanaticism, and a great deal of most intimate intercourse with the fanatics, I have come to the conclusion that the whole explanation of it lies in the fact that the emotional nature is allowed absolute control … everything effects our emotional nature: the state of our health, the weather, the sort of food we eat … and especially, more than anything else, the influence of other people upon us … . Emotions are more contagious than the most contagious disease in the universe. A cheerful person can cheer up a whole circle of unhappy people, and a depressed person can depress the most cheerful … simply by the mysterious, contagious power of emotion. In the whole history of religion this has been [the case] … I would therefore always urge every seeker after the deep things of God to ignore emotions and care only for convictions.[48]

The difference between a religious emotion and a religious conviction was that the latter was an indication of the Holy Spirit working to sanctify, while the former was a symptom of impressionable, some-times well-meaning, but deeply misguided faith. As in her early life, Smith acknowledged that she was as susceptible as others in allowing the emotions of her religious convictions to distract her from the

[47] Ibid. 52.
[48] Ibid. 155–64.

spiritual work at hand, encouraging believers to recognize the pitfalls of such purely emotional responses to faith. The story that Smith's archive of fanaticisms tells is one of seeking and trying to excise emotional religious errors without mistakenly eradicating faith in the process. She proposed that the line between genuine spiritual passion and unhealthy fanaticism was a fine one, as blurred as the intersections of the mainstream and the marginalized that she occupied as a popular, but challenged, religious reformer.

Hannah's letters and diaries reveal her to have been a tactful but forthright woman. As the boxes of newspaper clippings, posters and pamphlets outlining her every speaking engagement and public activity reveal, she was not completely detached from her reputation, but she was decidedly not afraid to speak her mind, believing that her religious message took precedence over widespread acceptance. This was especially true in her later years, when Hannah began to move away from formalized religious adherence, embracing an ever more syncretistic view of her Christian faith. Nonetheless Hannah's experimentation had its limits. Despite her openness to some fringe practices, including faith healing (she writes of a visit to a healer with her sister Mary who had been diagnosed with breast cancer), and spiritualism (she marvels about a mind cure doctor whom she believed to have miraculous powers), some traditions were too radical even for the open-minded Smith. These fell into quite a different category of fanaticism, one that was spiritually dangerous. She cautioned those seeking an authentic religious experience: 'beware impressions, beware emotions, beware of physical thrills, beware of voices, beware of everything, in short, that is not according to the strict Bible standard and to your own highest reason.'[49]

Defining a Higher Order

But how to cultivate such reason? For Hannah, the solution was not a movement away from the periphery, but instead, the cultivation of an inward transformation driven by practical Christian living and a balanced, rational approach to religious experience while relying on God's will and mercy. Attuned with her exposure to Quaker perfectionism and Holiness sanctification, this 'higher order' was aimed at

[49] Ibid. 164.

refining the moral and spiritual nature of the self, with the intention of broader social reform. In short, Smith, like Boardman, sought to reorder not just religious practice, but society at large, one individual spiritual transformation at a time.

Many pages of Smith's surviving correspondence enthusiastically discuss details from more than a decade of Higher Life meetings, starting in 1875 and hosted by Lady Mount-Temple, whose Broadlands estate in Hampshire served as a haven for the marginal movement and a forum for the cross-pollination of its unique religious ideals. The meetings, which were also known as the Keswick convention, were significant religious gatherings that promoted a deeper spiritual life and Christian sanctification. The first meeting was held in 1875 and became an annual gathering, which attracted a diverse group of evangelical Christians from different denominations.

Although challenged for its elitist tendencies and sometimes vague theological position, the community's emphasis on Hannah's brand of personal holiness and social responsibility resonated with many Christians, with lingering effects in the resulting Keswick movement through to the present day. The Broadlands meetings, which began as an annual convention of believers, gravitated toward Holiness views about sanctification, performing good works, and turning away from sinfulness through personal spiritual reflection and growth.[50] The movement especially gained traction in the 1890s, following the Smiths' return to England, and was uniquely open to female participation and leadership.[51]

Conclusions

Smith's work has left an enduring legacy, especially her influential publications and missives. Despite being a prolific female author and lay preacher, her role within a male-dominated paradigm and experimental Christianity kept her at the margins throughout her life. As has been argued here, there is not anything to indicate that Smith lamented this position, or that she wished to be embraced fully by

[50] See Charles F. Harford, ed., *The Keswick Convention: Its Message, Its Method and Its Men* (London, 1907).
[51] Alison M. Bucknall, 'Martha's Work and Mary's Contemplation? The Women of the Mildmay Conference and the Keswick Convention 1856–1900', in R. N. Swanson, ed., *Gender and Christian Religion*, SCH 34 (Woodbridge, 1998), 405–20.

the mainstream. Instead, her legacy of writings indicates an ardent hope that her message of Christian reform could transcend denominational and national boundaries. The essence of her theological view was a simple one: emphasizing personal spiritual growth through rational Christianity in preparation for salvation.

Although less well known today than her friends and contemporaries such as WCTU president Frances Willard (1839–98; a strict mainline Methodist), Smith's story sheds significant light on the intersections between the margins and mainstream in the Quaker and Holiness traditions. By embracing and negotiating liminal spaces, she challenged the boundaries of Christian expectations and experiences with her syncretistic approach. While labelled a fanatic sectarian by some, Smith appears to have found solace, purpose and strength in the peripheries, while fostering her 'higher order' with like-minded communities of believers.

Her close examination of, and experimentation with, diverse movements – from Quakerism, to Methodism, to Holiness traditions and beyond – underscores the dynamic nature of religious dialogue, as well as the fluidity of religious boundaries. Her legacy also compels us to re-evaluate how religious peripheries are defined: not as static spaces for inclusion or exclusion, but as fertile ground for understanding agency and authority, innovation and failure, acceptance and marginalization. Called a fanatic sectarian by some, Smith thought carefully about her own definitions of fanaticism and sectarianism. This interplay offers a broader understanding of religious identity and challenges us to see peripheries as integral to the tapestry of lived religious experience.

Friar Casimiro Brochtrup OFM: An Experience of the Catholic Church in the Brazilian Urban Context (1891–1945)

Dirceu Marroquim [iD]

Instituto Arqueológico Histórico e Geográfico Pernambucano

This article examines the role of the Catholic Church in the Brazilian city of Recife, in the aftermath of the Republic's Proclamation and the subsequent separation of church and state in Brazil. The study focuses on Friar Casimiro Brochtrup, OFM, who arrived in Brazil in 1894 and settled in Recife. His efforts in the impoverished Santo Amaro neighbourhood, particularly at Sítio da Macacheira, involved founding a church, chapels, schools and associations. The study aims to understand the Catholic Church's impact on urban territorialities amid ecclesiastical transformations and political shifts before the emergence of the theology of liberation in the late 1960s and early 1970s. It argues that the church's expansion from the late nineteenth to the early twentieth century involved territorial boundary expansion and rationalization of social assets. Drawing on diverse sources, including newspapers, ecclesiastical documents, reports and personal correspondence, this article illuminates the dynamic interactions between the Catholic Church, urban development and societal changes in Brazil during this period.

INTRODUCTION

In *The Next Christendom*, the historian Philip Jenkins made a paradigmatic statement: '[if] we wanted to visualize a "typical" contemporary Christian, we should think of a woman living in a village in Nigeria or a Brazilian favela.'[1] With this, Jenkins asserted that the centre of Christianity, including the Roman Catholic Church, had inexorably shifted 'southward' towards Africa, Asia and Latin America. Specific cases, such as the one discussed in this article, help shed new

Instituto Arqueológico, Histórico e Geográfico Pernambucano, Rua do Hospício, 130, Boa Vista, Recife, Pernambuco, Brasil, CEP: 50060-080. E-mail: dirceu_marroquim@yahoo.com.br.

[1] Philip Jenkins, *The Next Christendom: The Coming of Global Christianity* (Oxford, 2002), 2.

Studies in Church History 61 (2025), 520–540 © The Author(s), 2025. Published by Cambridge University Press on behalf of the Ecclesiastical History Society.
doi:10.1017/stc.2024.47

light on the larger picture and increase historical understanding of this shift.

The dawn of the twentieth century brought profound transform-ations in relations between church and state in most Latin American countries. Investments made by the Roman Catholic Church during the previous century, such as the establishment of the Latin American Pius College (1858) and the gradual improvement in training of priests, focused on the realities of South American countries and ultimately led to new forms of priestly action. This development manifested, on the one hand, the theological repositioning initiated by Pope Leo XIII (r. 1878–1903), and on the other hand, the territorial and administrative redefinitions implemented by Leo and his successor, Pius X (r. 1903–14). The Plenary Latin American Council (1899) is a further example of the implementation of these common norms.[2]

Sérgio Miceli has observed that 'at the end of the nineteenth and in the early twentieth centuries, patterns of relationships between church and state in Latin America and Brazil underwent profound disrup-tion.'[3] In some cases, such changes resulted in situations of extreme conflict, such as in Mexico (1917) and Uruguay (1919), while in Venezuela, where the separation of church and state was only partial, considerable resources were allocated to subsidizing ecclesiastical activity.[4] In Colombia, Peru, Bolivia, Paraguay and Argentina, there was no formal rupture, thus 'causing the Church to continue to receive institutional and financial benefits of all kinds in exchange for granting government authorities the power to interfere in the selection and appointment of ecclesiastical dignitaries.'[5] In Brazil, the separation of church and state was brought about by the Proclamation of the Republic in 1889, and was later reiterated in the first constitution of the new regime in 1891.

In the late nineteenth century, the Roman Curia began to establish direct contact with the countries of Latin America, both through official correspondence, encyclicals and apostolic letters, and through

---

[2] For further details of these developments, see Francisco J. R. Solans, 'The Creation of a Latin American Catholic Church: Vatican Authority and Political Imagination, 1854–1899', *JEH* 71 (2020), 316–36.
[3] Sérgio Miceli, *A Elite Eclesiástica Brasileira* (São Paulo, 2009), 21.
[4] Ibid.
[5] Ibid. 21.

diplomatic representations.[6] Encyclicals were written for Peru, Chile and also Brazil.[7] In addition, in 1900, in what Lisa Edwards sees as a 'redistribution of responsibilities more rationally and efficiently,'[8] new units of ecclesiastical administration were created simultaneously for several countries: Mexico gained seven new dioceses; Peru acquired four new ecclesiastical jurisdictions; and Chile and Venezuela each received two new dioceses.[9] The growth of the Roman Catholic Church in Brazil was such that, between 1890 and 1930, fifty-six dioceses, eighteen prelatures and three apostolic prefectures were created.[10]

This process of change and expansion also brought with it a need for an increasing number of priests. However, these were not necessarily forthcoming in Brazil, whose population Joseph Burnichon characterized in 1910 as 'a people moulded by Catholicism, still imbued with the Catholic faith, very attached to its religious traditions, but no longer supplying its clergy.'[11] This problem had long been recognized, for example in the instructions given to Monsignor Mário Mocenni, apostolic nuncio to Brazil in 1882. These 'lamented the corruption and ignorance of the Brazilian clergy' and recommended regular correspondence with local bishops, encouraging them to make use of the principles of the Council of Trent to encourage vocations. However, these instructions also anticipated the arrival of new priests from Europe to 'eradicate the grave disorders of the [Brazilian] clergy and to instill in them the true ecclesiastical spirit.'[12] Indeed, at the end of the nineteenth century and in the first decades of the twentieth, a considerable influx of religious men and women crossed the Atlantic to Brazil.

Several authors have sought to explain what was happening in Brazil in this period. The anthropologist Roger Bastide referred to the process as 'Romanization', arguing that this was the period when the Catholic Church in Brazil was becoming a 'Romanized Church'. Indeed, the

[6] E. L. Woodward, 'The Diplomacy of the Vatican under Popes Pius IX and Leo XIII', *Journal of the British Institute of International Affairs* 3 (1924), 113–38.

[7] Dilermano R. Vieira, *História do catolicismo no Brasil*, 2 vols (Aparecida, 2016), 2: 35.

[8] Ibid. 18.

[9] Lisa Edwards, *Roman Virtues: The Education of Latin American Clergy in Rome 1858–1962* (New York, 2011), 18.

[10] Ibid.

[11] Joseph Burnichon, *Le Brésil d'aujourd'hui* (Paris, 1910), 197.

[12] Edwards, *Roman Virtues*, 11.

new political regime in Brazil resulted in a movement in which 'German Franciscans replaced Brazilian Franciscans … . Monastic orders, often persecuted or expelled elsewhere, emigrated from France, Belgium, or Italy … . They included French Lazarists, German, Italian, Belgian Benedictines or Franciscans.' For Bastide, the result of this process was that 'in becoming Romanized, the Church denationalized itself.'[13]

Other authors have adopted the concept of 'Romanization', such as Ralph Della Cava in his *Miracle at Joaseiro* (1970). Cava spoke of 'the systematic integration of the Brazilian church, on both an ideological and institutional level, into the highly centralized structures of the Roman Catholic church directed from Rome.'[14] The 1889 military coup, which proclaimed the Republic in Brazil and led to the 1891 Constitution, was a crucial moment, for it marked the end of the so-called 'Padroado' (patronage), under which the Catholic Church had, since the fifteenth century, been accountable initially to the Portuguese king and then, from 1822, to the Brazilian emperor, and not necessarily to the Vatican. Riolando Azzi, on the other hand, proposed the concept of a 'Catholic Restoration' to describe the period from the 1920s onwards.[15] He argued that this period, characterized by the strengthening of the laity alongside an increasingly organized political militancy, began to create a space for the political mobilization of Brazilian Catholicism.

In this article, I will suggest that there are reasons for agreeing more with the analysis of Della Cava than with that of Azzi. However, I also make use of another concept employed by Edward Wright-Rios in his study *Revolutions in Mexican Catholicism* (2009): that of 'Catholic Resurgence'.[16] Through it, Wright-Rios emphasized the institutional dimension of the Catholic Church, which, since Pius IX, had manifested greater administrative centralism, and argued that priests and friars were figures with agency, whose social practices made a real impact in local contexts in Mexico. By considering the parallel transformations that occurred in Brazil, this article seeks to reveal the

---

[13] Roger Bastide, 'Religion and the Church in Brazil', in T. Lynn Smith and Alexander Marchant, eds, *Brazil: Portrait of Half a Continent* (New York, 1951), 334–55, at 342–3.
[14] Ralph Della Cava, *Miracle at Joaseiro* (New York, 1970), 216.
[15] Riolando Azzi, 'O início da Restauração Católica no Brasil (1920–1930)', *Revista Síntese* 4 (1977), 61–89.
[16] Edward Wright-Rios, *Revolutions in Mexican Catholicism* (Durham, NC, 2009), 43–137.

important interconnections between multiple aspects of the social history of the Catholic Church there.

This reconfiguration process, as will be shown below, was primarily a move toward occupying the peripheral areas of urban centres or territories that the Catholic Church had not yet reached systematically. Moreover, the presence of the Catholic Church in these areas was to be fundamental to the subsequent development of poor relief policies in the first half of the twentieth century in Brazil, an important consideration when shifting the focus from a history of the Catholic Church as centred on intellectual movements to one focused on the social practices of individuals and their interactions. Furthermore, the presence and impact of the Catholic Church, actively present on the peripheries of Brazilian urban centres before the advent of liberation theology in the 1960s and 1970s, is an historiographically underexplored subject.

This article seeks to shed new light on these developments by following the career trajectory of Casimiro Brochtrup (1868–1944), a Franciscan friar minor who arrived in Brazil from the newly united Germany in 1894.[17] For the purposes of this discussion, the periphery is understood as the areas of poverty surrounding the city of Recife, the capital of Pernambuco, a city which had considerable political importance during the period of Brochtrup's activity (1894–1944), with the Catholic Church acting as a fundamental pillar of structures of power.

Missionaries from Afar

More than three dozen male religious orders entered Brazil between 1880 and 1930.[18] The arrival of these new orders of missionary priests, each under the jurisdiction of a specific rule, both ended the predominance of the secular clergy, and significantly changed the ethnic composition of Brazilian Catholicism. Indeed, Serbin's analysis showed that 85.9% of regular priests in this fifty-year period had been born outside Brazil, and observes that, in consequence, 'once again, being a priest in Brazil meant

---

[17] See also Dirceu Marroquim, *Frei Casimiro Brochtrup: Igreja Católica, territorialidade e trabalhos sociais no Recife (1894–1944)* (São Paulo, 2022).
[18] Keneth P. Serbin, Padres, *Celibato e Conflito Social: Uma história da Igreja Católica no Brasil* (São Paulo, 2008), 95.

being white,' in a multi-ethnic country that had officially abolished slavery in 1888.[19]

This change in ecclesiastical profile had varying consequences in different Brazilian territories and local contexts, often reflecting the sometimes rigid outlook of priests who brought with them worldviews formed in completely different social, political and ecclesiastical contexts. The encyclical *Litteras a Vobis*, on clergy in Brazil, which was drafted by Leo XIII and addressed to the Brazilian episcopate in 1894, offers clues for understanding this process more clearly. Leo writes: 'By our apostolic providence, we have determined to restore the original observance of your institutions from the losses of past times.'[20] For the pope, this restoration meant for religious a closer adherence to the rules of the relevant order, or a return to them. He concluded his words to orders and congregations with an affirmation: 'the religious communities, both male and female, should be congratulated for receiving our commands willingly and for showing themselves ready for the restoration of the original institution of each one.'[21]

A comparison of the general censuses of 1872 and 1920 shows that the number of Brazilian priests increased by 35.65% over this period, while the number of foreign priests increased by 89.11%; however, no distinction is made in this census data between secular clergy and those who were members of religious orders.[22] Pernambuco experienced a significant change in its social framework, which can help explain other features of the region. In 1872, there had been 235 Brazilian priests and eight priests or members of religious orders who had come from abroad. In 1920, the number of Brazilian-born members of religious orders remained the same, but the number of foreign members of religious orders had increased to 129. The population in total had increased by 23.46%, but the total number of members of religious orders increased by 49.32%.[23] This reflects the transformation

---

[19] Ibid. 96.
[20] Leo XIII, *Litteras a Vobis* (Rome, 1894), §4.
[21] Ibid.
[22] To provide a slightly broader picture, I have considered here the current north-eastern Brazilian states, together with Rio de Janeiro (both capital and state), São Paulo and Minas Gerais. All the figures, including the total number of priests and nuns presented below, refer to these states: see José Oscar Beozzo, *Decadência e morte, restauração e multiplicação das ordens e congregações religiosas no Brasil 1870–1930* (São Paulo, 1983), 107.
[23] Ibid.

in Pernambuco, especially after 1889, when new structures were created in the Catholic Church.

Religious orders and congregations in Brazil were also shaped by political upheavals elsewhere that led to a diaspora. According to data collected by José Oscar Beozzo, in the nineteenth and twentieth centuries, 31.57% of the priests who came to Brazil were Italian, 26.31% were French, and 21.08% were either German or Dutch.[24] This migration was driven by a dual motivation: spreading Catholicism, and fleeing territories which were increasingly hostile to Catholic religious practices. The growth of religious orders in Brazil accelerated until the Second World War, although the rate of growth generally reflected the degree of anticlericalism in the order's society of origin.[25]

In Pernambuco, the influx was constituted by a range of different orders: Capuchins (arrival in 1841); Franciscans (1891); Congregation of the Priests of the Sacred Heart of Jesus (1893); Salesians (1894); Carmelites (1894); Benedictines (1895); Jesuits (1910); and Marist Brothers (1911). In order better to understand some of the nuances of this process, the case of the Franciscan friars coming to Brazil from Saxony (Germany), and in particular, that of Friar Casimiro Brochtrup, will now be explored.

The Province of the Holy Cross of Saxony Enters Brazil

In 1891, the Franciscan province of Saxony agreed to undertake a mission to Brazil. The number of Franciscan friars in Brazil had declined by 79% since the mid-nineteenth century, and it was therefore deemed necessary to bring priests to Brazil from elsewhere for the province of Santo Antônio do Brasil to be restored. Two of the order's friars, Camilo de Lélis and Joaquim do Espírito Santo, requested that new priests might be sent to Brazil, initially for missions among the indigenous people. While the Italian province declined the invitation, the province of Saxony accepted it.[26]

At this time, the province of Saxony was flourishing, with about 260 members and missions in the Netherlands, Belgium, the United

---

[24] Ibid. 120.
[25] Owen Chadwick, *A History of the Popes (1830–1914)* (Oxford, 2002), 487.
[26] Matias Teves OFM, *A Restauração da Província de Santo Antônio do Brasil. Revista do Instituto Arqueológico Histórico e Geográfico Pernambucano* (Recife, 1961), 430.

States and China.[27] The first Saxon priests arrived in Brazil from Bremen on 25 May 1891.[28] Dom Amando Bahlmann recalled years later that the voyage was quite uncomfortable: 'we were all very seasick, but almost every day we were able to celebrate Mass. With us, in third class, many Polish emigrants travelled.'[29] After landing in Salvador (Bahia) in the north-east, they travelled south, gaining an introduction to the Brazilian territory. A second missionary expedition arrived in Salvador in December 1891 with eight more friars; a third brought another sixteen in August 1892. The fourth expedition arrived in June 1893, the fifth in July 1894.

The friars who arrived in 1894 had more in common besides their dark brown habits and the rules of their order. Most of them had been born during a turbulent period in German history, in which successive wars had ultimately led to unification under Wilhelm I of Prussia and Chancellor Bismarck, who in the so-called *Kulturkampf* introduced a range of measures restricting or suppressing Roman Catholicism. This Protestantizing state project had prompted a reaction among Catholics who opposed it, and it was also condemned by the Vatican. After unification in 1871, the new German government expelled several religious orders from the country. The Province of the Holy Cross of Saxony was forced to move its headquarters to Harreveld in the Netherlands; it sent some of its members to the United States, where they founded a mission near Chicago, and others to China.[30] Another German province of the Friars Minor, Thuringia, also sent priests to the United States, in this case to New York City, in 1875.[31]

The expedition to Brazil was seen as paralleling the mission to the United States. Friar Gregório Janknecht, one of the organizers of the Brazilian mission and the man who had led the work of the order in North America, wrote to his superior that the Brazilian mission 'will be similar to the emigration to the United States in 1875'. Indeed, he

[27] Friar Hugo Fragoso, *Cadernos da Restauração* (Salvador, 1991), 6.

[28] Teves, *A Restauração da Província*, 430.

[29] Dom Amando Balhmann, *Memórias Inacabadas* (São Paulo, 1991), 59.

[30] David Blackburn, *The Catholic Church in Europe since the French Revolution: Comparative Studies in Society and History* (Cambridge, 1991), 782; Nicholas Atkin and Frank Tallett, *Priests, Prelates and People: A History of European Catholicism since 1750* (London, 2003), 188–93.

[31] See Joseph M. White, 'In Search of Holy Name Province, Order of Friars Minor', *U. S. Catholic Historian* 22 (2004), 113–25.

believed that 'in South America, we are given a field of action even more important and rewarding than in North America.'[32]

The friars who arrived in Salvador from the Netherlands in 1894 were thus products of a turbulent period. Some had experienced the militarism of German unification first hand before joining the Franciscan Order: Friar Ciríaco (1855–1941) and Friar Nicolau (1867–1942) had both been honoured by Emperor Wilhelm I for their military service, Friar Casimiro Brochtrup too had served in the army. These personal experiences shaped their ministry in Brazil.[33]

Friar Casimiro Brochtrup: Becoming a Missionary

Hermann Brochtrup was born on 10 March 1868, in Lüdinghausen, Westphalia, into a large but impoverished family of farmers.[34] He was educated at the local school and then enrolled in a teacher training college.[35] Called up for mandatory military service, he was not engaged in any military conflict, but he took the lead in caring for his comrades when some of them were afflicted with tuberculosis.[36] Unlike some of his colleagues who embarked for Brazil, Brother Brochtrup had had an independent life as a teacher before deciding, at the age of twenty-six, to become a Franciscan postulant.[37]

His formational journey began in Germany and concluded in Brazil. On joining the order, Hermann received the name Casimiro in honour of the saint, recognized for his connection with the poor and the sick, who had lived in Poland between 1458 and 1484.[38] With this new name, the young Roman Catholic committed to becoming one of the agents of the Catholic Church in Brazil. His ministry in the country was predominantly focused on the north-east region, known as the poorest area of Brazil, where he worked in the working-class suburbs but also ventured into the hinterlands.[39]

[32] A Missão no Brasil, *Revista Santo Antônio* (Salvador, 1951), 393.
[33] *Leituras Religiosas*, 12 December 1899, 555. Given his age, it is possible that Friar Ciríaco had fought in the Franco-Prussian War of 1870–1.
[34] Matias Teves OFM, *Entre os Mocambos do Recife* (Salvador, 1946), 29.
[35] Ibid.
[36] Ibid.
[37] Ibid.
[38] Ibid. 11.
[39] Recife, Archive of the Província Franciscana de Santo Antônio do Brasil, Casimiro Brochtrup, 'Crônica da Missão de S. Sebastião da Macaxeira' (version 3, [1936/7]), 2. Three

The position given to Casimiro Brochtrup by his superiors was that of missionary. His apostolic activity focused on evangelistic preaching in *Santas Missões* ('Holy Missions') in various regions of Brazil. He also left at least three written versions of 'The Chronicle of the Mission of São Sebastião da Macaxeira', a mission and social work foundation he established in Recife in 1926.[40]

In one version of the Chronicle of Macaxeira, Brother Casimiro wrote: 'Since 1918, I have led my life as a priest preaching missions and accompanying the bishops on Pastoral Visits.' A year after his return to Recife in 1924, having spent six months on a preaching mission in the hinterland, he experienced something 'like an inspiration from heaven'. This persuaded him that he should no longer work in the hinterlands, 'where the people showed so much faith,' but rather 'seek out the poor workers of Recife, who living in shanty towns were completely abandoned spiritually and in danger of losing the Catholic faith, as the preachers of the *nova-seita* [new sect] persecuted them.'[41] Friar Casimiro's sense was that the inhabitants of the shanty towns had been – or become – 'abandoned', not only in a spiritual sense, but also in relation to their poverty and morality.

In that same year of 1925, Friar Casimiro remembered: 'I was called to confess a poor worker in the Cordeiro neighbourhood and found him in an illicit union with a woman with whom he had four children, and I sought to marry him to that woman.'[42] Since there were no obstacles to performing the ceremony, Casimiro asked the couple to

---

versions of this text exist, distinguished by additions, deletions and omissions. Here, I mainly use the first and third versions. The first, composed in *c.*1934, consists of pages with many erasures and corrected words, and is clearly an initial attempt to construct a narrative. The words referring to public administration and politicians are harsher and without moderation. A consolidated edition of the first chronicle was made in the second version, in around 1935. The third includes significant changes, and was clearly written later, as it reaches the year 1936, which is beyond the chronological scope of the previous texts. All three versions can be found in the Archive of the Franciscan Province of Santo Antônio do Brasil.

[40] Teves, *Entre os Mocambos do Recife*, 35.

[41] Brochtrup, 'Crônica' (version 3), 1. The description 'spiritually abandoned' ('abandonados espiritualmente') is not included in version 1 of the manuscript. The term *nova-seita* or 'new sect' refers to preachers, primarily Pentecostals, who attempted to increase their influence in the outskirts of urban areas. In modern Brazil, there has been a noticeable connection between impoverished regions and the prevalence of Pentecostals. This correlation can also be observed through a historical lens.

[42] Brochtrup, 'Crônica' (version 3), 1. In versions 1 and 2, the protagonist was referred to as 'poor' without any mention of the term 'worker' ('operários pobrezinhos').

arrange for some people to serve as witnesses, only to receive the objection: 'Father, all the people in this street are adherents of the *nova-seita*.'[43] 'These words,' Casimiro wrote, 'cut me to the heart, and with more insistence, I heard the voice of God within me: Decide to care for the poor workers of Recife!'[44] This voice, or inspiration, prompted him to 'inquire about the spiritual state of people living in the "working-class neighbourhoods" ('bairros operários') of Recife'.[45] In December the following year, the friar would begin his social work in the city.

The question now was how to implement this vocation, but also to define the area in which he would operate. Casimiro's first step was to obtain authorization to start the work. He recalled that the provincial, Fr Eduardo, 'told me that there was no difficulty in obtaining this license,' and simply to 'make a written request to the Chapter stating your request'.[46] At the next meeting of their chapter, the friars of the Franciscan Province of Santo Antônio of Brazil approved Friar Casimiro's proposal. However, the approval of the archdiocese of Olinda and Recife was still necessary, and it was this that confirmed where the project would be based. Although there was some delay in obtaining the license from the local prelate, Casimiro had already decided on the location for his work: Macaxeira, located in Recife's Santo Amaro neighbourhood.

It was not the first time that Casimiro had been to Macaxeira. In a separate document, attached to the first version of his 'Crônica', there is mention of a holy mission he had been due to preach in Santo Amaro in 1924 by order of the metropolitan archbishop. However, due to the rainy season, it only lasted two days, as the priest fell ill: the rain was so heavy that 'there was no dry place, but everything was wet so that he could not kneel at the time of the blessing.'[47] The suspension of this apostolic work led to a disagreement between the archbishop and the friar.

Brother Casimiro wrote in his Chronicle that the parish priest of Piedade, João Olympio dos Santos, when 'asked by some ladies', had mentioned the need for more diligent work in the area. This locality

---

[43] Recife, Archive of the Província Franciscana de Santo Antônio do Brasil, Casimiro Brochtrup, 'Crônica da Missão de S. Sebastião da Macaxeira' (version 1, [c.1934]), 3.

[44] Brochtrup, 'Crônica' (version 3), 1.

[45] Ibid.

[46] Brochtrup, 'Crônica' (version 3), 1.

[47] Ibid.

was described by Brother Casimiro as a space located 'beside the Limoeiro line to the north of the cemetery [which] has about 800 shanties, and on the opposite side there are perhaps about 200 houses.' This one section of a neighbourhood alone housed a considerable number of people. In the 1913 census, the Santo Amaro neighbourhood was the fourth most populous in Recife, with 16,697 people, and the third in terms of the number of shanties. In absolute numbers, Santo Amaro was the seventh of fourteen neighbourhoods in terms of literate population, and the sixth in terms of the number of people without formal education. Moreover, in the early twentieth century, the state of Pernambuco, and with it its capital, had experienced intense industrialization, with the number of registered industrial enterprises increasing from 209 in 1880, to 791 in 1919. The number of industries almost quadrupled across various sectors, particularly in food, textile, clothing and ceramics. A notable rise in urban migration accompanied this, as people fleeing drought in rural areas sought employment opportunities.

The notion of a 'permanent mission', a term coined by Brother Casimiro himself, indicated that his proposal was for a sustained ministry rather than for a short-term intervention, as was more common. The experience described above, when Brother Casimiro attempted to conduct the wedding of a 'poor worker' on the outskirts of the city but was unable to find witnesses because the worker's neighbours belonged to the *nova-seita*, parallels the account of Father João Olympio, who warned that the youth were in danger of being corrupted by 'barefoot preachers' and ignorant propagators of harmful spiritualism.[48] These accounts highlight a growing concern over the influence of new religious beliefs and practices among marginalized populations, underscoring the challenge the Catholic Church faced in maintaining its presence and spiritual authority in urban outskirts.

At the same time, the terms used by both priests generalized and 'othered' people of different faiths or confessions, placing them in the position of a common enemy. Friar Casimiro couched his ministry in terms of a crusade confronting a social reality. This may be why the notion of a permanent mission seemed so apt. His social work initiatives were also a means by which he could confront the 'new sects'.

---

[48] Recife, Pernambuco, Archive of the Parish of Nossa Senhora da Piedade, João Olympio, *Livro de Tombo da Igreja Matriz da Piedade* (Recife, 1928), 1: 85.

The notion of *nova-seita* appears in Brother Casimiro's 'Crônica' as a generic concept referring to the range of denominations, often Pentecostal, that had, he said, 'opened worship houses on every street.' In general, the term 'new sect' had a pejorative character, especially when referring to Protestant groups. An example of this is the insult hurled by a layman of the church of Penha at a woman who refused – or was unable – to contribute to the church offering: 'You are a *nova-seita*, shameless! Even though you live near the church (of São Gonçalo), you have no shame.'[49] The Catholic press took a decidedly negative view of the 'new sects' and their practitioners. Similarly, an article on *nova-seita* in the magazine *Maria* claimed that 'Protestantism is a kind of Proteus; it changes its form, doctrine, and faith everywhere and for anyone, giving nonsense. Now, readers, take a look. In Brazil alone, the following new sects have sprung up from Protestantism.' It went on to list each of the Protestant groups operating in Brazil.[50]

This debate illuminates the complex historical connections between the rise of Pentecostalism in Brazil in the 1910s and 1920s, and the socio-economic landscapes of urban poverty. The emergence and spread of Pentecostalism can only be fully understood by considering the specific conditions of Brazil's urban centres, where marginalized communities often faced economic hardship, racial discrimination and social exclusion. Scholars such as John Burdick and R. Andrew Chesnut have explored the development and expansion of Pentecostalism through an intersectional lens encompassing class, race and gender dynamics.[51] Their studies reveal how Pentecostalism's appeal and growth among urban populations were shaped by these intersecting identities, historically constructed and continuously negotiated within the framework of Brazilian society. This approach demonstrates that Pentecostalism was – and is – not merely a religious phenomenon, but also a social movement deeply embedded in the lived experiences of the urban poor.

The testimonies of Friar Casimiro are particularly valuable as they underscore the importance of re-engaging with the social history of the Catholic Church from an interreligious and interdenominational perspective. This approach involves recognizing the diverse religious

[49] *Maria*, July 1923, 10.
[50] Ibid.
[51] John Burdick, *Blessed Anastácia* (New York, 1998); R. Andrew Chesnut, *Born Again in Brazil: The Pentecostal Boom and the Pathogens of Poverty* (New Brunswick, 1997).

expressions that emerged in impoverished urban settings and understanding how the Catholic Church interacted with, adapted to, or resisted these new forms of belief. Such analysis, which requires careful consideration of the different social positions occupied by marginalized communities in urban peripheries, helps us to empathize with their struggles and understand their search for meaning, community and social support. Revisiting these dynamics also sheds light on the complex interplay between religious institutions and the socio-economic realities faced by these communities, offering a more nuanced understanding of the role of the Catholic Church – and other religious groupings – in the broader religious landscape of urban Brazil.

FRIAR CASIMIRO AND HIS 'PERMANENT MISSION'

Describing the large, rough construction situated among the shanties of the Macaxeira site, a journalist from the *Jornal Pequeno* wrote: 'A crude wooden cross rises from the apex of an angle formed by two rafters, supporting the ridge, highlighting the facade of a shack, catching the attention of visitors to that poverty-stricken neighborhood.' The building was a 'misshapen house with irregular coverings, using a variety of materials,' with a roof made of thatch and walls made of 'wooden panels, boards of different shapes revealing their source, crates, and sacks of burlap'. It was surprising that such a fragile building had been able to withstand a winter.[52] On entering the premises, the journalist observed 'a large space/room, half of the shack. A burlap curtain marks the division'. The other half was divided into two additional rooms with a similar makeshift partition. An altar stood in the centre. The journalist concluded: 'There is both a chapel and a school.' This setting formed the backdrop to Brother Casimiro's social work.[53]

The first mass of his new ministry was celebrated outdoors in February 1927, on a platform raised by about 80 cm; on it was a temporary altar and the image of St Sebastian.[54] Brother Casimiro's work began by seeking 'the healing of souls through daily worship and frequent preaching,' but the engagement he had hoped for did not

---

[52] *Jornal Pequeno*, 6 October 1928, 1.
[53] Ibid.
[54] Brochtrup, 'Crônica' (version 1), 10.

materialize. A school was therefore started in the shack housing the church, for, as Casimiro recognized, 'catechism on its own would not yield a result if it did not start with education'.[55] He later recalled: 'in February I started with two primary schools, soon increased to four. There was no school in Macaxeira, except for some private ones, which were there to exploit poverty.'[56] This pivotal move underscored Brother Casimiro's realization that authentic spiritual engagement required a foundation of education, leading him to integrate schooling into his ministry in order better to serve and uplift the community of Macaxeira. Both the journalist's brief narrative and the priest's account reveal the precariousness of life for the inhabitants of Macaxeira at this time and the absence of any state provision for the area. Brother Casimiro's approach for attracting people to his work was to offer a service to the community, since more than spiritual activities would be necessary to ensure the continuity of the mission.

The article in the *Jornal Pequeno* vividly described the Franciscan friar's work in this poverty-stricken city area. Brother Casimiro sought resources to improve facilities and construct a church. The friar's ministry provided social assistance, some of which should have been the state's responsibility. It required funding, personal relationships, knowledge of bureaucratic intricacies, and an understanding of the operations of the state.[57] Brother Casimiro's efforts sought not only to fulfil spiritual requirements, but also to address critical social needs, highlighting his ability to navigate complex state systems and rally resources for a mission that extended far beyond the church walls. As such, Friar Casimiro's actions in his 'permanent mission' involved some of the social mobilization practices that had been recommended by the *Plenary Latin American Council* (1899), such as education and social care (along with a focus on rural ministry which was less relevant to his work).[58] The priest's actions confirm the impression that, in those years, the Catholic Church was expanding beyond its historical frontiers to reach into territories located in peripheral areas. Brochtrup founded at least ten Catholic groups of various kinds. These ranged from associations, such as the Our Lady of Perpetual Help Association;

[55] Ibid.
[56] Ibid.
[57] *Jornal Pequeno*, 6 October 1928, 1.
[58] For the Council, see Solans, 'The Creation of a Latin American Catholic Church', 332–5; Andrés Rivarola Puntigliano, 'The Geopolitics of the Catholic Church in Latin America', *Territory, Politics, Governance* 9 (2019), 455–70, at 459.

the Ladies of Charity; and the Infant Jesus of the Children; to the League of the Most Holy Names of Jesus, Mary and Joseph; and the well-known Apostolate of Prayer.[59] These organizations provided a range of collective experiences, such as commemorations, celebrations and cultural exchanges. From the statistical yearbook of Pernambuco for the year 1930, it can be seen that there were 168 devotional associations across the forty-one parishes of the archdiocese of Olinda and Recife, an average of about four associations per parish. In addition, there were thirty-four brotherhoods, based in older parishes and mostly near Recife.[60] However, there was also significant growth of evangelical churches of different denominations in this area during this period, as well as traditional manifestations of Afro-Brazilian religions. For a state whose leaders were openly Catholic and conservative, work like that of Friar Casimiro was therefore timely.

In addition to ecclesiastical initiatives such as frequent communion, the establishment of associations, and the annual celebration of festivals, Brother Casimiro's mission manifested a palpable concern with the long-term viability of Catholic engagement in the area. The idea of a 'permanent mission' involved more significant interaction with spheres of power, including the administrative elite, sometimes at the highest level. Friar Casimiro sought access to the public machinery of the state through the fostering of networks of relationship. He also attempted to establish strong relationships that were not dependent on those who held political power at any particular moment. While he was openly critical of some political leaders, he was also able to build up mutual relationships with them which could be sustained despite his criticism.[61] However, his primary focus was on establishing good relations with civil servants and other staff in public administration, and on establishing long-term relationships with those who were involved in the day-to-day implementation of political decisions. Through petitions, the acquiring of privileged information, and visits to local legislative offices, political activity in the territory became essentially the activities of the Catholic Church itself.

---

[59] These associations aimed to serve distinct groups, but they shared a common focus on providing care to poor populations through charitable action. Children and families received special attention in this context, particularly in the Association of the Infant Jesus of the Children and the League of the Most Holy Names of Jesus, Mary and Joseph: see Marroquim, *Frei Casimiro Brochtrup*, 190.

[60] Estado de Pernambuco, *Anuário Estatístico de Pernambuco* (Recife, 1931), 130.

[61] Teves, *Entre os Mocambos do Recife*, 75–97.

In 1937, after the political coup of the Estado Novo (New State), when Getúlio Vargas decreed a state of emergency and established a dictatorial regime, the scenario changed favourably for Brother Casimiro. The new governor of Pernambuco, Agamenon Magalhães, was a staunch Roman Catholic and chose the friar as his confessor. This relationship allowed the priest unrestricted access to the public sphere and its resources.

Friar Casimiro's ministry in Macaxeira illustrates the significant impact that combining education and social services with religious work could have on marginalized communities. Recognizing that spiritual activities alone were insufficient for meaningful engagement, he established schools within the church's modest facilities, understanding that education was essential for catechism to be effective. This approach addressed immediate needs and filled a void left by the lack of state services, demonstrating how the church could extend its influence beyond traditional spiritual boundaries to foster community development.

While his ability to navigate bureaucratic complexities and build relationships with political leaders like Governor Agamenon Magalhães was pivotal for securing resources, it also highlights the challenges inherent in relying on personal networks for community support. These connections enabled Friar Casimiro to advance his mission, but they also underscore the importance of having sustainable structures for social assistance that are not solely dependent on individual efforts. Friar Casimiro's work reflects both the potential of religious institutions to effect positive change and the necessity for broader, systemic solutions to address the needs of underprivileged and underserved areas like Macaxeira.

SHAPING THE LANDSCAPE

One result of Brother Casimiro's relationship to the new governor of Pernambuco was the transformation of the landscape of the former Sítio da Macaxeira (Macaxeira Ranch), including the replacement of shanties by houses. On 1 May 1941, the Santo Amaro neighbourhood celebrated the inauguration of a residential complex built with state resources, in partnership with civic and church agencies. The 'Social League Against the Slum', founded in 1939, sought to improve the quality of housing in the neighbourhood and to clear slums. The

League's regulations required applicants for the new housing to conform to regulations that aimed to improve living standards and morality. The celebration in 1941 also marked fifty years since the publication of *Rerum Novarum* (1891), the influential papal encyclical on social justice issues. The workers' village was named Leo XIII in honour of the encyclical's author.[62]

Friar Casimiro may well have attended the ceremony. Housing was one of his areas of expertise, and Leo XIII Village was just a short distance from the church and São Sebastião elementary school. However, the new housing was not unproblematic. The building programme had been preceded by a long process of demolishing slums and draining flooded areas. In addition, the number of new houses was less than the number of slum dwellings demolished, which created a difficult situation. Nonetheless, the new housing in many ways represented the culmination of Friar Casimiro's endeavours. Between 1926, when he began his social programme, and his death in 1944, the locality was almost completely transformed. The rural-urban landscape began to acquire masonry buildings instead of shacks and shanties. In this, the name of the Leo XIII Village represented much more than a tribute; this was a city project that sought to mitigate the hardships of life for a population which had been forcibly displaced from the shanty towns.

Friar Casimiro's relationship with Pernambuco's governor went beyond political patronage and their shared interests in the Catholic Church and its social doctrine. This is evident from an article written by Agamenon Magalhães after the friar's death on 25 May 1944, in which he recalled:

> Start here, Frei Casimiro told me, with your work against the slums. We responded to your appeal and began building the worker village .... The buildings multiplied, blessed by God and men, increasing the apostolic fervour of the missionary who was not afraid of poverty and lived through his sufferings.'[63]

Magalhães was clearly influenced by Casimiro as his confessor, and he here associates Friar Casimiro's ministry and his attempts at the 'Christianization' of the city with the implementation of the slum demolition initiative.

---

[62] *Jornal Pequeno*, 15 April 1941, 3.
[63] Teves, *Entre os mocambos do Recife*, 122.

Similarly, the priest who became Magalhães's confessor after Casimiro's death, Fr Romeu Pérea, later described his first contact with the politician: "'Did you know Frei Casimiro?" asked the Governor. "I did," replied the priest. Finally, he asked, "Was he a saint?"' The priest replied that he thought he had been, claiming that Friar Casimiro's role in opening catechism centres and setting up 'sufficient straw chapels in which to gather children to learn the true meaning of life,' made him the 'true precursor of the so-called Social League Against the Shantytown.'[64] Pérea also reported that Brother Casimiro had come to be known as the 'apostle of the shantytowns', whose ministry was not in the remote corners of the country but rather on the urban front lines. The construction of Friar Casimiro's reputation as a saint began very soon after his death, reflecting his renown during his life.

The chronicle book of the Santo Antônio Convent records that 'on April 15 [1944], Frei Casimiro fell gravely ill. Despite the greatest care from doctors and sisters, our esteemed brother in the habit did not survive the illness, passing away, surrounded by his brothers, on May 25.' The chronicler further wrote that with the death of their brother, a 'truly pious religious and extraordinarily zealous worker of great mortification' was lost. He added a reflection that the Franciscan himself would surely have endorsed: 'It is better to take the poor out of the quagmire of misery and make them illustrious Brazilian citizens than to build a palace.'[65] In seeking to make this vision a reality, Friar Casimiro witnessed a key historical process in the construction of early-twentieth-century Brazil, in which religion and state were closely entwined.

Conclusion

In August 1952, eight years after Casimiro Brochtrup's death in Recife, someone paid for the publication of a brief notice in the newspaper *Diário de Pernambuco*: 'To Friar Casimiro, I thank you for the cause achieved'.[66] The *Diário de Pernambuco* was not at that

[64] Romeu Peréa, *Diálogos com Agamenon Magalhães* (Recife, 1977), 20. The 'straw chapels' were rough wooden constructions with straw roofs.
[65] Recife, Arquivo da Província Franciscana de Santo Antônio do Brasil, *1º Livro de Crônicas do Convento de Santo Antônio do Recife* (Recife, 1944), 202.
[66] *Diário de Pernambuco*, 18 August 1952, 12.

time openly Catholic, as it once had been, but nonetheless published this reader's words of gratitude. Similar testimonies to the effective intercession of the Franciscan friar appear in other newspapers, alongside thanks to other figures well known in the hagiographies and imaginations of Roman Catholicism more widely: St Anthony, Our Lady of Perpetual Help, Saints Cosmas and Damian.[67]

Another tribute was recorded in the *Diário de Pernambuco* in July 1952, when the archbishop of Olinda and Recife visited the social institutions which had been set up by Brother Casimiro. He wrote: 'It has been 25 years since Friar Casimiro, a true apostle of Recife, founded the monumental and indelible work among the poorest workers in the capital of Pernambuco. He lived among these miserable people preaching the holy Gospel in a life of sacrifices.' The archbishop also noted that Casimiro had been accorded titles such as 'pious,' 'charitable,' 'untiring,' and 'apostle.'[68] On the centenary of the friar's birth, the famous Brazilian sociologist Gilberto Freyre called him 'perhaps a saint'.[69] The life of Friar Casimiro Brochtrup, in the aftermath of the proclamation of the Republic in Brazil in November 1889, illustrates the way in which the dimensions of political sociability are steeped in religious practices (and vice versa) and show how personal relationships within a network enable the undertaking of large-scale actions that impact the social life of an impoverished community, as was the case with Sítio da Macacheira. At the interface between religion, politics and piety, there is a complex history that can be told through various angles: by examining the political influence of religious institutions – such as how the Catholic Church has shaped governance, legislation and social policies – but also by investigating social movements rooted in piety, exploring how grassroots religious movements have led to social change or political action.

This leads to a final methodological reflection: the importance of the parish dimension. Numerous researchers have pointed out the potential of this ecclesiastical unit. This perspective also leads us to perceive more clearly how the presence of the Roman Catholic Church between the late nineteenth century and the early decades of the

---

[67] For further references, see *Maria*, 8 October 1948, 33; *Jornal Pequeno*, 21 December 1944, 2.

[68] *Diário de Pernambuco*, 30 July 1952, 3.

[69] Gilberto Freyre, 'Um franciscano talvez santo' ['A Franciscan perhaps a Saint'], *Diário de Pernambuco*, 10 March 1968, 2.

twentieth century resides, above all, in territorial expansion. There was a numerical growth of churches and chapels and an intensification in community life. The proliferation of Catholic lay associations, associated with a growing dependence on a priest leading these groups, illustrates a more effective presence of multiple Catholicisms in the territories. On the one hand, the church had growing political capital, and on the other, it represented a central element of local political stability. All this preceded – but in some ways formed the foundation for – the development of a liberation theology.

Returning to where we started, Philip Jenkins's recognition of the southward shift in contemporary Christianity requires research into the operations of the Catholic Church in peripheral areas as a long-term process. In Brazil, the occupation of these territories brought Roman Catholic social practices to the poorest strata of society. It is no coincidence that a survey published by the Datafolha Institute in 2019 on the demography of religions in Brazil found that 55% of Catholics consider themselves black and brown, 80% have no university education, and 67% earn up to three minimum wages. The story of Friar Casimiro Brochtrup helps to show why this is the case.

The Emergence of Hong Kong as a World Centre for Chinese Protestant Bible Publishing and Distribution, 1948–51

George Kam Wah Mak ⓘD
Hong Kong Baptist University

The Chinese Civil War (1946–9) and the Korean War (1950–3) contributed to the beginning of Hong Kong's evolution from a British colony occupying a geographically peripheral position in South China, to a world centre for Chinese Protestant Bible publishing and distribution in the Cold War era. In 1948, the China Bible House (CBH), the de facto national Bible society of China, decided to establish an emergency office in Hong Kong, responding to the prospect of the Communist takeover of China. Subsequently, as the Korean War unfolded, the CBH, owing to political pressure, desired to sever its connection with the emergency office in 1951. This resulted in the transition of the emergency office into the Hong Kong Bible House (HKBH), the British and American Bible societies' agency for Chinese Bible publishing and distribution. Thanks to the work of the HKBH, Hong Kong came to be the major source of Bibles for Chinese Protestants outside mainland China.

INTRODUCTION

In his study of Hong Kong as a global frontier in the Cold War era, Prasenjit Duara suggested that 'while the spread of economic and migrant networks from Hong Kong has been well documented', less

Department of Religion and Philosophy, Hong Kong Baptist University, Hong Kong.
E-mail: ggkwmak@hkbu.edu.hk.

The work presented in this article was fully supported by a grant from the Research Grants Council of the Hong Kong Special Administrative Region, China, through its General Research Fund (Project no. HKBU 12613322).

Studies in Church History 61 (2025), 541–562 © The Author(s), 2025. Published by Cambridge University Press on behalf of the Ecclesiastical History Society.
 doi:10.1017/stc.2024.52

noted has been the historical role of Hong Kong as a space of facilitation which allowed religious networks to fan out from China to South East Asia.[1] Ying Fuk-tsang, a noted historian of Chinese Christianity, is one of the handful of scholars who have paid attention to this overlooked role of Hong Kong. In his recent study of Protestant Christian literature and publishing work in post-war Hong Kong, Ying pointed out that Shanghai [上海] in East China, Hankou [漢口] in Central China, and Guangzhou [廣州] in South China had long been the centres for Chinese Protestant literature and publishing before the Communist takeover of China in 1949, with Shanghai as the most important. However, from the 1950s onwards, they were replaced by Hong Kong thanks to the migration of renowned, experienced Chinese Protestant writers and publishing professionals, as well as the relocation of Protestant publishing agencies from mainland China.[2] During the 1950s and 1960s, these people and agencies produced in Hong Kong many hundreds of Protestant publications including devotional literature, evangelistic writings and periodicals. Given the difficulty of sending books from Hong Kong to mainland China owing to the latter's political situation, these publications increasingly targeted Chinese living outside mainland China,[3] who, as suggested by the estimate of the American Bible Society (ABS), amounted to more than twenty million in total by late 1949.[4]

---

[1] Prasenjit Duara, 'Hong Kong as a Global Frontier: Interface of China, Asia, and the World', in Priscilla Roberts and John M. Carroll, eds, *Hong Kong in the Cold War* (Hong Kong, 2016), 211–30, at 211, 222.

[2] 邢福增 [Ying Fuk-tsang (Xing Fuzeng)], '文以載道：戰後(1950–1960年代)香港 基督教文字出版事業的發展與評檢' ['Wen yi zai dao: Zhan hou (1950–1960 niandai) Xianggang Jidujiao wenzi chuban shiye de fazhan yu pingjian'; 'Literature as a Vehicle for the Way: An Assessment of the Development of Protestant Christian Literature and Publishing Work in Post-war Hong Kong (1950s–1960s)'], in 黃文江 [Wong Man Kong (Huang Wenjiang)], 張雲開 [Zhang Yunkai] and 陳智衡 [Chen Zhiheng], eds, 變局下 的西潮：基督教與中國的現代性 [*Bianju xia de xichao: Jidujiao yu Zhongguo de xiandaixing; Western Tides Coming Ashore in a Changing World: Christianity and China's Passage into Modernity*] (Hong Kong, 2015), 543–65, at 543–4, 561–3; 邢福增 [Ying Fuk-tsang (Xing Fuzeng)], '戰前香港基督教文字出版事工研究 (1842–1941)' ['Zhan qian Xianggang Jidujiao wenzi chuban shigong yanjiu (1842–1941)'; 'A Study of Protestant Christian Literature and Publishing Work in Pre-war Hong Kong (1842–1941)'], in 國家宗教事務局宗教研究中心 [Guojia Zongjiao Shiwuju Zongjiao Yanjiu Zhongxin; Centre for Religious Studies, State Administration of Religious Affairs], ed., 基督教與中國文化 [*Jidujiao yu Zhongguo wenhua; Christianity and Chinese Culture*] (Beijing, 2013), 224–50.

[3] Ying, 'Literature as a Vehicle for the Way', 561–4.

[4] Philadelphia, PA, American Bible Society Archives [hereafter: ABS Archives], Janice E. Pearson, 'ABS Historical Essay #15, VII-F-2, Distribution Abroad, 1931–1966: China, 1931–1966' (1968), 207. The archival materials of the ABS are used with permission of the

According to Ying, at the same time, Hong Kong gained new status as the world's supply centre of Chinese Protestant Bibles. As early as the period from 1949 to 1952, twenty-eight editions of the Bible, twelve editions of the New Testament and nine editions of biblical portions, of which most were in Mandarin, and which in total amounted to 2,485,975 volumes, were published by the Hong Kong Bible House (HKBH). The HKBH was an agency which enabled the British and Foreign Bible Society (BFBS), the ABS and the National Bible Society of Scotland (NBSS), the three major Chinese Bible publishers and distributors in late Qing (1842–1911) and Republican China (1912–49), to continue their work among Chinese-speaking people after they were forced to withdraw from mainland China in 1951. The Chinese Bibles, New Testaments and biblical portions published by the HKBH were supplied not only to Hong Kong and Taiwan, but also to South East Asian countries, including Thailand, Indonesia and Malaya, as well as countries like New Zealand and the United States of America.[5]

As Bible publishing and distribution were not the focus of Ying's study, it is natural that he did not explore in depth why Hong Kong, a British colony occupying a geographically peripheral position at the southern end of China, became a world centre for Chinese Protestant Bible publishing and distribution. The brief account of the HKBH's work during the 1950s and 1960s in Ying's article is based on only a few published sources.[6] Building on Ying's account, this study draws on the archival materials of the Bible societies connected with the HKBH to argue that the Chinese Civil War (1946–9) and the Korean War (1950–3) were catalysts for the British and American Bible societies' desire to have an agency in Hong Kong for Chinese Protestant Bible publishing and distribution. This resulted in the establishment of the

American Bible Society, Philadelphia. While the ABS has an inventory of its archival materials for internal use, 'ABS Historical Essays' are not included in the inventory. This accounts for the lack of detail as to how and where the ABS Historical Essays cited in this article can be located in the ABS Archives.

[5] Ying, 'Literature as a Vehicle for the Way', 545–6, 564–5; David McGavin, 'Hongkong Bible House', *Bible Society Record* (December 1952), 152–3. Most of the Bibles, New Testaments and portions published by the HKBH in the 1950s were not distributed in Hong Kong. For instance, it was estimated that only ten per cent of the 700,000 volumes produced by the HKBH in 1959 were sold there. The remainder were supplied to churches in South East Asia and to the Chinese overseas diaspora: 師道弘 [Shih Tao Hung (Shi Daohong)], 教會事工平議 [*Jiaohui shigong pingyi*; *The Success & Failure of the Church*] (Hong Kong, 1964), 15.

[6] See Ying, 'Literature as a Vehicle for the Way', 546 n. 16, 561 n. 72, 565 n. 82.

'Emergency Office' of the Chinese Bible House (CBH) in Hong Kong in 1949, which, in 1951, became the HKBH. Thanks to the work of the Emergency Office, and subsequently of the HKBH, Hong Kong was set on the path towards becoming a world centre for Chinese Protestant Bible publishing and distribution in the Cold War era, in contrast to its pre-war peripheral role in Chinese Protestant Christianity as a Western Protestant missionary society or denomination's station in its South China mission, diocese or synod.[7]

THE CBH's HONG KONG 'EMERGENCY OFFICE': A CONTINGENCY MEASURE IN RESPONSE TO THE CHINESE CIVIL WAR

In Republican China, Chinese Bible publishing and distribution was mainly facilitated by three British and American Bible societies, namely the BFBS, the ABS and the NBSS, which had begun their work among the Chinese in the nineteenth century. For many years, they worked across the country without a clear division of territory, which unavoidably resulted in competition among them. This became more problematic when the Protestant church in China was making a transition from a mission to an indigenous church in the Republican era, since Chinese Protestants were generally unconcerned about 'whether their books come from an American office or a British office',[8] whereas Western missionaries usually supported a specific Bible society corresponding to their country of origin.[9] In 1932, delegates of the three Bible societies met in London to discuss 'how to reach fuller co-operation in view of the present position and problems in the world'.[10] One of the resolutions of this conference related to China, recommending that the three Bible societies should work together to encourage 'the formation of a China Bible Society, which, having the same basic principles as the co-operating Societies, shall share with them in the world-wide work of

---

[7] 邢福增 [Ying Fuk-tsang (Xing Fuzeng)], 香港基督教史研究導論 [*Xianggang Jidujiao shi yanjiu daolun*; *An Introduction to the Study of the History of Hong Kong Christianity*] (Hong Kong, 2004), 24–30, 180, 193.

[8] ABS Archives, RG#27 China Mission, 'China Matters: A Talk by Rev. Dr. G. Carleton Lacy, Agency Secretary of China Agency (now at home on furlough) Before the Committee on Foreign Agencies, Meeting in the Bible House, Oct[ober] 25, 1928'.

[9] ABS Archives, Eric M. North, 'ABS Historical Essay #15, Part V-F-2. Distribution Abroad 1861–1900. China' (1965), 42.

[10] James Moulton Roe, *A History of the British and Foreign Bible Society, 1905–1954* (London, 1965), 252.

the distribution of the Scriptures'.[11] In 1937, the BFBS and the ABS united their work in China under a single organization known as the CBH, which had its headquarters in Shanghai. With the integration of the NBSS's work in China into the CBH in 1946, the CBH was qualified to be considered as the national Bible society of China, since it functioned as the sole organization through which all three Bible societies carried out Bible publishing and distribution work in the country.[12]

Although it was the intention that the CBH would become a self-governing and self-supporting Bible society, it was not until December 1950 that Baen Lee [李培恩; Li Peien], former president of Hangchow University, was appointed as the first full-time Chinese general secretary.[13] Before his appointment, except during the Second Sino-Japanese War (1937–45), when E. S. Yu [俞恩嗣; Yu Ensi] and Chester S. Miao [繆秋笙; Miao Qiusheng] served, for a brief spell, as honorary general secretary (1942–4) and acting executive secretary (1944–5), respectively, the CBH's executive heads, known as 'secretaries', were Westerners representing the three Bible societies.[14] The first were George Carleton Lacy of the ABS, who resigned in 1941 on his election as bishop of the China Central Conference of the Methodist Church, and William H. Hudspeth of the BFBS, who was interned by the Japanese in October 1942 and released in 1945. They were followed by Ralph Mortensen of the ABS, who succeeded

---

[11] ABS Archives, Pearson, 'ABS Historical Essay #15, VII-F-2', 101.

[12] Cambridge, CUL, Bible Society's Library, Archives of the British and Foreign Bible Society [hereafter: BFBS Archives], 'Constitution and By-laws of the Chung Hua Sheng Ching Hui'. The materials of the BFBS Archives are used with permission of the Bible Society's Library, CUL. Although the BFBS Archives are represented on ArchiveSearch, the CUL's catalogue for archive collections, some sources in the BFBS Archives, such as this document, are uncatalogued. This accounts for the lack of detail as to how and where this document can be located in the BFBS Archives. ABS Archives, RG#1, Annual Reports, *One Hundred and Thirty-First Annual Report of the American Bible Society* (1947), 219.

[13] BFBS Archives, BSA/D8/4/5/4, Minutes of a Special Meeting of the Executive Committee of the China Bible House, 12 December 1950.

[14] Yu served as the CBH's honorary general secretary from 1942 to 1944 in response to the insistence of the Japanese authorities in occupied China that the CBH must have Chinese leadership. After his death in April 1944, Miao served as the CBH's acting executive secretary on a voluntary basis until the end of 1945: ABS Archives, Pearson, 'ABS Historical Essay #15, VII-F-2', 164–6, 171–2; BFBS Archives, BSA/D8/4/5/4, Minutes of the Executive Committee of the China Bible House, 7 February 1942; BFBS Archives, BSA/D8/4/5/3/1, Letter from C. S. Miao to J. C. F. Robertson, 12 May 1944; ABS Archives, RG#4.09, Minutes of Committee on Foreign Agencies, 24 September 1942.

Lacy but could not arrive in China until 1944, and David McGavin of the NBSS, who, after Hudspeth's relocation to Canada in 1947, also represented the BFBS.[15] These Western secretaries were members of the CBH's executive committee and also accountable to the Bible societies they represented. Moreover, the three Bible societies furnished most of the CBH's budget until 1951, when, as will be discussed below, the CBH severed its relationship with them and no longer received foreign financial support.[16]

Shortly after the end of the Second Sino-Japanese War, China was again embroiled in conflict, through a civil war which raged from 1946 to 1949 between the Chinese Nationalist Party (Kuomintang) and the Communist Party of China (CPC). In 1948, given the prospect of the Communist takeover of China which could put an end to Chinese Bible printing in the country, the CBH began to consider plans to produce 'with all speed the greatest possible stock' of Chinese Bibles.[17] One of the measures taken was to place an additional order for printing Chinese Bibles, New Testaments and biblical portions which amounted to two years' supply, and to deliver the books as speedily as possible. For example, a Lutheran mission aeroplane named 'St Paul' was chartered to 'make at least five trips transporting eighteen tons of Scriptures [from Shanghai] to Peiping [北平, now 北京; Beijing], Tientsin [天津; Tianjin], Sian [西安; Xian], Lanchow [蘭州; Lanzhou] and Chengtu [成都; Chengdu].'[18] This decision was made at a

---

[15] ABS Archives, Pearson, 'ABS Historical Essay #15, VII-F-2', 163–4, 166, 168, 223; BFBS Archives, BSA/C26/2, Minutes of a Meeting of the Overseas Administration Sub-Committee [hereafter: OASC] 'B', 16 October 1947; BFBS Archives, BSA/C26/3, Minutes of a Meeting of OASC 'B', 20 January 1949; ABS Archives, RG#1, Annual Reports, *One Hundred and Twenty-Seventh Annual Report of the American Bible Society* (1943), 201; George Henderson and David McGavin, *Bibles for China: An Account of Over 80 Years' Service by Two Bible Society Missionaries* (Edinburgh, 1969), 34.

[16] ABS Archives, RG#27 H-1-3, Foreign Agencies, 301-12-83, Hong Kong 1957–1964, Ralph Mortensen, 'China Bible House, 1949–1959'.

[17] Henderson and McGavin, *Bibles for China*, 34.

[18] BFBS Archives, BSA/D8/4/5/4, Minutes of the Meeting of the Executive Committee of the China Bible House, 10 November 1948; BFBS Archives, BSA/C26/3, Minutes of a Meeting of OASC 'B', 20 January 1949. It was reported that the plane also flew 'consignments of Scriptures' to Chongqing [重慶] and Kunming [昆明]: Edinburgh, Scottish Bible Society, Archives of the National Bible Society of Scotland [hereafter: NBSS Archives], *Forward in Unity: The Annual Report for 1948 of the National Bible Society of Scotland* (1949), 24. See also NBSS Archives, Letter from David McGavin to William C. Somerville, 3 December 1948. The materials of the archives of the NBSS are used with permission of the Scottish Bible Society, Edinburgh. Since the Scottish Bible Society does

time when John R. Temple, concurrently general secretary of the BFBS and the newly founded United Bible Societies, was visiting Shanghai in November 1948 as part of his final Far East tour. His 'wise words of counsel', for which the CBH's executive committee thanked him,[19] could have been a factor leading to the CBH's decision, as revealed in a letter written by Temple on his way to Hong Kong after visiting Shanghai:

> Many missionaries and business people are evacuating the country because of the Communist victories, and Shanghai itself is threatened. I was thankful to share with my colleagues the dangers: and *plan with them the sending of about 250,000 copies of the Scriptures to the threatened areas in planes flown to evacuate the missionaries.* Had I not been with them they would have hesitated to act in this way because of the expense. Hope the Committee [of the BFBS] will stand by me. It might be our last chance to get the Scriptures into Communist areas, and who knows how God can use them for the comfort and strengthening of His people in the hard days before them. They also may be used to convert many to the faith.[20]

Additionally, the CBH's standing committee decided at its meeting on 10 December to establish 'an auxiliary headquarters' in Hong Kong, 'as soon as conditions require, in order to ensure adequate printing of Scriptures, and to leave to the judgment of the Secretaries the decision of when to start.'[21] This decision was not surprising, as by the end of November 1948, the Communists had won the Liaoshen [遼瀋] campaign of the Chinese Civil War for control of Manchuria, while the Pingjin [平津] campaign was taking place in Peiping and

---

not have a catalogue of the NBSS Archives, no details can be provided as to how or where the archival materials of the NBSS cited in this article can be located in the NBSS Archives.

[19] BFBS Archives, BSA/D8/4/5/4, Minutes of the Meeting of the Executive Committee of the China Bible House, 10 November 1948. Temple attended the CBH's executive committee's meetings on 2 and 10 November as a guest.

[20] 'Copy of Dr. [John R.] Temple's Letter to Chairman of OASC 'B', 17th Nov[ember] 1948', in BFBS Archives, BSA/C26/3, China Enclosure (a) to Minutes of a Meeting of OASC 'B', 16 December 1948, emphasis added. According to McGavin, the cost of transportation for one full planeload of Chinese Bibles (weighing 6,600 pounds) to Peiping was £250, which 'may seem expensive' but 'is most reasonable', since 'a commercial plane with a similar load would cost three times as much': NBSS Archives, Letter from McGavin to Somerville, 3 December 1948.

[21] BFBS Archives, BSA/D8/4/5/4, Minutes of the Meeting of the Standing Committee of the China Bible House, 10 December 1948.

Tianjin, and the Huaihai [淮海] campaign in Xuzhou [徐州].[22] Given the proximity of Xuzhou to Nanjing [南京], the capital of Republican China, and Nanjing to Shanghai, if the Communists proved victorious in the Huaihai campaign, they would soon take over Shanghai, which could result in the closure of the CBH's headquarters.

Indeed, the idea of setting up an auxiliary headquarters in Hong Kong as a precautionary measure had been deliberated among the CBH's secretaries for some time. In a letter written on 9 December 1948 to William C. Somerville, the NBSS's general secretary, McGavin explained that he and Mortensen 'have been considering the advisability of arranging for printing to be done in Hongkong and it is felt that one of [them] ought to get down there to establish an auxiliary headquarters.' They also felt that 'it might be unwise to wait until the Communists, if they come, forbid us to continue further printing.'[23] Here McGavin and Mortensen shared a similar view with Temple, who believed that Hong Kong should be a base for Chinese Bible publishing and distribution if the Communists took over Shanghai. In a letter to William J. Platt, the BFBS's assistant general secretary, composed just two days before he died in Hong Kong on 30 November, Temple wrote:

> Two days after I had been in Shanghai my mind was made up to press for your taking hold of the China Field – the greatest job in Bible work … . But what if the Communists overrun China? … . The South will never be completely conquered by the Reds and we must have a base in Hong Kong with 2 or 3 hundred Gutzlaffs penetrating China – see G's story in [William] Canton's history [of the BFBS] … . I am sure it can be done, though it will cost money. If Shanghai falls to the Reds then I would urge that we find immediately a base in Hong Kong – the one stable secure place in the Far East … . Let us lead and fight the Reds with the 'Sword of the Spirit which is the Word of God'.[24]

---

[22] Hans van de Ven, *China at War: Triumph and Tragedy in the Emergence of the New China* (Cambridge, MA, 2017), 2. The Liaoshen, Pingjin and Huaihai campaigns were the three major military campaigns of the Chinese civil war.

[23] NBSS Archives, Letter from David McGavin to William C. Somerville, 9 December 1948. See also NBSS Archives, Letter from David McGavin to William C. Somerville, 25 November 1948.

[24] BFBS Archives, BSA/C26/3, Copy of Dr Temple's letter to Mr Platt, 27 November 1948. 'Gutzlaff' here refers to Karl Friedrich August Gützlaff (1803–51), an early Protestant missionary to China.

The three Bible societies' archival records, despite not stating explicitly their reasons for agreeing with the decision of the CBH's standing committee, hinted at why Hong Kong was considered as a suitable location for the CBH's auxiliary headquarters. As recorded in the minutes of the BFBS's Overseas Administration Sub-Committee 'B', which oversaw the society's work in China, of a meeting on 16 December 1948, Platt, who succeeded Temple as the society's general secretary, had had talks with Canon Henry August Wittenbach of the Church Missionary Society, who had been a prisoner of war in Hong Kong during the Japanese occupation of the city,[25] and with Harold Burgoyne Rattenbury of the Methodist Missionary Society. These two former China missionaries 'spoke of the advantages of Hongkong as a base, should the Communists' invasion envelop Shanghai and South China.' One of these advantages was the stability of the Hong Kong dollar, which was pegged to the pound sterling.[26] According to Wittenbach and Rattenbury, the Hong Kong dollar 'even in the Japanese occupation had been used, by underground channels, to support the Chinese Church on the mainland'.[27] This financial consideration reflected an earlier observation of William Shenton, a member of the sub-committee who retired from Hong Kong in 1936 after a legal career there.[28] Referring at the sub-committee's meeting on 20 May 1948 to discussions with friends who had recently returned to Britain from China, Shenton commented that 'the normal currency has been very largely superseded by Hongkong currency'.[29]

Another advantage of Hong Kong was its geographical location. In a letter to Arthur H. Wilkinson, another general secretary of the BFBS, dated 17 December 1948, McGavin indicated that Hong Kong was well-located for the Bible societies' work among the Chinese, suggesting that although printing in Hong Kong would cost more, the Bibles produced there would 'help to meet the need in southern areas

---

[25] Michael Poon, 'Introduction', in *Extract from H. A. Wittenbach's Report on his East Asia Tour 1953–1954*, online at: <http://anglicanhistory.org/asia/sea/wittenbach1953.htm>, accessed 9 September 2024.
[26] Tony Latter, *Hong Kong's Money: The History, Logic and Operation of the Currency Peg* (Hong Kong, 2007), 40, 43.
[27] BFBS Archives, BSA/C26/3, Minutes of a Meeting of OASC 'B', 16 December 1948.
[28] '"Good Old Days" In Hong Kong: Sir William Shenton Interviewed', *The Straits Times*, 11 April 1936, online at: <https://eresources.nlb.gov.sg/newspapers/digitised/article/straitstimes19360411-1.2.66>, accessed 9 September 2024.
[29] BFBS Archives, BSA/C26/2, Minutes of a Meeting of OASC 'B', 20 May 1948.

and in the many countries to the south from which come large orders for Chinese Scriptures'.[30] McGavin reiterated this view in a letter to I. C. Mawer, the BFBS's assistant secretary, a month later, in which he added that he expected to 'save something in shipping costs'.[31]

The availability of printing resources could also give Hong Kong an edge. Before the Chinese civil war, modern printing presses had already been available in Hong Kong.[32] Two notable examples of printing establishments there were the Hong Kong Printing Works of the Commercial Press, and that of the Chung Hwa Book Company, established in 1924 and 1933 respectively.[33] Indeed, in August 1949, the Hong Kong Printing Works of the Commercial Press was commended as 'a good printing plant' in a conversation between McGavin, Paul A. Collyer, the ABS's associate secretary, and Gilbert Darlington, the ABS's treasurer.[34] Also, it was not difficult for Hong Kong to have a supply of paper for Bible printing through import-ation, given that it was a port city. It is thus unsurprising that in late 1948, thirty tons of paper were ordered by the CBH from Sweden for shipment to Shanghai, but with the option of landing in Hong Kong.[35] In addition, as revealed in the report of McGavin's conversa-tion with Collyer and Darlington, Hong Kong had a supply of newsprint, a low-cost paper that could be used for printing cheap editions of the Chinese Bible for mass distribution.[36]

---

[30] BFBS Archives, BSA/D8/4/6/1, Extract of a letter from David McGavin to Arthur H. Wilkinson, dated 17 December 1948, received 29 December 1948. McGavin later reported to Platt that printing in Hong Kong 'costs anything from sixty per cent to one hundred per cent more than it does in Shanghai': BFBS Archives, BSA/D8/4/6/1, Letter from David McGavin to William J. Platt, 3 January 194[9] (incorrectly dated '1948').

[31] BFBS Archives, BSA/D8/4/6/5, Letter from David McGavin to I. C. Mawer, 17 January 1949.

[32] Christopher A. Reed, *Gutenberg in Shanghai: Chinese Print Capitalism, 1876–1937* (Vancouver, 2004), 26, 41–2, 159, 238–9.

[33] Sino United Publishing (Holdings) Limited, 'Corporate Profile', online at: <https://www.sup.com.hk/aboutus/history>, accessed 9 September 2024.

[34] ABS Archives, RG#27, 301-12-83, Foreign Agencies, G-1-6, 'Report of Conversation of David McGavin with P. A. Collyer and G. Darlington at Bible House, New York City, Aug[ust] 2, 1949'.

[35] BFBS Archives, BSA/D8/4/5/4, Minutes of the Meeting of the Standing Committee of the China Bible House, 10 December 1948.

[36] ABS Archives, RG#27, 301-12-83, Foreign Agencies, G-1-6, 'Report of Conversation of David McGavin with P. A. Collyer and G. Darlington at Bible House, New York City, Aug[ust] 2, 1949'; NBSS Archives, Letter from William C. Somerville to David McGavin, 22 June 1951.

Eventually, the CBH's executive committee decided that McGavin should go to Hong Kong 'for a period in order to start printing going there just in case work on the Shanghai presses should prove to be no longer possible'.[37] McGavin rather than Mortensen was sent to Hong Kong because 'it was felt that, since there were only two Westerners' in the CBH's national headquarters in Shanghai, and McGavin happened to be 'the British member of the staff', it would be better for him to proceed to Hong Kong.[38] McGavin travelled to Hong Kong in early January 1949 'to see what can be done and to prepare for the printing of the Scriptures in Hongkong',[39] setting up the CBH's 'auxiliary headquarters' there, which later came to be known as the 'Hongkong Emergency Office'.[40] At the CBH's executive committee meeting on 23 March 1949, McGavin reported that 'in view of the possible need for emergency headquarters in Hongkong early in January 1949, he had arranged for the use of the veranda of the Bible, Book and Tract Depot, Hongkong, as his temporary office'.[41] This arrangement was necessary because none of the Bible societies had 'any [office] accommodation of its own' in Hong Kong.[42] Moreover, he had placed an order for the printing of 500,000 Gospel portions in Hong Kong, in addition to receiving estimates for the printing of Bibles and New Testaments. Six cases of shells (paper matrices for printing) and three cases of zinc plates had also arrived in Hong Kong for safe keeping. The shells included those of the Mandarin Bible, the Wenli (literary Chinese) Bible, the Cantonese Bible, the New Testament in the Fuzhou [福州] dialect, and the New Testament in the Nasu language (the Eastern Yi [彝] language); while the zinc plates were all of the Mandarin Bible.[43]

---

[37] BFBS Archives, BSA/D8/4/6/5, Letter from Willliam C. Somerville to W[illiam] J. Platt, 10 January 1949.

[38] BFBS Archives, BSA/D8/4/6/1, Extract of a letter from McGavin to Wilkinson, dated 17 December 1948, received 29 December 1948.

[39] BFBS Archives, BSA/D8/4/6/1, Letter from McGavin to Platt, 3 January 194[9].

[40] BFBS Archives, BSA/D8/4/5/4, Minutes of the Meeting of the Executive Committee of the China Bible House, 24 February 1950.

[41] BFBS Archives, BSA/D8/4/5/4, Minutes of the Executive Committee Meeting of the China Bible House, 23 March 1949.

[42] BFBS Archives, BSA/D8/4/6/5, Letter from David McGavin to W[illiam] J. Platt, 12 January 1949.

[43] BFBS Archives, BSA/D8/4/5/4, Minutes of the Executive Committee Meeting of the China Bible House, 23 March 1949; 'Copy of Memo from Mr. D[avid] McGavin to Rev. W[illiam] J. Platt, 3rd Dec[ember] 1948', in BFBS Archives, BSA/C26/3, China Enclosure

The CBH's executive committee subsequently agreed to 'approve the purchase of substantial stocks of Bible paper wherever available at reasonable prices for the emergency printing of Bibles and New Testaments in Hongkong and/or Shanghai.'[44]

During the first year of its operation, the CBH's Hong Kong Emergency Office published the Gospels and the Acts of the Apostles in Chinese, as well as the complete Chinese Bible.[45] In early 1950, the CBH's executive committee noted that 'besides publishing Scriptures [it] was doing good work in arranging for the distribution of Scriptures to such places that could not be reached directly from China'.[46] McGavin reported on his work in Hong Kong for 1950 that 57,080 Bibles, 42,000 New Testaments, and one million portions of the Bible in Chinese were printed during the year ending 31 October 1950.[47] These books were dispatched not only to Guangzhou, where the CBH's South China agency was located, to supplement the CBH's work in that region,[48] but also to many other parts of the world to meet the needs of Chinese residents there, including Indo-China, Burma, Siam, Malaya, Indonesia, Japan, the United States of America, South America, the South Seas, and New Zealand. Korea was also among the destinations of the Chinese Scriptures published by the Emergency

(d) to Minutes of a Meeting of OASC 'B', 16 December 1948; BFBS Archives, BSA/D8/4/6/4, 'Packing List of Shipment from China Bible House, Shanghai, To: Bible Book & Tract Depot, Hongkong', enclosure to Letter from David McGavin to W[illiam] J. Platt, 14 February 1951.

[44] BFBS Archives, BSA/D8/4/5/4, Minutes of the Executive Committee Meeting of the China Bible House, 29 March 1949.

[45] According to McGavin, 'the first Bibles came off the press in mid-January' 1950: NBSS Archives, David McGavin, 'Hongkong "Emergency Office" 1950'. However, the title-verso page of edition 556 of the Chinese Bible printed in Hong Kong and published by the CBH indicates that the year of publication was 1949. This information has been ascertained from the copy kept in the Newberry Library, Chicago. It is possible that it was intended that the Bible edition concerned be published by the end of 1949 but that it was only actually possible to print it in early 1950. Nonetheless, two days before the end of 1949, McGavin wrote: 'The first supplies of the complete Bible ... to be printed in Hongkong are now being delivered': NBSS Archives, Letter from David McGavin to W. C. Somerville, 29 December 1949. This may explain the difference between McGavin's account and the front matter of edition 556.

[46] BFBS Archives, BSA/D8/4/5/4, Minutes of the Meeting of the Executive Committee of the China Bible House, 24 February 1950.

[47] NBSS Archives, David McGavin, 'Hongkong Emergency Office 1950'.

[48] NBSS Archives, Letter from David McGavin to W. C. Somerville, 14 August 1950.

Office: 'twenty-eight parcels containing 500 copies of Chinese New Testaments' were sent there for the use of the chaplain of the United Nations' Command in the Korean Campaign, Ivan L. Bennett, probably for work among Chinese prisoners.[49]

After the establishment of the People's Republic of China (PRC) in 1949, Hong Kong became an important source for supplying Chinese Bibles to Taiwan, as exporting them directly from Shanghai to Taiwan was no longer possible. Therefore, it is not surprising that an order for printing 100,000 Chinese New Testaments was placed by the CBH's Hong Kong Emergency Office for Taiwan in early 1951, while a quarter of a million copies of the Gospel of John were shipped to the island for 'the special work being done there by the Youth For Christ Team and the Every Creature Crusade'.[50]

The Chinese Scriptures published by the Hong Kong Emergency Office bore the imprint 'China Bible House'. This indicated its status as a branch of the CBH.[51] However, 1951 witnessed the publication of the first Chinese Bible with the imprint 'Hongkong Bible House',[52] which indicated the beginning of a new era for the Emergency Office.

---

[49] NBSS Archives, McGavin, 'Hongkong Emergency Office 1950'; McGavin, 'Hongkong Bible House', 152–3, at 153.

[50] NBSS Archives, Letter from David McGavin to W. C. Somerville, 28 March 1951. In addition, special orders of the Chinese New Testament had been printed and sent to Taiwan 'to aid the Evangelistic Campaign among Chinese soldiers' the previous year: NBSS Archives, McGavin, 'Hongkong Emergency Office 1950'.

[51] The strong connection between the CBH and its Hong Kong emergency office is manifested by the procedure adopted for the latter in 1950. First, all official invoices were issued by the CBH, Shanghai. Second, records of stock were kept in a series of record books, stock ledgers, receipts and issues journals, cash and bank records, and forms of Scriptures issued. Third, weekly reports were made to the CBH's Shanghai headquarters on the basis of the above records kept in Hong Kong: BFBS Archives, BSA/D8/4/5/4, Minutes of the Thirty First Meeting of the Administrative Committee of the China Bible House, 22 March 1950.

[52] According to the Bible publishing records in the Archives of the Hong Kong Bible Society, the first book published with the imprint 'Hongkong Bible House' was an edition of the Chinese-English New Testament, known as 'Edition 1001'. The first complete Chinese Bible printed under this imprint was 'Edition 1002', which contained a complete translation of the Chinese (Mandarin) Union Version. Hong Kong, Archives of the Hong Kong Bible Society, 'Edition Numbers', 28 June 1951–7 July 1958. This archival material is used with permission of the Hong Kong Bible Society. Since the Hong Kong Bible Society does not have a catalogue of its archives, no details can be provided of how or where this archival material can be located in its archives.

From an Emergency Office to the Bible Societies' Sole Agency for Chinese Bible Publishing and Distribution

Although the Korean War, which began on 25 June 1950, was originally a military conflict between North and South Korea, security concerns – and specifically its fear of a growing military threat from the United States – led the PRC to enter the war in October-November 1950.[53] As the war unfolded, the Communist Chinese government accelerated the implementation of its policy aimed at purging Western-imperialist influences from China – and thus from Chinese Christianity – in order to stabilize the nascent regime.[54] The consequent political pressure led to the severance of the CBH's relationship with the three foreign Bible societies and thus to the end of its foreign financial assistance. In 1951, the CBH was taken over by a Chinese board of directors; by that spring, all the CBH's foreign staff had withdrawn except Mortensen, who failed to secure an exit permit from the Communist Chinese government and remained in Shanghai until January 1953.[55] The CBH's board decided at its meeting on 14 March 1951 'in order to realise in their best effort the new movement of self-support', to 'receive from the year 1951 no more contributions from friends of the American Bible Society'. This was followed by its decision in May to 'cut completely the relationship with the U.S.A. and to decline acceptance of the £5,000 remitted by the British & Foreign Bible Society through the Kincheng Bank', which 'will be reported to the Government Bureaus concerned in order to express the Board of Directors' strong support' to the

---

[53] Hao Yufan and Zhai Zhihai, 'China's Decision to Enter the Korean War: History Revisited', *The China Quarterly* 121 (1990), 94–115, at 115.

[54] See 劉建平 [Liu Jianping], 紅旗下的十字架：新中國成立初期中共對基督教、天主教的政策演變及其影響 (1949–1955) [*Hongqi xia de shizijia: xin Zhongguo chengli chuqi Zhonggong dui Jidujiao, Tianzhujiao de zhengce yanbian ji qi yingxiang (1949–1955)*; *The Cross Under the Red Flag: The Policy Changes of the Chinese Communist Party Towards Protestantism and Catholicism and its Impact in the Early PRC (1949–1955)*] (Hong Kong, 2012); Fuk-tsang Ying, 'The CPC's Policy on Protestant Christianity, 1949–1957: An Overview and Assessment', *Journal of Contemporary China* 23/89 (2014), 884–901. For information about the CPC's implementation of its policy of aiming to purge Western-imperialist influences in other areas, see, for example, Jack Neubauer, 'Adopting Revolution: The Chinese Communist Revolution and the Politics of Global Humanitarianism', *Modern China* 47 (2021), 598–627.

[55] ABS Archives, Pearson, 'ABS Historical Essay #15, VII-F-2', 178–9; Roe, *A History of the British and Foreign Bible Society, 1905–1954*, 360.

Communist Chinese government for its stance against the United States in the context of the Korean War.[56]

Moreover, the CBH intended to sever its connection with the Hong Kong Emergency Office in May 1951. Baen Lee wrote to McGavin on 14 May 1951, informing him that 'it is the intention of the Board to have your office entirely separated from the C.B.H.' Lee indicated that at the board meeting on 11 May 'discussions were made as to how the Hongkong office may be made independent of China because the Board feels that close relationship at the present time is undesirable', although the minutes do not mention such discussions. He asked McGavin whether it was possible for the Emergency Office 'to become an agency of the BFBS, NBSS, or such organisation', suggesting that it would be 'much more convenient' for McGavin to 'take care of other areas than China for the supply of Chinese Bibles and Scriptures'. He also proposed that if the Emergency Office, after being separated from the CBH, received orders of Bibles for the overseas Chinese but could not supply them, it could order them from the CBH 'by paying cash', and the CBH 'can export such Scriptures as ordered upon the receipt of the remittance, especially earmarked for the purchase of Scriptures'.[57] A subsequent letter from Lee to McGavin, which was received by the latter in early June, explicitly requested that 'it is hoped that in the future you will change your letter heads ... . This will avoid the difficulty of misunderstanding by outside people'.[58] The separation was just a matter of time.

By the end of June 1951, all three Bible societies had reached a consensus that the name of the Emergency Office would be changed to the HKBH, which was originally suggested by McGavin as an unofficial name.[59] The HKBH was later officially confirmed as a joint agency of the three Bible societies under the BFBS's administration,

[56] BFBS Archives, BSA/D8/4/5/4, Minutes of a Special Meeting of the Board of Directors of the China Bible House, 14 March 1951; and Minutes of the Meeting of the Board of Directors of the China Bible House, 11 May 1951.

[57] NBSS Archives, Copy of Letter from Baen Lee to David McGavin, 14 May 1951; BFBS Archives, BSA/D8/4/5/4, Minutes of the Meeting of the Meeting of the Board of Directors of the China Bible House, 11 May 1951.

[58] BFBS Archives, BSA/D8/4/6/1, Letter from David McGavin to W. J. Platt, 6 June 1951.

[59] BFBS Archives, BSA/D8/4/6/1, Letters from David McGavin to W. J. Platt, 6 June 1951 and 27 June 1951; Letter from W. J. Platt to David McGavin, 18 June 1951; Letter from William C. Somerville to William J. Platt, 20 June 1951; and Letter from Paul A. Collyer to David McGavin, 2 July 1951.

being financially supported by them: the ABS and the BFBS each contributed forty-five per cent of the funding, and the remaining ten per cent came from the NBSS.[60] As indicated by the minutes of the NBSS's board meeting quoted by Somerville in a letter to Platt dated 11 July 1951, the renaming of the Emergency Office resulted from the Bible societies' acceptance of the CBH's recommendation that the Emergency Office should no longer be reckoned as part of the CBH.[61] The change of the Emergency Office's status could be understood as an outcome of mutual understanding, rather than a forced action due to the CBH's unilateral decision. Strictly speaking, the HKBH was not established as a successor to the CBH, as the CBH still operated at least till the end of the 1950s.[62] The HKBH's establishment should therefore not be regarded as a result of a move by the CBH from Shanghai to Hong Kong.[63]

The Korean War contributed to the renaming of the CBH's Hong Kong Emergency Office as the HKBH, which marked the office's beginning as the three Bible societies' sole agency for Chinese Bible publishing and distribution. However, it also gave rise to the possibility

---

[60] NBSS Archives, Letter from David McGavin to William C. Somerville, 4 July 1951; and Letter from William C. Somerville to William J. Platt, 11 July 1951. In 1955, the NBSS increased its share to one-third. Thus, each of the three Bible societies had an equal share in the HKBH: NBSS Archives, Letter from William C. Somerville to Laton Holmgren, 7 March 1955; and Letter from William C. Somerville to Douglas Lancashire, 7 March 1955.

[61] NBSS Archives, Letter from Somerville to Platt, 11 July 1951.

[62] ABS Archives, RG#27 H-1-3, Foreign Agencies, 301-12-83, Hong Kong 1957–1964, Mortensen, 'China Bible House, 1949–1959'. It has also been suggested that the CBH most probably came to an end during the Cultural Revolution: '中華聖經公會' ['Zhonghua Shengjing Gonghui'; 'Chinese Bible Society'], in 基督教大辭典 [Jidujiao da cidian; The Dictionary of Christianity], ed. 丁光訓 [Ding Guangxun] and 金魯賢 [Jin Luxian] (Shanghai, 2010), 841.

[63] Indeed, the suitability of relocating the CBH's headquarters to Hong Kong was questioned. For example, shortly before the CBH's standing committee decided to establish an auxiliary headquarters in Hong Kong, Somerville wrote to McGavin that 'it would be unwise to centre China Bible House in Hongkong itself as that is not China.' Somerville felt that anything centred in Hong Kong 'would be British and it would be "foreign" to the Chinese.' To him, Guangzhou, where the South China agency of the CBH was located, would be a much better option, 'if matters could be so arranged'. However, McGavin replied to him that centring the CBH's work in Guangzhou 'is hardly possible' simply because printing facilities there were 'very poor' and 'it is not possible to have our class of work done there': NBSS Archives, Letter from William C. Somerville to David McGavin, 2 December 1948; Letter from David McGavin to William C. Somerville, 17 December 1948.

that Hong Kong might be 'liberated' by the Communist Chinese government owing to the United Kingdom's involvement in the Korean War. This was one reason why McGavin suggested the advisability of shipping the shells and plates of the Chinese Bible from Hong Kong to some other place for safe-keeping.[64] However, the decision-makers at the headquarters of the three Bible societies had a more optimistic outlook for Hong Kong than McGavin. Eric North, the ABS's general secretary, wrote: 'I find it very difficult to think that anything would happen to Hong Kong until after something critical has happened about Formosa'.[65] Although he also suggested that duplicate sets of plates of the Chinese Bible could be sent to Japan for storage and, if necessary, printing, North felt that the situation in Hong Kong was unlikely to 'increase in difficulty unless British strategy involved negotiations for transfer of Hong Kong to Communist China', which he 'would really doubt'.[66] Platt of the BFBS, who agreed with North that Japan would be the best place for this purpose, also felt that 'things will settle down and there will be no incident beyond Korea'.[67] Somerville of the NBSS was less optimistic than his English and American counterparts, but still told McGavin that his feeling and hope were that 'there will be no war and that printing may be possible in Hongkong for a long time to come.'[68] Nonetheless, for safe keeping, two sets of shells for printing the Mandarin Bible and one for the Mandarin-English New Testament were shipped from Hong Kong to Canada, while three sets of shells for printing the Bible, the New Testament, and the Gospels and Acts in Mandarin were shipped to Japan.[69]

---

[64] BFBS Archives, BSA/C26/3, Minutes of a Meeting of OASC 'B', 22 February 1951; BFBS Archives, D8/4/6/4, Letter from David McGavin to W. J. Platt, 18 January 1951.
[65] BFBS Archives, BSA/D8/4/6/4, Letter from Eric M. North to W. J. Platt, 26 January 1951. Taiwan was at that time known as Formosa.
[66] BFBS Archives, BSA/D8/4/6/4, Letter from Eric M. North to W. J. Platt, 9 March 1951.
[67] BFSB Archives, BSA/D8/4/6/4, Letter from W. J. Platt to David McGavin, 6 February 1951.
[68] BFBS Archives, BSA/D8/4/6/4, Letter from William C. Somerville to David McGavin, 24 January 1951.
[69] BFBS Archives, BSA/D8/4/6/4, Letter from David McGavin to W. J. Platt, 27 August 1951; Letter from Ian H. D. Findlay to the Secretary of the BFBS in Canada (J. A. R. Tingley), 10 October 1951; Letter from J. C. F. Robertson to J. T. Watson, 1 October 1958.

Like the Emergency Office, the HKBH's chief concern in its early years was to print and distribute Chinese Bibles to Taiwan and the overseas Chinese, the majority of whom lived in South East Asia.[70] The printing of these Bibles was mainly done by the Printing Works of the Commercial Press, and sometimes by that of the Chung Hwa Book Company.[71] The former even allowed free storage of the plates and book stock of the HKBH.[72] As the BFBS reported in its periodical *The Bible in the World*, 'over a million copies of the Scriptures in Chinese' were printed in Hong Kong during 1951 for use among Chinese populations outside China.[73]

The work priorities of the HKBH could be due to three factors. First, opportunities arose from the influx of Chinese immigrants in countries neighbouring mainland China. For example, in the few months after the Communist takeover of China, more than twenty million Chinese left for Hong Kong, Taiwan and South East Asian countries. This, together with the fact that South East Asia was a major geographical destination for Chinese evangelicals as missionaries at that time,[74] gave rise to great demand for Chinese Bibles for special campaigns of evangelism, such as those among refugees and Chinese soldiers.

Second, the Korean War led to a prohibition on the importing of Chinese Bibles from Hong Kong to mainland China, which had previously been possible and had allowed the Hong Kong Emergency Office to supplement the work of the CBH. For example, according to a report from McGavin in November 1951, the CBH had ordered the printing of two editions of a cheap newsprint Chinese Bible to be sent

[70] ABS Archives, RG#27 H-1-3, Foreign Agencies, 301-12-83, Hong Kong 1957–1964, Mortensen, 'China Bible House, 1949–1959'.

[71] Archives of the Hong Kong Bible Society, 'Edition Numbers', 28 June 1951–7 July 1958.

[72] ABS Archives, RG#1, Annual Reports, *One Hundred and Thirty-Eighth Annual Report of the American Bible Society* (1954), 311; BFBS Archives, BSA/C28, Minutes of Asia Sub-Committee, 16 March 1967.

[73] BFBS Archives, BSA/G1/3/3, 'News and Notes: Hongkong Staff', in *The Bible in the World: Record of the Work of the British and Foreign Bible Society* (March–April 1953), 31. These figures correspond to those provided by McGavin, who reported that 'during the year he has seen through the press 65,000 Bibles, 200,000 Testaments and 800,000 Portions, mainly in Chinese, produced with funds supplied by the three Bible Societies': NBSS Archives, *The National Bible Society of Scotland Annual Report for 1951* (1952), 13.

[74] Joshua Dao Wei Sim, 'Making the South Seas a "Chinese" Mission Field: Chinese Evangelical Missionaries to Southeast Asia, 1920s to 1950s', *Mission Studies* 39 (2022), 304–30, at 305.

into mainland China. Unfortunately, after 1,500 copies were forwarded, the CBH had to request the HKBH to 'send no further supplies' until the CBH received an import permit from the Communist Chinese government. Once it became clear that the CBH could not expect to receive such a permit, it agreed that the HKBH should 'dispose of the books wherever they are required'.[75] Given the Bible societies' policy that they should not operate contrary to the laws of any country, the HKBH had to target the Chinese-speaking populations outside mainland China.[76]

Nevertheless, the HKBH initially continued to be able to do what Baen Lee proposed in the aforementioned letter from him to McGavin on 14 May 1951, namely ordering supplies of the Chinese Bible from the CBH, by which it provided additional funds for the CBH's work.[77] For instance, reflecting its position as a Bible supplier for the overseas Chinese, the HKBH ordered supplies of certain luxury Chinese Bible editions from the CBH in 1951 since, whereas these editions had 'little or no sale' in mainland China, there was 'a fair demand for these more expensive books' outside China, while the HKBH at that time restricted itself 'to the production of "Missionary" editions', as its priority was 'to meet the need from many quarters'.[78] However, in early 1954, the Communist Chinese government prohibited the export of Chinese Bibles since this was deemed to reflect the CBH's dependence on a foreign organization. Although the ban was lifted shortly afterwards, Douglas Lancashire, McGavin's successor, thought it unwise to continue importing Bibles from mainland China.[79]

A third factor was the sole agency rights of the Bible, Book and Tract Depot (BBTD) for the distribution of Chinese Bibles in Hong Kong before 1955, which meant that during its early years, the HKBH 'was unable to sell Scriptures direct to any person or organization in the

---

[75] BFBS Archives, BSA/D8/4/6/5, Letter from David McGavin to W. C. Somerville, 2 November 1951.
[76] Leslie Howsam and Scott McLaren, 'Producing the Text: Production and Distribution of Popular Editions of the Bible', in John Riches, ed., *The New Cambridge History of the Bible*, 4: *From 1750 to Present* (Cambridge, 2015), 49–82, at 75.
[77] ABS Archives, Pearson, 'ABS Historical Essay #15, VII-F-2', 185.
[78] BFBS Archives, BSA/D8/4/6/5, Letter from McGavin to Somerville, 2 November 1951.
[79] NBSS Archives, Letter from Douglas Lancashire to J. T. Watson, 11 February 1954; ABS Archives, Pearson, 'ABS Historical Essay #15, VII-F-2', 185.

Colony'.[80] An independent and interdenominational body, the BBTD was solely a distribution agency for Bibles and Bible portions issued by Bible societies, and Christian books and tracts in Chinese and English.[81] In 1948, a sole agency agreement had been drawn up between the CBH and the BBTD, and the BFBS obtained the BBTD's shares in 1949.[82] In November 1954, the BBTD decided to relinquish its sole agency rights, which allowed the HKBH to completely take over Chinese Bible distribution in Hong Kong in 1955 and to develop its work in the city.[83] Nonetheless, special business discount arrangements were continued in view of the BBTD's long-standing service to the Bible societies: the discount on Bibles supplied to the BBTD was increased from thirty per cent to thirty-five per cent after it relinquished the sole agency rights, while the discount to other Christian bookshops in Hong Kong was fixed at twenty-five per cent.[84]

CONCLUSION

Circumstances make the marginal begin to be central. Providing insights into a hitherto understudied aspect of the history of the British and American Bible societies, this study has attested to what Craig Browne and Philip Mar suggested about Hong Kong's peripherality: 'Hong Kong demonstrates that the periphery is not a static category and that the periphery can undergo major transitions in relation to a

[80] ABS Archives, RG#1, Annual Reports, *One Hundred and Thirty-Eighth Annual Report of the American Bible Society* (1954), 311.
[81] Milton T. Stauffer, Tsinforn C. Wong and M. Gardner Tewksbury, *The Christian Occupation of China: A General Survey of the Numerical Strength and Geographical Distributon* [sic] *of the Christian Forces in China, Made by the Special Committee on Survey and Occupation, China Continuation Committee, 1918–1921* (Shanghai, 1922), 451.
[82] BFBS Archives, BSA/C26/3, Minutes of a Meeting of OASC 'B', 20 October 1949; ABS Archives, RG#1, Annual Reports, *One Hundred and Thirty-Eighth Annual Report of the American Bible Society* (1954), 311; BFBS Archives, BSA/D8/4/6/4, 'Report on Hongkong & Formosa'.
[83] BFBS Archives, BSA/D8/4/6/4, Letter from Douglas Lancashire to W. J. Platt, 6 November 1954; BFBS Archives, BSA/C26/4, Minutes of a Meeting of OASC 'B', 18 November 1954. The BFBS's general committee passed the resolution on 6 December 1954: BFBS Archives, BSA/D8/4/6/4, Letter from J. T. Watson to Douglas Lancashire, 9 December 1954.
[84] ABS Archives, Pearson, 'ABS Historical Essay #15, VII-F-2', 186.

dominant center.'[85] Hong Kong, a location for a mission station in South China, was considered of relatively little weight in Chinese Protestant Christianity before the Communist takeover of China. Nevertheless, this study has shown that the British colony began to emerge as a world centre for Chinese Protestant Bible publishing and distribution at the turn of the 1940s and 1950s, thanks to two decisive wars for modern China, which led to the birth of the CBH's Hong Kong Emergency Office and subsequently the HKBH, through which the BFBS, the ABS and the NBSS maintained their presence among Chinese-speaking people, so as to continue their century-long work of Chinese Bible publishing and distribution. This reflects Hong Kong's role in Chinese Protestant Christianity in the 1950s: thanks to its peripheral autonomy as a British colony separated from the PRC, Hong Kong became a place for Western missionary societies and missionaries to continue to implement their visions for China.[86]

Moreover, the Chinese in China had been regarded as the central group and the overseas Chinese the relatively marginal group in the context of the Protestant mission effort among Chinese-speaking populations. Printing and distributing Chinese Bibles to Taiwan and the overseas Chinese as the HKBH's chief concern in its early years reminds us that since the PRC was inaccessible to Western Protestant missionary societies or denominations, the overseas Chinese, who used to be the marginal, began to be made central.

McGavin, who oversaw the Emergency Office's establishment, wrote to Platt shortly after its becoming the HKBH in 1952, expressing his view that 'it is a fact that, for supplying Scriptures to Chinese outside of China, the Hongkong Bible House has replaced the China Bible House.'[87] Indeed, to McGavin, the HKBH's significance was more than that, since its work 'is not that of a normal Bible Society Agency but is rather that of a manufacturing centre, producing Scriptures in various languages for the whole of South East Asia and even further afield',[88] as attested by its publication of not only the

---

[85] Craig Browne and Philip Mar, 'Hong Kong as a Dual Periphery', in Arthur Bueno, Mariana Teixeira and David Strecker, eds, *De-Centering Global Sociology: The Peripheral Turn in Social Theory and Research* (New York, 2023), 96–110, at 96.

[86] Ying, *An Introduction to the Study of the History of Hong Kong Christianity*, 82, 173–5.

[87] BFBS Archives, BSA/D8/4/6/1, Letter from David McGavin to W. J. Platt, 12 September 1952.

[88] BFBS Archives, BSA/D8/4/6/5, Letter from McGavin to Somerville, 2 November 1951.

Chinese Bible but also, for instance, the New Testament in the Lisu language and the Gospels and Acts in Vietnamese.[89] According to Atalanta Myerson, by the early 1960s, it was evident that Hong Kong was going to evolve into a major international printing centre.[90] As the process of such evolution overlapped with the later development of the HKBH, it is reasonable to ask whether the latter was among those contributing to the former. A foundation for further research into this question has been laid by this study, which itself has offered insights into the Christian dimension of the emergence of Hong Kong's global relevance in the Cold War era.

---

[89] McGavin, 'Hongkong Bible House', 152–3.
[90] Atalanta Myerson, 'East Asia', in William Roger Louis, ed., *The History of Oxford University Press*, 3: *1896 to 1970* (Oxford, 2013), 693–720, at 712.

Life on the Margins: The Clandestine Ukrainian Greek Catholic Clergy in the Soviet Union (1946–89)

Kateryna Budz

University of Edinburgh

During the Second World War, the West Ukrainian region of Eastern Galicia came under Soviet rule. In 1946, the Stalinist regime banned the church of most Ukrainians in the region, the Ukrainian Greek Catholic Church (UGCC), by 'reuniting' it with the Russian Orthodox Church (ROC). Whereas most Greek Catholic clergymen joined the ROC under state pressure, the opponents of 'reunion' endured arrests and other forms of persecution. The church of several million believers became a persecuted religious minority on the margins of Soviet society. Upon their return from the Gulag in the mid-1950s, the 'non-reunited' Greek Catholic priests usually encountered numerous bureaucratic obstacles when trying to settle down and secure their livelihoods. Based on archival and oral history material, this article focuses on the clandestine clergy's experiences of social marginalization.

In January 1980, a group of Ukrainian Greek Catholics from the village of Mshana in Western Ukraine wrote a document entitled 'The Life of the Ukrainian Catholic Church', which eventually reached its intended audience in the West.[1] The letter began with a

School of Divinity, New College, University of Edinburgh, Mound Place, Edinburgh, EH1 2LX. E-mail: katebudz@gmail.com.

[1] Quoted according to Ivan Hvat', 'The Ukrainian Catholic Church, the Vatican and the Soviet Union during the Pontificate of Pope John Paul II', *Religion in Communist Lands* 11 (1983), 264–94, at 283. An abridged and revised version of this document was also published in Serge Keleher, *Passion and Resurrection – the Greek Catholic Church in Soviet Ukraine, 1939–1989* (Lviv, 1993), 218–32. Galicia is a historic name of the region, whereas Soviets generally used the term 'Western Ukraine' or 'Western Oblasts of Ukraine'. For the purposes of this article, the terms 'Eastern Galicia', 'Galicia' and 'Western Ukraine' will be used interchangeably to refer to the territories of the former Galician metropolis that came under Soviet rule.

Studies in Church History 61 (2025), 563–585 © The Author(s), 2025. Published by Cambridge University Press on behalf of the Ecclesiastical History Society. This is an Open Access article, distributed under the terms of the Creative Commons Attribution licence (http://creativecommons.org/licenses/by/4.0), which permits unrestricted re-use, distribution and reproduction, provided the original article is properly cited.
doi:10.1017/stc.2024.53

brief description of how the Ukrainian Greek Catholic Church had been banned in the Soviet Union, from the arrests of the hierarchy in April 1945 to the illegal 'L'viv *sobor*' in March 1946.[2] By declaring the 'reunification' of the Ukrainian Greek Catholic Church with the Russian Orthodox Church, the Lviv pseudo-council signified the official liquidation of the UGCC.[3] Despite the fact that this pseudo-council declared 'the return of the Ukrainian people to the bosom of the Orthodox Church', wrote the authors of the document, some of the married clergy refused to repudiate the pope and endured state persecution as a result.[4] The document then outlined the situation of the recalcitrant clergy at the time when it was written:

> The priests of the Ukrainian Catholic Church – both those who returned from exile and the newly ordained, who acquired the necessary knowledge and wisdom in conspiratorial conditions, all of them, to this day, have no official registration to carry out pastoral work. However, all are 'registered' for persecution. For carrying out any aspect of pastoral work – confession, burial, etc., a priest is fined 50 roubles every time (at a time when the average monthly wage is approximately 70–90 roubles), and he is threatened with a prison sentence of seven years for carrying out pastoral work. For example, a priest named Dydych was fined 50 roubles three times for conducting burials. From time to time every priest is called to the office of religious affairs … and is ordered to sign a document stating that he will not carry out any pastoral work. Of course such a priest will never sign, but because of this he is punished: some lose their residence permits, some are fined or dismissed from work. Moreover, all priests who are not of pensionable age have to work somewhere in a government institution. The majority work as watchmen, stokers, yard-keepers or odd-job men.[5]

---

[2] Hvat', 'The Ukrainian Catholic Church', 281. 'The Ukrainian Catholic Church' is a common designation of the UGCC in diaspora, but it was also widely used by the Greek Catholics in the Soviet Union.

[3] Since no Greek Catholic bishop participated in the council, its decision was canonically void.

[4] Ibid. 281–2. At the same time, the article alleges that, unlike bishops and monks, most married clergymen, out of fear for their families, joined the Orthodox Church: ibid. 282.

[5] Ibid. 283.

Indeed, after March 1946, the Ukrainian Greek Catholic Church became a persecuted religious minority, with no legal status. The believers from Mshana captured this marginalization in their collective letter: 'We, Ukrainian Catholics have no rights. We do not exist in the Soviet Union, despite the fact that article 52 of the new Constitution of the USSR guarantees citizens of the USSR the right to profess any religion and to perform religious worship.'[6]

This article explores how the clergy of this supposedly 'non-existent' church described their experiences of social marginalization, that is, state discrimination based on their refusal to 'reunite', and navigated the challenges of life in Soviet society. It draws on both official Soviet documents and sources produced by the members of the Greek Catholic underground. Often contradicting each other, these two types of historical evidence contribute to a more comprehensive understanding of what it meant to be a clandestine Ukrainian Greek Catholic priest in the Soviet Union.

THE LIQUIDATION OF THE UKRAINIAN GREEK CATHOLIC CHURCH IN EASTERN GALICIA

The idea of a 'return' to Orthodoxy, declared by the Lviv pseudo-council in March 1946, referred to the foundation of the Greek Catholic Church at the Union of Brest in 1596. At that time, some Orthodox bishops of the Kyiv metropolis in the Polish-Lithuanian commonwealth switched allegiance from Constantinople to Rome. The Uniate Church, as it was then known, accepted Catholic dogmas but retained the specifics of the Eastern church, such as the Byzantine ('Greek') rite, married clergy and the Julian calendar.

As a result of the partitions of the Polish-Lithuanian common-wealth in the late eighteenth century, the territories with a Uniate presence were divided between the Roman Catholic Austrian empire and the Orthodox Russian empire. The church thrived under the Habsburgs, but was abolished by the Romanovs. The Russian tsars liquidated the Uniate Church in three steps: in 1795, 1839 and 1875.[7] Most notably, the Council of Polotsk (1839) under Tsar Nicholas I

---

[6] Ibid.
[7] Adam DeVille and Daniel Galadza, 'The "Lviv Sobor" of 1946: Perspectives on and Challenges to a Common Narrative', in eidem, eds, *The 'Lviv Sobor' of 1946 and its Aftermath: Towards Truth and Reconciliation* (Boston, MA, 2023), 1–16, at 7.

declared the 'reunification' of the Uniate Church with the Russian Orthodox Church.

Following the demise of Austria-Hungary and a short period of Ukrainian statehood in 1918–19, the Council of Ambassadors of the Entente officially recognized Polish claims to the territory of Eastern Galicia in March 1923. During the inter-war period, the region constituted the easternmost part of the Second Polish Republic. In September 1939, the Red Army entered Eastern Galicia under the slogan of 'liberation'. A period of German occupation followed, from 1941 to 1944, during which the church was allowed to operate and received back the property confiscated earlier by the Soviets. In summer 1944, however, the Soviets regained control of the region, which remained a part of the USSR until 1991. Soon after their return to power, the Soviet authorities started the liquidation of the Ukrainian Greek Catholic Church that united most Ukrainians in Eastern Galicia. As of 1938, the UGCC in Galicia, which consisted of the Lviv archeparchy, Stanyslaviv eparchy, Peremyshl eparchy and the apostolic administration of Lemkivshchyna, had 2,387 parishes, 2,352 eparchial and 143 monastic clergy, namely Basilians, Redemptorists and Studites.[8] In 1943, the number of believers was estimated at 3.6 million.[9]

The UGCC presented a hindrance to Soviet plans for the smooth integration of the newly annexed territories: Kathryn David views the abolition of the church as 'part of the process of making Galicians into Soviet Ukrainians'.[10] In Soviet Ukraine, the church was liquidated through the forced merger with the Russian Orthodox Church, first in Eastern Galicia (1946) and then in Transcarpathia (1949).[11] Greek Catholics were also forced into Orthodoxy in such Eastern bloc countries as Romania (1948) and Czechoslovakia (1950).

---

[8] Богдан Боцюрків [Bohdan Bociurkiw], *Українська Греко-Католицька Церква і Радянська держава (1939–1950)* [*Ukrains'ka Hreko-Katolyts'ka Tserkva i Radians'ka derzhava (1939–1950)*; *The Ukrainian Greek-Catholic Church and the Soviet State (1939–1950)*] (Lviv, 2005), 24.

[9] Ibid. 25.

[10] Kathryn David, 'Galician Catholics into Soviet Orthodox: Religion and Postwar Ukraine', *Nationalities Papers* 46 (2018), 290–300, at 290.

[11] In his pioneering study, Bohdan Bociurkiw explored in detail the abolition of the UGCC in Galicia and Transcarpathia. His book appeared in English in 1996: Bohdan R. Bociurkiw, *The Ukrainian Greek-Catholic Church and the Soviet State (1939–1950)* (Edmonton and Toronto, 1996).

The abolition of the UGCC in Galicia, which culminated in the Lviv pseudo-council of March 1946, was thoroughly planned. In April 1945, the Soviets launched a defamation campaign against the UGCC in Galicia, arresting the head of the church, Metropolitan Iosyf Slipyi, and other hierarchs who had remained in Soviet territory. A Greek Catholic priest, Havryil Kostelnyk, who was known for his anti-Vatican views, became the head of the newly created Initiative Group for the reunification of the Greek Catholic Church with the Orthodox Church. In cooperation with the Soviet security organs, Fr Kostelnyk conducted a 'reunion' campaign, convincing many clergy to join the Initiative Group. As of March 1946, 997 out of 1,270 Greek Catholic priests present in Galicia had joined the group.[12] At the same time, in early September 1946, 191 priests remained in opposition.[13] The Greek Catholic priests who refused to join the Russian Orthodox Church often endured long sentences in the Soviet labour camps.

The process of the liquidation of the UGCC has received a significant amount of scholarly attention, with a major focus on the Soviet state's repressive policy towards the church.[14] Some scholars have also dealt with the personal experiences of Greek Catholic clergy during the period of the post-war abolition of the UGCC. Thus, historian Svitlana Hurkina studied the fates of the Greek Catholic clergy of the Lviv archeparchy, looking at their convictions and their attitudes towards the Soviet state.[15] Nataliia Dmytryshyn compared the strategies of survival in Soviet society of four generations of underground

---

[12] Moscow, Государственный архив Российской Федерации (ГАРФ, м. Москва) [Gosudarstvennyi arkhiv Rossiiskoi Federatsii; State Archive of the Russian Federation; hereafter: GARF], f. 6991, op. 1, d. 33, l. 192. When citing sources from state archives, the contractions correspond to the Russian- or Ukrainian-language equivalents of collection, inventory, file and folio. Unless stated otherwise, translations from Ukrainian and Russian are my own.

[13] Київ, Галузевий Державний архів Служби безпеки України (ГДА СБУ, м. Київ) [Haluzevyi derzhavnyi arkhiv Sluzhby bezpeky Ukrainy; Sectoral State Archive of the Security Service of Ukraine; hereafter: HDA SBU], f. 16, op. 1, spr. 578, ark. 249.

[14] A detailed overview of the historiography relating to the abolition of the UGCC is provided, for example, in Іван Мищак [Ivan Myshchak], 'Ліквідація Греко-Католицької Церкви в Україні в повоєнні роки: історіографія' ['Likvidatsiia Hreko-Katolytskoi Tserkvy v Ukraini u povoienni roky: istoriohrafiia'; 'Liquidation of the Greek Catholic Church in Ukraine in the Postwar Years: Historiography'], *Історіографічні дослідження в Україні* [*Istoriohrafichni doslidzhennia v Ukraini; Historiographical Studies in Ukraine*] 17 (Kyiv, 2007), 270–87.

[15] Світлана Гуркіна [Svitlana Hurkina], 'Дві долі: греко-католицьке духовенство і радянська влада' ['Dvi doli: hreko-katolyts'ke dukhovenstvo i radians'ka vlada'; 'Two

Greek Catholic clergy.[16] This article explores the social marginalization of the 'non-reunited' Greek Catholic clergy compared to the pre-
Soviet era. It demonstrates that a key reason why the Soviet regime
specifically targeted clandestine clergy lay in their refusal to follow the
state scenario of forced Orthodoxization. Convinced that they had
made the right choice, many clandestine clergy endured state pressure
and learned to navigate the bureaucratic hurdles that complicated
both their pastoral work and their personal lives. Paradoxically, the
illegal status of the clandestine clergy often allowed them to evade the
control of the Soviet authorities, even if only for a short period of
time. The fact that Greek Catholics consistently protested against the
ban of the UGCC in the Soviet Union ensured the church's survival
underground for more than four decades, until its legalization
in 1989–90.

Obtaining a Residence Permit

As shown by David Shearer, under Stalin, passport and residency laws,
which had initially aimed at controlling migration, were used 'to
identify and exclude from strategic regions large numbers of populations considered socially or ethnically dangerous'.[17] In the five years
that followed the death of Stalin on 5 March 1953, four million Gulag

---

Fates: The Greek Catholic Clergy and the Soviet Authorities'], *Схід/Захід: істори-
ко-культурологічний збірник* [*Skhid/Zakhid. Istoryko-kulturolohichnyi zbirnyk; East-
West: Historical and Cultural Collection*] 11–12 (2008), 265–82; Світлана Гуркіна
[Svitlana Hurkina], '"Образ сили духу": греко-католицьке духовенство Львівської
архиєпархії після Другої світової війни і проблема персоніфікації релігійних
переконань та ідентичности' ['"Obraz syly dukhu": hreko-katolyts'ke dukhovenstvo
L'vivs'koi arkhyieparkhii pislia Druhoi svitovoi viiny i problema personifikatsii relihiinykh
perekonan' ta identychnosty'; '"The Image of Strength of Spirit": Greek Catholic Clergy of
the L'viv Archeparchy after the Second World War and the Problem of Personification of
Religious Beliefs and Identity'], *Україна модерна* [*Ukraina moderna; Modern Ukraine*]
11 (2007), 99–110.

[16] Наталія Дмитришин [Nataliia Dmytryshyn], 'Між опором і пристосуванням:
Греко-католицьке підпілля в системі радянського тоталітаризму' ['Mizh oporom
i prystosuvanniam: Hreko-katolyts'ke pidpillia v systemi radian'skoho totalitaryzmu';
'Between Resistance and Adaptation: The Greek Catholic Underground in the System
of Soviet Totalitarianism'], *Ковчег* [*Kovcheh; The Ark*] 5 (2007), 256–81.

[17] David Shearer, 'Elements Near and Alien: Passportization, Policing, and Identity in the
Stalinist State, 1932–1952', *JMH* 76 (2004), 835–81, at 844.

detainees were released, so that by 1960 the number of inmates was around one fifth of that in the time before the death of the Soviet leader.[18] As pointed out by Miriam Dobson, all former Gulag prisoners experienced problems in terms of accommodation and employment, with many being 'forced into a nomadic existence'.[19]

Among those released were several hundred Greek Catholic priests.[20] Upon their return to Ukraine, these clergymen faced numerous bureaucratic obstacles, particularly with regard to obtaining a residence permit and employment. Thus, Fr Vasyl Kulynych (1893–1981), who was released in 1954, lived for several years in various settlements of Lviv Oblast. However, in January 1957, he was ordered to leave Western Ukraine. The priest stayed for some time in Zaporizhzhia Oblast in south-eastern Ukraine, before moving in August 1958 to Khmelnytskyi Oblast in the west, where his daughter Lidia was working after graduating from a medical university. Then, in 1959, Fr Vasyl was able to return to Galicia with his daughter, having received a residence permit in Zhovkva (Lviv Oblast) through an acquaintance.[21]

Upon their return from exile in 1959, Fr Ivan Hrynchyshyn's family also experienced multiple problems with accommodation. Fr Ivan and his wife, Sofia, were not given back their house and were denied residence permits in Lviv; consequently, they moved in with Sofia's parents in Drohobych (Lviv Oblast). Although Sofia's father granted her the ownership of the house, she nonetheless did not receive the desired registration. Despite Sofia's numerous appeals to the Soviet authorities, including the militia and the first secretary of the city's executive committee, the Hrynchyshyns were forced to pay regular fines for not having residence permits. After they were evicted in the early 1960s, Fr Ivan Hrynchyshyn left for Vinnytsia Oblast, while his wife went to the CPSU Central Committee in Moscow, where she managed to arrange an appointment with General Barsukov.

[18] Miriam Dobson, *Khrushchev's Cold Summer: Gulag Returnees, Crime, and the Fate of Reform After Stalin* (Ithaca, NY, 2009), 109.
[19] Ibid. 110–11.
[20] Between 1944 and 1952, 182,543 persons were deported from Western Ukraine on charges connected to the nationalist underground: Amir Weiner, 'The Empires Pay a Visit: Gulag Returnees, East European Rebellions, and Soviet Frontier Politics', *JMH* 78 (2006), 333–76, at 337 n. 5.
[21] Bohdan Prakh, ed., *Dukhovenstvo Peremys'koii Ieparkhii ta Apostol's'koi Administratsii Lemkivshchyny*, 1: *Biohrafichni narysy (1939–1989)* [*Clergy of the Peremyshl Eparchy and the Apostolic Administration of Lemkivshchyna*, 1: *Biographical sketches (1939–1989)*] (Lviv, 2015), 270, 272.

However, even the latter's intervention did not bring the desired result, which Sofia Hrynchyshyn attributed to the prejudice of the USSR Prosecutor General Roman Rudenko against her as a priest's wife. Eventually, she managed to obtain a residence permit thanks to the intervention of the 'chief of the KGB'.[22]

Many other former detainees experienced problems with residence permits and, consequently, with employment throughout the Soviet period. As shown by a 1978 document entitled 'The denial of the right to work and the right to housing on political grounds', compiled by the Moscow human rights activists of the Helsinki group, prisoners of conscience, among others, commonly faced this type of discrimination upon their release.[23] The clandestine Greek Catholic priests were no exception. For example, the 1984 issue of the samizdat 'Chronicle of the Catholic Church in Ukraine' informed readers about the imminent danger of Fr Mykhailo Vynnytskyi's fourth arrest. Having returned to Lviv in early 1983, the priest, who together with a group of monks co-owned a house in the city, was denied a residence permit in June 1984. As a result, he lost his job as a stoker at the children's home where he had worked for more than a year.[24] Eventually, Fr Vynnytskyi was once again arrested. Over the course of his life, Fr Mykhailo Vynnytskyi (1926–2006), who had joined the Redemptorists in 1944 and been ordained priest in 1956, spent in total about twenty years in different places of detention: 1950–6, 1964–6, 1975–83 and 1985–7.[25]

It was not only former detainees who had difficulties with their registration, however. Fr Iosaphat Kavatsiv (1934–2010) attributed his numerous discharges from his place of residence to his active priestly work in the underground. In order to resolve the issue of his residence permit, the priest travelled to Moscow seven times and wrote

---

[22] Lviv, Архів Інституту історії Церкви (АІІЦ), м. Львів [Arkhiv Institutu istorii Tserkvy; Archive of the Institute of Church History; hereafter: AIITs], P-1-1-104, interview with Fr Ivan Hrynchyshyn, his wife, Ms Sofia, and daughter, Ms Vira Baisa, 10 November 1992, Drohobych. Interviewer: Borys Gudziak, 32, 44–46.

[23] Budapest, Open Society Archives, Radio Liberty Samizdat Collection, HU-OSA 300-85-9-85/AS3331, 1.

[24] Ibid., HU-OSA 300-85-9-133/AS5515/AS5537, 7.

[25] Borys Gudziak and Oleh Turii, eds, Життєві історії підпільної Церкви: збірка інтерв'ю [Zhyttievi istorii pidpil'noi Tserkvy: zbirka interviu; Life Stories of the Underground Church: A Collection of Interviews] (Lviv, 2022), 501 n. 56.

twenty-four complaints to different levels of the Soviet authorities. However, it was only after Fr Kavatsiv's article appeared in the newspaper *Izvestia* that the prosecutor of the Horodok Raion (that is, district) of Lviv Oblast considered his case. The priest then managed to obtain a residence permit through informal networks.[26]

Like former detainees and dissidents in general, the Greek Catholic clergy thus found it difficult to settle in Galicia, especially in the cities. Yet they often managed to overcome the bureaucratic hurdles imposed by the Soviet state by petitioning the political authorities or through resorting to informal networks.

THE ECONOMIC SITUATION OF THE CLERGY

In December 1956, the plenipotentiary of the Council for Russian Orthodox Church Affairs (CROCA) of the Ukrainian Soviet Socialist Republic, Hryhorii Korchevyi, reported that 426 Greek Catholic priests were present in Western Ukraine and Transcarpathia, 267 of whom had spent time in detention. In the four Western Ukrainian oblasts, those of Lviv, Stanislav, Drohobych and Ternopil, there were 308 'non-reunited' priests, among them 177 former detainees.[27] In his report, Korchevyi provided an evaluation of the situation of the Greek Catholic clergy:

> In their general education and religious training, almost all of these priests are fairly well-educated people and enjoy influence among a part of the believers in the Western Oblasts. In Lviv Oblast, almost half the Uniate priests live in Lviv without any particular occupation. In Stanislav oblast, most of the Uniate priests live in the cities of Stanislav and Kolomyia. About half of the Uniate priests are employed. Half of them live with relatives and work nowhere. According to the data of the Council's plenipotentiaries, a significant

---

[26] 'Спогади отця Йосафата Кавацiва' ['Spohady ottsia Iosafata Kavatsiva'; 'Memoirs of Father Iosafat Kavatsiv'], 24 February 2008, online at: <http://museum.khpg.org/1203888925>, accessed 8 November 2024.

[27] GARF, op. 1, d. 1378, l. 135. Established in 1943, the Council for Russian Orthodox Church Affairs (CROCA) was a government body in charge of the ROC. Other denominations were overseen by the Council for Religious Cult Affairs (CRCA), founded in 1944. The two institutions merged into one, the Council for Religious Affairs (CRA), in 1965.

part of the employed and almost all the unemployed Uniate priests live well, are well-dressed and well-nourished. The source of their livelihood is the money received for performing services for the believing population both in the cities and in the periphery, as well as from the donations of believers.[28]

Korchevyi's description gives the impression that the 'non-reunited' clergy were well-educated urban residents who enjoyed a respectable lifestyle, with good food and nice clothes. Moreover, the Soviet official's account suggests that half the priests did not need Soviet jobs in order to sustain a proper standard of living. Apart from the numbers of former detainees provided in the table, the republican plenipotentiary made no mention of the priests' recent experience in the Gulag. Nor did Korchevyi's narrative relate the high level of unemployment among the priests to their 'criminal' past.

In reality, however, it was generally difficult for priests to find a job in the 1950s, for example, in Lviv, due to new documentation requirements, such as passport and proof of registration. These apparently aimed to reduce the flow of rural population to the cities.[29] However, it also meant that priests who had previously been convicted and who struggled to obtain a residence permit had little chance of being employed in Soviet institutions. As highlighted by the regional CROCA plenipotentiary, P. Bibik, in his report for the second half of 1956, only twelve out of eighty-three 'non-reunited' Greek Catholic priests in Stanislav Oblast worked 'in institutions, organizations, and

---

[28] 'По своей общеобразовательной и духовной подготовке почти все эти сященники являются достаточно грамотными людьми и пользуются влиянием среди части верующего населения западных областей. В Львовской области почти половина униатских священников проживает в г. Львове без определенных занятий. В Станиславской области большая часть униатских священников проживает в гг. Станиславе и Коломые. Около половины униатских священников трудоустроена. Половина живет при родственниках и нигде не работает. По данным Уполномоченных Совета значительная часть трудоустроенных и почти все не работающие униатские священники живут хорошо, хорошо одеты, упитаны. Источником их существования являются средства, получаемые за совершение треб у верующего населения как в городах так и на периферии, а также от пожертвований верующих': ibid.

[29] Галина Боднар [Halyna Bodnar], *Львів. Щоденне життя міста очима переселенців із сіл (50-ті–80-ті роки XX ст.)* [*Lviv. Shchodenne zhyttia mista ochyma pereselentsiv iz sil (50-ti–80-ti roky XX st.*; *Lviv: Daily Life of the City through the Eyes of Immigrants from the Villages (50s–80s of the 20th Century)*] (Lviv, 2010), 148–9.

enterprises'; the rest lived from conducting religious services in unregistered churches, houses and elsewhere.[30] It is particularly revealing that none of the twelve employed clergymen had been prosecuted or detained.[31]

The economic well-being of the Greek Catholic clergy in the Soviet Union differed significantly from their situation in the pre-Soviet era. In the inter-war Second Polish Republic, Greek Catholic priests usually relied on several sources of income. They received a salary from the Polish state, which was also regulated by the Concordat of 1925.[32] Even though a Catholic priest's salary was typically lower than that of a teacher, the clergy had additional sources of income at their disposal. For example, a Greek Catholic parish priest had on average fifty-two hectares of benefice lands.[33] Moreover, the clergyman received sacramental fees from the faithful, even though in the aftermath of the First World War these did not amount to much.[34] Additional sources of income in inter-war Poland could include, among others, state payments for teaching catechism and income from the lease of parish land.[35]

The arrival and seizure of power by the Soviets in September 1939 changed this status quo. A professor of theology who contributed to Milena Rudnytska's compilation of testimonies about Soviet rule in Western Ukraine during 1939–41, reveals in his memoir that Greek Catholic priests were evicted from their parish houses and that church lands were first divided among the peasants and then collectivized.[36] Regarded as a 'non-working element', the clergy also had to pay disproportionately high levels of tax. Greek Catholic believers often helped to relieve the clergy's tax burden by contributing money to pay a church tax or providing a priest with a share of their crops. The anti-religious

---

[30] GARF, op. 1, d. 1504, l. 9.

[31] Ibid.

[32] Andrew Dennis Sorokowski, 'The Greek-Catholic Parish Clergy in Galicia, 1900–1939' (PhD thesis, University of London School of Slavonic and East European Studies, 1991), 113.

[33] Ibid. 112.

[34] Ibid. 113, 115–16.

[35] Ibid. 116.

[36] Мілена Рудницька [Milena Rudnytska], ed., *Західня Україна під большевиками, IX. 1939–VI. 1941: Збірник спогадів* [*Zahidnia Ukraina pid bolshevykamy, IX. 1939–VI. 1941: Zbirnyk spohadiv; Western Ukraine under the Bolsheviks, 9.1939–6.1941: A Collection of Memoirs*] (New York, 1958), 119.

drive of the new regime also resulted in arrests, deportations and death sentences for priests.[37]

During the so-called 'reunion' campaign of 1945–6, in contrast to the first Soviet occupation of Galicia, the Soviets did not treat all clergy as enemies of the regime. Specifically, those Greek Catholic clergy who agreed to join the Russian Orthodox Church were considered loyal, at least initially. These 'reunited' priests retained their former parishes, thus securing their livelihoods. However, in the mid-1950s, the economic status of the 'reunited' clergy was undermined by the 'non-reunited' clergy who returned from the Gulag. This caused numerous conflicts on a local level, for many religious communities preferred 'non-reunited' priests, who had an aura of martyrdom, to 'reunited' ones.[38] According to the CROCA plenipotentiary in Stanislav Oblast, Bibik, 'non-reunited' clergy conducted religious services 'at believers' houses and sometimes near the churches or even in unregistered churches'.[39]

Since the UGCC had been banned under Stalin, many hoped that following his death the church would be restored. Greek Catholics also closely observed international political developments. In 1956, a clandestine priest called Iakiv Biloskurskyi from Mshana (Ivano-Frankivskyi Raion, Lviv Oblast) abandoned his initial plan to get a job at a shoe factory, allegedly arguing before the 'reunited' priest Vanchytskyi that 'events in Hungary and Egypt would help to resolve the question about the Greek Catholic Church more quickly'.[40] A 1950 state security document had mentioned Fr Biloskurskyi's arrest.[41] Thus, in 1956, the priest must have been considering a job after his recent release. In the 1960s, the Second Vatican Council (1962–5), the release of Metropolitan Slipyi in 1963 and the legalization of the Greek Catholic Church in Czechoslovakia during the Prague Spring of 1968 all raised new expectations. However, Greek

---

[37] Ibid. 120–1.

[38] For more details on the relations between the 'reunited' and 'non-reunited' clergy after the latter's return from the Gulag, see Kateryna Budz, 'After "Reunion": Soviet Power and the "Reunited" and "Non-Reunited" Greco-Catholic Clergy in Eastern Galicia (1950s–1960s)', *Logos: A Journal of Eastern Christian Studies* 56 (2015), 357–89, at 363–7.

[39] GARF, f. 6991, op. 1, d. 1396, l. 73.

[40] '[С]обытия в Венгрии и Египте посодействуют скорейшому решению вопроса о греко-католической церкви': ibid. d. 1378, ll. 137–8.

[41] HDA SBU, f. 16, op. 1, spr. 806, ark. 96.

Catholics' hopes for legalization of their church remained unfulfilled until the late 1980s. Clandestine priests therefore had to resort to a broad array of survival strategies, including support from relatives, donations and state employment.

In his 1993 interview, Fr Volodymyr Senkivskyi (1908–2002) noted a slow improvement in his family's financial well-being after his release in 1956: 'When I came from Siberia, it was very hard at first. We had no money, we struggled for a long time. And later, the material situation improved a little bit, and we were living the way we do now'.[42]

Donations from other clergy and from believers seem to have played a crucial role, especially during the initial phase after the release of the Gulag returnees. The CROCA plenipotentiary of the Ukrainian SSR, Hryhorii Pinchuk, reported in August 1958 that in the regions of Transcarpathia, Drohobych and Lviv, the Roman Catholic clergy provided 'moral and material support' to their Greek Catholic counterparts.[43] Latin-rite clergy supported clandestine priests in Ukraine by giving them intention cards: believers' requests, typically accompanied by small donations, to celebrate a liturgy for a particular intention.[44] Due to this support, Fr Mykola Simkailo (b. 1952) was able to pay his colleagues at a fire station to cover his shifts, allowing the priest more time for his religious activities.[45]

Direct donations from believers were also common. According to Fr Damian (Hryhorii) Bohun, the number of intention cards was so great that some of them had to be sent abroad. While the clergy who received the cards said the masses, the clandestine priests kept the

---

[42] Gudziak and Turii, eds, *Життєві історії підпільної Церкви* [*Life Stories of the Underground Church*], 214. Fr Volodymyr Senkivskyi (1908–2002) was a married priest. In 1947, he 'reunited' with the ROC but was arrested in 1951 for connection to the nationalist underground. Upon his release, he ministered secretly as a Greek Catholic priest whilst holding secular employment: ibid. 193–4.

[43] Володимир Сергійчук [Volodymyr Serhiichuk], *Нескорена церква: подвижництво греко-католиків України в боротьбі за віру і державу* [*Neskorena tserkva: podvyzhnytstvo hreko-katolykiv Ukrainy v borot'bi za viru i derzhavu; The Unconquered Church: The Heroism of the Greek Catholics of Ukraine in the Struggle for Faith and State*] (Kyiv, 2001), 302–3, 309–10.

[44] AIITs, P-1-1-1160, interview with Fr Mykola Simkailo, 26 August 2000, Pidpechery. Interviewer: A. Kuzyk, 9–10.

[45] Ibid. 1, 10.

donations which came with those cards.[46] An interesting donation was reported by the CRA in 1981: S. Bartkiv from the village of Pyliava (Buchach Raion, Ternopil Oblast) handed over to M. Simkailo the Niva car which she had received in 1979 for being a 'leading worker on a collective farm'.[47] Siegelbaum's study shows that, even though the number of car owners increased during the Brezhnev era (1964–82), in 1980, only ten per cent of Soviet households owned a private car.[48] A 1983 survey showed a disproportionately high number of car owners among the intelligentsia (fifty-eight per cent) compared to workers (thirty-five per cent), especially given that the former constituted only fifteen per cent of the 1979 Soviet population.[49] Moreover, to purchase a car required on average eight years of savings.[50] Due to this generous donation, Fr Simkailo joined the small group of car owners in the Soviet Union. Paradoxically, a priest of the outlawed church thus drove a car that had been presented by the state to someone for their great contribution to the socialist economy.

As a priest of the younger generation, Fr Simkailo had a secular job. Overall, however, some state reports suggest that less than half of the 'non-reunited' clergy were officially employed. According to the CRA information, as of 1971, fifty-eight Greek Catholic priests lived in Ivano-Frankivsk (formerly Stanislav) Oblast. Of these, twenty-three were employed, twenty-six were not working 'due to old age and illness', four lived off their pensions, and the remaining five relied on the support of their 'relatives and children'.[51] As these data suggest, only a few 'non-reunited' priests had state pensions. The report provides no information on how the twenty-six priests who were too old or too ill to work survived.

The number of employed clergymen decreased over time. According to CRA information, in 1977, forty out of forty-nine 'non-reunited' Greek Catholic priests in Ivano-Frankivsk Oblast were sixty-one years

[46] Gudziak and Turii, eds, Життєві історії підпільної Церкви [Life Stories of the Underground Church], 299.

[47] Київ, Центральний державний архів вищих органів влади та управління України (ЦДАВО), Київ [Tsentral'nyi derzhavnyi arkhiv vyshchykh orhaniv vlady ta upravlinnia Ukrainy; Central State Archive of the Higher Organs of Power and Administration of Ukraine; hereafter: TsDAVO], f. 4648, op. 7, spr. 169, ark. 83, 89.

[48] Lewis H. Siegelbaum, Cars for Comrades: The Life of the Soviet Automobile (Ithaca, NY, 2008), 238.

[49] Ibid. 242.

[50] Ibid. 239.

[51] TsDAVO, f. 4648, op. 5, spr. 236, ark. 93.

old or older, that is, of pensionable age, which was sixty for men. Of these forty-nine, eleven were employed and eleven received pensions, while the remaining twenty-seven were 'dependent on relatives'.[52] The comparison of data on age and employment suggests that, as of 1977, less than one third of Greek Catholic priests aged above sixty received state pensions, with at least two priests of retirement age still working. The very low number of priests relying on state pensions may suggest that they had not had access to stable state jobs, and this may, in turn, have been related to earlier periods of detention. Indeed, just over half of the priests of which CRA was aware in 1977 (twenty-five out of forty-nine) had experienced a period of imprisonment and were consequently deemed to have a criminal record.[53] Even if their age and health allowed them to work, these priests often struggled to find jobs and were thus dependent on their relatives' support. Moreover, not all priests had children: ten of them – just over one fifth – were monks.[54] As evidence from an earlier period suggests, ordained monks could receive much-needed support from clandestine nuns. Thus, the Sisters Servants of Mary Immaculate in Kalush (Stanislav Oblast) cared for a Basilian monk, Fr Metodii Boletskyi (1910–53), after his release from Stanislav prison due to health problems, and until his premature death.[55] They then hosted another Basilian priest for about a year, a Gulag returnee, Fr Demian Bohun (1910–2008), who arrived in Kalush a few days after Fr Boletskyi died.[56]

STATE-EMPLOYMENT OF CLANDESTINE PRIESTS

Overall, the Soviet authorities wanted priests to leave their pastoral activities and to embrace civil jobs. However, secular employment did not necessarily help the Greek Catholic priests to avoid repression. Before his arrest in October 1949, Hryhorii Balahurak, a Basilian monk who also acted as a clandestine bishop, worked as a mechanic at an industrial cooperative or *artel* in Stanislav.[57] Frs Ivan Valnytskyi and Avksentii Kinashchuk, who were arrested at about the same time,

---

[52] Ibid. op. 7, spr. 52, ark. 67–8.
[53] Ibid. ark. 68.
[54] Ibid.
[55] Gudziak and Turii, eds, *Життєві історії підпільної Церкви* [*Life Stories of the Underground Church*], 553 n. 65.
[56] Ibid. 230, 282–3, 287.
[57] HDA SBU, f. 16, op. 1, spr. 717, ark. 118.

also had secular jobs in Stanislav: the former worked as an accountant at the city communal enterprise (*gorkommunkhoz*), while the latter was employed as a security guard at a tuberculosis sanatorium.[58]

During the post-Stalin era, Greek Catholic priests of working age who did not wish to serve in official Orthodox parishes also had to look for civil jobs. According to Soviet legislation, people who were unemployed for more than three months were considered 'parasites'.[59] As a punishment, they could be banished or assigned correctional labour for a period of two to five years.[60] In order to avoid possible accusations of 'parasitism', the 'non-reunited' clergy of working age had to look for state jobs. Despite being highly educated, clandestine bishops and active priests usually occupied low-qualified positions in Soviet institutions. Fr Volodymyr Sterniuk (a clandestine bishop from 1964) completed training to work as a paramedic on an ambulance in Lviv.[61] These studies lasted for about four years, between 1955 and 1959.[62] He retired from this job in 1967 and became head of the underground UGCC in 1972.[63] According to Fr Pavlo Vasylyk, who became a clandestine bishop on 1 May 1974, the new dignity did not grant him any privileges.[64] Having been employed as a collector of

---

[58] Ibid. ark. 120, 122.

[59] Sheila Fitzpatrick, 'Social Parasites: How Tramps, Idle Youth, and Busy Entrepreneurs Impeded the Soviet March to Communism', *Cahiers du monde russe* 47 (2006), 377–408, at 381.

[60] Joshua Rothenberg, 'The Legal Status of Religion in the Soviet Union', in Richard H. Marshall, ed., *Aspects of Religion in the Soviet Union 1917–1967* (Chicago, IL, 1971), 61–102, at 89.

[61] Севастіян Дмитрух [Sevastian Dmytrukh], *Життя як подвиг для Христа. Curriculum vitae монаха редемпториста, місцеблюстителя і правлячого архієрея Києво-Галицької митрополії Володимира Стернюка* [*Zhyttia iak podvyh dlia Khrysta. Curriculum vitae monakha redemptorysta, mistsebliustytelia i pravliachoho arhiiereia Kyievo-Halytskoi mytropolii Volodymyra Sterniuka; Life as a Feat for Christ: Curriculum Vitae of the Redemptorist Monk, Locum Tenens and Ruling Bishop of the Kyiv-Halych Metropolis Volodymyr Sterniuk*] (Lviv, 2007), 12.

[62] 'Слідами сповідника віри Володимира Стернюка' ['Slidamy spovidnyka viry Volodymyra Sterniuka'; 'In the Footsteps of the Confessor of Faith, Volodymyr Sterniuk'], 18 April 2016, online at: <http://ichistory.org.ua/2016/04/18/slidamy-spovidnyka-viry-volodymyra-sternyuka/>, accessed 6 September 2024.

[63] Дмитрух [Dmytrukh], *Життя як подвиг для Христа* [*Life as a Feat for Christ*], 12.

[64] 'Спогади Єпископа-Ординарія Коломийсько-Чернівецької єпархії Кир Павла Василика' ['Spohady Iepyskopa-Ordynariia Kolomyisko-Chernivets'koii ieparkhii Kyr Pavla Vasylyka'; 'Memoirs of the Bishop Ordinary of Kolomyia-Chernivtsi Eparchy Kyr Pavla Vasylyka'], 15 February 2008, online at: <https://museum.khpg.org/1203111955>, accessed 4 October 2023.

medicinal herbs for twenty-three years, Bishop Vasylyk used his work as an excuse to travel and to serve Greek Catholic communities all over Galicia and beyond.[65] Similarly, Fr Mykhailo Sabryha, a priest since 1974 and a bishop since 1986, worked at a bookshop for fifteen years, until he left this job in late 1989.[66] In Bishop Mykhailo Sabryha's words, it was 'God's mercy' that he was able to work in one place for such a long period.[67] As pointed out by Fr Kavatsiv, Greek Catholic priests often faced dismissals from work.[68]

Fr Mykhailo Havryliv's story illustrates how difficult it was for a Greek Catholic priest to find and keep a stable state job. A native of Galicia, Mykhailo Havryliv (b. 1949) studied at the Orthodox theological academy in Leningrad (now Saint Petersburg) and became an Orthodox priest in 1975. In December 1979, after serving for two years in Orthodox parishes in Galicia, Fr Havryliv left the Orthodox Church to join the clandestine UGCC. He then struggled to find a secular job. After two months, he was able, through personal connections, to find work as a disinfection technician. He stayed in that job for one year, later working as an electrician (for six months), a janitor (for three years), a hospital attendant (for six months), a manual labourer (for one month), a locksmith (for six months) and, finally, as a boiler operator or stoker.[69]

On the one hand, civil employment helped the priests to avoid arrests for 'parasitism'. On the other hand, state jobs left them with less time for pastoral activities. Overall, combining pastoral duties and full employment was a burdensome task. Fr Kavatsiv, for example, would usually hear confessions, conduct burials, baptize and perform other services nocturnally: 'This was done at night, and at 9 o'clock in the morning, wherever you were, you had to be at work'.[70] Leading a

---

[65] Ibid.

[66] AIITs, P-1-1-321, interview with Bishop Mykhailo Sabryha, 30 March 1994, Ternopil. Interviewer: Iaroslav Stotskyi, 18, 22, 30, 47.

[67] Ibid. 47.

[68] Спогади отця Йосафата Каваціва ['Memoirs of Father Iosafat Kavatsiv'].

[69] Свящ. Михайло Гаврилів [Fr Mykhailo Havryliv], *Кожна людина – це перш за все історія. Автобіографія українського католицького священика в сучасній Україні* [*Kozhna liudyna – tse persh za vse istoriia; Every Person is First of all a History: Autobiography of a Ukrainian Catholic Priest in Contemporary Ukraine*] (Rome, 1987), 11, 36–42, 71, 96, 119–24.

[70] 'Це робилося вночі, а рано на 9 годину треба було, де б не був, бути на роботі': Спогади отця Йосафата Каваціва ['Memoirs of Father Iosafat Kavatsiv'].

double life, as a clandestine priest by night and as a Soviet employee by day, required the utmost secrecy and measures of concealment.

State Attempts to Undermine the Reputations of Clandestine Clergy

While the state apparatus had a wide array of legal measures to curtail the activities of the 'non-reunited' priests, including fines, arrests and deportations, they also understood the need to undermine the clandestine clergy's moral authority. The flock admired their pastors precisely for their high moral values, so these came particularly under Soviet attack.

The representation of the Greek Catholic clergy as an 'anti-Soviet' element continued throughout the Soviet era. In the late 1980s, in their memorandum to the chairman of the Presidium of the Supreme Council of the USSR, a group of clandestine bishops and priests pleading for legalization described the 'bigoted propagandist war' that had been waged against their church for the previous forty years.[71] In particular, the Greek Catholic clergy found themselves labelled as '"slanderers" against reality', 'anti-Soviet' and 'nationalist-extremists'.[72]

Active clandestine priests were frequently slandered in the Soviet press. For example, an article which appeared in the Soviet Ukrainian newspaper *Vil'na Ukraina* in February 1988, began with the following sentence: 'Living in Lviv without a residence permit, Mykhailo Havryliv considers himself to be one of the holy fathers of the so-called Ukrainian Catholic Church (UCC)'.[73] The article mentioned that, during the second half of 1987, Radio Liberty had broadcast a series of programmes about the priest based on a memoir he had sent to the West.[74] The article speculated on Fr Havryliv's motives, which they proposed might be his vanity, his wish to receive a honorarium, or his obedience to the instructions of the Basilian priests. The author also

---

[71] 'нетерпимая пропагандистская война': HU-OSA 300-85-44-30, unpaginated.

[72] '"клеветников" на действительность', 'антисоветчиков', 'националистов-экстремистов': HU-OSA 300-85-44-30, unpaginated.

[73] Б. Дубовик [B. Dubovyk], '"Від власного кореспондента", або за що їм платять' ['"Vid vlasnoho korespondenta", abo za shcho im platyat'; '"From their own correspondent", or What They are Paid for'], *Vil'na Ukraina* [*Free Ukraine*], 23 February 1988, in HU-OSA 300-85-12-237.

[74] HU-OSA 300-85-12-237. A fragment of Fr Havryliv's autobiography (in Russian) can be found in HU-OSA 300-85-44-30, 13–48.

described the priest as hypocritical, since he continued to study at the Orthodox academy despite 'being a "convinced" Catholic'.[75]

After Fr Havryliv's autobiography was published in Rome in 1987, he became a well-known figure outside the USSR. Western observers monitored instances of state retaliation for Fr Havryliv's priestly activities.[76] For instance, following the Chornobyl nuclear disaster (26 April 1986), Fr Havryliv was made to dispose of radioactive waste without appropriate protective gear.[77] Later, as reported by the *Ukrainian Weekly* on 4 October 1987, Fr Havryliv received a draft notice to fight in Afghanistan.[78]

Another important figure who came under press attack was the clandestine bishop Pavlo Vasylyk. Following an open-air celebration of the Greek Catholic liturgy on 17 July 1988 in Zarvanytsia, the Marian shrine in Ternopil Oblast, on 6 August the local newspaper *Peremoha* published a hostile article on him. A month later, on 10 September, the same article was reprinted in another local newspaper, *Nadzbruchanska Pravda*. The author suggested that the bishop might have had a 'material and political interest' in the legalization of the church, also mentioning Vasylyk's two previous arrests 'for nationalist and anti-Soviet activities and for violation of the legislation on religious cults'.[79]

By attacking the most active Greek Catholic clergy, Soviet propaganda sought to compromise the legalization movement as a whole. By making allegations about the priests' supposed vanity, lust for money and hypocrisy, the Soviets tried to undermine the image of the clandestine priest as a highly moral person.

Apart from official Soviet propaganda, the state security organs tried to sow distrust among church members, both before and after the official liquidation of the UGCC. Resorting to the ancient strategy of divide and rule, security police skilfully used existing conflicts within

---

[75] HU-OSA 300-85-12-237.

[76] This is indicated on the photograph's caption. Waco, Texas, Keston Center, Keston Digital Archive, Photographs of Ukrainian Greek Catholic Priest Father Mykhailo Havryliv in Soviet Ukraine, online at: <https://digitalcollections-baylor.quartexcollections.com/Documents/Detail/photographs-of-ukrainian-greek-catholic-priest-father-mykhailo-havryliv-in-soviet-ukraine/1141742?item=1141747>, accessed 25 November 2024.

[77] Ibid.

[78] HU-OSA 300-85-12-237.

[79] І. Весняк [I. Vesniak], 'До якого храму веде "УКЦ"' ['Do iakoho khramu vede "UKTs"'; 'To which Temple does "UCC" Lead?'], *Nadzbruchanska Pravda* [*Truth from above Zbruch*], 10 September 1988, in HU-OSA 300-85-12-237.

the church. Thus, already during 1939–41, the Bolsheviks manipulated longstanding tensions amongst the Greek Catholic clergy, for example, between the adherents of Eastern and Western orientations, with an aim to 'disintegrate' the church.[80] Later, through their agent Mykola Muranyi, the state security organs tried to sever links between the Greek Catholics in Transcarpathia, where Muranyi acted as a clandestine Greek Catholic bishop, and Galicia.[81] Generally, rumours about some church figure being a Soviet state security agent created an atmosphere of suspicion in the underground church. For example, when the KGB summoned some clandestine priests and not others, it automatically cast doubts on the latter.[82] This artificially-created distrust led to the further marginalization of the clergy, now within the clandestine community itself.

Religious Inspiration of Resistance

Facing persecution and deprivation, clandestine Greek Catholics nonetheless believed that they were suffering for a just cause. With his pastoral letter 'Peace in Christ to the lost priests' (1953), Metropolitan Iosyf Slipyi rebuked the Greek Catholic clergy who had joined the Russian Orthodox Church: 'You have lost the right of priesthood, jurisdictions, all the honours and offices that you held in the Catholic Church. You were light, salt, and today you are the dung of the Gospel (Matt 5: 13). You have become springs without water and clouds driven by a snowstorm, for whom the gloom of darkness is preserved /2 Pet 2.17/'.[83] The

---

[80] Роман Скакун [Roman Skakun], '"Сторож братові своєму": агентура органів безпеки СРСР у середовищі греко-католицького духовенства в 1939–1941 роках' ['"Storozh bratovi svoiemu": ahentura orhaniv bezpeky SRSR u seredovyshchi hrekokatolyts'koho dukhovenstva v 1939–1941 rokakh'; "His Brother's Keeper": The Security Agents of the USSR among the Greek Catholic Clergy in 1939–1941, *Kovcheh* [*The Ark*] 8 (Lviv, 2018), 72–189.

[81] Роман Скакун [Roman Skakun] and Владимир Мороз [Vladimir Moroy], 'Николай Мурани – "Березовский" – "Сова": судьба агента и судьба Церкви' ['Nikolay Murani – "Berezovskiy" — "Sova": sud'ba agenta i sud'ba Tserkvi'; 'Nikolai Murani – "Berezovskiy" –"Sova": Fate of Agent and Fate of Church'], in Jaroslav Coranič, ed., *Gréckokatolícka Cirkev na Slovensku vo svetle výročí*, 7 vols (Prešov, 2009–24), 6b: 71–140, at 71.

[82] AIITs, P-1-1-946, interview with Fr Vitalii Dutkevych, 6 February 1999, Lviv. Interviewer: L. Kupchyk, 17.

[83] 'Ви стратили право священства, юриздикції, всі почесті і уряди, які ви займали в католицькій церкві. Ви були світлом, солею, а нині евангельським погноем /Мат.5.13/. Ви стали джерелами без води і хмарами гоненими

head of the UGCC then contrasted this with the example of the 'current sufferers', many of whom have already received 'a well-deserved crown of heavenly glory'.[84] Metropolitan Slipyi concluded his letter with a plea to the 'reunited' priests to return to the Greek Catholic Church.[85] Having spent about eighteen years in detention, from 1945 to 1963, Slipyi was and is generally recognized by the Ukrainian Greek Catholics as a confessor of the faith.

As Slipyi's letter implies, the clandestine priests generally juxtaposed their status as social outcasts and their inner sense of dignity. According to Bishop Mykhailo Sabryha, the clergy of the underground UGCC 'were mocked, [and] they were considered nothing, but they were proud to be Catholic priests'.[86] The hierarch's phrasing is reminiscent of the prophecy of Isaiah (53: 3):

> He was despised and rejected by others;
> a man of suffering and acquainted with infirmity;
> and as one from whom others hide their faces
> he was despised, and we held him of no account.

The self-perception of these Greek Catholic priests as sufferers for Christ was also shared by clandestine believers. Fr Mykhailo Havryliv, for example, contrasted the different attitudes of the Greek Catholics and the Orthodox to their clergy, arguing that Greek Catholic believers realized that a clandestine priest operating in secret faced the constant risk of arrest and thus held him in high esteem.[87] In contrast, Orthodox parishioners allegedly viewed the priest as 'an executor of their will':

> The priest is completely dependent on the church committee, and if he
> wants to break free from this power of the secular element, anonymous

---

хуртовиною для котрих збережена мряка темноти /2. Пет.2.17/': TsDAVO, f. 4648, op. 1, spr. 165, ark. 307. Metropolitan Slipyi refers to Matt. 5: 13 ('"You are the salt of the earth; but if salt has lost its taste, how can its saltiness be restored? It is no longer good for anything, but is thrown out and trampled under foot') and 2 Pet. 2: 17 ('These are waterless springs and mists driven by a storm; for them the deepest darkness has been reserved'). English-language quotations from the Bible are given according to the New Revised Standard Version (NRSV).

[84] TsDAVO, f. 4648, op. 1, spr. 165, ark. 308.

[85] Ibid., ark. 309.

[86] AIITs, P-1-1-321, interview with Bishop Mykhailo Sabryha, 42.

[87] Гаврилів [Fr Mykhailo Havryliv], *Кожна людина – це перш за все історія* [*Every Person is First of all a History*], 101.

letters, denunciations, slander, quarrels begin; everything ends with the intervention of the village council or raion executive committee, and either the priest is expelled or the church committee is re-elected – it all depends on who has more weight with the atheists, or rather the KGB.[88]

The clergy of the underground UGCC often perceived their afflictions as a sacrifice necessary for the survival of the church and of the Ukrainian people. Bishop Pavlo Vasylyk, who endured three arrests, spending a total of fourteen years in detention and banishment, stressed how many Ukrainian Greek Catholics 'were imprisoned for this great matter of struggle for the freedom of our people and Church'.[89] Similarly, in his memoir, Bishop Vasylyk wrote about 'a people who sacrificed itself for the sake of a Christian and national idea'.[90] The hierarch referred to Ukrainians as to 'God-loving people, chosen by the Lord for suffering'.[91] The idea of the chosen people resurfaces also in the interview with another active participant of the movement for legalization of the UGCC, Fr Mykola Simkailo. The priest compared the almost forty-four years of the church's underground existence with the forty years spent by the Israelites in the wilderness.[92] During the late Soviet period, this hitherto marginal group of illegal Greek Catholics stood in the vanguard of the Ukrainian national and religious revival, paving the way to legalization of the UGCC in 1989–90.

To conclude, despite the Soviet regime's efforts to curtail the religious activities of the 'non-reunited' clergy, including the imposition of fines, dismissals from work, arrests and evictions, the latter continued to serve the clandestine Greek Catholic communities. While the Soviet constitution officially declared freedom of conscience, the UGCC remained under ban from March 1946 until

---

[88] 'Священик повністю залежить від церковного комітету, і якщо хоче виламатися з-під цієї влади світського елементу, то починаються анонімки, доноси, наклепи, сварки; все закінчується втручанням сільради чи райвиконкому, і або священика виганяють, або переобирають церковний комітет - це вже залежить, хто має у безбожників, а точніше у КГБ, більшу вагу': ibid.

[89] АІІТs, P-1-1-455, interview with Bishop Pavlo Vasylyk, 18 February 1994, Kolomyia, Ivano-Frankivsk Oblast. Interviewer: V. Kachur, 24.

[90] Спогади Єпископа-Ординарія Коломийсько-Чернівецької єпархії Кир Павла Василика ['Memoirs of the Bishop Ordinary of Kolomyia-Chernivtsi Eparchy Kyr Pavlo Vasylyk'].

[91] Ibid.

[92] АІІТs, P-1-1-1160, interview with Fr Mykola Simkailo, 18.

December 1989. During this period, the 'non-reunited' clergy and their followers continued to profess the Catholic faith according to the Byzantine rite. They manifested their religious beliefs both in private, resorting to the utmost secrecy, and in public, through protests and open celebrations of the liturgy. While the most active priests endured numerous arrests, they also learned to skilfully navigate the hurdles of Soviet bureaucracy by relying on personal networks and by exploiting the weaknesses of the state system. Persecuted by the Soviet state, they were nonetheless highly respected by clandestine Greek Catholics.

Redefining Evangelicalism from the Margins: South Korean Student Evangelical Experiments, 1986–89

Dongjun Seo (iD)
Korean Bible University

Under the 1980s authoritarian regime of Doo-Hwan Chun, a young Christian group emerged from the evangelical majority of Korean Protestantism. On the margins of Korean evangelicalism, this group started to redefine what it meant to be evangelical and to challenge its conservative-leaning socio-political and missiological orientation. This theme of 'new evangelicals' or 'the evangelical left' has been covered by many scholars in relation to America and Latin America, but not in Asian contexts. This article illuminates the Korean story by analysing the new evangelical experiments of Korean students from 1986 to 1989. It looks at their socio-political and ecclesial background, the tensions between this group and mainstream evangelicalism, and their contribution to the wider Korean evangelical community. Based on in-depth research of Korean primary sources and oral interviews with its key members, this article explores how a new evangelical group at the margins of Korean evangelicalism challenged the centre.

INTRODUCTION

The second half of the twentieth century witnessed the emergence of a new brand of evangelicalism, which pursued a more engaged faith in society. In post-war America, 'new evangelicals' began, from the mid-1940s, to emerge from the tensions between two groups which were increasingly divided from the late nineteenth century onwards and which, by the 1920s, were generally known as modernists and fundamentalists.[1] This new evangelical group attempted to depart from the militant separatism of fundamentalism by taking a more positive attitude toward mainline Christianity, while distancing themselves from the theological ethos of modernists. From this new evangelical

32, Dongil-ro 214-gil, Nowon-gu, Seoul, Korea. Email: seodj59@gmail.com.

[1] George M. Marsden, *Understanding Fundamentalism and Evangelicalism* (Grand Rapids, MI, 1991), 56–61, 68–74; Brian Stanley, *The Global Diffusion of Evangelicalism: The Age of Billy Graham and John Stott* (Downers Grove, IL, 2013), 29–36.

Studies in Church History 61 (2025), 586–608 © The Author(s), 2025. Published by Cambridge University Press on behalf of the Ecclesiastical History Society.
doi:10.1017/stc.2024.51

movement, there emerged in the United States and elsewhere during the 1960s and 1970s those now widely described as 'the evangelical left' or 'progressive evangelicals' who urged more progressive socio-political engagement.[2] Most Latin American countries in the post-war period were in socio-political ferment under repressive military regimes. It was in this context that the Latin American evangelical left started to emerge from the 1960s.[3] This emergence of 'new evangelicals' or 'the evangelical left' has drawn scholarly attention and the theme has been covered by many scholars, particularly in relation to America and Latin America.[4] However, it has not been substantially analysed in relation to Asian countries, such as South Korea, which provide a compelling example of interactions between the various centres and peripheries of evangelicalism in different national contexts, and offer a useful comparison to the American or Latin American stories.

This article brings to the fore this Korean story by analysing a Christian student group that emerged from the evangelical majority of Korean Protestantism and experimented with new forms of evangelical socio-political engagement from 1986 to 1989. In Latin America especially, student experience and organizations were at the forefront of this new evangelicalism. This article focuses on one such organization in South Korea, which formed at the Seoul National University (SNU) and will hereafter be referred to as the SNU evangelical network.[5] Although this student group was on the periphery of Korean evangelicalism, its attempts to redefine evangelical identity challenged the prevailing evangelical interpretation of socio-political issues and Christian mission in significant ways. This article explores the socio-political and ecclesial background of its activities. It also looks

---

[2] Marsden, *Understanding Fundamentalism and Evangelicalism*, 74–6.

[3] David C. Kirkpatrick, *A Gospel for the Poor: Global Social Christianity and the Latin American Evangelical Left* (Philadelphia, PA, 2019), 33–52.

[4] For studies of the American evangelical left, see Peter Heltzel, *Jesus and Justice: Evangelicals, Race, and American Politics* (New Haven, CT, 2009); David Swartz, *Moral Minority: The Evangelical Left in an Age of Conservatism* (Philadelphia, PA, 2014); Brantley Gasaway, *Progressive Evangelicals and the Pursuit of Justice* (Chapel Hill, NC, 2015). For research on the Latin American context, see Raimundo C. Barreto Jr, 'Facing the Poor in Brazil: Towards an Evangélico Progressive Social Ethics' (PhD thesis, Princeton Theological Seminary, 2006); Kirkpatrick, *A Gospel for the Poor*; Jose Daniel Salinas, 'The Theological Revolution in Latin American Evangelicalism of the 1970s', in David W. Bebbington, ed., *The Gospel in Latin America: Historical Studies in Evangelicalism and the Global South* (Waco, TX, 2022), 41–61.

[5] Kirkpatrick, *A Gospel for the Poor*, 33–52.

at the tension between this group and mainstream evangelicalism, and its contribution to the wider Korean evangelical community. Based on in-depth research of Korean primary sources mostly unutilized in Anglophone scholarship, as well as on oral interviews with its key members, this article examines how a new evangelical group on the periphery of Korean evangelicalism challenged the centre. This study argues that the SNU evangelical network, despite its marginal position, created meaningful spaces for alternative perspectives within Korean evangelicalism.

Young Korean Evangelical Students in the Socio-Political Turmoil of the 1980s

In the 1980s, South Korea was in socio-political turmoil under the new authoritarian regime of Doo-Hwan Chun. General Doo-Hwan Chun had led a military coup on 12 December 1979, immediately after the fall of Chung-Hee Park's regime which had lasted eighteen years. In 1981, Chun established his own government. The emergence of the new authoritarian regime provoked a nation-wide pro-democracy movement. Over the course of the 1980s, the pro-democracy movement against Chun's authoritarian regime became more popular and radical than that against Park's regime in the 1970s.[6] Student groups continued to play a key role in the pro-democracy movement of the 1980s, as they had in the 1970s.[7] Like Park's regime, Doo-Hwan Chun's regime sought to suppress the pro-democracy movement. For instance, in May 1980, there were pro-democracy protests by citizens in the southern city of Gwangju, known as 'the Gwangju Uprising', which had originated in student protests. Observing the brutal suppression of these student protests by Chun's regime, many ordinary citizens became involved and the uprising developed into a city-wide pro-democracy movement.[8] However, armed troops dispatched by Chun's regime violently quelled the uprising, which resulted in 166

---

[6] Danielle Chubb, *Contentious Activism and Inter-Korean Relations* (New York, 2014), 101–13.
[7] 홍석률 [Seuk-Ryule Hong], 박태균 [Tae-Kyun Park] and 정창현 [Chang-Hyun Jung], 한국 현대사 [*Hanguk Hyeondaesa; The Contemporary History of South Korea*], 2 vols (Seoul, 2018), 2: 235–9, 241–3, 245–51.
[8] Gi-Wook Shin, 'Introduction', in idem and Kyung-Moon Hwang, eds, *Contentious Kwangju: The May 18 Uprising in Korea's Past and Present* (Lanham, MD, 2003), 10–27.

deaths, 64 missing and 3,139 injured.[9] A collective memory of the uprising and a feeling of the indebtedness to the Gwangju citizens' sacrificial efforts for the pro-democracy movement played a formative role in that movement throughout the 1980s.[10]

University campuses were a flashpoint of conflict between fervour for democratization and the zeal of the authoritarian government for suppressing disorder. Seoul National University's campus was a major site of such conflict. In May 1986, SNU students demonstrated against Chun's authoritarian regime, remembering the Gwangju Uprising, and were confronted by riot police. Against the backdrop of this growing tension between student protests and riot police, an evangelical Christian event called 'A Great March for Jesus' was held on the campus on 20 May. During the event, around 1,000 evangelical students gathered to proclaim God's sovereignty over their campus and over the socio-political turmoil of Korean society by prayer, praise of God and a march on the campus.[11] The event took place at the university plaza, in which university students often staged pro-democracy demonstrations.[12] This implies that the event was intended to provide an evangelical alternative to the student protests.[13] At the time, most mainstream evangelical churches and student ministry organizations were focusing on evangelism, and largely remained silent about socio-political issues except through prayer.[14] For instance, the Campus Crusade for Christ in Korea hosted the World Evangelization Crusade in Seoul in August 1980, three months after the Gwangju Uprising. The event succeeded in drawing a total

---

[9] Hong, Park and Jung, *The Contemporary History of South Korea*, 2: 216–7.
[10] Keun-Sik Jung, 'The Experience of the May 18 Uprising and the Communal Imagin-ation', in Georgy Katsiaficas and Na Kahn-Chae, eds, *South Korean Democracy: Legacy of the Gwangju Uprising* (New York, 2006), 134–57.
[11] 이종철 [Jong-Chul Lee], '80년대 기독 학생 운동사 (IV)' ['80nyeondae Gidok Haksaeng Undongsa (4)'; 'The Christian Student Movement in the 1980s (4)'], 복음과 상황 [*Bogeumgwa Sanghwang; Gospel and Context*] 14 [hereafter: *GC*] (December 1992), 128–35, at 129.
[12] Ibid. 129.
[13] '격동의 "86"' ['Gyeokdongui "86"; 'The Turbulent Year of "1986"'], 대학 기독 신 문 [*Daehak Gidok Sinmun; University Christian Newspaper*] [hereafter: *UCN*, 4 December 1986, 2; 김안식 [Ahn-Shik Kim], '역사의 현장에서 만난 예수님' ['Yeoksaui Hyeon-jangeseo Mannan Yesunim'; 'I Met Jesus in a Historic Moment'], *UCN*, 2 April 1987, 8.
[14] 'The Turbulent Year of "1986"', 2; 이종철 [Jong-Chul Lee], '80년대 기독 학생 운동 사 (III)' ['80nyeondae Gidok Haksaeng Undongsa (3)'; 'The Christian Student Movement in the 1980s (3)'], *GC* 13 (November 1992), 124–31, at 125.

attendance of 16,350,000 and in encouraging approximately 1,000,000 participants to volunteer for one-year-long overseas missions.[15] Yet no mention was made during the event of the oppressive measures taken by Chun's authoritarian regime against the uprising, or of its victims.

The conservative socio-political and missiological tone of mainstream Korean evangelicalism was partly rooted in the Western Protestant mission to Korea, which started in earnest from the late nineteenth century. Most Western Protestant missionaries came from America.[16] They were by and large pietistic in theology and quietist about socio-political issues.[17] The South Korean context after the liberation in 1945 from Japanese colonial power and the Korean War of 1950–3 stimulated this conservative tone among Korean evangelicals, largely due to a further influx of North Korean Protestant Christians into South Korea, most of whom were conservative in theology and in their stance toward socio-political issues. Their settlement and the subsequent expansion of their influence in South Korea contributed to the conservatism of Korean evangelicalism.[18] The post-liberation context also provided many Korean evangelicals with a strong rationale for acknowledging and even supporting authoritarian governments for the sake of national security against communist North Korea. While remaining silent about the pro-democracy movement which stood against these regimes, these churches primarily focused on the task of evangelization.

---

[15] Joon-Gon Kim, 'Korea's Total Evangelization Movement', in Bong-Rin Ro and Marlin L. Nelson, eds, *Korean Church Growth Explosion* (Seoul, 1983), 29, 35.

[16] Roughly seventy per cent of Western Protestant missionaries who came to Korea from 1884 to 1945 were American: 김승태 [Sung-Tae Kim] and 박혜진 [Hye-Jin Park], eds, 내한 선교사 총람 1884–1984 [*Naehan Seongyosa Chongnam 1884–1984; A List of Missionaries to Korea, 1884–1984*] (Seoul, 1994), 4–5.

[17] 이덕주 [Deok-Joo Rhie], 한국 토착교회 형성사 연구 [*Hanguk Tochakgyohoe Hyeongseongsa Yeongu; A Study of the Formation of the Indigenous Church in Korea*] (Seoul, 2001), 66–86; 김승태 [Seung-Tae Kim], '한말 일제 침략기 일제와 선교사와의 관계에 대한 연구 (1894–1910)' ['Hanmal Ilje Chimnyakgi Iljewa Seongyosawaui Gwangyee Daehan Yeongu'; 'A Study of the Relationship between the Japanese Empire and Protestant Missionaries during the Japanese Occupation, 1894–1910'], 한국 기독교와 역사 [*Christianity and History in Korea*] 6 (1997), 65–100.

[18] 윤정란 [Jung-Ran Yoon], 한국 전쟁과 기독교 [*Hanguk Jeonjaenggwa Gidokgyo; The Korean War and Protestantism*] (Seoul, 2015), 67–114; 강인철 [In-Cheol Kang], 한국의 개신교와 반공주의 [*Hangugui Gaesingyowa Bangongjuui; The Korean Protestant Church and Anti-Communism*] (Seoul, 2006), 405–567.

The 'Great March for Jesus' reflected the quietist socio-political and missiological tone of mainstream Korean evangelicalism, engaging in spiritual activity rather than political agitation. However, the context of the campus at the time meant that the 'Great March for Jesus' aroused resentment. Other university students disapproved of the fact that Christians were praising God in the month in which many were remembering the Gwangju Uprising and mourning its victims.[19] They also complained that the evangelical event took place in the same plaza as that used by the pro-democracy movement. As a result, they seized the main platform and drove evangelical students out of the university plaza.[20] This strong reaction from their fellow students aroused considerable uncertainty among the evangelicals, but they continued their rally by marching on the campus.[21] However, not long after they started to march, they heard some shocking news. During a demonstration against the government in another area of the campus, an SNU student had set himself on fire, crying: 'Let's remove the military regime from power'.[22] On learning this news, a group of evangelical Christians in the march split off to discuss in private approaches to societal issues.[23] Jong-Chul Lee, a key member of the group, recalled later that this incident, which 'was engraved deep' in their hearts, led them to recognize 'the void' in their understanding of political issues on the campus and in wider society.[24] This experience sparked intense discussions among the group members about their role as evangelical Christians in addressing societal issues. Following these discussions, a subset of students from this group, driven by their newfound awareness, decided to take concrete action. These students – who came from different departments across the campus and had all been raised in evangelical churches or involved in evangelical parachurch organizations, such as Korean chapters of Inter-Varsity Fellowship and Campus Crusade for Christ – concluded that the socio-political situation required a response on campus which differed from their current evangelical perspective.[25] As a result, they formed the

---

[19] Lee, 'The Christian Student Movement in the 1980s (4)', 129.

[20] Ibid.

[21] Ibid. 130.

[22] '군부 독재타도': ibid. All translations from Korean to English are mine unless otherwise noted.

[23] Ibid.

[24] Ibid.

[25] 'The Turbulent Year of "1986"', 2; Kim, 'I Met Jesus in a Historic Moment', 8; Jong-Chul Lee, interview by the author, Seoul, 12 July 2021; Keun-Joo Kim, interview by the author, Seoul, 18 May 2023.

Christian Culture Society and *University Christian Newspaper* to study, discuss and practise Christian social engagement, and to share with other evangelical students what they had learnt from their experience through the Society.[26] These students – comprising approximately twenty to thirty members and including key leaders such as Jong-Chul Lee (the *University Christian Newspaper*'s editor-in-chief), Wook Yoo and Eun-Seok Choi – together with their newly established organizations, constituted what we have termed the SNU evangelical network. This was the start of an endeavour by the SNU evangelical network to redefine evangelicalism.

Redefining Evangelicalism from the Margins

The attempt of the SNU evangelical network to redefine evangelicalism from the margins began by challenging the prevailing approaches to socio-political issues and Christian mission among mainstream evangelicals at the centre. The network criticized the understanding of the gospel and Christian mission among many mainstream evangelicals as partial. They saw it as paying attention only to individual salvation and evangelism, while being content to remain on the sidelines in terms of contemporary socio-political issues.[27] Furthermore, the network recognized that Korean evangelical churches had been influenced by more conservative American missionaries who insisted on the theological principle of separation between church and state.[28] In contrast, the network argued that through insisting on the principle of separation, the churches had remained silent about socio-political issues including violent and repressive measures by Chun's authoritarian government, and that remaining silent about the existence of an unjust authoritarian regime signified tacit approval.[29] Moreover, the network observed that although the Korean evangelical churches claimed the principle of separation between church and state, in reality they often took a pro-

---

[26] Wook Yoo, interview by the author, Seoul, 16 May 2023; Keun-Joo Kim, interview by the author, Seoul, 18 May 2023.

[27] '회개 운동은 철저한 비판적 현실 인식을 토대로 열매 맺어져야' ['Hoegae Undongeun Cheoljeohan Bipanjeok Hyeonsil Insigeul Todaero Yeolmae Maejeojyeoya'; 'A Repentance Movement Should Produce an Outcome Founded Upon a Critical Perspective of Reality'], *UCN*, 5 March 1987, 2; '정교분리 원칙 태동의 역사적 맥락' ['The Historical Context of the Principle of Separation between Church and State'], 복협 신문 [*Bokyeop Sinmun; Newspaper of the Association of Evangelical Youth and Students*] [hereafter: *NAEYS*], 4 December 1987, 4.

[28] 'The Historical Context of the Principle of Separation between Church and State', 4.

[29] Ibid.

government stance.[30] The network believed, however, that the Christian gospel and mission embraced more than individual salvation, and that Christian faith necessarily encompassed a societal dimension.[31] A 1988 article in the *University Christian Newspaper* highlighted this point:

> The core of the Gospel of Jesus Christ was to proclaim the Kingdom of God. His missional focus and historical awareness were to realise the Kingdom of God where the poor and the captives were hearing good news of liberty and where justice and peace were prevailing. … While traditional [evangelical] churches have remained at an elementary level of salvation by being preoccupied with the vertical dimension (of the Gospel), the Kingdom of God movement includes the horizontal dimension between human and human.[32]

In pursuing what has been termed a more holistic understanding of the gospel and Christian mission – a theological approach that integrated both individual spiritual salvation and active engagement with socio-political issues, in contrast to the mainstream evangelical focus primarily on individual salvation – the SNU evangelical network continued to hold an evangelical identity.[33] They believed that, in the words of a key member, 'the evangelicalism in which we believe can embrace all societal issues'.[34] At the same time, most members of the SNU network sought to distance themselves from the more liberal wings of Korean Protestant Christianity, such as groups following liberation and Minjung theologies, which adopted radical approaches to addressing socio-political issues and played a major role in the democratization movements of the 1970s and 1980s.[35] In this sense,

---

[30] Ibid.

[31] Wook Yoo, interview by the author, Seoul, 16 May 2023.

[32] '예수 그리스도의 복음의 핵심은 하나님 나라를 선언하는 것이었으며, 가난한 자와 억눌린 자가 해방의 소식을 얻게 되고 정의와 평화가 지배하는 하나님 나라를 실현하는 것이 그의 선교적 관심이고 역사의식이었다. …… 기존교회가 하나님과 인간이라는 수직적 관계에만 얽매여 구원의 초보에만 머문데 반해 하나님 나라 운동은 … 인간과 인간이라는 수평적 차원으로의 관계의 확장을 의미한다.' '88 무엇을 할 것인가?' ['88 Mueoseul Hal Geosinga?'; 'What Shall We Do in 1988?'], *UCN*, 15 March 1988, 2.

[33] Kirkpatrick, *A Gospel for the Poor*, 11–12.

[34] '우리가 믿는 복음주의라고 하는 것은 사회적인 문제를 모두 포괄해 낼 수 있다.' Wook Yoo, interview by the author, Seoul, 16 May 2023.

[35] Paul Y. Chang, *Protest Dialectics: State Repression and South Korea's Democracy Movement, 1970–1979* (Stanford, 2015), 49–110; Sebastian C. H. Kim and Kirsteen Kim, *A History of Korean Christianity* (New York, 2015), 246–55.

their endeavour to challenge a conservative-leaning socio-political and missiological orientation in mainstream evangelicalism through pursuing a holistic understanding of the gospel and Christian mission was not an attempt to abandon their evangelical identity, but to reinterpret and redefine it.

This attempt to redefine evangelicalism was influenced by many theological ideas. A list of Christian books recommended by the *University Christian Newspaper* displays a range of theological sources, which was notably broad considering the preponderance of Presbyterians in South Korean evangelicalism.[36] In 1982, Presbyterianism was the largest denomination within South Korean evangelicalism, constituting 56.3% of the entire Korean Protestant population, with Methodism following at 11.6%.[37] Despite this Presbyterian dominance, the list included Baptists (George E. Ladd and C. René Padilla), evangelical Anglicans (John Stott and Reuben A. Torrey III), a Mennonite (Ronald J. Sider), pre-Reformation Catholics (St. Augustine and Thomas à Kempis), post-Vatican II Catholics (Leonardo Boff and In-Seok Seo), a Dutch Reformed theologian (Bob Goudzwaard), as well as the Presbyterians Harvie M. Conn and Francis Schaeffer. This wide variety of writers with diverse denominational and theological backgrounds reflected the SNU evangelical network's effort to legitimize their work of redefining evangelicalism.

[36] The recommended books included: St. Augustine's *Confessions*; Thomas à Kempis's *The Imitation of Christ*; Bob Goudzwaard's *Idols of Our Time*; Harvie M. Conn's *Bible Studies on World Evangelization and the Simple Lifestyle*; George E. Ladd's *Gospel of the Kingdom: Scriptural Studies in the Kingdom of God*; James W. Sire's *The Universe Next Door*; John Stott's *Christian Mission in the Modern World*; Francis Schaeffer's *How Should We Then Live?*; *Evangelism, Salvation and Social Justice*, co-authored by Ronald J. Sider and C. René Padilla; Ronald J. Sider's *Rich Christians in an Age of Hunger*; Leonardo Boff's *The Lord's Prayer*; *Is Revolution Change?*, edited by Brian Griffiths; Reuben A. Torrey III's 토지와 자유 [*Land and Freedom*]; 해방신학의 올바른 이해 [*Understanding Liberation Theology*], edited by Bundo Publishing Editorial Team; Sam-Yeol Lee's 기독교와 사회이념 [*Christianity and Social Ideology*]; and In-Seok Seo's 성서의 가난한 사람들 [*The Poor in the Bible*]. See '한 권의 책을 권함' ['Han Gwonui Chaegeul Gwonham'; 'A Book Recommendation'], *UCN*, 2 April 1987, 5; '서평' ['Seopyeong'; 'A Book Review'], *UCN*, 16 October 1987, 6; '신입생을 위한 추천 도서' ['Sinipsaengeul Wihan Chucheon Doseo'; 'Book Recommendations for Freshmen'], *UCN*, 15 March 1988, 7; '서평' ['Seopyeong'; 'A Book Review'], *UCN*, 9 September 1988, 8; '서평' ['Seopyeong'; 'A Book Review'], *UCN*, 15 May 1989, 8.

[37] The Council for the Centennial Anniversary of the Korean Church, 한국 기독교 100 주년 기념 사업 요람 [*Hanguk Gidokgyo 100junyeon Ginyeom Saeop Yoram*; *A Booklet of the Memorial Enterprises of the Centennial Year of Korean Protestantism*] (Seoul, 1984), 47; Timothy S. Lee, *Born Again: Evangelicalism in Korea* (Honolulu, 2010), 141.

Three points should be noted in relation to the SNU evangelical network's embrace of this wide range of theological sources. First, the range arose from their search for a holistic understanding of the gospel and mission beyond a mainstream evangelical perspective, which was perceived as 'limited' or 'partial'. For instance, an article in the *University Christian Newspaper* in April 1987 recommended reading *Bible Studies on World Evangelization and the Simple Lifestyle* (1981), written by Reformed missiologist Harvie M. Conn.[38] That article also highlighted the need for Korean evangelical churches to adjust their view of the Christian gospel in a more holistic direction:

> The Gospel of the Kingdom of God ... has been interpreted with a focus on personal ethics. As a result, the understanding of evangelism and Jesus Christ has been reduced merely as verbal proclamation of the Gospel and as the Saviour, not the Lord. This interpretative tendency also has caused an extreme conflict among us between personal and social salvations, and a difficulty in understanding the relationship between evangelism and social responsibility. This book helps us to move from an extremely spiritualised understanding of the Gospel ... into an incarnated one.[39]

Second, a global evangelical impulse toward a more holistic approach to the gospel and Christian mission was observable. John Stott's *Christian Mission in the Modern World* (1975) was listed among the books recommended by the *University Christian Newspaper*. This was published the year after the 1974 International Congress on World Evangelization, held in Lausanne, Switzerland.[40] Stott, who was the chairman of the drafting committee for the Lausanne Covenant, acknowledged the missional significance of both evangelism and social justice in this book, as did the Covenant.[41] However, the Covenant's dual accent in Christian mission attracted contested interpretations

---

[38] Harvie M. Conn, *Bible Studies on World Evangelization and the Simple Lifestyle* (Phillipsburg, NJ, 1981).
[39] '하나님 나라의 복음 (은) ... 개인 윤리 중심의 성경해석으로 관념화되어 버린 나머지 전도는 구두선포만으로 예수 그리스도는 주 (Lord)가 아니라 구원자 (Savior)로 위축되어 이해되는 경우가 많았다. 그것이 개인구원과 사회구원의 극한 논리적 대립을 낳기도 하였고 복음전도와 사회적 책임의 관계 이해에 난관이 되기도 했다. 이 교재는 ... 지나치게 영화 (spiritualization) 된 복음의 구체화를 [돕는다].' 'A Book Recommendation', 5.
[40] John Stott, *Christian Mission in the Modern World* (Downers Grove, IL, 1975).
[41] Ibid. 15–34.

among global evangelical constituents.[42] Despite these differing interpretations, Stott's understanding of mission as expressed in both his book and the Covenant was broader than that which he had articulated at the 1966 World Congress on Evangelism held in Berlin.[43] *Christian Mission in the Modern World* was translated into Korean in 1981.[44] Books by representatives of the American and Latin American evangelical left also featured in the list. Anabaptist Ronald J. Sider came to broader evangelical prominence in the 1970s,[45] and Korean translations of Sider's *Rich Christians in an Age of Hunger* and *Evangelism and Salvation and Social Justice* were published in 1981 and 1987.[46] Inter-Varsity Press Korea expanded Sider's *Evangelism, Salvation and Social Justice* by adding an article written by C. René Padilla and the Wheaton Statement (titled 'Transformation: The Church in Response to Human Need') published by the Consultation on the Church in Response to Human Need in Wheaton, Illinois, in June 1983. Thus, the Korean version of *Evangelism, Salvation and Social Justice* had co-authors. The Latin American evangelical left had started to redefine evangelical understanding of the gospel and Christian mission from the 1960s, in distinction from the views of American and Latin American conservative evangelicals.[47] They developed a new evangelical theological formula of Christian mission which sought a more holistic approach, known as *misión integral* (complete mission), a term which the Ecuadorian C. René Padilla appears to have coined in 1973.[48] This attempt by the Latin American evangelical left to redefine

---

[42] Stanley, *The Global Diffusion of Evangelicalism*, 177–9.

[43] Ibid. 155.

[44] John Stott, 현대 기독교 선교 [*Hyeondae Gidokgyo Seongyo; Christian Mission in the Modern World*], transl. Myung-Hyuk Kim (Seoul, 1981). John Stott's commentary on the Lausanne Covenant had also been translated into Korean earlier in 1976, despite not being among the titles in the list recommended by the *University Christian Newspaper*: John Stott, *The Lausanne Covenant: An Exposition and Commentary* (Minneapolis, MN, 1975); idem, 선교에 대한 복음주의 입장 [*Seongyoe Daehan Bogeumjuui Ipjang; An Evangelical Perspective on Mission*], transl. 조종남 [Jong-Nam Cho] (Gyeonggi, 1976).

[45] Swartz, *Moral Minority*, 156–60.

[46] Ronald J. Sider, *Rich Christians in an Age of Hunger: A Biblical Study* (Downers Grove, IL, 1977); idem, 기아와 빈곤으로부터의 해방 [*Giawa Bingoneurobuteoui Haebang; The Liberation from the Starvation and Poverty*], transl. 권명달 [Myung-Dal Kwon] (Seoul, 1981); idem, *Evangelism, Salvation and Social Justice* (Bramcote, 1977); idem and Carlos René Padilla, 복음전도, 구원, 사회정의 [*Bogeumjeondo, Guwon, Sahoejeongui; Evangelism, Salvation and Social Justice*], transl. 한화룡 [Hwa-Ryong Han] (Seoul, 1987).

[47] Kirkpatrick, *A Gospel for the Poor*, 15–52.

[48] Ibid. 49; Salinas, 'The Theological Revolution in Latin American Evangelicalism', 41–61.

evangelicalism influenced the subsequent Korean attempt, primarily through the publication of translations of their books. For instance, *Is Revolution Change?* (1972), edited by the British Christian economist Brian Griffiths (another book recommended by the *University Christian Newspaper*), included chapters by Padilla and by the Puerto Rican Orlando E. Costas. This book was translated into Korean in 1989.[49] It argued that 'a violent and total revolution' was 'no panacea for society's problems'.[50] This stance against violent revolution resonated with two experiments conducted by the SNU evangelical network, which will be discussed in the next section. The 1987 translation of *Evangelism, Salvation and Social Justice* included a chapter on evangelism and social responsibility, written by Padilla. Although it was not included in the list of the books recommended by the *University Christian Newspaper*, Costas's *Christ Outside the Gate: Mission Beyond Christendom* (1982) was also translated into Korean and published in 1987.[51]

Third, the SNU evangelical network's acceptance of diverse theological ideas showed their eclecticism for the sake of social engagement. In interviews conducted by this author, members of the SNU evangelical network tended to hesitate to pick a particular theological idea which was most formative for them at that time.[52] This hesitation was in stark contrast to former members of the younger evangelical pastoral network. That network, primarily Presbyterian in nature, made its own attempts at redefining evangelicalism through the formation, in March 1988, of the Youth Evangelical Fellowship of Korea, which overlapped with the efforts of the SNU evangelical student group.[53] Most members of this pastoral network were actively involved in university student ministry, leading to close connections and collaborations with the SNU evangelical student network, notably through

---

[49] Brian Griffiths, ed., *Is Revolution Change?* (London, 1972); idem, ed., 혁명만이 변화인가? [*Hyeongmyeongmani Byeonhwainga?*; *Is Revolution Change?*], transl. 한화룡 [Hwa-Ryong Han] (Seoul, 1989).

[50] Griffiths, *Is Revolution Change?*, 7.

[51] Orlando E. Costas, *Christ Outside the Gate: Mission Beyond Christendom* (Maryknoll, NY, 1982); idem, 성문 밖의 그리스도 [*Seongmun Bakkui Geuriseudo; Christ Outside the Gate*], transl. 김승환 [Seung-Hwan Kim] (Seoul, 1987).

[52] Jong-Chul Lee, interview by the author, Seoul, 12 July 2021; Wook Yoo, interview by the author, Seoul, 16 May 2023; Keun-Joo Kim, interview by the author, Seoul, 18 May 2023.

[53] '복음주의 청년협 창립 강연회' ['Bogeumjuui Cheongnyeonhyeop Changnip Gangyeonhoe'; 'Inaugural Lecture for the Youth Evangelical Fellowship of Korea'], 크리스챤 신문 [*Keuriseuchyan Sinmun; Christian Press*], 27 February 1988, 11.

their frequent contribution of articles to the SNU evangelical network's *University Christian Newspaper*.[54] Unlike the eclectic approach of the student network, former members of this pastoral network recalled in interviews with this author that the Lausanne Covenant was the most important theological foundation in their journey of redefining evangelicalism.[55] The Youth Evangelical Fellowship of Korea, formed by the pastoral network, was also based on the Lausanne Covenant.[56] In the words of members of the network, the Covenant was 'the key theological foundation' and 'a ray of light' to them, and its impact was comparable with the explosion of 'a nuclear bomb'.[57] In contrast, former members of the SNU evangelical network were much less enthusiastic than the pastors' network in acknowledging the significance of the Covenant in their process of redefining evangelicalism.[58] Rather, in interviews, they tended to highlight that responding urgently to the context of socio-political turmoil was their most important agenda. One member of the pastors' network acknowledged this tendency among the SNU evangelical network, recognizing that the student network tended to accent more direct engagement in the socio-political context than the evangelical pastors' network.[59] The major interest of the pastors' network was to form a theological foundation for engagement through embracing the influence of theological ideas, particularly the Lausanne Covenant, and to provide other Christians with that foundation. The SNU evangelical network, on the other hand, laid its emphasis on urgent engagement in

---

[54] 구교형 [Ku Kyo-Hyung], 한국복음주의 사회선교운동 30년사: 하나님나라를 응시하다 [*Hangukbogeumjuui Sahoeseongyoundong 30nyeonsa: Hananim Narareul Eungsihada*; *Thirty Year History of the Korean Evangelical Movement for Social Mission: Looking at the Kingdom of God*] (Seoul, 2019), 57–8; 김회권 [Hae-Kwon Kim], '80년대 학원 선교의 반성과 전망' ['80nyeondae Hagwon Seongyoui Banseonggwa Jeonmang'; 'A Retrospect and Prospect of the Campus Ministry in the 1980s'], *UCN*, 5 March 1987, 4.

[55] Kyung-Min Kang, interview by the author, Seoul, 22 June 2021; Mun-Shik Lee, interview by the author, Yongin, 6 July 2021; Chul-Ho Han, interview by the author (via Zoom), Seoul, 19 July 2021; Chik-Han Koh, interview by the author (via Zoom), Seoul, 12 August 2021.

[56] 'Inaugural Lecture for the Youth Evangelical Fellowship of Korea', 11.

[57] '큰 신학적 토대', '하나의 빛', '핵폭탄': Kyung-Min Kang, interview by the author, Seoul, 22 June 2021; Chul-Ho Han, interview by the author (via Zoom), Seoul, 19 July 2021; Cheol-Soo Park, interview by the author, Yongin, 1 July 2021.

[58] Jong-Chul Lee, interview by the author, Seoul, 12 July 2021; Wook Yoo, interview by the author, Seoul, 16 May 2023; Keun-Joo Kim, interview by the author, Seoul, 18 May 2023.

[59] Mun-Shik Lee, interview by the author, Yongin, 6 July 2021.

the socio-political context, which led its members to draw on a range of theological ideas if they thought these ideas strengthened their responses to the context. Based on this eclecticism, some members of the SNU evangelical network embraced the influence of liberation theologians and social scientific analyses such as Marxism, and thus placed themselves at or even beyond what mainstream evangelicals regarded as the boundary of evangelicalism.[60] However, although all members of the SNU evangelical network agreed on the need to redefine evangelicalism, they differed on the issue of how far they were prepared to move toward the liberal end of the theological spectrum. This difference was a source of fragility in their collaboration, which became a major limitation of the emerging new evangelical group in the late twentieth century.

The issue of how far the new Korean evangelicals were prepared to move in their theology was particularly important, because most Korean Protestant Christians were evangelical. A 1982 government statistic estimated that, at that time, Protestants constituted around 20% of the whole population, with Roman Catholics roughly at 4%.[61] Over 90% of Korean Protestants, according to Timothy Lee's estimation, were evangelical in the early 1980s.[62] The Korean context contrasted thus with Latin America, where evangelical Christianity was a religious minority and Roman Catholics the majority. The experience of social isolation as a religious minority within a predominantly Catholic society had exerted an influence on the development of the Latin American evangelical left.[63] In contrast, the Korean counterpart emerged from a context where evangelical Christianity constituted the great majority of Korean Protestantism, and its

---

[60] '기초 공동체 운동의 심화 확산' ['Gicho Gongdongche Undongui Simhwa Hwaksan'; 'The Growth and Intensification of the Base Community'], *UCN*, 16 October 1987, 2; 'What Shall We Do in 1988?', 2; '운동권의 주체 역량 미비와 야권의 분열 속에서 여권의 순탄한 항해' ['Undonggwonui Juche Yeongnyang Mibiwa Yagwonui Bunyeol Sogeseo Yeogwonui Suntanhan Hanghae'; 'The Lack of Autonomy of the Pro-Democracy Movement Group, the Division of the Opposition Parties, and the Resulting Smooth Voyage of the Ruling Party'], *UCN*, 2 April 1987, 2; 이승재 [Seung-Jae Lee], '사회과학 방법론의 유물론적 기조와 그 수용 가능성' ['Sahoegwahak Bangbeomnonui Yumullonjeok Gijowa Geu Suyong Ganeungseong'; 'Socio-scientific Mythology's Materialistic Tendency and Its Acceptability'], *UCN*, 25 December 1988, 5.
[61] The Council for the Centennial Anniversary of the Korean Church, *A Booklet of the Memorial Enterprises*, 46.
[62] Lee, *Born Again*, 141.
[63] Kirkpatrick, *A Gospel for the Poor*, 33–52.

mainstream inclined to the conservative end of the spectrum in socio-
political and theological aspects. In the Korean context, a radical move
toward the liberal end, as defined by mainstream evangelicalism, was
more challenging and riskier than in Latin America. Mainstream
evangelical challenges to the radicalism of the new evangelical group
became more apparent after the 1980s, when the group gained more
influence over Protestant Christians. However, this challenge is
already observable in the case of the SNU evangelical network. For
instance, the fourth issue of the *University Christian Newspaper*
on 5 March 1987 contained many articles showing sympathy with
social scientific analyses, such as Marxism.[64] Amongst mainstream
evangelical students, this provoked serious concern about the periodical. For them, the tone of those articles sounded very similar to that of
the radical student pro-democracy movement and the periodical
looked as if it had embraced the influence of the radical student
movement without applying an evangelical filter.[65] Facing this challenge from mainstream evangelical students, the editorial board of the
periodical attempted to persuade their readers of the necessity of
accepting social scientific analyses of social structures.[66] In their view,
evangelical Christianity had not yet developed comparable analytical
tools for understanding social structures, making these social scientific
approaches necessary. The editorial board also stressed that this did not
mean completely embracing the analyses without any criticism from
the Christian perspective.[67] However, despite these arguments in
defence of the position taken by the journal, concerns among mainstream evangelical students about it persisted.[68]

In this way, the redefining work of the SNU evangelical network on
the periphery of the evangelical majority of Korean Protantism

---

[64] 박문재 [Mun-Jae Park], '우리는 무엇을 보며, 무엇을 들으려 하는가' ['Urineun
Mueoseul Bomyeo, Mueoseul Deureuryeo Haneunga'; 'What Should We Want to See and
Hear?'], *UCN*, 5 March 1987, 1; 'A Repentance Movement Should Produce an Outcome',
2; Kim, 'A Retrospect and Prospect of the Campus Ministry in the 1980s', 4; 김병연
[Byung-Yeon Kim], '아담 스미드와 칼 맑스 그리고 기독교' ['Adam Seumideuwa Kal
Malseu Geurigo Gidokgyo'; 'Adam Smith, Karl Marx, and Christianity'], *UCN*, 5 March
1987, 5.
[65] 'The Lack of Autonomy of the Pro-Democracy Movement Group', 2.
[66] Ibid.
[67] Ibid.
[68] '서울대 채플의 길' ['Seouldae Chaepeurui Gil'; 'The Way to Go for Seoul National
University's Chapel'], *UCN*, 2 April 1987, 4–5; '투고 환영' ['Tugo Hwanyeong'; 'Calling
for Contributions from Readers'], *UCN*, 9 September 1988, 4.

challenged the prevailing evangelical interpretation of socio-political issues and Christian mission. However, in redefining evangelicalism, the members of the SNU evangelical network varied on how far they were willing to travel. The differences among them produced a divergence between moderate and radical pathways of redefining evangelicalism. This divergence would later be reflected in the wider new evangelical movement. Two experiments conducted by the SNU evangelical network represented these two divergent pathways.

THE TWO DIVERGENT PATHWAYS OF NEW EVANGELICAL EXPERIMENTS

The more moderate pathway of redefining evangelicalism was symbolized by the formation in 1987 of the Association of Evangelical Youth and Students, and its launching of a campaign for a fair election. In 1987, one year after the SNU evangelical network started an endeavour to redefine evangelicalism, the June Uprising against Doo-Hwan Chun's regime occurred across Korea.[69] As a result of this nation-wide uprising, Chun's regime came to an end, although he nominated his political successor, Tae-Woo Roh. The constitution was revised in favour of a direct presidential election system which had been abolished in 1972 by Chung-Hee Park's regime. The SNU evangelical network saw the revival of a direct election system as 'an opportunity given by God for democratisation'.[70] At around the same time, in 1986, the National Citizens' Movement for Free Elections in the Philippines launched a nation-wide campaign to guard the presidential election from any attempts of election malpractice by dictator Ferdinand Marcos. The Filipino campaign directly inspired the SNU evangelical network to form the Association of Evangelical Youth and Students in November 1987 and to launch its campaign for a fair election.[71]

---

[69] 서중석 [Joong-Seok Seo], 한국 현대사 60년 [*Hanguk Hyeondaesa 60nyeon*; *The Contemporary History of South Korea – 60 Years*] (Gyeonggi, 2007), 196–201.

[70] '민주화를 위해 하나님이 주신 기회': Wook Yoo, interview by the author, Seoul, 16 May 2023.

[71] '복음주의 청년, 학생 협의회 발족 취지문' ['Bogeumjuui Cheongnyeon, Haksaeng Hyeobuihoe Baljok Chwijimun'; 'The Founding Document of the Association of Evangelical Youth and Students'], *UCN*, 19 November 1987, 1; '필리핀 남프렐의 공명 선거 운동' ['Pillipin Nampeurerui Gongmyeong Seongeo Undong'; 'A Filipino Fair Election

As the inclusion of the term 'evangelical' in its name shows, the association adhered to an evangelical identity. However, for its members, being evangelical implied neither remaining silent nor confining themselves to prayer about socio-political concerns (the position taken by most mainstream evangelical Christians), but rather a deep involvement in those issues. In other words, the association was founded on the basis of 'the absolute necessity of social practices based upon evangelical faith'.[72] What was meant by 'evangelical faith' here was a new or redefined form of evangelicalism, founded upon a more holistic understanding of the gospel and Christian mission than that held by most mainstream evangelicals.[73] The association recruited young evangelical Christians to train them as election observers and counting overseers, dispatching them to various electoral districts.[74] Young evangelical Christians who belonged to the youth groups of mainstream evangelical local churches and evangelical campus ministry organizations, such as Korean branches of the Intervarsity Fellowship and the Campus Crusade for Christ, enthusiastically participated.[75] As a result, the association succeeded in attracting around 2,000 young evangelical volunteers.[76] Reporting this success, they discerned that enthusiastic participation from young evangelical Christians was a sign of their 'thirst for social justice'.[77] Furthermore, this success was backed up by the association's moderate approach to social engagement. In an interview with the author, Wook Yoo, the president of the association and a key leader of the SNU evangelical network, said that the success of the association in attracting many young evangelical participants reflected the fact that

---

Campaign Launched by the National Citizens' Movement for a Free Election'], *NAEYS*, 27 November 1987, 4.

[72] '복음적 신앙에 기초한 사회적 실천의 절대 필요': '복음주의 청년, 학생 협의회 결성에 부쳐' ['Bogeumjuui Cheongnyeon, Haksaeng Hyeobuihoe Gyeolseonge Buchyeo'; 'Celebrating the Formation of the Association of Evangelical Youth and Students'], *NAEYS*, 27 November 1987, 1. See also '복음주의 청년, 학생 협의회 결성' ['Bogeumjuui Cheongnyeon, Haksaeng Hyeobuihoe Gyeolseong'; 'The Formation of the Association of Evangelical Youth and Students'], *NAEYS*, 27 November 1987, 1.

[73] 'The Formation of the Association of Evangelical Youth and Students', 1.

[74] 'The Founding Document of the Association of Evangelical Youth and Students', 1.

[75] '정의를 향한 교회의 뜨거운 몸짓' ['Jeonguireul Hyanghan Gyohoeui Tteugeoun Momjit'; 'Churches' Enthusiasm for Social Justice'], *NAEYS*, 4 December 1987, 1.

[76] '자원 봉사자 등록 상황' ['Jawon Bongsaja Deungnok Sanghwang'; 'The Status of Recruiting Volunteers'], *NAEYS*, 11 December 1987, 3.

[77] Ibid.

the association's approach to social engagement was not so radical even for mainstream evangelical Christians.[78]

For some members of the SNU evangelical network, the association's moderate approach represented 'the minimum' which could be expected of anyone with 'the least Christian conscience'.[79] They were open to the influence of more liberal theologies, such as liberation and Minjung theologies, as well as Marxist-type social scientific analysis, which many mainstream evangelical Christians viewed as boundaries which evangelicals should not cross. They thought that the task of redefining evangelicalism needed to go further than what the association proposed. In this regard, they had been conducting a more radical experiment in the form of a base community. Base communities were small groups of local Christians which aimed to live out the teachings of liberation theology.[80] In Latin America in 1978, there were over 100,000 base communities.[81] In April 1987, a pastor closely associated with the SNU evangelical network initiated a base community in a shanty town of Seoul. Some members of the student network were closely involved in the community from its start. The community consisted of around a dozen members. Living with poor neighbours in the town, they engaged in various relief activities, such as running daycare centres and tutoring poor children in the area.[82]

Those of the SNU evangelical network who were involved in the base community believed that this was an evangelical alternative to the radicalized student pro-democracy movement. At the time, the student leadership of the democratization movement was inclined to accept Marxist social analysis and sought the fundamental transformation of society by confronting imperialistic and capitalist

---

[78] Wook Yoo, interview by the author, Seoul, 16 May 2023.

[79] '최소한의 일', '최소한의 양심': Keun-Joo Kim, interview by the author, Seoul, 18 May 2023. See also '복협 공정선거운동을 돌아보며' ['Bokyeop Gongjeong Seongeo Undongeul Dorabomyeo'; 'A Retrospection on the Fair Election Campaign by the Association of Evangelical Youth and Students'], *UCN*, 25 December 1988, 2.

[80] Valerie Ann Macnabb and Martha W. Rees, 'Liberation or Theology? Ecclesial Base Communities in Oaxaca, Mexico', *Journal of Church and State* 35 (1993), 723–49.

[81] Ibid. 730.

[82] 임영환 [Young-Hwan Lim], '빈민 선교활동 보고' ['Binmin Seongyo Hwaldong Bogo'; 'A Report of Mission for the Poor'], *UCN*, 9 September 1988, 6; 이덕준 [Duk-Jun Lee], '나의 모친과 나의 동생들을 보라' ['Naui Mochingwa Naui Dongsaengdeureul Bora'; 'Behold, My Mother and My Brothers'], *UCN*, 15 May 1989, 7; '공부방 교사 모집' ['Gongbubang Gyosa Mojip'; 'We Are Looking for Volunteer Tutors'], *UCN*, 5 September 1989, 8.

forces.[83] However, for those of the SNU evangelical network participating in the base community, this pro-democracy movement with its Marxist influence tended to focus only on the political dimension of human life, whereas humans were complex beings with many other dimensions.[84] Complaining about this tendency, they advocated for the base community as a form of social engagement based on a more holistic understanding of humanity:

> There is now a tendency in universities ... to overstate politicisation concerning humanity. In other words, we are forced to perceive that the authentic practice was ... to make people conscientized and organised political agents by helping them recognise the structural evil in our context. ... However, a human being is ... a complex and holistic reality. ... If we stick merely to a political movement, the true liberation of humanity is not realised. ... The growth and intensification of the base community is ... a key to the transformation of society. The political movement might change an external dimension of human life, but the Community transforms its essence.[85]

However, although some of the SNU evangelical network saw the base community as an evangelical alternative to the radicalized student pro-democracy movement, many other evangelical Christians criticized their approach to social engagement as too radical and as beyond acceptable evangelical boundaries.[86] For many Korean evangelicals at the time, liberation theology was not a Christian theology, but rather a

---

[83] Chubb, *Contentious Activism and Inter-Korean Relations*, 101–13.

[84] 'What Should We Do in 1988?', 2.

[85] '현 대학에 있어 인간에 대한 관심이 ... 정치화에만 의미를 지나치게 부여하는 경향이 있다. ... 구조악으로 왜곡된 그들의 삶을 보여주며 의식화-조직화시켜 정치적 실천의 주체로서 이끄는 것, 이것만이 참다운 실천으로 강요 받고 있는 것이다. 그러나 ... 인간이란 존재는 ... 복잡한 총체적 실체이다. ... 우리가 정치운동에만 연연할 때 참 인간 해방은 올 수 없는 것이다. ... 공동체 운동의 심화, 확산이야말로 ... 사회변혁운동의 핵심이다. 정치운동은 외피만을 변화시키지만 공동체 운동은 삶의 실질을 변화시키는 것이다.' Ibid. See also '민족 구원을 위한 하나님의 부르심에 책임 있는 응답을' ['Minjok Guwoneul Wihan Hananimui Bureusime Chaegim Inneun Eungdabeul'; 'A Responsible Reply toward God's Call for Us to Save Our People Is Needed'], *UCN*, 16 September 1987, 3; 'The Growth and Intensification of the Base Community', 2.

[86] '약정 토론' ['Yakjeong Toron'; 'A Panel Discussion'], 새로운 지성 [*Saeroun Jiseong; New Thought*] 2 (1989), 23–53, at 29, 46, 48. For complaints about the criticism among those of the SNU evangelical network who favoured the base community, see '기독교 사회관 집담회' [Gidokgyo Sahoegwan Jipdamhoe; A Group Discussion of a Christian View of Society], *UCN*, 16 March 1989, 2.

socio-political ideology moulded by Marxism, which replaced a Christian concept of salvation by political liberation.[87] Thus, embracing the influence of liberation theology was seen as irreconcilable with being evangelical, because liberation and evangelical theologies had distinct frameworks.[88] Other members of the SNU evangelical network were also sceptical, for similar reasons, both about embracing liberation theology's influence and regarding the radical experiment by some members of their group.[89] Through involvement in the base community, some members of the SNU evangelical network attempted to redefine evangelicalism in a more radical way. However, in doing so, they were seen as crossing a boundary from evangelicalism to 'liberal' or 'radical' theology.

CONCLUSION

The SNU evangelical network emerged on the margins of Korean evangelicalism. On the campus in the 1980s where the student pro-democracy movement and governmental oppression confronted each other, evangelical students struggled with the prevailing evangelical approach to socio-political issues and Christian mission. As a result, they started an endeavour in 1986 to challenge the prevailing approach through their own redefining actions. The formation of the Association of Evangelical Youth and Students and its campaign for a fair election, and the base community, were different expressions of this endeavour. However, although the SNU evangelical network's experiments were pioneering, their direct influence remained limited. It failed to significantly alter conservative predominance among Korean evangelicals. The limited impact of these experiments can be attributed to the deeply entrenched conservative nature of Korean evangelicalism, which posed significant challenges for the SNU network in pursuing a more holistic approach to evangelical identity. Furthermore, the evangelical student endeavour did not last long, which contributed to the limited impact of their experiments. Facing the issue of moral failures among the network

---

[87] 한철하 [Chul-Ha Han], '성경이 가르치는 현실 참여' ['Seonggyeongi Gareuchineun Hyeonsil Chamyeo'; 'Biblical Teachings on Christian Socio-political Involvement'], 성경과 신학 [*Seonggyeonggwa Sinhak; Bible and Theology*] 1 (1983), 16–19; 손봉호 [Bong-Ho Son], '해방 신학' ['Haebang Sinhak'; 'Liberation Theology'], 성경과 신학 [*Seonggyeonggwa Sinhak; Bible and Theology*] 1 (1983), 248–54.
[88] 'A Panel Discussion', 46.
[89] Jeong-Soo Park, interview by the author, Anyang, 21 July 2021; Wook Yoo, interview by the author, Seoul, 16 May 2023.

leadership, their bond of trust and respect collapsed, and it resulted in the dissolution of the network in September 1989.[90]

Nevertheless, their pioneering work of redefining evangelicalism had an enduring impact upon specific segments of Korean evangelicalism, particularly in inspiring and shaping subsequent new evangelical movements and initiatives. For instance, their launch of a campaign for a fair election through the Association of Evangelical Youth and Students set a precedent for similar types of campaigns initiated by new evangelicals in the 1990s.[91] The periodical *Gospel and Context*, which published its first issue in January 1991 and subsequently became a flagship magazine of Korean new evangelicalism, originated in the *University Christian Newspaper* of the SNU evangelical network.[92] Those who had been members of the student network played a central role in the early stage of this periodical. The formative role of the SNU evangelical network in relation to the Korean new evangelical group was similar to the importance of student groups in shaping the Latin American evangelical left.[93]

The SNU evangelical network's experience also prefigured the divergent approaches which later emerged among new evangelical groups and their differing receptions among broader evangelicalism. Two experiments conducted by the SNU evangelical network exemplified the moderate and radical paths, along with their respective outcomes, that would be seen in future new evangelical efforts. These experiments were the Association of Evangelical Youth and Students' campaign for a fair election, and the base community. While the former was acceptable to mainstream evangelicals and gained some support from them, the latter was challenged and suspected. This pattern was repeated among new evangelicals in the 1990s. For instance, a campaign for fair elections initiated in 1991 by the Chris-

---

[90] Gyeonggi, Korea Democracy Foundation Open Archives, '기문연 대책위 활동 보고서' ['Gimunyeon Daechaegwi Hwaldong Bogoseo'; 'Report by the Task Force to Resolve the Christian Culture Society Members' Imprisonment'], online at: <https://archives.kdemo.or.kr/isad/view/00841425>, accessed 12 August 2023.

[91] '공정 선거 운동의 현 주소와 전망' ['Gongjeong Seongeo Undongui Hyeon Jusowa Jeonmang'; 'The Present and Prospect of Campaigns for Fair Elections'], *GC* 8 (1992), 138–44.

[92] Lee, 'The Christian Student Movement in the 1980s (4)', 134; Keun-Joo Kim, interview by the author, Seoul, 18 May 2023.

[93] Kirkpatrick, *A Gospel for the Poor*, 33–52.

tian Ethics Movement of Korea, which favoured the moderate way, gained significant support from mainstream evangelicals.[94] However, the periodical *Gospel and Context* which sought a more radical approach to socio-political and theological issues suffered in the 1990s, facing frequent challenges from mainstream evangelical readers, and finding itself struggling with chronic financial difficulties.[95] In contrast to Latin America, the Korean context was marked by the presence of an evangelical majority. Its mainstream had a conservative-leaning socio-political and missiological orientation. In this Korean context, the task of redefining evangelicalism was always under pressure. Those who took a radical move toward the liberal end of the evangelical spectrum had to face continuing challenges from mainstream evangelicalism. Facing these challenges, they tended to take one of three options: adopting a more moderate tone; continuing to redefine evangelicalism with a radical spirit on the margins of evangelicalism; or leaving the evangelical camp altogether. For instance, Jong-Chul Lee, a key figure in both the SNU evangelical network and the periodical *Gospel and Context*, departed in 1993 from the evangelical to the more liberal Christian camp, complaining about the rigidity of evangelical boundaries in which he felt ideological confinement.[96] Those who took a radical path while managing to maintain an evangelical identity were on the margin of the margins in the Korean context.

Ultimately, the story of the SNU network illustrates the complexities of redefining evangelicalism from the margins within a predominantly conservative evangelical context. While unable to alter the evangelical landscape fundamentally, these marginal experiments created small but significant spaces for alternative voices and approaches

[94] '공명 선거 캠페인을 위한 기독인 선언' ['Gongmyeong Seongeo Kaempeineul Wihan Gidogin Seoneon'; 'A Christian Declaration for Fair Election Campaign'], 크리스챤 신문 [*Keuriseuchyan Sinmun; Christian Press*], 9 February 1991, 10; '알립니다' ['Allimnida'; 'Notice'], 기독교 윤리 실천 운동 소식 [*Gidokgyo Yulli Silcheon Undong Sosik; A Newsletter of the Christian Ethics Movement of Korea*] 35 (1991), 3–12, at 12.

[95] '독자 투고' ['Dokja Tugo'; 'The Correspondence Column'], *GC* 13 (1992), 18–9, at 19; '독자 투고' ['Dokja Tugo'; 'The Correspondence Column'], *GC* 16 (1993), 18–9, at 19; 김호열 [Ho-Yeol Kim], '복음과 상황을 폐간하며' ['Bogeumgwa Sanghwangeul Pyeganhamyeo'; 'The Discontinuation of the Publication of *Gospel and Context*'], *GC* 62 (1997), 154–8.

[96] Lee Jong-Chul, interview by the author, Seoul, 12 July 2021.

within Korean evangelicalism. This demonstrates that limited and short-lived movements operating from the periphery can contribute to the ongoing dialogue and evolution of religious thought and practice, even in contexts where conservative traditions remain strong.

Christian Outlaws: Bible Smuggling across Cold War Europe

Mary Heimann [ID]
Cardiff University

Bible smuggling, the illicit transportation of religious contraband into the Communist countries of the Eastern bloc, was a marked Cold War phenomenon. At first a peripheral, amateurish pursuit, over the course of the 1970s and 1980s Bible smuggling developed into a transnational network of training camps and safe houses, which used recruitment practices and specially doctored objects and vehicles resembling those of state intelligence agencies. Bible smuggling also became a mode of perception. Professional Bible smugglers, reliant on student volunteers, preached a distinctive worldview. They developed their own literature, theology, moral codes, trade routes and criminal methods. Bestselling books, comics, advertisements and personal testimonies gradually came to shape how millions of conservative Christians, mainly evangelicals, viewed Communist Europe. Bible smuggling became a multi-million-dollar business and a televangelist staple which influenced US foreign policy. This article uncovers, for the first time, the scale, methods and significance of Cold War Bible-smuggling and argues for its enduring influence on conservative Christian thinking.

Whatever mental images the phrases 'born-again Christian', 'charismatic Protestant' and 'evangelical' may conjure up in most people's minds, they are unlikely to include a smuggler, a secret agent or a spy handler. Nevertheless, from the late 1960s, a distinct form of Cold War

School of History, Cardiff University, John Percival building, Colum Drive, Cardiff, United Kingdom of Great Britain and Northern Ireland. E-mail: HeimannM@cardiff.ac.uk.

My grateful thanks to the six anonymous Bible smugglers, of various nationalities, who were willing to share memories, photographs and documents with me and to be extensively interviewed for this project; to the Keston Trustees for awarding me a scholarship to consult the Keston Archives, Baylor College, Waco, Texas, *in situ* 7–11 November 2022; to Iulia Cindrea Nagy for helping me to locate relevant materials in the National Council for the Study of the Securitate Archives (CNSAS) in Bucharest, Romania; Gabija Strumylaite for assistance with the Lithuanian national security archive; and to Éva Mártonffyné Petrás for

Studies in Church History 61 (2025), 609–637 © The Author(s), 2025. Published by Cambridge University Press on behalf of the Ecclesiastical History Society. This is an Open Access article, distributed under the terms of the Creative Commons Attribution licence (http://creativecommons.org/licenses/by/4.0), which permits unrestricted re-use, distribution and reproduction, provided the original article is properly cited.
doi:10.1017/stc.2024.54

missionary work began to capture the imagination of evangelical pastors, low church congregations and Bible students across the United States, Canada, the United Kingdom, Scandinavia, the Netherlands, West Germany and Austria. This was Bible smuggling to the Communist world: the illicit transportation of Bibles and Christian literature, including pamphlets, hymnals and Sunday school missals, through the Iron Curtain to scattered Protestant communities in Poland, Hungary, Romania, Czechoslovakia, East Germany, Yugoslavia, Albania and the Soviet Union.[1]

Bible smuggling across Europe is a topic which has yet to be systematically researched, let alone incorporated into our understanding of East-West relations during the Cold War.[2] This is a serious omission, because Bible smuggling, although it only occasionally hit the headlines, came to frame how millions of evangelicals in the West –

help with the Hungarian State Protection Authority (Államvédelmi Hatóság, ÁVH). I am equally grateful to Esko Mäki-Soini for sharing Finnish sources, including his 'Rekkamiehen muistoja matkan verrelta' ('Memoirs of a Trucker along the Way'); and to staff at the Security Services Archive (Archív bezpečnostních složek) in Prague. An earlier version of this article was read to the annual meeting of the Keston trustees in November 2023 and printed in Keston Newsletter no. 39 (2024). I am grateful to David Brimage, Thom Loyd, Angela Muir and Michael Novotný, and to the anonymous reviewers for SCH, for helpful comments.

[1] Most smuggled religious materials were intended for Protestant pastors, ministers or churches, but some went to Roman Catholics, Jehovah's Witnesses and other non-Protestant groups. Jewish organizations also smuggled religious literature into the Soviet Union and other Communist countries: see Gal Beckerman, *When They Come for Us, We'll Be Gone: The Epic Struggle to Save Soviet Jewry* (New York and Boston, MA, 2010); Zoe Knox, *Jehovah's Witnesses and the Secular World* (London, 2018).

[2] There is, as yet, not a single scholarly monograph on the topic, and just one postgraduate (MA) dissertation. A handful of published articles exist, most of which were written by former Cold War Bible smugglers. See Joe Gouverneur, 'Underground Evangelism: Missions during the Cold War', *Transformation* 24 (2007), 80–6; Bent Boel, 'Bible Smuggling and Human Rights in the Cold War', in Luc van Dongen, Stéphanie Roulin and Giles Scott-Smith, eds, *Transnational Anti-Communism and the Cold War* (Basingstoke, 2014), 263–75; Francis Raška, 'Bibles for Communist Europe – A Cold War Story, Part 1', *Hungarian Review* 6/3 (May 2015), 40–62. Joseph Schneider, '*Through the Seams of the Iron Curtain: Clandestine NGO Support to Christian Religious Minorities in Communist-Controlled Eastern Europe, Central Europe and Russia, 1960–1989*' (MA thesis, Postgraduate Naval School, Monterey, CA, 2018), was written by a man who grew up in an American Bible-smuggling family stationed in West Germany. At least two private museums containing collections of artefacts from Cold War Bible smuggling across Europe exist, one in the Czech Republic and one in Sweden, but these are run by Bible-smuggling organizations and not open to the general public. For photographs, see also James Kapaló and Tatiana Vagramenko, eds, *Hidden Galleries: Material Religion in the Secret Police Archives in Central and Eastern Europe* (Abingdon, 2021).

especially in the English-speaking world – viewed the Communist regimes of the East.[3] Even after 1989 and the collapse of Communism in Central and Eastern Europe, some Bible-smuggling organizations survived, shifting the focus of their operations to China or North Korea, or reframing the enemy as Islam rather than Communism.[4] A number continue to recruit, raise money and smuggle internationally to the present day. Through their promotional materials, recruitment drives, published memoirs, sermons and online appearances, Bible smugglers perpetuate a view of the world in which Christians are understood to be a persecuted minority, itself a distinct strand in right-wing populism and Christian nationalism which is widely present across Europe and North America today.

From modest beginnings in the mid-1950s and early 1960s, Bible smuggling developed, over the course of the 1970s, into an international network of organizations which merit serious study in their own right. Some of the most prominent Cold War Bible-smuggling organizations operating during the 1960s, 1970s and 1980s were: Underground Evangelism, Open Doors, Jesus to the Communist World (later renamed Voice of the Martyrs), Eastern European Mission, *Dansk Europamission* ('Danish Mission to Europe'), *Licht im Osten* ('Light in the East'), Slavic Mission, The Team, and the organization which informs much of the present study, Operation Mobilisation (hereafter referred to as OM).[5] As OM's founder, an American

---

[3] The term 'evangelical', as used in the English-speaking world, is rather loose and malleable. It can refer to a specific church or union of churches or pressure group, as in the case of the National Association of Evangelicals; or to a theological tendency among members within a denomination, usually Protestant, who place particular emphasis on the importance of conversion, atoning grace through the crucifixion, the need to live by and spread the Good News, and the primacy of the Bible. The best working definition of 'evangelicalism' (sometimes referred to as 'Bebbington's Quadrilateral') can be found in David Bebbington, *Evangelicalism in Modern Britain: A History from the 1730s to the 1980s* (London, 1989), 2–17. See also David Bebbington and George Marsden, eds, *Evangelicals: Who They Have Been, Are Now, and Could Be* (Grand Rapids, MI, 2019). In Central and Eastern Europe, 'Evangel', or *evangelisch*, often misleadingly translated into English as 'evangelical', simply means a Christian in the reformed (usually Lutheran) tradition.

[4] On the crisis presented to Bible-smuggling organizations by the 1989 anti-Communist revolutions, see Gouverneur, 'Underground Evangelism', 80–6; on the shift to demonizing Islam, especially after the terrorist attacks of 11 September 2001, see ibid. 85.

[5] Eleven in-depth interviews by the present author with four former Bible smugglers, based in Finland, Canada, the USA and the former Czechoslovakia, were conducted (and recorded via Zoom) between 3 February 2022 and 28 February 2023. Two further interviews with a husband-and-wife team of Bible smugglers, one of whom had also worked

evangelical named George Verwer, later recalled, it was in Austria in 1961 (the same year in which the Peace Corps was founded), that 'God gave me a name – the name that has stuck Operation Mobilisation – OM' and 'showed me how to mobilize the church – bringing people together for a summer, for two years and to send them on outreaches. Then sending them back to their home churches or to another mission agency to energize, revitalize the church and spread the vision.'[6] The method which Verwer and his team perfected, of drawing on an ever-changing pool of volunteers from the West, recruited and managed by a small core of permanent staff based mainly in Western Europe, enabled an organization like OM to punch above its weight.

Bible smuggling became big business from the 1970s, attracting substantial donations and thousands of volunteers, mainly from North America, Scandinavia and the United Kingdom. Volunteers for short-term missions included Justin Welby, the future archbishop of Canterbury, who smuggled Bibles into Czechoslovakia in 1980 and into Romania in 1981 for Eastern European Mission.[7] By the 1980s, evangelical lobbyists and televangelists, whose most colourful claims about Christianity under Communist regimes came from Bible-smuggling testimonies and literature, had the ear of both US President Ronald Reagan and British Prime Minister Margaret Thatcher.[8] Today, the notion that much of the world remains 'starved' of Bibles,

---

on the ship *Logos* and was the only woman willing to be interviewed, were conducted in person in the UK on 10 August 2022.

[6] George Verwer, *Drops from a Leaking Tap*, rev. edn (Milton Keynes, 2009; repr. Croydon, 2012), 19–20.

[7] Andrew Atherstone, *Archbishop Justin Welby: The Road to Canterbury* (London, 2013), 25. See also the archbishop's Facebook tribute to celebrate the sixtieth anniversary of Open Doors, online at: <https://www.facebook.com/watch/?v=10153800972067502>, accessed 20 October 2024. Eastern European Mission, originally a Dutch Bible-smuggling organization set up by Hank Paulson (a pseudonym), was associated with Brother Andrew's Open Doors: see Hank Paulson and Don Richardson, *Beyond the Wall: The People Communism Can't Conquer* (Ventura, CA, 1982); and <https://www.eem.org>, accessed 21 October 2024.

[8] On evangelical influence in foreign affairs, see especially Angela Lahr, *Millennial Dreams and Apocalyptic Nightmares: The Cold War Origins of Political Evangelicalism* (Oxford, 2007); Lauren Turek, *To Bring the Good News to All Nations: Evangelical Influence on Human Rights and U.S. Foreign Relations* (London and Ithaca, NY, 2020); Melani McAlister, *The Kingdom of God Has No Borders: A Global History of American Evangelicals* (Oxford, 2018). On scholarly interpretations of the end of the Cold War which focus on the role of Christianity as a force for opposition, see especially Michael Weigel, *The Final Revolution: The Resistance Church and the Collapse of Communism* (Oxford, 2003); John Burgess, *The East German Church and the End of Communism* (Oxford, 1997).

which need to be shipped or smuggled abroad, often at great personal risk, remains a common rallying cry at US televangelist campaigns, for example during 'Bible-thon' fundraisers organized through Jimmy Swaggart's SonLife broadcasting network, which aim to get tens of thousands of 'Expositor's Study Bibles' into Ethiopia, South Sudan, Uruguay, Venezuela and elsewhere.[9]

The publication, in 1967, of two important English-language Bible-smuggling memoirs helps to explain the timing of the boom years in Bible smuggling, which was most intensive in the 1970s and 1980s. These memoirs were *God's Smuggler* by 'Brother Andrew' (the Dutch founder of Open Doors, whose real name was Anne van der Bijl, but whose code-name as a smuggler was 'Andrew');[10] and *Tortured for Christ* by Romanian pastor Richard Wurmbrand, the founder of Jesus to the Communist World (later renamed Voice of the Martyrs).[11] *God's Smuggler* describes how, in 1957, in what was to become the first of many crossings into Communist territory, Brother Andrew had driven his blue Volkswagon Beetle, 'literally bulging with tracts, Bibles, and portions of Bibles', to the border with Yugoslavia.[12] Waiting anxiously for the Communist border guards to inspect his documents, for 'the first of many times' he said what became known as 'the Prayer of God's Smuggler'. 'Lord,' prayed Brother Andrew, 'in my luggage I have Scriptures that I want to take to Your children across this border. When You were on earth, You made blind eyes see. Now, I pray, make seeing eyes blind. Do not let the guards see those things You do not want them to see.'[13] The guards failed to find Brother Andrew's stash and let him through. So began his long 'career for God', first as a smuggler, and subsequently as the director of the Bible-smuggling organization Open Doors.

---

[9] 'The November Bible-Thon is Live Today!' claims once such post (2 November 2024), which publishes a toll-free telephone number and online site for cash donations; see online at: <https://www.facebook.com/sonlifebroadcastingnetwork> and <www.shopjsm.org>, accessed 5 November 2024.

[10] In Dutch, the name 'Anne' can be male or female.

[11] The first editions of these works were Brother Andrew [van der Bijl], with John and Elizabeth Sherrill, *God's Smuggler* (London and New York, 1967) and Richard Wurmbrand, *Tortured for Christ (Today's Martyr Church)*, foreword by the Rev. W. Stuart Harris (London, 1967).

[12] Brother Andrew [van der Bijl], with John and Elizabeth Sherrill, *God's Smuggler*, 1st British edn (London, 1968; first publ. 1967), 101.

[13] Ibid.

God's Smuggler by Brother Andrew was a runaway success. It was brought out in hardback, paperback, anniversary, illustrated, junior, and other editions. Within a generation, the book had sold over ten million copies and been translated into thirty-five languages.[14] This exceptional commercial success was helped by the publication, in 1972, of a comic book version, drawn by Al Hartley (a former Marvel comic book illustrator and the creator of Archie comics), as one of the first in a new 'Spire Christian Comic' series which sought to present the Christian message in accessible, teen-friendly vernacular.[15] The very phrase 'God's Smuggler' came to be used rather like a franchise, for example in *God's Smuggler to China*, the bestselling paperback first published by another member of Open Doors International, 'Brother David', in 1981.[16] Bible smuggling, or at least a romanticized version of it, was being actively advertised and promoted.

As the author of *God's Smuggler*, van der Bijl became a legend in his own lifetime. He appeared on television talk shows; as a guest preacher during evangelical tours and missions around the world; and, latterly, in Facebook, YouTube and Vimeo videos.[17] He was presented not only as *God's Smuggler* but also as *God's Agent* or *Secret Agent* in libraries of Christian books with series titles such as 'Christian heroes' or 'Heroes of the Cross'.[18] Profits from the sales of these works were used to support not only missionary organizations, such as Youth With A Mission (YWAM), but even Keston College, originally set up in London in 1969 (as the 'Centre for the Study of Religion and Communism')

---

[14] To contextualize, Joy Adamson's *Born Free*, which was first published in 1960, sold five million copies and was translated into twenty-five languages.

[15] The other title which launched the Spire Christian Comic series, *The Cross and the Switchblade*, similarly sought to make Christianity seem exciting, modern and relevant to teenagers and pre-teens. Al Hartley went on to create an entire run of Christian 'Archie' comics, ubiquitous in evangelical circles in the 1970s, in which 'the Gang' dealt with Christian themes. See also Jason Sacks et al., *American Comic Book Chronicles: the 1970s* (Raleigh, NC, 2014).

[16] Brother David, with Dan Wooding and Sara Bruce (Open Doors International), *God's Smuggler to China: A Cry to the Chinese to Let Us Love Them* (London, 1981).

[17] For a Facebook video about Brother Andrew, the Bible Smuggler, see online at: <https://www.facebook.com/opendoorsfans/videos/brother-andrew-the-bible-smuggler/1731386523708530/>, accessed 19 July 2023. A 'family-friendly' cartoon video about Brother Andrew's life, entitled 'Secret Smuggler: the story of Brother Andrew', can be found on *Vimeo*, online at: <https://vimeo.com/401393042>, accessed 19 July 2023.

[18] Brother Andrew, with Dan Wooding, *Brother Andrew God's Agent (Heroes of the Cross)* (Basingstoke, 1983); Janet and Geoff Benge, *Christian Heroes Now and Then: Brother Andrew God's Secret Agent* (Seattle, WA, 2005).

to monitor religious persecution in 'Communist Lands', which took pride in its accuracy in reporting and avoidance of sensationalism.[19] By the time of van der Bijl's death in 2022, Open Doors, which recruits young people from the USA and around the world, claimed to be helping Christians in 'more than 60 countries', and to be distributing '300,000 Bibles and 1.5 million Christian books, training materials, and discipleship manuals' per year.[20] The organization's annual turnover, as published in 2015, was an impressive $116.3 million. In 2023, the Open Doors official website described itself as 'a global membership organisation with 25 national bases', including in the USA, Canada, Austria, Poland, Denmark, Finland and France. The website includes such features as 'Prayer Alerts', a 'prayer generator to pray for a specific country or person' and a 'World Watch List 2023 Interactive Map' which comes with 'a series of engaging prayer ideas' to 'help you pray for Christians who are risking it all for Jesus.'[21]

The other major Bible-smuggling blockbuster, also first published in 1967, was *Tortured for Christ* by Richard Wurmbrand (also known as Nicolai Ionescu). *Tortured for Christ* gives a gruesome account of the fourteen years its author, an evangelical convert from Judaism, spent in a Romanian prison, in which he describes being beaten, tortured and otherwise abused, but nonetheless full of the joy of God. After being brought out of Romania by the Norwegian Mission to the Jews and the Hebrew Christian Alliance in 1964, Wurmbrand was granted asylum in the United States where, in 1966, he testified to the US Congress on

---

[19] The Centre, renamed Keston College, relocated to Oxford and subsequently became the Keston Institute. In 2007, the Keston Institute's archive and library were moved to the Keston Center for Religion, Politics and Society at Baylor College in Waco, Texas. Michael Bourdeaux, who founded the Keston Centre, judged Wurmbrand's 'Voice of the Martyrs' and Joe Bass's 'Underground Evangelism' to be 'prone to the wildest exaggeration and generalisation'; Keston was nevertheless dependent on their financial support. See Michael Bourdeaux, *One Word of Truth: The Cold War Memoir of Michael Bourdeaux and Keston College* (London, 2019), 103, 214–16. See also Julie de Graffenried and Zoe Knox, eds, *Voices of the Voiceless: Religion, Communism and the Keston Archive* (Waco, TX, 2019). Further information about Keston's funding and development was drawn from a conversation by the author on 4 November 2023 with Xenia Dennen, now director of the Keston Institute, who worked with the late Michael Bourdeaux at Keston.

[20] Daniel Silliman, 'Died: Brother Andrew, Who Smuggled Bibles into Communist Countries', *Christianity Today*, 27 September 2022, 10.

[21] See the Open Doors Youth page, online at: <https://www.opendoors.org>, accessed 11 January 2022.

the 'Communist Exploitation of Religion'.[22] His testimony, which consisted largely of a plea to Americans patriotically to help Christians behind the Iron Curtain, together with the promotion of his own organizations and forthcoming book, included a dramatic gesture which was captured for the *New York Times*.[23] Before the Senate subcommittee and the press, Wurmbrand took off his shirt to show, in evidence, the knife-wound scars on his own neck, chest and back. Stripped to the waist, he declared: 'I show you the tortured body of my country, of my fatherland, and of my church.'[24] As Melani McAlister has noted, Wurmbrand 'reprised his famous shirt removal' a year later, in the film version of *Tortured for Christ*, in which he repeated and amplified his warnings about the persecution of Christians around the world.[25]

The central message of Wurmbrand's memoir is that real saints, true believers, genuine followers of Christ, were not to be found in the compromised, liberal and affluent Western denominations, but rather in the so-called 'underground church' in the Eastern bloc whose members were risking all for Christ.[26] The Bible-smuggling organization which he set up, and which retains his emphasis on physical suffering, continues to report large profits. In its report of 31 December 2022 to the Evangelical Council for Financial Accountability (ECFA), Voice of the Martyrs disclosed \$103,714,450 in annual revenue, mainly from donations.[27] It advertises aggressively on Facebook, Twitter, Instagram and YouTube; and a range of merchandise can be bought through its website, including study packs, the film version

---

[22] *Communist Exploitation of Religion: Hearing before the Subcommittee to Investigate the Administration of the Internal Security Act and other Internal Security Laws of the Committee on the Judiciary United States Senate Eighty-Ninth Congress. Testimony of Rev. Richard Wurmbrand, May 6, 1966* ([Washington, DC], 1982).

[23] The photograph, from the *New York Times* (7 May 1966), is reproduced in McAlister, *The Kingdom of God Has No Borders*, 106.

[24] *Communist Exploitation of Religion*, 99. See also the very interesting discussion of this episode in McAlister, *The Kingdom of God*, 105–7.

[25] McAlister, *The Kingdom of God*, 105.

[26] Richard Wurmbrand, *Tortured for Christ*, paperback edn (Orpington, 2009; first publ. 1967), 144–6. This theme became increasingly pronounced in Wurmbrand's pamphlets, interviews and sermons during the 1980s.

[27] See 'The Voice of the Martyrs: Data for the year ended December 31, 2022, ECFA', online at: <https://www.ecfa.org/MemberProfile.aspx?ID=12238>, accessed 20 January 2022.

of *Tortured for Christ*, tapes, books and 'Bible bags', with the legend: 'This book is illegal in 52 countries'.[28]

'With the arrival in the West of Pastor Richard Wurmbrand and the publication of Brother Andrew's *God's Smuggler*', recalled Michael Bourdeaux, the Anglican priest who founded Keston College in 1969, 'Bible smuggling became a headline issue in the Christian press.'[29] The appeal of joining what was presented as a worldwide crusade, in which the principal weapon was nothing more than the gospel, captured the essence of the missionary impulse in which so many evangelical Christians had been raised. The notion, especially shocking to Protestant sensibilities, that people living in traditionally Christian countries like Poland, Czechoslovakia or East Germany were 'starved' of Bibles, which therefore needed to be supplied to them like so many Red Cross or care packages, carried a simple, electrifying message. The gospel taught that the Good News should be spread to all nations (Mark 13: 10; Mark 16: 15; Matthew 28: 19–20). There were also specifically theological and historical resonances in the English-speaking world where, even today, stirring tales of William Tyndale, Reformation Bible smuggling and Protestant martyrdoms are aimed at young evangelicals.[30] The timing was also fortuitous: in the second half of the twentieth century, Eastern Europe was being looked at with fresh eyes, as a new missionary field, at just the time that traditional European missionary and colonial endeavours in Africa and Asia were being compromised by a string of independence and anti-colonial movements which often included anti-Western and anti-missionary feeling. To work on the margins, operating across Cold War borders, was also to recapture the centre ground, to recover traditional missionary endeavour at a time when the secularizing West seemed to evangelical Christians to be losing its way.

---

[28] See the following websites and social media: <https://www.persecution.com/>; Facebook: <https://www.facebook.com/vomusa/>; Twitter or X: <https://twitter.com/vom_usa>; Instagram: <https://www.instagram.com/vom_usa/>; YouTube: <https://www.youtube.com/user/voiceofthemartyrsusa>, all accessed 4 June 2022.

[29] Bourdeaux, *One Word of Truth*, 214.

[30] See, for example, Lori Rich, *William Tyndale: The Smuggler's Flame* (Tain, 2004), part of the Torch Blazers series, online at: <https://www.christianfocus.com>, accessed 5 November 2024; 'William Tyndale: Life and Death of the Father of the English Bible' (updated 23 August 2023), Bible Study Tools, online at: <https://www.biblestudytools.com/bible-study/topical-studies/translator-william-tyndale-strangled-and-burned-11629961.html>, accessed 5 November 2024; the Reformation Graphic Novel Set, online at: <https://www.cph.org/reformation-graphic-novel-set>, accessed 5 November 2024.

Bible smugglers, like CIA operatives, were acutely aware of the effect which the dissemination of works like Boris Pasternak's *Doctor Zhivago* (1957) or Alexsandr Solzhenitsyn's *Gulag Archipelago* (1973) could have on public opinion in the West. They did their best to promote their own perceptions of the Eastern bloc as missionary territory ripe for Christian conversion, for example through such blockbusters as Danish Bible smuggler Hans Neerskov's *Mission: Possible* (first published in English translation in 1975) and Sergei Kourdakov's *Forgive me, Natasha* (1973), the conversion story of a KGB officer who relished persecuting Christians until he 'found' God through the heroic example of the young Christian girl he tortured to death.[31] Books initially brought out by Bible-smuggling organizations, in this case Underground Evangelism, were taken up by evangelical publishers, such as Revell and Lakeland, and turned into bestsellers. The most popular were further exploited in film, study packs and other media suitable for classrooms, prayer-groups and Bible-study camps. To become a smuggler for God was to pursue a path which was, in its own way, as exciting for a young Christian as becoming a hippie, experimenting with drugs or joining in consciousness-raising could be to a non-Christian. As David Babcock, a Wesleyan from Colorado who ended up working for OM in Germany and Austria, later remembered, in 1970, a 'time of radical student movements', he had been 'nineteen – eager, resolved, committed, and young.' Although he was 'not involved in political movements', his life 'would soon be filled with equally radical commitment to Christ and to missions', leading to 'adventure, heartache and an ocean between "home" and my new "home"', and what turned out to be forty-six years of living abroad and working undercover for OM.[32] Thanks to the ubiquity of Bible-smuggling memoirs and comic books, which included information about how to contact Bible-smuggling organizations like Open Doors, Voice of the Martyrs, Underground Evangelism or OM, by the 1980s, a stint abroad with a missionary and Bible-smuggling organization was becoming as natural an opportunity for a young Christian from a Bible college or an evangelical church as a

---

[31] Sergei Kourdakov, *Forgive Me, Natasha* (Basingstoke, 1973; first paperback edn 1975). On the Danish European Mission, see Boel, 'Bible Smuggling and Human Rights in the Cold War', 263–75.

[32] David and Brenda Babcock, *Stones of Remembrance: Mapping God's Faithfulness through 46 Years* (Mosbach, 2015), 13, 71.

gap year with Outward Bound, VSO or the Peace Corps might seem to a student from a Liberal Arts college.

EVANGELICAL ESPIONAGE

Those who took part in the 'secret work' of illegally transporting Christian literature across the Iron Curtain and distributing it to safe houses in the Soviet Union and the Eastern bloc in the 1960s, 1970s and 1980s, knew that to leave a paper trail could put both themselves and their contacts at risk. Smugglers were warned by their handlers against bringing any potentially incriminating piece of paper with them on a trip: pockets and vehicles were scoured for receipts, alibis were concocted and rehearsed, maps and lists of contacts' names and addresses committed to memory. The very qualities that made for a successful drop – those which got Bibles and Christian literature to the right contacts without arousing the notice or suspicion of border guards or the secret police – are the same qualities which should have left little or no trail for the historian.

Bible smuggling did leave traces in the historical record, however. When Bible smugglers were caught, they left traces in Communist Ministry of Interior (secret police) files, which characteristically included 'crime scene' photographs, prison mug shots, lists of confiscated materials, photographs and detailed descriptions of hiding places, reports of police interrogations, witness testimony and formal trial proceedings.[33] Sometimes, Bible smugglers were filmed, together with their captured loads of contraband literature, for newsreels and propaganda films trumpeting the work of the Communist authorities in protecting the Socialist commonwealth from the perfidious methods of the West.

Occasionally, high-profile cases hit the press. One of the most celebrated cases of a Western Bible smuggler being caught and tried by the Communist authorities in the East was that of David Hathaway, an evangelical pastor from Yorkshire who became involved with

---

[33] The present study draws on unpublished materials from Czechoslovak, Romanian, Hungarian and Lithuanian Ministry of Interior archives, and from the Keston archives held at Baylor College in Waco, Texas. For those without easy access to secret police archives, sample photographs of Bible-smuggling busts can also be seen online, as part of the 'Hidden Galleries' project, at: <http://hiddengalleries.eu>, accessed 27 May 2022. Another helpful resource is de Graffenried and Knox, eds, *Voices of the Voiceless*.

Joe Bass's Underground Evangelism in the early 1960s and worked as a Bible smuggler from 1961 to 1972, during which time he claims to have delivered some 150,000 copies. Hathaway used his Crusader Tours company, which advertised trips to the Holy Land, as a cover for a Bible-smuggling operation into Hungary, Romania and Yugoslavia. On 21 June 1972, he was caught at the Czechoslovak border with Germany at Rozvadov with nearly 3,000 concealed Bibles, together with religious literature deemed by the authorities to be seditious.[34] His autobiographical memoir *Czech-Mate* (1974) describes his arrest, trial and imprisonment in Czechoslovakia, together with the campaign mounted by his wife, evangelical circles, the British press and, finally, Parliament, to press for his early release from a five-year prison sentence.[35] Hathaway, whose case came to the attention of the British Cabinet, was brought home in 1973, after serving less than a year of his sentence, through the intervention of the then opposition leader and former prime minister, Harold Wilson. The affair was noted with interest by the US Embassy in Prague and thoroughly monitored by the Czechoslovak secret police, the StB, whose main file runs to over 300 pages and includes photographs, lists, interrogation reports and witness statements from each of the passengers on his tour bus.[36]

Other cases were kept out of the public eye, but can be reconstructed through secret police archives, unpublished documents and the memories of former Bible smugglers, six of whom have been interviewed, repeatedly and at length, for the present study.[37]

---

[34] David Hathaway, *Czech-Mate* (London, 1974), 8–9.

[35] See also 'Czechoslovakia (Rev David Hathaway)', HC Deb., 29 January 1973 (vol. 849, cols 938–9) online at: <https://hansard.parliament.uk/Commons/1973-01-29>, accessed 6 December 2021.

[36] Plzeň, Czech Republic, Archiv bezpečnostních složek [Ministry of Interior Archive], Fond V-Plzeň, sig. V-8558, folder entitled 'Plzeň David Gordon Hathaway'. Hathaway was charged, convicted and sentenced under Czechoslovak Law 140 (29 November 1961). See 140 trestní zákon (29. listopadu 1961) [Criminal Law 140 (29 November 1961)], *Sbírka zákonů Československé socialistické republiky* [*Collection of Laws of the Czechoslovak Socialist Republic*] 65 (8 December 1961), 485–508. Compare also the collection of newspaper clippings about the case in Waco, TX, Baylor College, The Keston Archive, Czechoslovak Subject Files 1946–1989, Box 1, Folder 5 (Individuals: Hathaway, David); Kew, TNA, FCO 28/1765, 'Detention of British Subjects in Czechoslovakia: Reverend David Hathaway (1 January 1972–31 December 1972); and FCO 28/2226 'Detention and Release of British Subject, Reverend David Hathaway, in Czechoslovakia' (1 January 1973–31 December 1973).

[37] The Bible smugglers interviewed, five men and one woman, were of various nationalities (American, Canadian, Czech, English, Finnish) and included volunteers, team leaders,

These interviews with Bible smugglers, which were undertaken by the present author in 2022, constitute the first, and to date only, such interviews to have been conducted by any scholar. The resulting collection of interviews, which were recorded, covers the recollections of workers, at all levels, with responsibility for different aspects of OM. Most had never before discussed their involvement in this secret work, and spoke on the understanding that their identities would not be revealed. The interview technique was to begin with open-ended, standardized questions (such as to ask for a brief biography, including nationality, schooling, parents' occupation, religious upbringing, political outlook, conversion experience, first involvement with Bible smuggling), and to follow up, in subsequent interviews, with more targeted, and sometimes probing, questions about smuggling techniques, institutional conventions, theological rationale, motivations, expectations, and other aspects of the work. Cross-checking, with written records, was undertaken wherever possible. Some interviewees provided additional proof, such as photographs, documents and videos.

In early 1987, according to Czechoslovak secret police reports, guards at the Czechoslovak-West German border control station at Strážný in the Czechoslovak Socialist Republic began to notice a pattern: a spate of Ford camper-vans, in which people of various citizenships travelled, always in twos or in threes.[38] The vehicles, they observed, had Swiss, British or Dutch registration plates and were claimed to be borrowed from friends rather than owned by those who drove them. There were other common features. Drivers and passengers had their visas issued in Vienna. They gave as their temporary address in Czechoslovakia a campsite or a private residence, but never a hotel. They usually left the territory of the Czechoslovak Socialist Republic within forty-eight hours, thus avoiding the need to register with the police.

---

mechanics, long-distance lorry drivers and pastors working for OM. Some were married and some unmarried; most were in their 70s at the time of interview. All interviews were conducted by the present author and were recorded, in person or via Zoom, between 2 February 2022 and 28 February 2023.

[38] Adolf Sebera, 'Brief Summary of the Findings: Discovery of a Dead Space (Compartment) in a Vehicle which traveled [*sic*] Canadian Citizen Edward BUKOWSKI and American Citizen Hans KOEBELE, across the Strážný Department of Passport Control (DPC) – Report', unpublished translation of unpublished report, dated 24 February 1987. Interviewee's private collection.

On 2 February 1987, a beige camper-van, driven by a Canadian citizen who was accompanied by an American, pulled into Strážný station for the customary customs declaration, passport check and compulsory currency exchange. The fact that it fitted the observed pattern – an international crew of two or three, the vehicle not owned by either the driver or the passenger, the Czechoslovak visas issued in Vienna – raised the alarm. Using the excuse of customs regulations, the border guards asked the two foreigners to unload their luggage for inspection. When nothing was found, it was decided to move the van to the back of the station, away from West German view, for a more thorough search.

The vehicle inspection started with the engine, which was clear. Next, the ceiling was unscrewed, and the upholstery removed. The dashboard and areas around the driver's and passengers' seats were searched. Finally, the living area, with its fridge, gas cooker with a pressurized gas bottle, folding table, two benches and cabinets with drawers, was examined.[39] The drawers in the cabinets could not be completely removed because they had a stop inside. When the officers got out their tape measures, they found that there was discrepancy of between 15 and 20 cm between the side of the vehicle and the end of the inserted drawers. This suggested that there must be a double wall, concealing what they referred to as a 'dead space'. Guards and police officers applied themselves to the pillars of the door frame, at the bottom of which they found a vent hole. Shining a torch into the vent hole showed the area, which was about 20 cm deep, to be empty. One of the officers noticed further vent holes at the top which appeared to be blocked: when these were poked with a screwdriver, polystyrene pieces fell out. Since it seemed odd that vent holes should be blocked, the officer unscrewed the door jam on the driver's side, revealing three more screw holes. Shining a light into these holes, the spines and sheets of thin booklets wrapped in plastic could plainly be seen.[40]

'Within a few minutes', the driver afterwards reported to his superiors at OM, 'each of the seven guards were looking down the shaft with a flashlight, and they were very excited with the discovery of some literature.'[41] The foreigners were ordered into the building,

---

[39] Sebera, 'Brief Summary of the Findings', fol. 3.
[40] Ibid., fol. 4.
[41] Hans Koebele, 'Trip #287H- Strážný, ČSSR' (27 February 1987), unpublished typescript report, fol. 2. Author's private collection.

where they were taken separately for questioning. As one of the guards took notes, a different guard – one who spoke English – asked questions such as: '"What kind of books are they?" "Where did you meet this man?" "Who is the owner of the vehicle?"'. 'I gave him a 45-second Gospel presentation', the American passenger explained in his written report for the OM leadership, 'and then two other guards came in. He told the guards what I had just said, and they simply laughed.'[42]

Next, the combined expertise of border and passport control was brought to bear on the Canadian driver, by now under armed guard, who was asked several times whether he knew how to open the hidden space in the camper-van. The police report states that he replied that he 'wouldn't open it: let the guards figure it out for themselves'. In the end, the secret compartment was forced open, damaging the opening mechanism and revealing a cache of Christian literature, calendars and cassette tapes. The smugglers were handcuffed and taken into custody. The camper-van, with its contraband, was sent to a specialist unit in České Budějovice, where the prisoners were also sent for interrogation by the secret police.[43] Full details of the case, including a series of photographs showing the stages of opening the hidden compartment, were reported to state security, the Ministry of Interior, the intelligence services, border patrol, terrain border patrol, state border surveillance, České Budějovice headquarters and the Sušice border guard station.[44] A preliminary police report suggested that the van was part of a smuggling ring, run from Vienna, involving 'the organized transportation of objectionable literature to the ČSSR [Czechoslovak Socialist Republic]' and 'other socialist countries', mainly using paid students as mules.[45] This information, it judged, was of interest to the rest of the Warsaw Pact.

At the same time that the Communist authorities in Czechoslovakia were building up a picture of OM's smuggling ring based in Vienna, the team members at OM, whose European centre was indeed

---

[42] Ibid., fol. 2.

[43] Sebera, 'Brief Summary of the Findings', fol. 5.

[44] Samples of this sort of classic police coverage can be viewed via the 'Hidden Galleries' project, online at: <http://hiddengalleries.co>, accessed 27 May 2022. See also the book arising from this project: James Kapaló and Tatiana Vagramenko, eds, *Hidden Galleries: Material Religion in the Secret Police Archives in Central and Eastern Europe* (Abingdon, 2021).

[45] Sebera, 'Brief Summary of the Findings', fol. 5.

based in Vienna (but with specialist camps, garages and workshops dotted across Austria, West Germany, the UK and Scandinavia), were gathering intelligence of their own. Its handbook for new recruits, known simply as 'The Rules', explained, in the section entitled 'What to do when you return to Wien if you have been caught': 'We do NEED to have accurate information about what happened in order to assess the situation'.[46] Having returned from a drop, and only once they were certain of not being followed, smugglers were to report either to a team leader or the travel coordinator. Next, they would be given a 'verbal debriefing', which might be taped. The recruit would be told which details could not be shared, even within the organization, for security reasons. The returnee would then be isolated from the rest of the team until he or she had written a full report of the trip, including details of exactly what had happened at the border, during the arrest and interrogation, and what the cell conditions were like in the prisons where they had been held.[47] It was deemed especially important for the team leadership to glean information about 'any special tools [or] equipment' which had been used by the authorities to detect or open secret hiding-places; to find out 'what information' they knew about OM; and to bring to light 'any mistakes in the planning'. Only by receiving this constant stream of intelligence, and updating its methods accordingly, could OM expect to continue to outwit the Communist authorities and transport Bibles and religious literature to their intended recipients behind the Iron Curtain.

Working for a Bible-smuggling organization in the 1970s and 1980s in many ways resembled working for the intelligence services. Those who were recruited to smuggle contraband religious literature from West to East, in what were euphemistically known as 'trips across the bridge', were trained never to carry a name, address, or anything which would incriminate themselves, local believers, or the OM leadership. All addresses and information about safe houses and dead-letter drops were to be encoded and memorized. If too difficult to remember, they were written on little slips of paper which could be easily swallowed. 'Trippers', as smugglers were known within the organization, were never to leave a country between 21:00 and 08:00 hours, since this could arouse suspicion, and

---

[46] 'Introduction: What to do when you return to Wien if you have been caught', *The Rules*, fol. 1. This typed document is unpublished, unpaginated and undated, and was made available to the author by a former member of OM who wishes to remain anonymous.
[47] Ibid., fols 1–2.

never to enter a Communist country after 21:00 hours local time. They were to refer to vehicles by code-names, and to themselves and others in the team by pseudonyms.[48] When seeking to communicate across the many different languages which might be used in a single trip – for example, Czech, Hungarian, Romanian, Ukrainian and Russian – the Bible, which was conveniently available in all languages, was sometimes used as a key to encrypt and decipher coded messages.[49]

Addresses for illicit Bible and literature drops were normally learned by heart. Target countries were referred to only by code-names. 'When you go to Paul', read the relevant instructions, 'you are to stay at least 48 hours. In Steve, stay at least 3 nights. In Mannfred, stay at least 4 nights (or 5 days). When you go to Eric, stay at least 2 nights. Staying this long in Eric means that you will need to register with the police'.[50] Host contacts were not told the details of the trippers' plans, or even the month or year in which to expect a cache of Christian literature mysteriously to appear in a barn, field or vacant lot. In general, everyone was given 'as little information as possible, to allow them plausible deniability, and to protect the network and operations'; information was to be given out on a strictly 'need to know' basis.[51]

Cover stories were concocted, memorized and rehearsed in Vienna before 'crossing the bridge'. 'Trippers' were drilled to 'know the name of two or three major cities' and 'specific places, such as a mountain area or a popular lake' so that, if 'asked at the bridge' (that is, the border), they could 'name one quickly without fumbling around'. Twenty-five kilometres before arriving at a border, trippers were required to 'sanitize' the vehicle, which meant 'removing and destroying any receipts that could link them to their home base location, or to the location of their travel and contacts.'[52] The Rules also required that, upon arrival in the target country, no vehicle be parked within 500 metres of a contact

---

[48] Schneider, 'Through the Seams of the Iron Curtain', fols 46–7.
[49] Unpublished interviews by the author with a former Team Member of OM (3 February 2022; 10 February 2022; 15 March 2022).
[50] Point 19, 'Crossing the Bridge', *The Rules*.
[51] Interviews by the author with a former Team Member of OM (3 February 2022; 10 February 2022; 15 March 2022). See also Schneider, 'Through the Seams of the Iron Curtain', 39; Thomas Henderson, *Tripping: A True Story of Bible Smugglers and How the East German Stasi Tried to Stop Them*, 3rd edn (n.pl. [USA], 2020; first publ. 2016), 36, 62; Genovieva Sfatcu Beattie, with Stephen Beattie, *Caught with Bibles: A True Story from Communist Romania* (Sisters, OR, 2009), 62–3. See also Babcock and Babcock, *Stones of Remembrance*, 192.
[52] Henderson, *Tripping*, 13; Schneider, 'Through the Seams of the Iron Curtain', 44.

address. On the return trip, the vehicle was not to stop again for any reason until it was at least 50 kilometres away from the drop point.[53] On exiting the country, driver and passengers were to be 'ready with an excuse, if asked' as to why they had not gone to whichever 'particular place' they had said, on entry, that they intended to visit.[54]

Like intelligence officers, Bible students and pastors who signed up for the Bible-smuggling way of life were taught not to attract attention to themselves. Drivers and passengers whose mission was to deliver Bibles were instructed to dress 'neatly' and to look 'clean-cut and unobjectionable', with short hair and unmemorable clothes. 'It might be good,' suggested the Rules, 'if one person is seated in the back making sandwiches, sewing or involved in some other activity while at the bridge. This may distract from the vehicle'.[55] Other calculated distractions included having a pretty young woman as a passenger, changing a baby's nappy, or creating a chaotic family scene just as the border was reached.

To turn a law-abiding Christian into a smuggler, intelligence operative or secret agent was not straightforward. One of the first hurdles to be overcome was the natural reticence of believers to lie, dissemble or break the law. 'Before you go', advised the leadership, 'make sure you have all spiritual doubts settled.' A small doubt, they cautioned, 'will mushroom in the hours of waiting that you will have to do' if arrested or imprisoned.[56] Long-distance drives, across multiple border checks, could be hard on a tripper's nerves: groups were picked partly for their ability to keep calm under pressure. Training on how to handle interrogations included the advice: 'Give the appearance that you are naïve and that you want to be as co-operative as you can'; but also: 'be determined in your own mind that you are not going to tell them anything they cannot obtain from your passport and visa.'[57] Special care had to be taken to train students from Bible colleges, raised to tell the truth, to throw border guards and secret police off the scent. If asked

---

[53] Henderson, *Tripping*, 147; Schneider, 'Through the Seams of the Iron Curtain', 44; Lloyd Sparks, *Detour: My Brief but Amusing Career as a Bible Smuggler* (Bloomington, IN, 2011), 140–4, 146–7.
[54] Point 16, 'Crossing the Bridge', *The Rules*.
[55] Point 11, 'Crossing the Bridge', *The Rules*.
[56] Item 2, 'Thoughts on Imprisonment', *The Rules*. See also Babcock, 'The Ethics of Smuggling' in idem, *Stones of Remembrance*, 75–9; Henderson, 'A Word from the Author', in idem, *Tripping*, 5–7.
[57] Item 4, 'Helpful Things to Remember', *The Rules*.

'"Do you have religious literature with you?" you are to answer "No"', instructed the Rules. 'The Bible is not merely religious literature, it is the living word of God. Remember, concealment of the truth is not lying.'[58] Young trippers setting out to 'cross the bridge' were further reminded: 'you don't have to say the whole truth. For example, if it is your intention to go to Ostend, you can say you were going to Brussels, since you must pass through Brussels on your way to Ostend'. Or, again, 'Ask yourself the real meaning of the words they use. For example, "Do you know Mr Y?" Psychologists say that it takes about seven years to really get to know a person. Sometimes you can truthfully answer "No".'[59] Such tricks were calculated to make trippers appear calm and assured, helping to make their cover stories more plausible to the border police.

Before leaving to cross the bridge, and as part of their overall preparation, trippers were expected to 'realize and come to terms' with the 'fact that they could be imprisoned in one of the countries they travelled to'. They were therefore subjected to training of various kinds, including physical fitness, simulated interrogations, and what one team leader whom I interviewed referred to obliquely as 'pressure'.[60] It was well understood by handlers that worry about families at home could tempt otherwise steadfast smugglers to talk. Trippers were therefore required to write an 'Emergency Letter' to be delivered to their parents in case of arrest. 'If your parents are too emotional', ran the instructions, 'you may choose to write another relative ... If you are a regular tripper, you may also want to write a letter to a close Christian friend with whom you have shared about the work. Immediately upon receiving this letter, they would know to start praying for you.'[61] In the emergency letter left for family, which the Rules stated could not be shown to a Western consular officer or journalist until two weeks after a tripper had failed to return from a Communist country, it was to be clearly stated that 'you are not with O.M. or ANY OTHER ORGANIZATION. Make it clear that this trip was your own idea.'[62] The emergency letter was also required to include a clause stating that it was the tripper's wish to be represented by the organization's legal team, rather than by a different

---

[58] Item 14, 'Crossing the Bridge', *The Rules*.
[59] Items 12 and 14, 'Interrogation', *The Rules*.
[60] Interviews by the author with a former Team Member of OM (3 February 2022; 10 February 2022; 15 March 2022). See also Henderson, *Tripping*, 44.
[61] Point 3, 'Interrogation Preparation', *The Rules*.
[62] Point 5, 'Interrogation Preparation', *The Rules*.

lawyer or their country's own consular services.[63] Western consular staff were to be told exactly the same cover story as the one concocted for the Communist authorities. This detail is significant: it means that both honesty and allegiance to one's own country were to be sacrificed to what was evidently perceived to be a higher good, the missionary task of saving souls. In this respect, Bible smuggling needs to be sharply distinguished from state-sponsored book smuggling, such as that under-taken by the CIA and other Western intelligence agencies.

As with the intelligence services, the priority at OM was to protect the organization, rather than the individual. The most important thing for trippers to remember, if caught and questioned, was to deny the very existence of the organization which had sent them. The second most important thing was to keep silent about the secret mechanisms – 'gizmos' as OM called them – which opened and closed hidden spaces for concealing Bibles, pamphlets, hymn books, cassette tapes, micro-fiche, rolls of film, parts of printing presses, medicines and other illicit materials, such as ink for photocopiers. 'Whatever answer you give', insisted the Rules, 'it must not betray the vehicle'.[64]

It is easy to see why the OM leadership was so concerned to protect its specially doctored vehicles. Smuggling techniques, which mostly made use of false bottoms, double walls and camouflage, grew increas-ingly sophisticated over the course of the 1970s and 1980s. Some audaciously constructed camper-van and lorry shells – especially those with complex opening mechanisms – could take months, even years, to design, test and build; and it could take just as long to raise the money to pay for them. Back in the 1960s, simple items reminiscent of contemporary James Bond films had been used: gas cannisters adjusted so that the amount of propane was reduced, leaving space for secreting books and pamphlets; oil drums given a false bottom, leaving room for paper to fill the bottom quarter, while oil filled the remaining three-quarters. Private Bible-smuggling archives, one housed in Sweden and another in the Czech Republic, contain common personal objects, such as a handbag, briefcase or thermos flask, provided with secret compartments suitable for carrying a microfiche or small machine parts.[65] These simple adaptations in

[63] Ibid.
[64] Item 13, 'Crossing the Bridge', *The Rules.*
[65] See, for example, the *Ljus i Öster* [Light in the East] secret archive kept in Stockholm, Sweden, which holds photographs of a variety of objects which were used for smuggling.

some cases enabled entire printing presses to be smuggled, piece by piece, and reassembled on the other side of the Iron Curtain. Specially tailored underclothes, rather like long johns but with multiple hidden pockets, could be worn for concealing Bibles, or bags of printer ink, under outer clothes and an overcoat.[66]

By the 1980s, far more elaborate smuggling vehicles were being designed and purpose-built by OM in specialist garages: for example, entire lorries encased in a false outer shell began operating out of Finland. To give some idea of scale: one large Ford transit van, outfitted by the team with a false floor and wall compartment, and operated by an electronic opening mechanism, was able to conceal and transport 1,400 Bibles.[67] This compares very favourably with the number of illicit books that the CIA was able to smuggle into the Eastern bloc, even at the height of its Book Distribution Programme, which ran from 1956 to 1991. In a recent study, Alfred Reisch suggests that in 1968, 'the best year' for the secret Cold War Book Distribution Programme, a total of some 328,000 books were distributed to 'individuals and institutions' across the Eastern bloc.[68] This was roughly equivalent to 234 Ford vanloads per year. OM had a range of vehicles – some of them able to carry much larger loads than the Ford – at their disposal: these included not only cars, vans and camper-vans, but also articulated lorries and vast, ocean-going ships. Moreover, OM was just one Bible-smuggling organization amongst many. The Bible-smuggling organization Open Doors, for example, claimed to have delivered 'a million' Bibles to China, by barge and tugboat, in just one night in 1981 in an international operation code-named 'Project Pearl'.[69]

Some are shown in a Finnish retrospective article by a former smuggler: Esko Mäki-Soini, 'Rekkamiehen muistoja matkan varrelta' ['A Trucker's Memories Along the Way'] (4 January 2018), online at: <http://suuressamukana.fi/rekkamiehen-muistoja-matkan-varrelta/>, accessed 20 April 2022.

[66] One such set is displayed in a glass case at the Keston Institute, Keston Center, Baylor College, Waco, TX.

[67] Henderson, *Tripping*, 13–22, as summarized in Schneider, 'Through the Seams of the Iron Curtain', 40.

[68] Alfred Reisch, *Hot Books in the Cold War: The CIA-funded Secret Western Book Distribution Program behind the Iron Curtain* (Budapest, 2013), 266.

[69] Brother David, with Dan Wooding and Sara Bruce, *God's Smuggler to China* (London, Sydney, Auckland and Toronto, 1981), 310, 322–3. See also 'Project Pearl', online at: <https://www.billionbibles.com/china/project-pearl.html>, accessed 7 November 2024;

Operation Mobilisation (OM), though staffed by amateurs and funded through voluntary donations, appears to have been rather more adept at breaching the Iron Curtain than the USA's lavishly funded Central Intelligence Agency. It was certainly just as creative: indeed, it is not always clear which organization drew inspiration from the other.[70] Driving instructions for Bible drops organized by OM included a complicated system of reconnaissance, undertaken up to a year, or even two years, before the final drop at a safe house. Methods used by the team to transport Bibles into Communist countries included floating large plastic rubbish bags filled with Christian literature down an Albanian river; sending pamphlet-balloons across the Iron Curtain (a trick also used by the CIA); anchoring boats – and, eventually, large ocean-going sea liners – offshore from which lifeboats could be launched or to which locals discretely come aboard.[71] One of the large ships, *Logos*, in use from 1970 to 1988, was joined by a second ocean-going ship, *Doulos*, from 1977; later, *Logos II*, *Logos Hope* and *Doulos Hope* were added to the fleet.[72] Another tactic was to create ever smaller, miniature Bibles of durable, heat-resistant plastic. Not only could a larger number of 'Bible units', as OM referred to them, be crammed into every available space on board a specially adapted vehicle; but the miniature Gospels were small enough to be concealed in a hand and tough enough to withstand being hidden in a toilet or a

---

and Brother David with Paul Hattaway, *Project Pearl* (Oxford and Grand Rapids, MI, 2007).

[70] On the Cold War as a religious or 'spiritual' war, together with the use of Christian propaganda, especially in the 1950s and 1960s, as official Western strategies to weaken and discredit the Eastern bloc, see, for example, Uta Balbier, *Altar Call in Europe: Billy Graham, Mass Evangelism and the Cold-War West* (New York, 2022); Michael Graziano, *Errand into the Wilderness of Mirrors: Religion and the History of the CIA* (Chicago, IL, 2021); Jonathan Herzog, *The Spiritual-Industrial Complex: America's Battle against Communism in the Early Cold War* (Oxford, 2011); Dianne Kirby, ed., *Religion and the Cold War* (Houndmills, 2003); Giuliana Chamedes, *A Twentieth-Century Crusade: The Vatican's Battle to Remake Christian Europe* (Cambridge, MA, 2019).

[71] The method of sending balloons across the Iron Curtain containing pamphlets or leaflets was also used by the CIA, for example in Hungary in 1956 in the weeks preceding the 'uprising' or 'revolution' in Budapest: see 'Meeting at the White House (7 November 1956)', as cited in US State Department, *Foreign Relations of the United States, 1955–1957*, 25: *Eastern Europe* (Washington, DC, 1990), 423 n. 177.

[72] See the interview by the present author with a former volunteer with OM (10 August 2022) about life on the ship and her motives for joining. Author's private archive. Details of OM's 'ship ministry' in 2024 can be viewed online at: <https://www.om.org/eng/ships/the-ships>, accessed 22 January 2024.

mug of hot coffee.[73] Small wonder that, as early as 1973, the Stasi had set up at least three counter-smuggling operations – code-named 'Apostle', 'Transport' and 'Container' – to deal with the seven Bible-smuggling channels which they had identified operating in East Germany alone.[74] After the Helsinki Final Act (1975), which achieved wide agreement on security and human rights, the election of Karol Wojtyla as Pope John Paul II (1978) and the rise of the Solidarity movement (1980), the Romanian *Securitate*, Czechoslovak *StB*, East German Stasi, and Hungarian *Államvédelmi Hatóság* or ÁVH, were all increasingly preoccupied with monitoring, and seeking to infiltrate, covert operations run by book smugglers, including those run by what they referred to as Bible-smuggling 'cults'.[75]

CHRISTIAN OUTLAWS

Bible-smuggling organizations operating in Europe in the 1960s, 1970s and 1980s created what was in effect a shadow Christian intelligence and espionage service. This distinctively Bible-centred intelligence agency, however, worked for no state. It did not even work for any particular church or denomination: a smuggler's home church was often just as much in the dark about its member's secret activities as anyone else. Bible-smuggling organizations like Open Doors, Underground Evangelism, Voice of the Martyrs and Operation Mobilisation set their own priorities: to transport Bibles and religious literature across the Iron Curtain and into the hands of scattered communities of marginalized Christians. They made their own rules and had their own ethical codes. These included finding it

---

[73] Schneider, 'Through the Seams of the Iron Curtain', 54. This was confirmed in interviews by the author with a former smuggler and mechanic for OM (19 April 2022; 22 April 2022; 6 May 2022; 17 May 2022; 23 May 2022); a sample miniature Bible was sent to the author by that interviewee's wife, and is now held in the author's private archive.

[74] Schneider, 'Through the Seams of the Iron Curtain', 57.

[75] See, for example, Bucharest, Consiliul Național pentru Studierea Arhivelor Securității [National Council for the Study of Security Archives; hereafter: CNSAS], Ministerul de Interne [Ministry of Interior], 11195, Fond Documentar, Informări si rapoarte promovate în anii 1971, 1974, 1978, 1979, 1980, 1981 linia/problemei 'CULTE-SECTE' [Documentation Collection, Information and Reports from the years 1971, 1974, 1978, 1979, 1980, 1981 concerning/problem 'CULTS-SECTS'], D 012389, vol. 1, fols 1–46. On the wider context, see, for example, Jonathan Bolton, *Worlds of Dissent: Charter 77, The Plastic People of the Universe and Czech Culture* (Cambridge, MA, 2012); Peter Sarros, *U.S.-Vatican Relations, 1975–1980: A Diplomatic Study* (Notre Dame, IN, 2020).

morally acceptable to mislead not only Communist authorities in states which were hostile to missionary work, but also their own governments in the West, which did not restrict the printing or dissemination of Bibles and religious tracts. Bible smugglers showed equal disregard for international rules and conventions. It was not only in the Communist 'Eastern bloc' but also in the 'free world' that customs declaration forms were required to be filled out, visa regulations adhered to, passports and vehicle registration documents checked. Consular officers from the Bible smugglers' countries of origin often found themselves forced to agree with the Communist authorities that their own compatriots had broken the laws or ignored the customs of the state they were visiting.[76] Bible smugglers, in short, lived on the edge and were a law unto themselves.

The people Bible-smuggling organizations recognized as their own were Christians of a certain disposition, which we might broadly describe as 'evangelical' in the stress they placed on the importance of conversion, atoning grace through the crucifixion, the need to live by and spread the Good News, and the primacy of the Bible.[77] We might also consider them 'fundamentalist' in the weight they put on the precise wording of the gospel. This spiritual outlook had little to do with nationality. The mental maps which Bible smugglers had in their heads were not the standard geopolitical maps to be found in an atlas. Indeed, the borders which were shown on published maps were the very ones which smugglers made it their business to subvert. The Bible smugglers' view of the world more closely resembled that of the earliest days of the church, when essentially the whole world was hostile to Christianity, with just a few pockets of believers, scattered here and there, keeping the flame alive. In their heroism, and sometimes martyrdom, Bible smugglers could feel themselves to be preserving the faith, protecting the truth, passing on revelation as transmitted from the earliest Christians. This sense of kinship with the apostles could sometimes be quite literal. Richard Wurmbrand, for example, who worked for Underground Evangelism before setting up his own series of missionary organizations

[76] In the Hathaway case, for example, the British Consul in Prague agreed that Hathaway had broken Czechoslovak law and would need to serve the sentence meted out by the court. See Prague, Ministry of Interior Archive, Archiv bezpečnostních složek [Security Services Archive], Fond V/Plzeň, V-8558, 'Plzeň, David Gordon Hathaway' for interrogation, court prosecution and related records. See also David Hathaway, *Czech-Mate* (London, 1974).
[77] See Bebbington, *Evangelicalism in Modern Britain*, 2–17.

to the 'Communist world', claimed that it was only after his experiences in the 'secret church' that he was able to 'understand texts of the Bible' which had previously passed him by. Formerly, he had not been clear as to 'why it is written in the Bible that a man named Simon was called Peter. Simeon was called Niger and so on. Everyone is called other than his mother called him'. In light of his own experience, he now understood the extensive use of nicknames in the New Testament to be codenames used by the apostles to avoid blowing each other's cover. As he explained in his testimony to the US Senate subcommittee on Communism and religion in 1966: '"In every village," ... he too, "was called by another name. I was called Valentin, Georgescu, Ruben. In every village I had another name, and so I could preach."'[78] The same close reading of the Bible in light of his new experiences also made clear to him that Jesus, too, had used techniques of espionage such as dead-letter drops. As Wurmbrand explained:

> I did not understand in earlier times why Jesus, when He wishes to have the last supper, said: 'Go in[to] town and you will see a man with a pitcher and go after him and where he enters prepare the supper.' Why does he not give an address, a number and a street? Now we know it when we make secret prayer meetings. We never give the address. We don't know if that man is not the informer of the secret police. We tell the man to wait in a public garden or somewhere, and one with a flower here, or with a necktie passes, go after him. We don't introduce ourselves to each other, and if somebody asks the name of the other one, we know that he is the informer of the secret police. And so we have developed a technique of secret church work.[79]

To Bible smugglers, the existential struggle of the twentieth century was not over whether the USA or the Soviet Union, NATO or the Warsaw Pact, would 'win' the Cold War, but rather whether men and women, wherever they lived and however they had been raised, would choose to follow God or Satan.[80] In this sense, Bible smugglers were levellers, judging Western materialism to be as empty as Communist atheism. Bible-smuggling organizations took no heed of official Western policies such as *détente*; they were equally unmoved by the Soviet policy

---

[78] *Communist Exploitation of Religion*, 3.

[79] Ibid. 3–4.

[80] Crucial to this perspective was Billy Graham's essay on communism: Billy Graham, 'Satan's Religion', *American Mercury* 79 (1954), 41–6, at 41–3.

of *perestroika* ('restructuring') under Communist Party General Secretary Mikhail Gorbachev. Their own shifts in missionary priorities, methods and approach were determined behind closed doors, without regard to the diplomatic niceties or the political goals even of their own governments, let alone those of the declared enemies of God.

It will have been noticed that Bible-smuggling organizations, which linked like-minded Christians across international and political boundaries, had many qualities which we might associate with a cult. The intensity of commitment, the secrecy and the separation from ordinary society all point in that direction. However, although Bible smugglers, like spies, sought to make themselves invisible and their covert operations undetectable, they also needed publicity to raise money, attract recruits and to protect their secret missions. Furthermore, however marginal they might have seemed to outsiders, their own sense of themselves was as fully and deeply Christian, intrinsically part of a wider apostolic, Christian and Protestant tradition spanning centuries.

Western Bible smugglers saw themselves as bringing the light of the gospel to places of darkness. To them, the struggle was ideological and spiritual, not material. In contrast, evidence from the secret police archives suggests that the threat which Communist regimes perceived to come from Bible smuggling was not so much spiritual or even ideological, but rather political. Communist regimes, Western assumptions notwithstanding, did not seem to fear penetration of ideas per se; at any rate, it was not the gospel of Jesus Christ which made them tremble. What the Communist authorities went to extraordinary lengths to seek to prevent, contain and destroy was rather the creation of rival structures, parallel channels of communication, and effective networks for the distribution of goods and services. When Bible smugglers were caught, it was not their Christian literature which preoccupied border guards and the secret police so much as the mechanisms used to conceal it. Communist police, in short, were not so much concerned about the importation of Bibles as by the way they were concealed, imported and distributed.[81]

[81] See, for example, CNSAS, Ministerul de Interne [Ministry of Interior], 11195, Fond Documentar, Informări si rapoarte promovate în anii 1971, 1974, 1978, 1979, 1980, 1981 linia/problemei 'CULTE-SECTE' [Documentation Collection, Information and Reports from the years 1971, 1974, 1978, 1979, 1980, 1981 concerning/problem 'CULTS-SECTS'], D 012389, vol. 1, fols 1–46.

CONCLUSION

Bible smuggling was predicated on the idea that Communist-controlled East-Central Europe was a territory 'starved' of Bibles and, by implication, knowledge of Christ. This increasingly widespread perception led to the creation of a secret Cold War army of Protestant missionaries, rugged individuals whose sense of mission to convert the world was not limited by state borders, denominational boundaries or even conventional Christian morality. The fact that Bible-smuggling networks criss-crossed Cold War Europe suggests that the Iron Curtain was considerably more porous than is popularly believed.[82] As intelligence-gathering institutions, Bible-smuggling organizations like Open Doors, Underground Evangelism, Voice of Martyrs and Operation Mobilisation played a central role in discovering and publicizing conditions in Communist prisons, the existence of underground churches in formally Communist countries, and high-profile cases of Communist conversions to Christianity. In so doing, they influenced public opinion, and sometimes even foreign policy, in the West.

Bible smuggling was arguably more about perception than reality. Smugglers took part in a cosmic drama in which they acted out their beliefs that Christianity was under existential threat; and sought to persuade the world of that perception. Although the phrase 'the culture wars' has only come to prominence in the anglophone world relatively recently, the decades from the 1960s to the 1980s can, in many ways, be seen as a series of victories for the Liberal-left over traditional Christian attitudes towards sexuality, gender, the family and other emotive topics. The so-called 'fall' of Communism in Europe in 1989 was a decisive moment. For some Bible smugglers, it was devastating: almost overnight, their life's work was made irrelevant.[83] Others managed to weather the storm, turning to China, North Korea or the Middle East as places to target with Bibles. In the East, contacts with the West continued, not only among the

---

[82] Specialists are already aware. See, for example, van Dongen, Roulin and Scott Smith, eds, *Transnational Anti-Communism and the Cold War*; Simo Mikkonen and Pia Koivunen, eds, *Beyond the Divide: Entangled Histories of Cold War Europe*, rev. edn (New York and Oxford, 2018; first publ. 2015).

[83] Gouverneur, 'Underground Evangelism', 83; interviews by the author with a former smuggler and mechanic for OM (19 April 2022; 22 April 2022; 6 May 2022; 17 May 2022; 23 May 2022). Recording in author's private archive.

high-profile dissident groups who were to come to power after the anti-Communist revolutions in 1989/90, but also in the minority Protestant circles which were scattered across Central and Eastern Europe, and were disproportionately influential in seeking to discredit, and eventually overthrow, the Communist regimes.[84] This may help to explain why Pentecostals, Baptists and other evangelical groups were often at the forefront of religious revival in the 1990s: these were groups whose contacts were already in place, and which did not have to shake off accusations of collaboration or compromise with the previous regime.

Bible smuggling today remains a tried and tested method to raise funds, galvanize followers and missionize to Christians living under hostile regimes. Seen as marginal, even laughable, by those on the liberal side of the culture wars, on the evangelical side, Bible smugglers remain central to heroic narratives of Christian missionary endeavour. For those who made a career out of Bible smuggling across Europe in the 1960s, 1970s or 1980s, the political Cold War may have ended, but the spiritual Cold War has not. Christ himself, they remind themselves, was an outcast who was reviled by the authorities and executed like a criminal. His apostles learned more than how to bless, pray and live Christian lives. As the New Testament shows, they also learned how to deflect police questioning, move undetected around hostile territory, and keep in secret contact with one another. What we might think of as God's secret service remains as necessary today, in their own view, as it was during the Cold War.

The mentality which was spread through Cold War Bible smuggling, in which Christians are imagined as a suffering and persecuted minority, did not disappear at the end of the Cold War. Popular evangelical notions of a world in which Bibles need to be smuggled to needy Christians around the world left a rich legacy of Bible-smuggling testimony and memoirs. This message is amplified today through Mega-church fundraisers, online charity drives and advertising campaigns in Christian newspapers, magazines, radio and on social media. As the 'culture wars' continue to sharpen political differences between 'traditional Christian' and 'progressive Liberal' values, the Bible has become a highly politicized symbol in what is presented as an existential struggle. It is not only the liberal Left, watching the rise of

---

[84] See, for example, Sparks, *Detour*, 148–9.

Christian nationalism across Europe and America, which fears for the future. The Christian film 'Disciples in the Moonlight' (2024) imagines a 'not-too-distant' dystopian America in which 'Christians are persecuted, the Bible is banned as "hate speech"' and the 'government has issued its own "inclusive, welcoming" and censored version of the Bible'.[85] The film, which appears under the banner 'Christians are persecuted and the Bible is banned', carries endorsements by former US Vice-President Mike Pence. Soon, it suggests, it will no longer be oppressed Christians abroad, but rather outlawed Christians at home, who will need Bibles smuggled to them, in the dead of night, by God's secret agents. In this new Cold War, shaped and prepared by decades of Bible-smuggling organization, training, fundraising, literature and intelligence work, the enemy is no longer abroad, but within.

---

[85] Kathryn Post, 'In "Disciples in the Moonlight", US Christians are persecuted and the Bible is banned', *RNS*, 16 July 2024, online at: <https://religionnews.com/2024/07/16/in-disciples-in-the-moonlight-us-christians-are-persecuted-and-the-bible-is-banned/>, accessed 20 October 2024.

CORRIGENDUM

Introduction – CORRIGENDUM

Catherine Cubitt

DOI: https://doi.org/10.1017/stc.2024.26 Published online by Cambridge University Press: 08 June 2022

Upon publication of this introduction, a typographical error was found to have been made to an author's name: Dickinson should have been spelled Dickerson. This section of the introduction should thus read: 'Jamaica and the United States of America (Kinghorn, Wang, Manger and Dickerson)'.

Additionally, an author was missed when listing those authors covering France, Germany and Italy. The authors listed here should be: Sabapathy, Methuen, Maghenzani, Cubitt and Gravanis.

REFERENCE

Cubitt C. (2024). Introduction *Studies in Church History*, 60, 1–16. doi:10.1017/stc.2024.26

Studies in Church History 61 (2025), 638 © The Author(s), 2025. Published by Cambridge University Press on behalf of the Ecclesiastical History Society. doi:10.1017/stc.2024.28